The Wiley Handbook on Violence in Education

Wiley Handbooks in Education

The Wiley Handbooks in Education offer a capacious and comprehensive overview of higher education in a global context. These state-of-the-art volumes offer a magisterial overview of every sector, sub-field and facet of the discipline-from reform and foundations to K-12 learning and literacy. The Handbooks also engage with topics and themes dominating today's educational agenda-mentoring, technology, adult and continuing education, college access, race and educational attainment. Showcasing the very best scholarship that the discipline has to offer, The Wiley Handbooks in Education will set the intellectual agenda for scholars, students, researchers for years to come.

The Wiley Handbook on Violence in Education: Forms, Factors, and Preventions
by Harvey Shapiro (Editor)

The Wiley Handbook of Global Educational Reform
by Kenneth J. Saltman (Editor) and Alexander J. Means (Editor)

The Wiley Handbook of Ethnography of Education
by Dennis Beach (Editor), Carl Bagley (Editor), and Sofia Marques da Silva (Editor)

The Wiley International Handbook of History Teaching and Learning
by Scott Alan Metzger (Editor) and Lauren McArthur Harris (Editor)

The Wiley Handbook of Christianity and Education
by William Jeynes (Editor)

The Wiley Handbook of Diversity in Special Education
by Marie Tejero Hughes (Editor) and Elizabeth Talbott (Editor)

The Wiley International Handbook of Educational Leadership
by Duncan Waite (Editor) and Ira Bogotch (Editor)

The Wiley Handbook of Social Studies Research
by Meghan McGlinn Manfra (Editor) and Cheryl Mason Bolick (Editor)

The Wiley Handbook of School Choice
by Robert A. Fox (Editor) and Nina K. Buchanan (Editor)

The Wiley Handbook of Home Education
by Milton Gaither (Editor)

The Wiley Handbook of Cognition and Assessment: Frameworks, Methodologies, and Applications
by Andre A. Rupp (Editor) and Jacqueline P. Leighton (Editor)

The Wiley Handbook of Learning Technology
by Nick Rushby (Editor) and Dan Surry (Editor)

The Wiley Handbook on Violence in Education

Forms, Factors, and Preventions

Edited by Harvey Shapiro

WILEY Blackwell

This edition first published 2018
© 2018 John Wiley & Sons, Inc.

The right of Harvey Shapiro to be identified as the author of the editorial material in this work has been asserted in accordance with law.

Registered Office(s)
John Wiley & Sons, Inc., 111 River Street, Hoboken, NJ 07030, USA

Editorial Office
101 Station Landing, Medford, MA 02155, USA

For details of our global editorial offices, customer services, and more information about Wiley products visit us at www.wiley.com.

Wiley also publishes its books in a variety of electronic formats and by print-on-demand. Some content that appears in standard print versions of this book may not be available in other formats.

Library of Congress Cataloging-in-Publication Data applied for

9781118966679 [Hardback]

Cover Design: Wiley
Cover Image: © Spencer Starnes / EyeEm/Gettyimages

Set in 10/12pt Warnock by SPi Global, Pondicherry, India

Printed in the United States of America

10 9 8 7 6 5 4 3 2 1

Contents

Notes on the Editors

Book Editor

Harvey Shapiro, PhD, is Clinical Associate Professor in the Graduate School of Education of the College of Professional Studies at Northeastern University. His primary areas of scholarship are interpretations of violence in education, ethical leadership, interdisciplinarity, the philosophies of Giorgio Agamben, Jacques Derrida, and John Dewey, and modern Hebrew literature. In addition to his work that has appeared in *Educational Theory*, *Educational Philosophy and Theory*, the *Philosophy of Education Society Yearbook*, the *International Journal of Jewish Education Research*, *Jewish Education*, *Shofar: An Interdisciplinary Journal of Jewish Studies*, and the *Journal of Modern Jewish Studies*, he is the author of *Educational Theory and Jewish Studies in Conversation: From Volozhin to Bucascz* (Lexington Books, 2013). Prior to his appointment at Northeastern University in 2008, Dr. Shapiro served as Dean of the Graduate School of Education at Hebrew College in Newton, Massachusetts, principal of Cohen Hillel Academy in Marblehead, Massachusetts, principal of the Stephen S. Wise Middle School in Los Angeles, California, and Director of the UAHC Swig Camp Institute in Saratoga, California.

Section 2 Editor, "Group and Gang Violence in Education"

Emily E. Tanner-Smith, PhD, is an Associate Professor in the Department of Counseling Psychology and Human Services at the University of Oregon. Her research focuses broadly on adolescent development, and seeks to identify effective programs and policies for promoting healthy youth development. As an applied research methodologist with emphasis in systematic reviewing and meta-analysis, her recent work has focused on the social epidemiology, prevention, and treatment of adolescent substance use and delinquency. Her recent research appears in the *Journal of Developmental and Life-course Criminology, Journal of Youth and Adolescence, Prevention Science*, and *Review of Educational Research*.

Section 3 Editor, "Bullying, Sexual Violence, and Suicide in Education"

Dorothy L. Espelage, PhD, is Professor of Psychology at the University of Florida. She is the recipient of the APA Lifetime Achievement Award in Prevention Science and the 2016 APA Award for Distinguished Contributions to Research in Public Policy, and is a Fellow of APS, APA, and AERA. She earned her PhD in Counseling Psychology from Indiana University in 1997. Over the last 22 years, she has authored over 170 peer- reviewed articles, six edited books, and 70 chapters on bullying, homophobic teasing, sexual harassment, dating violence, and gang violence. Her research focuses on translating empirical findings into prevention and intervention programming and she has secured over $10 million of external funding.

Notes on Contributors

Lynn A. Addington, PhD, is a professor in the Department of Justice, Law, and Criminology at American University. Her research focuses on violent victimization with an emphasis on adolescents and school environments. Her recent publications have appeared in *American Behavioral Scientist, Homicide Studies, Journal of Quantitative Criminology, Justice Quarterly*, and *Trauma, Violence and Abuse*. She is the coeditor (with James P. Lynch) of *Understanding Crime Statistics: Revisiting the Divergence of the NCVS and UCR* (2007).

Anastasia Alexis received her EdM in Counseling Psychology, with a concentration in School Counseling, from Boston University's School of Education. She also holds a BA in Social Work from the University of Southern Maine. Anastasia's research interests include the impact of shame, stigma, and vulnerability on adolescent development, particularly within minority populations.

Chelsey Bowman, EdM, is a doctoral student in Counseling Psychology at Boston University School of Education. As a member of the Social Adjustment and Bullying Prevention Lab, Chelsey researches the impact of a range of victimization forms, including bullying, dating violence, and sexual assault, on the health and well-being of K–12 and college students. She intends to utilize her research to develop, inform, and enhance prevention programs and counseling services for adolescents and young adults.

Deron Boyles, PhD, is Professor of Philosophy of Education in the Department of Educational Policy Studies at Georgia State University. His research interests include school commercialism, epistemology, critical pedagogy, and the philosophy of John Dewey. His work has been published in such journals as *Social Epistemology, Journal of Thought, Education & Culture, Philosophical Studies in Education, Inter-American Journal of Philosophy, Educational Foundations, Journal of Curriculum Theory*, and *History of Education*.

Kristeen Cherney, MA, is a PhD student in Rhetoric and Composition at Georgia State University, where she also teaches first-year writing courses with themes of literacy and primary research. Her research interests include disability studies, literacy studies, archival research methods, and activist rhetorics. Cherney's work has been featured in *Praxis: A Writing Center Journal* and The Digital Rhetoric Collaborative. Her dissertation aims to investigate the intersections between autism rhetorics and literacy studies.

Kendra J. Clark, BS, is a doctoral student in sociology at the University of Colorado Boulder. She is also affiliated with the Institute of Behavioral Science at the University of Colorado Boulder. Her work is concentrated in the area of crime and deviance, with specific research interests in gangs, juveniles, incarceration, and restrictive housing.

Nadine M. Connell, PhD, is an Assistant Professor of Criminology in the School of Economic, Political and Policy Sciences at the University of Texas at Dallas. Her research has been published in several peer-reviewed journals, such as *Youth Violence and Juvenile Justice* and the *American Journal of Public Health*. Her research interests include school violence, juvenile delinquency prevention, program and policy evaluation, and capital punishment.

Dewey G. Cornell, PhD, is a forensic clinical psychologist who holds the Linda Bunker Chair as Professor of Education in the Curry School of Education at the University of Virginia. Dr. Cornell has authored more than 200 publications in psychology and education, including studies of school climate and safety, bullying, and threat assessment. He is principal developer of the Virginia Student Threat Assessment Guidelines and the Authoritative School Climate Survey.

Hilary Cremin, PhD, is a Senior Lecturer at the Faculty of Education, University of Cambridge. She researches and teaches peacebuilding, in and through education, in settings in the United Kingdom and elsewhere. She has worked in the public, private, and voluntary sector as a schoolteacher, educational consultant, project coordinator, and academic. Hilary has been the principal investigator in a number of prestigious externally funded research projects, and has published her work extensively over a number of years. Her latest book, with Terence Bevington, is *Positive Peace in Schools: Tackling Conflict and Creating a Culture of Peace in the Classroom* (2017).

F. Chris Curran, PhD, is an Assistant Professor of Public Policy at the University of Maryland, Baltimore County (UMBC) School of Public Policy. His research focuses on issues of school discipline and safety, early elementary education, and teacher labor markets.

Lisa De La Rue, PhD, is an Assistant Professor in the Department of Counseling Psychology at the University of San Francisco. Her research is informed by ecological frameworks that seek to delineate the gendered, cultural, and contextual associations between trauma, interpersonal violence, and adolescent risk behavior. She is also engaged in research in the area of school-based interventions, and looking at ways to empower youth-led activism.

Dorothy L. Espelage, PhD, is Professor of Psychology at the University of Florida. She is the recipient of the APA Lifetime Achievement Award in Prevention Science and the 2016 APA Award for Distinguished Contributions to Research in Public Policy, and is a Fellow of APS, APA, and AERA. She earned her PhD in Counseling Psychology from Indiana University in 1997. Over the last 22 years, she has authored over 170 peer-reviewed articles, six edited books, and 70 chapters on bullying, homophobic teasing, sexual harassment, dating violence, and gang violence. Her research focuses on translating empirical findings into prevention and intervention programming and she has secured over $7 million of external funding.

Joey Nuñez Estrada Jr., PhD, is an Assistant Professor at San Diego State University. Research interests include street gang culture, school violence, school-based intervention, resiliency, and youth empowerment. He specializes in data-driven school-based models to reduce gang activity and school violence. His work has been published in major academic journals and he is a recipient of the American Educational Research Association (AERA) Division E Counseling and Human Development Outstanding Research in Counseling Award.

Katherine Evans is an Assistant Professor of Education at Eastern Mennonite University, teaching courses in special education, restorative justice, and educational theory. With a PhD in Educational Psychology and Research from the University of Tennessee, her research, teaching, and scholarship focus on the ways in which restorative justice in education can supplant zero tolerance policies and exclusionary school discipline practices.

Michael E. Ezell, PhD, is Associate Professor of Sociology at Northern Illinois University. His research interests include serious youthful offenders, life course criminology, victimization, and quantitative methods. He is the author of *Desisting from Crime: Continuity and Change in Long-Term Crime Patterns of Serious Chronic Offenders*. His other publications have appeared in *Journal of Research in Crime and Delinquency*, *Crime & Delinquency*, *Homicide Studies*, *Law & Society Review*, and *Sociological Methodology*.

Benjamin W. Fisher, PhD, is an Assistant Professor in the Department of Criminal Justice at the University of Louisville. Broadly, his research focuses on issues related to school safety, with particular emphases on the impacts of school security measures, exclusionary school discipline, and school climate, as well as inequalities within these areas of focus.

Anjali J. Forber-Pratt, PhD, is an Assistant Professor in the Department of Human and Organizational Development at Vanderbilt University. Her research looks at issues related to identity development, school safety, social-emotional learning, gangs in schools, and school climate particularly for individuals who are different in some way, with a large focus on disability. She was recognized as a White House Champion of Change in 2013 for her work for persons with disabilities.

James Alan Fox, PhD, is the Lipman Family Professor of Criminology, Law, and Public Policy at Northeastern University. He has written 18 books, including *Violence and Security on Campus: From Preschool through College*. He has published widely in both scholarly and popular outlets, and, as a member of its Board of Contributors, his column appears regularly in *USA Today*. He also served on President Clinton's advisory committee on school shootings and on the US Department of Education expert panel on Safe, Disciplined and Drug-Free Schools.

Emma E. Fridel, BA, BS, is a doctoral student in the School of Criminology and Criminal Justice at Northeastern University, specializing in the area of atypical homicide. She received a BS in Biology and a BA in Chinese from Duke University.

Joseph H. Gardella, MS, is a graduate student in a PhD program in the Department of Human and Organizational Development at Vanderbilt University. He is a community psychologist who focuses on education settings with particular attention to behavior management and violence prevention in schools that implement prosocial approaches to education.

Alex Guilherme, PhD, works in the School of Humanities, Pontifícia Universidade Católica do Rio Grande do Sul, Porto Alegre, Brazil. He is the leader of a research group registered with the Brazilian Ministry of Education focusing on education and violence. He has published extensively on Martin Buber, dialogue, and peace education. He is the coauthor of *Buber and Education: Dialogue as Conflict Resolution* (2014) and of *New Perspectives in Philosophy of Education* (2013).

Danielle Guttman, PhD, NCSP, is a school psychologist in Aldine Independent School District in Houston, Texas. She conducts psychological evaluations for special education eligibility and consults with school staff to address behavioral concerns in the classroom. She was formerly a postdoctoral research associate at the Alberti Center for Bullying Abuse Prevention at the University at Buffalo, the State University of New York. Her research interests include school-wide prevention approaches and social-emotional learning.

Edwin Hernandez, MA, is a doctoral candidate in the Social Science and Comparative Education program and a research associate at the Institute for Immigration, Globalization, and Education at UCLA's Graduate School of Education & Information Studies. His research interests include issues around access and equity for low-income and minority youth, with a focus on how school culture shapes students' experiences in urban schools and the role of institutional agents in the educational trajectory of under-represented students.

Richard Hernandez, MS, is a first-year doctoral student at the University of Texas at Dallas. His research interests revolve around police behavior, juvenile delinquency, and life-course criminology.

Robert A. Hernandez, MSW, University of Southern California, has research interests that include vulnerable youth populations, adolescent social issues, adolescent gang intervention, strength-based resiliency, and youth empowerment models of practice. In particular, his work examines risk and protective factors within communities that are associated with vulnerable youth populations residing in trauma-exposed communities. He has focused on advancing marginalized populations through a range of practice approaches addressing violence-related trauma through violence reduction, prevention, and intervention strategies.

Melissa K. Holt, PhD, is an Assistant Professor of Counseling Psychology at Boston University's School of Education. She co-leads the Social Adjustment and Bullying Prevention Lab, and has particular expertise in the relation between bullying and suicide. More broadly, Dr. Holt's research focuses on how victimization at school, at home, and in the community affects youth functioning in multiple domains.

Jun Sung Hong, PhD, is an Assistant Professor at Wayne State University, School of Social Work in Detroit, Michigan and at Sungkyunkwan University, Department of Social Welfare in Seoul, South Korea. His research interests are school violence (bullying/peer victimization), school-based intervention, juvenile delinquency, child welfare, and cultural competency in social work practice.

Adrian H. Huerta, PhD, is a Provost's Postdoctoral Scholar in the Rossier School of Education at the University of Southern California Pullias Center for Higher Education. He has published his work in *Journal of College Student Development*, *Journal of the First-Year Experience & Students in Transition*, and *Journal of Latino/Latin American Studies*. Adrian's research area connects college access, gangs, and school discipline for Latino male students using qualitative methods.

Sheila M. Katz, PhD, is an Assistant Professor in the Department of Sociology at the University of Houston. Her qualitative sociological research focuses on gender, poverty, domestic violence, inequalities, grassroots activism, reproductive justice, and higher education. Her first book, *Reformed American Dreams: Welfare Mothers, Higher Education, and Activism*, will be published by Rutgers University Press in 2018. She serves on the boards of the National Center for Student Parent Programs and the journal *Social Problems*.

Gabriel Keehn, BS, is a doctoral student in educational policy at Georgia State University. His main areas of interest are in the philosophy of education, particularly the political aspects of educational philosophy. He has also worked on Plato, recent Continental theory, and Lacan. His dissertation focuses on the theory and history of individualist-anarchist education.

Douglas Kellner, PhD, is George Kneller Chair in the Philosophy of Education at UCLA and is author of many books on social theory, politics, history, culture, and education, including *Herbert Marcuse and the Crisis of Marxism, Camera Politica, Critical Theory, Marxism, and Modernity; Jean Baudrillard: From Marxism to Postmodernism and Beyond*; works in social theory and cultural studies such as media culture; a trilogy of books on postmodern theory with Steve Best; and a trilogy of books on the media and the Bush administration. His most recent books are *Media Spectacle and Insurrection, 2011: From the Arab Uprisings to Occupy Everywhere* and *American Nightmare: Donald Trump, Media Spectacle, and Authoritarian Populism*.

Sang Hyun Kim, PhD, is Assistant Professor of Philosophy of Education in the Department of Education at Kyungpook National University. His primary areas of scholarship are ethics and education, democratic education, and authority and freedom in education.

Steve W. Kim, MSW, is cofounder of Project Kinship, a non-profit organization in Orange County, California that aims to promote hope, health and well-being among formerly incarcerated individuals and their families. He has dedicated his life to serving marginalized populations impacted by root causes of trauma and focuses on school-based and re-entry services. He is highly regarded for human rights work in the field of forensic social work and leads a multidisciplinary team on capital cases.

Ralph W. Larkin, PhD, is an Adjunct Professor of Sociology at John Jay College of Criminal Justice. He has published three books: *Suburban Youth and Cultural Crisis* (1979), *Beyond Revolution: A New Theory of Social Movements* (with Daniel Foss, 1986), and *Comprehending Columbine* (2007). He has published articles on education, youth, sociology of religion, and social movements. He also has published several articles about Columbine and rampage shootings.

Jeoung Min Lee, MS, MSW, is a doctoral student in the School of Social Work at Wayne State University, Detroit, Michigan. She is interested in risk/protective factors associated with bullying and school-based bullying prevention and intervention programs.

Jessica Nina Lester is an Assistant Professor of Inquiry Methodology in the School of Education at Indiana University. She teaches research methods courses and focuses a good deal of her research on the study and development of qualitative methodologies. She situates much of her research within discourse studies and disability studies, with a particular focus on education and mental health contexts.

Patricia L. Maarhuis, PhD, is a researcher, educator, and artist at Washington State University in Health and Wellness Services. Her publications include chapters in the *Handbook of Research on the Facilitation of Civic Engagement through Community Art* (2017) and *Poetic Inquiry II: Seeing, Understanding and Caring* (2015), and coauthored articles on high-risk health behaviors (*Addictive Behaviors Journal*, 2017). Patricia has exhibited arts-informed research nationally and internationally. She studied at Washington State University and Western Washington University.

Laura J. McGuire, EdD, earned her doctorate in Educational Leadership for Change from Fielding Graduate University. Her dissertation, "Seen but Not Heard: Pathways to Improve Inclusion of LGBT Persons and Sexual Trauma Survivors in Sexual Health Education," addressed the marginalization of sexual minorities in health education internationally. She was the first Sexual Violence Prevention and Education Program Manager at the University of Houston. She writes, consults, and teaches on sexual health education and sexual trauma recovery.

Justine Medrano, MS, earned her Master of Science in Criminology from the University of Texas at Dallas and is currently pursuing a Master of Science in Psychology. Her research interests include corrections, re-entry, juvenile delinquency, and co-occurring disorders. She hopes to be a mental health professional focusing on re-entry issues.

Claudia Mitchell, PhD, is a James McGill Professor in the Faculty of Education, McGill University where she is the Director of the McGill Institute for Human Development and Well-being. She is also Honorary Professor at the University of KwaZulu-Natal. She was awarded the 2016 SSHRC Gold Medal for the impact of her international research on girlhood studies, youth sexuality and HIV and AIDS, gender violence, and teacher identity. She is a cofounder and editor-in-chief of the award-winning journal *Girlhood Studies: An Interdisciplinary Journal*.

Relebohile Moletsane, PhD, is Professor in the School of Education, University of KwaZulu-Natal in Durban, South Africa where she focuses on rural education, sexual and reproductive health education, and girls' education. She is the co-principal investigator (with Claudia Mitchell) on the Networks for Change and Wellbeing project (www.networks4change.co.za/). She is the author of the research report *The Need for Quality Sexual and Reproductive Health Education to Address Barriers to Girls' Educational Outcomes in South Africa*, which she completed as a 2014 Echidna Global Scholar at the Brookings Institution's Centre for Universal Education.

Alyssa Murphy, BA, is a master's student at Boston University's School of Education, where she is enrolled in the Counseling Psychology program with concentrations in School Counseling and Child and Adolescent Mental Health Counseling. She earned a BA in Psychology from The College of the Holy Cross in 2012. Alyssa is particularly interested in the availability and use of mental health services in K–12 schools.

Amanda Nickerson, PhD, NCSP, is a professor of school psychology and director of the Alberti Center for Bullying Abuse Prevention at the University at Buffalo, the State University of New York. Her research focuses on school violence and bullying, and the critical role of schools, peers, and families in preventing violence and building social-emotional strengths of youth. She has published more than 85 journal articles and book chapters, and written or edited five books.

Elizabethe Payne, PhD, is Director of the Queering Education Research Institute© (QuERI), currently housed at Hunter College, CUNY. She is a Distinguished Lecturer at Hunter, and a sociologist of education specializing in LGBTQ issues. She has worked on New York State anti-bullying policy and with the US Department of Justice on the application of Title IX to LGBT student anti-harassment cases. She founded QuERI in 2006. For more information, see www.queeringeducation.org.

F. Alvin Pearman II, PhD, is Assistant Professor of Urban Education in the Center for Urban Education at the University of Pittsburgh. His research focuses on the intersection of urban schooling, social inequality, and racial stratification. His current research on education examines the impact of city-wide income inequality on schooling outcomes, the influence of neighborhood gentrification on disciplinary patterns in schools, and the role of neighborhood environments in shaping the efficacy of early-childhood interventions.

Margaret Price, PhD, is Associate Professor of English at Ohio State University. Her research interests within rhetoric and composition include discourse analysis, disability studies, and digital composition. Her book, *Mad at School: Rhetorics of Mental Disability and Academic Life*, was published by University of Michigan Press in 2011. Price also publishes scholarly articles, creative essays, fiction, and poetry in venues including *College Composition and Communication, Profession, Disability Studies Quarterly, Bitch: Feminist Response to Pop Culture*, and *Ms.* magazine.

David C. Pyrooz, PhD, is Assistant Professor of Sociology and Faculty Associate of the Institute of Behavioral Science at the University of Colorado Boulder. He studies gangs and criminal networks, life course and developmental criminology, and incarceration and re-entry. He is the author of *Confronting Gangs: Crime and Community* and the editor of the *Handbook of Gangs*.

David Ragland, PhD, is the codirector and cofounder of the Truth Telling Project of Ferguson, MO. He has been a board member for the Peace and Justice Association, a United Nations representative for the International Peace Research Association, and a professor at the United Nations Mandated University for Peace. His interests as a researcher and activist include the Black Lives Matter Movement, police brutality, racism, and the intersection of race, law, and power.

Ryan Randa, PhD, is an Assistant Professor of Criminal Justice and Criminology at Sam Houston State University. His research interests include fear of crime, victimization, and influences on adaptive behaviors. His recent work in this area has appeared in *Crime and Delinquency, Journal of Criminal Justice, Youth Violence and Juvenile Justice, Victims and Offenders*, and *Security Journal*.

Jordan Riddell, BA, is a graduate assistant at the University of Texas at Dallas and is working on completing his Master of Science in Criminology. His research interests include juvenile delinquency and antisocial behavior.

Richard Riner is doctoral student in the Criminology Program at the University of Texas at Dallas. His research interests revolve around policing policy, domestic violence, and procedural justice.

Shannon Robinson is a doctoral student in Philosophy of Education in the Department of Educational Studies at The Ohio State University. Her primary interests are social justice, liberal education, ethics, and educational policy.

A.G. Rud, PhD, is Distinguished Professor at Washington State University. His books include *Albert Schweitzer's Legacy for Education* (2011), and he has coedited *The Educational Significance of Human and Non-Human Animal Interactions: Blurring the Species Line* (2016), *Teaching with Reverence: Reviving an Ancient Virtue for Today's Schools* (2012), and *John Dewey at 150: Reflections for a New Century* (2009). Rud has two coedited books and a coauthored book forthcoming. He was educated at Dartmouth College and Northwestern University.

Claudia W. Ruitenberg, PhD, is an Associate Professor in the Department of Educational Studies at the University of British Columbia. She is the author of *Unlocking the World: Education in an Ethic of Hospitality* (2015), coeditor (with D.C. Phillips) of *Education, Culture and Epistemological Diversity: Mapping a Disputed Terrain* (2012), and editor of (among other titles) *Reconceptualizing Study in Educational Discourse and Practice* (2017). From May 2017 she will be Academic Director of UBC Vantage College, an innovative program for international first-year students.

Harvey Shapiro, PhD, is Clinical Associate Professor in the Graduate School of Education of the College of Professional Studies at Northeastern University. His primary areas of scholarship are interpretations of violence in education, interdisciplinarity, the philosophies of Giorgio Agamben, Jacques Derrida, and John Dewey, and modern Hebrew literature. In addition to his work that has appeared in *Educational Theory*, *Educational Philosophy and Theory*, the *Philosophy of Education Society Yearbook*, the *International Journal of Jewish Education Research*, *Jewish Education*, *Shofar: An Interdisciplinary Journal of Jewish Studies*, and the *Journal of Modern Jewish Studies*, he is the author of *Educational Theory and Jewish Studies in Conversation: From Volozhin to Bucascz* (Lexington Books, 2013). Prior to his appointment at Northeastern University in 2008, Dr. Shapiro served as Dean of the Graduate School of Education at Hebrew College in Newton, Massachusetts, principal of Cohen Hillel Academy in Marblehead, Massachusetts, principal of the Stephen S. Wise Middle School in Los Angeles, California, and Director of the UAHC Swig Camp Institute in Saratoga, California.

Amy Shuffelton, PhD, is Associate Professor of Cultural and Educational Policy Studies at Loyola University Chicago. Her research interests include democratic education, the role of parents in the public sphere, and gun violence in schools.

Melissa J. Smith, PhD, is Assistant Professor of English Education at University of Central Arkansas and Assistant Director of Research at the Queering Education Research Institute© (QuERI). Her research interests include teacher ally identity and social justice English education. She has also published research about educators' responses to LGBTQ-inclusive professional development and educators' experiences working with transgender elementary school students.

Emily E. Tanner-Smith, PhD, is an Associate Professor in the Department of Counseling Psychology and Human Services at the University of Oregon. Her research focuses broadly on adolescent development, and seeks to identify effective programs and policies for promoting healthy youth development. As an applied research methodologist with emphasis in systematic reviewing and meta-analysis, her recent work has focused on the social epidemiology, prevention, and treatment of adolescent substance use and delinquency. Her recent research appears in the *Journal of Developmental and Life-course Criminology, Journal of Youth and Adolescence, Prevention Science,* and *Review of Educational Research.*

Samantha VanHout is a doctoral student in the Counseling Psychology/School Psychology Program at the University at Buffalo, the State University of New York. She received her bachelor's degree in psychology with a minor in counseling from Ithaca College. Her clinical and research interests include school crisis prevention, bullying, childhood trauma, and parent–child attachment.

Bryan R. Warnick, PhD, is Professor of Philosophy of Education in the Department of Educational Studies at The Ohio State University. His primary areas of scholarship focus on questions related to ethical and political aspects of education, learning theory, and educational technology.

Michalinos Zembylas, PhD, is Professor of Educational Theory and Curriculum Studies at the Open University of Cyprus. He is Visiting Professor and Research Fellow at the Institute for Reconciliation and Social Justice, University of the Free State, South Africa and at the Centre for Critical Studies in Higher Education Transformation at Nelson Mandela Metropolitan University. He has written extensively on emotion and affect in relation to social justice pedagogies, intercultural and peace education, human rights education, and citizenship education.

Acknowledgments

I would like to thank Emily Tanner-Smith, an expert on adolescent delinquency, school crime, substance use, adolescent behavior, and applied research methods, for serving as editor of Section 2, "Group and Gang Violence in Education." I would also like to thank Dorothy L. Espelage, an expert on bullying, homophobic teasing, sexual harassment, and dating violence, for serving as editor of Section 3, "Bullying, Sexual Violence, and Suicide in Education." It has been a privilege to have them as colleagues in the creation of this book. I would also like to express my gratitude to the 59 contributors, representing a wide range of specializations, for their excellent chapters and for their continued scholarship and work to make learning, growth, support, community, care, and safety hallmarks of education. Finally, I would like to thank the College of Professional Studies at Northeastern University for its encouragement and support throughout this project.

Introduction

Context, Form, Prevention, and Response: A Multidisciplinary Approach to Violence in Education

Harvey Shapiro

Violence in education has reached new levels of frequency and lethality in recent decades, as have the intensity and reach of the alarming media spectacles of violent incidents and their aftermaths. The violence in education that we have witnessed points to a crying need to understand and come to terms with its multiple forms and contextual factors as we address a continuing dilemma: We want our schools to be places of learning, inspiration, community building, and growth. Yet, how do we pursue these aspirations in the context of increasing security measures that can foster more tension and even confrontational school climates? We hope the *Handbook on Violence in Education: Forms, Factors, and Preventions*, in providing a multidisciplinary understanding of violence in education, will help educators, policy makers, and community leaders respond to this difficult entanglement of educational purpose and security.

The phenomenon of violence is fraught with complexity and dissensus on how to prevent and respond to it (Bernstein 2013). And, there is no universally accepted way to interpret it, categorize it, or to understand the relationships among its wide range of forms, including physical, verbal, linguistic, social, legal, religious, political, structural, and symbolic violence, to name but some. Moreover, there is no scholarly consensus on whether violence is increasing or decreasing. Of course, this unsettled nature of discourse on violence is long-standing: "The problems of violence still remain very obscure" (Sorel 1925, 47). French philosopher George Sorel's oft-quoted 1906 remark, invoked in Hannah Arendt's 1969 iconic *On Violence* (1969), has enduring veracity, challenging our thinking, research, and efforts to respond. Thus, discussions on violence continue to intensify.

Rather than seeking a singular definition or proposing universal responses and prevention measures, however, the very structure of this volume reflects violence's phenomenological heterogeneity – the plurality of its forms and contributing factors. While the book's framework honors the centripetal semantic force of the word "violence," it also demonstrates its multiple usages across contexts. There is, then, a common attribution of "violent" to experiences of rampage and targeted school shootings, group and gang violence, bullying, cyberbullying, sexual violence, domestic abuse, and suicide. It will be argued, furthermore, that even education's systemic oppression, marginalizations, and exclusions can be considered violent. Therefore, we consider and explicate this paradox of violence's phenomenological, formal divergence and its conceptual, semantic convergence.

The Wiley Handbook on Violence in Education: Forms, Factors, and Preventions, First Edition.
Edited by Harvey Shapiro.

In examining the vast and pressing subject of violence in education, we address two variables: The *distinctive* forms of violence in education and *common* factors that traverse these forms. Violence, indeed, has multiple prevalent *forms*. While we show relationships between these distinctive forms, we also provide nuanced inquiries into each form's particular dynamics, risks, and contexts, as well as into response and prevention measures. At the same time, despite the multiplicity of forms, we consider their common *factors*: The individual, the community, race and racism, socioeconomic class and classism, gender identity, sexual orientation, homophobia, sexism, school climate, the media, and sociopolitical contexts. Each of these factors can contribute to outbreaks of multiple forms of violence. So, rather than simply including a section on prevention and response measures in general, we consider how different forms of violence call for distinctive kinds of responses and prevention strategies, while also showing how some interventions and prevention programs can address multiple forms of violence.

The focus of this volume is on violence in education in the United States, though we also include international research on violence in education, most explicitly in Chapters 21 and 29, recognizing the critical value of a global perspective when examining assumptions and recommending policies. The accelerated frequency and increasing lethality of violence in education in the United States present particular kinds of challenges to this democracy and cause critical, growing concerns for a wide array of stakeholders.

To address the complexities of violence in education, we approach it from a wide range of conceptual and disciplinary angles. The volume's contributors are experts from the fields of sociology, psychology, criminology, philosophy of education, forensic psychology, literary theory, critical theory, and educational policy. This distinctive multidisciplinarity is intended to expose violence's stratified nature, as we triangulate our inquiries and discourses to achieve a deeper understanding of its contexts and to provide direction toward more efficacious responses and prevention measures.

In a book that seeks to help prevent violence and to respond to it more effectively and appropriately, one might expect advocacy for more surveillance, better lockdown drills, increased firearms training for school personnel, more school security personnel and resource officers, renewed, consistent zero tolerance measures, and more thorough profiling of would-be shooters. The absence of these kinds of recommendations in this volume is not incidental. To be sure, we examine the particularities of perpetrators and the experiences of victims, bystanders, and communities, and offer well-researched recommendations for response and prevention programs. But this volume also recurs to a motif of situated, contextualized violence in education. We offer, then, a wide range of studies that examine violence with both closely focused and wide-angle lenses.

We approach the subject of violence as complex, deeply situated in schools, communities, the broader society, and culture. This embedded, contextually driven nature of violence is suggested in Arendt's (1969) invaluable insight:

> [T]he greater the bureaucratization of public life, the greater will be the attraction of violence. In a fully developed bureaucracy there is nobody left with whom one could argue, to whom one could present grievances, on whom the pressures of power could be exerted. Bureaucracy is the form of government in which everybody is deprived of political freedom, of the power to act; for the rule by Nobody is not norule, and where all are equally powerless we have a tyranny without a tyrant. The crucial feature in the students' rebellions around the world is that they are directed everywhere against the ruling bureaucracy. (81)

As we will see in Section 4, what Arendt refers to as "bureaucratization of public life" is analogous to what today we call neoliberal corporatization, privatization, and marketization of education as contexts of violence.

Violence does not take place in a vacuum. If it did, it would be a mere coincidence, for example, that the United States ranks higher in the number of most violent crimes than the total number of those crimes in Western countries. The official claims and conclusions of the University of Massachusetts at Dartmouth's President (2013) and of the Virginia Attorney General's office (2013) are not entirely true, as much as we might like to think so: The "responsibility for these atrocious acts [of the Boston Marathon bombing] rests solely with the people who possessed the grotesque ability to place bombs alongside innocent men, women and children" (Caret 2013) and "[Seung-Hui] Cho was the lone person responsible for the Virginia Tech shooting" (Virginia Tech 2013).

That our educational systems themselves are settings conducive to violence, and even contribute to it, may seem counterintuitive. Yet we ask how education's often overly punitive and competitive structure and practices, and its political and socioeconomic circumstances, among other factors, might constitute a kind of cultural petri dish for resentment, anxiety, hostility, and violence (Klein 2012), sometimes expressed in shootings, vengeful attacks, gang affiliation, bullying, gender-based violence, and even suicide.

In his book, *Violence*, Slovenian philosopher and cultural critic Slavoj Žižek (2008) underscores this contextual nature of violence:

> At the forefront of our minds, the obvious signals of violence are acts of crime and terror, civil unrest, international conflict. But we should learn to step back, to disentangle ourselves from the fascinating lure of this directly visible "subjective" violence, violence performed by a clearly identifiable agent. We need to perceive the contours of the background which generates such outbursts. A step back enables us to identify a violence that sustains our very efforts to fight violence and to promote tolerance. (1)

Žižek contrasts "subjective violence" (the violence that has the agency of a particular individual or group) with "systemic" or "objective" violence. He refers to the latter as "the often catastrophic consequences of the smooth functioning of our economic and political systems." Though both are given the attribution of "violent," Žižek explains,

> subjective and objective violence cannot be perceived from the same standpoint: subjective violence is experienced as such against the background of a non-violent zero level. It is seen as a perturbation of the "normal," peaceful state of things. However, objective violence is precisely the violence inherent to this "normal" state of things. Objective violence is invisible since it sustains the very zero-level standard against which we perceive something as subjectively violent. Systemic violence is thus something like the notorious "dark matter" of physics, the counterpart to an all-too-visible subjective violence. It may be invisible, but it has to be taken into account if one is to make sense of what otherwise seem to be "irrational" explosions of subjective violence. (2)

As I have argued, these explosive, most visible forms of violence often are treated as exceptions to the norm, as aberrations and anomalies (Shapiro 2014, 2015). When we consider a school shooter an exception, considering him an absolute abnormality against the background of a "normal," "non-violent" society, we assume that he is not a product of that society; we disavow any connection. But as contemporary Italian philosopher Giorgio Agamben compellingly demonstrates, the exception is not simply an exclusion, but a case of removal, "taken outside (*ex-capere*), and not simply excluded" (1998). The excepted perpetrator, once considered *a part* of the community and its norms, is now *apart* from them. I argue that the consequences of this logic of exceptionality are grave, for they can preclude examination of the normative conditions that may contribute to physically violent acts.

What sets this volume apart from other fine work on violence in education, then, are its attention both to violence's distinctive forms and to its common factors, its multidisciplinary scope and vision, and its attention to violence's contextual nature. The reader will find that these pages also are replete with proposals for responding to and preventing violence in education. But the violence we witness and that is most visible is often generated by broader, more hidden phenomena that provide a context for its more overt forms. So, while specific issues of gun violence, bullying, sexual violence, school safety, and gang violence are addressed directly and extensively, this book shows how these forms of violence are situated in a larger culture – in its linguistic, social, economic, political, and axiological structures and norms. Thus, this is not what often is a kind of response to "an SOS call" (Žižek 2008) of spectacles of physical violence, that considers it, over-simplistically, to be the product of "evil" or "deranged" perpetrators. For we show that there is also an elusive, even invisible, sustaining violence of the larger social sphere.

The *Handbook on Violence in Education: Forms, Factors, and Preventions* contains four sections. Section 1 addresses rampage and targeted school shootings, considering the recent growth in the frequency and lethality of these disturbing, shattering events. This increase has created a new concern that seemingly peaceful, intact communities and institutions may be vulnerable to deadly shootings. The section also shows how common misconceptions have led to prevalent problematic responses and prevention measures. It thus provides new perspectives on the contexts of school shootings, the role of cultural conceptions of masculinity, a case study of a rampage shooter, and productive, restorative modes of response, recovery and prevention.

In the introduction to Section 1, I note how it addresses school shooters' "relationships to their educational, communal, and political environments and to the times in which we live." The contributors, then, examine a "crisis of masculinities" (Kellner), "contextual issues that might make violence more likely" (Cherney and Price), "sociocultural processes" (Rud and Maarhuis), "social-political" conditions (Larkin), differences in "perception and reality of school violence" in the context of historical and current crime data (Fox and Fridel), and "historical, political, linguistic, and social understandings of this devastating phenomenon" (Shapiro). And, while addressing the threat of school shootings, the contributors also point to systemic modes of prevention such as "helping families to raise healthy, well-adjusted children," "improving school and community services, so that all youth receive the benefits of good education, health care, and freedom from crime" (Cornell), and "maintaining a school climate that is conducive for learning" (Fox and Fridel).

In Section 2, researchers and scholars from the fields of communication studies, sociology, criminology, social psychology, and education provide new perspectives, meta-analyses, critiques, and recommendations to address group and gang violence in education. Section 2's editor, Emily Tanner-Smith, points out how this underresearched, exceedingly complex phenomenon has often generated ineffective and destructive policies and practices with disproportionately deleterious, marginalizing effects on young people of color.

In her introduction to Section 2, Tanner-Smith sets the keynote for the contextual nature of group and gang violence, explaining the need for a "socioecological framework for understanding the multitude of individual, peer, family, school, and community-based risk/prospective factors for youth gang involvement." The contributors to this section point us to new policy approaches that show the promise of fostering an inclusive, safer, and healthier educational setting for all. Such approaches become compelling when considered against the backgrounds of "a complicated, interdependent system of relationships between community characteristics (including crime rates), school characteristics (including school climate)" (Ezell), "a socioecological framework to highlight the systemic failures that push vulnerable high-risk youth to flee toward gangs" the ways in which gangs, schools, and violence interact and how these interactions are related to youths' life outcomes (Estrada, Jr. et al.), "the relationship between those who are committing acts of violence and those who are being victimized" (Clark, Pyrooz, and Randa), "a latent 'school social disorder'" (Fisher et al.), "public discourse," (Lester and Evans), "school security–school crime relationships" (Addington and Tanner-Smith), and "contextual factors that may be contributing to these behaviors" (Connell et al.).

Section 3 considers bullying and sexual violence in education. This section's editor, Dorothy L. Espelage, notes that there is much at stake in addressing these public health concerns. The contributors show how bullying and sexual violence are not only harmful to victims, witnesses, perpetrators, and the school community when they occur, but, left without proper, timely intervention and prevention, the risk of long-term psychological problems is high. This section provides precise definitions, current literature reviews, and new recommendations for intervention and prevention as alternatives to practices that have been proven to have minimal success.

A contextual understanding of violence, thus, continues in Section 3, as Espelage's introduction describes the "association between bullying and school climate." The section's contributors consider the contexts of the "peer, school, family, and larger societal issues that are associated with bullying perpetration and/or victimization for youths" (Nickerson, Guttman, and VanHout), "cultural norms for sexuality and gender expression" (Payne and Smith), "rape culture," "our patriarchal culture," and "sexist, racist, heteronormative, misogynistic frameworks" (Katz and McGuire), "social challenges," "reproduction of many of the very norms and cultural factors that marginalize the girls in the first place and that should be challenged," (Moletsane and Mitchell), "familial characteristics and the home environment (Holt et al.), "a climate where students feel safe, are connected and engaged with their school, and feel comfortable in their physical environment (Hong, Espelage, and Lee), "peer and school norms," and "social connectedness" (Forber-Pratt and Espelage).

Section 4 explores the nature of structural, systemic violence in education. Structural violence includes deliberate, habitual, implicit, and often unnoticed educational inequities and aggressive conduct based on gender, race, socioeconomic class, sexual orientation, and race, among others. Calling these dimensions violent may seem to be an overextension of the term. Yet, the contributors offer conceptions of violence that include our often unseen, self-reproducing social, political, economic, and linguistic frameworks. While the previous sections also address these more elusive, but powerful, contextual dimensions of forms of violence, Section 4 focuses specifically on the very nature of schools, social media, racism, police violence, gender violence, cultural norms of male honor, and peace education.

Introducing Section 4, I explain that the contributors expose, and seek to depose, forms of violence that are suppressing human expression, that are objectifying, conflict producing, and supposedly honorific. The section thus shows how violence is situated in social meanings that exist in American society (Warnick, Kim, and Robinson), in discourse itself (Ruitenberg), in cultural conceptions of male honor (Shuffelton), in "symbolic subsumptions of unique individual beings under pre-established categories and headings" and "contemporary economic, neoliberal ideologies" (Keehn and Boyles), and in "the continued injustices perpetrated on historically marginalized communities" (Ragland). Responses are proposed that include "public pedagogy" (Ruitenberg), the educational place for "emotion as potentially … supportive of resistance to inequity" (Zembylas), "a well-established culture of peace and democracy that can address power imbalances and structural and cultural violence" (Cremin and Guilherme), and "critical," "truth-telling" "voices and approaches from the margins extending and reaching out to the broader public to offer authentic experiences that inform us of the most pressing concerns of this society" (Ragland).

With penetrating analyses and new proposals, the *Handbook on Violence in Education* offers the opportunity to take a fresh look at this troubling, complex phenomenon. We hope that this volume's multidisciplinary, multilevel vision of violence's forms and factors will help us respond with sober, well-informed, well-grounded efforts for understanding, preventing, and responding.

References

Agamben, Giorgio. 1998. *Homo Sacer: Sovereign Power and Bare Life*. Translated by Daniel Heller-Roazen. Stanford, CA: Stanford University Press.

Arendt, Hannah. 1969. *On Violence*. New York: Harcourt.

Bernstein, Richard J. 2013. *Violence: Thinking Without Banisters*. Oxford: Polity Press.

Caret, Robert L. 2013. University of Massachusetts President's Statement on Task Force Report, August 15, 2013. http://www.umassd.edu/media/umassdartmouth/officeofthechancellor/pdfs/rlc_taskforce_statement.pdf (accessed March 10, 2017).

Klein, Jessie. 2012. *The Bully Society: School Shootings and the Crisis of Bullying in America's Schools*. New York: NYU Press.

Shapiro, H. 2015. "When the Exception Is the Rule: School Shootings, Bare Life, and the Sovereign Self." *Educational Theory* 65(4), 423–440.

Shapiro, H. 2014. "Exposing and Deposing the Nexus: School Shootings and the Sovereign Exception." *Philosophy of Education Society Yearbook* 15, 260–268.

Sorel, George. 1925. *Reflections on Violence*. London: George Allen and Unwin,. https://archive.org/details/reflectionsonvio00soreuoft (last accessed October 3, 2017).

Virginia Tech. 2013. University Statement on Decision by the Supreme Court of Virginia, October 31, 2013. https://vtnews.vt.edu/articles/2013/10/103113-president-statement.html (last accessed October 3, 2017).

Žižek, Slavoj. 2008. *Violence: Six Sideways Reflections*. New York: Picador.

Section 1

School Shootings
Section Editor: Harvey Shapiro

Section 1 Introduction

Broadening the Context, Refocusing the Response

Harvey Shapiro

Sandy Hook, Columbine, Sparks, Red Lake, Oak Creek, Columbine, and, even more recently, Toqueville High School (in Grasse, France) and South Carolina's Townville Elementary School, Benton, Kentucky's Marshall County High School, and Parkland, Florida's Marjory Stoneman Douglas High School. This partial list of school shootings continues to present us with questions of "how": *How* could this happen – and in a school or college campus, of all places? *How* might education respond? *How* can we prevent what has become an increasing frequency of rampage and targeted school shootings? *How* can we help our children, school personnel, and communities heal in the wake of such trauma? *How* can we begin to understand? Asking these questions, we seek guidance for coping, comprehending, preventing, and responding.

Rather than considering these questions from the perspective of one discipline alone, we respond to these questions from a wide range of conceptual and disciplinary angles. The authors of this section are experts from the fields of criminology, sociology, philosophy, education, social theory, cultural studies, ethics, and forensic psychology. Without presuming to have conclusive answers explaining these tragedies, this section's contributors provide compelling contextual understandings and new directions for policy and practice, revealing a complex matrix of often overlooked factors that contribute to school shootings and suggesting thoughtful, well-grounded measures for prevention and response.

Equally important, the authors address prevalent misconceptions, misrepresentations, questionable, counterproductive responses, and their unintended, but harmful consequences. When we hear of a school shooting we become preoccupied, justifiably, with issues of school security, mental health, response time, and deterrence. These important concerns, however, can foreclose responses to pervasive underlying problems. By beginning to expose the latter, we offer new, ambitious, hopeful directions for understanding, preventing, and responding to the scourge of this form of devastating violence.

We all sense with empathy the deep pain, anger, and resolve of survivors and their loved ones. Their quests for safer school environments are exemplified in Sandy Hook Elementary School parents' and Newtown, Connecticut's community leaders' continuing campaign to educate school personnel and students to "know the signs of planning a shooting," asserting that "gun violence is preventable when you know the signs" (Sandy Hook Promise 2015). The ability to recognize signals of a potentially imminent

The Wiley Handbook on Violence in Education: Forms, Factors, and Preventions, First Edition.
Edited by Harvey Shapiro.
© 2018 John Wiley & Sons, Inc. Published 2018 by John Wiley & Sons, Inc.

repetition of anything akin to the seismic shock of the 2012 rampage school shooting and similar tragedies may be of great value.

As will become evident in this section's chapters, there are other actions that could prove efficacious. For example, at this writing, the Connecticut Supreme Court has consented to hear an appeal of the Newtown victims' families on their previously dismissed wrongful-death lawsuit against the manufacturer of the AR-15 assault rifle used by Adam Lanza in his December 14, 2012 shooting rampage at their children's school. Also named in the lawsuit are the weapon's distributor and the store where the weapon had been purchased by the shooter's mother (Altimari 2017). One online retailer markets the AR-15 assault rifle with the service mark, "Shoot now. Pay later[SM]" (GrabAGun.com 2017). Also used in the San Bernardino, California and Aurora, Colorado shootings, the large-magazine AR-15 is called "America's Rifle" by the National Rifle Association (Altimari 2017).

Despite the complexity of school shootings' contexts and circumstances, there are significant, indisputable facts. As sociologist Ralph Larkin points out in Chapter 4, included among these are "that rampage school shooters are almost all male" and "that the vast majority of school shootings happen in the United States." And these additional points are beyond contention:

- The number of rampage school shootings worldwide has increased in recent decades, from six in the 1970s, to 11 in the 1980s, to 36 in the 1990s, to 57 between 2000 and 2013 (Böckler et al. 2013).
- Since 1925, the United States has had 76 rampage school shootings. The country with the next largest number is Germany, with 8 during the same period (Böckler et al. 2013).
- These do not include the significant number of planned attacks that were averted (Madfis 2012). On February 1, 2017, for example, police in Florida arrested two teenagers for allegedly plotting what could have been a mass shooting the next day in their school. Other students reported overhearing them say that the attack would be "bigger than Columbine" (Hanna and Ansari 2017).

This section's contributors provide new ways of interpreting and responding to these and many other alarming facts. Much recent research has minimized the shooters' relationships to their educational, communal, and political environments and to the times in which we live, searching instead for a typology of common psychological profiles and proposing intensified security measures. The media, too, often overlooks relational, contextual understandings, tending to focus, instead, on spectacularized images and perpetrators' mental illnesses and manifestos. Thus, a common response has been increased security measures, lockdown drills, the arming of staff, and defensive protocols. And there have been distorted, even false, characterizations in academia, as well, such as this recent one in a social science and policy journal: "These days, it is *not uncommon* for a teenager or a young man to walk into his present or former school on a shooting rampage" (Frank 2016, emphasis added). After reading these chapters, we hope our readers with recognize the inaccurate or misdirecting nature and effects of such depictions and hyperbolic claims.

In Chapter 1, criminologists James Fox and Emma Fridel argue that caricaturing school shootings as not being *uncommon* is the source of *common* misconceptions that schools today are unsafe places. They show how this disproportionally inflated understanding of the risk of school shootings has spawned widespread counterproductive responses, such as oversurveillance, zero tolerance measures, the increasing ubiquity of school security personnel, more simulated drills and lockdowns, firearms for staff, student profiling, and unwarranted, draconian punishments. The authors demonstrate how the unintended, but harmful, consequences of such increased measures are heightened fear, tension, a confrontational school climate, achievement declines, increased dropout rates, and psychological problems. They provide a broader perspective on school shootings, suggesting compelling alternative approaches and measures that consider school architectural design, the size of the student body, and school climate.

In Chapter 2, Dewey Cornell, a forensic clinical psychologist, responds to the shortcomings of widespread profiling, metal detection, and surveillance measures, presenting his well-developed, increasingly utilized, evidence-based threat assessment approach to prevention. The Virginia Student Threat Assessment Guidelines is showcased as an appropriate way to recognize and respond to students' threats of violence, while placing those threats in the context of the actual relative infrequency of violent crimes in educational settings. Arguing compellingly for the heterogeneity of student threats, Cornell shows how these threats are not generalizable and require thoughtful consideration of each individual context, avoiding a knee-jerk alarm when a student makes a threat or fits a kind of profile. Beyond threat assessment, Cornell then argues for broader prevention measures: Support for families' child-rearing efforts, strengthening student services, addressing socioeconomic inequities, and considering the particular context of an individual student's conduct.

In Chapter 3, Douglas Kellner, an expert in cultural studies and a critical educational theorist, builds on his work on the cultural linkages between masculinity and school shootings. He demonstrates that school shootings take place within the context of two interdependent, critical sociocultural fault lines – "a crisis of masculinities and an out-of-control gun culture" – showing how these intersecting crises are disseminated in the form of media spectacles. Kellner argues for responses that include such ambitious undertakings as reconstructing the cultural meaning of masculinity, addressing the need for more restrictive gun laws, and designing curricula of empathic compassion, caring, and media literacy.

In Chapter 4, sociologist Ralph Larkin expands on his research on rampage school shootings, considering their sociocultural meanings. In a focused case study of a school shooter, he suggests profound linkages between cultural conceptions of masculinity and rampage school shootings. In doing so, he exposes what is easily obscured by those who overemphasize a perpetrator's mental illness. Larkin argues that the shooter is heavily influenced by a growing American sociocultural script, situated within "subcultures of hate" and fueled by the gun lobby. Far from being senseless acts or vengeful, uncontrolled outbursts, these are carefully planned forms of self-advertisement and expressions of ideological affinity with previous perpetrators. And, rather than propose more security measures, Larkin proposes a broader agenda that includes addressing the gun-lobby-supported subcultures' "scripts for rampages." He then goes further, calling for the need to "support feminist and LBGT organizations that offer a more expansive and peace-oriented view of masculinity," and, even more broadly and ambitiously, "to make America a more inclusive and egalitarian society, so that fewer young men feel isolated and rejected."

In Chapter 5, I explain the problematic communal and institutional disavowals of shooters' being formed within institutions and social milieus. Shooters are often "ex-cepted," cast out as disconnected human aberrations. Examining school shootings from the standpoint of a critique of instrumental violence, I argue that school shootings emerge in conceptual, socio-cultural, and political contexts in which governmental, military, and police violence are deemed justifiable. This kind of instrumental justification for state violence, then, extends to juridical, social, psychological, and physical violence throughout our society. In the name of the law (the Second Amendment), the gun lobby invokes the purportedly unfettered right to bear arms. In the name of a "stand your ground" law, a shooter claims the right to kill. In the name of justice and honor, a vengeful shooter sprays his bullets. These examples are but extensions of instrumental justifications for state-sponsored violence such as when, in the name of sovereign democracy, a government colonizes, tyrannizes, suppresses, or presumes hegemony over people's lives (and deaths). I seek, then, to open a field for human action and educational response that might free us from instrumental justifications of violence and from the logic of the exception.

Kristeen Cherney and Margaret Price, in Chapter 6, continue the emphasis on socio-cultural contexts by exposing the myth that there are recognizable mental health profiles that indicate a potential perpetrator. Cherney and Price, representing the fields of rhetoric and discourse analysis, show how an isolated, decontextualized approach, often exacerbated by media reports on the perpetrators' psychological diagnoses, is ineffective, unsupported by research evidence, and fraught with collateral problematic consequences, including stigmatizing those with mental illnesses.

In this section's final chapter, A.G. Rud and Patricia Maarhuis turn our attention toward recovery, resilience, and hope. They argue for a "pivot" toward "the interaction between continual social reconstruction, as well as adjustment and growth for individuals, communities, and spaces of associated living." The authors address a glaring gap in the literature on school shootings, as they examine instances of "purposeful enactment of relational aesthetic response by teachers and administrators, working together in wake of these devastating violent acts to reconstruct their community anew." Drawing on John Dewey's pragmatism and theory of aesthetic experience, they consider artistic responses of young survivors, from whom much can be learned about resiliency, community, and hope. Going well beyond conventional increased security measures, new kinds of questions are posed for us in the wake of school shootings: "Who are we in this place? Who are we together? How are we to teach and learn after this shooting?"

Respecting the survivors and the memories of the innocent, no simplistic solutions are offered. Rather, this section's contributors provide bold new directions for understanding, responding, and preventing school shootings. In careful, multidisciplinary analyses and innovative proposals, this first section of the *Handbook on Violence in Education* addresses the scourge of these atrocities and tragedies that occur in what should be among our society's most comforting, inspiring, and safe spaces for learning and growth.

References

Böckler, N., Seeger, T., Sitzer, P., and Heitmeyer, W. 2013. "School Shootings: Conceptual Framework and International Empirical Trends." In *School Shootings: International Research, Case Studies, and Concepts for Prevention*, edited by N. Böckler et al. New York: Springer.

Frank, T. 2016. "The US in a Changing World Order." *Society* 53(5), 531–537.

GrabAGun.com. 2017. http://grabagun.com/firearms/ar-15-ar10-and-other-ar/complete-ar-rifles.html (accessed April 3, 2017).

Hanna, J. and Ansari, A. 2017. "Florida Teens Accused of Planning School Shooting." CNN, January 27, 2017. http://www.cnn.com/2017/01/27/us/florida-school-shooting-plot/index.html (last accessed October 3, 2017).

Altimari, D. 2017. "Sandy Hook Parents File 1st Argument to Supreme Court in Gun Lawsuit Case." *Hartford Courant*, March 1, 2017. http://www.courant.com/news/connecticut/hc-sandy-hook-supreme-court-lawsuit-20170301-story.html (last accessed October 3, 2017).

Madfis, E. 2012. "Averting the Unlikely: Fearing, Assessing, and Preventing Threats of Rampage Violence in American Public Schools." Unpublished doctoral dissertation. Northeastern University, Boston, Massachusetts.

Sandy Hook Promise. 2015. Know the Signs Programs. http://www.sandyhookpromise.org/prevention_programs (last accessed October 3, 2017).

1

The Menace of School Shootings in America

Panic and Overresponse

James Alan Fox and Emma E. Fridel

The Changing Landscape

There was a time, not very long ago, when the "three Rs" was a catchy reference to the trilogy of basic skills (i.e., reading, 'riting and 'rithmetic). But over the past quarter century, several major shockwaves involving multiple-victim school shootings have put the concern for student safety and security on par with scholastics. In the modern-day climate of fear, the "three Rs" has also become about risk, readiness, and response with regard to gun violence.

For many generations of students, schools were seen as a place of safety. Although schoolyard fistfights and bullying had long been commonplace, gun violence was hardly a serious problem. By the early 1990s, however, middle schools and high schools, particularly those in urban locations, confronted the spillover of gang-related gun violence from the city streets to the school hallways. The spike in gang violence within schools prompted the US Congress to pass legislation establishing schools as "gun-free zones," with heavy penalties for possessing a firearm at or within close proximity of a school.

The focus of concern and the locus of fear changed suddenly and dramatically in 1996 when a 14-year-old student from rural Moses Lake, Washington, who was obsessed with a school shooter in a fictional Stephen King tale, mimicked the actions of his hero by killing his algebra teacher and two classmates during a classroom hostage-taking. The Moses Lake massacre then set the stage for a series of multiple homicides at the hands of alienated adolescents over the next five years (as reflected in the first eight cases of multiple-victim school homicides listed in Table 1.1), including the infamous and massive shooting spree at Columbine High. The surge in bloodshed impacting schools across the country impelled the venerable CBS anchorman Dan Rather (2001) to declare school shootings an emerging epidemic.

The string of deadly school shootings occurred during the time frame when the now-expired federal assault weapons ban was still in force. President Bill Clinton and many Americans had hoped the 1994 prohibition against certain military-style weapons would reduce the scourge of mass killings that had surfaced at post offices, restaurants, and shopping malls as well as schools. However, with the notable exception of the Columbine High assailants, all of the young school shooters of this era had used

The Wiley Handbook on Violence in Education: Forms, Factors, and Preventions, First Edition.
Edited by Harvey Shapiro.
© 2018 John Wiley & Sons, Inc. Published 2018 by John Wiley & Sons, Inc.

Table 1.1 Multiple-victim school shootings, 1992–2016.

Date	School, location	Shooter(s), age(s)	Victims killed			Victims wounded	Total victims
			Students	Staff	Others		
February 2, 1996	Frontier Junior High School Moses Lake, WA	Barry Loukaitis, 14	2	1	0	1	4
February 19, 1997	Bethel Regional High School Bethel, AL	Evan Ramsey, 16	1	1	0	2	4
October 1, 1997	Pearl High School Pearl, MS	Luke Woodham, 16	2	0	1	7	10
December 1, 1997	Heath High School West Paducah, KY	Michael Carneal, 14	3	0	0	5	8
March 24, 1998	Westside Middle School Jonesboro, AR	Mitchell Johnson, 13 Andrew Golden, 11	4	1	0	10	15
May 21, 1998	Thurston High School Springfield, OR	Kipland Kinkel, 15	2	0	2	25	29
April 20, 1999	Columbine High School Littleton, CO	Eric Harris, 18 Dylan Klebold, 17	12	1	0	23	36
March 5, 2001	Santana High School Santee, CA	Charles "Andy" Williams, 15	2	0	0	23	15
March 21, 2005	Red Lake High School Red Lake Indian Reservation, MN	Jeffrey Weise, 16	5	2	2	5	14
October 2, 2006	West Nickel Mines School Nickel Mines, PA	Charles Roberts IV, 32	5	0	0	5	10
February 27, 2012	Chardon High School Chardon, OH	Thomas "TJ" Lane III, 17	3	0	0	3	6
December 14, 2012	Sandy Hook Elementary School Newtown, CT	Adam Lanza, 20	20	6	1	2	29
October 24, 2014	Marysville-Pilchuck High School Marysville, WA	Jaylen Fryberg, 15	4	0	0	3	7
September 28, 2016	Townville Elementary School Townville, SC	Jesse Osborn, 14	1	0	1	3	5

Note: Incidents with 4+ victims and at least two deaths (not including the assailant) semi-automatic handguns or long guns, which were not illegal under the federal ban but still sufficiently capable of causing substantial death and injury.

The series of school massacres energized gun control advocates, but did little to silence gun rights proponents. One ultra-conservative group exploited the shootings as political fodder to attack Clinton's gun control efforts. Assembling a map showing the era's school shootings as falling almost precisely on two straight lines that intersected at Hope, Arkansas (Clinton's birthplace), the Cutting Edge Ministries claimed there was a conspiracy involving Clinton and a handful of young assailants designed to turn public opinion against the Second Amendment and the right of private gun ownership.

The September 11, 2001 terrorist attack on America then shifted public discourse and political debate from school safety to national security. Meanwhile, schools enjoyed a respite of several years from shooting rampages. Unfortunately, any notion that the carnage was a problem of the past was quickly dispelled early in the 2006–2007 school year when three frightening incidents occurred within a week. Unlike the student-perpetrated shootings of the 1990s, two of the cases involved adult intruders who capitalized on the vulnerability of schools by taking children hostage. The October 2, 2006 siege upon a one-room Amish schoolhouse in rural Pennsylvania was particularly tragic, as five girls were killed and five others wounded before the 32-year-old assailant turned the gun on himself.

This second wave of bloodshed prompted President George W. Bush, a strong gun rights supporter, hurriedly to convene a special White House summit on school violence. However, the elephant in the room – guns and gun control – was explicitly off limits for the conference proceedings, replaced with the overarching theme of character education.

The focus on school safety then gave way, at least for a period of several years, to worries about the nation's economic crisis following the 2008 stock market plunge. The economy did eventually recover, of course. And, sadly, the issue of school safety reemerged with a vengeance in December 2012, when the nation collectively mourned the deaths of 20 children and 6 adults at a Newtown, Connecticut elementary school (Sandy Hook) at the hands of a local resident who had attended the school during his formative years.

The Sandy Hook massacre, and the issue of school shootings in general, dominated the news and the national discourse, so much so that the Associated Press named it the top news topic of the year. The carnage at Sandy Hook eclipsed another Sandy, the devastating hurricane that stormed the eastern coast. Hurricane Sandy actually resulted in five times as many deaths of Americans as did the shooting with a similar name. However, unlike the storm, the Connecticut school massacre claimed the lives of young children, causing it to have a decidedly different impact on the nation's consciousness.

The other significant distinction between the two Sandys surrounded the source of the devastation, one being of natural origin and the other resulting from the deliberate actions of one deeply disturbed gunman. The belief that the massacre was preventable gave new life to the debate over gun control as well as related issues of access to mental health treatment and the adequacy of school security.

Perception and Reality of School Violence

Each multiple-victim shooting has reinforced a sense that schools are under siege. While calling the spate of school shootings an "epidemic" may have been more hyperbole than reality, there is little question that the level of fear and anxiety over school safety has spread wide and fast, particularly in the immediate aftermath of the most high-profile episodes. With impressions especially impacted by the double-digit death tolls at Columbine and Sandy Hook, there remains pervasive concern among school officials and parents of school-age children that school violence is definitely a significant problem, if not reaching epidemic proportions.

Notwithstanding the unmitigated horror and outrage associated with the 13 school-yard massacres over the past two decades presented in Table 1.1, the overwhelming majority of school homicides involve a single victim and single perpetrator.

Unfortunately, no "official" (i.e., "known to the police") national data series for school crime exists. However, there are available several sources of data pertaining to school violence, based either on student/staff surveys or news media reports, all of which vary with regard to their coverage, completeness, and accuracy. Arguably, the most accurate data available come from incident reports of school-associated violent deaths initially maintained by the National School Safety Center – a private organization established in 1984 initially through federal funding directed by President Ronald Reagan. Then, in 2010, the data collection and reporting were assumed by the Centers for Disease Control. Although these data are not exactly "official," school-related homicides are presumably always reported in some media outlet somewhere, and thus relatively easy to identify.

Between the 1992–1993 and 2014–2015 school years, there were a total of 235 shootings at primary and secondary schools in the United States in which at least one victim was killed. These included shootings by students (such as the Columbine massacre) as well as assailants not directly connected with the school setting (such as the Sandy Hook mass murder). Overall, these shooting incidents claimed of the lives of 317 people, 217 of whom were students. Nearly half of the remaining victims were administrators, faculty, or other school employees, and the others included parents and individuals not connected with the school. Over 70% of the shootings took place at a high school, and the remainder were slightly more likely to have occurred at a middle school than at an elementary school. In terms of location, nearly 40% of the shootings occurred in the South, which is slightly above its share of the population, with all other regions roughly proportional to their population shares as well.

In terms of victim characteristics, over 70% of the victims were male, reflecting the large share of cases involving conflict between two male students, sometimes over gang rivalries. In shooting incidents involving multiple victims, cases in which the victims were less likely to have been specifically targeted, the gender split was virtually even. Just over half the victims were 15 to 19 years old; however, focusing on student victims alone, older adolescents accounted for 70% of the victims, consistent with the predominance of shootings at high school.

Table 1.2 displays annual counts for several measures based on these shooting episodes (see also Figure 1.1). In addition, the rate of homicide victimization per million students is calculated based on annual public and private school enrollment figures. Contrary to the impression that many Americans have formed from watching media saturation surrounding high-profile school massacres, the number of incidents and of victims – both overall and students only – were appreciably larger in the early 1990s, when concerns about school violence were not center stage in public discourse. In reality, schools are not only safe relative to other settings in which children typically spend their time, but are growing safer.

Without minimizing the pain and suffering that these incidents cause the victims, their families, and their entire communities, the rate of victimization is remarkably low.

Table 1.2 School shootings and mass shootings, 1992–1993 through 2014–2015.

School year	Fatal shootings			Fatal multiple-victim shootings			Students killed per million
	Incidents	Total victims	Student victims	Incidents	Total victims	Student victims	
92/93	33	35	27	2	4	1	0.55
93/94	31	32	21	1	2	0	0.42
94/95	12	12	10	0	0	0	0.20
95/96	17	21	16	4	8	5	0.32
96/97	12	14	10	2	4	1	0.19
97/98	18	27	21	5	14	13	0.40
98/99	4	17	16	2	15	14	0.30
99/00	9	10	5	1	2	1	0.09
00/01	11	12	5	1	2	2	0.09
01/02	2	2	1	0	0	0	0.02
02/03	6	7	6	1	2	1	0.11
03/04	21	26	12	5	10	3	0.22
04/05	9	15	8	1	7	5	0.15
05/06	5	5	4	0	0	0	0.07
06/07	8	12	10	1	5	5	0.18
07/08	3	4	4	1	2	2	0.07
08/09	6	6	4	0	0	0	0.07
09/10	5	5	3	0	0	0	0.05
10/11	4	5	1	1	2	0	0.02
11/12	2	4	3	1	3	3	0.05
12/13	4	30	20	2	28	20	0.36
13/14	7	7	4	0	0	0	0.07
14/15	6	9	6	1	4	4	0.11
Total	235	317	217	32	114	80	0.18

At its height in 1992–1993, partially reflecting the spillover effect of gang violence, the homicide risk for students was one in 2 million. After that, the rate declined steadily throughout the 1990s. Since 2000, the risk has remained relatively flat – with the exception of the 2012–2013 academic year during which 20 students and 6 adults were killed at Sandy Hook – with an average risk as low as one in 10 million.

Part of the reason for the disconnect between incidence and public awareness involves the changing nature of school-related lethal violence between the early and late 1990s, specifically the emergence of mass shootings and multiple-victim homicides. Whereas single-victim homicides, particularly those that occurred during the early 1990s when the rate was at its highest, tended to be publicized only locally, the string of multiple

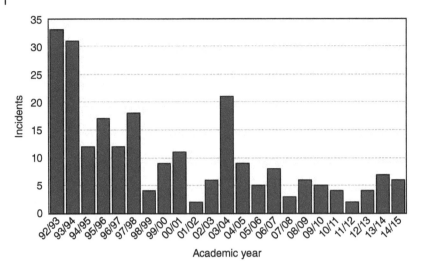

Figure 1.1 Fatal shooting incidents in schools, 1992–1993 through 2014–2015.

homicides that took place between 1996 and 2001 became a national obsession. Each new incident attracted massive publicity across the country (and internationally), creating an unprecedented sense of urgency and alarm. The media focus, including cover photos in prominent magazines, also placed the young assailants in the limelight, making them undeserving heroes in the eyes of at least a few similarly minded youngsters. Thus, although Dan Rather's characterization of the school shooting problem as an epidemic may have been overstated in terms of the risk, the description was unfortunately on target in terms of the contagion effect (Coleman 2004). Moreover, not only did the media exposure encourage copycat murders and countless aborted attempts (see Towers et al. 2015), it had a powerful impact on policy and practices related to school safety and security, not necessarily for the better.

Even though the increased level of concern expressed by parents of school-age children was understandable, their fears were also well out of proportion to the actual risk. Table 1.3 places the risk of school homicide in context with other causes of death for children, based on mortality data from the National Center for Health Statistics (NCHS) for the years 1999 to 2013. Clearly, swimming pools and bicycles represent a far greater peril for the safety of children than their classmates. This would suggest a greater benefit in having more lifeguards at pools rather than more armed guards at schools. Likewise, requiring all children to wear bicycle helmets would certainly be more advantageous that equipping them with bullet-resistant backpacks. Focusing specifically on homicide, the bottom panel of the table confirms that school is in fact a very safe place for children. Less than 1% of murders of children and adolescents occur at school, where they typically spend more than one-quarter of their waking hours during a calendar year.

The exclusive focus here on school-associated homicides does not mean that non-fatal shootings are unimportant. In fact, non-fatal school shootings far outnumber those in which a student or staff member is killed. Specifically, of the 86 shootings in elementary and secondary schools from 2013 through 2015 identified in the crowd-source database maintained by Everytown for Gun Safety (2015), a gun control

Table 1.3 Cause of death by age group, 1999–2013.

Cause of death	Age group			
	5–9	10–14	15–19	Total
Pool drowning	777	417	447	1,641
Lightening and other storms	56	87	108	251
Animal attack	80	40	26	146
Bus accident	16	33	37	86
Bicycle accident	533	980	887	2,400
Firearm accident	221	486	1,268	1,975
Accidental fall	231	317	1,215	1,763
School shooting	*25*	*13*	*75*	*113*
Homicide	650	1,601	21,797	24,048
Percent at school	3.8%	0.8%	0.3%	0.5%

advocacy group that grew out of Mayors Against Illegal Guns, only 19 (or 22%) resulted in the death of one or more victims.

It has been noted, based on the Everytown tally, that there was, on average, about one school shooting per week in the United States in the three years after the December 2012 Sandy Hook massacre (including suicides, accidental shootings, cases without injury to anyone, and all school types from preschool through college). Of course, that claim can be misinterpreted to suggest a far worse situation than exists in reality, as the public tends to imagine the worst (horrors like Sandy Hook) when confronted with this statistic. Not only is the typical school shooting in the Everytown database significantly less serious than the kind of multiple-victim rampage that dominates the news, but with the limited window of just three years, it is not possible to draw any conclusions about whether the rate is increasing, decreasing, or is relatively unchanged.

The Brady Center to Prevent Gun Violence has been gathering data on school shootings, including non-fatal incidents, since 1998. Unfortunately, the less severe incidents reported only in local newspapers are easily overlooked, especially in the earlier years when these news outlets were not digitized and searchable. This would explain the fact that, over time, an increasing share of the Brady Center cases were non-fatal. Thus, it is not possible to identify trends reliably because the availability of information in less serious, non-fatal school shootings has changed over time. The apparent rise in the number of school shootings since the late 1990s in the Brady Center data may reflect an increase in data completeness rather than any change in the actual incidence.

Fear and Overresponse

The string of school shootings that marked the late 1990s changed the face of public education, and had many Americans questioning their faith in the notion that schools were safe places for children to grow intellectually and socially. Each episode of schoolyard terror – at least those that were highlighted, if not hyped, by the national media – incited widespread fear, dread, and anxiety. Each recurrence of the seemingly same old story of some alienated adolescent running amok in the hallways of his school intensified concerns that school shootings were not just an occasional and frightening aberration, but a new and persistent crime wave that should place schools everywhere on high alert.

In reaction to the flurry of school shootings in the late 1990s, the Gallup polling organization incorporated school violence and safety as a regular theme in its ongoing program of research measuring changes in public opinion. Gallup had not examined the issue since 1977, when a quarter of parents surveyed across America indicated a concern for their children's safety at school. Twenty years later, Gallup routinized its questioning regarding school violence and safety in surveys coinciding with the start of each school year, as well as at exceptional points in time immediately following certain widely publicized school rampages.

Figure 1.2 summarizes the overall results of the series of Gallup polls related to a question presented to parents about whether they fear for the safety of their oldest child while he or she is at school. Clearly, the Columbine shooting had a strong effect on the respondents' sense of security for their children, as the majority of respondents (55%) surveyed on the day following the April 20, 1999 massacre indicated feeling fearful.

As Americans faced new challenges during the decade after Columbine (precipitated by the 9/11 attack on America), the school-related fears of parents gradually subsided, despite a spike of 45% in the survey taken immediately after the multiple shooting at Santana High School in Santee, California. By the late 2000s, as the level of panic and media hype dissipated, the percentage of parents worried about their child's safety settled back to 26%, just about the same level as a decade earlier.

The December 2012 massacre at Sandy Hook – the deadliest school massacre in the United States except for the 1927 bombing of a Michigan elementary school that killed 45, including 38 children – resulted in but a modest jump in the percentage being fearful (from one-quarter to one-third). Perhaps Americans have grown somewhat accustomed to, although surely not tolerant of, the occasional incident of multiple fatalities of students.

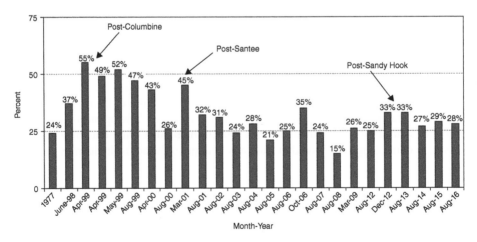

Figure 1.2 Percent of parents fearful of oldest child's safety while at school. *Source:* Data from Gallup News Service.

Despite the relatively low statistical risk, the extensive, sensationalized, and ubiqui-tous news coverage of certain high-profile school shootings (particularly those in largely white, suburban communities) has raised the level of panic and fear. Because of advances in communications technology and the emergence of 24-hour news channels with fleets of satellite trucks, dreadful images of mass murder can be transmitted live to viewers far and wide, making it seem as if the horror is taking place in their own backyards (Heath and Gilbert 1996).

Bracy and Kupchik (2009) examined the way in which school shootings and violence were portrayed in the media between 2000 and 2006. They observed that the media repeatedly reminded the public about the Columbine massacre, suggesting that such shootings were a random, unpredictable, and growing menace. They also found that stories were presented out of context, as they failed to include the data on the degree of risk, particularly ignoring the rarity of such episodes. At the same time as the media were exploiting this issue, students themselves were reporting that they were experiencing less crime in schools than previously. Despite the safer reality, security issues remained a major priority for school systems and families alike.

Target Hardening

The immediate response to deadly shootings in schools is typically a call for enhanced physical security (see Lassiter and Perry 2009; Trump 2011). In the short term, access control and close surveillance may calm the fears of an anxious public. Yet, in the long run, it is equally important to avoid transforming comfortable places for learning into imposing fortresses.

Despite the safer reality, school systems around the country reacted aggressively to prevent another Columbine. As a result, the majority of middle and high school chil-dren spend a large portion of their day in a locked building with armed guards, video surveillance, and random inspections of their possessions.

Table 1.4 identifies the most common methods implemented by middle and high school administrators to address the perceived need to bolster security at their facilities. These figures are based on observations by students, aged 12 to 18, at schools across the country concerning the prevalence of technology and supervision aimed at reducing the danger they face in their daily efforts to get an education. As such, the data reflect the percentage of students reporting the existence of safety strategies at their schools, not the percentage of schools that employ such methods.

Codes of conduct, visitor sign-in, and hallway supervision are nearly universal, part of the educational environment for at least 90% of middle school and high school students. Nearly 70% of our young people spend their school days under the watchful eyes of security guards or armed police officers. It is of note that the widespread use of these measures has not diminished in the years since the 1999 Columbine massacre, even though the incidence of fatal school shootings has declined.

Based on student reports, the use of security cameras doubled, from 38% in 2001 to 77% in 2013, while the extent to which students confront locked entrances and exits increased from 49% to 76%. Although not quite so dramatically, nearly all the other measures of school security increased over the 12-year time span. With consistently over half of all students reporting locker checks, a grim picture of life in a secured environment emerges.

Table 1.4 Percentage of students aged 12–18 who reported selected security measures at school.

Security measure	2001 %	2003 %	2005 %	2007 %	2009 %	2011 %	2013 %	2015 %
Metal detectors	8.7	10.1	10.7	10.1	10.6	11.2	11.0	12.3
Locker checks	53.5	53.0	52.9	53.6	53.8	53.0	52.0	52.9
Security cameras to monitor the school	38.5	47.9	57.6	66.0	70.0	76.7	76.7	82.5
Security guards and/or assigned police officers	63.6	69.6	67.9	68.8	68.1	69.8	70.4	69.5
Other staff/adult supervision in the hallway	88.3	90.6	89.8	90.0	90.6	88.9	90.5	89.5
Students required to wear badges or picture ID	21.2	22.5	24.7	24.3	23.4	24.8	26.2	23.9
A code of student conduct	95.1	95.3	95.1	95.9	95.6	95.7	95.9	95.7
Locked entrance or exit doors during the day	48.8	52.8	54.2	60.9	64.3	64.5	75.8	78.2
A requirement that visitors sign in	90.2	91.7	92.7	94.3	94.3	94.9	95.8	90.2

Although generally effective in protecting a student population, most security measures serve only as a minor inconvenience for those who are determined to cause mayhem (see Fox and Burstein 2010; Rocque 2012; Trump 2000). At the time of the mass shooting, Columbine High School had both a video surveillance system and armed police, neither of which deterred Dylan Klebold and Eric Harris from carrying out their murderous plan. Two unarmed security guards monitoring a metal detector at the entrance to Red Lake Senior High School on the first day of spring 2005 did not prevent 16-year-old Jeffrey Weise from killing five fellow students and a teacher. He simply shot one of the guards to death and sent the other one scrambling before walking through the metal detector on his way to infamy. In the West Side Middle School shooting in Jonesboro, Arkansas, 11-year-old Andrew Golden politely asked to be excused from class, pulled a fire alarm, and then ran to join his 13-year-old partner, Mitchell Johnson, to ambush students and teachers as they streamed out of the building.

Security cameras, access control measures, random searches and the like are designed not only to protect students from harm but to reassure students (and their parents) and alleviate fear. But absent a significant threat, tight security instead projects a feeling of impending danger. A fortress-like environment can be a constant reminder of the risk, however small.

To avoid the negative impact on school climate, surveillance systems in school buildings should be as unobtrusive as possible. This is a lesson that architects of Sandy Hook's new elementary school, replacing the demolished building where the December 2012 massacre took place, have incorporated into their plans. The Sandy Hook reconstruction uses landscape design to create natural and aesthetic separation between the school and visitors, including pushing the building back from the road to provide for more open space. Visitors must cross one of three bridges to reach the front entrance, and first-floor rooms are elevated from ground level. The open space and building configuration allows for easier means of egress should an emergency evacuation ever become necessary.

Apart from Sandy Hook, another promising covert security measure involves the use of acoustic detection systems, technology developed for the military to identify gunfire. For example, the Guardian Indoor Gunshot Detection system employs small and well-disguised sensors throughout the building that would immediately alert first responders of a shooting as well as the shooter's location and movements. It is extremely unlikely that the Guardian system will ever be triggered in any school where it might be installed. Even so, should the unthinkable in fact occur, the speed and efficiency of police response would likely save lives and reduce injuries.

Zero Tolerance

Reacting to the high rate of gun violence involving youth, Congress enacted the Gun-Free Schools Act of 1994, requiring schools that receive federal aid to expel any student in possession of a firearm on school property for at least one year. This zero tolerance approach did not end with firearms, however. States soon expanded their no-nonsense posture to other weapons or could-be weapons, including knives, penknives, and plastic knives as well as scissors and even nail files (Pinard 2003). Hoping to send a stern message, school administrators further broadened mandatory suspension or expulsion policies to include possession of drugs, alcohol, and tobacco, and ultimately to many other violations of school rules and codes of conduct (Hirschfield 2008).

The zero tolerance approach is designed, ostensibly, to achieve several objectives. Most fundamentally, mandatory sanctions are often believed to achieve the greatest deterrent effect, as punishment certainty (rather than severity) tends to carry the greatest weight in the calculus of decision making. At the same time, it is hoped that removing all serious violators of the student code of conduct, no matter what their intent or exact purpose, would create a calmer school climate, ensuring the safety and well-being of the overwhelming majority of the student population. In addition to the stated objectives, school administrators embraced zero tolerance because it eliminated any second-guessing that could potentially follow from discretionary use of sanctions. Similarly, it was also widely assumed to alleviate professional responsibility and civil liability should an underresponse in disciplining a troublemaker lead to more serious acts of aggression. Despite these presumed benefits, zero tolerance lacks the essential element of discretion and level-headed reasoning about the difference between menace and mistake.

The rigid application of zero tolerance punishment has resulted in countless instances of excessive or misplaced punitiveness. A 5-year-old Massachusetts kindergartener was suspended for bringing his souvenir toy gun to school. A 7-year-old Maryland boy was suspended after he nibbled away at his breakfast pastry until it was left shaped like a gun. A Colorado girl, who mistakenly grabbed her mother's lunch bag from the kitchen counter when rushing off to school, was punished after she learned of her error and volunteered the small paring knife that her mother had packed for slicing an apple. A high school junior in Chicago was expelled, taken to jail, and charged with misdemeanor battery for shooting a paper clip at a classmate that inadvertently struck a cafeteria worker instead (see Skiba and Peterson 1999).

Notwithstanding the many inane examples of overreaction to innocuous behavior, the zero tolerance approach would still be defensible were there evidence that it had an appreciable deterrent effect. Sponsored by the American Psychological Association, a special task force undertook a meta-analysis of existing research on the effectiveness of zero tolerance policies (Skiba et al. 2008). The review revealed no real evidence that zero tolerance increased school safety or reduced inconsistency in the application of school discipline. On the contrary, zero tolerance policies were found to breed a hostile school climate and a decline in academic achievement linked to increased school exclusions. Not only do zero tolerance policies fail to deter misbehavior, they may even contribute to higher rates of misbehavior and school dropout for the students they punish.

It is critical that however the student code of conduct is enforced and discipline is applied, respect for student rights and a commitment to fairness remains essential for maintaining a positive school climate. Unfortunately, instead of promoting an atmosphere of mutual respect, many school administrators have used court rulings as a crutch to defend random locker searches, use of metal detectors, drug-sniffing dogs, and similarly aggressive tactics in the name of safety. The change in approach is visible in areas beyond security and sanctions. Out of concern for protecting a vulnerable population from harm, the rules pertaining to search and seizure in the context of a school setting have been gradually relaxed. Apparently, when it comes to conducting student searches, the courts have applied lower standards, replacing probable cause with reasonable suspicion (Campbell 2003).

Given the range of negative repercussions that derive from decidedly punitive disciplinary practices, some schools have instead opted for a restorative justice framework for handling school-based infractions. According to Zehr (2002), the restorative justice approach engages various local stakeholders (victims, offenders, and other members of the affected community) in a collective dialogue about the harm caused by the transgressions as a critical step in the healing process. Thus, rather than focusing on just punishing the person responsible, the restorative justice model addresses the needs and concerns of all those impacted in some significant way. Instead of emphasizing measures to deter and punish wrongdoing, it strives to allow victims, offenders, and others to achieve a sense of closure while at the same time pursuing personal accountability for misbehavior (see Morrison, Blood, and Thorsborne 2005).

Several evaluations of the effects of adopting a restorative justice approach in schools have been quite promising (see Karp and Breslin 2001). Most importantly, this philosophy on discipline fosters a positive school climate based on connectedness and trust, rather than a negative climate based on suspicion and disrespect. In the long run, the positive approach leads to healthy, safer school environments in which both the intellectual growth and social development are immovably center stage. At a minimum, restorative justice lays a path toward restoring justice in school discipline.

School Resource Officers

As early as the 1960s, long before school violence became a serious national concern, police officers were occasionally assigned to public schools as a special form of community policing (Girouard 2001). But by the late 1990s, President Bill Clinton, responding to a disturbing string of school shootings (including one in his home state of Arkansas), pushed for having more police officers placed in public schools. In 1999, the US Department of Justice created the "COPS in Schools" program. With federal funding, the number of school resource officers (SROs) increased by 50% between 1999 and 2005 (US Department of Justice 2008).

There are, of course, many advantages to having police regularly assigned to school settings, including the ability to respond quickly to potentially deadly incidents. However, Columbine High School, for example, had school resource officers on duty the day in 1999 when two alienated adolescents turned their school into a war zone. Columbine was a fairly large campus with nearly 2,000 students enrolled, and the officers couldn't be everywhere at once.

Despite the many benefits of employing school resource officers, their presence has led to a criminalization of student misbehavior. Rule infractions that would otherwise be resolved informally within the school context by school personnel have resulted in formal sanctions (arrest and prosecution). Many more students, particularly minorities, are being processed through the criminal justice system in what has been termed the school-to-prison pipeline. Youngsters who might otherwise have had only a school disciplinary record are being saddled with the lasting effects of a criminal record instead.

As law enforcement officers, SROs should arguably be held to the more rigorous standard of "probable cause" for searches, yet, just like school officials, SROs can conduct searches with only "reasonable suspicion" (*S.W., 171 N.C. App. 335*, 2005). Even more disconcerting is when aggressive police tactics are employed in response to relatively minor issues. It is not surprising, therefore, that a 2015 video of a South Carolina SRO pulling a 16-year-old female student out of her seat and wildly tossing her across the classroom before arresting her for being disruptive in math class instantly went viral and sparked widespread public outrage (as well as the officer's termination) (Ford, Botelho, and Conlon 2015).

Extreme actions and overresponse only serve to alienate students further from the school personnel, making them less likely to reach out for support in times of emotional distress. Instead, school officials should protect students' rights and treat them with respect. Policies and practices designed to promote a safer school environment have inadvertently created disciplinary procedures that are capricious, exclusionary, and excessively punitive. Although undoubtedly well-meaning, the approach to school discipline has become decidedly mean-spirited.

Preparing for the Worst

First introduced selectively following the 1999 Columbine massacre, lockdown drills have become commonplace in schools across America, especially in the wake of 2012 Sandy Hook shooting spree. A number of states have gone so far as to mandate that all schools drill their faculty and students on how to act should there be an actual shooting on campus. Called "active shooter drills" in the more recent lexicon, these exercises sometimes include fake blood and blanks fired in the hallway for added realism. At the extreme, one tactical approach has a trainer chasing students from classroom to classroom, pointing a large flashlight as if it were a firearm and shouting, "Bang, bang, you're dead." Some schools arm their pretend intruder with a fake, but realistic-looking, gun.

Emergency drills are nothing new to schools, of course. Simulated exercises to prepare pupils for fire and other natural catastrophes have been commonplace for generations. Yet the aggressive nature of shooting drills makes them qualitatively different and exceptionally more traumatizing to children, especially younger ones. These simulations reinforce the notion that schools are dangerous places where the bad guy is coming to shoot you.

The psychological harm that may come from these simulations is not warranted in light of the low probability that such an event will occur. It is one thing to prepare the faculty and staff for what to do and how to instruct the students in the case of a violent episode; it is quite another to involve impressionable youngsters whose innocence need not be compromised. Furthermore, it is questionable whether children would recall their escape lessons amid the hysteria associated with an actual shooting.

School administrators could take an important lesson in moderation from the airline and cruise industries. Commercial airlines train their flight crews to handle disaster situations, but passengers are only asked to watch a brief demonstration of grabbing hold of oxygen masks, without actually having to practice this maneuver. Cruise ships require that guests don life jackets and learn the location of their muster stations, but no one has to step foot inside a lifeboat or suffer the unsettling experience of being lowered into the water. In the case of a catastrophe in the air or at sea, passengers will be directed where to go and told what to do. Schools would be wise to take the same low-key approach to the unlikely event of a shooting. The faculty and staff need to be adequately trained, and the students just reminded to listen to instructions from staff members.

Exploiting the elevated level of fear prompted by school shootings, several companies designed and successfully marketed bullet-resistant backpacks and blankets. Anxious parents, wanting to protect their kids from harm, were willing to pay a high price for an additional measure of protection. Students have also been advised to fill their backpacks with heavy textbooks that also might shield them in the event of a shooting. Actually, the best advice in such cases might be to drop the heavy bag of books and run as fast as possible.

Armed Protection

In January 2013, in the immediate aftermath of the Sandy Hook massacre, the National Rifle Association, hoping to deflect criticism as well as efforts to tighten gun control laws, promoted a "more guns" national strategy for school safety. The so-called School Shield Program would furnish every school in America, regardless of size or grade level, with trained sharpshooters (Hutchinson 2013). In subsequent months, lawmakers in many states sponsored legislation to arm schoolteachers and train them to shoot. More than a few of these initiatives became law. And, based on a nationwide poll by the Gallup organization, nearly two-thirds of Americans see merit in this idea (Newport 2012).

Supporters of firearms-for-faculty laws argue that ever since the early 1990s, when the US Congress established schools as gun-free zones, an armed assailant, be it a student-insider or a stranger-intruder, could be assured of facing little opposition. The belief is that arming teachers and administrators might serve as a powerful deterrent to anyone contemplating a Columbine-style school shooting. It is hard to imagine, however, that a vengeful student, who is willing to die by police gunfire or by his own hand, would be dissuaded by knowing that the faculty were armed. He may even welcome the chance to shoot it out with the principal at high noon in the school cafeteria.

More importantly, we want faculty to educate their students, not execute them. For schoolteachers, especially the ones who are frustrated when dealing with the belligerent bully seated in the back of the classroom, marksmanship should just be about As and Bs, not guns and ammo. Concealed chalk is fine, a concealed Glock is not.

If armed guards and armed teachers are indeed worthy strategies for protecting children, then what should schools do to protect the students before and after school? Expanding this approach would dictate providing weapons to coaches, athletic directors, and even bus drivers. The slope behind the school is treacherously slippery.

Bullying

Despite their relative safety, schools can still feel dangerous to children, particularly in the face of harassment and intimidation. In fact, most bullying in school does not involve actual violence or fighting, but rather the constant threat of violence, which can make school halls and bathrooms tremendously fear-provoking.

Bullying at school or in the schoolyard is hardly a new concern for students and their parents, or for teachers and administrators. Harassing behavior – from teasing to intimidation, from targeted vandalism and malicious pranks to shoving and fighting – has been a problem for decades, if not centuries, likely for as long as there have been schools. Previously dismissed as normal and relatively harmless child's play – "boys being boys," "girls being catty" – in recent years bullying has taken on an entirely different meaning, occasionally with devastating repercussions.

Chronic bullying has frequently been cited as an underlying precipitant for suicide and homicide. Several high-profile cases of school homicide have involved a victim of long-term bullying seeking payback with a gun. In October 1997, for example, 16-year-old Luke Woodham of Pearl, Mississippi, used a rifle from home to murder two female classmates (one of whom was his former girlfriend) and wound seven other students at his high school. He had also killed his mother with a knife and baseball bat. In what apparently was meant to be a suicide note (were it not for the fact he lived), Woodham wrote, "I am not insane! I am angry. I kill because people like me are mistreated every day. I do this to show society – push us and we will push back. I have suffered all my life. No one ever truly loved me."

Woodham was not the only beleaguered student to have avenged repeated bullying with a counter-assault. Anne Lenhardt (pers. comm., February 13, 2009) assembled case profiles of 15 young assailants involved in 13 episodes of school homicide in the United States between 1996 and 2005. She found that 73% of the 15 perpetrators had apparently been the victims of bullying and persecution. Of course, bullying itself is hardly sufficient to produce the level of rage seen in school rampages; it is usually harassment in combination with poor coping skills that produces this extreme response. Lenhardt's results show that 71% of attackers felt rejected and isolated by peers, 64% had poor coping skills, and 64% demonstrated an exaggerated need for attention and respect.

For too many years, schools often responded to reports of bullying by placing the blame on the shoulders of victims, implicitly assuming that they were somehow responsible for their own victimization, if only because they failed to stand up for themselves. In cases where a student had to be transferred from one class or homeroom to another to prevent further harassment, it was usually the victim and not the bully who was displaced.

In the past couple of decades, however, school administrators have come to take – or have been compelled by law to take – a more progressive and enlightened view of the causes of and solutions to bullying. Rather than focusing just on the victims and offenders, schools have had far greater success by addressing the broader school climate (Fox and Burstein 2010).

Despite the range of promising tools for bullying suppression, there are significant hurdles to their successful application in school settings. Most of all, the school climate must be amenable to changing norms surrounding intimidation and aggression. Intolerance of acts of bullying must be the perspective widely embraced and shared by both staff and students, not something merely imposed upon students by administrative decree.

Unfortunately, even when students and teachers appear, at least superficially, solidly unified against bullying, certain deeply rooted prejudices that favor bullies over victims remain somewhat resistant to change. A study of perceptions and attitudes among middle school students and teachers in Pennsylvania (Crothers and Kolbert 2004) found relatively weak confidence in the utility of anti-bullying curricula and role-playing strategies. Rather, both groups seemed to prefer an approach that encourages victims to be more assertive and to stand up for themselves. Apparently, the long-standing "blame the victim" viewpoint suggesting that victims are in some way responsible for their mistreatment remains largely impenetrable.

Notwithstanding the widespread adoption of various school-based anti-bullying curricula, the empirical evidence with regard to their preventive value is disappointing. An analysis of anti-bullying interventions implemented over a 25-year time period, from 1980 to 2004, concluded that the effectiveness of bullying prevention programs was modest at best, and mostly had an impact om knowledge and attitudes rather than actual bullying behavior (Merrell et al. 2008).

Regardless of the approach to prevention and enforcement, it remains extremely difficult to convince bullies that their actions are disadvantageous to themselves, besides being injurious to the targets of their abuse. Even with threats of punishment, some students see bullying as a positive thing – for themselves, that is.

All too often, bullies gain from their use of power over weaker classmates. Not only do they come away with their victim's lunch money or property, but they are typically admired for their supremacy. Researchers at the University of Virginia found that bullies are, based on peer nominations, overwhelmingly considered to be the more popular students in class (Thunfors and Cornell 2008).

Of course, the problem of bullying and its solution goes way beyond the schoolyard. In our competitive society – in sports, in corporate America, and especially in politics – we admire aggressors and pity pushovers. Schools need to change, but then so does society.

School Size and Climate

Public schools, especially high schools, vary widely in terms of their enrollments, from a couple of hundred to several thousand. Whereas college students can make a choice between attending a large or a small campus, their younger and less mature counterparts at the secondary school level are generally assigned to attend whatever school lies in their district no matter the size or their emotional readiness. For some adolescents, attending a sprawling school with thousands of students can be quite daunting and a significant threat to their sense of comfort and well-being. Confronting a sea of unfamiliar faces, students can easily feel alienated, depersonalized, and disconnected from the school environment.

Columbine High School and Marysville-Pilchuck High School, for example, enrolled nearly 2,000 and 1,200 students respectively at the time of their mass shooting incidents. Large enrollment can also have an impact on the effectiveness of oversight. With so many students to supervise, teachers, guidance counselors, and coaches have tenuous emotional links to their charges, and thus have more difficulty identifying warning signs and addressing issues like depression and anxiety, academic failure, and the potential for violent behavior. In 2013, the national average of students per guidance counselor was a whopping 470, nearly twice the recommended number as per the American School Counselor Association (2014). Even worse, more than one in five US high schools did not employ any guidance counselors during the year prior (US Department of Education 2014). Furthermore, Haller (1992) found that school size was significantly related to problems of disorder and truancy, even after controlling for race, disadvantage, achievement level, and location.

Despite the negative effects of large school size, the United States has a long tradition of consolidating small schools for the sake of economic efficiency. A century ago, for example, there were more than a quarter of a million public schools in the United States, a number which has since plummeted to just about 100,000 (Snyder and Dillow 2012). As the number of schools declined, school size naturally increased. Due to the large variation in school size, averages tend to be deceptive: in 1995–1996, elementary and secondary schools had an average of around 500 students each, yet less than 2% of students attended districts with fewer than 500 students (Snyder, Hoffman, and Geddes 1998). In contrast, during the 2009–2010 school year, only 6.5% of districts enrolled over 10,000 children, yet these schools accounted for over half of the nation's school population (Snyder and Dillow 2012).

Expanding school enrollment may have been necessary a half-century ago when million upon millions of baby boomers flooded our nation's schools. In fact, US school enrollment nearly doubled (from 28 million to 51 million) between the 1949–1950 and the 1972–1973 school years (Snyder and Dillow 2012). With the exception of slight increases between 1985 and 2006, however, school enrollments have remained fairly stable since the 1970s. In light of this, it would seem reasonable and prudent to control enrollments and school size.

While completely dismantling massive schools is not a viable solution to reducing school violence, large schools should make efforts to develop smaller internal communities to foster a sense of attachment and school spirit for students. Many universities have developed a "residential college" or "house system" model for precisely this purpose in response to large enrollment sizes, where students can number in the tens of thousands. While most high schools cannot incorporate the residential component of these university models, they can sort students into subschools with their own academic advisors, deans, and guidance counselors so that students have a more personal relationship with adults in their support networks.

Discussion

For millions of Americans, the notion of terrorism evokes frightful images of hijacked airliners crashing into the Twin Towers of New York City and suicide bombers wreaking devastation upon countless innocents. However, years before the identities of Osama bin Laden and al-Qaeda became widely recognized, another form of terror – based not on religious fundamentalism but on adolescent rage – had surfaced in once-obscure places like Moses Lake, Washington; Pearl, Mississippi; and Jonesboro, Arkansas. And the word "Columbine," once reflecting the colorful beauty of the Colorado state flower, has become linked to the horror of children being gunned down in the halls of their school. Adding to the irony, the diary of one of the young shooters from Columbine High described a fantasy about following up the massacre by flying an airplane into the skyline of New York; of course, the journal entry was made years before the Twin Towers collapsed.

It may seem a stretch to characterize school shootings as a form of terrorism. Yet, the issues of international terror and schoolyard terror are remarkably similar. Prompted by a string of school massacres in the late 1990s, school administrators were eager to profile dangerous students, just as airport security officials strived to identify violent extremists among those who boarded commercial airplanes. And while the US Congress voted to permit airline pilots to carry weapons in the cockpit to guard against a possible in-air takeover, state legislators around the country debated the wisdom of arming school teachers. Moreover, the fine balance between privacy and security that troubles many Americans with regard to the ongoing "War on Terror" has been a thorny matter as well at educational institutions of all levels, from elementary schools to colleges."

As widespread fear and apprehension over the safety of students pushed school security onto the national agenda, the body of research and scholarship on the topic of school violence and its prevention grew dramatically. While at one time the theme would have seemed far too narrow, in 2002 the *Journal of School Violence*, an interdisciplinary quarterly on theory, research, and practice focused only on violence and disorder in schools, released its inaugural issue. In addition, based on key terms included in the *Social Science Abstracts*, the focus on school violence in particular rose significantly after the late 1990s' string of school rampages. Whereas 1% of all violent-related scholarly articles published between 1985 and 1999 concerned school violence, the percentage doubled to 2% from 2000 through 2014.

The growth in interest and concern has also been reflected outside of the academic literature. As one measure, the *New York Times*, widely considered the newspaper of record, has published more than 1,500 articles containing the phrase "school shooting" since the early 1990s, a pattern that reveals the impact of the most high-profile incidents. As shown in Figure 1.3, the count of *Times* articles increased in the late 1990s when several multiple-victim shootings took place, and then spiked in 1999 following the Columbine massacre. After a steady decline through the 2000s, the number of articles soared once again in late 2012 into 2013 in the aftermath of the Sandy Hook shooting spree. Meanwhile, a cottage industry emerged for school security hardware, technology, guidebooks, and consulting.

Whatever the enduring impact of the Columbine massacre on public consciousness and the operation of schools at all academic levels, the shooting spree at Sandy Hook became the new watershed in terms of school safety and security. Not only was the victim count double that of Columbine, but the tender age of the victims seared through

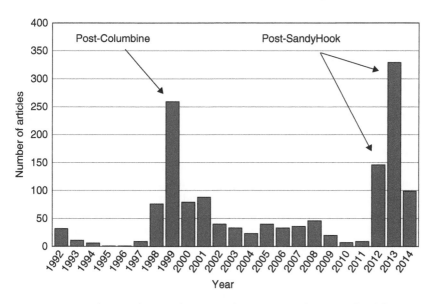

Figure 1.3 Annual count of *New York Times* articles containing the term "school shooting."

the public consciousness. Hopefully, there will never be another episode as devastating at the Sandy Hook shooting. Even so, there will continue to be enough isolated incidents in which schoolchildren are slain that the impact will endure.

While attention to tragic school shootings is certainly appropriate, the hyperfocus on isolated cases of gun violence in school and the fortress-like approach to security carry significant drawbacks in terms of maintaining a school climate that is conducive to learning. Certain preventative measures, particularly those that are disproportionate to the actual risk, can serve as constant reminders for impressionable youngsters that schools are under siege. In addition, regarding school shootings as the "new normal" can become a self-fulfilling prophesy by which disgruntled, alienated adolescents continue to perceive violence as the best way to resolve conflict. In the long run, a low-key approach may be the most effective in promoting a safe school environment and alleviating fears.

References

Bracy, Nicole L. and Kupchik, Aaron. 2009. "The News Media on School Crime and Violence: Constructing Dangerousness and Fueling Fear." *Youth Violence and Juvenile Justice* 7, 136–155.

Campbell, Christopher Z. 2003. "The Effective Use of School Resource Officers: The Constitutionality of School Searches and Interrogations." *School Law Bulletin* 34(1): 13–17. DOI: 10.1177/1541204008328800.

Coleman, Loren. 2004. *The Copycat Effect: How the Media and Popular Culture Trigger the Mayhem in Tomorrow's Headlines.* New York: Paraview Pocket Books.

Crothers, Laura M. and Kolbert, Jered B. 2004. "Comparing Middle School Teachers' and Students' Views on Bullying and Anti-Bullying Interventions." *Journal of School Violence* 3(1), 17–32.

Everytown for Gun Safety. 2015. "Analysis of Recent Mass Shootings." http://every.tw/1WIarom (last accessed October 4, 2017).

Ford, Dana, Botelho, Greg, and Conlon, Kevin. 2015. "Spring Valley High School Officer Suspended after Violent Classroom Arrest." CNN. http://www.cnn.com/2015/10/27/us/south-carolina-school-arrest-video/ (last accessed October 4, 2017).

Fox, James Alan and Burstein, Harvey. 2010. *Violence and Security on Campus: From Preschool through College*. Santa Barbara, CA: Praeger.

Girouard, Cathy. 2001. *School Resource Officer Training Program*. Office of Juvenile Justice and Delinquency Prevention Fact Sheet, 5.

Haller, Emil J. 1992. "High School Size and Student Indiscipline: Another Aspect of the School Consolidation Issue?" *Educational Evaluation and Policy Analysis* 14, 145–156.

Heath, Linda and Gilbert, Kevin. 1996. "Mass Media and Fear of Crime." *American Behavioral Scientist* 39(4), 379–386.

Hirschfield, Paul J. 2008. "Preparing for Prison? The Criminalization of School Discipline in the USA." *Theoretical Criminology* 12, 79–101.

Hutchinson, Asa. 2013. "Report of the National School Shield Task Force, April 2, 2013." In the Matter of: *S.W., 171 N.C. App. 335, 2005*.

Karp, David R., and Breslin, Beau. 2001. "Restorative Justice in School Communities." *Youth & Society* 33, 249–272.

Lassiter, William L. and Perry, Danya C. 2009. *Preventing Violence and Crime in America's Schools: From Put-downs to Lock-downs*. Santa Barbara, CA: Praeger.

Merrell, Kenneth W., Gueldner, Barbara A., Ross, Scott W., and Isava, Duane M. 2008. "How Effective Are School Bullying Intervention Programs? A Meta-analysis of Intervention Research." *School Psychology Quarterly* 23, 26–42.

Morrison, Brenda, Blood, Peta, and Thorsborne, Margaret. 2005. "Practicing Restorative Justice in School Communities: Addressing the Challenge of Culture Change." *Public Organization Review* 5, 335–357.

Newport, Frank. 2012. "To Stop Shootings, Americans Focus on Police, Mental Health: Democrats Substantially More Likely to See Assault Gun Ban as Effective." *Gallup News Service*. http://www.gallup.com/poll/159422/stop-shootings-americans-focus-police-mental-health.aspx (last accessed October 4, 2017).

Pinard, Michael. 2003. "From the Classroom to the Courtroom: Reassessing Fourth Amendment Standards in Public School Searches Involving Law Enforcement Authorities." *Arizona Law Review* 45,1067–1124.

Rather, Dan. 2001. *CBS Evening News* (accessed March 5, 2016).

Rocque, Michael. 2012. "Exploring School Rampage Shootings: Research, Theory, and Policy." *The Social Science Journal* 49, 304–313.

Skiba, Russell and Peterson, Reece. 1999. "The Dark Side of Zero Tolerance: Can Punishment Lead to Safe Schools?" *The Phi Delta Kappan* 80, 372–376.

Skiba, Russell, Reynolds, Cecil R., Graham, Sandra, Sheras, Peter, Conoley, Jane C., and Garcia-Vasquez, Enedina. 2008. "Are Zero Tolerance Policies Effective in the Schools? An Evidentiary Review and Recommendations." *American Psychologist* 63(9), 852–862. DOI: 10.1037/0003-066X.63.9.852.

Snyder, Thomas D. and Dillow, Sally A. 2012. "Digest of Education Statistics 2011 (NCES 2012-001)." National Center for Education Statistics, Institute of Education Sciences, US Department of Education.

Snyder, Thomas D., Hoffman, Leff, and Geddes, Claire. 1998. "State Comparisons of Education Statistics: 1969–70 to 1996–97 (NCES 98-018)." National Center for Education Statistics, US Department of Education.

Towers, Sherry, Gomez-Lievano, Andres, Khan, Maryam, Mubayi, Anuj, and Castillo-Chavez, Carlos. 2015. "Contagion in Mass Killings and School Shootings." *PLoS ONE* 10(7), e0117259. DOI: 10.1371/journal.pone.0117259.

Trump, Kenneth S. 2000. *Classroom Killers? Hallway Hostages?: How Schools Can Prevent and Manage School Crises.* Thousand Oaks, CA: Corwin.

Trump, Kenneth S. 2011. *Proactive School Security and Emergency Preparedness Planning.* Thousand Oaks, CA: Corwin.

Thunfors, Peter and Cornell, Dewey. 2008. "The Popularity of Middle School Bullies." *Journal of School Violence* 7, 65–82.

US Department of Education. 2014, March. *Civil Rights Data Collection: Data Snapshot (Teacher Equity).* US Department of Education Office for Civil Rights.

US Department of Justice, Office of Community Oriented Policing Service. 2008. "COPS in Schools." http://www.cops.usdoj.gov/Default.asp?Item=54 (accessed February 3, 2016).

Zehr, Howard. 2002. *The Little Book of Restorative Justice.* Intercourse, PA: Good Books.

2

Threat Assessment

Dewey G. Cornell

Programs and Evaluations: Threat Assessment

A series of highly publicized school shootings in the 1990s stimulated widespread fear that schools had become dangerous places (Cornell 2006). After the 1999 shooting at Columbine High School in Colorado, reports by the Federal Bureau of Investigation (FBI) (O'Toole 2000) and US Secret Service and Department of Education (Fein et al. 2002) recommended that schools adopt a threat assessment approach to violence prevention. Although threat assessment was an unfamiliar concept to most educators at the time, it has become widely recognized as a violence prevention strategy (American Psychological Association 2013). The Secret Service developed threat assessment as a systematic approach to evaluate whether a person poses a threat to government officials (Borum et al. 1999). Threat assessment has also become widely used to prevent workplace violence (Meloy, White, and Hart 2013), to protect public figures and celebrities from stalkers (Hoffman, Meloy, and Sheridan 2013), and to prevent domestic violence (Kropp and Cook 2014).

Threat assessment is a kind of risk assessment used when an individual threatens to commit a violent act or engages in threatening behavior. The practice of threat assessment has evolved to include the identification, assessment, and management of threats (Borum et al. 2010). In school settings, the somewhat ominous connotation of a "threat assessment" contrasts with its emphasis on resolving interpersonal conflicts and problems before they escalate into violence. Especially in schools, a threat assessment might be more appropriately termed a "safety assessment" or "behavioral assessment."

A typical threat assessment begins when a student is reported to have threatened to harm someone or engaged in some kind of behavior that suggested a threat of violence. In such situations, the dilemma faced by school authorities is to avoid overreacting to minor student misbehavior or underreacting to a potentially lethal situation. A threat assessment team will gather information to determine whether the student poses a serious risk of violence. Threat assessment moves from an initial assessment phase into an intervention or management phase depending on the seriousness of the threat and the nature of the underlying problem or conflict. Students might make a threatening statement as an immature expression of frustration or anger, but lack genuine

The Wiley Handbook on Violence in Education: Forms, Factors, and Preventions, First Edition.
Edited by Harvey Shapiro.

intent to harm someone. Other students might be capable of violence, but the threat could be ameliorated through counseling, conflict mediation, or some other intervention that resolves the underlying problem. In the most extreme cases, there may be a very serious threat that requires law enforcement intervention to prevent an imminent attack.

Prevalence of Threats and Violence in Schools

Threats are a common occurrence in schools, so it is important to assess them carefully, recognizing that they may have widely different meanings and significance. School-age children and youth engage in a great deal of verbal aggression, and may make threats simply as an expression of anger or frustration. A survey of 4,400 high school students found that approximately 12% reported being threatened with harm by another student in the past 30 days (Nekvasil and Cornell 2012). Nearly three-quarters did not believe the threat was serious and only about one-quarter reported the threat to school authorities. Similarly, acts of physical aggression, harassment, and bullying are common in schools. According to the Youth Risk Behavior Survey, 20% of female and 18% of male high school students nationwide reported being bullied at school in the past 12 months (Centers for Disease Control and Prevention 2014). Sixteen percent of boys and 8% of girls in grades 9–12 reported being in a physical fight at school during the previous 12 months (Robers et al. 2014).

In contrast, schools experience comparatively low rates of serious violent crime, which includes robbery, forcible rape, and aggravated assault. According to the National Crime Victimization Survey (NCVS), serious violent crime is consistently lower at school than away from school. In 2012, the rate of serious violent crime was 3.4 crimes per 1,000 students (ages 12–18) at school versus 6.5 crimes per 1,000 students outside of school (Robers et al. 2014). Also noteworthy is that crime rates have declined markedly in the past two decades, from a high point in 1993 of 22.1 at school and 41.4 outside of school.

It would be a mistake to regard threat assessment as an approach solely intended to prevent school shootings. It is true that public dismay over a series of shootings at schools was the impetus for the recommendation that schools use this approach, but, as described in this chapter, threat assessment has broader value as a more general violence prevention strategy and alternative to zero tolerance disciplinary practices. The massive media attention given to school shootings, and the understandable public reaction of shock and dismay, has created the mistaken belief that shootings constitute an epidemic that places many schools at risk (Cornell 2006). After the 1999 shooting at Columbine High School, a Gallup poll found that two-thirds of Americans believed that a similar shooting was "very likely" or "somewhat likely" to happen in their own community (Saad 1999). A similar surge in parental fear followed the shootings at Sandy Hook Elementary School in Newtown, Connecticut (McCarthy 2014).

In fact, the rate of school homicides is extraordinarily low. In the 10-year period from 2001 to 2011 there were 200 homicides of school-age children in US schools, an average of about 20 per year (Robers et al. 2014). Although 20 homicides is a tragic and unacceptable amount, it means that in the nation's 120,000 schools, the average school will have a student homicide every 6,000 years (120,000 ÷ 20). It is not practical to institute a program to prevent events that are so infrequent, and it would be quite difficult to conduct research demonstrating that such a program was effective, if its only purpose was to prevent homicides. With no program at all, the average school can expect to avoid a student homicide with greater than 99.999% certainty. This probability is important for school administrators and mental health professionals to remember when considering whether a student in their office who has threatened to kill someone at school will actually carry it out.

Although 20 student homicides per year is a distressingly large number, it represents less than 1% of the annual homicides of youth aged 5–18 in the United States (Modzeleski et al. 2008). A study of homicide locations found that schools are much safer than other locations (Nekvasil, Cornell, and Huang 2015). In a 37-state sample of 18,875 homicide incidents recorded in the Federal Bureau of Investigation's National Incident Based Reporting System (NIBRS), only 49 incidents, comprising less than 0.3% of the total, took place in schools. The majority (52%) of homicides took place in residences and 30% took place in parking lots or roads. Homicides were ten times more likely to occur in restaurants than in schools, yet "restaurant violence" has not been identified as a national safety concern and there have been no public calls to post law enforcement officers in restaurants or to arm restaurant staff (Nekvasil, Cornell, and Huang 2015).

Consequences of School Violence Fear

It is important to recognize that schools are comparatively safe from severe forms of violence, because the fear of school violence has serious consequences (Cornell 2015). One major consequence is that school authorities have diverted billions of dollars from their school budgets to institute new security measures such as metal detectors, alarm systems, surveillance cameras, remodeled building entrances, and electronic door locks (Linskey 2013; Sheriff 2015). Multiple|studies have concluded that security measures such as metal detectors do not increase school safety and, on the contrary, make students feel less safe at school (Bachman, Randolph, and Brown 2011; Gastic 2011; Hankin, Hertz, and Simon 2011).

There is a further, less obvious cost to the safety of the community when law enforcement agencies are required to pull officers from community patrols in order to post guards at school entrances. Research has found that there is little evidence that schools with increased security personnel are safer or that they promote better student behavior, although more research is needed (Petrosino, Guckenburg, and Fronius 2012). Although well-trained school resource officers (SROs) can serve valuable functions beyond school security (Clark 2011), the presence of law enforcement officers can result in arrests and criminal charges against students for minor misbehavior such as disorderly conduct and simple assault (Morgan et al. 2014; Theriot 2009). In *The School Discipline Consensus Report*, the Council of State Governments Justice Center (Morgan et al. 2014) called for school systems to prohibit the use of law enforcement officers to police misbehavior that could be more appropriately handled through school discipline. They recommended a selective, specialized process of identifying and training school-based officers who can promote a safe and supportive environment and help reduce the risk of youth involvement in the juvenile justice system.

Zero Tolerance

Another consequence of the misperception that schools are dangerous places was the institution of zero tolerance discipline practices. Concern over school violence propelled the federal government to enact the Gun-Free Schools Act of 1994, which required states to pass legislation mandating schools to expel for at least one year any student found with a firearm at school. Although the federal law permitted school authorities to make exceptions in extenuating circumstances, state laws and local school policies were often less flexible and extended zero tolerance for firearms into a general philosophy of school discipline that applied to other weapons, and to drugs, fighting, and other infractions (American Psychological Association 2008). Under zero tolerance, students could be automatically suspended even if the violation was accidental or posed no serious threat to others. For example, students have been suspended for misbehavior such as pointing their fingers like a gun or pretending to shoot someone with a pencil (Rubinkam 2013). This practice contrasts directly with a threat assessment approach that considers the circumstances and seriousness of the student's behavior.

Many education authorities have criticized zero tolerance practices as fueling a nationwide increase in school suspensions (Losen and Martinez 2013; Morgan et al. 2014). There is no evidence that zero tolerance policies improve student behavior or increase school safety, but considerable evidence that school suspension does not achieve its stated objectives of reforming misbehaving students or deterring other students from breaking school rules (American Psychological Association 2008). A longitudinal study following one million Texas students from grades 6 through 12 found that suspensions did not have a positive impact on students, and instead increased the likelihood of school failure, dropout, and juvenile court involvement (Fabelo et al. 2011). Although a correlational study, this investigation controlled for numerous student and school factors that might explain that finding and demonstrated a persistent association with school suspension. Even among schools with similar at-risk student enrollments, the school administration's decision to use suspension as a disciplinary practice was associated with negative outcomes. Other studies have found that schools with high suspension rates have lower graduation rates than other schools, even after controlling for differences in school demographics (Lee et al. 2011; Losen and Martinez 2013).

Profiling

The fear of school violence also sensitizes school authorities to be on the lookout for dangerous students. There has been great interest in developing a psychological profile or set of warning signs that could be used to identify a student who is going to carry out a school shooting. The Federal Bureau of Investigation was asked to investigate the possibility of developing a profile of school shooters that could be used to prevent further attacks (O'Toole 2000). The FBI's profiling unit, along with several panels of experts in mental health and education, studied the problem of school shootings and ultimately rejected the use of profiling (O'Toole 2000). The FBI's experts on profiling agreed that although the use of a psychological profile to identify a school shooter is intuitively appealing, it is impractical. Psychological characteristics that seem to accurately describe many violent individuals are not specific indicators and can be found among many non-violent individuals. For example, many students who committed school shootings were victims of bullying and enjoyed playing violent video games, but the vast majority of bully victims and video game players are not going to engage in a school shooting. As the FBI report concluded, "Trying to draw up a catalogue or 'check-list' of warning signs to detect a potential school shooter can be shortsighted, even dangerous. Such lists, publicized by the media, can end up unfairly labeling many non-violent students as potentially dangerous" (O'Toole 2000, 2).

The US Department of Education distributed a useful guidebook to schools on school safety (Dwyer, Osher, and Warger 1998). The guidebook featured 16 warning signs of student violence that included items such as history of discipline problems, drug use and alcohol use, feelings of being persecuted, uncontrolled anger, and excessive feelings of rejection. These items may merit intervention as mental health concerns, but they are not reliable predictors of imminent violence. The federal guidebook recognized the limitations of a warning signs approach and cautioned, "Unfortunately, there is a real danger that early warning signs will be misinterpreted" (Dwyer, Osher, and Warger 1998, 7). The guidebook urged school authorities to refrain from using the warning signs as a basis for punishing students or excluding them from school.

Violence Prevention versus Prediction

A common objection to threat assessment is that violence is so difficult to predict that threat assessment is futile. This objection is based on the mistaken assumption that prevention requires prediction. Although there is only a moderate ability to identify individuals who subsequently commit serious acts of violence (Fazel et al. 2012), the unpredictability of violence in individual cases does not mean violence cannot be prevented on a larger scale. There are many examples of public health programs that have been successful in saving lives from seemingly unpredictable dangers (Mozaffarian, Hemenway, and Ludwig 2013). For example, motor vehicle accidents seem unpredictable, but traffic safety laws, driver training, and well-designed cars reduce the rate of accidents. Another example is the public health campaign to reduce tobacco smoking that has saved millions of lives. By identifying risk factors like smoking, prevention programs can have widespread effects without knowledge of which individuals have been saved. The American Psychological Association (2013) report on gun violence recommended a similar application of prevention principles to risk factors for violence.

Prevention can be undertaken on three levels or tiers (O'Connell, Boat, and Warner 2009). The first level is primary or universal prevention, which includes efforts to address the underlying environmental conditions and general factors that lead to the negative outcome such as a disease, injury, or, in this case, violence. Universal interventions are aimed at the general population. The secondary, or selective, level is aimed at individuals who are deemed to be at risk for the negative outcome, and the tertiary, or indicated, level is for those who already demonstrate the negative outcome and are in need of treatment to prevent recurrence or worsening.

Threat assessment can be regarded as a method of identifying the appropriate level of prevention needed for a specific student. For example, a male student who threatens to "kill" another male classmate would need different interventions depending on the seriousness of his threat. If the two boys were roughhousing and playfully making threats to one another in the hallway, the appropriate intervention might be to make the boys stop their disorderly behavior and to admonish them that threatening language was not appropriate. This is a form of primary prevention that can be applied to all students. On the other hand, if the boy made the threatening statement because he was angry, it would be useful to interview him and find out what he was upset about and what he meant in making a threat. In most cases like this, the boy would calm down and explain that he did not have any intention to kill his classmate but was upset over some problem or conflict between them. A school counselor might work with the boys to resolve the problem, which is a form of secondary prevention addressing anger and conflict as risk factors for violence. Finally, under different circumstances, the boy might have made a threat that was not so easily resolved. If the boy was not amenable to discussing his threatening statement, the threat assessment would expand to include a more careful exploration of the boy's intentions, the history of his conflict with the classmate, and an investigation to determine whether he had engaged in any actions that showed he was planning or preparing to carry out the threat. An intervention to stop an impending or imminent act of violence would constitute tertiary prevention.

True violence prevention efforts must begin well before there is a gunman in the parking lot. Violence prevention can begin at a primary level by helping families to raise healthy, well-adjusted children who will be less prone to violence. Primary prevention can also be aimed at improving school and community services, so that all youth receive the benefits of good education, health care, and freedom from crime. Secondary prevention can ameliorate risk factors for violence that range from behavioral problems, bullying, and mental disorders, to social and economic disadvantages that are the seedbed for much criminal violence. As in the example above, tertiary prevention might be undertaken to avert an imminent act of violence in someone who is actively planning and preparing to carry out an attack, or it might be designed to prevent further violence in an individual who has already engaged in violent behavior.

Virginia Student Threat Assessment Guidelines

The Virginia Student Threat Assessment Guidelines were developed in response to the FBI (O'Toole 2000) and US Secret Service and Department of Education (Vossekuil et al. 2002) recommendations for school-based threat assessment teams. The Virginia model was intended to provide school authorities with a standard and systematic approach for responding to student threats of violence. In 2002, the threat assessment guidelines were formulated, reviewed by a board of national experts in psychology and risk assessment, and field-tested in 35 Virginia schools for one year. The guidelines were refined and then published in a 145-page manual, *Guidelines for Responding to Student Threats of Violence* (Cornell and Sheras 2006).

The Threat Assessment Team

A threat assessment team typically consists of a school administrator (such as the school principal or assistant principal), several mental health professionals, and a law enforcement representative. Teachers provide valuable information in cases involving their students but in most schools are not expected to serve on the teams. The entire team is not engaged in every threat assessment, because the model is designed to resolve simple cases quickly and efficiently, reserving most intensive effort and full team involvement for only the most serious cases.

The law enforcement representative for the team is usually a school resource officer (SRO) or another police officer who is available to work with the school. The SRO can advise the team whether a student's behavior has violated the law and can conduct a criminal investigation and take appropriate action in the most serious cases. The SRO's everyday role is to be a member of the school community who encourages law-abiding behavior and establishes positive relationships with students (Clark 2011). School resource officers can take a preventive approach to crime by identifying potentially volatile conflicts between students or groups of students.

Depending on the school's staffing pattern, a threat assessment team should include one or more mental health professionals (e.g., school counselor, psychologist, social worker). A mental health professional may be involved at multiple stages in a threat assessment. In the most common, transient cases that, by definition, do not involve serious, substantive threats, the mental health professional may work in tandem with the team leader to interview witnesses and clarify that the identified student does not pose a threat of violence. Many student threats are simply figures of speech or expressions of anger that can be easily resolved.

In the most serious cases, a school psychologist or another suitably qualified mental health professional member conducts a mental health evaluation of the student. These evaluations have two main objectives. The first objective is to screen the student for mental health problems that demand immediate attention, such as psychotic symptoms or suicidality. The second objective is to assess why the student made the threat and to provide recommendations for dealing with the problem or conflict that stimulated the threatening behavior.

Mental health professionals also may conduct interventions such as counseling a distressed student or resolving conflicts between students. There is a large body of evidence that school-based interventions can reduce aggressive behavior (Wilson and Lipsey 2007). There are several comprehensive lists of evidence-based programs, such as the National Registry of Evidence-based Programs and Practices (Substance Abuse and Mental Health Services Administration 2014) and Blueprints for Healthy Youth Development (Center for the Study and Prevention of Violence 2014), that identify effective programs in areas such as social competence training, cognitive-behavioral counseling to improve social interaction and problem-solving skills, and conflict resolution programs. In all cases, there should be follow-up monitoring to ensure that a plan is working.

A school-based team is preferable to an external team for four reasons. First, a threat assessment requires an immediate response. School authorities cannot wait for outside experts to begin an investigation. In some schools, students have been suspended for weeks awaiting evaluations by external teams. Second, threat assessment requires careful consideration of contextual and situational factors that are familiar to school staff but not to outsiders. Third, most student threats are not serious enough to warrant the use of an outside team. Finally, threat assessment should not be limited to an initial assessment, but should involve an ongoing process of intervention and follow-up. An effective threat assessment team will implement a response to a serious threat that is intended to reduce the risk of violence and will continue to monitor the student's status.

Nevertheless, in a complicated case involving a serious threat of violence, the school-based team can certainly consult with outside mental health experts and other resources in the community.

Steps in a Threat Assessment

The Virginia model uses a seven-step decision tree designed to help teams work efficiently. See Figure 2.1 for a flow chart illustrating the seven steps. The first three steps of the assessment are a triage phase to determine whether the case can be quickly and easily resolved as a transient threat or will require more extensive evaluation and intervention as a substantive threat. In the simplest cases, a threat can be resolved the same day, but in more complex cases, there may be a comprehensive assessment of the student, interviews with witnesses, meetings with parents, and the formulation of an intervention plan. It is important that teams use a graduated process so that they do not overreact to threatening statements that are not serious threats.

The team leader usually begins by interviewing the student who made the threat with a standard set of questions that can be adapted to the specific situation. The interviewer is concerned with determining the context in which the threat was made and what the student meant and intended in making the threat. If necessary, the team leader or other team members also interview witnesses to the threat and make notes on a standard form.

At step 2, the team must distinguish between serious threats that pose a continuing risk or danger to others and those that are not serious because they can be quickly resolved and do not pose a continuing risk. Less serious threats are termed *transient* threats, which can be readily identified as expressions of anger or frustration, or per- haps inappropriate attempts at humor. If a threat is judged to be transient, it is resolved at step 3 without further assessment. The student may receive a reprimand or other disciplinary consequence, but there is no need to take protective action because the threat is not serious. Ideally, the student will apologize and explain or make amends for his or her behavior. Our research has found that approximately three-quarters of threat cases can be resolved as transient threats (Cornell et al. 2015).

Any threat that cannot be resolved as transient is regarded as a substantive threat, which means that it involves a sustained intent to harm someone beyond the immediate incident. These substantive threats are usually more detailed and specific than transient threats. There may be evidence of planning or preparation to carry out the threat. Another indication may be an effort to recruit accomplices or to invite an audience. In each case, the team must consider the total circumstances and make reasoned judg- ments based on all available information, such as the student's prior history of violent behavior and mental health status. The guidelines assist the team in its investigation, but do not provide a prescription or formula.

At step 4, a substantive threat is classified as serious or very serious based on the intended severity of injury. A threat to hit or fight someone is classified as a serious substantive threat. A threat to kill, sexually assault, or severely injure someone is very serious. Step 5 is the final step for serious substantive threats. In these cases, the team must take action to prevent the threat from being carried out. Immediate protective actions include cautioning the student about the consequences of carrying out the threat, providing supervision so that the threat is not carried out at school, and contact- ing the student's parents. A team member should also meet with the intended victim(s)

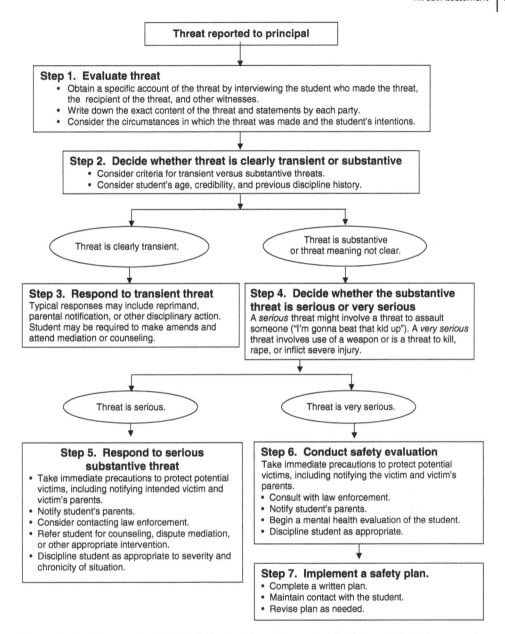

Threat reported to principal

Step 1. Evaluate threat
- Obtain a specific account of the threat by interviewing the student who made the threat, the recipient of the threat, and other witnesses.
- Write down the exact content of the threat and statements by each party.
- Consider the circumstances in which the threat was made and the student's intentions.

Step 2. Decide whether threat is clearly transient or substantive
- Consider criteria for transient versus substantive threats.
- Consider student's age, credibility, and previous discipline history.

Threat is clearly transient.

Threat is substantive or threat meaning not clear.

Step 3. Respond to transient threat
Typical responses may include reprimand, parental notification, or other disciplinary action. Student may be required to make amends and attend mediation or counseling.

Step 4. Decide whether the substantive threat is serious or very serious
A *serious* threat might involve a threat to assault someone ("I'm gonna beat that kid up"). A *very serious* threat involves use of a weapon or is a threat to kill, rape, or inflict severe injury.

Threat is serious.

Threat is very serious.

Step 5. Respond to serious substantive threat
- Take immediate precautions to protect potential victims, including notifying intended victim and victim's parents.
- Notify student's parents.
- Consider contacting law enforcement.
- Refer student for counseling, dispute mediation, or other appropriate intervention.
- Discipline student as appropriate to severity and chronicity of situation.

Step 6. Conduct safety evaluation
Take immediate precautions to protect potential victims, including notifying the victim and victim's parents.
- Consult with law enforcement.
- Notify student's parents.
- Begin a mental health evaluation of the student.
- Discipline student as appropriate.

Step 7. Implement a safety plan.
- Complete a written plan.
- Maintain contact with the student.
- Revise plan as needed.

Figure 2.1 Decision tree for the Virginia Student Threat Assessment Guidelines.

of the threat, both in an effort to resolve the underlying dispute or problem and to warn them. If the intended victim is a student, that student's parents should be contacted as well. For serious substantive threats, threat assessment ends here.

Step 6 is the response to a very serious substantive threat. The team takes protective actions and warns potential victims as in step 5, but there is a more comprehensive assessment of the student that leads to a more formal intervention plan. Ordinarily, a mental health professional such as the school psychologist will conduct a mental health evaluation of the student with two goals. The first goal is to assess the student's mental state and need for immediate mental health services, such as whether the student has delusional ideas that could motivate aggressive action. Another concern is whether the student might be so depressed or suicidal that he or she might take desperate action without concern for the consequences. In such cases, the team seeks immediate treatment from available community resources. A second goal of the mental health evaluation is to determine the reasons for the threat and develop a plan for addressing the problem or conflict underlying the threat. For example, is the student a victim of bullying or involved in some other peer conflict?

In most threat assessment cases, there is no need to suspend the student from school, but in the case of a very serious substantive threat, a brief suspension for safety reasons may be advisable as a safety precaution until the team can complete its evaluation. There is both the risk that the student may engage in aggressive behavior at school and the risk that others in the school might act aggressively or provocatively toward the student. Suspensions do not guarantee safety, and in several school shootings, the student had been suspended prior to the attack. Suspensions must be carefully considered because they may add stress to the situation and leave the student unsupervised outside of school. Threat assessment teams always make safety their first priority and must weigh the pros and cons of school suspension or any other disciplinary action.

While the mental health evaluation is being conducted, the school resource officer may undertake a law enforcement investigation to determine appropriate legal action. The officer may conduct a search for weapons, interview witnesses, and generally look for evidence that the student was engaged in planning or preparing to carry out the threat. In the most severe cases, the student may be arrested and charged with an offense.

At step 7, the team synthesizes its findings into a written safety plan designed both to protect potential victims and to address the educational needs of the student who made the threat. Threats are regarded as symptoms of a problem that a student is unable to resolve and the safety plan is designed to resolve that problem. The plan should include provisions for monitoring the student and making sure that it is effective. If the student has been referred for counseling or mental health services, there should be a provision to share information about the student's attendance and progress. For students who are receiving special education services, there may be changes in the student's Individualized Education Program (IEP). An IEP might include behavior support plans to help a student deal with anger or interpersonal conflict, or improve social skills.

Research on the Virginia Student Threat Assessment Guidelines

Many school systems have developed their own threat assessment procedures, but there is little research on their effectiveness (e.g., Van Dreal 2011; Van Dyke and Schroeder 2006). The Virginia Student Threat Assessment Guidelines has been examined in a series of studies involving hundreds of schools and is the only threat assessment program recognized as an evidence-based practice in the National Registry of Evidence-based Programs and Practices (NREPP; 2013). The first two studies were field tests that demonstrated that school-based teams could carry out threat assessments in a practical, efficient manner without violent outcomes (Cornell et al. 2004; Strong and Cornell 2008). Notably, in 397 threat assessment cases, nearly all of the students were permitted to return to school and few of the students received long-term suspensions or transfers to another school. Students receiving special education services made more threats than students in general education, but they did not receive disproportionately higher rates of school suspension (Kaplan and Cornell 2005).

A key feature of this program is to train school teams to take an individualized approach to evaluating student threats rather than a more rigid zero tolerance approach that does not consider the context and meaning of the student's behavior. Studies have repeatedly demonstrated that staff training in the Virginia Guidelines has a substantial effect on the attitudes and knowledge of school personnel across disciplines (Allen et al. 2008; Cornell, Allen, and Fan 2012; Cornell, Gregory, and Fan 2011; Cornell et al. 2004, 2009; Strong and Cornell 2008). After training, school personnel showed decreased fears of school violence and reduced support for a zero tolerance approach. They showed knowledge of the threat assessment principle and the ability to classify cases reliably. These changes were observed across groups of school principals, psychologists, counselors, social workers, and school-based police officers.

Four controlled studies have been conducted to date. The first controlled study was a retrospective comparison of 95 high schools reporting use of the Virginia Guidelines, 131 schools reporting use of locally developed procedures, and 54 schools reporting no use of a threat assessment approach (Cornell et al. 2009). Students at schools using the Virginia Guidelines reported less bullying at their school, greater willingness to seek help for bullying and threats of violence, and more positive perceptions of school staff members than students in either of the other two groups. School records indicated that there were one-third fewer long-term suspensions, after controlling for school size, minority composition and socioeconomic status of the student body, neighborhood violent crime, and the extent of security measures in the schools (Cornell et al. 2009).

The second controlled study showed that 23 high schools using the Virginia Guidelines experienced a 52% reduction in long-term suspensions and bullying infractions, but 26 control group schools showed no statistically significant change over a two-year period (Cornell, Gregory, and Fan 2011). For bullying infractions, the control group had a slight increase, while schools using the Virginia Guidelines had a decline of 79%.

The third study was a randomized controlled study of 40 schools where half of the schools were randomly assigned to receive threat assessment training and 20 delayed training for one year and served as a control group (Cornell, Allen, and Fan 2012). During one school year, there were 201 students identified as making threats of violence (approximately half in each group). The critical issue was how school authorities would respond to these threats and the extent to which they would rely on school suspension or transfer as a response. Compared with control students, students in schools using the Virginia Guidelines were approximately four times more likely to receive counseling services and two-and-a-half times more likely to receive a parent conference. Notably, students in the intervention group were about one-third as likely to receive a long-term suspension and one-eighth as likely to be transferred to a different school.

Although the results of randomized controlled study were strongly supportive of the model, researchers observed a wide range of implementation fidelity (Cornell, Allen, and Fan 2012). Schools that more closely complied with the model achieved more positive results than schools that followed it less closely. Some of the difficulties arose when the team leader did not oversee the process or new school staff joined the team who had not participated in the training. It is helpful for schools to review the manual and to complete a documentation form to help assure compliance with the Virginia Guidelines model.

The fourth study examined suspension rates in secondary schools that had adopted the Virginia Guidelines across the state of Virginia (JustChildren and Cornell 2013). Among Virginia's 663 secondary schools (middle, high, or combined schools), the 398 schools that used the Virginia Guidelines recorded 15% fewer short-term suspensions and 25% fewer long-term suspensions per year than the other 265 schools. This study was particularly concerned with the racial disparity between black and white students, since black students across all schools were twice as likely as white students to be suspended from school. A noteworthy finding was that short-term and long-term suspension rates were lower for both white and black students in schools using the Virginia Guidelines, and the lower rate for black students substantially reduced the racial disparity in long-term suspensions.

In 2013, the Virginia legislature required that all public schools establish threat assessment teams. (The legislation did not require that schools use the Virginia Student Threat Assessment Guidelines, and schools were free to use other threat assessment models.) A study examining the statewide implementation of threat assessment in its first year found that the average rate of threat assessment cases was approximately 6.1 per 1,000 students (Cornell et al. 2015). Descriptive information was collected on a sample of 1,470 cases from 810 schools. The most common threat made by students was a threat to kill (20%), followed by unspecified threats to harm (19%), hit or fight (18%), stab or cut (13%), or shoot (11%). The majority (64%) of threats were aimed at another student, 16% targeted a teacher, 8% were directed at another school staff member, and the remaining threats were aimed at other individuals or broader groups, such as threatening to blow up the school.

The school threat assessment teams made determinations of the seriousness of the threat and took appropriate disciplinary action and, if necessary, protective actions to prevent the threat from being carried out. Most of the threats were resolved without serious disciplinary consequences. Only 47% of students received a school suspension and 2% were expelled. A small number were charged with an offense by law enforcement (3.6%). The majority of students (80%) were able to return to their school, with the others transferred to another school, placed on homebound instruction, or receiving some other disposition.

In almost all cases (96%), there was no attempt to carry out the threat. In the remaining cases, 2% of students made an attempt to carry out a threat that was averted by school authorities or law enforcement. The most serious of these cases was a student who was apprehended after bringing a loaded firearm to school. There were also 2% of cases in which the student was reported to have carried out the threat, which in almost all cases was a threat to hit or strike someone. The most serious of these cases involved a student stabbing a classmate with a pencil and a student who superficially cut another student with a sharp object.

Overall, this initial assessment of threat assessment cases showed positive results, with schools responding to students in a differentiated manner rather than applying a zero tolerance approach. Almost all students were able to return to their schools and there were few serious incidents of violence. It should be noted that the results cannot be clearly attributed to the threat assessment process because the study did not have a control group of schools not using threat assessment. However, the purpose of the study was to examine the implementation of an approach that has been previously examined in controlled studies. Future studies are needed to compare different models of threat assessment and to identify best practices leading to the most favorable outcomes.

In conclusion, threat assessment is a promising approach to violence prevention in schools. Although originally conceived as a way to prevent school shootings, threat assessment has wider applications in dealing with student conflicts, bullying, and other forms of aggressive behavior. Threat assessment represents a shift in emphasis from violence prediction to violence prevention, and can help school authorities to determine the appropriate level of intervention in a multi-tiered prevention model. As a discipline tool, it provides schools with an alternative to zero tolerance discipline that can reduce the use of school suspension.

References

Allen, K., Cornell, D., Lorek, E., and Sheras, P. 2008. "Response of School Personnel to Student Threat Assessment Training." *School Effectiveness and School Improvement* 19, 319–332. DOI: 10.1080/09243450802332184.

American Psychological Association. 2013. "Gun Violence: Prediction, Prevention, and Policy." Retrieved from http://www.apa.org/pubs/info/reports/gun-violence-prevention.aspx (last accessed October 19, 2017).

American Psychological Association Zero Tolerance Task Force. 2008. "Are Zero Tolerance Policies Effective in the Schools? An Evidentiary Review and Recommendations." *American Psychologist* 63, 852–862. DOI:10.1037/0003-066X.63.9.852.

Bachman, R., Randolph, A., and Brown, B.L. 2011. "Predicting Perceptions of Fear at School and Going to and from School for African American and White Students: The Effects of School Security Measures." *Youth & Society* 43, 705–726.

Borum, R., Cornell, D. Modzeleski, W., and Jimerson, S.R. 2010. "What Can Be Done about School Shootings?: A Review of the Evidence." *Educational Researcher* 39, 27–37. DOI: 10.3102/0013189X09357620.

Borum, R., Fein, R., Vossekuil, B., and Berglund, J. 1999. "Threat Assessment: Defining an Approach to Assessing Risk for Targeted Violence." *Behavioral Sciences & the Law* 17, 323–337.

Center for the Study and Prevention of Violence. 2014. *Blueprints for Healthy Youth Development*. http://www.blueprintsprograms.com/ (last accessed October 5, 2017).

Clark, S. 2011. "The Role of Law Enforcement on Schools: The Virginia Experience – A Practitioner Report." *New Directions for Youth Development* 129, 89–101. DOI: 10.1002/yd.

Cornell, D. 2006. *School Violence: Fears versus Facts*. Mahwah, NJ: Lawrence Erlbaum.

Cornell, D. 2015. "Our Schools Are Safe: Challenging the Misperception That Schools Are Dangerous Places." Invited commentary for *American Journal of Orthopsychiatry* 85, 217–220. DOI: 10.1037/ort0000064.

Cornell, D., Allen, K., and Fan, X. 2012. "A Randomized Controlled Study of the Virginia Student Threat Assessment Guidelines in Grades K–12." *School Psychology Review* 41, 100–115.

Cornell, D., Gregory, A., and Fan, X. 2011. "Reductions in Long-term Suspensions Following Adoption of the Virginia Student Threat Assessment Guidelines." *Bulletin of the National Association of Secondary School Principals* 95, 175–194.

Cornell, D., Maeng, J., Huang, F., Burnette, A., Datta, P., and Heilbrun, A. 2015. *Threat Assessment in Virginia Schools: Technical Report of the Threat Assessment Survey for 2013–2014.* Charlottesville, VA: Curry School of Education, University of Virginia.

Cornell, D. and Sheras, P. 2006. *Guidelines for Responding to Student Threats of Violence.* Longmont, CO: Sopris West.

Cornell, D., Sheras, P., Gregory, A., and Fan, X. 2009. "A Retrospective Study of School Safety Conditions in High Schools Using the Virginia Threat Assessment Guidelines versus Alternative Approaches." *School Psychology Quarterly* 24, 119–129.

Cornell, D., Sheras, P. Kaplan, S., McConville, D., Douglass, J., Elkon, A., McKnight, L., Branson, C., and Cole, J. 2004. "Guidelines for Student Threat Assessment: Field-test Findings." *School Psychology Review* 33, 527–546.

Dwyer, K., Osher, D., and Warger, C. 1998. *Early Warning, Timely Response: A Guide to Safe Schools.* Washington, DC: US Department of Education.

Fabelo, T., Thompson, M.D., Plotkin, M., Carmichael, D., Marchbanks, M.P., and Booth, E.A. 2011. *Breaking Schools' Rules: A Statewide Study of How School Discipline Relates to Students' Success and Juvenile Justice Involvement.* New York: Council of State Governments Justice Center.

Fazel, S., Singh, J.P., Doll, H., and Grann, M. 2012. "Use of Risk Assessment Instruments to Predict Violence and Antisocial Behaviour in 73 Samples Involving 24 827 People: Systematic Review and Meta-analysis." *BMJ* 345, e4692.

Fein, R.A., Vossekuil, B., Pollack, W.S., Borum, R., Modzeleski, W., and Reddy, M. 2002. *Threat Assessment in Schools: A Guide to Managing Threatening Situations and Creating Safe School Climates.* Washington, DC: US Department of Education and US Secret Service, National Threat Assessment Center.

Gastic, B. 2011. "Metal Detectors and Feeling Safe at School." *Education and Urban Society* 43, 486–498.

Hankin, A., Hertz, M., and Simon, T. 2011. "Impacts of Metal Detector Use in Schools: Insights from 15 Years of Research." *Journal of School Health* 81, 100–106.

Hoffmann, J., Meloy, J.R., and Sheridan, L. 2013. "Contemporary Research on Stalking, Threatening, and Attacking Public Figures." *International Handbook of Threat Assessment*, 160.

JustChildren and Cornell, D. 2013. *Prevention v. Punishment: Threat Assessment, School Suspensions, and Racial Disparities.* Legal Aid Justice Center, Charlottesville, VA. https://www.justice4all.org/wp-content/uploads/2013/12/UVA-and-JustChildren-Report-Prevention-v.-Punishment.pdf (last accessed October 5, 2017).

Kaplan, S. and Cornell, D. 2005. "Threats of Violence by Students in Special Education." *Behavioral Disorders* 31, 107–119.

Kropp, P.R. and Cook, A.N. 2014. "Intimate Partner Violence, Stalking, and Femicide." *International Handbook of Threat Assessment*, edited by J.R. Meloy and J. Hoffmann, pp. 179–194. New York: Oxford University Press.

Lee, T., Cornell, D., Gregory, A., and Fan, X. 2011. "High Suspension Schools and Dropout Rates for Black and White Students." *Education and Treatment of Children* 34, 167–192.

Linskey, A. 2013. "Newtown Rampage Spurs $5 Billion School Security Spending." *Bloomberg Business*, November 14. http://www.bloomberg.com/news/articles/2013-11-14/schools-boosting-security-spending-after-newtown-massacre (last accessed October 5, 2017).

Losen, D.J. and Martinez, T.E. 2013. *Out of School and off Track: The Overuse of Suspensions in American Middle and High Schools.* Los Angeles, CA: The UCLA Center for Civil Rights Remedies at The Civil Rights Project.

McCarthy, J. 2014. *Fear for Child's Safety Nearly Back to Pre-Sandy Hook Levels.* Gallup, August 13. http://www.gallup.com/poll/174827/fear-child-safety-nearly-back-pre-sandy-hook-levels.aspx (last accessed October 5, 2017).

Meloy, J.R., White, S.G., and Hart, S. 2013. "Workplace Assessment of Targeted Violence Risk: The Development and Reliability of the WAVR-21." *Journal of Forensic Sciences* 58, 1353–1358. DOI: 10.1111/1556-4029.12196.

Modzeleski, W., Feucht, T., Rand, M., Hall, J., Simon, T., Butler, L., et al. 2008. "School-associated Student Homicides – United States, 1992–2006." *Morbidity & Mortality Weekly Report* 57(2), 33–36.

Morgan, E., Salomen, N., Plotkin, M., and Cohen, R. 2014. *The School Discipline Consensus Report: Strategies from the Field to Keep Students Engaged in School and out of the Juvenile Justice System.* The Council of State Governments Justice Center, New York. http://csgjusticecenter.org/wp-content/uploads/2014/06/The_School_Discipline_Consensus_Report.pdf (last accessed October 19, 2017).

Mozaffarian, D., Hemenway, D., and Ludwig, D.S. 2013. "Curbing Gun Violence: Lessons from Public Health Successes." *JAMA: Journal of the American Medical Association* 309, 551–552. DOI:10.1001/jama.2013.38.

National Registry of Evidence-Based Programs and Practices. 2013. *Virginia Student Threat Assessment Guidelines.* http://nrepp.samhsa.gov/landing.aspx.

Nekvasil, E. and Cornell, D. 2012. "Student Reports of Peer Threats of Violence: Prevalence and Outcomes." *Journal of School Violence* 11, 357–375.

Nekvasil, E., Cornell, D., and Huang, F. 2015. "Prevalence and Offense Characteristics of Multiple Casualty Homicides: Are Schools at Higher Risk than Other Locations?" *Psychology of Violence* 5(3), 236–245.

O'Connell, M.E., Boat, T., and Warner, K.E. 2009. *Preventing Mental, Emotional, and Behavioral Disorders among Young People: Progress and Possibilities.* Washington, DC: Institute of Medicine; National Research Council. National Academies Press.

O'Toole, M.E. 2000. *The School Shooter: A Threat Assessment Perspective.* Quantico, VA: National Center for the Analysis of Violent Crime, Federal Bureau of Investigation.

Petrosino, A., Guckenburg, S., and Fronius, T. 2012. "'Policing Schools' Strategies: A Review of the Evaluation Evidence." *Journal of Multidisciplinary Evaluation* 8, 80–101.

Robers, S., Kemp, J., Rathbun, A., and Morgan, R.E. 2014. *Indicators of School Crime and Safety: 2013* (NCES 2014-042/NCJ 243299). National Center for Education Statistics, US Department of Education, and Bureau of Justice Statistics, Office of Justice Programs, US Department of Justice, Washington, DC.

Rubinkam, M. 2013. "Kids' Recent School Suspensions Renew Debate over Zero Tolerance." *Huffington Post.* http://www.huffingtonpost.com/2013/02/19/kids-school-suspensions_n_2717996.html.

Saad, L. 1999. "Public Views Littleton Tragedy as Sign of Deeper Problems in Country." *Gallup*, April 23. http://news.gallup.com/poll/3898/public-views-littleton-tragedy-sign-deeper-problems-country.aspx (last accessed October 5, 2017).

Sheriff, N. 2015. "Guns in Schools: Using Threat Assessments to Prevent School Violence." *Aljazeera America*, January 28. http://america.aljazeera.com/articles/2015/1/28/how-to-stop-school-shootings.html (last accessed October 5, 2017).

Strong, K. and Cornell, D. 2008. "Student Threat Assessment in Memphis City Schools: A Descriptive Report." *Behavioral Disorders* 34, 42–54.

Substance Abuse and Mental Health Services Administration. 2014. SAMHSA's National Registry of Evidence-based Programs and Practices. US Department of Health and Human Services. http://nrepp.samhsa.gov/Index.aspx (last accessed January 15, 2014).

Theriot, M.T. 2009. "School Resources Officers and the Criminalization of Student Behavior." *Journal of Criminal Justice* 37, 280–287.

Van Dreal, J. 2011. *Assessing Student Threats: A Handbook for Implementing the Salem-Keizer System*. Lanham, MD: Rowman & Littlefield.

Van Dyke, R. and Schroeder, J. 2006. "Implementation of the Dallas Threat of Violence Risk Assessment." In *The Handbook of School Violence and School Safety*, edited by S.R. Jimerson and M.J. Furlong, pp. 603–616. Mahwah, NJ: Lawrence Erlbaum.

Vossekuil, B., Fein, R.A., Reddy, M., Borum, R., and Modzeleski, W. 2002. *The Final Report and Findings of the Safe School Initiative: Implications for the Prevention of School Attacks in the United States*. Washington, DC: US Secret Service and US Department of Education. http://www.secretservice.gov/ntac/ssi_guide.pdf.

Wilson, S.J. and Lipsey, M.W. 2007. "School-based Interventions for Aggressive and Disruptive Behavior: Update of a Meta-analysis." *American Journal of Preventive Medicine* 33, 130–143. DOI: 10.1016/j.amepre.2007.04.01.

3

School Shootings, Societal Violence and Gun Culture

Douglas Kellner

School shootings and gun violence are a plague on our schools and society in the USA today. I have been writing about school shootings and an out-of-control gun culture since the Virginia Tech shootings on April 16, 2007 which was inspired by the Columbine High shootings of April 20, 1999. My initial studies produced *Guys and Guns Amok: Domestic Terrorism and School Shootings from the Oklahoma City Bombings to the Virginia Tech Massacre* (Kellner 2008), and since then I have periodically tracked school and other mass shootings and the continued plague of gun violence and a virulent gun culture in the United States.

As I began writing this study on Wednesday June 1 as my semester teaching at UCLA was winding down, I walked by the television and was shocked to see gun violence had struck my own UCLA campus. Initial reports indicated that two were dead in the shooting that took place in the fourth-floor office in an engineering building close to where I taught in the Graduate School of Education and Information Studies. Reports indicated that the two people were shot and killed, and rumors swirled through the campus and media for the next hours suggesting the possibility of another shooter, or shooters, loose on campus.

At 9.49 a.m. UCLA's BruinAlert system told students and faculty to avoid the Engineering School area and to lockdown in place. Around 10.00 a.m., Los Angeles Police Department (LAPD) forces arrived, accompanied by SWAT teams and police helicopters, sealed off the campus, and went into tactical lockdown. The first responders were directed to the fourth-floor office of a building called Engineering IV, where the gunshots had been heard. The police announced that two bodies had been found, and soon after it was revealed that one victim was a professor and that the shooter had apparently taken his own life.

Two handguns and a suicide note were found near the two bodies and the police announced that the victim was a professor in the engineering department and that the shooter was apparently a student. There were initially reports, however, that a second shooter could still be active on campus and the lockdown remained in place until noon. When the lockdown order was given, students and teachers discovered that few of the classrooms had secure locks, leading students to take creative measures to bolt their doors, and students and faculty anxiously barricaded themselves in their rooms or offices until the all-clear signal was given after noon.

The Wiley Handbook on Violence in Education: Forms, Factors, and Preventions, First Edition.
Edited by Harvey Shapiro.
© 2018 John Wiley & Sons, Inc. Published 2018 by John Wiley & Sons, Inc.

The suicide note at the UCLA crime scene indicated that the shooter had killed a second victim in Minnesota. It was discovered that this was the shooter's wife, from whom he was apparently separated, whose body was found in her apartment (Giaritelli 2016). Apparently, the shooter killed his wife, loaded up his car with weapons, and drove to UCLA to shoot the engineering professor and another UCLA professor whose name was found on a "kill list" found in the shooter's home, but who was not on campus that day. In the meantime, gun violence continued to erupt throughout the LA area and the entire nation on a daily basis, culminating in a mass shooting in Orlando, Florida on June 12, 2016 that left around 50 dead and more than 50 wounded, appraised one of the worst mass shootings in US history.[1]

School shootings and domestic terrorism have been proliferating on a global level in the 2000s, as in recent years there have been rampage shootings in Finland, Germany, Greece, Brazil, and other countries as well as the United States. Although there may be national differences, in all cases the shootings feature young men in crisis who explode with rage, using guns and violence to resolve their crises and creating a media spectacle and celebrity through their deadly actions. Media coverage of the phenomenon rarely, if ever, roots rampage killing in male rage and crises of masculinity, and fails to see how the violence is a pathological form of resolving crises in masculinity, in which men in crisis use the media to gain celebrity and to overcome feelings of powerlessness and alienation. The media and academic discussions also largely tend to ignore the connection between crises in masculinity and guns, and thus fail to see how the plague of school shootings is a form of "guys and guns amok."

Crises in Masculinities

By "crises in masculinities," I refer to a dominant societal connection between masculinity and being a tough guy, assuming what Jackson Katz (2006) describes as a "tough guise," a mask or facade of aggressive assertiveness, to cover up vulnerabilities. The crises erupt in outbreaks of violence and societal murder, as super-angry men act out their rage, which can take extremely violent forms such as political assassinations, serial and mass murders, school and workplace shootings, and other forms of societal violence.

Each shooting has its own specific dynamics and each killer has his own history and grievances (it's almost always men, so I use masculine pronouns). Yet the shootings have in common crises in masculinities and an out-of-control gun culture. "Loser" males immerse themselves in gun culture to express their rage, choose targets or venues, and a gun rampage can result. Sometimes the shooters have specific targets, for example, the UCLA shooter who had grievances against his former engineering professor, or the Orlando mass shooter who targeted the gay and lesbian community. School shootings, by contrast, are often more indiscriminate, with shooters like the Columbine, Virginia Tech, or Sandy Hook killers opening fire and shooting whoever was in their pathway (see Kellner 2008, 2013, 2014).

---

1 Actually, there were many massacres of Native Americans in an earlier period of US history (see Nelson 2016).

Crises in masculinities are grounded in deteriorating socioeconomic possibilities for men and are aggravated by our current economic troubles and fevered political situation with presidential candidates targeting minorities and exacerbating tensions around race, gender, sexuality, religion, and other issues. Crises of masculinity and accelerating gun violence are also produced in part by a media which repeatedly shows violence as a way of solving problems. Explosions of male rage and rampage shootings are also connected to the escalation of war and militarism in the United States, from the long nightmare of Vietnam through the military interventions of the Bush–Cheney administration in Afghanistan and Iraq and the Obama administration's intervention in Libya and the ongoing war in the Middle East against ISIS and other terror groups, as well as to accelerating social violence in the media and society at large.

To be sure, there is a tradition of social scientists and activists who have explored connections between crime, violence, and masculinity. In *Masculinities and Crime* (2003) and other writings, James Messerschmidt explores the link between masculine socialization and the overwhelming prevalence of male perpetration of crime – including violent crime. Emphasizing the social construction of gender, class, race, and crime, Messerschmidt stresses how these factors are interrelated, and that men learn violent behavior both as a means of "doing masculinity" and to assert dominance over women and other men, behavior that socially reproduces structures of capitalism and patriarchy.

Messerschmidt and Raewyn W. Connell (Connell and Messerschmidt 2005) critically interrogate the concept of "hegemonic masculinity," whereby dominant models of an assertive – and sometimes violent – masculinity are constructed that reinforce gendered hierarchies among men and reinforce men's power over women. Hegemonic masculinity is the dominant form of masculinity in a culture at a specific period, and in the United States over the past century hegemonic masculinity is associated with military heroism, corporate power, sports achievement, action adventure movie stars, and being tough, aggressive, and macho – ideals reproduced in corporate, political, military, sports, and gun culture, as well as in Hollywood film, video games, men's magazines and other forms of media culture, and sites like the frat house, locker room, board room, male-dominated workplaces, bars, and hangouts where men congregate.

In *The Macho Paradox* (2006), Jackson Katz explores how this conception of violent masculinity helps produce violence against women. Calling upon men to question such behavior and to seek alternative masculinities, Katz challenges them to confront violence against women and to struggle against it. All of these scholars share a critical relation to dominant conceptions of a hegemonic hyper and violent masculinity and all of them search for alternative modes of masculinity, a project that I share.

In this chapter, I argue that school shooters, and other gun killers, share male rage. They attempt to resolve crises of masculinities through violent behavior, exhibit a fetishism of guns or weapons, and engage in gun violence orchestrated as media spectacle. The combination of male rage and crisis, mental health issues, and obsession with guns is lethal and can lead to the mass shootings that have plagued our era.

Yet there are many causes of the rise of school violence and events like the Columbine and Virginia Tech school shootings (Kellner 2008), so I do not want to advocate a reductive causal approach. Complex historical events like the Iraq invasion (Kellner 2005) or the Virginia Tech and Sandy Hook shootings (Kellner 2008, 2013) require a multiperspectivist vision and interpretation of key factors that constitute the constellation from which events can be interpreted, explained, and better understood. Thus, addressing the causes of problems like societal violence and school shootings involves a range of apparently disparate things such as critique of male socialization and construction of ultra-masculine male identities, the prevalence of gun culture and militarism, and a media culture that promotes violence and retribution while circulating and sensationalizing media spectacle and a culture of celebrity. Such a constellation helps construct the identities, values, and behavior that incite individuals to use violence to resolve their crises of masculinity through creation of an ultra-masculine identity and its associated gun violence.

Accordingly, solutions that I suggest to the problems of school violence and shootings range from more robust and rational gun laws, to better school and workplace security with stronger mental health institutions and better communication between legal, medical, and school administrations, to the reconstruction of masculinity and the reconstruction of education for democracy (Kellner 2008, 2014). In addition, we must consider examining better ways of addressing crime and violence than prisons and capital punishment, draconian measures aimed increasingly today at youth and people of color. Today our schools are like prisons, while in a better society schools would become centers of learning and self-development, while prisons could also be centers of learning, rehabilitation, and job training and not punitive and dangerous schools for crime and violence (see Davis and Mendietta 2005).

Guns in America, School Shootings, and Media Spectacle

To grasp the magnitude of societal violence and school shooting requires a critical theory of society focusing on problems of the present age. Escalating gun violence in schools and other sectors of society today in the United States is a national scandal and serious social problem. The United States has been experiencing epidemic levels of gun violence annually. According to the US Centers for Disease Control and Prevention, firearm violence claims over 30,000 lives a year, and for every person who dies from a gunshot wound, two others are wounded, meaning that every year there are more than 100,000 Americans who become victims of gun violence (National Center for Injury Prevention & Control 2011).[2]

Gun ownership is rampant in the United States and gun violence is epidemic. According to an article published after the April 2012 Oikos University school shooting in Oakland: "The United States has 90 guns for every 100 citizens, making it the most heavily armed society in the world" (MacInnis 2007). US citizens own 270 million of the world's 875 million known firearms, according to the Small Arms Survey 2007 by the Geneva-based Graduate Institute of International Studies. About 4.5 million of the 8 million new guns manufactured worldwide each year are purchased in the United States, the report said (*Press TV* 2012).

The massacre at Virginia Tech in 2007 was the twenty-fifth school shooting on an American campus since the Columbine school shootings in 1999. That figure represents more than half the number of shootings at schools across in the world in the same time

---

2 For useful statistics on gun violence in the United States, see Law Center to Prevent Gun Violence at http://smartgunlaws.org/gun-law-statistics-and-research/(last accessed October 5, 2017).

span (Infoplease 2016). Deadly school shootings at a wide range of schools have claimed over 400 student and faculty lives since Columbine. As publicists for a new edition of Lieberman's *The Shooting Game* (2006) indicate: "In March and April of 2006, 16 deadly Columbine-style plots were hatched by over 25 students arrested across the U.S.A. from the heartland up to North Pole, Alaska. As the fall semester began, there were more deadly shootings in Montreal, Colorado, Wisconsin and even a tiny Amish school in Pennsylvania."[3] This alarming trend has continued to the present with no end in sight.

My studies of school shootings in the past decades suggest that many school shooters have orchestrated shootings as media spectacles to dramatize personal grievances or to lash out against supposed tormentors, gaining their short bursts of celebrity and fame. In the case of the Virginia Tech shootings, it was clear that the alienated student and frustrated writer Seung-hui Cho carried out "The Virginia Tech Massacre" in which he was star, director, and producer. His multimedia dossier revealed that he was imitating images from films and carrying out a vengeance drama in the tradition of the Columbine School shooters, whom he cited as "martyrs" (Kellner 2008). And the Orlando shooter Omar Mateen posted on Facebook the day of the attack to publicize the attack, posted during the attack, and called his ex-wife to see how the media was presenting the event (Smith and Ackerman 2016).

The following year, in the February 14, 2008 shootings at Northern Illinois University, a former student, Steven Kazmierczak, leaped from behind the curtain onto a stage in a large lecture hall. Armed with a barrage of weapons and dressed in black, he began randomly shooting students in a geology class, killing five before shooting himself. While his motivations were never made clear, it is striking that he was obviously creating a highly theatrical spectacle of violence in the tradition of the Columbine and Virginia Tech shootings.[4]

My notion of media spectacle builds on French theorist Guy Debord's conception of the society of spectacle, but differs significantly from Debord's concept. For Debord, spectacle "unifies and explains a great diversity of apparent phenomena" (Debord 1970, #10). Debord's conception, first developed in the 1960s, continues to circulate through the Internet and other academic and subcultural sites today. It describes a media and consumer society, organized around the production and consumption of images, commodities, and staged events.

For Debord, "spectacle" constituted the overarching concept to describe the media and consumer society, including the packaging, promotion, and display of commodities and the production and effects of all media. Using the term "media spectacle," I am largely focusing on various forms of technologically constructed media productions that are produced and disseminated through the so-called mass media, ranging from radio and television to the Internet and the latest wireless gadgets. Every medium, from music to television, from news to advertising, has multiple forms of spectacle, involving such things in the realm of music as the classical music spectacle, the opera spectacle, the rock spectacle, and over the last decades the hip-hop spectacle. The forms and circulation of the spectacle evolve over time and multiply with new technological developments.

---

3 The quote can be found at http://www.goodreads.com/book/show/1901337.The_Shooting_Game (last accessed October 5, 2017).
4 See the "Timeline of School Shooting" at http://www.infoplease.com/ipa/A0777958.html (accessed June 14, 2016).

On my account, there are many levels and categories of media spectacle (Kellner 2003a). Some media spectacles, like Dayan and Katz's *Media Events* (1992), are recurrent phenomena of media culture that celebrate dominant values and institutions, as well as its modes of conflict resolution. They include media extravaganzas like the Oscars and Emmys, or sports events like the Super Bowl or World Cup, which celebrate basic values of competition and winning. Politics is increasingly mediated by media spectacle. Political conflicts, campaigns, and those attention-grabbing occurrences that we call "news" have all been subjected to the logic of spectacle and tabloidization in the era of the media sensationalism, infotainment, political scandal and contestation, seemingly unending cultural war, and the phenomenon of the War on Terror which has characterized the post-9/11 epoch (see Kellner 2003b).

Spectacles of terror, like the 9/11 attacks on the Twin Towers and Pentagon, differ significantly from spectacles that celebrate or reproduce the existing society as in Guy Debord's "society of the spectacle," or the "media events" analyzed by Dayan and Katz (1992), which describe how political systems exploited televised live, ceremonial, and preplanned events. Spectacles of terror are highly disruptive events carried out by oppositional groups, or individuals who are carrying out politics or war by other means. Like the media and consumer spectacles described by Debord, spectacles of terror reduce individuals to passive objects, manipulated by existing institutions and figures. However, the spectacles of terror produce fear which terrorists hope will demoralize the objects of their attack, but which are often manipulated by conservative groups, like the Bush–Cheney administration, to push through right-wing agendas, cut back on civil liberties, and militarize the society.

I argue that what domestic terrorists like Timothy McVeigh (Oklahoma City bombings) and shooters such as those who perpetrated the massacres at Columbine, Virginia Tech, Sandy Hook etc. have in common is that the perpetrators created media spectacle to act out their grievances and in so doing achieved celebrity (Kellner 2008). This achievement of celebrity through acts of violence transformed into media spectacles no doubt promoted copycat shootings, now on a global level. Indeed, school shootings can be seen as a form of terrorism, although there are often significant differences. Certain forms of terrorism have specific political objectives while school shootings are more grounded in individual grievances or crises. Both, however, use violence to obtain goals and aim at media spectacle to get publicity for their actions, and in some cases celebrity. Both are obviously forms of terror and use violence to generate fear and destruction. And in most cases, terrorism and school shootings are carried out by men, using guns and violence to resolve their crises of masculinity through creating media spectacles (Kellner 2008).

My cultural studies approach to guns and school shootings reads events like school shootings in their sociohistorical context and uses a critical theory of society to help situate, interpret, and trace the effects of certain texts, artifacts, or events (see Hammer and Kellner 2009; Kellner and Durham 2012). Critical theory is historical theory, contextualizing its object in its historical matrix, and so I felt the need to ground my studies of guns and school shootings in the contemporary moment in the context of the history of guns in the United States and controversies over guns and their regulation. In 2000, Michael A. Bellesiles published *Arming America: The Origins of a National Gun Culture* with the prestigious Alfred Knopf publishers. It was garnished with an impressive array of reviews and won the Bancroft Award as the best historical study of the year. The book, however, was highly controversial and provoked a firestorm of criticism.

Right-wing gun advocates and their academic minions ferociously attacked Bellesiles's scholarship. It turns out he made mistakes, among other things, in his sample and inter-pretation of probate records, which resulted in him underestimating the number of guns privately held in colonial America. With the ensuing scandal and fierce attacks, Bellesiles was stripped of the Bancroft prize and eventually lost his job at Emory University.[5]

Bellesiles's history describes the origins of a national gun culture and the ways that the gun became central to American life and concepts of masculinity. He seems to have underestimated the extent of early colonial gun culture and gun culture after the Revolution, but convincingly depicts the explosion of gun culture at the time of the Civil War, with the mass production of guns and the manufacture and marketing of guns in the post-Civil War period. He also convincingly reproduces the debates over guns at the time of the Constitutional Convention when Federalists fought for a centralized federal government with a federally controlled standing army, while anti-Federalists supported state militias (Bellesiles 2000, 208ff.). As Bellesiles argued: "The Constitutional Convention hammered out a document full of compromise and barely obtained concessions. On one point at least there was no disagreement: Congress should arm the militia" (2000, 213). Bellesiles sets out the debates over whether the militia should remain under the direct control of state or federal government, whether or not to have a standing army, and what gun rights should be included. The result was the Second Amendment to the Bill of Rights which held: "A well-regulated Militia, being necessary to the security of a free State, the right of the People to keep and bear Arms, shall not be infringed" (2000, 217).

The context of the Second Amendment suggests an original intent to bestow the right to bear arms within the confines of a militia, itself to be regulated by the federal govern-ment (i.e., as in the phrase "*well-regulated* Militia" in the Second Amendment; empha-sis mine). Some have argued that until the last few decades, the Second Amendment was largely read as supporting gun rights within militias, but not in terms of individual rights to bear firearms. But recently, accordingly to legal scholars and commentators, the Second Amendment has been interpreted by law professors, the courts, and the public to provide individual gun ownership rights to citizens, though controversies over the meaning of the Second Amendment continue to this day.[6]

I fear that initially Bellesiles and his impressive array of reviewers wanted to believe that gun culture was not so deeply entrenched in American history and that an earlier period could be pointed to as an ideal to emulate, whereas the problem of guns and violence may be more deeply rooted and intractable than liberals want to acknowledge. Both Bellesiles and Cramer (2006) emphasize the tremendous violence of the Indian wars that continued into the nineteenth century, the ferocity of the Civil War, and the eventual triumph of gun culture in the United States. They also point out how the

---

5 For Winkler's account of the promotion and limitations of Bellesiles's scholarship, see Winkler (2011, 22–31).

6 See Liptak (2007). Liptak notes: "There used to be an almost complete scholarly and judicial consensus that the Second Amendment protects only a collective right of the states to maintain militias. That consensus no longer exists – thanks largely to the work over the last 20 years of several leading liberal law professors, who have come to embrace the view that the Second Amendment protects an individual right to own guns." Liptak suggests that opinions over the last two decades by liberal law professors helped produce a decision whereby a federal appeals court struck down, in March 2007, a gun control law on Second Amendment grounds. Winkler (2011) documents how the militia argument for interpreting the Second Amendment and gun rights has been replaced by interpreting the Second Amendment in terms of private gun ownership.

federal government, from the beginning, regulated gun ownership and use, preventing at different times gun ownership by blacks, indentured servants, Indians, and other stigmatized and oppressed groups. Together, the books present a national history of gun culture that has bequeathed serious problems to the present age.

Building on these studies, Adam Winkler argues in *Gun Fight* (2011) that Americans have had the right to bear arms from the beginning of the Republic, but that there is also a long tradition of gun control. Recognizing that the Second Amendment, with its talk of militias, is "maddeningly ambiguous," Winkler notes that a balance between gun control and gun rights has marked US history up until the current era when gun rights groups began to dominate the discourse. Winkler points out that the National Rifle Association (NRA) strongly supported gun control until the 1970s, and that even the Ku Klux Klan started off as a gun control group – wanting to keep guns out of the hands of newly freed African American slaves.

Winkler begins his book by claiming that both "gun grabbers" and "gun nuts" pursue extremist objectives, either wanting to abolish gun ownership completely, or resisting even minimal gun control.[7] Winkler follows a 2011 Supreme Court ruling *District of Columbia v. Heller* that expands Second Amendment constitutional interpretation to move from a right to bear arms within militias to private gun ownership rights, and documents the fierce battles still going on, between gun rights and gun control proponents, recognizing that the gun rights forces backed by the NRA have the upper hand.

Obviously, properly understanding the role of guns and gun culture in the epidemic of school shootings requires taking seriously the need for gun control and reforming of laws concerning access to fire arms. Yet since I believe that school shootings have multiple causes, there need to be multiple solutions which ultimately involve a restructuring of school and society, including new concepts of masculinity, better mental health facilities and treatment in schools and society, better gun control, and a curriculum in schools that involves peaceful conflict resolution, courses in non-violence and peace studies, and teaching compassion and empathy, while attempting to overcome or diminish societal alienation.

Yet, clearly, more rational policies about access to guns is one of the solutions to the problem. It is heartening that groups of people appalled by the Virginia Tech shootings have long campaigned to close gun show loopholes where people can purchase firearms without adequate back ground checks. But ABC's *20/20* on April 10, 2009 broadcast a segment where young men bought scores of weapons on the floor of the gun show, or even in the parking lot, without showing any identity or having any checkup, so this loophole of gun shows in many states is glaring. Likewise, a *60 Minutes* report on April 12, 2009 showed the startling increase in gun sales and increase in NRA

---

7 Interestingly, Barbara Kopple's HBO documentary *Gun Fight* (2011), with the same title and year of release as Winkler's book, has quite a different take on the debate between gun control and gun rights forces in the United States. While Winkler presents the two camps as extremist and diametrically opposed, Kopple's film shows gun control forces who are extremely reasonable, showing major figures in the Brady Center gun control camp as moderate. In the film *Gun Fight*, they insist that they are simply advocating that the gun show loopholes be closed where individuals can buy guns from private dealers at gun shows without any background check, registration, or paper trail. By contrast, Winkler presents the Brady group as extreme "gun grabbers" whose goal is banning and seizing all guns (35), a position at odds with their portrayal in Kopple's *Gun Fight*. It thus appears that Winkler's attempt to brand gun control advocates as unabashedly absolutist in a desire to ban guns completely is problematic.

membership after Obama's election in 2008, as if gun enthusiasts feared that the government was suddenly going to pull their rifles from their "cold dead hands."[8]

Barbara Kopple's 2011 HBO documentary *Gun Fight* also demonstrates how easy it is to purchase guns without background checks at gun shows from private owners, or using "straw purchasers" with a friend who can easily pass a background check to buy guns from those excluded because of age, mental health issues, or a criminal background, as did a friend of the Columbine shooters who bought guns for them at a gun show (Cullen 2009, 90, 122). And Katie Couric's 2016 documentary *Under the Gun* explored issues of gun violence and gun control in the contemporary US context and argued that a large majority of gun owners actually support reasonable gun safety measures that the National Rifle Association (NRA) rejects.

We also need to examine the role of the Internet as a source of ammunition and firearms, where anyone can assume a virtual identity and purchase lethal weapons and ammo; it is perhaps not coincidental that the Virginia Tech and Northern Illinois University shooters both bought weapons used in their shootings from the same online business.[9]

On the political front, however, neither Democrat nor Republican administrations have been able to effectively address the issue of gun control. As I note below, there were efforts at rational gun safety legislation by the Obama administration, but it was blocked by the Republican-controlled Congress and lobbying by the National Rifle Association (NRA) which has opposed all gun safety legislation and targeted politicians to advocate gun safety legislation. The issue, however, is being addressed during the 2016 presidential election, as Hillary Clinton called for a ban on assault rifles the day after the Orlando mass shooting, and the Democrats have supported several rational gun safety measures in their 2016 platform, but Republican candidate Donald Trump claims he is a big guns right supporter, brags about carrying lethal weapons, and has followed the directives of the Republican Party which for years has been loath to call for any gun control, following the dictates of one of their major funders, the NRA.

Indeed, the problem of escalating gun violence and random shootings is a larger problem than gun control alone. With discernible and accelerating alienation, frustration, anger, and even rage in the schools, universities, workplaces, public spaces, and communities of contemporary US society, we clearly need better mental health facilities and monitoring of troubled individuals. Yet, we also need the monitoring of institutions like schools and the provision of mental health facilities to ensure that people are getting adequate treatment and that we are not breeding a generation of killers.

Schools and universities, for example, have been scrambling to ensure that they have in place counseling and monitoring programs to deal with troubled students, as well as safety plans for how to deal with violence and crises. Schools should be assessed

---

8 On the April *60 Minutes report, see* http://www.cbsnews.com/stories/2009/04/09/60minutes/
main4931769.shtml (accessed April 15, 2012). See also, "Gun Sales: Will The 'Loophole' Close?," *CBS News*,
July 26, 2009 at http://www.cbsnews.com/2100-18560_162-4931769.html (accessed April 15, 2012).

9 See "Gun Dealer Sold to Both Va. Tech, NIU Shooters," *USA Today*, February 16, 2008 at http://www.
usatoday.com/news/nation/2008-02-16-gundealer-niu-vatech-shooters_N.htm (accessed April 16, 2012).
Interestingly, Eric Thompson's company, TGSCOM Inc., which sold Cho and Kazmierczak weapons through
his website (www.thegunsource.com) offered customers weapons at cost for two weeks to help citizens get
the weapons they needed for their own self-defense. See "Owner of Web-based Firearms Company that Sold
to Virginia Tech and NIU Shooters to Forgo Profits to Help Prevent Future Loss of Life," April 25, 2008,
TGSCOM Inc. at http://www.thegunsource.com/Article.aspx?aKey=Guns_at_Cost (accessed April 16, 2012).

concerning how well they are caring for their students and whether they are providing a secure learning environment. After the Columbine shootings, there were strong demands for more student safety in schools, but often this led to increased surveillance, metal detectors, and harassment of students – which in many cases increased student alienation and maybe increased the possibility of violence, requiring serious assessment of how well violence prevention programs have or have not worked in schools (see Muschert 2007; Muschert et al. 2014).

To be sure, in an era of war and growing poverty, there is likely to be increased societal violence, so that problems of random and targeted shootings will no doubt be a problem that we will face in the years to come. It is important, however, to address the issue of crises of masculinities, social alienation, and eruptions of societal violence and not use simplistic categories like mental health (i.e., "he's just crazy") to explain the issue, since mental illness is a complex phenomenon that has a variety of causes and expressions. It is also important not to look for scapegoats like the Internet, media, prescription drugs, or any one factor that may well contribute to the problem of rampage shooting but is not the underlying cause. Rather, we need to see the seriousness of the problems of school and rampage shootings and come up with an array of responses that will produce a more productive and humane society.

Beyond the Culture of Male Violence and Rage

In the remainder of the chapter, I argue that dealing with problems of school and societal violence will require reconstruction of male identities and critique of masculinist socialization and identities, as well as changing gun laws and effecting stricter gun control. Unfortunately, the media, our rancorous political culture, gang culture, sports, and military culture generate ultra-macho men as an ideal, producing societal problems such as violence against women and gang murder (see Katz 2006; Kellner 2008). Katz urges young men to renounce these ideals and behavior and construct alternative notions of masculinity, and he concludes that reconstructing masculinity and overcoming aggressive and violent macho behavior and values provides "a vision of manhood that does not depend on putting down others in order to lift itself up. When a man stands up for social justice, non-violence, and basic human rights – for women as much as for men – he is acting in the best traditions of our civilization. That makes him not only a better man, but a better human being" (2006, 270).

Major sources of violence in US society include cultures of violence caused by poverty; masculinist military, sports, and gun culture; ultra-masculine behavior in the corporate and political world; high school bullying and fighting; general societal violence reproduced by media and in the family and everyday life, and in prisons, which are schools for violence. In any of these cases, an ultra-violent masculinity can explode and produce societal violence, and until we have new conceptions of what it means to be a man that include intelligence, independence, sensitivity, and the renunciation of bullying and violence, societal violence will no doubt increase.

In both the corporate and political world, Donald Trump has been a paragon of bullying. His reality TV show *The Apprentice*, which first made him a major public figure for a national audience (2004–2010), featured contests to see which applicant would win and get a job with the Trump organization, and each "contest" concluded with Trump barking "You're fired" to the loser. His 2016 presidential campaign has exhibited bullying toward his opponents, Republican and Democrat, and scapegoating of immigrants, Muslims, people of color, the disabled, women, and other targets, including a judge who is ruling on a course in which former students are claiming that Trump University is fraudulent. The issue, however, was addressed during the 2016 presidential election, as Hillary Clinton called for a ban on assault rifles, the day after the Orlando mass shooting, and the Democrats supported several rational gun safety measures in their 2016 Platform, but Republican candidate Donald Trump claims he is a big guns right supporters, brags about carrying lethal weapons, and has followed the dictates of the Republican Party which for years have been loath to call for any gun control, following the dictates of one of their major funders, the NRA – and Trump won the election intensifying the crisis of an out-of-control gun culture.

Lee Hirsch's film *Bully* (2011) has called attention to the phenomenon of bullying in schools, and *Bully* shows intense bullying taking place on school buses, playgrounds, classrooms, and neighborhoods. Focusing on five victims of bullying from various regions in the United States, two of whom committed suicide, Hirsch's film puts on display shocking physical mistreatment of high school students by their peers. In an allegorical mode, the wildly popular film *The Hunger Games* (2012) also presents a stark view of a dystopic world in which only the strongest survive and violence is valorized as the key to survival, although this time the hero is a young woman.

Sports culture is another major part of the construction of American masculinity that can take violent forms. In most of the high school shootings of the 1990s, jocks tormented young teenage boys who took revenge by asserting a hyper-violent masculinity and going on shooting rampages. Ralph Larkin (2007, 205ff.) provides a detailed analysis of "Football and Toxic High School Environments," focusing on Columbine. He describes how sports played a primary role in the school environment, how jocks were celebrities, and how they systematically abused outsiders and marginal youth like Columbine shooters Eric Harris and Dylan Klebold.

The "pattern of sports domination of high schools," Larkin suggests, "is apparently the norm in America" (2007, 206). Larkin notes how football "has become incorporated into a hyper-masculinized subculture that emphasizes physical aggression, domination, sexism, and the celebration of victory." He notes that, more "than in any other sport, defeat in football is associated with being physically dominated and humiliated" (208). Further, it is associated with militarism, as George Carlin, among others, has noted in his comedy routine:

> In football the object is for the quarterback, also known as the field general, to be on target with his aerial assault, riddling the defence by hitting his receivers with deadly accuracy in spite of the blitz, even if he has to use the shotgun. With short bullet passes and long bombs, he marches his troops into enemy territory, balancing this aerial assault with a sustained ground attack that punches holes in the forward wall of the enemy's defensive line.
>
> In baseball the object is to go home! And to be safe! (Carlin, cited in Larkin 2007, 208)

Larkin argues that football culture has "corrupted many high schools," including Columbine where "the culture of hyper masculinity reigned supreme" (209). Hence, he concludes that: "If we wish to reduce violence in high schools, we have to de-emphasize the power of sports and change the culture of hyper masculinity. Football players cannot be lords of the hallways, bullying their peers with impunity, sometimes encouraged by coaches with adolescent mentalities" (210).

Hyper-masculinity in sports is often a cauldron of homophobia and many of the school shooters were taunted about their sexuality and responded ultimately with a berserk affirmation of compensatory violence. Yet hyper-masculinity is found throughout sports, military, gun, gang, and other male subcultures, as well as the corporate and political world, often starting in the family with male socialization by the father, and is reproduced and validated constantly in films, television programs, and other forms of media culture.

Obviously, media culture is full of violence. The case studies in Chapter 3 of *Guys and Guns Amok* (Kellner 2008) show that Timothy McVeigh, the two Columbine shooters, and many other school shooters were allegedly deeply influenced by violent media culture. Yet, while media images of violence and specific books, films, TV shows, or artifacts of media culture may provide scripts for violent masculinity that young men act out, it is the broader culture of militarism, gun culture, extreme sports, ultra-violent video and computer games, subcultures of bullying and violence, and the rewarding of ultra-masculinity in the corporate and political worlds that are major factors in constructing a hegemonic violent masculinity. Media culture itself obviously contributes to this ideal of macho masculinity, but it is a contested terrain between different conceptions of masculinity and femininity, and between liberal, conservative, and more radical representations and discourses (Kellner 1995).

After dramatic school shootings and incidents of youth violence, there are usually attempts to scapegoat media culture. After the Virginia Tech shootings, the Federal Communication Commission (FCC) issued a report in late April, 2007 on "violent television programming and its impact on children" that called for expanding governmental oversight on broadcast television, but also extended content regulation to cable and satellite channels for the first time and banned some shows from time slots where children might be watching. FCC Commissioner Jonathan S. Adelstein, who is in favor of the measures, did not hesitate to invoke the Virginia Tech shootings: "particularly in sight of the spasm of unconscionable violence at Virginia Tech, but just as importantly in light of the excessive violent crime that daily affects our nation, there is a basis for appropriate federal action to curb violence in the media" (cited in cited in Gillespie 2007).

In a *Los Angeles Times* op-ed piece, Nick Gillespie, editor of *Reason*, noted that the report itself indicated that there was no causal relation between watching TV violence and committing violent acts. Further, Gillespie argued that given the steady drop in incidents of juvenile violence over the last 12 years, reaching a low not seen since at least the 1970s, it is inappropriate to demonize media culture for acts of societal violence. Yet, in my view, the proliferation of media culture and spectacle requires renewed calls for critical media literacy so that people can intelligently analyze and interpret the media and see how they are vehicles for representations of race, class, gender, sexuality, power, and violence (on critical media literacy see Funk, Kellner, and Share 2016).

In the wake of the Columbine shootings, fierce criticism and scapegoating of media and youth culture erupted. Oddly, there was less finger pointing at these targets after the Virginia Tech massacre –perhaps because the Korean and Asian films upon which Cho modeled his photos and videos were largely unknown in the United States, and perhaps because conservatives prefer to target jihadists or liberals as nefarious influences on Cho (Kellner 2008, ch. 1). I want to avoid, however, the extremes of demonizing media or youth culture and asserting that it is mere entertainment without serious social influence. There is no question but that the media nurture fantasies and influence behavior, sometimes sick and vile ones, and to survive in our culture requires that we are able to critically analyze and dissect media culture and not let it gain power over us. Critical media literacy empowers individuals so that they can produce critical and analytical distance from media messages and images. This provides protection from media manipulation and avoids letting the most destructive images of media gain power over us. It also enables more critical, healthy, and active relations with our culture. Media culture will not disappear and it is simply a question of how we will deal with it and whether we can develop an adequate pedagogy of critical media literacy to empower our youth.

Unfortunately, there are few media literacy courses offered in schools in the United States from kindergarten through high school. Many other countries such as Canada, Australia, and the United Kingdom have such programs (see Kellner and Share 2007). To address problems of societal violence raised in these studies requires a reconstruction of education and society, and what Herbert Marcuse referred to as "a revolution in values" and a "new sensibility."[10] The revolution in values involves breaking with values of competition, aggression, greed, and self-interest and cultivating values of equality, peace, harmony, and community. Such a revolution of values "would also make for a new morality, for new relations between the sexes and generations, for a new relation between man and nature" (Marcuse 2001, 198). Harbingers of the revolution in values, Marcuse argued, are found in "a widespread rebellion against the domineering values, of virility, heroism and force, invoking the images of society which may bring about the end of violence" (198).

The "new sensibility" in turn would cultivate the need for beauty, love, connections with nature and other people, and more democratic and egalitarian social relations. Marcuse believes that without a change in the sensibility, there can be no real social change, and that education, art, and the humanities can help cultivate the conditions for a new sensibility. Underlying the theory of the new sensibility is a concept of the active role of the senses in the constitution of experience that rejects the Kantian and other philosophical devaluations of the senses as passive, merely receptive. For Marcuse, our senses are shaped and molded by society, yet constitute in turn our primary experience of the world and provide both imagination and reason with its material. He believes that the senses are currently socially constrained and mutilated and argues that only an emancipation of the senses and a new sensibility can produce liberating social change.

Ultimately, addressing the problem of societal violence and gun control requires a democratic reconstruction of education and society, new pedagogical practices, new social relations, values, and forms of learning, which I have addressed in other books and articles (Kellner 2008, 2013). Here, I want to conclude with some comments on gun safety and the need to take rational action on the plague of violent gun murders in the United States.

Gun Safety and the Hopes for a More Secure Future

Barack Obama has noted that one of his biggest frustrations as President was failing to get Congress to pass meaningful gun safety legislation. He made consoling comments to the nation on over 15 occasions after mass shootings during his presidency, and tried to get gun safety measures passed in Congress, but was limited to passing executive

---

10 See "A Revolution in Values" in Marcuse (2001), and on the new sensibility see my introduction to the volume of collected papers of Marcuse, *Art and Liberation* (Marcuse 2006).

orders to get some rational public safety measures concerning gun control in place without being able to pass any significant gun legislation. While there was intense media discussion and calls for urgent gun safety reform during the early months of 2013 following the Sandy Hook Elementary School shooting, so far there has been no significant legislation on the national level, and the pro-gun constituency of the Republican Party, which controls Congress, makes it unlikely that serious reform will take place in the immediate future. While the Obama administration pressed for gun law reform that would mandate and expand background checks, while banning assault rifles and high-capacity cartridges, the NRA and gun lobby continued to block legislation at the national level. Although a bipartisan committee in the Senate attempted to advance a bill that would expand background checks, so far it has been blocked and there has since been little concrete action on the gun safety issue on the national stage. On the state level, however, there have been many significant gun safety laws passed in states including New York, Connecticut, Maryland, and even Colorado, and significant debates to change local gun laws throughout the country, although there continue to be fierce debates over changes in gun laws on the state, local, and national level.

The major mass shootings over the past decade, including the Orlando Florida massacre in June 2016 and the 2018 Parkland, Florida school shooting massacre, involved AR-15-style assault rifles with high-capacity magazines that made possible shooting 30 rounds of ammunition, quickly reloading, and shooting another torrent of deadly bullets. These assault rifles and high-capacity magazines were banned in the 1990s during the Clinton administration, but during the George W. Bush administration the ban expired (2004) and has allowed mass shooters ever since to buy lethal assault rifles.

The United States has suffered a plague, reaching epidemic proportions of school shootings, as well as terrorist mass shootings, accidental shooting in the home, sometimes by toddlers, and gang and gun violence in hot spots like Chicago (Healy et al. 2016). Every day there are an appalling number of deaths from gun violence and this is intolerable. However, it would be a mistake to wait and expect politicians on the national or local level to solve the problem of mass shootings and gun safety reform. This is an issue that concerns every individual who cares about their fellow citizens and wants to see a reduction in gun violence. We need an informed discussion to pressure politicians on the national, state, and local level to move toward seeing the real extent of the problem of gun violence, and the need for serious steps to address the cycle of mass shootings. The debate over school shootings and gun violence would include multiple dimensions such as mental health issues, crises of masculinities, and a culture of violence in the media and other sectors of US life. We need new conceptions of what it means to be a man that include intelligence, independence, sensitivity, and the renunciation of bullying and violence. And we need rational gun legislation without which there is no doubt but that gun violence will increase, and Americans will not live a life or in a society worthy of human beings.

References

Bellesiles, Michael A. 2000. *Arming America: The Origins of a National Gun Culture.* New York: Alfred A. Knopf.

Connell, Raewyn W. and Messerschmidt, James W. 2005. "Hegemonic Masculinity. Rethinking the Concept." *Gender & Society* 19(6), 829–859.

Cramer, Clinton E. 2006. *Armed America. The Story of How and Why Guns Became as American as Apple Pie*. Nashville, TN: Nelson Current.

Cullen, Dave. 2009. *Columbine*. New York: Hachette.

Davis, Angela, with Mendietta, Eduardo. 2005. *Abolition Democracy. Beyond Empire, Prisons, and Torture*. New York: Seven Stories Press.

Dayan, Daniel and Katz, Elihu. 1992. *Media Events: The Live Broadcasting of History*. Cambridge, MA: Harvard University Press.

Debord, Guy. 1970. *The Society of the Spectacle*. Detroit: Black and Red.

Funk, Steven, Kellner, Douglas, and Share, Jeff. 2016. "Critical Media Literacy as Transformative Pedagogy." In *Handbook of Research on Media Literacy in the Digital Age*, edited by Melda N. Yildiz and Jared Keengwe, pp. 1–30. IGI Global.

Giaritelli, Anna. 2016. "UCLA Shooter's Suicide Note about Cat Led Police to Kill List." *Washington Examiner*, June 2. http://www.washingtonexaminer.com/ucla-shooters-suicide-note-about-cat-led-police-to-kill-list/article/2592881 (last accessed October 16, 2017).

Gillespie, Nick. 2007. "The FCC's Not Mommy and Daddy." *Los Angeles Times*, May 2, A23.

Hammer, Rhonda and Kellner, Douglas, eds. 2009. *Media/Cultural Studies: Critical Approaches*. New York: Peter Lang.

Healy, Jack, Bosman, Julie, Blinder, Alan, and Turkewitz, Julie. 2016. "One Week in April, Four Toddlers Shot and Killed Themselves." *New York Times*, May 5. http://www.nytimes.com/2016/05/06/us/guns-children-deaths.html?_r=0 (last accessed October 5, 2017).

Infoplease. 2016. "A Time Line of Recent Worldwide School Shootings." http://www.infoplease.com/ipa/A0777958.html (accessed June 12, 2016).

Katz, Jackson. 2006. *The Macho Paradox*. Naperville, IL: Sourcebook.

Kellner, Douglas. 1995. *Media Culture*. London and New York: Routledge.

Kellner, Douglas. 2003a. *From September 11 to Terror War: The Dangers of the Bush Legacy*. Lanham, Md.: Rowman & Littlefield.

Kellner, Douglas. 2003b. *Media Spectacle*. London and New York: Routledge.

Kellner, Douglas. 2005. *Media Spectacle and the Crisis of Democracy*. Boulder, CO: Paradigm Press.

Kellner, Douglas. 2008. *Guys and Guns Amok: Domestic Terrorism and School Shootings from the Oklahoma City Bombings to the Virginia Tech Massacre*. Boulder, CO: Paradigm Press.

Kellner, Douglas. 2013. "The Sandy Hook Slaughter and Copy Cat Killers in a Media Celebrity Society: Analyses and Plans for Action." *Logos*, Winter, 12(1). http://logosjournal.com/2013/kellner/(last accessed October 5, 2017).

Kellner, Douglas. 2014. "Diagnosing and Preventing School Shootings." In *Responding to School Violence. Confronting the Columbine* Effect, edited by Glenn W. Muschert, Stuart Henry, Nicole L. Bracy, and Anthony A. Peguero, pp. 189–214. Boulder, CO and London: Lynne Rienner.

Kellner, Douglas and Durham, Meenakshi Gigi, eds. 2012. *Media and Cultural Studies. Key Works*, 2nd ed. Malden, MA and Oxford: Blackwell.

Kellner, Douglas and Share, Jeff. 2007. "Critical Media Literacy, Democracy, and the Reconstruction of Education." In *Media literacy. A Reader*, edited by Donald Macedo and Shirley R. Steinberg, pp. 3–23. New York: Peter Lang.

Larkin, Ralph W. 2007. *Comprehending Columbine*. Philadelphia: Temple University Press.

Lieberman, Joseph. 2006. *The Shooting Game: The Making of School Shooters*. Santa Ana, CA: Seven Locks Press.

Liptak, Adam. 2007. "A Liberal Case for the Individual Right to Own Guns Helps Sway the Federal Judiciary." *New York Times*, May 7, A18.

MacInnis, Laura. 2007. "U.S. Most Armed Country with 90 Guns per 100 People." *Reuters*, August 28. https://www.reuters.com/article/us-world-firearms/u-s-most-armed-country-with-90-guns-per-100-people-idusl2834893820070828 (last accessed October 16, 2017).

Marcuse, Herbert. 2001. *Toward a Critical Theory of Society: Collected Papers of Herbert Marcuse, Volume* 2, edited by Douglas Kellner. London and New York: Routledge.

Marcuse, Herbert. 2006. *Art and Liberation: Collected Papers of Herbert Marcuse, Volume 4*, edited by Douglas Kellner. London and New York: Routledge.

Messerschmidt, James. 2003. *Masculinities and Crime: Critique and Reconceptualization of Theory*. Lanham, MD: Rowman & Littlefield.

Muschert, Glenn W. 2007. "Research in School Shootings. *Sociology Compass* 1(1), 60–80.

Muschert, Glenn W. Henry, Stuart, Bracy, Nicole L., and Peguero, Anthony A., eds. 2014. *Responding to School Violence. Confronting the Columbine Effect*. Boulder, CO and London: Lynne Rienner.

National Center for Injury Prevention & Control, US Centers for Disease Control and Prevention. 2011. *Web-Based Injury Statistics Query & Reporting System (WISQARS) Injury Mortality Reports, 1999–2009, for National, Regional, and States* (September). http://www.cdc.gov/injury/wisqars/(accessed June 14, 2016).

Nelson, Laura J. 2016. "The Worst Mass Shooting? Comparing the Orlando Tragedy with Other Massacres in U.S. History." *Los Angeles Times*, June 16, A2.

PressTV. 2012. "US Shooting Suspect Was Teased." *PressTV*, April 6. http://www.presstv.ir/usdetail/234881.html (accessed April 17, 2012).

Small Arms Survey. 2007. http://www.smallarmssurvey.org/publications/by-type/yearbook/small-arms-survey-2007.html (last accessed October 16, 2017).

Smith, David and Ackerman, Spencer. 2016. "Law Enforcement Officials Continue the Investigation at Pulse Gay Nightclub Thursday in Orlando, Florida." *The Guardian*, June 16. https://www.theguardian.com/us-news/2016/jun/16/orlando-attack-facebook-post-pulse-nightclub-shooting (accessed July 27, 2016).

Winkler, Adam. 2011. *Gun Fight: The Battle Over the Right to Bear Arms in America*. New York: W.W. Norton.

4

Learning to Be a Rampage Shooter

The Case of Elliot Rodger

Ralph W. Larkin

Three incontrovertible facts outline causal issues of school rampage shootings: first, almost all rampage shooters are male; second, the overwhelming majority of shootings are committed in the United States; third, before the 1970s school rampage shootings were extremely rare. They doubled from 3 to 6 from the 1960s, nearly redoubling from 6 to 11 in the 1980s, more than tripling to 36 in the 1990s, and increasing by half again to 57 in the first decade of the twenty-first century (Böckler et al. 2013). Of the more than 100 school rampage shootings listed by Böckler et al., only three were committed by females.

According to Böckler et al. (2013), of 129 school rampage shootings worldwide between 1925 and 2011, 76 (58.9%) were committed in the United States. Schildkraut (2014) documented four US school rampage shootings in the year 2012, which resulted in 39 deaths and 9 injuries, including the Newtown shootings in which 27 deaths and 1 injury were recorded. The list by Böckler et al. also does not cover the numerous rampages in the United States that have occurred in other venues such as shopping malls, churches, movie theaters, airports, bars, post offices, military sites, immigration centers, and workplaces. Schildkraut documented 64 such rampage shootings in the United States between January 2000, and January 2013, two of which were committed by women. All such rampage shootings occurred in public venues. These statistics do not include domestic rampage shootings by husbands, boyfriends, live-in partners, and estranged husbands or sexual partners.

Although rare, rampage shootings have become a major social problem for several reasons: Perpetrators use their acts as spectacles to advertise their grievances and achieve notoriety (Kellner 2008). They often engage the media through the publication of manifestoes, videos, and pictures, such as in the cases of Columbine, Virginia Tech, and most recently in the Emmanuel AME Church in Charleston, South Carolina and Umpqua Community College. Because they take place in public venues, they undermine the public sphere by creating the perception that participation in social events and activities in public spaces is unsafe and unpredictable; almost all victims of rampage shootings are innocent and happen to be at the wrong place at the wrong time. Rampage shootings have generated heated debates on numerous volatile social issues, including gun rights and control, media violence, school security, mental health care, parenting, police profiling, and racism.

The Wiley Handbook on Violence in Education: Forms, Factors, and Preventions, First Edition.
Edited by Harvey Shapiro.
© 2018 John Wiley & Sons, Inc. Published 2018 by John Wiley & Sons, Inc.

This case study of Elliot Rodger is used to examine how social context influences the motivation of rampage shooters to engage in and justify the slaughter of innocent people. The popular notion, abetted by psychologists (e.g., Fast 2008; Langman 2009), that such perpetrators are mentally ill obscures the fact that however mentally deranged a given rampage shooter is, he is acting out a cultural script that has influenced him to become a rampage shooter.

Just prior to his rampage, Elliot Rodger posted numerous videos on YouTube in which he talked to the camera about his motivations. He also posted online his 140-page manifesto, entitled "My Twisted World," which is primarily autobiographical, but also details his feelings, mind-set, and worldview at various times throughout his life. These materials plus local media, police reports, and an hour-long televised interview with Elliot's father, Peter Rodger, by Barbara Walters constitute the primary data sources for this paper.

Alienated American Men Learn to Kill

The model rampage shooter is an American male under the age of 30. Elliot Rodger fits into these categories. What is it in American culture that prompts young men with real or imagined grievances to rampage and kill innocent people that they do not know? Rampages are both acts of revenge and a form of self-advertisement. They are a particular form of masculine acting out. As Kimmel and Mahler (2003) noted, in many cases rampage shooters attempted to "out masculine" those whose predatory behavior they were avenging. However, rarely were the actual perpetrators targeted. One of the defining characteristics of a rampage shooting is that even if there were specific targets, at some point in time shooting becomes random (Muschert 2007; Newman 2004).

Kellner (2008) indicated that one of the aspects of American exceptionalism has been the association of masculinity with guns, violence, and independence, which were identified with the Western frontier. Masculinity is a homosocial performance (Connell 2005); that is, one's masculinity is judged by other men. This is the ideological context in which American masculine identity has been forged. Several investigators have noted that American males have highly ambivalent attitudes toward women, marriage, and family (Ehrenreich 1983; Faludi 1999; Kimmel 1996). Rampage shootings by Mark Lepine (Montreal, 1989; Elgin and Hester 2003), Luke Woodham (Mississippi, 1997; Bellini 2001), Mitchell Johnson and Andrew Golden (Arkansas, 1998; Newman 2004), Seung-Hui Cho (Virginia Tech, 2007; Kellner 2013), and Elliot Rodger were motivated at least in part, by misogyny. Many school rampage shooters wrote manifestoes, produced videos, or made political statements. Nearly all included right-wing rants.

Not only are rampage shootings the most masculine of crimes, with the male participation rate above 95%, but they are also committed primarily by middle-class males (Kellner 2008). One understudied aspect of the motivation of rampage shooters is what Kalish and Kimmel (2010) referred to as "aggrieved entitlement":

> Feeling aggrieved, wronged by the world – these are typical adolescent feelings, common to many boys and girls. What transforms the aggrieved into mass murders is also *a sense of entitlement*, a sense of using violence against others, making others hurt as you, yourself, might hurt. Aggrieved entitlement inspires revenge

against those who have wronged you; it is the compensation for humiliation. Humiliation is emasculation: humiliate someone and you take away his manhood. For many men, humiliation must be avenged, or you cease to be a man. Aggrieved entitlement is a gendered emotion, a fusion of that humiliating loss of manhood and the moral obligation and entitlement to get it back. (454, emphasis added)

Elliot Rodger is a classic example of aggrieved entitlement, which led to what Katz identified as "righteous slaughter" (1988, 12). The question arises, where did Elliot Rodger get his sense of entitlement? How did he come to the point where he could blame others, specifically women, for his troubled state of existence? Finally, how did he come to justify the murder of innocent others?

Howard Becker (1963) viewed social deviance as a learned process. In his classic study of jazz musicians, he demonstrated that learning how to smoke marijuana was an initiation rite into a deviant subculture. Since the Columbine shootings, virtual communities of rampage shooter fans have emerged on the Internet (Paton and Figeac 2015; Schildkraut and Elsass 2016). Rampage shooters become cult heroes; they engage in extensive planning and interact with virtual communities on the Internet. They often study other rampage shootings, especially Columbine. Potential rampage shooters also purchase weaponry (and sometimes costumes), view media, read books, and access websites that reinforce their worldview and provide legitimations for their behavior (Larkin 2009). Then many make their own multimedia contributions to the lore of rampage shootings, as did the Columbine and subsequent shooters (Larkin 2007; Schildkraut and Elsass 2016).

Columbine was a cultural watershed. It changed rampage shootings from isolated local events to internationally reported news and media frenzies (Muschert 2002). Immediately after the shootings on April 20, 1999, Eric Harris and Dylan Klebold worship sites sprang up on the Internet (Larkin 2007). Debates on bullying, the rightness or wrongness of the shootings, parenting, availability of weapons, and myriad of other topics related to the Columbine shootings filled Internet chat rooms. Schildkraut and Elsass (2016) reported that since Columbine, each mass shooter has collected a following on social media websites, with a group called "Columbiners" as the most numerous. In this paper, I will examine the socialization process engaged in by Elliot Rodger.

Rodger's Day of Retribution

Elliot Rodger's "Day of Retribution" rampage began when he stabbed to death his two roommates and one of their friends who was visiting (Ellis and Sidner 2014; Santa Barbara County Sheriff's Office 2015). All three victims were from Asian American backgrounds. On Saturday afternoon, May 27, Elliot drove his BMW 328i luxury coupé through the Isla Vista neighborhood just north of the University of California, Santa Barbara (UCSB) campus. He drove to the Alpha Phi sorority house, which he had determined contained the "hottest" and prettiest women at UCSB (Rodger 2014a), exited his car, and banged on the door. When there was no response, he returned to his car and shot and killed two women who were nearby. As he drove away, he shot at pedestrians and hit and injured two bicyclists and a skateboarder with his car. He shot randomly at passersby, injuring several and killing a student who was walking out of a delicatessen.

He then exchanged fire with Santa Barbara County Sheriffs and hit another bicyclist. His car careened into several parked cars and came to a stop. Sheriff's deputies approached the car and found Rodger dead of a self-inflicted gunshot wound. In the car they found three pistols and over 400 rounds of ammunition (Santa Barbara County Sheriff's Office 2015).

Precursors to the Rampage

Elliot's rampage was the culmination of two years of increasingly violent confrontations after he enrolled in Santa Barbara Community College (SBCC). These outbursts resulted from his inability to have any relations, much less sexual relations, with women. His parents secured an apartment for him in the Isla Vista student ghetto adjacent to UCSB (Rodger 2014a). Although his parents thought that moving him from his home in Los Angeles to Santa Barbara would give him space to grow and develop independently, Elliot's loneliness and isolation increased along with his feelings of frustration and failure to have sexual relations with his female ideal.

Although Elliot was certainly intelligent enough to achieve in college, and his autobiography shows considerable writing skill, he was unable to complete all but a few courses. He kept dropping them because they included pretty girls to whom he was attracted but afraid to approach, or they were attended by couples showing affection to each other. In the three years that he attended college at Pierce College, Moorpark College, and SBCC, it is doubtful that he accrued enough credits to complete a single semester (Rodger 2014a).

Elliot described several instances in which he splashed people with his drinks: in two cases, he threw coffee or tea on couples embracing and fled; in another, he threw a latte at two girls sitting at a bus stop when he smiled at them from his car and they did not respond (Rodger 2014a). Police reported numerous instances where he exchanged hostile insults with passersby and confrontations with couples (Santa Barbara County Sheriff's Office 2015). He fantasized about stabbing young couples while they were engaged in intercourse. In his second year in Santa Barbara, Elliot had to be restrained by one roommate from hitting the other when the first one bragged about his sexual conquests after Elliot admitted that he was a virgin.

In the summer before his rampage, he observed a coed group of college students playing kickball in an open field. They seemed to be having fun, which enraged him. He left and bought a super soaker gun, filled it with orange juice, returned to the field, and started spraying the players. When the players responded to his attack, he ran to his car and drove away. His response to their anger was, "I was giddy with ecstatic, hate-fueled excitement. I wished I could spray boiling oil at the foul beasts. They deserved to die horrible, painful deaths just for the crime of enjoying a better life than me" (Rodger 2014a, 107).

However, the most violent episode occurred about 10 months before his rampage when he decided to crash a party in Isla Vista (Rodger 2014a). Because of his social phobia, he felt that he had to consume considerable quantities of liquor before he could interact with his peers. It was a large party that Elliot estimated at over 100 people. Already fairly drunk, he began consuming free beer. He noticed a "hot" girl talking to an

Asian male, which enraged him. He felt that because he was half Asian, girls were not attracted to him. He insulted the Asian male. Later, while partygoers ignorant of his presence were enjoying themselves on a 10-foot-high ledge, he started insulting them. The partiers responded in kind. He then tried to push two girls off the balcony; instead, others intervened and pushed him off the balcony. Elliot broke his leg in the fall (Santa Barbara County Sheriff's Department 2013).

Learning the Basic Social Categories

Elliot Rodger, age 22 at his death, was the eldest son of Li Chin and Peter Rodger. According to Elliot, his father came from a distinguished upper-class British family (Rodger 2014a). His mother was of Chinese descent, born in Malaysia. He wrote that his mother moved to London to work as a nurse on movie sets. His father was a film producer. Elliot was born in London; shortly thereafter, the Rodgers immigrated to the United States. Elliot was raised mostly in Topanga Canyon, one of the most hip, affluent, New Age communities in the Los Angeles area. It supposedly has a "countercultural vibe" (Morgan 2014). Because of his father's Hollywood connections, Elliot was often in the company of the Los Angeles elite: moguls, movie stars, and successful business persons (Rodger 2014a). He attended red carpet ceremonies for movie premieres, which reinforced his belief that wealth, beauty, and sexuality are closely associated.

Although Elliot described his life prior to the age of nine as idyllic, an alternative perspective was provided by his parents and adults who knew him as a youngster. His father, in the wake of the murders, described Elliot as "an enigma to the family – distant, remote, unknowable" (Rodger 2014b). A family friend described him as the most withdrawn individual that he had ever met (Nagourney and Cieply 2014). By his own admission, Elliot had difficulty with relationships. He described himself as jealous and often mentioned his envy and hatred of others because of capabilities that they had that he did not. He hated other boys who were more athletic and sociable, and most especially as he got older, who were sexually active.

Masculine Role Failure

Elliot was painfully aware of his inability to achieve in traditional masculine activities. He was thin and small of stature. As a pre-teenager, he practiced basketball shooting for hours on end in the hopes that playing basketball would make him taller (Rodger 2014a). Shortly thereafter, Elliot saw that skateboarding became the chosen sport among schoolmates that he considered "cool" (Rodger 2014a). As was the pattern, he asked his parents buy him a skateboard. His parents, happy to see that their isolated son was interested in a sport, immediately bought him a customized skateboard. A third effort to use sports as a way of being cool was taking up hacky sack, a fad among his peers. He abandoned all of his efforts when he came to the conclusion that most people were better than he.

To compensate for his social inferiority, he hounded his parents for the latest technological gizmos, computer games, bikes, clothes, or other material objects that he associated with being cool and hip (Rodger 2014a). They consistently granted his wishes, which included the purchase of the late-model BMW that he used in his rampage. Elliot characterized his relationships with his mother and father as supportive and loving (Rodger 2014a). Throughout his manifesto, which is a year-by-year biography, he described numerous instances where his parents showed him love, care, and support. For example, he was bullied in school. His parents, especially his father, attempted to enroll him in schools where bullying would be at a minimum and, if necessary, he would receive personal support. When he graduated from middle school, his parents enrolled him in an all-boys Catholic school, where, by his account, he was bullied viciously. His parents enrolled him in the local public high school; however, he was so petrified that he begged his father not to send him there. After a week of isolation, loneliness, and harassment, he suffered a panic attack, freezing in the middle of the hallway, unable to move (Nagourney and Cieply 2014). His parents then enrolled him in a small alternative high school where he received supportive services.

The Intersection of Class and Masculinity: Elliot the "Gentleman"

The fundamental categories that occupied Elliot's consciousness were class and gender. He was highly sensitized to the fact that he came from a family of high status and privilege. He considered himself a member of the upper class. His desires for the trappings of class status were central to his view of himself as a man. He repeatedly referred to himself as a "gentleman," which had a very specific meaning:

> On the morning of the first day [of attendance at SBCC], I donned my fabulous Armani Exchange shirt and put on my new Gucci sunglasses that my mother gave me. I admired myself in the mirror for a few moments, and began to feel a surge of enthusiasm. I wanted everyone to see me looking like that. I was hopeful that some girls would admire me. I said to myself that there was no way I could possibly have trouble with getting girls now. I ... set off for my college with the confidence that I would appear as a superior gentleman to all of the students there. I *was* a superior gentleman. That was what I was born to be, and it was now time to show it to the world. (Rodger 2014a, 99, emphasis in original)

To Elliot, gentlemanliness was associated with the accoutrements of social class and commodity branding: Ray-Ban and Gucci sunglasses, Armani shirts, Hugo Boss outfits, and a late-model BMW. Yet none of these high-end commodities seemed to attract the attention of women; he railed against women who were attracted to men who wore T-shirts and cut-off jeans. His concept of gentleman also was meant to separate him from the "brutes" that teased and harassed him with sexualized comments like "faggot." His focus on social class was a compensation for his failure as an American male. In all the traditional masculine expectations, he was decidedly a loser. Elliot was less socially competent, less physically skilled, shorter, and slighter than his peers. However, because of his inherited social status, he had convinced himself that he was "chosen"; he was destined for greatness and celebrity. He felt he was entitled to be admired by men and loved by women.

Yet, his social relationships with his peers were fraught with conflict. He feared abandonment by the few friends that he had (Rodger 2014a) and had highly sensitized himself to any potential slight. He also rejected former friends when they developed competencies with which he could not compete, especially after puberty when his friends started having relationships with females. Once his friends began engaging in sexual relations, his relationships with them deteriorated as he grew to envy and hate them.

Racial Hatred

A third social category that bedeviled Elliot Rodger was race, which was also tied to class, sexual status, and masculinity. Although Elliot passed as white, he was highly sensitive about his mixed-race background, which played out in his relationships with others from non-white backgrounds. Elliot was openly racist. In his manifesto, he admitted hating and fearing African Americans and Hispanics. When Elliot moved to Santa Barbara, he had two white roommates; however, they had a friend who was African American who visited often. In the first few days, Elliot asked if the three of them were virgins, admitting his own virginity. All three indicated that they had lost their virginity years before. Elliot recorded the following reaction:

> How could an inferior, ugly black boy be able to get a white girl and not me? I am beautiful, and I am half white myself. I am descended from British aristocracy. *He* is descended from slaves. I deserve it more ... If this ugly black filth was able to have sex with a blonde white girl at the age of thirteen while I've had to suffer virginity all my life, then this just proves how ridiculous the female gender is. They would give themselves to this filthy scum, but they reject *ME?* The injustice! (Rodger 2014a, 83, emphasis in original)

In his second year in Santa Barbara, he took on new roommates. This was his comment:

> Their names were Ryan and Angel, and to my dismay they were of Hispanic race ... They ... seemed like rowdy, low-class types. My first impression of them soured me, but I tried to be pleasant and not show it. The two of them acted cordial to me on the first day, but after observing them for a bit, I had a bad feeling that they would be trouble to live with ... And they were to be my housemates for a whole year! ... I was hoping I would get decent, mature, clean-cut housemates. Instead I got low-class scum. (Rodger 2014a, 89)

Sex and Sexism

Elliot Rodger was raised in one of the most openly sexual communities in the world. Topanga Canyon was one of the last remaining bastions of the 1960s counterculture, and was at the forefront of the sexual revolution in the 1970s (Morgan 2014). When Elliot arrived at college, it's hard to think of a more sexualized environment than UCSB, with its isolated student ghetto in unincorporated county territory, mild weather, and campus beach. The campus is notorious for its high rate of sexually transmitted diseases (STDs), although rates are in dispute (Dankner 2013; UCSB Associated Students 2011). Elliot Rodger was essentially correct when he surmised that if he could not lose his virginity in Isla Vista, he could not lose it anywhere.

Apparently, Elliot was extremely naive about sexuality. According to his testimony, his parents never talked to him about sex (Rodger 2014a), although his father claimed that he did (Rodger 2014b). Elliot claimed that his first awareness of sexuality occurred when he was 13 years old when he saw a pornographic video that traumatized him:

> I saw an older teenager watching pornography. I saw in detail a video of a man having sex with a hot girl. The video showed him stick his penis inside a girl's vagina … The sight was shocking, traumatizing, and arousing. All of these feelings mixed together took a great toll on me.
>
> … Finding out about sex is one of the things that truly destroyed my entire life. Sex … the very word fills me with hate. Once I hit puberty, I would always want it, like any other boy … But I would never get it. Not getting any sex is what will shape the very foundation of my miserable youth. This was a very dark day. (Rodger 2014a, 69–70)

From this point on through his narrative, Elliot discussed his troubled relationships with women (Rodger 2014a). For him, being able to have sexual relationships with women was central to his sense of his masculinity. However, in the entire narrative, he never describes an instance where he attempted to initiate a conversation with a woman. Repeatedly, he hung out at malls, in eateries and college cafeterias, on campus quads, and took long walks hoping to meet up with a woman. However, because of his lack of social skills, his highly ambivalent feelings about sex, and his fear and loathing of women, he never made contact.

As time wore on, and the people around him were having sexual relationships while he still remained a virgin – or, in his words, an "incel" or involuntary celibate – he became increasingly depressed, angry, and agitated. He would go online to incel websites and commiserate with other male virgins. He began acting out violently against others whom he perceived were sexually active. His frustration with his own inability to interact with women evolved into hatred of people who had heterosexual relationships.

Although his autobiography contains numerous episodes where he has conflicts with men over sexuality, there is no episode where he describes a woman insulting, taunting, harassing, or rejecting him. He refers to himself throughout the document as a "kissless virgin." His narrative is devoid of any interaction with women other than members of his own family. When he found out that his sister, four years his junior, had become sexually active, he became jealous of her. He provides no evidence of any attempt to introduce himself or become friendly with a woman who could possibly be a sexual partner, much less having one of his male friends become a wing man to act as an intermediary to help him initiate a relationship with a woman. He bitterly lamented his isolation, loneliness, lack of love, and virginity.

Elliot Rodger increasingly saw himself as a person who was excluded from one of the great pleasures of humanity. His only solace in his life was the computer game World of Warcraft (WoW), which he played every waking moment he could (Rodger 2014a). He alternated between immersing himself in WoW and attempting to attract women by dressing in designer clothes and frequenting some agora where young people hung out. When he went out in public, he was more alone than ever because he saw other people, especially young couples, having a good time while he could only observe and wish it for himself. He desired sex, fantasized about it, yet was frightened and disgusted by it

(Rodger 2014a) – so much so, he perseverated, repeating behaviors that ended in his failure to make contact with sexually attractive women. As a consequence, he became increasingly frustrated and angry.

In contradiction to his own failures as an American male, he constructed a self-image of a superior being: "I am Elliot Rodger ... Magnificent, glorious, supreme, eminent ... Divine! I am the closest thing there is to a living god" (Rodger 2014a, 135). Elliot's reason for his lack of sexual experience was because the human race was too bestial. Women had something wrong with them because they were attracted to stupid athletic men. His actual relations with women were nonexistent. He did not even have a female friend with whom he had a platonic relationship. Therefore, his concept of women emerged from several sources: corporate media, especially the film industry, Internet chat rooms with like-minded males, and the computer game World of Warcraft.

WoW is a multiplayer role-playing first-person online game in which players individually or collectively engage in quests (Wikipedia 2015). In those quests, players have to defeat or kill numerous enemies who stand in the way. It is the most popular massively multiplayer online role-playing game (MMORPG) ever released. The setting of the game tends to mix a number of fantasy genres, including Gothic, steam punk (fantasy nineteenth-century industrial imagery), and science fiction. The game contains numerous fantasy beings such as griffons, ogres, dragons, and elves. Elliot Rodger was an early adapter who began playing the game at age 13. He played the first version that was released in 2004 and played obsessively as a teenager. He stopped playing for a couple of years when he was a college student, but resumed after his nineteenth birthday. However, he stopped playing shortly thereafter:

> WoW no longer became a sanctuary where I could hide from the evils of the world, because the evils of the world had now followed me there. I saw people bragging online about their sexual experiences with girls ... and they used the term "virgin" as an insult to people who were more immersed in the game than them ... I couldn't stand to play WoW knowing that my *enemies*, the people I hate and envy so much for having sexual lives, were now playing the same game as me. (Rodger 2014a, 74–75, emphasis in original)

Feminist WoW gamer Angela Washko stated, "I have found that most of the servers that I have participated in ... are overwhelmingly misogynistic, homophobic and racist" (Washko, pers. comm., 2014). Anita Sarkeesian (2015), a feminist critic of computer games, noted that in video games, sexualized female bodies are portrayed as playthings for males and victims of male violence. Because of her criticism of the sexism of such games, she has been subject to numerous threats of rape and murder by her detractors.

In addition to inhabiting the sexist world of MMORPG, Elliot frequented a website called puahate.com, short for "pickup artist hate." It was inhabited by young men who were sexually inexperienced and who expressed hostility toward sexually active heterosexuals. It was on this website that Elliot Rodger could express his misogynistic and misanthropic opinions and receive support from like-minded males. Through WoW and puahate.com, Elliot could express his hatred against women and sexually active people while receiving support for his views, although his opinions on puahate.com generated controversy because of his extreme views. Elliot's computer history revealed a fascination with Nazis and the Third Reich (Santa Barbara County Sheriff's Office 2015).

Not just any woman was good enough for Elliot Rodger. The term "beautiful blonde" occurs repeatedly in his narrative. She must be beautiful by Hollywood standards. It is clear from his writings that his image of female beauty is hegemonic. She must look like a model and, of course, be blonde. Excluded from Rodgers' narrative are any internal characteristics, such as a sense of humor, intelligence, compassion, caring, or athleticism. She is a trophy that Elliot wants to be seen with in public to validate his masculinity. Because this was not happening, Elliot needed to develop a rationale that explained his "victimization" by women:

> I realized that I would be a virgin forever, condemned to suffer rejection and humiliation at the hands of women because they don't fancy me, because their sexual attractions are flawed. They are attracted to the wrong type of male. I always mused to myself that I would rather die than suffer such an existence, and I knew that if it came to that, I would exact my revenge upon the world in the most catastrophic way possible. (Rodger 2014a, 101)

As he became increasingly frustrated, he became delusional. He concocted a get-rich scheme that he thought could not fail because of his inherent superiority. He was going to win a lottery. He first tried the Megamillions lottery and lost twice after waiting for payoffs to exceed $500 million. Then he tried the Powerball lottery (Santa Barbara County Sheriff's Office 2015). However, in order to do so, he drove to Arizona on four separate occasions, a drive of approximately 350 miles, to buy tickets. When he lost after spending $700 on tickets, he fell into a depression, realizing that his dreams of instant wealth were never going to be realized and that his life was going to end in his Day of Retribution.

Because women were not attracted to him and he saw himself as the ideal of masculinity, he concluded that women did not have the intelligence to choose a proper mate. He, as a superior being, should be allocated that right:

> Women should not have the right to choose who to mate with [*sic*]. That choice should be made for them by civilized men of intelligence. If women had the freedom to choose which men to mate with, like they do today, they would breed with stupid, degenerate men, which would only produce stupid, degenerate offspring. This in turn would hinder the advancement of humanity. Not only hinder it, but devolve humanity completely. Women are like a plague that must be quarantined. When I came to this brilliant, perfect revelation, I felt like everything was now clear to me, in a bitter, twisted way. I am one of the few people on this world who has the intelligence to see this. I am like a god, and my purpose is to exact ultimate Retribution on all of the impurities I see in the world. (Rodger 2014a, 117)

The fundamental contradictions in Elliot's life between social status and masculinity percolated into an ideology in which "civilized" men such as he practice eugenics in the betterment of the human race. His lack of performance in traditional masculine practices such as sports, physical prowess, attractiveness to women, and dominance are effaced in a fantasy in which he is rich and powerful. In his fantasy, social class trumps masculine performance. Women become the passive instruments of masculine dominance, just as in WoW.

From Misogynist to Misanthrope

As Elliot's frustration increased, he began to develop an ideology that would justify his rampage. At age 18 he wrote:

> I delved more into learning as much as I could from books at Barnes & Noble. I expanded on the political and philosophical ideals I concocted when I was seventeen, and I soon became even more radical about them than I ever was before. It was all fueled by my wish to punish everyone who is sexually active, because I concluded that it wasn't fair that other people were able to experience sex while I have been denied it all my life. I started to have the desire to create a world where no one is allowed to have sex or relationships [*sic*]. I again saw that as the perfect, fair world. Reproduction can be accomplished without sex, through artificial insemination. Sex is evil, as it gives too much pleasure to those who don't deserve it. (Rodger 2014a, 65)

Elliot had come to the conclusion that his "magnificent" self had been rejected by women and derided by men; therefore, there was something inherently wrong in the human species: "Humanity is a disgusting, depraved, and evil species. It is my purpose to punish them all. I will purify the world of everything that is wrong with it. On the Day of Retribution, I will truly be a powerful god, punishing everyone I deem to be impure and depraved" (Rodger 2014a, 135).

Similarly to Eric Harris, one of the Columbine shooters, Elliot Rodger assumes a God-like status that can exact retribution from a sinful, depraved, and ignorant human species (Larkin 2007). Both Harris and Rodger were fascinated by Nazi ideology and the concept of a Superman dictating to the masses (Santa Barbara County Sheriff's Office 2015). Because he has been excluded from one of the major sources of human pleasure through no apparent fault of his own, the problem lay in flawed human nature. His studies led him to a misanthropic ideology that justified killing other lesser beings.

He began to fantasize about what he would do if he ruled the world. He wished to purify the species by eliminating sexuality from the human experience (Rodger 2014a). Realizing that the rest of humanity might not be so sanguine about desexualizing human relationships, he proposed a totalitarian regime with him as dictator:

> In an ideal world, sexuality would not exist. It must be outlawed. In a world without sex, humanity will be pure and civilized … The human race will evolve to an entirely new level of civilization, completely devoid of all the impurity and degeneracy that exists today.
>
> In order to completely abolish sex, women themselves would have to be abolished … The first strike against women will be to quarantine all of them in concentration camps. At these camps, the vast majority of the female population will be deliberately starved to death … I would have an enormous tower built just for myself, where I can oversee the entire concentration camp and gleefully watch them all die. *If I can't have them, no one will*, I'd imagine thinking to myself as I oversee this. Women represent everything that is unfair with this world, and in order to make the world a fair place, they must all be eradicated. (Rodger 2014a, 136, emphasis in original)

However, his motives are not merely for the improvement of the species. He seeks vengeance against the entire female sex for not granting him sexual access and secondarily against men who desire women. He wants to deny them the sexual pleasure that he has been denied.

Discussion and Conclusion

Because rampage shootings occur in venues usually not associated with violence, such as schools, shopping malls, and churches, they tend to violate the hegemonic ideology that violence is associated with minorities and urban areas (Kalish and Kimmel 2010). In order to rationalize the cause of rampage shootings the media characterize them as "senseless." While running loops of the most sensational footage they can obtain, almost universally, they declare the perpetrators mentally ill (Cullen 2004; Fast 2008; Langman 2009). Although psychologists often examine context, social context is used to legitimize mental illness, which is presumed as the causal factor.

The problem with this kind of theorizing is that it tends to fog over more salient social factors that are involved in the motivation of rampage killers. Classifying rampage shooters according to mental illness cannot answer such questions that prefaced this study: Why are nearly all rampagers male, why are they mostly young Americans, and why have rampage shooters emerged as a social problem since the 1980s? In this case study, a young American male rampage shooter wrote a manifesto and posted videos describing his life and his motivation for his rampage shooting. Was he mentally ill? Yes; he was diagnosed early on as having severe psychological and social problems. Peter Langman (2014), a profiler of rampage shooters, classified him as a "psychotic psychopath."

Elliot Rodger's thought process obviously severely deviated from the norm. He displayed delusions of grandeur and lacked compassion. However, psychological typologies ignore important factors in his motivation. He was raised in a highly sexualized and class-conscious atmosphere in which sex, beauty, race, and money were highly valorized. It is clear from his manifesto that Elliot incorporated those aspects into his consciousness. Typologies also ignore his social and sexual phobias and his highly ambivalent attitude toward women, all of which played a part in his motivation to rampage. Langman (2014) also failed to address issues of American masculine sexuality and violence in relationship to his rampage.

So, what did we learn from the rampage of Elliot Rodger? First, he learned that he was socially identified as a "loser" as an American male. Because of his sexual and social phobias, he was invisible to females, especially those who were potential sexual partners. Given hegemonic notions of masculinity, Rodger blamed women not only for his own victimization, but for his own inadequacies. Borrowing from right-wing misogynist ideologies, he came to define women as stupid, dangerous, and exclusionary. Although he hated anybody who was sexually active, women were the putative cause of his misery. Why? Because he was a man and he was petrified of sexual intimacy to the point where he was incapable of establishing a relationship with a female peer.

In line with the hegemonic ideology that is played out in Hollywood where Elliot Rodger was an onlooker, sexuality was associated with the somatic norm images promulgated by the media and with wealth, status, and celebrity. In a final act of desperation, associated with his delusions of grandeur, he thought he was destined to win a national lottery, become rich, and have all the women he wanted. This delusion, fashioned out of media hype, was exploded by the reality that he was a loser: small of stature, a racial hybrid, a virgin, a failure at school, unathletic, unable to obtain a "beautiful blonde woman with a great body," and a sucker for all of what it means to be a man and a "winner," including false hopes generated by lotteries. However deranged he was, his dreams were fashioned out of those aspects of American culture that celebrate masculine dominance, materialism, and celebrity. To him, he had nothing left to lose. His Day of Retribution was also derived from American subcultures of violence that justify rampage shootings as a means of getting even with an unjust society and dying in a blaze of glory for one's cause (Gibson 1994). In this act, Elliot Rodger observed a postmodern tradition sensationalized in previous rampage shootings at Columbine, Virginia Tech, Aurora, and Sandy Hook.

Early on, school rampage shooters were influenced by the media (Larkin 2009). However, prior to Columbine, the influence was from the media to the rampagers. In 1975, Michael Slobodan (Brampton, Canada), after his rampage went home and dressed in combat fatigues. In 1992, John McMahon (Napa, CA) shouted, "I am a New Jack City hustler!" before he began his rampage. Wayne Lo (Simon's Rock College, 1992) wore a sweatshirt that read, "Sick of it all." Jamie Rouse (Linville, TN, 1995), Barry Loukatis (Moses Lake, WA, 1996), and the Columbine shooters were influenced by the movie *Natural Born Killers*. Precursors to Columbine included Gang Lu, a graduate student at the University of Iowa, who went on a rampage after he was denied an honor for his doctoral dissertation in 1991. He wrote letters to news outlets praising Clint Eastwood for his movies that suggested using guns to settle arguments. Luke Woodham (Pearl, MS, 1997) wrote a "manifesto" that, among other things claimed revenge for being hated, ridiculed, and unloved.

The Columbine shootings, because of their intensive and extensive media coverage, made it obligatory for would-be rampage shooters to communicate their motives to the media (Larkin 2009; Muschert 2002). Klebold and Harris, the Columbine shooters, produced numerous videotapes, webpages, diaries, and short stories that revealed their ideologies and motivations (Larkin 2007). The role expectations of rampage shooters have evolved over time, and have become more complex and media aware. Numerous post-Columbine rampages have been inspired by movies, TV programs, Internet websites, books, and video games that contain the ideologies of the cultures of violence (Kellner 2008; Larkin 2009).

Elliot Rodger was typical of post-Columbine rampage shooters: he played first-person shooter video games, and chatted with like-minded individuals on websites that promulgated authoritarian and misogynist ideologies. He bought guns and ammunition with money supplied to him by his parents and meticulously planned his rampage. Similar to the Columbine shooters, when his plans went awry, he improvised.

The subcultures of hate provide the scripts for rampages; here in the United States, the gun lobby provides them the wherewithal. In America, anyone who is contemplating a shooting rampage can go on the Internet to learn how it is done, receive encouragement from like-minded individuals, and easily purchase high-powered weaponry. In the words of the Nike commercial stolen from the youth movement of the 1960s, they can "Just do it!"

It was established at the outset that rampage shootings are attacks on social institutions (Muschert 2007; Newman 2004); therefore, it is a politicized crime, primarily supported and abetted by right-wing hate groups, violent subcultures, and the gun lobby (Kellner 2008). It is clear that the major policy difference between the United States and other countries is universal access to guns. Revenge fantasies are featured in the media. On the Internet, frustrated young men can interact with virtual hate communities and learn legitimations for mass murder. Lax gun control legislation and enforcement allows them easy access to the weapons they desire. The overwhelming prevalence of mass shootings by men in the United States is due to hypocrisy related to the crisis of masculinity. Certain right-wing hate groups tacitly encourage rampage shootings by vilifying their political opposition, promulgating racist, sexist, anti-Semitic, and antigovernment views and suggesting that violence is the answer to conflict (Gibson 1994; Ridgeway 1995). To a man, they believe in unrestricted access to guns. They have been able successfully to obstruct any form of meaningful gun control. Therefore, every few weeks Americans are subjected to another horrific rampage shooting, to which the gun lobby claims that the solution to the problem is to arm more people.

The absurdity of this position fails to pass what jurists refer to as the "straight face test," (McElhaney 2011). Two armed officers were present at the Columbine massacre, one of whom exchanged fire with Eric Harris (Larkin 2007). In 2012, New York City police exchanged fire with a shooter in front of the Empire State Building. Nine bystanders were wounded all by police bullets (Barron 2012). Clearly, the reason why the United States has so many more rampage shootings than any other country is because of lax gun laws and the proliferation of weaponry that permit virtually anybody who wants to obtain a gun the ability to do so, through legal, semi-legal, or illegal means. Gun control legislation has been made more difficult by the Supreme Court in *Washington, DC vs. Heller* (54 U.S. 570 [2008]), which enshrined the Second Amendment as an individual right irrespective of maintaining a "well regulated militia."

The battle to eliminate rampage shootings is difficult because of the strength of the culture of violence, supported by the political right, of which the gun lobby is an integral part. If we want to reduce the incidence of rampage shootings, we must continue the fight for reasonable gun control legislation and enforcement. We must also align ourselves with those individuals and organizations that oppose violence, hate, and an ideology of masculinity as controlling women and violence. We need to support feminist and LGBT (lesbian, gay, bisexual, transgender) organizations that offer a more expansive and peace-oriented view of masculinity. We should promote educational efforts aimed at instituting peaceful conflict resolution, promoting gender equality, preventing bullying, and developing peaceful campuses. Because of their power, right-wing terror organizations, neo-Nazi groups, skinhead and motorcycle gangs, which have engaged in more terrorism than Muslim jihadist groups, tend to be under-surveilled (Scott 2015). Law enforcement needs to be pressured to prosecute their illegal activities. We need to do everything we can within a free society to limit the power of hate groups that influence alienated young males. On the positive side, we need to make America a more inclusive and egalitarian society, so that fewer young men feel isolated and rejected and feel the need to lash out at a social system that has excluded them.

References

Barron, James. 2012. "Gunman Dies after Killing at Empire State Building." *The New York Times*, August 24.

Becker, Howard Saul. 1963. *Outsiders: Studies in the Sociology of Deviance.* London: Free Press of Glencoe.

Bellini, Jon. 2001. *Child's Prey.* New York: Pinnacle.

Böckler, Nils, Seeger, Thorsten, Sitzer, Peter, and Heitmeyer, Wilhelm. 2013. "School Shootings: Conceptual Framework in International Empirical Trends." In *School Shootings: International Research, Case Studies, and Concepts for Prevention*, edited by Nils Böckler, Thorsten Seeger, Peter Sitzer, and Wilhelm Heitmeyer, pp. 1–26. New York: Springer.

Connell, R.W. 2005. *Masculinities.* Berkeley: University of California Press.

Cullen, Dave. 2004. "The Depressive and the Psychopath." Slate.com. http://www.slate.com/articles/news_and_politics/assessment/2004/04/the_depressive_and_the_psychopath.html (last accessed October 6, 2017).

Dankner, Danielle. 2013. "Questions You Were Too Embarrassed to Ask Your Doctor." *The Bottom Line*, October 24. https://thebottomline.as.ucsb.edu/2012/10/questions-youre-too-embarrassed-to-ask-your-doctor (last accessed October 6, 2017).

Ehrenreich, Barbara. 1983. *Hearts of Men: American Dreams and the Flight from Commitment.* New York: Doubleday Anchor.

Elgin, Peter and Hester, Stephen. 2003. *The Montréal Massacre: A Story of Membership Categorization Analysis.* Waterloo, ON: Wilfrid Laurier University press.

Ellis, Ralph and Sidner, Sara. 2014. "Deadly California Rampage: Chilling Video, But No Match for Reality." CNN, May 28. http://edition.cnn.com/2014/05/24/justice/california-shooting-deaths/index.html (last accessed October 6, 2017).

Faludi, Susan. 1999. *Stiffed: The Betrayal of the American Man.* New York: William Morrow.

Fast, Jonathan. 2008. *Ceremonial Violence: A Psychological Explanation of School Shootings.* Woodstock, NY: Overlook Press.

Gibson, James William. 1994. *Warrior Dreams.* New York: Hill & Wang.

Kalish, Rachel and Kimmel, Michael. 2010. "Suicide by Mass Murder: Masculinity, Aggrieved Entitlement, and Rampage School Shootings." *Health Sociology Review* 19(4), 451–464. DOI: 10.5172/hesr.2010.19.4.451.

Katz, Jack. 1988. *Seductions of Crime.* New York: Basic Books.

Kellner, Douglas. 2008. *Guys and Guns Amok.* Boulder, CO: Paradigm Press.

Kellner, Douglas. 2013. "School Shootings, Crises of Masculinities, and the Reconstruction of Education: Some Critical Perspectives." In *School shootings: International Research, Case Studies, and Concepts for Prevention*, edited by Nils Böckler, Thorsten Seeger, Peter Sitzer, and Wilhelm Heitmeyer, pp. 497–518. New York: Springer Science + Business Media.

Kimmel, Michael S. 1996. *Manhood in America.* New York: Free Press.

Kimmel, Michael S. and Mahler, Matthew. 2003. "Adolescent Masculinity, Homophobia, and Violence: Random School Shootings, 1982–2001." *American Behavioral Scientist* 46, 1439–1458.

Langman, Peter. 2009. *Why Kids Kill: Inside the Minds of School Shooters.* New York: Palgrave Macmillan.

Langman, Peter. 2014. "Elliot Rodger: A Psychotic Psychopath?". *Psychology Today*. http://www.psychologytoday.com/blog/keeping-kids-safe/201405/elliot-rodger-psychotic-psychopath (last accessed October 6, 2017).

Larkin, Ralph W. 2007. *Comprehending Columbine.* Philadelphia, PA: Temple University Press.

Larkin, Ralph W. 2009. "The Columbine Legacy: Rampage Shootings as Political Acts." *American Behavioral Scientist* 52(9), 1309–1326.

McElhaney, Jim. 2011. "No Laughing Matter: Failing the Giggle Test Might Leave You Crying." *ABA Journal*, November 1. http://www.abajournal.com/magazine/article/no_laughing_matter_failing_the_giggle_test_might_leave_you_crying (last accessed October 6, 2017).

Morgan, Susan. 2014. "California Dreamy: A New Generation of Crunchy Creatives Has Moved into L.A.'s Perennially Hippie-Chic Topanga Canyon." *W Magazine*. https://www.wmagazine.com/story/topanga-canyon-california (last accessed October 23, 2017).

Muschert, Glenn W. 2002. "Media and Massacre: The Social Construction of the Columbine Story." Unpublished doctoral dissertation. University of Colorado, Boulder, Colorado.

Muschert, Glenn W. 2007. "Research in School Shootings." *Sociology Compass* 1(1), 60–80.

Nagourney, Adam and Cieply, Michael. 2014. "Before Brief, Deadly Spree, Trouble Since Age 8." *New York Times*, October 22. Accessed March 25, 2015.

Newman, Katherine S. 2004. *Rampage: The Social Roots of School Shootings*. New York: Basic Books.

Paton, Nathalie and Figeac, Julien. 2015. "Expressive Violence: The Performative Effects of Subversive Participatory Media Uses." *ESSACHESS. Journal for Communication Studies* 8(1), 231–256. https://www.essachess.com/index.php/jcs/article/viewFile/160/332 (last accessed October, 2017).

Ridgeway, James. 1995. *Blood in the Face*, 2nd ed. New York: Thunder's Mouth Press.

Rodger, Elliot. 2014a. My Twisted World: The Story of Elliot Rodger. https://www.documentcloud.org/documents/1173808-elliot-rodger-manifesto.html (last accessed October 23, 2017).

Rodger, Peter. 2014b. "The Secret Life of Elliot Rodger." In *2020*, edited by Barbara Walters. YouTube: ABC News.

Santa Barbara County Sheriff's Department. 2013. Police Report Altercation 13 – 10081. Santa Barbara, California: Santa Barbara County Sheriff.

Santa Barbara County Sheriff's Office. 2015. Isla Vista Mass Murder, May 23, 2014: Investigative summary.

Sarkeesian, Anita. 2015. "Feminist Frequency: Tropes versus Women in Video Games." Feminist Frequency. http://feministfrequency.com/tag/tropes-vs-women-in-video-games/(last accessed October 6, 2017).

Schildkraut, Jaclyn. 2014. Rampage Shooters: 2000–2014. https://lccn.loc.gov/2015036730.

Schildkraut, Jaclyn and Elsass, H. Jayme. 2016. *Mass Shootings: Media, Myths, and Realities*. Santa Barbara, CA: Praeger.

Scott, Shane. 2015. "Homegrown Extremists Tied to Deadlier Toll Than Jihadists in U.S. since 9/11." *New York Times*, June 24. (accessed July 7, 2015).

UCSB Associated Students. 2011. "Is It UCSB or UCSTD?" *The Daily Nexus*, November 1. http://dailynexus.com/2011-11-01/ucsb-ucstd/(last accessed October 6, 2017).

Wikipedia. 2015. "World of Warcraft." https://en.wikipedia.org/wiki/World_of_Warcraft (last accessed October 6, 2017).

5

The Logic of the Exception

Violence Revisited[*]

Harvey Shapiro

> *For no ethics can claim to exclude a part of humanity no matter how unpleasant or difficult that humanity is to see.*
>
> Giorgio Agamben, *Remnants of Auschwitz*, p. 64

A recurring claim following school shootings is that the cultural, political, and educational milieus must be absolved. For example, the fact that the Boston Marathon bomber attended the University of Massachusetts, Dartmouth, is relegated to the category of incidental:

> [T]here is nothing that UMass Dartmouth could have done to prevent the outrageous, depraved actions that cost four people their lives and injured scores more. This is a sensible, fair-minded finding in that responsibility for these atrocious acts rests solely with the people who possessed the grotesque ability to place bombs alongside innocent men, women and children. (Caret 2013)

This assertion by the university's president underscored the conclusion of that institution's official report on the tragedy. Similarly, in the wake of the 2007 Virginia Tech shooting, the state's attorney general's office summarized the findings of its official investigation with this statement: "[Seung-Hui] Cho was the lone person responsible for this tragedy" (Burgos 2013).

These kinds of understandable conclusions are part of a prevalent discourse that characterizes school shootings as anomalous acts or, when common factors are identified, as perpetrated by isolated mentally ill individuals. The assertion of disconnection between place and shooter often yields explicit and implicit rhetorical questions: How could some*one* so violent "belong" to this peaceful, ordinary community? How could some*thing* so violent occur in a place such as this? This stark contrast between perpetrator and place often frames the outrage, leading to media spectacles of stark black and white contrasts, as the "unthinkable" stands out in sharp relief from the ordinary.

---

[*] This chapter is a revised and expanded version of Harvey Shapiro, "When the Exception Is the Rule: School Shootings, Bare Life, and the Sovereign Self" *Educational Theory*, 2015, 65(4), 423–440.

The Wiley Handbook on Violence in Education: Forms, Factors, and Preventions, First Edition.
Edited by Harvey Shapiro.
© 2018 John Wiley & Sons, Inc. Published 2018 by John Wiley & Sons, Inc.

In one sense, these contrasts are compelling. Yet they also conceal the relationships of shooters to their educational, communal, and political environments, and to the times in which we live. I argue that denying such relational, contextual dimensions relegates school shooters to the problematic status of "exceptions." This assertion of exceptionality distorts certain historical, political, linguistic, and social understandings of this devastating phenomenon, implying a definitive separation between normal and exceptional, between what is *expected* in the course of human events and what is *excepted* as a sociohistorical aberration.

To show these prevailing binaries and what they conceal, I will draw on the interwar writings of Walter Benjamin (1978) on the nexus between violence and law, and on Giorgio Agamben's (1998, 2002, 2005) extensions and radicalizations of Benjamin's notions of the "sovereign decision" and the "state of exception." I maintain that exposing the rhetorical structures of exceptionality will help us consider alternative responses to the increased frequency and lethality of shootings that have plagued our educational institutions in the United States in recent decades.

I will first show how responses to school shootings – from gun enthusiasts and the gun lobby, in particular – tend to both appropriate and, paradoxically, dismiss certain kinds of violence. In doing so, they imply a specific vision of the self: Individuals are sovereign, able to exert power over bodily life, and able to remove themselves from community norms, as they claim what Agamben (using political theorist Carl Schmitt's terminology) calls the "sovereign exception" (1998, 28, 34, 66). Second, I will suggest how Benjamin's concept of "divine violence" (1978, 294, 297, 300) can inform education's efforts to challenge binaries of good and evil, urban and suburban, individual and community, justice and law, normal and exceptional, that confound our deliberations and long-term responses to shootings.

"Form-of-Life," Bare Life, and Sovereign Power

Let us begin to clarify the relationship of shooters (and, as we will see, of the gun lobby and governments) to life itself. In our parlance, the term "life" is fraught with multiple meanings. Its semantic range comes into sharper relief when we consider the classical Greek distinction between *zoē* and *bios*. As Agamben explains, *zoē* "expressed the simple fact of living common to all living beings (animals, humans, or gods)" whereas *bios* "signified the form or manner of living peculiar to a single individual or group." *Zoē*, then, connotes "that naked presupposed common element" – corporeal, biological life – "that it is always possible to isolate in each of the numerous forms of life" (Agamben 2000, 2–3). In contrast, the concept of form-of-life (akin to *bios*, rather than *zoē*) is "a life that can never be separated from its form, a life in which it is never possible to isolate something such as naked life" (8–9). So, a form-of-life includes strong sociocultural and personal dimensions as "the form or way of living proper to an individual or a group" (1998, 9). In a form-of-life, our values, beliefs, and norms are confluent and coincident with living itself; they are inextricable from biological life. "Bare life," on the other hand, is the term Agamben, following Benjamin, uses for what remains when all non-biological qualities of life are removed, after "stripping away of predicates and attributes" (de la Durantaye 2009, 203). Bare life is produced, with violence, in this removal (Agamben 1998, 10; 2000, 6–7).

As Agamben argues, this violent capacity to strip life bare is an implicit foundational assumption of sovereign power: "the inclusion of bare life in the political realm constitutes the original – if concealed – nucleus of sovereign power. It can even be said that the production of a biopolitical body is the original activity of sovereign power" (1998, 11). And, as we will see, bare life is created by sovereign power even as sovereignty's very power is created by the production and appropriation of bare life. This severance of bare life from form-of-life is thus an act of violence by governments, groups, and individuals who arrogate to themselves the status of sovereignty. So, before turning to the meaning of violence in Benjamin and Agamben, let us first consider the notion of sovereignty.

An image that Agamben invokes to describe sovereignty's extraction of bare life from form-of-life is the frontispiece of Thomas Hobbes's political treatise *Leviathan* (published in 1651), a canonical urtext of modern political philosophy (Hobbes 1991). A mythic image dominates the scene, shown in Figures 5.1 and 5.2. The giant, crowned

Figure 5.1 Frontispiece in *Leviathan* by Thomas Hobbes, illustration by Abraham Bosse (London, Andrew Crooke, 1651). The British Library Board, 522.k.6 frontispiece.

Figure 5.2 Detail from frontispiece in *Leviathan*.

sovereign, bearing sword and scepter, looks down on what appears to be a city devoid of people. Despite being situated far from the city and behind a hilly range, the sovereign's gaze, stature, and reach suggest omniscience and omnipotence. Equally significant, on looking more closely, we see that, with the exception of his head, the sovereign's upper body and arms are fully constituted by miniscule people facing him – a "body … formed out of all the bodies of individuals" (Agamben 1998, 74). For Agamben, this image is paradigmatic of modern notions of sovereign power controlling bare life and extracting it from any given form-of-life. As shown in Figure 5.1, this extraction is evident as we see only the residual spatial outlines of a form-of-life in the empty city streets and buildings – akin to a ghost town. Agamben argues that modern politics is structured around this depiction of sovereign power.

But in this control over bare life, the citizen's body (the *corpus*) bears a "two-faced" quality: subjection to the sovereignty of the state or ruler *and* the personal sovereignty of individual liberty (Agamben 1998, 73). Thus, two seemingly dissonant processes coexist, particularly in modern democracies:

> Everything happens as if, along with the disciplinary process by which State power makes man as a living being into its own specific object, another process is set in motion that in large measure corresponds to the birth of modern democracy, in which man as a living being presents himself no longer as an *object* but as the *subject* of political power. These processes … converge insofar as both concern the bare life of the citizen, the new biopolitical body of humanity. (Agamben 1998, 13, emphasis in original)

Agamben is devoted to exposing the ambiguous zone of indistinction between the qualities of totalization and individualization – a zone that defines the modern relationship between the human body, the sovereign nation-state, and, as we will see, the sovereign self.

The most extreme manifestations of sovereign power's producing bare life are the genocidal events of our era. Agamben gives extensive attention to the concentration camp as a paradigm for the sovereign's production of bare life. Yet, as he argues, we should also consider biotechnological "advances" that record and influence so many aspects of our lives and that, without much stretch of the imagination, could be appropriated by sovereign power. Or, consider the concerns with "right to life" and with the personal right to bear arms in the interest of bodily protection and the inevitably concomitant interest of wielding power over others.

State of Exception

The assumption of sovereign power over human beings' bodies, then, has the potential of producing bare life. He who is sovereign can subject a body to power – through force, harm, killing, or removal. Doing so, as we will now show, following Agamben, is to relegate human beings to the status of "exceptions" (Agamben 2005, 52). I now turn to this latter concept, after which I suggest how gun violence, such as school shootings, is a form of this extraction of bare life from form-of-life that reflects a larger biopolitical ethos. I then argue that the gun lobby also assumes a notion of power in which what is at stake is control over biological life rather than the free expression of a form-of-life.

In its etymological sense, to be ex-cepted (*excapare*), is to be "taken outside," excluded. Yet, as Agamben explains, in being ex-cepted, one remains included in the sovereign's control; it is a kind of inclusive exclusion. The very word "exception" refers to that which "is taken outside (*ex-capere*), and not simply excluded" (1998, 18).

Carl Schmitt, who infamously became the ideologue of the German Third Reich, is an important source of influence and object of critique in Benjamin's and Agamben's interpretations of sovereignty and of the sovereign's decision on a "state of exception": "Sovereign is he who decides on the state of exception" (Schmitt, 2005, 5). The sovereign invokes the exception in matters that are considered the extreme emergency, suspending and bypassing constitutional law, thereby purportedly restoring the state's security and viability (Agamben, 1998, 17). Following Benjamin, Agamben shows that this suspension of the law (that is, the sovereign's invoking the state of exception) exposes a legal vacuum and paradox. Schmitt had suggested that though the sovereign's capacity to suspend the law implies his standing outside of the political and juridical order, he is nonetheless an essential dimension of the order and therefore included within it. Agamben highlights this inside–outside paradox and contradiction: The law relates to the exception by suspending its own application (1998, 18). The sovereign is the one who makes a decision on who shall be "taken outside" the limits of the law. There is then no legal or ethical status for one removed from the *nomos*.

This paradox is elucidated by Benjamin in his much discussed 1921 essay, "Critique of Violence." In the essay, which is frequently invoked in recent scholarship on state-sponsored violence, law enforcement, national states of emergency, and "ethical" uses of violence, Benjamin contests the prevalent justifications of violence as a means to an end. Any consideration of an "ethics" of violence, he argues, must evaluate it separately from ends that it might be serving. The enigma of a violence as "pure" means, then, becomes the essay's focus.

A contemporary example Agamben cites to illustrate a state of exception's production of bare life is President George W. Bush's military order of November 13, 2001, "Detention, Treatment, and Trial of Certain Non-Citizens in the War Against Terrorism":

> [I]t is not practicable to apply in military commissions under this order the principles of law and the rules of evidence generally recognized in the trial of criminal cases in the United States district courts ... I have determined that an extraordinary emergency exists for national defense purposes, that this emergency constitutes an urgent and compelling government interest, and that issuance of this order is necessary to meet the emergency. (Bush 2001, 57833–57834)

The order has been much debated and contested by constitutional law scholars. For example, Raven-Hansen (2004), argues:

> I suggest that the war on terrorism provides no reason to depart from the conventional rule of lawmaking – the procedures a government under the rule of law conventionally follows in making law. Instead, I argue that the exigencies of that war especially require observance of the rule of lawmaking when the executive asserts liberty-and life-threatening military powers at home. (832)

Asking the question in his article's title, "Detaining Combatants by Law or by Order?," Raven-Hansen suggests an interpretation that places the military order outside "the rule of lawmaking" (832), beyond legal limits. The order goes on to prohibit any review by the judiciary, declaring that

> any individual subject to this order ... shall not be privileged to seek any remedy or maintain any proceeding, directly or indirectly, or to have any such remedy or proceeding sought on the individual's behalf, in (i) any court of the United States, or any State thereof, (ii) any court of any foreign nation, or (iii) any international tribunal. (Bush 2001, 57835–57836)

Agamben (2005) points out the order's unprecedented nature: "What is new about President Bush's order is that it radically erases any legal status of the individual, thus producing a legally unnamable and unclassifiable being" (2005, 3). Moreover, this extra-legal declassification of human beings, paradoxically, "captures" them in a "sovereign sphere ... in which it is permitted to kill without committing homicide" (1998, 78). Or, in a more familiar vein: It is permitted to torture without regard for legal constraints or juridical frameworks.

The military order violated the international law of the UN Convention against Torture and Other Cruel, Inhuman or Degrading Treatment (United Nations, 1984, Part 1, Articles 1 & 2), the UN Declaration of Human Rights, the International Convention of Civil and Political Rights, the European Convention for the Protection of Human Rights and Fundamental Freedoms, and the Geneva Convention (Ramsey 2006, 104).

Disregarding this international legal consensus, the Bush administration suggested that "cruel, inhuman or degrading treatment was permissible" and redefined "what counts as torture" (Ramsey 2006, 106). White House counsel Alberto Gonzales's memorandum to President Bush, then, constituted an overt suspension of international law: "The war on terror is a new kind of war ... this new paradigm renders obsolete Geneva's strict limitation on questioning of enemy prisoners and renders quaint some of its provisions" (Ramsey 2006, 106). These are instances, then, when the state's use of violence is taken outside of the rule of law, ex-cepting human beings and stripping them of their form-of-life, producing them as bare life in a sovereign decision. I argue that such exceptions are not made by the state alone.

The gun lobby, too, appropriates this kind of presumed sovereign exception. For the gun lobby, Hobbes must be read reflexively and not as a covenant between a person and a government. Sovereignty lies within and it is expressed outwardly with the gun. Loss of the gun is the loss of an individualized internal sovereignty. The obligation of a social contract, therefore, is appropriated as an obligation to the sovereign self, to a presumed self-contained, self-identical bare life and body of the individual perpetrator of violence himself. Thus, sovereignty and its power to decide on the exception are reflected both in the exercise of governmental power *and* in the individual's sovereign disposition toward himself and others as extrajuridical exceptions.

For Agamben, what is unique "in our age" is that the exception "ultimately begins to become the rule," deferring and progressively replacing the norms of communities and the constituted law: "The state of exception thus ceases to be referred to as an external and provisional state of factual danger and comes to be confused with the juridical rule itself" (1998, 168). In this inversion of rule and exception, "the exception everywhere becomes the rule ... and exclusion and inclusion, outside and inside ... right and fact, enter into a zone of irreducible indistinction" (1998, 9).

This interpretation of modern sovereignty's Janus-faced quality (collective and individual) finds support from fellow philosopher, Jacques Derrida – with whom, ironically, Agamben frequently takes issue. In a late interview, Derrida argues that this attitude toward the self is characteristic of "modern notions of subjectivity as autonomous":

> In an entire realm of our lives we act as though we still believed, at bottom, in the sovereign authority of the I, of consciousness, etc., and employ the language of this "autonomy" ... either in our souls or our bodies, whether the body of each individual, the body of society, the body of the nation, or the body of the discursive and juridical-political apparatus. (Weber 2008, 636)

Citing Derrida, Weber makes clear how, in the context of a modern "metaphysics of sovereignty," the "'autonomous self' thus invokes a kind of indivisible exceptionalism in which the sovereign wields "power over the life and death of its subjects" (Weber 2008, 637). So there is, as Derrida points out, a pervasive set of "ethical, legal or political practices that are informed by a distinct logic, namely by a certain metaphysics of sovereignty (autonomy and omnipotence of the subject – whether individual or statist)" (637). As will be significant in my argument below, in this logic (which Derrida deconstructs), violence is instrumental in seeking to preserve, defend, and protect the bare life of the self, and to control and reduce the bare life of those who, in some way, may be seen as a threat to one's *corpus*.

From Gun Culture to the Gun Lobby to the Shooter's Exceptionality

It would be inaccurate to suggest that inherent in what historically has come to be called America's "gun culture" is a domination of bare life and a disregard for a form-of-life. Indeed, for many, guns are integral to a form-of-life (Kohn 2004). Many see gun owner-ship as an expression of American individualism (Bellah et al. 1985), self-reliance, and a highly valued "American exceptionalism" (Lipset 1997). And, though we are familiar with the devastatingly tragic archetype of the lone gunman, guns constitute a social and cul-tural practice (Kohn 2004, 39). However, I suggest that, increasingly, much of the gun culture's and gun lobby's contemporary rhetoric has isolated bare life rather than asserting its own form-of-life as its concern and, in the process, has arrogated a certain exceptiona-lity to itself. This exceptionalism is then appropriated by perpetrators of violence.

In the National Rifle Association's history, for example, we see this transition from concern with form-of-life to control over bare life. Indeed, for its first 100 years, the NRA's charter opened with a statement promoting "marksmanship and organized shooting matches" (Sierpien 2006, 1). But in recent decades it has transformed itself from an organization that supported gun enthusiasm to a political action organization. In this transformation, the control of one's own and others' bare lives becomes para-mount – hence the emphasis on fundamentalist interpretations of the Second Amendment. Guns are embraced and supported in a discourse of physical security and insecurity. The language of gun supporters does not emphasize the sustaining of a form-of-life, but rather power over bare life.

Consider Sarah Palin's infamous political call to arms prior to the shooting of Representative Gabrielle Giffords: "Don't Retreat, Instead – RELOAD!" (Palin 2010, emphasis in original). Or consider Jesse Kelly's campaign ad to defeat the Democratic congresswoman: "Get on Target for Victory in November/Help remove Gabrielle Giffords from office/Shoot a fully automatic M15 with Jesse Kelly" (Safier 2010). Following the attempted assassination of Giffords (and the killing of a number of other innocents), we can see how Palin again invoked the language of bare life to criticize her detractors as perpetrating a "blood libel" (Engels 2012, 122; Palin 2011).

This isolation of bare life from form-of-life has enabled a relation of exception on several levels. First, the gun lobby excepts the perpetrator of mass shootings from itself. That much political discourse tends to isolate the mass shooter as a non-systemic, iso-lated, criminal, mentally ill element is well documented. Ronald Reagan famously (and infamously) offered a keynote for this sentiment, claiming that "we must reject the idea that every time a law's broken, society is guilty rather than the lawbreaker. It is time to restore the American precept that each individual is accountable for his actions" (Reagan 1968). No form-of-life is indicated here, no social theory or context is sought; instead, this formulation simply isolates the body of the shooter, the perpetrator's bare life. He is thus *ex*cepted, *de*contextualized, *dis*owned.

This process involves several steps. In the view of the NRA, for example, the mass shooter is *included* among those who have the right, purportedly guaranteed by the Second Amendment, to possess automatic weapons *up until* the point when he engages in his heinous act. At that point, what had been a relation of inclusion becomes a relation of exclusion. But in order to be excluded, the shooter had to be included in the larger class of those who have that right to bear arms. The gun lobby casts out the rampage shooter as an exception.

This is not an unfamiliar position for many shooters. In their video transcripts, the Columbine shooters discussed a "revolution of the dispossessed" (Langman 2014). In German school shooter Sebastian Bosses's suicide note, he declares that he is doing this for the sake of "revolution of the rejected!" (Böckler, Seeger, and Wilhelm Heitmeyer 2010, 280). One Columbine shooter wrote: "I am in eternal suffering ... hoping that people can accept me ... that i can accept them" (286). The perpetrator, then, is ex-cepted both by those who lobby for freedom to buy guns (including automatic assault rifles) without restriction, and by those to whom he had proclaimed grievances for exclusion.

What can be learned from the exception? Kierkegaard (2009), through the character in his book *Repetition*, argues that there is much to be discovered in "the dialectical battle through which the exception emerges from the universal, the extended and incredibly complicated procedure through which the exception fights for and asserts its legitimacy." When a community or collectivity (what Kierkegaard might refer to as the "universal") "breaks with the exception," there is a violent "rupture." The "vigorous and determined exception" is, in fact, "an offshoot of [the universal]." In this ex-cepted condition, there is much to be learned of the universal: "The exception thus explains the universal and itself, and when one really wants to study the universal, one need only examine a legitimate exception, because it will present everything much more clearly than the universal would itself ... If one cannot explain [exceptions], then neither can one explain the universal" (Kierkegaard 2009, 78).

For our purposes, we can consider the "universal" as the ethos and norms of a group, community, nation, or even a world order. If Kierkegaard is right, we can learn much about the broader collective by understanding those whom it has excepted: those on the fringes, what Bauman (2004) refers to as "wasted lives," "things excluded – thrown out of focus, cast in the shadow, forced into the vague or invisible background – no longer belong[ing] to 'what is'" (Bauman 2004, 18).

In Agamben's terms, considering persons or a group an exception is to relate to them as "included solely through its exclusion" (1998, 18). He exposes this kind of relation of inclusive exclusion primarily as a function of the political relationship of sovereignty to law and violence. And it is not difficult to recognize that this complicity of inclusion and exclusion is what the gun lobby seeks to conceal by simply placing the shooter into the category of "bad apples." But the shooter is not simply an example of a figurative bad apple; he is, rather, made an exception from the rule. Exposing this complicit, paradoxical relation can reveal much:

> As long as the state of exception and the normal situation are kept separate in space and time, as is usually the case, both remain opaque, though they secretly institute each other. But as soon as they show their complicity, as happens more and more often today, they illuminate each other, so to speak, from the inside. (Agamben 2002, 49–50)

Our educational institutions and systems, instead of seeking to learn from the exception – in this case the school shooter – often think they can control it through securing a separation, keeping a distance, in what Lynn Davies (2016) calls the "'securitisation' of responsibility for education" (5). Thus, there is little exposure of what Kierkegaard and

Agamben argue is the complicity between "nomal" and "exceptional." Böckler, Seeger, and Wilhelm Heitmeyer (2010, 261) note that this "expectation of control" is but an "illusion": society's illusion and expectation of control is due to the "safety imperative" of modern society, according to which all risks are controllable (261).

We must expose the relation to exception's dual status of inclusion and exclusion to reveal its complicity with gun violence, for ironically, if not surprisingly, this logic of the exception, of isolating bare life, is appropriated by the shooter as well. In a sense, the shooter is mirroring the exclusive sovereignty of the gun and the gun lobby. The shooter becomes sovereign over the bare life of victims, extracting their bare life from their form-of-life by extinguishing the former. In doing so, the gunman produces and controls the bare life of victims, and perhaps also exposes his own biological being as subjected to suicidal death. He becomes a bare life, an empty shell that has no form-of-life, no sense of the possible. For the gun lobby, it is vital to distinguish this "exceptionality" of the school shooter or criminal from the "normality" of an unfettered right to bear arms.

Educational institutions and school systems, too, are complicit in the logic of the exception. Consider when students are automatically suspended or summarily expelled. While, in some extreme cases, these measures may be appropriate, often these are exclusionary trigger policies, what Agnich and Hale (2015) call "hair-trigger policies that remove students from the classroom, take kids away from their teachers, school counselors, and staff at the very moment they could use the guidance and mentoring of caring adults" (82). Disproportionate, implicitly racist zero tolerance policies and school-to-prison incarcerations are yet further examples of educational systems' applying the logic of the exception – taking young people outside, ex-cepting them, seeking to dispose of them in a forced exile (Keisch and Scott 2015; Kerby 2012).

A further example of this relation of exception – of isolating and disavowing connections to perpetrators of violence – is the highly racialized public discourse on school shootings. As DeLeon (2012) has demonstrated, "because Whiteness is not popularly associated with deviance, blackness is often constructed as its binary opposite. Poor African American communities, for example, are constructed as dens of rampant sexuality and crime, poor work ethic and morally lax" (153). Moreover, the white school shooter is often depicted as "calculating, intelligent and conniving" (153), whereas urban crime, in contrast, is excepted from the norm, "constructed as random, wild and tied to 'ghetto' issues like gangs, reputation and revenge" (153). As exceptions, "perpetrators of urban crime are constructed as criminals, deviant or dangerous in relation to supposedly White innocence" (153).

The dominant societal culture thus fosters a view of the white shooter as an isolated individual exception and of the violence in communities of color as an isolated collective exception. Furthermore, this kind of discourse privileges certain sites as "safe" or "away," creating a binary relation between urban – where violence is "commonplace" – and suburban or rural – where violence "should not" or "does not" happen. It is therefore education's task to address and reconceive all of these manifestations of the logic of the exception, most notably those that isolate acts of violence in a kind of conceptual, ethical quarantine.

This logic of the exception is akin to what Edward Said (1978) calls "orientalism," in which the West assumes a "positional superiority" over the East (90). Consider, for example, US Navy Seal Marc Luttrell's characterizing himself as a "special breed of warrior," whereas those whom he fights are "lawless," "wild mountain men" (2007, 9, 6, 10, 13) – the "righteous and valiant" against the "dangerous and unpredictable" (McClennen 2012, 187–188).

Divine Violence

In the notion of "divine violence," Agamben sees the possibility of deposing the dominance of this ubiquitous distinction between "the state of exception" and "the normal case" (1998, 41) – for our purposes here, in responses to school shootings. For, as we will see, divine violence exposes "a zone in which it is no longer possible to distinguish between exception and rule" (42). In making his case, Agamben builds upon Benjamin's project of shattering instrumental justifications of sovereign violence. Benjamin argues in his "Critique of Violence" that an instrumental justification does nothing to suggest the meaning or "criterion for violence itself as a principle, but, rather, the criterion for cases of its use," that is, its intended outcomes (1978, 277). Thus, the very state of exception creates the context and assumed license to exercise violence instrumentally. Violence, as instrument, serves the state of exception and is justified by a sovereign decision – individual, collective, or statist – to declare or assume the need for exceptional means to achieve noble ends.

Of course, decoupling instrumentality and violence would be anathema to the gun lobby's motivation and argument. After all, the gun is an instrument in service of individual security and control. It is the vehicle for command and control, the apparatus that allows one to target, to lock and load, putting bare life in its crosshairs. But, in the notion of divine violence we might begin to see how education can help undo this nexus between life, liberty, and pursuit of happiness, on the one hand, and the freedom to possess and use instruments of violence and death, on the other.

The problem is that instrumental justifications for violence often control and subordinate its very ends. This violent conflation of means and ends is summarized by Hannah Arendt (1969) (who knew Benjamin's work well): "The very substance of violent action is ruled by the means–end category, whose chief characteristic, if applied to human affairs, has always been that the end is in danger of being overwhelmed by the means which it justifies and which are needed to reach it'" (1969, 4). Violence – of the school shooter, war criminal, terrorist, a state's unjust war, or corporal disciplinarian – overwhelms its ends; it takes on a life of its own that resists being subordinated. Its source of legitimation is an end external to it, but this very legitimation lets it thrive as an annihilating power.

To elucidate how we might expose such seemingly instrumental violence, note that, as previously mentioned, divine violence is a response to the prevailing state of exception. The state of exception that has increasingly become the rule has become shrouded in habitual acceptance. Divine violence has the potential to remove the many layers of this opaque conceptual and prereflective acquiescence and to make this exceptional state transparent.

We have come to accept the exceptionality of violence, whether used by states, groups, or individuals. The common assumption is that violence is necessary as an instrument of control, protection, and sovereign power. We can consider Benjamin's essay on violence itself an act of divine violence for it exposes the instrumentalism of mythic justifications of violence – the spread of democracy, the need for "honor," the display of vengeance, the "justice" of *lex talionis* ("an eye for an eye"). Such justifications are often expressed in mythic symbols and images: the flag, military fatigues, slogans (for example, "stand your ground"), and maxims (for example, "make yourself memorable"). Benjamin seeks to expose the need for a "violence" (that is, "divine violence") that annihilates the very justifications of violent force, whether juridical, social, psychological, emotional, or physical. So, he takes on the task stated in a challenging formulation: "individuating a different kind of violence that certainly could not be either the legitimate or illegitimate means to those ends" and is not related to those ends "as means at all" (Benjamin 1978; Agamben 2005, 62).

In a brief, but significant, passage, Benjamin explicitly asserts the relationship between divine violence and education: "This divine power is attested not only by religious tradition but is also found in present-day life in at least one sanctioned manifestation. The *educative* power, which in its perfected form stands outside the law, is one of its manifestations" (1978, 250, emphasis added). The concept of divine violence here demands a great deal from educational theorists accustomed to a means–ends logic, for it is not a vehicle for implementation of a new norm, temporary or permanent (as is the state of exception). Divine violence is neither instrumentally serving an end nor is it an emotional outburst or expression, but it has an effect in "exposing" and "deposing" the linkages between violence, norms, and sovereignty, "unmasking the fiction" of their nexus (Agamben 1998, 41–42; 2005, 62). Thus, it does not stake a claim but reveals a relationship between force and the *nomos* (for instance, "stand your ground" and its emergence out of what is claimed to be justified instrumental violence, having invoked a state of exception). By exposing the dependence of the logic of exception on this nexus, divine violence deposes the sovereign individual or sovereign ruler excepting himself.

It is important to clarify that "divine violence" is not violent in the sense that we are accustomed to using the term. This is a paradoxically powerful non-violence that assertively "posits itself without insisting on its moment of foundation" (Blumenthal-Barby 2009, 729). Divine violence, then, is neither transgressive nor conservative, neither ordaining nor upholding. Important for Agamben is that divine violence suggests no foundational or transcendent principle. Education, if indeed a form of divine violence, exposes the static linkages among law, violence, and exceptionalism in the sovereign state and the sovereign self, and thus calls for an iterative reconstructing of the relationships between individual and communal forms of life.

The concept of divine violence suggests the responsibility of education to expose less than transparent paradoxes, revealing contradictions in what is commonplace, in what we have come to accept as seemingly unchallengeable norms. For example, teaching the principle of *lex talionis* may involve showing the counterintuitive effect of its causing more violent crime; or teaching responsibility toward one's own community may also involve exposing how we can seem to absolve ourselves from more extensive responsibilities toward communities geographically remote from us; or teaching citizenship virtues may also involve showing how a pedagogical emphasis on citizenship can contribute (intentionally or not) to a xenophobic disposition toward non-citizens in general, and toward undocumented immigrants in particular.

Exposing what Agamben calls "the paradoxes of the state of exception" is a most exacting educational responsibility, for doing so shows how it has become increasingly "impossible to distinguish transgression of the law from execution of the law, such that what violates a rule and what conforms to it coincide without any remainder" (1998, 37–38).

One of Agamben's examples resonates with the paradoxes surrounding school shootings: "A person who goes for a walk during the curfew is not transgressing the law any more than the soldier who kills him is executing it" (38). The instituting of the curfew is an "exceptional" measure, that is, outside the normative law. Likewise, the soldier who kills is exercising another exceptional measure. There is no transgressing or executing of a law, but an invoking of a state of exception in both cases.

In the name of the law (the Second Amendment), the gun lobby invokes the right to bear arms. In the name of the "stand your ground" law, a shooter claims the right to kill. In the name of the sovereign self's need for protection and security, a shooter claims to seek justice or to neutralize a perceived threat. In the name of honor, a shooter carries out a massacre. In the name of sovereign democracy, a government colonizes, tyrannizes, or seeks dominion over others. In each of these examples, the "execution of the law" and the "transgression of the law" become indistinguishable. The state of exception that all of these conflations reveal is the "point at which the juridical stops and a sovereign unaccountability begins; it is where the dam of individual liberties breaks and a society is flooded with the sovereign power of the state" (de la Durantaye 2009, 338).

Divine violence, first, exposes this paradox of the pervasive state of exception's legally transgressive, but, in fact, extrajuridical execution. Next, it calls for undoing the paradoxical nexus between norm and exceptional decision. It invokes a pedagogical power to unravel the accepted thicket of intertwined strands that assert control in the name of freedom, punishment in the name of responsibility, banishment and exclusion in the name of security, violent vengeance in the name of honor, and domination in the name of sovereign autonomy. But such divine violence cannot simply follow a prescriptive protocol or a deskilled pedagogical path. It involves a free use of educational imagination that no precedent can provide.

Conclusion: Education and the "Real State of Exception"

Benjamin presents us with a political and educational challenge that transcends his own historical situation in Nazi Germany. In his "Eighth Thesis on the Philosophy of History" (first published in 1940), he surprisingly asserts that we also have a responsibility to create a state of exception, but of a different kind than those described above:

> The tradition of the oppressed teaches us that the "state of exception" in which we live is not the exception but the rule. We must attain to a conception of history that is in keeping with this insight. Then we shall clearly realize that it is our task to bring about a real state of exception, and this will improve our position in the struggle against Fascism. (Benjamin 1968, 257)

What, then, is this "real state of exception," and how does it depart from and undo that state of exception so fraught with appropriations of violence? Quoting Heidegger, Agamben explains that it involves assuming a "freedom" that "reveals" being "capable of being, with possibilities that gape open" (Agamben 1999, 200). As Agamben points out here, there is a kind of "cobelonging of capacity and incapacity" that balance each other in our authentic choices (200). Human beings do not have to be or not to be a particular "essence," but rather, need to recognize "the simple fact of one's own existence as possibility or potentiality" (1993, 43). There is, then, no determined destiny toward which we are progressing in a kind of "servitude to continuous linear time" (2007, 114–115). Rather, to live freely is to live in "liberation from" such predeterminations. Choosing one's "own freedom in the moment" (105) involves recognizing the coexistence and interdependence of our potentiality and our impotentiality. In a provocative statement, Agamben argues that "To be free is … to be capable of one's own impotentiality, to be in relation to one's own privation" (1999, 183). Although a full elucidation of Agamben's theory of potentiality and impotentiality is beyond the scope of this chapter, I suggest that a critical educational goal is to teach that our freedom is not exercised in deciding to do something against another, but to *not* do it. To decide the "not" is the act of a free student.

The "real state of exception" to which Benjamin alludes is unlike a state of martial law, a state of siege, or an emergency, for these latter soon become permanent states of exception that justify themselves by their very exceptionality, perpetuating acts of violence and extractions of bare life. The "real state of exception" is fraught with the capacity, the potentiality, to be open to both the possible and the not-possible. The difference between the problematic and the real states of exception is summarized well by Samuel Weber (2008). When confronted with a sense of insecurity, when experiencing a perceived threat, a government, an institution, a collective, or an individual can do one of two things: "It can either insist on preserving and protecting what cannot simply be protected: the given, actual self-identity of the institution or the individual." This would be to decide on the state of exception that produces violence. Or "it can offer an opportunity to transform that self-identity by no longer simply protecting it, as it was, but opening it to a transformation, to the heterogeneity that it has always contained, but also sought to reduce and dissimulate" (Weber 2008, 638). Our educational task is to provide this latter perspective, this "real state of exception," that resists any semblance of monolithic predetermination and desperation.

For Agamben, the real state of exception is a "point of departure for any discourse on ethics" (1993, 43), though at first glance his formulation appears merely nihilistic: "that there is no essence, no historical or spiritual vocation, no biological destiny that humans must enact or realize." But as we read on and consider this claim, his point becomes clearer: "This is the only reason why something like an ethics can exist, because it is clear that if humans were or had to be this or that substance, this or that destiny, no ethical experience would be possible – there would be only tasks to be done" (1993, 43). He argues, therefore, that divine violence deposes the grounding of ethical decisions in prescriptive juridical duty, in a determinate legal responsibility, or justifications of violence, invoking a state of exception. In so doing, it exposes a real state of exception, an ethical freedom.

Our pedagogical challenge, then, is to expose and depose the language of non- responsibility and exceptionality when it comes to school violence and violence's other forms and contexts. The problem, which of course can never be isolated, is not simply people and not simply guns, but the increasing disposition toward bare life and relations of exception. So I end with an open question: Is there a vision of community and responsibility that does not strip bare our forms-of-life, that does not isolate bare life? This is a question that must invoke a kind of divine violence in which education seeks to conduct meaningful emancipatory conversations about and responses to patterns of devastating violence.

By exposing the extraction of bare life and modern efforts to assume power over it with violence and the threat of violence, we reveal a certain reality. What has been rhetorically posed as a struggle for law and security – that is, the Second Amendment – is also the exercising of a sovereign exception by individuals and groups. Agamben shows us that, in this process of appropriating the sovereign exception, form-of-life has become bare life. The object of concern has become the assumption of power to arrogate the sovereign exception over life, to assume an imperial disposition toward the other, and to cast the other as a potential threat to one's own bodily existence. We can only expose this reality by getting past the public health and gun safety discourse. To be sure, physical, mental, and societal health are at stake whenever there is a threat of violence and whenever violence is an available means for wielding power and control. Yet, I have sought here to demonstrate the need for political, philosophical, and educational conversations that move beyond this discourse, exposing the unrecognized, pervasive "state of exception in which we live," and opening a field for human action that frees itself from instrumental justification of violence and an illusory fatalism.

References

Agamben, Giorgio. 1998. *Homo Sacer: Sovereign Power and Bare Life*. Translated by Daniel Heller-Roazen. Stanford, CA: Stanford University Press.

Agamben, Giorgio. 1999. *Potentialities: Collected Essays in Philosophy*. Edited by Daniel Heller-Roazen, Editor. Stanford: Stanford University Press.

Agamben, Giorgio. 2000. *Means Without End: Notes on Politics*. Translated by Cesare Casarino and Vincenzo Binetti. Minneapolis, MN: University of Minnesota Press.

Agamben, Giorgio. 2002. *Remnants of Auschwitz*. Translated by Daniel Heller-Roazen. New York: Zone Books.

Agamben, Giorgio. 2005. *State of Exception*. Translated by Kevin Attell. Chicago: University of Chicago Press.

Agamben, Giorgio. 2007. *Infancy and History: Essays on the Destruction of Experience*. Translated by Liz Heron. New York: Verso.

Agamben, Giorgio. 1993. *The Coming Community*. Translated by Michael Hardt. Minneapolis, MN: University of Minnesota Press.

Agnich, Laura E. and Hale, Meghan. 2015. "Committing Mass Violence to Education and Learning. *Contexts* 14(2), 82–83.

Arendt, Hannah. 1969. *On Violence*. New York: Harcourt.

Bauman, Zygmunt. 2004. *Wasted Lives: Modernity and Its Outcasts*. Cambridge: Polity Press.

Bellah, Robert N., Madsen, Richard, Sullivan, William M., Swidler, Ann, and Tipton, Steven M. 1985. *Habits of the Heart: Individualism and Commitment in American Life*. Berkeley and Los Angeles: University of California Press.

Benjamin, Walter. 1978. "Critique of Violence." In *Walter Benjamin, Reflections*. Edited by Peter Demetz. Translated by Edmund Jephcott. New York: Schocken Books. First published 1921.

Benjamin, Walter. 1968. "Theses on the Philosophy of History." In *Illuminations*. Edited by Hannah Arendt. Translated by Harry Zohn. New York: Houghton Mifflin Harcourt. First published 1940.

Blumenthal-Barby, Martin. 2009. "Pernicious Bastardizations: Benjamin's Ethics of Pure Violence." *MLN* 124(3), 729.

Böckler, Nils, Seeger, Thorsten, and Heitmeyer, Wilhelm. 2010. "School Shooting: A Double Loss of Control." In *Control of Violence: Historical and International Perspectives on Violence in Modern Societies*, edited by Wilhelm Heitmeyer, Heinz-Gerhard Haupt, Stefan Malthaner, and Andrea Kirschner, pp. 261–294. New York: Springer.

Burgos, Evan. 2013. "Va. Tech Cleared in Wrongful-Death Lawsuit over 2007 Massacre." *NBC News*. October 31. http://www.nbcnews.com/news/other/va-tech-cleared-wrongful-death-lawsuit-over-2007- massacre-f8C11505007 (last accessed March 1, 2017).

Bush, George W. 2001. "Military Order of November 13, 2001 – Detention, Treatment, and Trial of Certain Non-Citizens in the War Against Terrorism." Federal Register 66, no. 222. November 16, 2001: 57833–57837.

Caret, Robert L. 2013. "University of Massachusetts President's Statement on Task Force Report." August 15. http://www.umassd.edu/media/umassdartmouth/officeofthechancellor/pdfs/rlc_taskforce_statement.pdf (accessed March 1, 2017).

Davies, Lynn. 2016. "Security, Extremism and Education: Safeguarding or Surveillance?" *British Journal of Educational Studies* 64(1), 1–19. DOI: 10.1080/00071005.2015. 1107022.

de la Durantaye, Leland. 2009. *Giorgio Agamben: A Critical Introduction*. Stanford, CA: Stanford University Press.

DeLeon, Abraham P. 2012. "'A Perverse Kind of Sense': Urban Spaces, Ghetto Places and the Discourse of School Shootings." *Urban Review: Issues and Ideas in Public Education* 44(1), 152–169.

Engels, Jeremy. 2012. "The Rhetoric of Violence: Sarah Palin's Response to the Tucson Shooting." *Symploke* 20(1–2).

Hobbes, Thomas. 1991. *Leviathan or the Matter, Forme, & Power of a Common-wealth, Ecclesiastical and Civill*. Edited by Richard Tuck. Cambridge: Cambridge University Press. First published 1651.

Keisch, Deborah M. and Scott, Tim. 2015. "U.S. Education Reform and the Maintenance of White Supremacy through Structural Violence." *Landscapes of Violence* 3(3), Article 6. http://scholarworks.umass.edu/lov/vol3/iss3/6 (last accessed October 6, 2017).

Kerby, Sophia. 2012. "1 in 3 Black Men Go to Prison? The 10 Most Disturbing Facts about Racial Inequality in the U.S. criminal Justice System." *American Prospect*, March 17. http://www.alternet.org/story/154587/1_in_3_black_men_go_to_prison_the_10_most_disturbing_facts_about_racial_inequality_in_the__u.s._criminal_justice_system (last accessed October 6, 2017).

Kierkegaard, Søren. 2009. *Repetition and Philosophical Crumbs*. Translated by M.G. Piety. Oxford: Oxford University Press.

Kohn, Abigail A. 2004. *Shooters: Myths and Realities of America's Gun Cultures*. Oxford: Oxford University Press.

Langman, Peter 2014. School Shooters .info, July 29. https://schoolshooters.info/sites/default/files/columbine_basement_tapes_1.0.pdf (last accessed October 6, 2017).

Lipset, Seymour Martin. 1997. *American Exceptionalism: A Double-Edged Sword*. New York: W.W. Norton.

Luttrell, Marc. 2007. *Lone Survivor*. New York: Back Bay Books.

McClennen, Sophia A. 2012. "Neoliberalism as Terrorism; or State of Disaster Exceptionalism." In *Terror, Theory, and the Humanities*, edited by Jeffrey R. Di Leo and Uppinder Mehan, pp. 178–195. Ann Arbor: University of Michigan Publishing.

Palin, Sarah. 2010. Twitter post. March 23, 2010, 10.31 a.m. https://twitter.com/sarahpalinusa/status/10935548053 (last accessed October 6, 2017).

Palin, Sarah. 2011. "America's Enduring Strength." Facebook post. January 12, 2011, 3.52 a.m. http://www.facebook.com/note.php?note_id=487510653434 (last accessed October 6, 2017).

Ramsey, Maureen. 2006. "Can the Torture of Terrorist Suspects be Justified?" *The International Journal of Human Rights* 10(2), 103–119.

Raven-Hansen, Peter. 2004. "Detaining Combatants by Law or by Order? The Rule of Lawmaking in the War on Terrorists." *Louisiana Law Review* 64(4), 831–850.

Reagan, Ronald. 1968. "Excerpts of a Speech by Governor Ronald Reagan, Republican National Convention, Miami, FL (July 31, 1968)." Ronald Reagan Library, Simi Valley, California.

Safier, David. 2010. "Jesse Kelly Event: Is This Wording Intentional?" BlogforArizona.com, June 12. http://blogforarizona.net/jesse-kelly-event-is-this-wording-intentional/ (last accessed October 6, 2017).

Said, Edward. 1978. *Orientalism*. London: Routledge & Kegan Paul.

Schmitt, Carl. 2005. *Political Theology, Four Chapters on the Concept of Sovereignty*. Translated by George Schwab. Chicago: University of Chicago Press. First published 1922/1934/.

Sierpien, Jeffery. 2006. "Frontline Strategies of the National Rifle Association." PhD dissertation. Naval Postgraduate School, Monterey, CA.

United Nations. 1984. *UN Convention Against Torture and Other Cruel, Inhuman or Degrading Treatment*. http://www.ohchr.org/EN/ProfessionalInterest/Pages/CAT.aspx (last accessed October 6, 2017).

Weber, Samuel. 2008. "Toward a Politics of Singularity: Protection and Projection." In *Religion: Beyond a Concept*, edited by Hent de Vries, pp. 626–646. New York: Fordham University Press.

6

Student Profiling and Negative Implications for Students with Disabilities

Kristeen Cherney and Margaret Price

The threat of school violence is real, but programs to help identify potential threats by profiling students have been proven ineffective, and have also supported an erroneous popular discourse around school violence that focuses on "fixing" or removing violent individuals, rather than contextual issues that might make violence more likely. Exacerbating the issue is the mainstream media, "with its 24/7 coverage and its intense focus on the killers and their backgrounds. As a result, administrators, teachers, school personnel, and students are left to identify safety threats on their own by creating profiles of the generic would-be perpetrator. Yet one has to wonder: What does the profile of a student shooter look like? Due in part to accounts spread via popular media, many observers are quick to assume that violence and mental health issues go hand in hand. As a result, media coverage and subsequent bias have increased the threat for anyone with a mental illness of stereotypical student profiling in educational institutions. Not only does this draw attention away from more useful, research-based solutions for evaluating at-risk students (as well as faculty and staff), but it also leads to the unwarranted targeting of students with mental health disabilities.

This chapter aims to investigate the history of student profiling in educational settings and examine how it has led to a mainstream discourse of connecting mental health disabilities with violence. We do not offer a set of criteria for profiling, as doing so further inflicts stigmatization. Instead, we advocate for an inclusive approach that creates safer spaces for all students.

Popular Media and the Urge to Profile

Profiling students and other individuals who commit violent crimes in schools and on college campuses has been fueled by some of the investigations spawned from recent acts of school violence. In fact, "mass shootings can increase mental health stigma, reinforce negative stereotypes that people with mental illness are dangerous and violent" (Rosenberg 2014, 107). No one could argue that shooters do not have problems they are grappling with. However, the notion that there is a consistent mental health would-be shooter profile that would prevent acts of violence is supported by little evidence.

The Wiley Handbook on Violence in Education: Forms, Factors, and Preventions, First Edition.
Edited by Harvey Shapiro.
© 2018 John Wiley & Sons, Inc. Published 2018 by John Wiley & Sons, Inc.

School officials are encouraged – often by popular media reports – to look for warning signs of a would-be shooter. Though not always explicitly stated, media accounts of the state of violence in schools can understandably cause pressure to find preventative measures, including profiling. Take, for example, the following passage from a 2014 news article:

> Parents worried about their children's safety while at school might not just be over-protective. While the number of school-related deaths are starting to decrease, incidents of theft and violence – including student violence against teachers – are on the rise in America's schools, according to a federal report released Tuesday. And schools are beefing up security, including video cameras and armed security guards, as a result. (Bidwell 2014)

Rhetorically, news articles such as these support underlying fears surrounding violence, thereby pressuring officials to put profiling measures in place. Fear combined with popularized accounts of profiling increase the likelihood of mental health stigmatization. When a shooter's mental health issues are highlighted, people are more likely to target students with mental disabilities as potential threats.

Meanwhile, scholarly research into violent behavior indicates that its roots are extremely complex and, moreover, that certain traits (such as being white, male, and young) are more likely to be part of a school shooter's profile than a specific kind of diagnosed mental illness. But if there is no set profile, then what can be done? Institutions thus find themselves in a conundrum, driven by conflicting points of view that would govern how policies are set. In somewhat oversimplified terms, the question is whether or not to try to predict individuals' behavior through profiling. There is also the common belief that "if schools are able to address students' mental health issues successfully, it is possible that they might prevent future violent acts" (Dikel 2012, 2). Following this logic, *if* there is evidence that mental illness is causally linked to mass shootings, then – from the school's standpoint – it would only make sense to target students with existing mental health issues as a way to stop violence. And yet, though profiling is a tempting approach to take, it is not an accurate or ethical one. Indeed, profiling is exemplified by popular accounts of mass shooters that cannot be replicated as a reliable tool to prevent school violence.

For example, in 2012, at Sandy Hook Elementary School in Newtown, Connecticut, Adam Lanza shot and killed 20 children and six adults. He had previously killed his own mother, and would later kill himself. At the time, this massacre was considered one of the most horrific mass shootings in US history. Immediately following the event, popular media accounts pointed to Lanza's mental state. For instance, *Newsweek* reporter Matthew Lysiak (2014) wrote that Lanza was "twisted with mental illness." The *New York Times* declared that Lanza was "completely untreated … for psychiatric and physical ailments like anxiety and obsessive-compulsive disorder" (Cowan 2014). *Psychology Today* ran an imploring headline: "Was Adam Lanza an Undiagnosed Schizophrenic?" (Turndorf 2012), while *The Telegraph* declared: "Childhood of Sandy Hook Killer Was Filled with 'Crippling' Mental Health Issues" (Millward 2104). Headlines like these increase anxieties over whether undiagnosed mentally ill individuals are "lurking" among ordinary members of society.

Certainly, no one could dispute the fact that Lanza was mentally ill. However, this relatively clear piece of information becomes murkier when that information is translated into the assumption that *all* mentally ill individuals are potentially dangerous. Some of the popular discourse around school shootings has caused unfounded generalizations among campus leaders, who may deem people with mental health histories to be potential threats. In what follows, we offer brief descriptions of some of the best known (and most heavily covered) school shootings in order to suggest some insights about how popular media typically cover school shootings. Examining the profile-inducing and mental-illness-focused rhetoric surrounding these incidents can help us better understand how responses to violence in schools have evolved.

In the immediate aftermath of the 2007 shooting by Seung-Hui Cho at Virgina Tech University, the *New York Times* ran the headline, "Before Deadly Rage, a Life Consumed by a Troubling Silence" (Kleinfield 2007). Meanwhile, the *Wall Street Journal* reported, "From Disturbed High Schooler to College Killer" (Golden 2007). Another example comes from the 2008 shooting at Northern Illinois University by Steven Kazmierczak. Although Kazmierczak did not have as obvious a mental health history as Cho, popular media accounts seemed determined to link him with mental health issues. One ABC News article noted that the 27-year-old "had most recently been studying mental health issues at the University of Illinois, and had taken a job at a prison, according to his academic adviser" (Friedman 2008). The persistent investigations into mental health as the assumed leading cause of a violent act places all students with mental disabilities under unfair surveillance and stigma. As Price (2011) writes in *Mad at School*:

> Such representations function as case studies of the killers, and as records of mental pathology escalating "inevitably" toward extreme violence. Each killer is relentlessly individuated, and the tiniest details of his life taken apart and reconstructed in a narrative aimed to show that he was a "time bomb that sputtered for years before he went off" ("Framing"). Through these representations ... disorders [are] taken as evidence of the progression of each [shooter's] life toward its violent conclusion. (143)

Thus, although Kazmierczak's atypical profile was puzzling to some, it demonstrates both the complexity of profiling potential killers and the problematic stigma that popular accounts tend to generate with regard to mental illness. This can compound the confusion surrounding the issue, leaving schools at a loss as to what sorts of policies should be pursued in response.

The 1999 shooting at Columbine High School in Littleton, Colorado greatly expanded national and international concern for school safety. It was also, at the time, one of the most widely discussed incidents of school violence in modern history. In April of that year, students Eric Harris and Dylan Klebold killed 13 people and injured 24 others before killing themselves. In 2009, the Associated Press ran the headline: "Columbine Shooters Mentally Ill, Not Bullied" (Rubinkam 2009). This headline, run with the accompanying article nearly 10 years after the Columbine mass shooting, perhaps reflects the epitome of much of the public's stance on school rampage shootings: it is not bullying, bad parenting, violent video games, or vulgar music that is to blame, but rather mental illness. The article also acts as a veiled advertisement for child psychologist Peter Langman's 2009 book *Why Kids Kill: Inside the Minds of School Shooters* in which he explores the mental states of Harris and Klebold, among other student shooters. The Associated Press declares that Langman set off on a "decade-long inquiry" to fulfill an "ethical obligation to learn all he could about the psychology of school shooters" (2009). It is not clear whether this "ethical obligation" was to fully explore the reasons behind school shootings or if Langman's "obligation" was more focused on warning the public about mentally ill students. Since the 1990s (especially after the Columbine shooting), the stereotype of the mentally ill student as being more prone to violent acts has become established in popular discourse as common sense. However, there is no scientific support for any established "profile" that indicates mentally ill individuals are more prone to violence.

Mental illnesses are often understood within an ableist framework. Therefore, when a student is profiled based on his or her mental state, the focus tends to move quickly to deviance. Watts and Erevelles (2004) expand on the concept of the deviant student, writing that such a student is the result of "normalizing structures" within ableist social constructs. We can also think of ableism as "society's pervasive negative attitude about disability" (Hehir 2007, 9), or simply as society's expectation that everyone needs to conform to a certain standard. As Hehir (2007) put it: "an ableist perspective asserts that it is preferable for a child to read print rather than Braille, walk rather than use a wheelchair, spell independently rather than use a spell-checker, read written text rather than listen to a book on tape, and hang out with nondisabled kids rather than disabled kids" (9). Based on these assumptions – which can take the form of implicit bias as well as more explicit acts of discrimination – such students may be wrongly perceived as automatic risk factors in school shootings. Thus, they may be stigmatized by various means, or may undergo increased surveillance. There have even been calls for students' records of "emotional or mental disturbance" to follow them from school to school, despite the fact that this would violate laws protecting students' privacy (see Price 2011, 159–162).

The assumption that all people with mental health disabilities are predisposed to violence represents a cluster of misinterpretations. First, just because many school shooters have histories of mental health diagnoses does not mean that one can generalize that such a diagnosis is an inherent and automatic characteristic of violence. Second, although the link between mental health diagnosis and tendency to violence does exist, it has been strenuously debated by social scientists in a range of fields; it is contextualized by many other factors, including gender and age (most school shooters are young men); and, ironically, is not as strong as the likelihood that people with serious mental illnesses will be, or have been, the victims of violence. Finally, this complex web of issues is complicated even further by issues of race, ethnicity, citizenship, and religion. As Price (2011) points out, although most school shooters are young white males, "no one ponders the stigmatizing effect of this fact on white males in general, although there is considerable hand-wringing about what is wrong with 'our youth,' with both 'us' and 'youth' implicitly marked as white" (2011, 150) (see also Brandzel and Desai 2008; Watts and Erevelles 2004). In short, profiling in ways that make quick assumptions about a predictive link between mental illness and violence meets an emotional need but does not stand up to what research into violent behavior actually shows (Metzl and MacLeish 2015).

Profiles offer a kind of catharsis for a horrifying event, rather than an actual solution. If schools truly wanted to reduce violence on campus, it would make far more sense to focus on crimes such as sexual assault, or crimes related to alcohol use. While a school shooting is incredibly devastating and frightening, its frequency – given how many millions of students and faculty inhabit campuses in the United States every day – is not unlike the frequency with which a student is hit by a bolt of lightning. Ironically, the expensive "preparedness" literature surrounding school shootings trades on this frightening, bolt-of-lightning quality – sometimes by featuring bright-colored images of actual bolts of lightning, as is true of the cover of the DVD *Shots Fired on Campus* (see Price 2011, 164–165).

Schools regularly report statistics on campus safety to help ensure they are gaining all the appropriate resources. Also, "school violence statistics are often used to promote public awareness and inform parents and students of the safety status of their schools" (US Department of Justice 2002, 2). Such statistics are not meant to create student profiles, nor do they suggest that mentally ill students are sources of threat assessment. The inaccurate link between mental health and school violence has been created as a result of the expansive media coverage of school violence. In the next section, we discuss the history of violence in schools as well as the history of profiling.

History of Profiling and Violent Acts in Schools

Violence in schools has led to increased post-secondary education campus security measures within the pre-K–12 overall educational environment. Once considered open spaces, many public schools are now enclosed by fences. These are sometimes even guarded by law enforcement officers. "More than one-quarter of schools also reported having security staff present on campus routinely carrying a firearm" (National Center for Education Statistics (2015). Often, all visitors – even parents – are checked through systems that may include background checks. Many schools undergo "drills" for practice in case of a shooting, much like fire or tornado drills. Much of the public is convinced that schools are more dangerous than ever, perhaps as a result of these boosted security measures in addition to alarmist news stories.

Another consideration is the debate over campus carry laws: this particularly applies to college campuses, where more freedom persists than in secondary schools. In the wake of college campus shootings, some university officials have appealed for more liberal campus carry laws. Such laws would allow instructors, and students of a certain age (usually 21), to carry guns on campus for protection. While some people feel safer with their guns, having open-carry laws on campus can inadvertently create a false sense of safety. Also, firearms can be a dangerous combination with students who drink, or who are going through personal struggles. As *Armed with Reason* (DeFilippis 2015) notes, "the college students most likely to carry firearms in public may be predisposed to detrimental behavior." Furthermore, students who experience increased aggression are the ones who are most likely to own guns – a dangerous combination that no school official would want to see.

In 2016, a bill to allow campus carry across Georgia state colleges and universities was presented to Governor Nathan Deal for approval. Often touted as a "pro-gun governor" (Li and Spies 2016), Deal ended up vetoing the bill. In his explanation for the veto, Deal expressed the following concerns:

> In order to carry a weapon onto a college, there is no requirement that the armed individual actually be a student, only that they possess a license to carry a weapon. Since most, if not all, of our colleges are open campuses, this bill will allow any licensed gun owner to bring a concealed weapon onto the campus and neither police nor other law enforcement personnel will be allowed to even ask the individual to produce evidence of his license ... If the intent of HB 859 is to increase safety of students on college campuses, it is highly questionable that such would be the result. (Office of the Governor 2016)

Deal also noted in his response that even James Madison and Thomas Jefferson – who were also pro-Second Amendment – viewed colleges as inappropriate places to carry weapons. Despite the surprising veto of HB 859, campus carry is still an issue that has been discussed in other states. In fact, such a bill was successfully passed in the state of Texas, where "the law gives public universities some discretion to regulate campus carry" (University of Texas at Austin 2016). At the public school level, there have even been discussions about allowing teachers to carry weapons on school property (Council of State Governments Justice Center 2014). The argument here is that if there were to be a mad shooter on campus, the death toll could be minimized if more people were armed.

The anxiety surrounding potential violence in education is, of course, heightened in the wake of an incident. Metzl and MacLeish (2015) have identified four common assumptions that the public tends to make following mass shootings: "(1) that mental illness causes gun violence, (2) that psychiatric diagnosis can predict gun crime, (3) that shootings represent the deranged acts of mentally ill loners, and (4) that gun control 'won't prevent' another Newtown [Connecticut school mass shooting]." These assumptions also contribute to the widespread fear that violence is increasing in educational settings. Although the number of school-based multiple-homicide events has increased, there still is less than one chance in a million of a school-related violent death" (US Department of Justice 2002, 1). Anxieties over a connection between mental health and gun violence is not proven, yet this perception remains. What is more concerning is the unfounded perception that increased mental illness cases – which are prompted by increased access to diagnostic testing and treatment – could indicate future influxes in violence.

The late twentieth century saw a rise in affixing blame upon mental health and mental disabilities. Representing school shootings primarily as functions of mental illness is certainly misleading in that it increases stigmatization. In *Mad at School* (2011), Price explains:

> In these representations [of school shootings], madness is generally assumed to be the *cause* of the shooters' actions. My rereading makes an alternative argument: that in fact, madness operates in the representations as a *mechanism* through which the shooters are placed in a space of unrecoverable deviance.

This move enables such accounts to separate Cho and Kazmierczak – and by extension, madness itself – from everyone else. By individuating the shooter and detailing every nuance of their "odd" or "disturbed" behavior, these representations reify the belief that madness and sanity are two extremely separate spaces – one dangerous, one safe. (144–145)

Indeed, it is the perception of madness in relation to mental illness that continues to fuel the stigma and the way mainstream society looks for would-be threats in schools. School violence is not a twentieth- or twenty-first-century phenomenon, but its assigned blame to mental disabilities is relatively modern. Responses to school shootings in the late 1990s compounded the issue that we see today.

Student Profiling in Educational Institutions

In response to the 1998 Thurston High School mass shooting by 15-year-old Kip Kinkel in Springfield, Oregon, then-President Bill Clinton "directed the Secretary of Education and the Attorney General to prepare a guidebook of 'early warning signs' for potential school violence to be distributed to every school in the country" (Frontline 1999). The idea of such a manual was to help keep students and school personnel safe by creating an easy-to-use checklist that could profile students who might be prone to violence.

President Clinton's initiative was in response to a spate of school shootings that had occurred in the late 1990s. Since then, "lists of warning signs have been extremely popular" (Frontline 1999). After all, it is seemingly easy to assess a student based on a checklist. The more check marks made, the more dangerous that person might seem. Action might be taken against the students who have the most check marks on any such lists. In 1999, Frontline found common traits in student checklists produced by the American Psychological Association, the National Center for the Prevention of Crime, and the National School Safety Center. Just some of the items that could be checked off in the organizations' lists included: "chronic feelings of isolation or rejection, frequent angry outbursts, social withdrawal or depression, fascination with or possession of weapons, alcohol or drug dependency, history of bullying behavior, and lack of interest in school or poor school performance" (Frontline 1999).

Yet these attempts are prime examples of student profiling. Profiling can be implemented from the top (such as school boards and administration), but perhaps the most consequential form is through instructors, as these individuals have the most direct contact with students. In fact, in 1999, Frontline analyzed previously used checklists by the National School Safety Center, stating that, "Some checklists have been criticized as unhelpfully vague or misleadingly predictive – a danger that arises mainly when warning signs lists are informally adapted as profiling tools" while "other checklists and warning signs approaches have been challenged as dangerously likely to identify and label too many students, or as insufficiently based on peer-reviewed research to be considered valid."

In this sense, a checklist is a profile, much like a profile checklist for a passport application, or for a driver's license. A checklist can offer a few concrete facts, but one that profiles students to try to assess risk of violence is often based on assumptions that do not reflect current findings about what factors are *causally* linked to violence, rather than correlatively. In other words, it is one thing to discover that a school shooter is often also mentally ill; it is a very different thing to claim that therefore all mentally ill people are more likely to be school shooters. One might as well erroneously conclude that maleness (another trait that most school shooters exhibit) is predictive of school shooting, and therefore males should not be allowed on any campuses.

While student profiling is often promoted with good intentions, it often feeds into an ableist agenda, through which students with mental disabilities are wrongly targeted. The "loner," for example, is sometimes perceived as having autism or another disability, while the "socially awkward" might be inaccurately perceived as having social anxiety. These profiles might identify students with mental illnesses to others, but mental illness and violence are not strongly linked – particularly not in comparison to the links between violence and other traits, including being male.

Effects of Profiling Rhetoric on Mental Health Stigmatization

Despite the lack of clear causal link between mental illness and violence, stigmatization of mental health patients continues from mainstream profiling rhetoric. Metzl and MacLeish (2015) note that "notions of mental illness that emerge in relation to mass shootings frequently reflect larger cultural stereotypes and anxieties," which might include social class, race, and other cultural differences. We saw this in the cases of Cho and Kazmierczak, where case studies also stigmatized "other aspects of the men's lives, including race, class, religion, and even body size" (Price 2011, 149). There is certainly a danger as "these issues become obscured when mass shootings come to stand in for all gun crime, and when 'mentally ill' ceases to be a medical designation and becomes a sign of violent threat" (Metzl and MacLeish 2015). In turn, mentally ill students who might disclose their disabilities might undergo targeting through increased surveillance despite displaying no signs of violent behavior.

School shooters are usually assumed to have some form of mental illness. However, such a classification can be broken down further into other types of profiling, such as race and personality differences. There is no question that race continues to be a common factor in profiling, on and off school campuses. Patterson (1999) wrote, shortly after the Columbine massacre, of his concerns about a prevalent double standard in the way Americans broadly regard violent students. He argues that the "terrorist act of white, middle-class teen-agers creates an orgy of national soul-searching," while poor and working-class non-white students who commit violence are not assumed to indicate anything in particular about mainstream American culture (which is, in turn, assumed to be white). Patterson would likely agree that the public seems to try and find excuses for deviant behavior among whites, while non-white students who commit the same acts of violence are more prone to heightened profiling schema due to the normative misconception that white people are not prone to violence. He adds: "This is not to suggest that race and class are irrelevant to discussions of violent crime but rather that there is a disturbing double standard in the way we discuss the problems of different groups of people and in the way we label deviant behavior" (1999).

Indeed, race and class are just some of the issues bound up in the way we react to violence; it also stems from the way we profile students based on mainstream profilers of shooters. As noted during the June 2016 mass shooting of the Pulse nightclub in Orlando, Florida, there was confusion about the "motives" of the shooter, Omar Mateen. Based on his race (Mateen was born in the United States to parents originally from Afghanistan), terrorism was slated as the primary motive. Indeed, Mateen did pledge his faith to ISIS during 911 calls during the shootings (NPR 2016). At the same time, questions also arose about Mateen's mental health, including speculation that he could be bipolar. The *Washington Post* investigated Mateen's mental health with the title: "Troubled. Quiet. Macho. Angry. The Volatile Life of the Orlando Shooter" (Sullivan and Wan 2016).

Another example was the November 2016 attack at Ohio State University (OSU), where 18-year-old student Abdul Razak Ali Artan "rammed his car into a group of people on the Columbus campus and then got out and charged at passersby with a knife" (CNN 2016). Almost immediately after the attack, media accounts pointed to the possibility of terrorism ties, despite the fact that law enforcement agencies – including the FBI (Federal Bureau of Investigation) and local officials – stated it was not possible to make such links at the time (McCarthy 2016). Despite the fact that investigators of the OSU case specifi- cally cautioned against assuming terrorism, mainstream accounts quickly settled on the label. This is a far cry from attitudes toward white shooters, as they are often perceived as more representative of mainstream society. As a result, white shooters are often per- ceived as "mentally ill," and people of color are perceived as "terrorists."

The problem with stigmatizing students who have mental health disabilities is twofold: not only do such students fall victim to unjustified targeting, but schools may mistakenly focus on mentally disabled students who are labeled as being "quiet," "impulsive," "emotional," "socially awkward," or "depressed." It is certainly important to reach out to students who exhibit signs of untreated mental illness, but this does not warrant automatic suspicion that *any* student with a mental illness could be a perpetrator of school violence. Dikel (2012) writes: "If we examine the profiles of these killers, which often include histories of mental illness, it is easy to assume, with the benefit of hind- sight, that their crimes were inevitable or predictable. This assumption is ill advised; it suggests that these murderers can be identified in advance and should be incarcerated or hospitalized" (1). Not only does such an approach not work, but it also sets a dangerous precedent in how mentally ill students receive treatment. Such a misconstrued focus creates a dangerous environment for disabled students who may be targeted. As Price (2011) explains in her research on Cho and Kazmierczak:

> My concern is not to argue whether or not they *were* mentally ill; they certainly were labeled as such by various doctors and institutions, and based on the information available, both were in great distress. Rather, I want to look at how madness is constructed in the representations of Cho and Kazmierczak that appeared in various media, including mainstream news, academic discourse, online blogs and discussion groups, and government reports. (144)

Indeed, this persistent focus on madness as mental illness continues to fuel the rhetoric of mental health disabilities as precursors to violence. The various media outlets Price dis- cusses reveal a common framework in such discussions of school shooters: mental illness.

How Profiling in Schools Furthers Stigmatization of Mental Health

Despite the fact that consistent framing of mental illnesses in violent acts has created profiling rhetoric, mainstream society continues to create profiles of people with mental health disabilities. In the following section, we discuss the multitude of problems that persist with student profiling in consideration of mental health stigmatization. School administrators should review these issues carefully when compiling a plan to address student violence.

There Is No Evidence That Profiling Works for *Any* Student

The more schools try to profile students, the more officials come under fire for stereotyping. Yet for the sake of purportedly increasing safety, profiling continues – despite the overwhelming evidence showing that profiling is ineffective in preventing school shootings. Not only does the FBI look down on the idea of a profile of a student shooter (also see Chapter 2, this volume), but the agency also states that "School shootings are rarely impulsive acts ... they are typically thought out and planned in advance" (FBI n.d.a). The FBI also recommends that educators monitor student behavior as a whole, rather than creating profiles of individuals. According to the FBI, 27% of school shooters are "motivated by suicide or depression." This is lower than the "34% motivated by attempt to solve a problem," or the "61% motivated by desire for revenge." At the same time, "75% felt bullied/persecuted/threatened by others." While some students with mental health issues are bullied, this is not the only cause of being bullied, nor do the vast majority of students who are bullied commit such a horrendous act. Rather than advocating for specific monitoring of a specific student population (such as students with mental health disabilities), the FBI's argument on monitoring overall behavior is in line with a more inclusive space.

Despite its cautions about profiling, the agency offers "clues to a student's personality" which can come from observing behaviors such as:

- displaying difficulties coping with "stresses encountered in everyday life";
- expressing extreme anger or rage;
- displaying intentional lack of empathy for peers, teachers, and administration;
- having difficulty taking constructive criticism;
- "demonstrating and expressing a desire or need for control, attention, respect, admiration, confrontation, or other needs";
- viewing other students as inferior. (FBI n.d.b, 12)

These "clues" seem like encouragement to profile, especially with regard to mental health issues. While the "clues" offer a first step to increasing awareness of student behavior, such traits rarely indicate a student is violent. It seems likely that administrators trying to apply the FBI's recommendations will end up profiling individual students, often on the basis of apparent mental health difficulties.

Other types of experts also downplay the potential effectiveness of any profiling tools. Dikel (2012), a child and adolescent psychiatrist, agrees with such cautions set forth by the FBI. He writes: "for every violent perpetrator of mass killings who has a history of mental health disorders and/or psychological and social stressors, there are hundreds of individuals who have similar profiles who do not become violent" (1). Furthermore, while some students with mental illnesses do commit acts of violence, Dikel points out that these occurrences are "rare." He argues that, on the whole, "an individual who has a mental health disorder (with the exception of a paranoid delusional disorder) generally does not have an increased risk of violence" (2). Metzl and MacLeish (2015) further point out that "little population-level evidence supports the notion that individuals diagnosed with mental illness are more likely than anyone else to commit gun crimes." Furthermore, "common psychiatric diagnoses, including depressive, anxiety, and attention-deficit disorders, have no correlation with violence whatsoever" (Metzl and MacLeish 2015).

Profiling Can Have Legal Repercussions

A final issue to consider is the possibility of legal repercussions for schools that implement student profiling techniques. Frontline reported in 1999 that school administrators were warned about the possible "legal liability problems with student profiling," and that they were warned that using any lists as a means of targeting students could get them into trouble" (1999). Certainly, no school wants to find themselves in the middle of legal battles; but what is more important is to consider the circumstances that could cause such legal troubles in the first place. Profiling students is not only unethical, but it can also cause emotional and mental damages to those who are the unfair victims of such targeting. Legal action between families and schools would then only add to the damage already done to both parties involved.

Solutions to Help Prevent Violence Without Profiling Students

Profiling students with mental health issues detracts from the larger needs at hand: taking effective, research-based action to prevent school shootings and promoting better supports for mental health on campuses. The following are solutions that can help mitigate the fear of school shootings while also preventing unjust stigmatization of mentally disabled students.

Avoiding Influence of Exaggerated Threats

School safety should always be a priority. Yet it is also worth detecting when safety measures become extreme reactions to exaggerated threats. Borum et al. (2010, 27) write: "The fear of school shootings is greatly exaggerated in comparison with other risks such as riding in a car." In other words, while the threat of school violence is real, it is slim compared to other everyday dangers school administration ought to address. According to the Centers for Disease Control and Prevention (2016), 17 students aged 5 to 18 were homicide victims on campus during the 2009–2010 school year. Far more students will die in automobile or alcohol-related accidents on campus than from a school shooting. Over 3,000 teenagers between the ages of 13 and 19 were killed in car accidents in

2010 (Insurance Institute for Highway Safety 2017). In addition, students on college campuses are much more likely to encounter sexual violence than gun violence.

There are also issues surrounding the exaggeration of threats associated with the zero tolerance policies many public schools have adapted. While these are intended to identify threats and ultimately place a purportedly dangerous student outside of the school for the safety of the other students, there are also questions of the efficacy and non-inclusiveness of such a policy. As Fidel and Fox write: "zero tolerance lacks the essential element of discretion and level-headed reasoning about the difference between menace and mistake" and "the rigid application of zero tolerance punishment resulted in countless instances of excessive or misplaced punitiveness" (see Chapter 1, this volume)

Discourse Surrounding School Violence and Mental Health: Next Steps to Prevent Further Stigma[1]

Measures taken by schools to prevent the stereotyping and bullying of students are positive steps toward inclusiveness. However, as we have discussed throughout this chapter, these do not guarantee the prevention of stigma given the pervasiveness of profiling rhetorics against mentally disabled individuals in mainstream society. What further continues to fuel the stigmatization of mentally ill students are decontextualized statistics, such as these reported by Dikel (2012, 2): "Research indicates that approximately 18% of children and adolescents have a mental health disorder, and that approximately 5% are severely emotionally disturbed." In an average class size of 25 students, this could potentially mean that nearly five have mental illnesses, while one student might have a particularly severe disorder. Depending on disclosure, instructors might then inadvertently focus on mentally disabled students as potential threats, rather than creating universal platforms for their classes as safe spaces for emotional expression. This can work more effectively than relying on profiles for behavioral warning signs.

In addition to reaching out to any student in need, schools can benefit from changing the ways they handle mental health. These can include improving student support services (especially mental health services and counseling), faculty and staff awareness of mental health issues and the lack of a link to violent threats, and stress management for all. School counselors and student support staff are often relied on as resources. However, as Dikel (2012) points out, "School counselors, social workers and psychologists may provide counseling services, but in general, they do not provide mental health diagnostic and treatment services" (3). Raising awareness of students who need help across the board can help schools guide parents to appropriate resources that are also available outside of the school – including diagnostic resources that schools may be unable to provide.

Finally, Dikel also argues that schools should not diagnose mental health problems with Individualized Education Programs (IEPs), which are prescriptive educational plans made for students needing support services. IEPs are sometimes prepared for

---

1 Resources to help improve campus climates with regard to mental health are available from the Bazelon Center (2006; focused on students) and from Price and Kerschbaum (2017; focused on faculty).

students with mental illnesses, but they can also be implemented for students with learning disabilities that are related to other forms of disability. Furthermore, IEPs can help students who need services for serious emotional disturbances (SEDs). Detailed accommodations – rather than listing the behavior – in students' IEPs is one approach schools can take. As Hehir (2007, 12) points out: "For large numbers of students with serious emotional disturbance, their IEPs are more likely to include inappropriate responses to control the most common symptom of their disability – acting-out behavior – than to provide the accommodations and support the students need to be successful in education."

In this chapter, our mission was to point out mainstream discourse that influences the way non-violent students with mental health disabilities are wrongly stigmatized. This is attributed to profiling rhetoric that is further fueled through mainstream media coverage of school shootings and other violent acts, and is subsequently shared across other forms of media, such as social media and personal websites. Identifying the rhetoric of profiling can decrease the instances of mental health stigmatization in schools, while also freeing up efforts for school officials to focus on policies that may help decrease violent acts without creating unnecessary – and ineffective – profiling tools.

References

Bazelon Center. 2006. "Effective Mental Health Services Integrated with Schools: What Works." *Way to Go: School Success for Children with Mental Health Needs.* http://www.bazelon.org/wp-content/uploads/2017/01/Way_to_Go.pdf (last accessed October 23, 2017).

Bidwell, Allie. 2014. "Report: School Crime and Violence on the Rise." *U.S. News and World Report,* June 10. http://www.usnews.com/news/articles/2014/06/10/incidents-of-school-crime-and-violence-on-the-rise-for-students-and-teachers (last accessed October 9, 2017).

Borum, Randy, Cornell, Dewey G., Modzeleski, William, and Jimerson, Shane R. 2010. "What Can be Done About School Violence? A Review of the Evidence." *Educational Researcher* 39(1), 27–37. DOI: 10.3102/0013189X09357620.

Brandzel, Amy L. and Desai, Jigna. 2008. "Race, Violence, and Terror: The Cultural Defensability of Heteromasculine Citizenship in the Virginia Tech Massacre and the Don Imus Affair." *Journal of Asian American Studies* 11(1), 61–85. DOI: 10.1353/jaas.2008.0005.

Centers for Disease Control and Prevention. 2016. "School-Associated Violent Death Study." https://www.cdc.gov/violenceprevention/youthviolence/schoolviolence/savd.html (last accessed October 9, 2017).

CNN. 2016. "Investigators Believe Ohio State Attacker was Inspired by ISIS." http://www.cnn.com/2016/11/29/us/ohio-state-university-attack/index.html (last accessed October 17, 2017).

Council of State Governments Justice Center. 2014. "Arming Teachers and K–12 Staff: A Snapshot of Legislative Action." https://csgjusticecenter.org/wp-content/uploads/2014/03/NCSL-Arming-Staff-Brief.pdf (last accessed October 9, 2017).

Cowan, Alison Leigh. 2014. "Adam Lanza's Mental Health Problems 'Completely Untreated' Before Newtown Shootings, Report Says." *New York Times*, November 21. http://www.nytimes.com/2014/11/22/nyregion/before-newtown-shootings-adam-lanzas-mental-problems-completely-untreated-report-says.html?_r=0 (last accessed October 9, 2017).

DeFilippis, Evan. 2015. "Why Campus Carry is a Bad Idea: Or Why Alcohol, Hormones, and Guns Don't Mix." Armed with Reason, November 29. http://www.armedwithreason.com/why-campus-carry-is-a-dangerous-idea-or-why-alcohol-hormones-and-guns-dont-mix/(last accessed October 9, 2017).

Dikel, William. 2012. "School Shootings and Student Mental Health: What Lies Beneath the Tip of the Iceberg." https://www.nsba.org/sites/default/files/School%20Shootings%20and%20Student%20Mental%20Health.pdf (last accessed October 9, 2017).

Golden, Daniel. 2007. "From Disturbed High Schooler to College Killer." *Wall Street Journal*, August 20. https://www.wsj.com/articles/SB118756463647202374 (last accessed October 9, 2017).

FBI. n.d.a. "The School Shooter: A Quick Reference Guide." http://www.broward.edu/safety/Documents/FBITheSchoolShooterAQuickReferenceGuide.pdf (last accessed October 9, 2017).

FBI. n.d.b. "The School Shooter: A Threat Assessment Perspective." https://www.fbi.gov/stats-services/publications/school-shooter (accessed July 27).

Friedman, Emily. 2008. "Who Was the Illinois School Shooter?" ABC News, February 15. http://abcnews.go.com/US/story?id=4296984&page=1 (accessed October 9, 2017).

Frontline. 1999. "Profiling' School Shooters: The Killer at Thurston High." http://www.pbs.org/wgbh/pages/frontline/shows/kinkel/profile/(last accessed October 9, 2017).

Hehir, Thomas. 2007. "Confronting Ableism." *Educational Leadership*, February 8–14.

Insurance Institute for Highway Safety, Highway Loss Data Institute. 2017. "Teenagers: Fatality Facts." http://www.iihs.org/iihs/topics/t/teenagers/fatalityfacts/teenagers (last accessed October 9, 2017).

Kleinfeld, N.R. 2007. "Before Deadly Rage, a Life Consumed by a Troubling Silence." *New York Times*, April 22. http://www.nytimes.com/2007/04/22/us/22vatech.html?_r=0 (last accessed October 9, 2017).

Li, Olivia and Spies, Mike. 2016. "Pro-Gun Governor Vetoes Campus Carry Bill in Georgia." *The Trace*, May 3. https://www.thetrace.org/2016/05/republican-governor-nathan-deal-vetoes-campus-carry-bill/(last accessed October 9, 2017).

Lysiak, Matthew. 2014. "Why Adam Lanza Did It." *Newsweek*, January 17. http://www.newsweek.com/why-adam-lanza-did-it-226565 (last accessed October 9, 2017).

McCarthy, Ciara. 2016. "Ohio State University Attack: 'Too Soon' to Determine Terrorism Link." *The Guardian*, November 30. https://www.theguardian.com/us-news/2016/nov/30/ohio-state-university-attack-terrorism-link (last accessed October 19, 2017).

Metzl, Jonathan M. and MacLeish, Kenneth T. 2015. "Mental Illness, Mass Shootings, and the Politics of American Firearms." *American Journal of Public Health* 105(2), 240–249. DOI: 10.2105/AJPH.2014.302242.

Millward, David. 2014. "Childhood of Sandy Hook Killer was Filled with 'Crippling' Mental Health Issues." *The Telegraph*, November 21. http://www.telegraph.co.uk/news/worldnews/northamerica/usa/11247242/Childhood-of-Sandy-Hook-killer-was-filled-with-crippling-mental-health-issues.html (last accessed October 9, 2017).

National Center for Education Statistics. 2015. "Indicators of School Crime and Safety: Key Findings." https://nces.ed.gov/programs/crimeindicators/key.asp (last accessed October 9, 2017).

NPR. 2016. "3 Hours in Orlando: Piecing Together an Attack and its Aftermath." Accessed September 20. http://www.npr.org/2016/06/16/482322488/orlando-shooting-what-happened-update (last accessed October 9, 2017).

Office of the Governor. 2016. "Deal Issues 2016 Veto Statements." Governor Nathan Deal Office of the Governor, May 3. https://gov.georgia.gov/press-releases/2016-05-03/deal-issues-2016-veto-statements (last accessed October 9, 2017).

Patterson, Orlando. 1999. "When 'They' Are Us." http://www.nytimes.com/1999/04/30/opinion/when-they-are-us.html (last accessed October 19, 2017).

Price, Margaret. 2011. *Mad at School: Rhetorics of Disability and Academic Life*. Ann Arbor: University of Michigan Press.

Price, Margaret and Kerschbaum, Stephanie L. 2017. *Promoting Supportive Academic Environments for Faculty with Mental Illnesses: Resource Guide and Suggestions for Practice*. http://tucollaborative.org/sdm_downloads/supportive-academic-environments-for-faculty-with-mental-illnesses/(last accessed October 23, 2017).

Rosenberg, Jessica. 2014. "Mass Shootings and Mental Health Policy." *Journal of Sociology and Social Welfare* 41(1), 107–121.

Rubinkam, Michael. 2009. "Book: Columbine Shooters Mentally Ill, Not Bullied." Associated Press, March 13. http://www.deseretnews.com/article/705290742/Book-Columbine-shooters-mentally-ill-not-bullied.html?pg=all (last accessed October 9, 2017).

Sullivan, Kevin and Wan, William. 2016. "Troubled. Quiet. Macho. Angry. The Volatile Life of the Orlando Shooter." *The Washington Post*, June 17. https://www.washingtonpost.com/national/troubled-quiet-macho-angry-the-volatile-life-of-omar-mateen/2016/06/17/15229250-34a6-11e6-8758-d58e76e11b12_story.html (last accessed October 9, 2017).

Turndorf, Jamie. 2012. "Was Adam Lanza an Undiagnosed Schizophrenic?" *Psychology Today*, December 20. https://www.psychologytoday.com/blog/we-can-work-it-out/201212/was-adam-lanza-undiagnosed-schizophrenic (last accessed October 9, 2017).

US Department of Justice Office for Victims of Crime. 2002. "Reporting School Violence." https://www.ncjrs.gov/ovc_archives/bulletins/legalseries/bulletin2/ncj189191.pdf (last accessed October 9, 2017).

University of Texas at Austin. 2016. "Campus Carry." University of Texas at Austin. https://campuscarry.utexas.edu/(last accessed October 9, 2017).

Watts, Ivan E. and Nirmala Erevelles. 2004. "These Deadly Times: Reconceptualizing School Violence by Using Critical Race Theory and Disability Studies." *American Educational Research Journal* 41(2), 271–299. DOI: 10.3102/00028312041002271.

7

Aftermath of School Shootings

A Model for Relational Aesthetic Response, Reconstruction, and Associated Living

A.G. Rud and Patricia L. Maarhuis

Introduction

Duncan-Andrade (2009) explores concepts of hope for traumatic events or difficult circumstances in education. Material hope – an element of critical hope, the enemy of hopelessness – is a pragmatic and compassionate response that "teachers can cultivate in their students, and it comes from the sense of control young people have when they are given the resources to deal with the forces that affect their lives" (6). He addresses the need for reflection on pedagogical practice and harsh realities – specifically about connecting academic rigor, classroom experience, and events in the community and in students' lives. In one example, he attends to the response of a fourth grade teacher and her class to a shooting at their school:

> Today was an almost unbearably sad day at school. According to my students (all of which were SOBBING) two young men were sitting in a car yesterday afternoon. Some men in a car rolled up, got out and shot one in the eye (his head exploded) there was a 3-month old in the back seat (she was left "unharmed") the other got out and ran (they call him "baby" Marcus) the guys ran after him and shot him in the back and then more when he fell. ... For an hour and a half the kids all just talked and cried. I felt ill-equipped to handle a crisis like this but, we got through it. ... I said as little as possible, I cried with the kids, we all consoled each other, and others began sharing different stories of violence and loss. In the end, I did what I thought (and hope) was best, tried to empower them with the belief that they must work to become the warriors who combat the senseless violence and madness. ... We're making cards, and going to send a little money to the families. The kids all seem to feel a little better. How would you handle this? It looks as if many teachers didn't say or do much. Feeling a bit weary today. (2009, 6)

Duncan-Andrade concludes that an effective teacher, like the one described above, is a "*material* resource: an indispensable person who can connect schooling to the real, *material* conditions of urban life" (2009, 7, emphasis in original).

Tragically, between 2013 and 2015 and across 38 states, 160 school shootings took place in the United States with nearly 53%, or 84 incidents, in K–12 schools.

The Wiley Handbook on Violence in Education: Forms, Factors, and Preventions, First Edition.
Edited by Harvey Shapiro.
© 2018 John Wiley & Sons, Inc. Published 2018 by John Wiley & Sons, Inc.

(Everytown for Gun Safety 2016). Simply put, school shootings, which continually undermine the positive growth and learning of individuals and communities, continue to occur in the United States and, at the same time, these individuals and communities attempt to re-establish harmony, recover, and restabilize their schools. While ongoing school shootings will never be acceptable, focus on the development of post-crisis strategies – specifically an aesthetic response – can assist teachers and administrators toward hopeful and pragmatic educational responses in the aftermath of shootings.

Purpose

Our aim in this chapter is to further discussion about planning and policy development post-school shooting, for the purposeful enactment of relational aesthetic response by teachers and administrators, who must work with violent and disturbing incidents. First, we review a Deweyan theoretical model of steps in the aesthetic response to school shootings, based on educational strategies, relational aesthetic response, and associated living practices found in the analysis of the three identified communities (Maarhuis and Rud 2017). Second, we summarize previous research results on aesthetic responses to school shootings in three communities – Columbine High School (CHS), Red Lion Junior High School (RLJHS), and Sandy Hook Elementary School (SHES) – where those who are affected try to come to terms with what has happened and have the task of returning to teaching in the aftermath of a school shooting (Maarhuis and Rud 2017). And last, we build upon these findings through exploration of potential strategies that address ongoing recovery in the aftermath of a school shooting, which are based on national guidelines (National Education Association (NEA) n.d.).

This chapter is a pragmatic shift toward developing strategies for post-shooting aftermath, recovery, and return to teaching and learning, as opposed to the more common focus on prevention or in-crisis response. Investigation into these responsive aesthetic works can assist educators in finding an ameliorant as well as a means to teach and learn about these ongoing violent events as engaged acts of material hope. This contributes to the development of practices for meaning making about difficult and violent events at schools, for effective and artful response to tragedy that considers sociocultural processes and rebuilding community, and for pragmatic response by educators to incidents of shootings at school.

Significance

The significance of this research project is threefold. First, school shootings in the United States continue to occur (Everytown 2016) and there is a need for teachers and school administrators to effectively respond and recover in the aftermath of shooting incidents. Second, there are basic guidelines and steps for normalizing the school environment in the later aftermath of a crisis, general calls to develop a re-entry plan that gradually reintroduces school routine, and the stated need for appropriate post-shooting classroom activities (Department of Education 2007; National Education Association n.d.). Despite this, there are few research studies addressing the development of effective educational response strategies in the later aftermath of and recovery from a shooting incident. In part, this chapter addresses this gap in the literature. Third, the model and research analysis addresses the complex combination social relationships, identity, place/space, and aesthetic response. This research provides a theoretical model and pivot to think through the interaction between continual social reconstruction, as well as adjustment and growth for individuals, communities, and spaces of associated living.

Research Questions

Initial analysis of themes found in the three collections of aesthetic responses at CHS, RLJHS, and SHES was used to address the following two primary research questions (Maarhuis and Rud 2017):

1) How do artists experience, make meaning, and relate to these acts of violence?
2) How do artists and community members interpret, translate, and educate about what happened?

Two more research questions are addressed in this chapter:

3) How can the theoretical aesthetic response model inform the national guidelines for school crisis (National Education Association n.d.)?
4) How can the aesthetic response model be applied within the national guidelines (National Education Association n.d.) for the aftermath of school crisis?

Background and Summary Literature Review

A non-exhaustive review of the literature about violence as an ongoing presence in K–12 schools and about responses and recovery is provided below. A non-exhaustive review of the literature on the philosophy of John Dewey (1922, 1958, 2005, 2011, 1916), is provided in the "Theoretical Framework" section. Review of the literature regarding aesthetic response to three selected research sites is provided in earlier publications and presentations, with summaries given in this chapter (Maarhuis and Rud 2015a, 2015b, 2015c, 2017).

Shooting violence is an ongoing presence in K–12 schools (Everytown 2016). School shootings and other forms of serious violence leave students with a lasting feeling of "shock, apprehension, and grief" (Alvarez 2007, 1114). Those exposed to lethal school violence, whether directly as victims or indirectly as members of the school and local community, encounter multiple psychological effects, including post-traumatic stress disorder (PTSD), anxiety, fear, and depression (Daniels and Bradley 2011). Shootings at school, no matter what the circumstances, create instability and insecurity for all students and educators in the learning environment (Cornell and Mayer 2010) and decrease academic success, in particular, decreased enrollment and standardized test scores for math and English (Beland and Kim 2015). Additionally, Newman et al. (2004) found that student attendance was negatively impacted in schools where a shooting took place. Violence has long-term impact on people's social engagement and interaction patterns. While these long-term impacts include a rise in positive social solidarity after the school shooting, this can also be followed by various negative phenomena such as strengthened group divisions between youth and adults, social stigmatization, and feelings of collective guilt (Nurmi, Räsänen, and Oksanen 2011).

Despite calls for a broad and transdisciplinary approach to school violence and shooting response (Cornell and Mayer 2010), the literature review found that most articles dealt with threat assessment, prevention programs, and immediate crisis response to single school shootings:

- Threat assessment and attacker profiles (Borum et al. 2010; Cornell et al. 2009; Schuster 2009; Vossekuil et al. 2004).
- Prevention programs, school climate, and lethal violence (Daniels and Bradley 2011; Department of Education 2007; Wike and Fraser 2009; Zucker et al. 2010).
- School environments and social dynamics (Farmer et al. 2007; Hurford et al. 2010; Hyman and Perone 1998; Steffgen, Recchia, and Viechtbauer 2013; Thompson and Kyle 2005).
- School security, enforcement, and safety (Blair and Schweit 2014; Daniels and Bradley 2011; Gray, Lewis, and Ralph 2015; International Association of Chiefs of Police 2009; Jimmerson et al. 2012; Noonan and Vavra 2007; Wallace 2015).
- Immediate crisis response by school administrators, teachers, and first responders (Brock et al. 2009; Daniels et al. 2010; Department of Education 2007; International Association of Chiefs of Police 2009; Jordon 2003; National Education Association n.d.; Noonan and Vavra 2007; Rider 2015).

Given this strong emphasis in research and policy on threat assessment, prevention programs, and immediate crisis response, Warnick and colleagues (2010) ask an important question: "How does it change the role of teachers or administrators if they come to see their job as the being responsible for anticipating and responding to school shootings?" (386). They conclude that "Educators would need to continually see students and their idiosyncrasies – their depressions, their humiliations, their resiliences, and their admirations – as potential threats rather than, say, as potential areas of talent to cultivate or as expressions of individuality" (Warnick, Johnson, and Rocha 2010, 387). And, the literature about school safety, profiling, and threat assessment often does not address the complexity and difficult trade-offs involved with attempting to prevent school shootings. Interestingly, although general characteristics are known, there is "no accurate or useful 'profile' of students who engaged in targeted school violence," including school shootings (Vossekuil et al. 2004, 19).

School administrators and teachers are profoundly affected by school violence. There is pervasive fear among school employees following a school shooting, which is compounded by feelings of unpredictability: "our school could be the next one" (Ardis 2004, 133). Newman et al. (2004) found that teachers felt neglected following school shootings, with few activities and services provided specific to their needs. Further, this study reported that teachers who are worried about violence are more likely to leave the teaching profession and experience negative long-term consequences including illness, divorce, burnout, and career change.

The underlying school climate plays a critical role in how a teacher recovers and on his or her career path after witnessing a school shooting (Mooney 2013). Duffy and Mooney (2014) found that school cultures have a major impact on teacher morale, relationships between teachers and students, and absenteeism. A school's organizational climate contributes to teachers' abilities to engage students actively in the classroom and to continue to be involved in teaching despite witnessing violence. Importantly, Galand, Lecocq, and Philippot (2007) found that the impact of various forms of school violence on teacher disengagement was moderated by teachers' reports of well-being. According to this study, well-being was related to supportive colleagues and strong administrative leadership. Therefore, teachers who experienced violence in their schools were less likely to disengage from their work when they had a supportive work environment. Daniels, Bradley, and Hays (2007) conclude that because many teachers do not receive the appropriate support, the school district administration must be aware of the potential impact of school violence on school personnel and increase resources and support.

Less research has been conducted on and administrative attention given to the development of effective educational response strategies for the later aftermath of and recovery from a shooting incident. One case study (Dishman, Lewis, and Pepper 2011) focused on a principal's prioritized response to the recovery from a school shooting: Healing staff, students, community, and oneself through anticipating the short- and long-term effects of the crisis. Resuming school in order to re-establish a familiar routine was a key objective in the crisis response. Although the study mentions community forums, the setting up of temporary memorials, and involvement of parents and community members in the short- and long-term response, there is little attention to ideas of aesthetic response and reconstruction.

From a psychological and mental health perspective, Jaycox and colleagues (Jaycox, Stein, and Wong 2014) look at the role school can play in addressing the ongoing needs of children exposed to traumas, violence, and disasters. In specific school shooting examples, the authors clarify the challenges that need to be addressed in developing and implementing psychological and education interventions in the immediate and post-crisis aftermath of a school shooting. The authors note that, early on in the crisis, individuals and the community are open to intervention efforts but that it is often premature to implement effective mental health programs. As well, standard classroom education and crisis mental health intervention are identified as competing priorities in the aftermath of a school shooting. A long-term view of response and recovery is encouraged via intervention efforts to support students, for training and support of teachers, for funding, and for capacity building.

Similarly, Craig (2008) focuses on how violence and trauma in general influence how children learn, how to manage the emotional demands of teaching, and how to create a trauma-sensitive school. Artwork, music, and other aesthetic and meaning-making experiences are frequently referenced in examples of students dealing with trauma in the classroom, in educator responses to those students experiencing trauma, and in options for effective teaching and problem-solving trauma-based concerns in the classroom. In more recent writing, Craig (2016) builds on previous work by specifically addressing the "failure of zero-tolerance policies" (6) toward violence and disruptive student behavior following the Columbine High School shootings in 1999. The author specifically addresses teachers' role in trauma-sensitive schools, by recognizing the "emotional work of teachers" (88) as impacting teacher attrition and resilience, and by discussing the need for administrators and school districts to adopt a trauma-sensitive approach when managing the necessary changes to school policies and practices. Again, creative works, along with other aesthetic and meaning-making experiences, are integrated into instruction adaptation, positive behavior supports, relationship building, school routines, and school-wide responses.

Review of the literature did find some evidence for aesthetic responses in the aftermath of school shootings that focused on renewal, restoration, and transformation through civic and individual engagement as well as cultural practices, rituals, and meaning making. In her qualitative research with parents of students involved in the Columbine High School shooting, Mears (2008) noted three themes in the parents' recommendations for preparation and response –*location*, *intention*, and *connection* – which speak to the interaction between spaces/places and the experience of identity. In terms of location, she notes:

> The loss of a sense of place was profound. Because of the shootings, families expressed that their sense of location had been disrupted, for the school and community they knew before no longer existed. School was no longer a place of safety. The community now had risk that had not been recognized before … Parents and students alike struggled to recover a sense of place that would allow them to rebuild their lives. (2008, 167)

Linked to a sense of place, the parents' sense of connection was disturbed. Mears concludes:

> Lethal school violence on the scale of the Columbine shootings causes enormous disconnection. All expressed a feeling of being alienated or distanced from others, even from family and friends, who had not lived the experience. The feelings of isolation, of being misunderstood, of being harshly judged, of being disconnected from their prior assumptions, were commonly expressed. Recovery requires reconnection, with friends and family, with those outside of the community, and with self. (2008, 167)

In general, relational community and individual responses was important to the reinterpretation of the experiences of school shootings into artful form, meaning making, ritual, or community involvement (Turunen et al. 2014; Warnick, Johnson, and Rocha 2010). As well, group cultural practices were important to the process of community and individual meaning making and reclamation (Anderson and Dolmage 2009). Littlefield et al. (2009) conclude that communities may experience the process of renewal differently depending on culture practices and traditions, type of community leadership and participation of elders, availability of community resources, pre-incident social justice concerns, and power structures.

In sum, review of the literature found evidence of shooting violence as an ongoing presence in K–12 schools, which creates instability and insecurity for all students and educators in the learning environment and decreases academic success. Most articles dealt with threat assessment, prevention programs, and immediate crisis response to single school shootings. Less research has been conducted on the development of effective educational response strategies for the later aftermath of and recovery from a shooting incident. Research indicated the need for education-based responses that can be integrated directly into classroom projects and school or community activities, given the schools' long-term and primary mission of education. And last, review of the literature found some evidence for aesthetic responses in the aftermath of school shootings that focused on renewal, restoration, and transformation through civic and individual projects that included cultural practices, rituals, and meaning-making efforts. The aesthetic responses were expressed in classroom projects and school- or community-based activities.

Theoretical Framework

This chapter draws upon a number of Dewey's most basic concepts, in which experience is a major theme. Dewey (1958, 2005) was concerned with the significance of experience and its pragmatic role in philosophy, culture, scientific method, psychology, ethics, education, and learning. In *Art as Experience* (first published 1934), Dewey (2005) systematically considered the interrelationship between experience and art. His main concern was to explain aesthetic experience – as generated by works of art and as emergent from everyday life. Dewey examines an array of artistic mediums and examples of various artistic works, but always with reference to relational communication and generation of new modes of experience.

We discuss how a school shooting, whether experienced directly or indirectly, is *an experience* in that one undergoes – to a greater or lesser degree – an intensified change. Likewise, engagement in a transactional aesthetic response is *an experience* as seen through involvement in reclamation, restoration, and re-presentation in the aftermath of a shooting. Other Deweyan theoretical concepts, including poiesis, impulse, habit, and motivation, are discussed within the findings, analysis, and aesthetic response model.

Experience

The ordinary interactions of beings, things, and environs is understood as being situated in a particular context. Experience is transactional and relational. "The nature of experience is determined by the essential conditions of life ... The first great consideration is that life goes on in an environment; not merely in it but because of it, through interactions with it" (Dewey 2005, 12). Human beings are not separate from objects, events, and other beings. Moreover, the temporality of experience is a result and a consequence of "continuous and cumulative interaction of the organic self within the world" (Dewey 2005, 229).

An Experience

Broadly stated, *an experience* (Dewey 2005) is generative in that the one who is experiencing undergoes a transformation or adaptation of the self, perspective, attitude, and/or knowledge. This change may be positive or negative depending on the circumstances. In terms of aesthetics and artwork, *an experience* is "an intensified form of unified and flowing creativity: the imaginative transference of the expression of Self and Other – in and through medium – to create a work that is itself a prolonged interaction ..., a process in which both [the object and the artist] ... acquire a form and order they did not at first possess" (67–68).

Transactional

Artful works generated in response to a school shooting create *an experience* for the viewer and one that is *transactional*: a display of artful objects or actions in order to create a purposefully intensified aesthetic environment that is designed for relational interaction and communication. It is not only an internal subjective experience – a matter of what registers in one's senses, memory, or consciousness – but a relational manifestation that includes events, happenings, places, and objects that compose our sphere of existence and a system of meaning making (Jackson 1998). An experience that is transactional is also a form of "dramatic rehearsal" for imaginative deliberation that allows the viewer to move beyond his or her own perspective (Fesmire 2003, 70).

Poiesis

Artful works give rise to an intensified opportunity for ethical and moral reflection – even interruptions in thinking – on cultural discourse and simple subject–object binaries (Dewey 2005), especially in regard to difficult, even traumatizing, experiences such as school shootings. This pushes individual and collective artful works beyond reductional singularity and embeds them within acts of poiesis (Levine 2009). Etymologically derived from ancient Greek, *poiesis* means "to make"; however, it also is a moment of *ecstasis*, when over time there is movement away from one state of "being" to shift and become another through relational aesthetics (Bourriaud 2002; Dewey 2005).

Relational Aesthetics

Engaging poiesis shifts the metaphoric work of art from a static object to a transactional event or an interpretive re-presentation. Relational aesthetics are made evident in the responsive poiesis of artful interpretation, dialogue, bearing witness, and reflection (Bourriaud 2002). Basically, it is what comes out of the unstoppable desire to "do something" in the wake of tragedy and loss. This opens the capacities of the broader community to be present with, to be changed by, and to compassionately respond to the experiences of another (Jackson 1998). The work of art is "recreated every time it is esthetically experienced" (Dewey 2005, 113). Fundamentally, the works of art made in response to school shootings are relational and aesthetic experiences in that emotion and embodied senses serve to unify and intensify an experience for all involved.

Order and Harmony?

Clearly, Deweyan thought provides a cohesive structure through which to understand aesthetic responses to school shootings; however, how does one reconcile Dewey's consistent reference to order, harmony, and unity (1958, 2005) with experiences of disruption, suffering, and confusion? Analysis on CHS and RLJHS data found evidence of aesthetic responses that depicted suffering, loss, sadness, and chaos. Some of the created visual forms were highly challenging and were not harmonious. So, when using Deweyan philosophy, how does one understand works that do not depict what is harmonious and orderly? How do notions of "transformation" regarding difficult and violent experiences figure into Dewey's thinking?

When one digs deeper into Deweyan thought and is recentered on dialogic process, the use of "order and harmony" becomes clearer. The actual process of creation and the specific form of the work of art is purposeful and ordered, even though the experience depicted in the artwork may be brutal and the works of art may produce feelings of dissonance and discord. Dewey clarifies: "Since the artist cares in a peculiar way for the phase of experience in which union is achieved, he does not shun moments of resistance and tension. He rather cultivates them, not for their own sake, but because of their potentialities, bringing to living consciousness an experience that is unified and total" (2005, 14). Thus, the artist uses chaos, pain, tension, and discord and converts it into an art form – through the use of a particular medium – so that interest, reflection, and transformation can take place. It is essential to remain focused on the artist's purposeful creation of the artwork and the resulting communication or transactional experience through the medium. Without the use of some order and harmony within the process of creativity, the artist and the audience cannot have a fully transactional experience. Given this perspective, Deweyan ideas of unity and harmony can be used for a broad understanding of the difficult experiences and artful works.

Schools and Associated Living

In his most celebrated work, *Democracy and Education* (first published 1916), Dewey frames the process of education as a social function within a community and centered in a particular environment, context, and activities. In terms of communal society and education, he addresses the questions: Who are we and how are we together? Teaching and learning at a school is a "mode of associated living," which binds its community members in common identities, experiences, and interests (Dewey 2011, 47).

Then again, schools are also a place of vulnerability. Parents drop off very young children at school for the day. Students mill through open and crowded hallways to find their classrooms and exercise in outdoor playgrounds. Educators teach dozens of students at a time in side-by-side rooms with unlocked doors. At present, US communities find – with chilling frequency but random location – that this place of associated living also can be the location of a highly violent and disruptive event: a school shooting.

Model for Aesthetic Response

Informed by the Deweyn concepts discussed above and based on the findings in answer to research questions 1 and 2 above, we identified seven steps of aesthetic response to school shooting incidents and developed the aesthetic response model (Maarhuis and Rud 2017) (see Figure 7.1). Applied analysis is provided with examples of the artful conduct and aesthetic response that took place at the RLJHS, post-school shooting

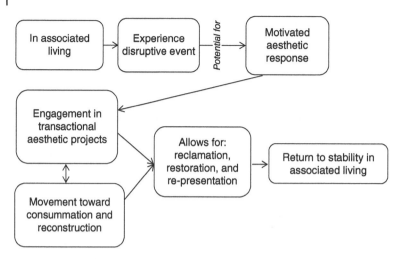

Figure 7.1 The aesthetic responses and artful conduct within stepped phases and observed in analysis of three school shooting settings.

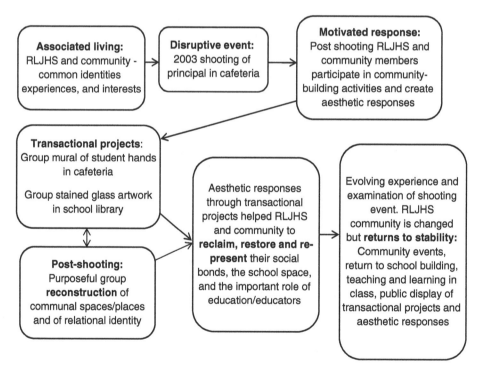

Figure 7.2 The application of the stepped phases of aesthetic response to the RLJHS (Red Lion Junior High School) 2003 shooting incident with specific examples.

(see Figure 7.2). Adler and Obstfeld (2007) apply a Deweyan model of conduct to creative behavior in a work setting with engineering projects. Our research project uses similar elements of thinking but we expand the application to aesthetic engagement in works of art in response to violent incidents.

Consummation, Time, and Rhythm

The practice of associated living is where Dewey (2011) centered his ideas of aesthetic experience, as noted in the first step of the aesthetic response (see Figures 7.1 and 7.2). In the first step of the model, associated living is enacted through a combination of communal practices, communication, and social spaces of civic engagement that connect and unite people in common interests and actions. In the next step, the disruptive experience of a school shooting shifts individual and community conduct into the next phase of motivated care (step 3), and then on to the engagement in transactional aesthetic projects (step 4). This engaged movement reflects passage of time, a productive rhythm of stepped response, and the desire for generative communication – toward potential consummation and resumption of associated living or the return to stable communal relationships and common interests and actions post-school shooting (steps 5, 6, and 7).

Aesthetic response is present in the dynamic movement toward potential consummation. The basic elements of artful conduct – "habit, sense, and imagination" (McClelland 2005, 49) – moves one through the seven steps. Given our focus on transactional aesthetic projects, we also consider Deweyn concepts of motivated response, impulse, context, and engaged social creative behaviors within the aesthetic response model.

Motivated Care

Dewey's writing establishes the premise that responsible people, who are engaged in associated living in a community, take motivated action in difficult situations in ways that attempt to "ameliorate them and render them productive" (Hickman 1990, 200). Through our analysis we concluded that violent deaths of students at school violate social contracts and shatter relational bonds of a whole community. The response of motivated care and production of social artifacts in transactional projects is an experiential reply to the wound of school shootings, and is a means to engage purposeful power and energy toward the development of an effective and pragmatic aftermath. The engagement in transactional art acts as a means to channel feeling and thinking. The work of art and the artifacts create an accessible milieu, where it is safe to explore the possibility of consummation and reconstruction.

Impulse

The experience of a school shooting, directly or indirectly, produces varying degrees of interruption in our relationships and regular activities and one that releases *impulse* or affective response (grief, horror, crying, and fear). Dewey (1922) understands emotions, such as fear, as qualitatively different experiences: "There is no one fear having diverse manifestations ..." (154). Importantly, the individual experiences of emotions are understood as qualitatively embedded within relationships of associated living, which provided the impetus and direction to respond to the disruptive context of the school shootings through social creative behavior and transactional projects.

Context

Dewey (2005) examined human response, aesthetic expression, and adaptation in the context of ever-changing environments and new experience. In terms of disturbing experiences, like a school shooting, he describes the active process of impulse and actions to reconstruct and come back into relationship with new circumstances:

> Life is interruptions and recoveries ... [A] novel factor in the surroundings releases some impulse which tends to initiate a different and incompatible activity, to bring about a redistribution of the elements of organized activity ... Now at these moments of a shifting in activity conscious feeling and thought arise and are accentuated. The disturbed adjustment of organism and environment is reflected in a temporary strife which concludes in a coming to terms of the old habit and the new impulse. (2005, 179)

In terms of disturbing experiences, like a school shooting, the active process of impulse and actions works to reconstruct social environments and to help the community and individual to come back into relationship with new circumstances. Themes common to the three research sites, in terms of response and adaptation, included an evolving sense of living and evolving experience of the impact of the shooting experience.

Engagement in Social Creative Behaviors

After a disturbing event, it is impulse – combined with intelligence and habit – that is channeled into motivated care and engagement in transactional aesthetic projects or social creative behaviors. But what explains the passionate attention, the strength and tenacity of the aesthetic responses? For this, our analysis requires the depth of other Deweyan ideas: direction, care, intensity, and persistence. These ideas explicate motivated care and the specific elements of the creative social behavior, exploratory search, and resolution efforts.

Transactional Aesthetic Projects

Creativity in organizational settings, such as a school or community center, can be an individual activity but it is still a distinct form of social or relational activity, as a communicative or transactional project. A project is defined as a "temporary endeavor undertaken to create a unique product or service (Duncan 1996 cited in Adler and Obstfeld 2007, 11). Transactional aesthetic projects are driven by and made manifest through motivated care and affect as well as through the elements of our experience (see steps 4 through 7 in Figures 7.1 and 7.2).

Object of Care

The affective aspect of engaging in a task goes beyond mechanical stimulus–response to a particular object: "[It] ... is something called out *by* objects, physical and personal; it is response *to* an objective situation (Dewey 1958, 390). In pragmatic fashion, Dewey designates an engaged context of "caring" about the object (i.e., victims of violence), which influences the direction of creativity and task (i.e., a specific work of art) (Adler and Obstfeld 2007). Also, positive and negative emotions impact decision making and goals within the task differently; most notably, in reduction of uncertainty or anxiety and resolution from feeling of sadness (Raghumathan and Pham 1999), as noted in the themes common to the three research sites.

Intensity and Persistence

Care and passion about an object or situation (i.e., victims of a school shooting) is the intrinsic foundation of motivation for creative work and provides intensity and persistence of effort (Adler and Obstfeld 2007), especially for difficult tasks such as responding to school shootings. Caring effort, as found in intensive and persistent reflection and action, is necessary to attain a desired aim (Prawat 1998). Dewey (1958) describes the unique role artwork plays in emotional expression: "art should select and assemble objective things in such ways as to evoke emotional response of a refined, sensitive and enduring kind; it is intelligible that the artist himself is one capable of sustaining these emotions, under whose temper and spirit he performs his compositions of objective materials" (1958, 390)

Consummation and Reconstruction

We now turn toward the potential consummation and reconstruction through individual and community engagement in transactional aesthetic projects as the last steps in the aesthetic response model. As one engages in transactional aesthetic projects, the experience is not singular achievement but can be productive and instrumental over time (Dewey 1958), just like the aesthetic responses to the school shootings at CHS, RLJHS, and SHES. There is a maturation in perspective and cognitive, physical, and emotional responses. Dewey describes this movement: "[experience] has a developing movement toward its own consummation. I have emphasized the fact that every integral experience moves toward a close, an ending, since it ceases only when the energies active in it have done their proper work" (2005, 42).

Consummation of experience through engagement in responsive reconstruction is contextual and on a continuum of negative to positive emotions, depending on conditions.

In terms of reconstruction, the focus is on the prefix "re-" – indicating an ongoing experience in regard to expression and consummation (Dewey 2005): "For 'taking in' in any vital experience is something more than placing something on the top of consciousness over what was previously known. It involves reconstruction which may be painful. Whether the necessary undergoing phase is by itself pleasurable or painful is a matter of particular conditions" (Dewey 2005, 42).

Within ongoing phases of reconstruction and aesthetic response, Dewey (2005) incorporates the concepts of time and rhythm as the individual and community evolve through vital experiences, emotion, and change. In this situation words like "ending" and "close" refer to the end of a particular response or quality of emotion, to which there is a movement or reconstruction onto the next experience. This is not conclusive stasis or even a return to a previous state of harmony and order. Rather, it coincides with the results found in our analysis of the three research sites of individuals and communities as changed by the experience of school shootings but also evolving, adapting, and returning to associated living.

A surface reading of Deweyan philosophy may lead one to focus on its consensual and consummatory nature, whereas acts of disruptive violence such as school shootings challenge this *telos* toward aesthetic consummation and reclamation. However, the steps of the aesthetic response fully utilize the complexity of Dewey's thinking by engaging concepts of continual experience and context within evolving consummation through transactional aesthetic response, as a means to further the process of reconstruction. Moreover, understanding the puzzling relations of consummatory experience as embodying wholeness, energy, and integration, and the actuality that traumatic and disturbing experience precludes wholeness, helps to understand and appreciate the power of aesthetic reclamation and recovery of associated living in the longer term aftermath of disruptive violence (pers. comm., R. Hildreth, April 18, 2015).

Responsive and transactional aesthetic projects to school shootings are material markers of consummation within the ongoing integration of context, change, and individual and communal experience (Maarhuis and Rud 2017). Associated living is a combination of communal practices, communication, and social spaces of civic engagement, democracy, and education that works to connect and unite people in common interests and actions (Dewey 2011). As well, associated living in the aftermath of a school shooting can be purposefully engaged through practices of "social solidarity" (Ryan and Hawdon 2008). The social communication and civic engagement in aesthetic responses are active steps toward potential responsive reconstruction of the bonds of associated living.

In sum, through the stepped model of aesthetic response there is potential for reclamation, restoration, and re-presentation of experience through the doubled reconstruction of communal spaces, places, and of relational identity after shooting incidents. Additionally, in teaching and learning about violent events, Deweyan philosophy and arts-based inquiry address some of the curricular concerns regarding issues of harm and one's duty to care for students, who may be adversely affected by the brutal realities of school shootings (Fesmire 2003). This potential informs post-crisis response in the aftermath of a school shooting and the use of aesthetic response and associated living practices by administrators and educators as a means to return to teaching and learning. We believe exploration into these artworks goes far to assist educators and activists in finding (i) a social ameliorant, (ii) a means to transform the experience after disruptive and violent events, and (iii) a means to integrate both mental health and education objectives into the later aftermath and recovery from a shooting by focusing on school reconstruction and redesign as well as engagement in artful curriculum and classroom projects.

Methods of Inquiry

This exploratory and theoretical research project utilizes an arts-based education research (ABER) methodology (Barone and Eisner 1997) that employs the arts as a primary way of understanding experience and is based on Deweyan philosophy (2005).

Methods

For the first two research questions, we utilized educational criticism, a form of ABER in which qualities, meanings, and significance of some situation or object are researched, analyzed, and interpreted through the lens of aesthetic critique (Barone and Eisner 1997). We explored the aesthetic dialogue of artworks to understand experience as well as educational and sociocultural contexts in the aftermath of school shootings.

We made a purposeful selection of three sites – a high school, a junior high school, and an elementary school – that experienced shooting events and had a public display of aesthetic response via multiple media sites and types. Aesthetic dialogue of artworks were explored to better understand the experiences and sociocultural contexts in the aftermath of school shootings. Our methods were a dialogic process with emergent, collaboratively constructed, and ongoing meaning making (Paulus, Woodside, and Ziegler 2008). Applied analysis took place during review of data sources and the litera-ture, regular researcher conversations, and exchanges of notes and model design. Additionally, there was ongoing discussion with colleagues and audience members at national conference presentations (Maarhuis and Rud 2015a, 2015b, 2015c).

For the third and fourth research questions, we conducted a non-exhaustive review of the literature on effects of school shootings on academic outcomes, educational response strategies, as well as best practices and recommendations for educational response and later recovery. Again, our methods were a dialogic process with emergent, collaboratively constructed, and ongoing meaning making (Paulus, Woodside, and Ziegler 2008). Analysis took place during individual review of the literature review, regular researcher conversations, and exchanges of notes and graphics.

Data Sources and Materials

For the first two questions of this research project, the data sources for analysis and development of the aesthetic response model were digital and news media descriptions of works of art and aesthetic expression made in response to school shootings at CHS in 1999, RLJHS in 2003, and SHES in 2012 (Maarhuis and Rud 2017). Specifically, we analyzed relational and aesthetic content of the CHS redesign and aesthetic responses by students and community members, the RLJHS cafeteria and library redesign, the SHES construction and design as well as the Newtown Documentation Project Galleries (n.d.) and the Healing Newtown Arts Center (Newtown Cultural Arts Commission 2012). Researcher journal, graphs, and observation notes were kept throughout the process of data recording, analysis, and interpretation.

For the third and fourth research questions of this research project, a non-exhaustive review of the literature was conducted pertaining to the potential application of the aesthetic response model in the later aftermath of a school shooting. Databases such as ERIC: Educational Resource Information Center, WorldCat, JSTOR, Google Scholar, PubMed Central, Sagepub, and Elsevier were accessed, utilizing keywords including *post-school shooting, recovery, response, trauma, education, guidelines, recommenda-tions,* and *academic outcomes.*

Results

Research Questions 1 and 2

How do artists experience, make meaning, and relate to these acts of violence? How do artists and community members interpret, translate, and educate about what happened? In short, there was evidence for motivated aesthetic response (Maarhuis and Rud 2017). A review of the three sites found that, on an individual, community, and organizational level, there was evidence of a motivated care and active response to the shootings through the use of artful projects – in addition to other works such as annual commemorative events and memorial sites.

Columbine High School

The massacre in April, 1999 at CHS claimed the lives of 12 students and one teacher with 21 additional people injured, and three others being injured while attempting to escape the school (Jefferson County Sheriff n.d.; Report of Governor Bill Owns' Columbine High School Review Commission 2001). The complex and well-planned attack also involved a fire bomb to divert firefighters, propane tanks converted to bombs placed in the cafeteria, 99 explosive devices, and bombs rigged in cars. In the immediate aftermath, the perpetrators committed suicide.

Although initial reconstruction took place in the summer of 1999, the CHS community engaged a lengthy community-based approach to reconstruct and redesign school buildings, the school mascot and graphics, works of art, and surrounding acreage for years following the shooting. Overall public response, across all media and aesthetic forms, to the shooting was vast and, at times, contentious (*Fleming v. Jefferson County* 2001). Our analysis was limited to general school building renovations and student-generated art projects and exhibitions.

While aesthetic response at the shooting sites began immediately and many projects were completed within one year of the attack, the CHS aesthetic response took many years to come to fruition. For example, the CHS Memorial Garden (Columbine High School Memorial Foundation 2007) was not opened until 2007 – a full eight years after the shooting.

The CHS underwent extensive redesign and renovation, including new windows, furniture, tile floor covering and carpets, greenery, works of art, and coordinated color schemes (McDowell 1999a, 1999b, 1999c, 1999d). Hundreds of student-made ceramic tiles were put up along hallways, some of which are dedicated to classmates who died in the rampage (Kurtz 1999a, 1999b). Figure 7.3 shows how memorials dedicated to particular students were incorporated into the surroundings.

The library and cafeteria were considerably changed with the library floor being taken out, creating a two-story light-filled atrium above the cafeteria. Rectangular sculptural images with graphics of aspen trees by artist Virginia Wright-Frierson are suspended from the ceiling (Molinsky 2012) (Figure 7.4). The location of the artwork is poignant and fitting. Before the school was remodeled, the school library –where many students died – was located above the cafeteria (Kurtz 1999c).

Even the school mascot, a 1776 Revolutionary Rebel soldier, was revised and no longer carries a gun (Newsweek 2003). Additionally, changes were not all visual as multiple senses were attended to in the redesign. For example, the school's fire alarm siren was replaced with a sound different from the one that went off for hours on the day of the shootings (Urist 2014).

Though the original building was not demolished, extensive work was required due to damage inflicted during the attack and insistence by families of victims and community members. Overall, there was an intense desire to create a completely different spatial and aesthetic experience for returning students. Renovation had three primary goals: the building redesign worked to blunt the psychological impact for returning students, to honor those who were lost, and to reclaim the place as a school (Kenworthy 1999).

Figure 7.3 Columbine student Rachel Scott was killed outside of the school, but that area is now a hallway leading into the new library. This design - inspired by a drawing in Scott's journal - was embedded in the floor on the spot where she died. Retrieved from http://www.wnyc.org/story/290110-can-trauma-be-healed-with-design/. *Source:* Courtesy of Eric Molinsky.

Figure 7.4 Sculptural images with graphics by artist Virginia Wright-Frierson in the Columbine High School cafeteria. Retrieved from http://www.wnyc.org/story/290110-can-trauma-be-healed-with-design/. *Source:* Courtesy of Eric Molinsky.

Additionally, numerous student aesthetic responses, art shows, and exhibits were organized – some of them officially sanctioned with works screened by CHS teachers, administrators, and community leaders (Chandler 2000; Gazette 1999). Works portrayed individual experiences of the incident and had themes of healing and images from nature.

Figure 7.5 In solidarity, the Columbine High School community aesthetically responded to the Sandy Hook Elementary School shooting. Embracing Newtown online gallery. Posters, banners, quilts, and arts, p. 2. Retrieved from http://embracingnewtown.com/index.php?album=Posters-Banners-Quilts-and-Art&page=2. *Source:* Courtesy of Newtown Public Schools.

While some members of the community desired a unified response, several CHS students organized an exhibit of "uncensored and unaffiliated" student art at a local gallery to provide an alternative perspective (Fletcher 2000, para. 8).

There were four main experiential themes found in narratives and image expressions: the need to reclaim identity, individual and communal; a range of emotional positive and negative experiences; the ongoing impact of the shooting experience; and honoring those who were killed and injured. The negative emotions expressed in response to the shootings were primarily of sorrow, unease, tension, hyper-vigilance, shock, descriptions of crying and sadness, nostalgia, solidarity, and a loss of innocence. Many responses expressed the negative psychological impact of the shooting experience and PTSD. Some aesthetic responses focused entirely on positive or "happy" experiences and a repetition of symbols of solidarity. Many expressed hope and happiness in the future with remembrances of past joy.

Later on, the CHS community responded to the shootings at Sandy Hook Elementary School by producing artworks in solidarity (Figure 7.5).

Red Lion Junior High School

On the morning of April 24, 2003, hundreds of students at RLJHS witnessed the shooting to death of their principal, Dr. Eugene Segro, by Jimmy Sheets, a 14-year-old student (Landauer 2012). Without warning, Sheets calmly walked into the cafeteria, shot Segro, and then shot himself. The perpetrator left no indication of a motive for the shooting.

In the months following the 2003 shooting, members of Red Lion community participated in multiple community-building activities, public memorials, and created aesthetic responses. Along with over 45 other students, Heather Gisiner helped create stained glass artwork in honor of Principal Segro that hangs in the library. After the shooting, she had recurring nightmares involving a gunman. Kim Preske, a former substitute teacher at RLJHS, engaged in artwork as part of her PTSD therapy and struggles with negative emotions (Landauer 2012). When students returned to the building – including many who had witnessed the shooting – they were invited to dip their hands in black paint and make handprints on the cafeteria wall in an effort to reclaim their school (York Daily Record 2012). The permanent wall display has a marker that states "Hands touched by Dr. Segro."

Graphic themes in aesthetic responses included images from nature, the human body – specifically, student handprints – and a symbol of teaching and learning – an open book. There were paper assemblages, paintings, and glasswork that used universal symbols, popular culture images, and print words.

The RLJHS aesthetic response differs from the CHS and SHES response in multiple ways. Most notably, no significant renovations were made to the school building as there was virtually no damage. As well, no formal archive of aesthetic responses was found outside of those noted in local newspaper accounts. Overall, the public aesthetic responses, though highly meaningful and genuinely heartfelt, were of a much smaller number and scale. This may be due to the fewer number of victims and relatively contained nature of the attack.

Sandy Hook Elementary School
Adam Lanza shot off the door lock at Sandy Hook Elementary School and entered the school on December 14, 2012. Despite security systems in place and heroic intervention from faculty and staff, Lanza killed 20 children and 6 adults in less than 11 minutes. As police closed in, Lanza shot himself. Very little is known about specific motives or reasons for this violent act (Connecticut State Police 2013).

The unprecedented national and international responses to the horrifying Sandy Hook shooting incident have quieted but are still unfolding. Different from the CHS and RLJHS incidents, the student victims and many witnesses to the shooting were very young, only 6 to 8 years old. Given this, no aesthetic expressions made directly by the students are publically available. Analysis was limited to the new SHES, the Newtown Documentation Project (n.d.), and the Healing Newtown Arts Center (Newtown Cultural Arts Commission 2012).

New school. The new SHES opened in fall 2016 (Svigals + Partners n.d.) and is seen as a milestone that marks the step toward seeing the school return to the center of community life (Ryser 2015). Planning for the new school began just weeks after the shootings occurred as an interactive community process (Smith 2014). There was strong community involvement in development and design of the building and environment with numerous open forums, a large committee overseeing the project, a "Kids Build" educational program, and ongoing use of social media and news outlets to enhance open communication (Ryser 2015) (see Figures 7.6, 7.7, and 7.8).

The two primary themes used in the design narrative were a strong sense of community solidarity and the regenerative and healing elements of nature (Talarski 2014). These extended the meaning of the school structure and the act of building from merely solid brick and mortar to a deeper response of connectedness and rebirth. The lead architect noted: "Nature was the heart of our inspiration because nature has a deeply healing effect on people." "This is much more than just a building that provides for basic functional needs. This reaches into our aesthetic and spiritual needs" (Ryser 2015, para. 11).

The design team lists specific themes constructed into building and landscape design as canopies that connect, bridges and threshold, tree houses and a new horizon, the inner forest, layers of transparency, and building as a book or hand (Svigal + Partners n.d.) (see Figures 7.7 and 7.8). The unusual design has gently sloping wings that open like arms, with the multiple building sections extending like the fingers of an open hand tucked into wooded landscape and courtyards. The heavily

Figure 7.6 Sandy Hook community design meeting: Retrieved from http://www.svigals.com/wp-content/uploads/2015/06/SHS-Design-Narrative-2016.pdf. *Source:* Courtesy of Svigals + Partners.

Figure 7.7 Exterior of the new Sandy Hook Elementary School designed by Svigals + Partners (2016). Gallery, Photo 4. Retrieved from http://www.svigals.com/project/sandy-hook-school-newtown-ct/. *Source:* Courtesy of Robert Benson Photography.

Figure 7.8 Arts integration. Svigals + partners focused on security, design, and educational mission with input from students and community members. Retrieved from http://www.svigals.com/project/sandy-hook-school-newtown-ct. *Source:* Courtesy of Svigals + Partners.

windowed upper story gives the feel of a softly-lit tree house (Figure 7.9). Artwork within the building and as part of the landscape reflects the themes of nature and connected social relationships.

Additionally, security concerns were balanced with design themes (Rhodes 2014; Talarski 2014). For example, in the courtyards there are rain gardens that are part of the nature theme but also are an element of the school's security system by acting as a "bridge" for visitors to cross, by not allowing an easy approaching to classrooms, and by providing alternative evacuation routes.

The Newtown Documentation Project Galleries. Thousands upon thousands of heart-felt aesthetic expressions including cards, banners, artwork and more were sent to Newtown Connecticut after the 2014 tragedy in an extraordinary outpouring of care, sorrow, and a desire to help. In an effort to bear witness and acknowledge the relational

Figure 7.9 Interior of the new Sandy Hook Elementary School designed by Svigals + Partners. Gallery, Photo 7. Retrieved from: http://www.svigals.com/project/sandy-hook-school-newtown-ct/. *Source:* Courtesy of Robert Benson Photography.

connection, Newtown community members documented these expressions in a web-based gallery (Newtown Documentation Project Galleries n.d.). Hundreds of digital pages of poems, posters, books, banners, quilts, scrapbooks, maps, paper chains, paintings, drawings, and photos are featured on the site, along with thousands of letters from across the world (see Figures 7.10 through 7.14).

Six graphic themes were images from nature, the human body, universal symbols, religious symbols, play, and buildings. The experiential expressions included nine themes: extensions of condolence and blessings, calls to be strong and courageous, statements of love and of being with the victims, reassurance that the victims are in heaven or with God, a lack of knowing what to say, inclusions in thoughts or prayer, reassurance of change for the better, and acknowledgment of the magnitude of unfathomable loss. Some narratives included expressions of empathy and relational connection, as the writer/artist had also experienced significant loss or of parents expressing thankfulness for their children and families.

Healing Newtown Arts Center. Within days of the shooting incident, Newtown was inundated with donated works of art and hundreds of offers for arts services, funding, music and theater performances, and supplies (Crevier 2013). Out of this generosity came the Newtown Arts Center, which eventually evolved into an Arts Action Team

Figure 7.10 Embracing Newtown online gallery. Volunteer favorite art, p. 7. Retrieved from http://embracingnewtown.com/index.php?album=Volunteer_Favorite_Art/. *Source:* Courtesy of Newtown Public Schools.

Figure 7.11 Embracing Newtown online gallery. Volunteer favorite art, p. 1. Retrieved from http://embracingnewtown.com/index. php?album=Volunteer_Favorite_Art/. *Source:* Courtesy of Newtown Public Schools.

Figure 7.12 Volunteers work at sorting the hundreds of thousands of pieces of mail that flooded into Newtown from around the world after the Sandy Hook School shooting. *Hartford Courant News*, 2013. Retrieved from http://www.courant.com/news/connecticut/hc-in-newtown-preserving-worlds-reaction-to-sandy-hook-tragedy-20140127-story.html. Cloe Poisson/*Hartford Courant*. Copyright © 2013. Hartford Courant. Used with permission.

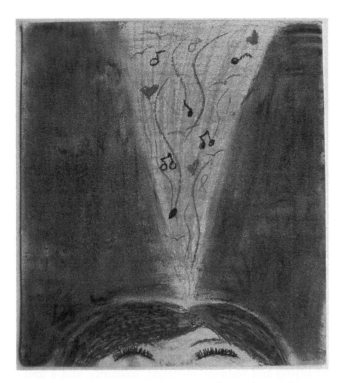

Figure 7.13 Embracing Newtown online gallery. Volunteer favorite art, p. 12. Retrieved from http://embracingnewtown.com/index.php?album=Volunteer_Favorite_Art/. *Source:* Courtesy of Newtown Public Schools.

Figure 7.14 Embracing Newtown online gallery. Volunteer favorite art, p. 1. Retrieved from http://embracingnewtown.com/index.php?album=Volunteer_Favorite_Art/. *Source:* Courtesy of Newtown Public Schools.

and Arts Space (Cultural Alliance of Western Connecticut n.d.). This organization hosts a gallery of artworks and provides ever expanding art-based opportunities for children and adults.

While there is acknowledgment of and memorials to the shooting incident, there is an even stronger emphasis on social relationships and building a community identity and healthy associated living practices within the arts organizations program and events.

Common Themes

Although there was variation in type of settings, populations, length of time passed, media coverage, amount of digital information available, and magnitude of the impact on communities, the three school shooting sites had multiple common themes (Maarhuis and Rudd 2017).

These themes were found across multiple art forms, media, design, and construction of the aesthetic responses to the tragic events. The common themes were found in the school spaces as well as the individual and community aesthetic responses and include:

1) Engagement: multiple senses and modes of aesthetic experience.
2) Use of nature in graphic artwork.
3) Use of human form in graphic artwork.
4) Use of universal and religious symbols in graphic artwork.
5) Expression of a wide range of emotions (shock, sorrow, unease, tension, hyper-vigilance, descriptions of crying and sadness, nostalgia, solidarity, and a loss of innocence, hope for the future, remembrances of past joy).
6) Strong involvement: local and extended community members.
7) Relational connection with victims to the local and extended community.
8) Evolving identity: sense of community and individual.
9) Evolving sense of living in association.
10) Evolving experience of impact.

Evidence for Motivated Aesthetic Response

Based on the common themes, there was evidence of motivated aesthetic response. A review of the three sites found that – on an individual, community, and organizational level – there was evidence of a motivated care and active response to the shootings through the use of artful projects, in addition to other works such as annual commemorative events and memorial sites (Maarhuis and Rud 2017).

Analysis of common themes as well as individual and community actions found a doubled or amplified reconstruction through the productive process of relational aesthetic response to school shootings (Maarhuis and Rud 2017). There was potential for reclamation, restoration, and re-presentation of social relationships in associated living through aesthetic responses in and about (i) spaces/places (school buildings, gardens, community centers) and (ii) the experience of social identity (community and individual) after the disruptive shooting incident. Each of the sites had many specific examples of reconstruction through purposeful involvement in aesthetic projects of reclamation, restoration, and re-presentation. Additionally, these findings informed the development of the aesthetic response model. The findings suggest that engagement in responsive aesthetic works and artful projects potentially can ameliorate the trauma and disruption of school shootings and promote recovery in the later aftermath of a shooting incident (Maarhuis and Rud 2017).

Research Questions 3 and 4

We now shift to a discussion about pragmatic application of Aesthetic Response in the later aftermath of a school shooting via research questions 3 and 4: How can the theoretical model of Aesthetic Response inform the national guidelines for school crisis (National Education Association n.d.)? How can the model of Aesthetic Response be applied within the national guidelines (National Education Association n.d.) for the aftermath of school crisis?

Informing the National Guidelines
The current NEA School Crisis Guide (National Education Association n.d.) provides highly specific information and step-by-step guidance for being prepared before a crisis as well as being responsive during a crisis. In contrast, the section of the guide that focuses on response in the later aftermath of a crisis is significantly shorter and addresses issues such as long-term mental health needs, handling donations, managing long-term reminders and benchmarks, long-term communications and media strategies, evaluating the school response, and a post-incident review of the school crisis plan. Outside of simple directives – "provide classroom activities for teachers to use with students," "Take care of staff," and "Take care of students" (p. 28) – there is little to no guidance or specified steps outlined for administrators and teachers regarding the reclamation, restoration, and re-presentation of social relationships in associated living and through aesthetics, specific to the school building and design or the experience of social and school identity after the shooting incident. The guidelines do provide highly abbreviated statements about an educational or curricular responses: "Classroom activities should be developmentally appropriate, help students express grief, feel safe and look forward to a positive future. Students can express their feelings through art and writing" (28); however, no detailed direction about trauma-sensitive curricula or educationally based expressions and aesthetic response is provided. The digital site of "sample activities" referenced in the guide could not be located (28). As well, attention to design and aesthetics of the school building is given one short paragraph in terms of considerations of "operational issues that make staff and student feel more comfortable" (28) with examples such as changing the "look" of affected parts of the building.

Despite this lack of inclusion in the guidelines, our literature review points to effective educational and administrative strategies, curricula, and procedures that include aesthetic responses and practices of associated living in the later aftermath of a school shooting. These research efforts indicate specific engagement in aesthetic response and works of art in the post-crisis aftermath as a potential means to work toward the alignment of mental health and education goals and objectives within school design and reconstruction as well as aesthetically focused curricula. Specifically, the literature review pointed to a need for purposeful translation and alignment of post-crisis intervention and objectives to be in line with the educational mission, goals, and objectives of the school. Jaycox and colleagues (2014, 287) call for "reestablishing social supports" and directing school teachers and staff to "actively work to help students ... to restore social and emotional equilibrium and order to the learning environment." Further, in her study with parents about impacts of a school shooting and what could be done to promote recovery, Mears (2008) describes the importance of intention – positive and non-exploitive – when individuals and the community respond to crisis. Notably, purposeful and planned aesthetic responses by community members, teachers, and administrators in the aftermath of a school shooting can work to establish positive social solidarity and appropriate displays of intention, motivated care, and acts of support.

Application in the National Guidelines

The aesthetic response model has implications for teacher and school administrator training, for consistent application of all three phases of the national response and recovery guidelines, for application of effective educational strategies in post-shooting recovery, and for the potential reconstruction of relationships and identity within associated living practices at school.

First, in conjunction with preparation before a crisis as well as being responsive during a crisis, the use of the aesthetic response model in the later aftermath can assist a community and school to return to the practices of stable associated living by working to rebuild social bonds and a sense of place in and outside the classroom. Rossen and Hull (2013) emphasize motivated care, transactional projects, and the importance of associated living through opportunities for meaning making. They note:

> When we make meaningful contributions to the welfare of others, we improve our own feelings of self-worth. Helping others strengthens resiliency, and providing guided opportunities for participation in activities that support the welfare of others is an important principle of compassionate teaching for educators. Such supervised opportunities can provide solace, create mutual trust, and affirm the self-worth of those involved. Participation can also be meaningful if extended to families and other throughout the school and community. (2013, 32)

The relational reconstruction and purposeful steps taken to return to associated living through aesthetic response has the potential to smooth the transition back to classroom teaching and learning, positively affect school climate, contribute to a more integrated and transdisciplinary approach, and contribute to decreasing the negative effects of shootings on student performance and education outcomes.

Second, and more specifically related to the education practices in the aftermath of school violence, the utilization of the aesthetic response model can help to support teachers in their return to the routine of classroom instruction in a timely manner (Newman et al. 2004) with transactional projects and curricula that are appropriate to the primary mission of the school and the full context of the aftermath of a shooting. Researchers and educators (Craig 2008, 2016; Rossen and Hull 2013) call for the utilization of artful works, aesthetic and meaning-making experiences within trauma-sensitive and trauma-responsive instruction and instruction adaptation. This also provides a support for teachers as they struggle to return to the difficult work of teaching and learning in the aftermath of violent experiences.

Third, the use of the aesthetic response model and transactional projects, along with other research and educational practices noted in the literature review, can provide administrators and policy makers a theoretical framework and applied approach for the later aftermath of a school shooting. Consequently, this framework and approach can allow for ongoing research of various practices in the aftermath of a shooting and, in turn, assist administrators and policy makers to pragmatically expand the section of the NEA guide (National Education Association n.d.) that focuses on an educational response in the later aftermath of a crisis, not just immediate crisis and mental health responses. Expansion of research and dissemination on relational and aesthetic responses in the later aftermath of a school shooting will provide needed guidance to future administrators and will emphasize the importance of including procedures and practices of associated living, adapted instruction and curricula, and the ongoing support of teachers and students in the full context of the learning environment. The dissemination and training about crisis guidelines and efficacious policies and procedures in teacher, principal, and superintendent training is essential for consistent and effective response to the later aftermath of school shootings.

Conclusion

At the beginning of this chapter, we drew upon Duncan-Andrade's (2009) ideas about material hope – an element of critical and materialized hope. Again, at closing, we reflect on another of his ideas, "Socratic hope," which is a type of teacher–student relationship and humanizing practice conducted in solidarity to "painfully examine our lives and actions within an unjust society and to share the sensibility that pain may pave the path to justice" (2009, 7). Further, he draws upon Cornel West by noting that young people want "to be able to perceive in palpable concrete form how these channels will allow them to vent their rage constructively and make sure that it will have an impact" (West 2004 cited in Duncan-Andrade, 2009, 7). While Duncan-Andrade focuses his analysis on the experiences of despair, rage, and indignation in response to social injustices, it is our desire that the use of the aesthetic response model is a pragmatic means to bring about the practices of materialized hope and Socratic hope that can allow for critical as well as artful examination of the broad and ongoing range of contexts, emotions, and responses within the aftermath of a school shooting.

Aesthetic response to school shootings is born out of great suffering but there is evidence of the potential to shift into new thinking and conduct about relational identity, associated living and educational response. The engagement in aesthetic response through transactional projects communicates thoughts, feelings, and ideas about *who we are* and *how we are to be* now that this shooting has happened. Through this process, there is a potential means to return to the everyday experience of going to school and a return to some form of stable associated living. It is a process through which we attend to the desire to understand and interpret: Who are we in this place? Who are we together? How are we to teach and learn after this shooting?

References

Adler P.S. and Obstfeld, D. 2007. "The Role of Affect in Creative Projects and Exploratory Search." *Industrial and Corporate Change* 16(1), 1–32.

Alvarez, H.K. 2007. "The Impact of Teacher Preparation on Responses to Student Aggression in the Classroom." *Teaching and Teacher Education* 23, 1113–1126.

Anderson, M. and Dolmage, R.W. 2009. "Making Meaning of a School Community's Traumatic Experience: The Sacred and the Profane." *Education Law Journal* 19(1), 1–33.

Ardis, C. 2004. "School Violence from the Classroom Teacher's Perspective." In *School Crime and Policing*, edited by W.L. Turk, pp. 131–150. Upper Saddle River, NJ: Pearson Education.

Barone, T. and Eisner, E.W. 1997. "Arts-based Educational Research." In *Complementary Methods for Research in Education*, edited by R.M. Jaeger, 2nd ed., pp. 72–116. Washington, DC: American Educational Research Association.

Beland, L. and Kim, D. 2015. "The Effect of High School Shootings on Schools and Student Performance." *Educational Evaluation and Policy Analysis* 38(1), 113–126.

Blair, J.P. and Schweit, K.W. 2014. *A Study of Active Shooter Incidents, 2000–2013*. Texas State University and Federal Bureau of Investigation, US Department of Justice, Washington, DC. Retrieved from Homeland Security Digital Library. https://www.hsdl.org/?abstract&did=757920.

Borum, R., Cornell, D.G., Modzeleski, W., and Jimerson, S.R. 2010. "What Can Be Done About School Shootings? A Review of the Evidence." *Educational Researcher* 39(1), 27–37.

Bourriaud, N. 2002. *Relational Aesthetics*. Translated by S. Pleasance, F. Woods, and M. Copeland. Dijon: Les presses du reel France.

Brock, S.E., Nickerson, A.B., Reeves, M.A., Jimerson, S.R., Lieberman, R.A, and Feinberg, T.A. 2009. *School Crisis Prevention and Intervention: The PREPaRE Model*. Bethesda, MD: National Association of School Psychologists.

Chandler, M.V. 2000. "Death and Violence Rarely Visit Exhibition Spaces." *Rocky Mountain News*, April 16. https://www.highbeam.com/doc/1G1-81053163.html (accessed December 12, 2015).

Columbine High School Memorial Foundation. 2007. *Columbine High School Memorial Garden*. Littleton, CO. http://www.columbinememorial.org/default.asp (accessed December 15, 2015).

Connecticut State Police, Department of Emergency Services and Public Protection. 2013. SHES Shooting Reports (CFS 1200704559). http://cspsandyhookreport.ct.gov/(last accessed October 10, 2017).

Cornell, D.G. and Mayer, M.J. 2010. "Why Do School Order and Safety Matter?" *Educational Researcher* 39(1), 7–15.

Cornell, D., Sheras, P., Gregory, A., and Fan, X. 2009. "A Retrospective Study of School Safety Conditions in High Schools Using the Virginia Threat Assessment Guidelines versus Alternative Approaches." *School Psychology Quarterly* 24(2), 119–129.

Craig, S.E. 2008. *Reaching and Teaching Children Who Hurt: Strategies for Your Classroom*. Baltimore, MD: Brookes.

Craig, S.E. 2016. *Trauma-sensitive Schools: Learning Communities Transforming Children's Lives, K–5*. New York: Teachers College Press.

Crevier, N.K. 2013. "Organizations Are Here for the Long Haul as Newtown Moves Forward." *The Newtown Bee*, December 12. http://newtownbee.com/news/0001/11/30/organizations-are-here-long-haul-newtown-moves-for/181422 (accessed December 20, 2015).

Cultural Alliance of Western Connecticut. n.d. http://www.artswesternct.org/index.php/ get-involved/front-end-social-feeds/vimeo-feeds/item/4502-the-newtown-healing-arts-center.

Daniels, J.A. and Bradley, M.C. 2011. *Preventing Lethal School Violence.* New York: Springer.

Daniels, J.A., Bradley, M.C., and Hays, M. 2007. "The Impact of School Violence on School Personnel: Implications for Psychologists." *Professional Psychology: Research and Practice* 38(6), 652–659.

Daniels, J.A., Volungis, A., Pshenishny, E., Gandhi, P., Winkler, A., Cramer, D.P., Bradley, M. C. 2010. "A Qualitative Investigation of Averted School Shooting Rampages." *The Counseling Psychologist* 38(1), 69–95.

Department of Education. 2007. *Practical information on Crisis Planning: A Guide for Schools and Communities* (Report No. ED-01-CO-0082/0006). Office of Safe and Drug-Free Schools, Washington, DC. http://www2.ed.gov/admins/lead/safety/ emergencyplan/crisisplanning.pdf (last accessed October 10, 2017).

Dewey, J. 1916. "Force and Coercion." *International Journal of Ethics* 26, 359–367.

Dewey, J. 1922. *Human Nature and Conduct.* New York: Henry Holt & Company.

Dewey, J. 1958. *Experience and Nature.* New York: Dover Publications.

Dewey, J. 2005. *Art as Experience.* New York: Perigee. First published 1934.

Dewey, J. 2011. *Democracy and Education.* Hollywood, FL: Simon & Brown. First published 1916.

Dishman, M.L., Lewis, J.L., and Pepper, M.J. 2011. "A Student [Came] Down and Said 'There's a ... guy in the ... English classroom with a gun'": Recovering from Violent Invasion. *Journal of Cases in Educational Leadership* 14(1), 48–58.

Duffy, J.O. and Mooney, E. 2014. "The Ethical Relationship between School Violence and Teacher Morale." *Pedagogy and the Human Sciences* 1(4), 22–38.

Duncan-Andrade, J. 2009. "Note to Educators: Hope Required When Growing Roses in Concrete." *Harvard Educational Review* 79(2), 1–13.

Everytown for Gun Safety. 2016. *Analysis of School Shootings: January 1, 2013 – December 31, 2015* (Research report). New York. http://everytown.org/article/schoolshootings/ (accessed December 15, 2015).

Farmer, T.W., Farmer, E.M.Z., Estell, D.B., and Hutchins, B.C. 2007. "The Developmental Dynamics of Aggression and the Prevention of School Violence." *Journal of Emotional and Behavioral Disorders* 15(4), 197–208.

Fesmire, S. 2003. *John Dewey and Moral Imagination.* Bloomington: Indiana University Press.

Fleming v. Jefferson. November 1, 2001. United States District Court, Denver, Colorado. COUNTY SCHOOL DIST. NO. R-1, No. Civ.A. 99-D-1932., 70 F.Supp.2d 1094. http:// www.leagle.com/decision/20011264170FSupp2d1094_11129.xml/FLEMING%20v.%20 JEFFERSON%20COUNTY%20SCHOOL%20DIST.%20NO.%20R-1 (last accessed October 10, 2017).

Fletcher, H. 2000, April 27. "The Kids Are All Right." *Westword News.* http://www. westword.com/news/the-kids-are-all-right-5062464 (last accessed October 10, 2017).

Galand, B., Lecocq, C., and Philippot, P. 2007. "School Violence and Teacher Professional Disengagement." *The British Journal of Educational Psychology* 77(2), 465–477.

Gazette 1999, May 9. "Auction Will Benefit Columbine High School Fund." https://www. highbeam.com/doc/1P2-5936426.html (last accessed October 10, 2017).

Gray, L., Lewis, L., and Ralph, J. 2015. *Public School Safety and Discipline: 2013–14* (First Look Report). US Department of Education, Washington, DC. https://nces.ed.gov/pubs2015/2015051.pdf (last accessed October 10, 2017).

Hickman, L. 1990. *John Dewey's Pragmatic Technology*. Bloomington: Indiana University Press.

Hurford, D.P., Lindskog, R., Cole, A., Jackson, R., Thomasson, S., and Wade, A. 2010. "The Role of School Climate in School Violence: A Validity Study of a Web-based School Violence Survey." *Journal of Educational Research & Policy Studies* 10(1), 51–77.

Hyman, I.A. and Perone, D.C. 1998. "The Other Side of School Violence: Educator Policies and Practices That May Contribute to Student Misbehavior." *Journal of School Psychology* 36(1), 7–27.

International Association of Chiefs of Police (IACP). 2009. *Guide for Preventing and Responding to School Violence*, 2nd ed. US Department of Justice, Washington, DC. http://www.theiacp.org/portals/0/pdfs/schoolviolence2.pdf (last accessed October 10, 2017).

Jackson, P.W. 1998. *John Dewey and the Lessons of Art*. London: Yale University Press.

Jaycox, L.H., Stein, B.D., and Wong, M. 2014. "School Intervention Related to School and Community Violence." *Child and Adolescent Psychiatric Clinics of North America* 23(2), 281–293.

Jefferson County Sheriff. n.d. "Columbine High School Incident." http://www.cnn.com/SPECIALS/2000/columbine.cd/Pages/TOC.htm (last accessed October 10, 2017).

Jimmerson, S.R., Nickerson, A.B., Mayer, M.J., and Furlong, M.J., eds. 2012. *Handbook of School Violence and School Safety. International Research and Practice*, 2nd ed. New York: Routledge.

Jordan, K. 2003. "A Trauma and Recovery Model for Victims and Their Families after a Catastrophic School Shooting: Focusing on Behavioral, Cognitive, and Psychological Effects and Needs." *Brief Treatment and Crisis Intervention* 3(4), 397–411.

Kenworthy, T. 1999. "As Crews Work on Columbine, Memory Vies with a Makeover." *Washington Post*, June 16. https://www.highbeam.com/doc/1P2-590169.html (last accessed October 10, 2017).

Kurtz, H. 1999a. "Hand-painted Tiles to Decorate Columbine High School Renovation Project." *Rocky Mountain News*, July 20. https://www.highbeam.com/doc/1G1-67416449.html (last accessed October 10, 2017).

Kurtz, H. 1999b. "Columbine High School Students Heal Through Their Art." *Rocky Mountain News*, August 12. https://www.highbeam.com/doc/1G1-67418188.html (last accessed October 10, 2017).

Kurtz, H. 1999c. "Groups Plan to Raze Library, Raise Columbine High School Memorial." *Rocky Mountain News*, December 7. https://www.highbeam.com/doc/1G1-67429127.html (last accessed October 10, 2017).

Landauer, B. 2012. "Finding Their Way Out: Red Lion School Shooting Still Haunts Some." *York Daily Record*, October 9. http://media.ydr.com/interactive/rlheals/(accessed December 15, 2015).

Levine, S.K. 2009. *Trauma, Tragedy, Therapy: The Arts and Human Suffering*. Philadelphia, PA: Jessica Kingsley.

Littlefield, R., Reierson, J., Cowden, K., Stowman, S., and Long Feather, C. 2009. "A Case Study of the Red Lake, Minnesota, School Shooting: Intercultural Learning in the Renewal Process." *Communication, Culture and Critique* 2, 361–383.

Maarhuis, P. and Rud, A. 2015a. "Philosophical Perspectives on School Shootings: Demands of Honor, Sovereign Exception, Aesthetic Reclamation, and Civic Response." Paper presentation. Philosophy of Education Society (PES), Memphis, TN, March.

Maarhuis, P. and Rud, A. 2015b. "Dewey, School Violence, and Aesthetic Response." Paper presentation. American Educational Research Association (AERA), Chicago, IL, April.

Maarhuis, P. and Rud, A. 2015c. "Material Hope: Dewey, School Shootings, and Aesthetic Reclamation." Paper presentation. Northwest Association of Teacher Educators Conference (NWATE), Pullman, WA, June.

Maarhuis, P. and Rud, A. G. 2017. "Dewey, School Violence, and Aesthetic Response." In *Handbook of Research on the Facilitation of Civic Engagement Through Community Art*, edited by L.N. Hersey. Hershey, PA: IGI Global.

McClelland, K.A. 2005. "John Dewey: Aesthetic Experience and Artful Conduct." *Education and Culture* 21(2), 44–62.

McDowell, R. 1999a. "Construction Crews Repair Columbine." Associated Press Online, June 16. https://www.highbeam.com/doc/1P1-23230560.html (accessed December 12, 2015).

McDowell, R. 1999b. "Columbine High School Students Design Wall Tiles." Associated Press Online, July 7. https://www.highbeam.com/doc/1P1-23222614.html (accessed December 22, 2015).

McDowell, R. 1999c. "Columbine High School: A School Again." Associated Press, The Columbian, August 7. https://www.highbeam.com/doc/1P2-23425728.html (accessed December 22, 2015).

McDowell, R. 1999d. "Painful Reminders of Agony at Columbine High School Erased with Bright, Colorful Renovations." *The Buffalo News*, August 8. https://www.highbeam.com/doc/1P2-23138526.html (last accessed October 10, 2017).

Mears, C.L. 2008. "A Columbine Study: Giving Voice, Hearing Meaning." *The Oral History Review* 35(2), 159–175.

Molinsky, E. 2012. "Can Trauma Be Healed with Design?" *Studio 360*, May 3. (Public Radio International.) http://www.studio360.org/story/290110-can-trauma-be-healed-with-design/(accessed December 4, 2015).

Mooney, E.J. 2013. "The Effects of Witnessing a School Shooting on a Teacher's Career: A Narrative Study." Doctoral thesis. Northeastern University Libraries Digital Repository Service. https://repository.library.northeastern.edu/files/neu:1090 (last accessed October 10, 2017).

National Education Association (NEA). n.d. *School Crisis Guide: Help and Healing in a Time of Crisis*. Health Information Network, Washington, DC. http://neahealthyfutures.org/wp-content/uploads/2015/05/schoolcrisisguide.pdf (last accessed October 10, 2017).

Newman, K.S., Fox, C., Harding, D.J., Mehta, J., and Roth, W. 2004. *Rampage: The Social Roots of School Shootings*. New York: Basic Books.

Newsweek. 2003. "More than Sixty Interviews with Columbine High School Students and Community Members." *Press Release Newswire*, October 26. http://www.prnewswire.com/news-releases/newsweek-more-than-sixty-interviews-with-columbine-students-and-community-members-reveal-a-school-that-dwells-simultaneously-in-its-past-and-present-72707057.html (last accessed October 10, 2017).

Newtown Cultural Arts Commission (NCAC). 2012. *Healing Newtown Arts Center*, Cultural Alliance of Western Connecticut. http://www.newtownartscommission.org/healing-newtown-httpwww-healingnewtown-org/(last accessed October 10, 2017).

Newtown Documentation Project Galleries. n.d. *Embracing Newtown, Connecticut.* http://embracingnewtown.com/index.php (last accessed October 10, 2017).

Noonan J.H. and Vavra M.C. 2007. *Crime in Schools and Colleges: A Study of Offenders and Arrestees Reported Via National Incident-Based Reporting System Data.* (The CARD Report). US Department of Justice, Federal Bureau of Investigation, Criminal Justice Information Services Division, Washington, DC. https://www.fbi.gov/about-us/cjis/ucr/nibrs/crime-in-schools-and-colleges-pdf (last accessed October 10, 2017).

Nurmi, J., Räsänen, P., and Oksanen, A. 2011. "The Norm of Solidarity: Experiencing Negative Aspects of Community Life after a School Shooting Tragedy." *Journal of Social Work* 12(3), 300–319.

Paulus, T., Woodside, M., and Ziegler, M. 2008. "Extending the Conversation: Qualitative Research as Dialogic Collaborative Process." *The Qualitative Report* 12(2), 226–243.

Prawat, R.S. 1998. "Current Self-regulation Views of Learning and Motivation Viewed through a Deweyan Lens: The Problems with Dualism." *American Educational Research Journal* 35, 199–226.

Raghumathan R. and Pham, M.T. 1999. "All Negative Moods Are Not Equal: Motivational Influences of Anxiety and Sadness on Decision Making." *Organizational Behavior and Human Decision Processes* 79(1), 56–99.

Report of Governor Bill Owns' Columbine High School Review Commission. 2001. *The Columbine High School Massacre.* Littleton, CO.

Rhodes, M. 2014. "The New SHES Is All About Invisible Security." *Wired*, November 14. http://www.wired.com/2014/11/new-sandy-hook-elementary-school-invisible-security/(last accessed October 10, 2017).

Rider, C.F. 2015. "Teachers' Perceptions of Their Ability to Respond to Active Shooter Incidents." Doctoral dissertation. University of Southern Mississippi Aquila Digital Community (Paper 62). http://aquila.usm.edu/dissertations/62/(last accessed October 10, 2017).

Rossen, E. and Hull, R., eds. 2013. *Supporting and Educating Traumatized Students: A Guide for School-based Professionals.* New York: Oxford University Press.

Ryan, J. and Hawdon, J. 2008. "From Individual to Community: The "Framing" of 4–16 and the Display of Social Solidarity." *Traumatology* 14(1), 43.

Ryser, R. 2015. "Little Fanfare, but Great Hopes, as Sandy Hook School Construction Begins." *Connecticut Post*, February 14. http://www.newstimes.com/local/article/Little-fanfare-but-great-hopes-as-Sandy-Hook-6080232.php (last accessed October 10, 2017).

Schuster, B. 2009. "Preventing, Preparing for Critical Incidents in Schools." *National Institute of Justice Journal*, 262. US Office of Justice Programs, Washington, DC. http://www.nij.gov/journals/262/pages/critical-incidents-in-schools.aspx (last accessed October 10, 2017).

Smith, L. 2014. "Building the New Sandy Hook Elementary." *Slate.* http://www.slate.com/articles/life/culturebox/2014/12/the_new_sandy_hook_elementary_school_designing_and_building_the_newtown.html (last accessed October 10, 2017).

Steffgen, G., Recchia, S., and Viechtbauer, W. 2013. "The Link between School Climate and Violence in School: A Meta-analytic Review." *Aggression and Violent Behavior* 18, 300–309.

Svigals + Partners n. d. *The New Sandy Hook School.* http://www.sandyhook2016.com/index.html (last accessed October 10, 2017).

Talarski, C. 2014. "Design after Disaster: A New Sandy Hook school." Online radio interview, September 11. WNPR–Connecticut Public Radio. http://wnpr.org/post/design-after-disaster-new-sandy-hook-school#stream/0 (last accessed October 10, 2017).

Thompson, S. and Kyle, K. 2005. "Understanding Mass School Shootings: Links between Personhood and Power in the Competitive School Environment." *Journal of Primary Prevention* 26(5), 419–438.

Turunen, T., Haravuori, H., Pihlajamaki, J.J., Marttunen, M., and Punamäki, R. 2014. "Framework of the Outreach after a School Shooting and the Students Perceptions of the Provided Support." *European Journal of Psychotraumatology* 5, 1–9.

Urist, J. 2014. "The Architecture of Loss: How to Redesign after a School Shooting." *The Atlantic*, November 20. http://www.theatlantic.com/education/archive/2014/11/the-architecture-of-loss-how-to-redesign-after-a-school-shooting/382952/(last accessed October 10, 2017).

Vossekuil, B., Fein, R.A., Reddy, M., Borum, R., and Modzeleski, W. 2004. *The Final Report and Findings of the Safe School Initiative: Implications for the Prevention of School Attacks in the United States.* United States Secret Service and the United States Department of Education, Washington, DC. https://www2.ed.gov/admins/lead/safety/preventingattacksreport.pdf (last accessed October 10, 2017).

Wallace, L.N. 2015. "Responding to Violence with Guns: Mass Shootings and Gun Acquisition." *The Social Science Journal* 52, 156–167.

Warnick, B.R., Johnson, B.A., and Rocha, S. 2010. "Tragedy and the Meaning of School Shootings." *Educational Theory* 60(3), 371–390.

Wike, T.L. and Fraser, M.W. 2009. "School Shootings: Making Sense of the Senseless." *Aggression and Violent Behavior* 14, 162–169.

York Daily Record Opinion. 2012. "Our Take: Red Lion Suffers in Silence." *York Daily Record*, April 25. http://webcache.googleusercontent.com/search?q=cache:1ScA_tSEKegJ:www.ydr.com/opinion/ci_20442844/+&cd=2&hl=en&ct=clnk&gl=us (accessed December 15, 2015).

Zucker, M., Spinazzola, J., Pollack, A.A., Pepe, L., and Barry, S. 2010. "Getting Teachers in on the Act: Evaluation of a Theater- and Classroom-based Youth Violence Prevention Program." *Journal of School Violence* 9, 117–135.

Section 2

Group and Gang Violence in Education

Section Editor: Emily E. Tanner-Smith

Section 2 Introduction

Group and Gang Violence in Education

Emily E. Tanner-Smith

On March 17, 2005, 15-year-old Deliesh Allen-Roberts was shot in the head by a stray bullet outside Locke High School in Los Angeles, CA. She died one week later. She was shot by an 18-year-old former student of the school, an alleged member of the Bacc Street Crips gang, who was shooting at a car passing the school (*People v. Dejuan Hines* 2008). On August 5, 2006, 16- and 17-year-olds David Gamero and Juan Quito were stabbed in the parking lot of Springbrook High School in Silver Spring, MD by members of the Mara Salvatrucha (MS13) gang. The stabbing occurred after a verbal altercation with another member of MS13 at school, who allegedly called other gang members to the school for backup (Vogel 2006). These two incidents symbolize the threats associated with gang violence at school feared by many students, parents, teachers, and school administrators: namely, that gangs can make schools unsafe learning environments due to violent interactions or altercations between gang members that occur on school property (e.g., "turf wars" that occur in areas like parking lots, school buses, and football fields) or the potential diffusion of gang violence to innocent student bystanders.

Although there is no universally agreed upon definition of youth gangs (Curry 2015), one popular definition of youth street gangs is "any durable, street-oriented youth group whose involvement in illegal activity is part of its group identity" (Klein and Maxson 2006, 4).

According to the 2012 National Youth Gangs Survey, an estimated 29.6% of law enforcement agencies in the United States reported gang activity in their jurisdictions, with gang prevalence being substantially higher in urban areas (Egley, Howell, and Harris 2014). Despite consistent declines in gang prevalence during the 1990s and early 2000s, gang activity has remained relatively consistent in the past decade (National Youth Gang Center 2015). Most youth gang activities occur in communities surrounding schools, but their presence certainly can diffuse to the students and schools in those communities. National estimates from the School Survey on Crime and Safety found that, in 2013, 12% of students aged 12–18 reported that gangs were present in their school – again, with prevalence being higher in urban (18%) than suburban (11%) or rural (7%) schools (Zhang, Musu-Gillette, and Oudekerk 2016).

Gang presence in schools is troubling given the large body of research that suggests gang membership is associated with delinquency and victimization (Curry, Decker, and Egly 2002; Papachristos et al. 2015; Peterson, Taylor, and Esbensen 2004; Pyrooz, Moule, and Decker 2014; Schreck, Miller, and Gibson 2003); violence (Jennings et al. 2011;

The Wiley Handbook on Violence in Education: Forms, Factors, and Preventions, First Edition.
Edited by Harvey Shapiro.
© 2018 John Wiley & Sons, Inc. Published 2018 by John Wiley & Sons, Inc.

Matsuda et al. 2013), incarceration rates (Gilman, Hill, and Hawkins 2014), substance use and distribution (Esbensen and Huizinga 1993; Fagan 1989; Swahn et al. 2010), poor social/emotional/mental health (Gilman, Hill, and Hawkins 2014; Harper and Robinson 1999), as well as high school dropout and poor academic performance (Pyrooz 2014). Despite debate as to the causal relationship between gang membership and these negative outcomes (i.e., selection vs. facilitation effects; see Thornberry et al. 2003), it is clear that gang membership can be disruptive and detrimental to healthy adolescent development.

Drawing on criminological theories of social bonding, social strain, and social learning, a large body of research has established risk factors for gang participation, such that youth who are male, African American, have prior histories of delinquency, have histories of peer rejection, or histories of school failure are at higher risk of gang participation (Bjerregaard and Cochran 2012; Dishion, Nelson, and Yasui 2005; Howell 2010; O'Brien et al. 2013). Yet, as noted in this volume, social ecological theories can be useful for identifying larger meso- and macro-level risk and protective factors for gang participation. Indeed, gangs may yield greater power (and be an attractive option for some youth) in school settings that are perceived to be unsafe, whereby existing gang members can prey on student fears through the promise of safety and security (Thompkins 2000).

Schools have responded to concerns about gangs in a variety of policy and programming efforts. One of the most widely applied gang prevention programs, the Gang Resistance Education and Training (GREAT) program (Peterson and Esbensen 2004) is a school-based program delivered by law enforcement officers that addresses a range of risk factors such as school commitment and performance, association with peers/peer influences, prosocial activity involvement, empathy, self-control, perceived guilt, neutralization techniques, and moral disengagement. The GREAT program activities typically focus on skills development through the use of problem-solving exercises and cooperative learning strategies (Esbensen 2015). Other school-based policy responses are more deterrence based, including zero tolerance type policies or school surveillance and security policies aimed at monitoring and punishing misbehavior on school property. These types of exclusionary school policies tend to disproportionately affect not only gang members, however, but also racial/ethnic minority youth, propagating what has been termed the "school to prison pipeline" (Garcia and De Lissovoy 2013; Pinnow 2013; Rios 2010; Rios and Galicia 2013).

The goal of this section of the handbook is to focus on the issue of group and gang violence in educational settings, an important but understudied social institution in the field of gang violence research. By summarizing and synthesizing the current evidence on gang violence in education, and exploring the potential effects of different school-based policy responses to gangs, the chapters in this section should advance new and innovative research in this area. The eight chapters in this section highlight key theories from the fields of communication, community psychology, criminology, and sociology.

First, Michael Ezell provides an overview of the relationship between gang membership and school crime and violence, discussing some of the challenges associated with defining gangs, defining gang crime, and establishing causal relationships between gang membership and crime. This chapter highlights the numerous methodological challenges associated with conducting research on group and gang violence, particularly when examining the correlates and consequences of gangs on crime in school environments.

Next, Joey Nuñez Estrada Jr., Adrian Huerta, Edwin Hernandez, Robert Hernandez, and Steve Kim present a socioecological framework for understanding the multitude of individual, peer, family, school, and community-based risk/prospective factors for youth gang involvement. This chapter highlights the importance of acknowledging the potential benefits of gang involvement – including physical protection and a sense of identity – particularly for marginalized youth of color residing in high-risk environments. Drawing on this socioecological framework, the authors call for educational researchers to place renewed emphasis on understanding how complex trauma and systemic marginalization can affect students' emotional and behavioral development.

In Chapter 10, Kendra Clark, David Pyrooz, and Ryan Randa review the evidence base regarding the relationships between gangs, schools, and violence, including an in-depth review of state-level gang-related school legislation measures. This chapter also reviews recent evidence regarding gang prevention program effectiveness, with particular focus on the findings from the GREAT II school-based gang and violence prevention program. This chapter highlights the need for reform in school policies and practices designed to reduce gang violence, particularly the use of ambiguous zero tolerance policies that are punitive and disproportionately burdensome to marginalized youth. More promising school-based prevention and intervention approaches will be those that are proactive and supportive, rather than reactive and punitive.

In the next chapter, Benjamin Fisher, F. Chris Curran, Alvin Pearman II, and Joseph Gardella use data from the Educational Longitudinal Study to examine whether various school gang prevention policies and programs are associated with students' perceived safety and exposure to fighting and drugs at school. This chapter presents correlational evidence that school uniform policies may be associated with decreased gang activity and negative outcomes associated with gangs at schools, and suggests that other dress code policies and targeted gang prevention programs may have minimal impact on student outcomes. This chapter highlights the importance of understanding whether and how individually targeted and/or whole-school approaches to gang activity may affect school safety, and how school contextual factors may moderate program effectiveness.

In Chapter 12, Jessica Nina Lester and Katherine Evans use archival data from the *New York Times* to conduct a discourse analysis of zero tolerance policies in schools. This chapter highlights the changing public discourse around zero tolerance policies, beginning in the early 1990s with a discourse demanding zero tolerance policies, shifting later to a discourse of debate around zero tolerance policies, and most recently shifting to a discourse deconstructing and criticizing zero tolerance policies. The findings from this chapter illustrate the value of using discourse analysis to disrupt media narratives that may perpetuate inequalities and reify negative images of youth, including historically marginalized youth of color, and the importance of examining how discourses may influence educational policies.

In the following chapter, Lynn Addington and Emily Tanner-Smith investigate another specific type of school policy response for addressing gang activities in schools: school surveillance and security policies. The authors use national data from the School Survey on Crime and Safety to examine whether schools' use of security personnel as a surveillance mechanism leads to reduced gang-related crime in schools. This chapter presents correlational evidence that school security measures may have minimal impact on gang-related crime in schools, and that some school security policies could have unintentional harmful consequences due to net-widening effects. This chapter highlights the need to carefully attend to unintentional adverse effects that may result from school-based policies intended to reduce gang-related crime, and to examine the need for more comprehensive school policy responses.

In Chapter 14, Lisa De La Rue and Anjali Forber-Pratt provide a critical discussion of the different types of disciplinary strategies schools may use to address issues of gang involvement and gang violence. This chapter problematizes punitive school strategies such as zero tolerance, law enforcement, and surveillance policies, which often criminalize students and disproportionately affect students of color. The authors discuss alternative approaches schools might use, including more therapeutic intervention strategies aimed at promoting positive youth development. This chapter outlines how punitive school policies can perpetuate the school-to-prison pipeline, highlighting the need for more therapeutic and contextually informed policies.

Finally, Nadine Connell, Richard Riner, Richard Hernandez, Jordan Riddell, and Justine Medrano discuss short school-based intervention approaches that can be used to address risky behaviors at school, such as substance use and violence (including gang violence). This chapter reviews several promising short school-based prevention programs that may be of interest to school administrators, and discusses a critical appraisal tool that may be useful for practitioners tasked with selecting school-based prevention programs.

The chapters in this section of the handbook make important contributions to the burgeoning literature on group and gang violence in educational settings, and call attention to several specific areas that deserve further study. First, gang membership is a fluid process, so future research should attend to the issue of youth's level of embeddedness in gangs, and how gang embeddedness trajectories may affect subsequent outcomes (e.g., Pyrooz, Moule, and Decker 2014). Second, as social media and technology become increasingly focal in the lives of students, more research will be needed to investigate their role as both sites for gang crime, organization, or socialization but also as potential sites for prevention and intervention efforts.

Third, more rigorous research is needed to evaluate and test the effects of gang prevention and intervention efforts – for instance, those efforts drawing on the Office of Juvenile Justice and Delinquency Prevention (OJJDP) comprehensive gang strategy model (2009), which emphasizes the importance of social intervention, opportunities provision, suppression, organizational change and development, as well as community mobilization (Gebo, Bond, and Campos 2015). Schools can take a range of approaches depending on their needs, including whole-school, classroom-based, or individually targeted programming. But there are a variety of structural barriers that must be acknowledged, foremost of which is that many teachers and administrators may not have appropriate training or expertise to deliver or maintain these gang prevention programs. Thus, more research is needed to examine the potential role of community-oriented and problem-oriented policing strategy approaches and how those might be used to garner interagency collaboration between schools and police systems, while avoiding traditional, potentially ineffective suppression strategies (Braga and Weisburd 2012). Research in this area should attend to potential adverse or unintentional harmful effects of such programs delivered in schools, particularly as they might lead to the diffusion of gang activities outside of schools and into surrounding communities.

Youth gang involvement is a complex social phenomenon, and to date there has been limited empirical research examining the prevalence of gang-related activity in school or the effectiveness of school-based responses to gang-related crime. Given the multitude of individual, peer, family, community, and school-level risk and protective factors for gang involvement and persistence, strategies that are punitive and suppression-focused will likely have limited effectiveness, and may have disproportionately harmful effects on historically marginalized youth of color. The chapters in this section of the handbook advance the literature in this field by highlighting potentially promising avenues of research and policy aimed at improving the well-being and safety of all students.

References

Bjerregaard, Beth and Cochran, Joseph A. 2012. "The Role of School-Related Bonding Factors and Gender: Correlates of Gang Membership among Adolescents." *Women & Criminal Justice* 22(1), 30–53. DOI: 10.1080/08974454.2012.636289.

Braga, Anthony A. and Weisburd, David L. 2012. "The Effects of Focused Deterrence Strategies on Crime: A Systematic Review and Meta-Analysis of the Empirical Evidence." *Journal of Research in Crime and Delinquency* 49(3), 323–358. DOI: 10.1177/0022427811419368.

Curry, G. David. 2015. "The Logic of Defining Gangs Revisited." In *The Handbook of Gangs*, edited by Scott H. Decker and David C. Pyrooz, pp. 7–27. Chichester, UK: John Wiley & Sons.

Curry, G. David, Decker, Scott H., and Egley, Jr., Arlen. 2002. "Gang Involvement and Delinquency in a Middle School Population." *Justice Quarterly* 19(2), 275–292. DOI: 10.1080/07418820200095241.

Dishion, Thomas J., Nelson, Sarah E., and Yasui, Miwa. 2005. "Predicting Early Adolescent Gang Involvement from Middle School Adaptation." *Journal of Clinical Child and Adolescent Psychology* 34(1), 62–73. DOI: 10.1207/s15374424jccp3401_6.

Egley Jr., Arlen, Howell, James C., and Harris, Meena. 2014. *Highlights of the 2012 National Youth Gang Survey. OJJDP* Juvenile Justice Fact Sheet. Washington, DC: Office of Juvenile Justice and Delinquency Prevention.

Esbensen, Finn-Aage. 2015. "The Gang Resistance Education and Training (G.R.E.A.T.) Program: An Evaluator's Perspective." In *The Handbook of Gangs*, edited by Scott H. Decker and David C. Pyrooz, pp. 369–391. Chichester, UK: John Wiley & Sons.

Esbensen, Finn-Aage and Huizinga, David. 1993. "Gangs, Drugs, and Delinquency in a Survey of Urban Youth." *Criminology* 31(4), 565–589. DOI: 10.1111/j.1745-9125.1993.tb01142.x.

Fagan, Jeffrey. 1989. "The Social Organization of Drug Use and Drug Dealing among Urban Gangs." *Criminology* 27(4), 633–670. DOI: 10.1111/j.1745-9125.1989.tb01049.x.

García, José and De Lissovoy, Noah. 2013. "Doing School Time: The Hidden Curriculum Goes to Prison." *Journal for Critical Education Policy Studies* 11(4), 49–68.

Gebo, Erika, Bond, Brenda J., and Campos, Krystal S. 2015. "The OJJDP Comprehensive Gang Strategy: The Comprehensive Gang Model." In *The Handbook of Gangs*, edited by Scott H. Decker and David C. Pyrooz, pp. 392–405. Chichester, UK: John Wiley & Sons.

Gilman, Amanda B., Hill, Karl G., and Hawkins, J. David. 2014. "Long-term Consequences of Adolescent Gang Membership for Adult Functioning." *American Journal of Public Health* 104(5), 938–945. DOI: 10.2105/AJPH.2013.301821.

Harper, Gary W. and Robinson, W. LaVome. 1999. "Pathways to Risk among Inner-City African-American Adolescent Females: The Influence of Gang Membership." *American Journal of Community Psychology* 27(3), 383–404.

Howell, James C. 2010. *Gang Prevention: An Overview of Research and Programs. Juvenile Justice Bulletin.* Washington, DC: Office of Juvenile Justice and Delinquency Prevention.

Jennings, Wesley G., Khey, David N., Maskaly, Jon, and Donner, Christopher M. 2011. "Evaluating the Relationship between Law Enforcement and School Security Measures and Violent Crime in Schools." *Journal of Police Crisis Negotiations* 11(2), 109–124. DOI: 10.1080/15332586.2011.581511.

Klein, Malcolm W. and Maxson, Cheryl L. 2006. *Street Gang Patterns and Policies.* Oxford: Oxford University Press.

Matsuda, Kristy N., Melde, Chris, Taylor, Terrance J., Freng, Adrienne, and Esbensen, Finn-Aage. 2013. "Gang Membership and Adherence to the 'Code of the Street." *Justice Quarterly* 30(3), 440–468. DOI: 10.1080/07418825.2012.684432.

National Youth Gang Center. 2015. "National Youth Gang Survey Analysis." https://www.nationalgangcenter.gov/Survey-Analysis/Prevalence-of-Gang-Problems (accessed February 5, 2015).

O'Brien, Kate, Daffern, Michael, Chu, Chi Meng, and Thomas, Stuart D.M. 2013. "Youth Gang Affiliation, Violence, and Criminal Activities: A Review of Motivational, Risk, and Protective Factors." *Aggression and Violent Behavior* 18(4), 417–425. DOI: 10.1016/j.avb.2013.05.001.

Office of Juvenile Justice and Delinquency Prevention (OJJDP). 2009. "OJJDP Comprehensive Gang Model: A Guide to Assessing Your Community's Youth Gang Problem." https://www.nationalgangcenter.gov/Comprehensive-Gang-Model/Assessment-Guide (accessed June 8, 2016).

Papachristos, Andrew V., Anthony A. Braga, Eric Piza, and Leigh S. Grossman. 2015. "The Company You Keep? The Spillover Effects of Gang Membership on Individual Gunshot Victimization in a Co-offending Network." *Criminology*, 43(4): 624–649. DOI:10.1111/1745-9125.12091.

People vs. Dejuan Hines, Los Angeles County Superior Court No. TA078425. (2008).

Peterson, Dana and Esbensen, Finn-Aage. 2004. "The Outlook is G.R.E.A.T. What Educators Say about School-Based Prevention and the Gang Resistance Education and Training (G.R.E.A.T.) Program." *Evaluation Review* 28(3), 218–245. DOI: 10.1177/0193841X03262598.

Peterson, Dana, Taylor, Terrance J., and Esbensen, Finn-Aage. 2004. "Gang Membership and Violent Victimization." *Justice Quarterly* 21(4), 793–815. DOI: 10.1080/07418820400095991.

Pinnow, Rachel J. 2013. "An Ecology of Fear: Examining the Contradictory Surveillance Terrain Navigated by Mexican Youth in a U.S. Middle School." *Anthropology & Education Quarterly* 44(3), 253–268. DOI: 10.1111/aeq.12033.

Pyrooz, David C. 2014. "From Colors and Guns to Caps and Gowns? The Effects of Gang Membership on Educational Attainment." *Journal of Research in Crime and Delinquency* 51(1), 56–87. DOI: 10.1177/0022427818348316.

Pyrooz, David C., Moule Jr., Richard K., and Decker, Scott H. 2014. "The Contribution of Gang Membership to the Victim–Offender Overlap." *Journal of Research in Crime and Delinquency* 51(3), 315–348. DOI: 10.1177/0022427813516128.

Rios, Victor M. 2010. "Navigating the Thin Line between Education and Incarceration: An Action Research Case Study on Gang-Associated Latino Youth." *Journal of Education for Students Placed at Risk* 15(1–2), 200–212. DOI: 10.1080/10824661003635283.

Rios, Victor M. and Galicia, Mario G. 2013. "Smoking Guns or Smoke & Mirrors?: Schools and the Policing of Latino Boys." *Association of Mexican American Educators Journal* 7(3), 54–66.

Schreck, Christopher J., Miller, J. Mitchell, and Gibson, Chris L. 2003. "Trouble in the School Yard: A Study of the Risk Factors of Victimization at School." *Crime & Delinquency* 49(3), 460–484. DOI: 10.1177/0011128703049003006.

Swahn, Monica H., Bossarte, Robert M., West, Bethany, and Topalli, Volkan. 2010. "Alcohol and Drug Use among Gang Members: Experiences of Adolescents Who Attend School." *Journal of School Health* 80(7), 353–360. DOI: 10.1111/j.1746-1561.2010.00513.x.

Thompkins, Douglas E. 2000. "School Violence Gangs and a Culture of Fear." *The Annals of the American Academy of Political and Social Science* 567(1), 54–71. DOI: 10.1177/000271620056700105.

Thornberry, Terrence P, Krohn, Marvin D., Lizotte, Alan J., and Smith, Carolyn A. 2003. *Gangs and Delinquency in Developmental Perspective.* New York: Cambridge University Press.

Vogel, Steve. 2006. "Teenager Gets 4 1/2 –Year Term in Summer School Stabbings." *The Washington Post*, May 25, B5.

Zhang, Anlan, Musu-Gillette, Lauren, and Oudekerk, Barbara A. 2016. *Indicators of School Crime and Safety: 2015* (NCES 2016-079/NCJ 249758). Washington, DC: National Center for Education Statistics, US Department of Education and Bureau of Justice Statistics, Office of Justice Programs, US Department of Justice.

8

The Distinguishing Features, Trends, and Challenges of Group and Gang Violence in Education

Michael E. Ezell

Introduction

In analyzing over one hundred years of gang research, Pyrooz and Mitchell (2015, 44) argued that 1993 was the year gang literature shifted from being "little gang research" to "big gang research," and marked the approximate genesis of the exponential growth in publications on gangs and gang behavior we still experience 20 years later. This rapid expansion was fueled in large part by a number of individual-level, longitudinal surveys allowing respondents to self-nominate their gang membership during each wave of the survey.

Indeed, the research accumulated during the last two decades has provided valuable evidence on a number of key questions related to gang membership, including the prevalence and duration of gang membership, the risk factors associated with it, the effects of it on both criminal offending and victimization, and the consequences of it (Krohn and Thornberry 2008; Pyrooz and Mitchell 2015). However, one of the research areas concerning the impact of gangs and gang membership that has not benefited equally during this expansion in research concerns the specific, direct contribution that gangs and gang members make to both criminal events occurring in schools, including violent crimes, and the general environments of schools.

In this chapter, I first discuss two broad challenges relevant to examining the relationship between gangs and school crime/violence: the problem of defining both gangs and gang crime; and determining the causal relationship between gangs and school crime/violence. Following that, the trends in the presence of gangs are discussed, followed by a brief review of studies examining the relationship between gangs and school crime/violence. The final section of the chapter discusses several important distinguishing features of both gangs and gang membership. It should be noted that the unqualified use of the term "gang" will be used herein to denote groups known as "street gangs," which are the gangs most relevant to the school environment because they are the "gangs" populated with the same individuals found in the school setting – adolescent youths.

The Wiley Handbook on Violence in Education: Forms, Factors, and Preventions, First Edition.
Edited by Harvey Shapiro.

Particular Challenges

The Problem of Defining Gangs

The problem of defining gangs is a paradox – street gangs are seen by nearly everyone as being qualitatively different from all other youth social groups, yet there is no agreed-upon definition of "gang" able to validly identify street gangs themselves and to distinguish them from other social groups. Simply stated, "There is little, if any, consensus as to what constitutes a gang and who is a gang member, let alone what gangs do, either inside or outside the law" (Esbensen et al. 2001, 106). Several recent excellent discussions of this issue are available in Curry (2015), Curry, Decker, and Pyrooz (2014), Decker et al. (2014), Howell and Griffiths (2016), and Klein and Maxson (2006).

In fact, this widespread disagreement over how to define gangs includes differences both between and within the following key groups: gang researchers, law enforcement agencies, and legislatures. This definitional ambiguity and disagreement has significant consequences, including determining the true size and nature of the gang problem, measuring trends in gang behavior across time, properly allocating resources, and systematically comparing research findings on "gangs," along with concerns over fairly punishing individuals for gang activity (Esbensen et al. 2001; Huff and Barrows 2015; Klein and Maxson 2006; Maxson and Matsuda 2011).

The definitional debate has often centered on the specific characteristics necessary to separate out gangs from other qualitatively distinct social groups, especially separating them from adolescent delinquent peer groups and adult criminal groups such as organized crime. Two of the key complications to this "separation" goal are (i) variations in gang characteristics across time and place, and (ii) whether or not to include "criminal activity" in the definition.

On the first problem, given that gangs have been argued to be an "inherently amorphous phenomena" (Katz and Jackson-Jacobs 2004, 98), the necessary definitional characteristics are open to disagreement. However, the variety of definitions often share a number of characteristics. After distilling the key characteristics in 23 different definitions of gangs, Howell and Griffiths (2016, 56–59) noted that criminal activity was the most commonly appearing characteristic (in 18 definitions), along with "organized" (in 14 definitions), "territory/turf" (13), "meetings/continuous" (11), "name/identity" (10), "colors/dress/symbols" (9), and "leadership" (6).

Criminal activity is seen by some as the key defining characteristic separating street gangs from other (non-criminal) social groups, but others see the inclusion of criminal activity as problematic because it yields a tautological relationship between gangs and criminal behavior (Klein and Maxson 2006). Further, defining a gang simply on the basis of "criminal activity committed by a group of three or more people" would not separate street gangs from many adolescent delinquent peer groups nor from many adult criminal groups. In addition, during the last 30 years, the diffusion of gang culture into general adolescent youth culture via music, movies, and television has served to further muddy the waters over differentiating real street gangs from groups that mimic or simply look like possible street gangs (Howell and Griffiths 2016).

The one more recent definition of street gangs enjoying a degree of widespread consensus is the "Eurogang" definition, which defines a street gang as "any durable, street-oriented youth group whose involvement in illegal activity is part of its group identity," and is argued to be a definition containing "the minimal necessary elements to recognize a street gang" (Klein and Maxson 2006, 4). More recently, however, the problem of defining gangs has been largely circumvented through the widespread use of the "self-nomination" method, transferring the problem of defining a gang/gang member to the survey respondents themselves (Decker et al. 2014, 579). Sometimes this is done without supplying any definition at all and merely asking variants of two questions: "Have you ever been in a gang?" and "Are you currently in a gang?" (Decker et al. 2014, 579). Additional questions may follow inquiring about certain other features, thereby allowing the subsequent application of a more "restrictive" definition of gang membership (see, for example, Esbensen et al. 2001). The self-nominating method of measuring gang membership is of course dependent upon each respondent's understanding of what a gang is, which is potentially influenced by respondents both applying stereotypes/myths of "gangs" and being willing to self-report membership in an oft-stigmatized group (Katz and Jackson-Jacobs 2004; Matsuda, Esbensen, and Carson 2012).

While several empirical studies provide evidence supporting the self-nomination method (e.g., Decker et al. 2014; Esbensen et al. 2001; Thornberry et al. 2003), recent research also demonstrates how prevalence estimates of gang membership are sensitive to the specific definition employed. Using a single, representative sample of youth respondents, Matusda, Esbensen, and Carson (2012, 19) compared the results generated from three different definitions of self-reported gang membership/involvement ("Are you currently a gang member," "Do you consider your group of friends to be a gang," and questions operationalizing the "Eurogang" definition). Among the group of respondents defined as a gang member by one or more of the definitions, an astounding 67% of the "gang members" were identified as a gang member by only one of the definitions, 33% of the "gang members" were identified as gang members by two or more of the definitions, but only 9% of the original "gang member" group was defined as a gang member according to all three definitions.

A final issue pertaining to defining gang members concerns the growing evidence supporting the existence of two different, yet potentially overlapping, gang problems (Curry 2015). One of these gang problems concerns the adolescent gang problem described in the survey results of self-reported gang members, while the other gang problem concerns the adult gang problem described by law enforcement data. More specifically, compared to law enforcement data, self-reported survey data indicate higher rates of gang membership among Caucasians, females, younger adolescents, and adolescents from both two-parent and non-poor households (Curry, Decker, and Pyrooz 2014; Pyrooz and Sweeten 2015). Pyrooz's (2014) study of the longitudinal patterns of gang membership using the 1997 cohort of National Longitudinal Survey of Youth (NLSY97) sheds considerable light on this issue. After examining distinct trajectories of gang membership across age, Pyrooz concludes that the strong age-grading patterns of gang membership helps in part to create the dual realties of the gang problem. More specifically, as the NLSY97 respondents became older, the characteristics of the active adult gang members become more similar to law enforcement data. Further, the gang problem described by law enforcement is not only more criminally involved, but is also argued to be more involved in acts of violence (Pyrooz and Sweeten 2015). These findings that the characteristics and nature of the gang problem may be conditioned by the "dual realities" of the gang problem require consideration when considering the specific gang problem in the adolescent school environment.

The Problem of Defining Gang Crime

Beyond the challenge of defining gangs is the challenge of defining gang crime – distinguishing the crimes committed for the gang from those committed by a gang member engaging in "individualistic" crime for any variety of idiosyncratic reasons. In fact, when gang crime is counted, it is generally counted using one of two definitions: "gang related" or "gang motivated" (Greene and Pranis 2007; Huff and Barrows 2015). The key to differentiating between those two crime types involves understanding the "motivation" or "intent" for committing the crime (Klein 2016), and the distinction between them is central to understanding the impact of the gang itself. Gang-motivated crime, a narrower definition, is crime "committed at the direction of, for the benefit of, or in association with a street gang" (Bureau of Justice Assistance 1997, 30). Gang-related crime, on the other hand, is a broader definition of gang crime – as "any crime in which a gang member is the suspect, offender, or victim, regardless of motivation or circumstances" (Bureau of Justice Assistance 1997, 30). Thus, gang-related crime is defined merely on the basis of the involvement of a gang member, whereas gang-motivated crime specifically serves either a function of the gang or benefits the gang itself (Greene and Pranis 2007). It is important to note that unless clearly defined, the term "gang-related crime" can potentially be misinterpreted as meaning "gang-motivated crime."

Importantly, in most empirical studies the crime committed by gang members is defined using the gang-related crime definition. Surveys, for example, overwhelmingly tend to measure types of crimes but not the underlying intent or motivation behind those crimes. Law enforcement agencies, on the other hand, generally only record whether a crime event involves a gang member for a very limited number of crimes, with gang-motivated crimes rarely measured for crimes other than homicide (Egley, Howell, and Harris 2014; Klein and Maxson 2006; Maxson 1999). Studies examining the application of these two definitions of homicide are illustrative: across various studies, only about 50–60% of gang-related homicides can be classified as gang-motivated homicides (Maxson 1999), and thus the size of the gang crime problem could vary substantially depending on the definition employed (Klein 1995; Shelden, Tracy, and Brown 2013).

The volume of gang crime therefore depends on the definition of gang crime applied. In the school setting, not only will using the "gang-related" definition yield significantly higher "gang crime" counts, but that definition is only associational (Huff and Barrows 2015). Thus, a study finding that gang members commit more crimes than non-gang members is not necessarily evidence of a causal gang effect; as described below, it could be spuriously due, in part or in whole, to the specific types of people more likely to join gangs (i.e., those with higher criminal propensity) and/or due to the specific types of places where gangs are more likely to exist (i.e., socially disadvantaged areas with higher crime rates). The gang-related definition of gang crime is certainly easier to measure, but it is more ambiguous with respect to whether the crime is actually due to the gang itself. The measurement of criminal behavior by gang members in the school setting thus needs greater attention paid to the issue of gang-related versus gang-motivated (Arciaga, Sakamoto, and Jones 2010).

The Problem of Determining Causality

Although gangs and gang membership are associated with a wide variety of negative outcomes, what is not clear "is the causal role of gang membership in the genesis of these risky behaviors and outcomes" (Decker, Melde, and Pyrooz 2013, 372). For example, the central question for gang membership is, "what would each person's behavioral outcome been had they not participated in a gang?," but the "readily observable counterfactual" needed to make that comparison is missing (Decker, Melde, and Pyrooz 2013, 376). Thus, because gangs and gang membership are not "treatments" (or "exposures") subject to random assignment in an experimental design, researchers are left with little choice other than to use observational data that is causally elusive. Indeed, determining the causal effect of either gangs and/or gang membership is arguably the key problem not only for gangs in schools, but in the whole gang literature.

Not unlike other areas of criminology where research is conducted using observational data out of necessity, studies on gang behavior are often critically evaluated with respect to meeting several criteria for causality, with two of the criteria proving problematic: (i) establishing causal order, and (ii) eliminating the possible influence of rival/confounding/selection-based causes of the observed association.

With respect to causal ordering, the cause (gang/gang behavior) needs to precede the effect in time. The widespread use of cross-sectional data on the topic of gangs creates uncertainty as to whether an observed outcome existed before the period of gang activity (Katz and Jackson-Jacobs 2004; Klein and Maxson 2006; Krohn and Thornberry 2008). For example, does prior criminal victimization lead to gang membership, does gang membership lead to criminal victimization, or is there a reciprocal relationship? Because gangs, gang membership, and crime all unfold across time, even the notorious link between gangs and crime is argued to be causally ambiguous. Katz and Jackson-Jacobs (2004) critically noted much uncertainty surrounding the relationship between gang activity and crime because crime may cause gang activity as much as gang activity causes crime.

With respect to eliminating rival/confounding causes of observed relationships, it is imperative to recognize that neighborhoods with gangs are different from neighborhoods without gangs on a number of other characteristics besides gangs; similarly, gang members are different from non-gang members on a variety of other characteristics besides gang membership. Indeed, research has shown that gangs and gang membership are more likely to occur in "riskier" people and places, and thus crime would be more likely to occur in those people and places even in the absence of any effect of gang activity (e.g., see Curry, Decker, and Pyrooz 2014; Decker, Melde, and Pyrooz 2013; Esbensen et al. 2010; Klein and Maxson 2006). The argument that certain people may "self-select" into gang activity highlights the need for researchers to always consider, and control for, rival explanations of observed associations. Doing so, however, is difficult because of both the research designs (e.g., lacking either non-gang places or people and/or longitudinal data) and measurement deficiencies in available data (e.g., lacking specific measures for rival arguments). The importance of this is clear, however. A recent meta-analysis of 1,649 effect size estimates of the association of gang membership and crime (Pyrooz et al. 2016, 382) found that while only about half of all the estimates included any control variables, the estimates were 33% larger in the absence of any control variables; and further, the estimates were significantly weaker "when modeled prospectively rather than contemporaneously."

Researchers have also recently begun discussing the possible methodological problems arising as a result of the dynamically changing, and relatively short, typical patterns of gang membership. Gang membership is often only a year or less in duration, and since the dynamic patterns of gang membership do not necessarily align with the specific time periods measured in surveys, those survey data can be "inherently misaligned" and render a "confounding of gang and nongang time" (Decker, Melde, and Pyrooz 2013, 378–379), as well as causing additional problems for maintaining the proper temporal ordering of causes and effects (Gibson et al. 2012).

All of the methodological issues described above are critically important for examining the relationship between gang activity and school violence. For example, causal ordering is a problem when considering the specific nature and direction of the relationship between gangs and fear in schools (see Chapter 10, this volume; also see Gottfredson 2013; Thomkins 2000; Yiu and Gottfredson 2014). In terms of rival hypotheses, schools without gang activity are likely to be different from schools with gang activity on a number of other rival/confounding factors besides gang activity itself (e.g., see Gottfredson 2013; Yiu and Gottfredson 2014). Laub and Lauritsen's (1998, 145) literature review on the relationship between school violence and neighborhood characteristics argued that neighborhood characteristics are the "strongest predictors of school violence rates," but noted that rates of school violence are also likely to be "influenced by school policies regarding discipline, security, and dropping out." The qualitative research of both Mateu-Gilbert and Lune (2003) and Brunson and Miller (2009) highlights the dynamic, reciprocal relationship between neighborhood and school conflicts, with conflicts in one "spilling over" into the other location. Indeed, the relationship between gang activity and school violence is likely to be a complicated, interdependent system of relationships between community characteristics (including crime rates), school characteristics (including school climate), and individual characteristics of gang members themselves. Although not specifically on the topic of school violence, the words of Curry (2015, 12) resonate: "The causal question, whether we are studying the individual behaviors of gang members, the collective behavior of gangs, or the criminal rates of gang neighborhoods, is not going to be possible to address without an understanding of the dimension of time."

Trends in Gang Prevalence

As noted above, one consequence of the lack of a stable, universal definition of a gang is that it complicates understanding time trends in the prevalence of gangs and gang membership. Indeed, prior to 1996, the problem of measuring the presence of gangs was conducted by a series of different researchers at different time points and places (Curry, Decker, and Pyrooz 2014). However, gang researchers generally agree that, beginning largely in the 1980s, there was an increasing presence of gangs over time in the United States, with large cities (populations over 100,000) being the first to experience the increase in gangs, and that the spread of gangs continued into the 1990s (Howell and Griffiths 2016; Klein and Maxson 2006). Despite general agreement on the proliferation of gang problems from the 1980s into the mid-1990s, scholars do not agree on its precise causes; however, the diffusion of gang culture is generally argued to be one important cause (Howell and Griffiths 2016).

Since 1996, determining the prevalence of gang problems has been largely under-taken and documented by the National Gang Center's National Youth Gang Survey (NYGS), a "nationally representative sample of law enforcement agencies" reporting on gang problems within their jurisdictions (Howell and Griffith 2016, 147). However, besides using a definition of gangs that has changed across time (see Sanders 2017), the NYGS has also been criticized for using a broad definition allowing each jurisdiction to apply its own definition of a "street gang," possibly allowing for both wide differences between jurisdictions and the inclusion of groups that might not truly be street gangs; that said, the NYGS is still noted by its critics to be "the best we have" (Klein and Maxson 2006, 43).

Based on the NYGS results since 1996, Howell and Griffiths (2016) note several key trends. First, the percentage of jurisdictions reporting gang problems peaked in the very first year of the survey (1996) at approximately 40%. Second, the percentage of jurisdictions with gang problems then declined until around 2001 (at 23.9%) when the percentage began rising again until the mid-2000s, before leveling off (at around 33–34%) for the rest of the decade. According to the 2012 survey, the percentage of jurisdictions with gang problems were reported to be roughly 30% (Egley, Howell, and Harris 2014). Several other key points in the trends of the NYGS data noted by Howell and Griffiths (2016, 151) are that the gang proliferation process was one that displayed a "cascading" nature from larger cities to smaller cities and then to rural counties, that the "consistency" of the gang problem is a function of city size (smaller cities and areas tend to have a more variable gang presence), and that gang experiences vary across place. A final trend noted is that the overall nature of the gang problem varies as a function of city size, with smaller cities having fewer gangs and gang members, less gang violence, and gangs that are more transient, all of which are important points to remember when considering the presence of gangs in schools.

Gang Presence in Schools

Determining the extent and nature of gang presence in schools is difficult for a variety of reasons, including the "problem of defining gangs" and because school officials may be reluctant to admit the presence of gangs in their schools (Gottfredson 2013; Holmes, Tewksbury, and Higgins 2011; Naber et al. 2006; Yiu and Gottfredson 2014). The research of Naber et al. (2006, 63) found that even within the same schools, the answer to whether or not gangs are present in schools "depends not only on 'whom' you ask but also on 'how' the question is asked." The school principal and law enforcement agency responsible for the same school did not always agree on whether there was a gang presence in the school, and the presence of gangs dropped substantially (from about 7% of schools to just 2%) if both parties were required to agree.

The presence of gangs in schools has been most commonly measured through the School Crime Supplement (SCS) to the National Crime Victimization Survey (NCVS) (Naber et al. 2006). The SCS is a biennial set of supplemental questions concerning issues related to crime and safety at schools asked to the NCVS respondents between the ages of 12 and 18 who were enrolled in school during the survey time (Zhang, Musu-Gillette, and Oudekerk 2016). Some of the SCS survey questions ask about the presence of street gangs "at school"; however, the NCVS design itself has changed across time, as have the specific SCS gang presence question(s) and the definition of the term

Table 8.1 Percentage of SCS respondents reporting gang presence at school during the school year.

	1989	1995	2001	2003	2005	2007	2009	2011	2013
Gang presence %	15.3	28.5	20.1	20.9	24.2	23.2	20.4	17.5	12.4

Source: 1989 (Chandler et al. 1998) and 1995–2013 (Zhang, Musu-Gillette, and Oudekerk 2016)

"at school," which taken together complicate interpreting changes across time (see Beres and Griffith 2004; Howell and Lynch 2000).

Nonetheless, Table 8.1 contains the estimates of the presence of gangs at school for each of the SCS survey years since the first time it was measured (1989). Beginning at 15.3% in 1989, there was a sharp increase to 28.5% in 1995, followed by a decline to 20.1% in 2001. Another small increase to 23–24% in 2005 and 2007 was followed by a strong decline to 12.4% in 2013, its lowest recorded level according to the most recently available data.

It is also important to note that the typical SCS question concerning gangs ("Are there any street gangs at your school?") involves student respondents nominating other students, rather than themselves, as gang members; thus, similar to the self-nomination method, the entire problem of defining a street gang is transferred to the respondent. According to Howell and Lynch (2000), the three most common characteristics students use to identify gangs are (i) the group has a name, (ii) the group members spend time with each other, and (iii) the presence of group-identifying items or clothing. It is worth pointing out that these three characteristics would not necessarily distinguish a street gang from other non-gang groups at school. As argued by Naber et al. (2006), it is imperative to remember that the "problem of defining gangs" is a major obstacle to understanding how gang activity impacts the school environment.

Studies Examining Gangs and School Crime

Few empirical studies have specifically examined the link between gangs and school crime; this lack of research is especially important when considering that gangs and gang members are often logically assumed to be associated with increased levels of criminal activity, especially acts of violence, occurring at school (Parks 1995; Thompkins 2000). Such logical expectations, however, warrant further empirical examination and validation, with a special need for longitudinal studies designed to address some of the limitations of the few existing studies on this topic. Indeed, the understanding of the association of gangs and school violence has not generally progressed much beyond the conclusion of Parks' (1995) review of this issue about 20 years ago, "there is little empirical support for a causal relationship between school violence and youth gang-related behaviors," and we "need to re-evaluate the true impact of this particular behavior on our schools and the violence issue generally" (Parks 1995, 42) – conclusions arguably still pertinent today.

Parks (1995) provides an excellent, extensive review of this topic, so I concentrate here on studies not included in her review and focus specifically on the main limitations of this literature: it is generally dated (e.g., from the 1980s), based on small and/or geographically limited samples with limited external validity (e.g., St. Louis and Chicago), and uses research designs with limited internal validity (more ethnographic than quantitative, lacking good comparison groups, indirect examinations, and/or lacking multivariate analyses).

For example, two key studies using ethnographic data from the 1980s on either just a few schools in Chicago or across a number of schools in St. Louis came to opposite conclusions. In the two Chicago schools studied, gangs "wielded significant influence in the public school system, establishing zones of control within individual schools," controlled drug sales in the schools, and were argued to be a main reason other students dropped out (Hutchinson and Kyle 1993, 131); the study in St. Louis concluded that "these schools are not controlled by omnipotent gangs who hold the students and adult populations in terror" (Decker and Van Winkle 1996, 204). Forber-Pratt, Aragon, and Espelage's (2013, 16) qualitative study of the effect of gang presence on victimization and bullying in one middle school concluded that the "hierarchy of the gang system creates fear not just from students walking to and from school, but also from the teachers and administrators who do not want to cross paths with the gang leaders for fear of retaliation," and argued that bullying becomes more violent when mixed with gang presence. However, given that it was a case study of a single school specifically selected because it was an outlier with respect to victimization, those findings may be due solely to that specific school and/or community setting.

Three other often cited studies examining the link between gang presence and crime in schools use the SCS data to examine the association between gang presence in schools and victimization rates (Chandler et al. 1998; Howell and Lynch 2000; Ralph et al. 1995). These studies found a strong association between gangs and victimization rates: victimization rates were significantly higher for students who reported the presence of gangs in their schools. However, these studies were largely bivariate examinations that "indirectly" examined the link between gangs and victimization at school. Although the victimization rates were higher at schools with a gang presence, the data did not indicate who (gang or non-gang youth) in fact was committing the crime nor their underlying motivations (i.e., gang-related vs. gang-motivated). Recalling that riskier people and places/schools are more likely to be gang-involved, these results are more suggestive of a possible relationship than strong evidence of a causal effect. In addition to noting the potential complex causal ordering between fear, gangs, school climate, and school crime, Howell and Lynch (2000, 7) also note that, "Both gangs and criminal victimization in school are products of disorder in schools ... and a host of other factors in the school, family, community, peer group, and individual domains ... this could account for the positive relationship." Indeed, studies using the SCS data have even been criticized as possibly "exaggerating" the gang problem in schools and failing to provide strong evidence supporting the claim that gangs were responsible for reduced safety in schools (Beres and Griffith 2004).

Overall, the evidence is mixed and causally vague. For example, when examining the criminal behavior patterns of comparable gang and non-gang at-risk youth in Cleveland, Huff (1998) found that while gang members were more criminally active and significantly more likely to bring guns and knives to school, there were no significant differences between the two groups in terms of assaults on teachers, assaults on students, or on drug sales on school grounds. Among public school principals in 2009–2010, 16.4% reported any occurrence of gang activities at their school, but only

5.2% reported the occurrence of any "gang-related" crime (Neiman 2011). In this volume (Chapter 13), Addington and Tanner-Smith found that gang-related crime occurring at schools was relatively low compared to the overall volume of crime. Conversely, the National Gang Intelligence Center (2013, 38) contends that gangs "maintain a significant presence in educational facilities at every level" and that gangs "pose a moderate or serious threat" in many public school systems. Similarly, Joseph's (2008) study of two northeastern secondary schools found that gang members were more likely to be involved in acts of violence at school. The current body of methodologically limited research examining gangs and school crime is not only sparse but also mixed in conclusions (see also Clark, Pyrooz, and Randa, Chapter 10 in this volume). Additional rigorous research is needed for more conclusive answers.

Distinguishing Features of Gangs and Gang Membership

Risk Factors of Gang Membership and Reasons for Joining

One key feature of the "big gang research" era has been to examine the risk factors associated with gang membership. A number of key findings reviewed here have generally been consistently noted across detailed reviews of this research found in Esbensen et al. (2010), Howell (2010), Howell and Egley (2005), Howell and Griffiths (2016), Klein and Maxson (2006), and Krohn and Thornberry (2008). First, this body of research has largely focused on five risk factor (or developmental) domains, namely characteristics related to the individual, family, school, peer groups, and community context (Howell and Egley 2005); however, there is variability across studies with respect to which specific domains are examined, the specific measures included for any given domain (e.g., attachment to school vs. achievement in school), whether temporal ordering of the variables can be determined, and the varying prevalence of risk factors, all of which make comparisons across studies difficult (see Howell and Griffiths 2016; Klein and Maxson 2006). Second, the research has tended to find that while the risk of joining a gang involves all five of the domain areas, certain domains and certain measures within a given domain seem to be more important (Krohn and Thornberry 2008). For example, whereas risk factors within the school and family domains have been found to predict gang membership, risk factors within the individual and peer group domains have been found to be more consistently and strongly related to the risk of joining a gang, while within the peer group domain, associating with delinquent peers has routinely emerged as one of the most highly predictive risk factors (Howell and Griffiths 2016; Klein and Maxson 2006; Krohn and Thornberry 2008). Third, while many significant predictors have been reported in prior research, the independent impact of most risk factors is small (see Krohn and Thornberry 2008).

Yet, fourth and perhaps most importantly, this body of research has consistently found that gang membership is more strongly associated with the accumulation of multiple risk factors than it is with any specific risk factor, and is even more strongly related to the accumulation of risk factors across multiple life domains (Howell and Griffiths 2016; Klein and Maxson 2006; Krohn and Thornberry 2008). Fifth, while gang membership is known to be more likely among those with more risk factors in their backgrounds, gang membership can still not be predicted accurately at the individual level (Klein and Maxson 2006). Thus, while no one single risk factor accurately predicts gang membership, the accumulation of risk is simply the best known predictor to date (Decker, Melde, and Pyrooz 2013). Sixth, the important role of protective factors, which potentially offset the impact of known risk factors, is not as commonly studied and may also be important for understanding why prediction at the individual level is not accurate (Howell and Egley 2005; Howell and Griffiths 2016; Thornberry et al. 2003). Thus, there is an important need for continued research on this important topic, especially replicable research designs that employ longitudinal data with similar measures and multivariate analysis (Howell and Griffiths 2016; Klein and Maxson 2006; Krohn and Thornberry 2008).

Finally, studies report that the same risk factors predicting gang membership often also predict criminal offending, meaning gang members can look similar to other criminally involved individuals who do not report gang membership (Howell 2010; Howell and Griffiths 2016). A study by Esbensen et al. (2010) found a large number of risk factors predicted both gang membership and violent offending, but none uniquely predicted gang membership. Furthermore, becoming a gang member required more risk factors compared to becoming a violent offender, meaning that "youths who are gang members experience the most risk" (175). Coupling that finding with the argument that the underlying risk process generating gang membership is more likely to occur in structurally disadvantaged neighborhoods that would be more likely to have troubled schools (e.g., Howell 2010; Howell and Griffiths 2016; Thornberry et al. 2003) reinforces the need to always critically examine studies investigating the association between gangs or gang membership and criminal/negative outcomes for the presence of both control variables and multivariate analyses.

While the studies above are based on quantitative analyses of survey data, other qualitative studies have examined the reasons gang members give for why they joined their gangs. Although there is no one single reason that overwhelmingly dominates the reasons provided, they do tend to consistently highlight the role of the perceived need for protection, the role of family and friends, and the desire for status, identity, fun/excitement, and/or a surrogate family (Curry, Decker, and Pyrooz 2014; Howell and Griffiths 2016). Indeed, studies have also found that these reasons can often combine and intersect in powerful ways that result in the decision to join a gang being a complex one as youth are both "pushed" and "pulled" into joining a gang, and that gang membership can be perceived as positive or beneficial to gang members in terms of protection, fun/excitement, and status/identity (see Estrada et al., Chapter 9 in this volume; see also Decker and Van Winkle 1996; Thornberry et al. 2003; Ward 2013). A key point often made in studies on this issue is that the vast majority of youth voluntarily "chose" to join the gang rather than the myth/stereotype that youth are either pressured into or forced to join the gang (Howell and Griffiths 2016).

The Life Course of Gang Membership: Prevalence, Duration, and Termination

The collection of longitudinal surveys of youth has been key for investigating the "life course" of gang membership, including the prevalence, duration, and termination of gang membership (Krohn and Thornberry 2008). Klein and Maxson's (2006) extensive review of a large number of studies examining the prevalence of gang membership provides several important conclusions. First, the prevalence of gang membership varies across a number of key dimensions, including the population the sample is selected from (e.g., national vs. school vs. high-risk samples), the definition of "gang" employed, whether one is asking if the youth is "currently" a gang member versus "ever" a gang member, and across race and gender (Klein and Maxson 2006).

Second, samples that are "high risk" have higher estimates of gang membership than nationally representative samples. Indeed, perhaps the best overall ranges of "ever" being a gang member are somewhere between 5–10% in nationally representative samples and 15–30% in high-risk samples. For example, Pyrooz's (2014) analysis of six waves of the National Longitudinal Survey of Youth estimated the prevalence of gang membership at 8%, while high-risk samples in Seattle and Rochester have estimated the prevalence of gang membership at about 15% and 31%, respectively (Hill et al. 1999; Thornberry et al. 2003). More generally, Klein (2016) posits that in most US cities, only 1–2% of all youth would likely be current gang members at any point in time. A recent analysis of the NLSY97 data by Pyrooz and Sweeten (2015) lends empirical support to this assertion. According to their analyses, 2.0% of youth between the ages of 5 and 17 in the United States were gang members in 2010. A final key point of Klein and Maxson's review (2006) was that most youth, including 70% or more of those living in high-risk areas, never report any gang membership.

The finding that the estimates of gang membership are consistently higher for "ever" being a gang member compared to "currently" being a gang member helps to illustrate a key, general pattern of gang membership: most youth cycle into and out of active gang membership in a relatively short period of time. Stated differently, the average duration of gang membership is quite short. Most individuals report gang membership only during adolescence, with an average duration of two years or less for most, while only a few youth report gang membership lasting four or more years (Curry, Decker, and Pyrooz 2014; Pyrooz 2014; Pyrooz, Sweeten, and Piquero 2013; Thornberry et al. 2003). In fact, a number of studies report finding somewhere between 50% and 70% of youth gang members are active for only one year or less (e.g., see Appendix A of Pyrooz, Sweeten, and Piquero 2013), findings that directly refute a prominent myth about gang membership being a lifelong commitment (Howell and Griffiths 2016). Pyrooz and Sweeten's recent analyses of the NLSY97 (2015) lend further support to many of these patterns, most notably the strong age-grading of the prevalence of gang membership that peaks during early adolescence and the extremely high turnover rate of youth gang membership.

Recognizing that most gang members tend to leave the gang shortly after joining has generated increased interest in the process of leaving gangs. Much of this research focuses on the method through which gang members leave the gang (i.e., "how"), their motives for leaving the gang (i.e., "why"), the consequences of leaving, and the factors that may complicate the process of leaving (Pyrooz and Decker 2011). Carson and Vecchio's (2015) comprehensive review of this topic highlights that most ex-gang members simply walk or drift away without any violence toward themselves or others (2015, 264), that the exit process is generally more gradual than abrupt (264) and happens without consequence (265), that it results from a variety of interwoven "pushes" and "pulls" in terms of why they left the gang (261), that it varies based on the degree to which individuals are "embedded" within the gang and have "enduring ties" to the gang (267–268), and also, unfortunately, that attending school may in fact help facilitate continued ties to the gang (268).

Different Types of Gang Members

The significant variability between gang members with respect to their relative involvement in gang activities and commitment to the gang is long-standing in gang research (Decker et al. 2014). This known heterogeneity in gang involvement has been typically handled by classifying members using one of two dichotomies: core/fringe or stable/transient (Pyrooz, Sweeten, and Piquero 2013, 243). Using these classifications, the majority of gang members qualify as transient/fringe or peripheral, terms highlighting the fact that most gang members have short durations of active gang membership (less than 1 year) and are "less involved with antisocial peers, unstructured activities, and offending and victimization" (Carson and Vecchio 2015, 267). In contrast, the much less prevalent core/stable gang members have longer periods of active gang membership and are much more involved in gang associations and activities.

More recently, Pyrooz, Sweeten, and Piquero (2013, 243) developed the concept of "gang embeddedness" as a way of differentiating between gang members in terms of the "varying degrees of involvement, identification, and status among gang members – the adhesion of the gang member to the gang." Their study created a measure of gang embeddedness in terms of gang contacts, gang positioning, gang importance, gang friends, and gang assaults, and they found considerable heterogeneity among gang members on this measure. Other recent work applying this concept has also found considerable differences in gang embeddedness between "never," "current," and "former" gang members (Decker et al. 2014). Sweeten, Pyrooz, and Piquero's study on gang embeddedness found it to be important in terms of the duration of gang membership and contemporaneous criminal offending levels, noting that "embeddedness in gangs matters as much if not more than gang membership itself" (2013, 490). When examining the effect that gangs may have on the school climate, it is thus important to remember the considerable individual differences in gang embeddedness and that most gang members are more likely to be more fringe/peripheral rather than the more core gang members.

Gang Membership and Criminal Behavior

As one of the primary defining characteristics of a street gang (Klein and Maxson 2006), there is perhaps no better known feature of gang life than its association with criminal behavior; for even if gang members only spend a small amount of their time actually engaging in crime, this small part of gang life is also argued to be a centrally important part of it, helping to explain why "One of the strongest established facts to emerge from gang research over the past five decades is that gang members commit a lot of crime – and substantially more than similarly aged peers from the same community" (Maxson and Matsuda 2011, 258). Here I review several key themes found in reviews and studies examining the association between gangs, gang membership, and crime (Curry, Decker, and Pyrooz 2014; Decker and Van Winkle 1996; Greene and Pranis 2007; Klein and Maxson 2006; Krohn and Thornberry 2008; Maxson and Matsuda 2011; Pyrooz et al. 2016; Sanders 2017; Shelden, Tracy, and Brown 2013; Ward 2013).

First, gang members both commit more crime than non-gang members and commit a disproportionate share of criminal offenses, especially in terms of serious crimes, with these findings quite robust across time, place, research designs, and measurement approaches (see Klein and Maxson 2006). Second, not all gangs and not all gang members are alike with respect to their patterns of criminal activity. The amount and nature of the crime committed varies extensively across gangs and gang members, with some more criminally involved than others, both in terms of frequency and crime types, a fact which refutes a common misconception that all gangs and all gang members are alike (Howell 2007; Ward 2013). Third, most gangs and gang members do not specialize in offending, rather they are generalists engaging in many different types of crime (Klein and Maxson 2006). Yet, the relative rank ordering of the crime they engage in (from most to least often) is also quite illustrative. Much of the crime committed is relatively minor – property crimes are generally more common than violent crimes – while the crimes they generally engage in least often are the forms of serious violence they are notoriously associated with, especially the crimes of homicide and drive-by shootings (Decker and Van Winkle 1996; Ward 2013).

As highlighted above, perhaps most debated in the literature is the theoretical discussion and empirical investigation with respect to whether the association between gang membership and crime (and other negative outcomes) is causal, spurious, or perhaps some of both. In brief, three models have been described to account for the strong association between gang membership and elevated criminal activity (for more details, see Curry, Decker, and Pyrooz 2014; Krohn and Thornberry 2008; Thornberry et al. 2003). First, the selection model argues that the association between gang membership and crime is spuriously due to the particular types of criminally prone individuals who join gangs. This model posits that individuals with an already strong and unchanging predisposition to engage in crime select into gangs and thus entry into the gang does not change their criminal behavior. The facilitation model, on the other hand, argues that the effect of gangs on criminal behavior is causal – gangs cause changes in the behaviors of individuals *while* they are in them. Importantly, both before and after gang membership, gang members are argued to be no different, on average, than non-gang members. The third model, known as the enhancement model, is a blending or mixing of the other two models. Gangs both select more criminally prone individuals into the gang environment and the gang environment serves to further enhance their criminal behaviors while they are gang members, and thus this model explains the association as both spurious and causal.

In fact, now more than 30 separate studies examine this methodologically complicated topic, and the results of reviews of these studies reveal two important and generally consistent findings (Curry, Decker, and Pyrooz 2014; Krohn and Thornberry 2008). First, the evidence is most consistent with the enhancement model and is least consistent with the pure selection model. Second, of the two effects in the enhancement model, the facilitation effect is larger than the selection effect. These results mean the gang context likely changes people more than gangs selecting the most criminally prone individuals. However, individuals who are more criminally active are also more likely to select into gangs, and thus there is always a need to pay close attention to pre-existing differences between those who do and do not join gangs. The recent meta-analysis by Pyrooz et al. (2016) of 1,649 estimates (found in 179 different studies) of the association between gang membership and crime also supports these general conclusions, including both the argument that joining a gang changes criminal behavior patterns and that there is an important need to control for other differences between gang members and non-gang members, as well as concluding there is a pressing need to uncover the precise group process mechanism(s) responsible for this effect (see also, Decker, Melde, and Pyrooz 2013).

Gang Membership and Violent Victimization

A number of studies in the last 20 years have also examined the relationship between gang membership and violent victimization. The findings of this body of research generally indicate that gang members are at a significantly heightened risk of violent victimization (Decker, Melde, and Pyrooz 2013; Taylor 2008), although Gibson et al.'s (2012) review raised concerns over methodological shortcomings in this literature. The fact that youth often report joining gangs for protection yet are more likely to be victimized as a result of joining a gang has been called "an unfortunate irony" (Klein and Maxson 2006, 83). In fact, Carson and Vecchio's (2015, 262) recent review of the literature on leaving the gang indicates that the various manners of violence one is exposed to in gang life is one form of "disillusionment" that can help to push gang members out of the gang.

Conclusion

Since the onset of the era of "big gang research," we have learned much about gangs, gang members, and gang life, but many questions still remain (Decker, Melde, and Pyrooz 2013; Pyrooz and Mitchell 2015). The intense research focus since the 1990s has helped to better understand the realities pertaining to street gangs (rather than assuming the stereotypes or myths), including the length of gang membership, the participation rates of youth of different ages, races/ethnicities, and gender, the structure/organization of gangs, and how gang membership is related to both offending and victimization (see e.g., Howell 2007; Howell and Griffiths 2016). Rather than as an attempt to minimize the negative impact of gangs and gang behavior, Howell argues this improved understanding of both the realities and complexities of gangs and gang behavior is a necessary important first step in the effort to effectively respond to gangs.

As argued in this chapter, however, the relationship between gangs and the school environment, especially its influence on school crime and violence, has not progressed as significantly as the broader research. The extant literature on this specific topic has not as effectively nor as convincingly been able to determine the true causal impact of gangs and gang members on the nature and amount of school crime, and the existing evidence on this understudied topic can be argued to be not only limited and mixed in findings, but also now quite dated. Thus, further research on this topic is warranted, and ideally this research not only employs rigorous and methodologically diverse research designs (quantitative and qualitative), but also is explicitly comparative. The comparative angle is critical for understanding how the impact of gangs may vary across both person and place. The importance of the topic of gangs and school crime cannot be understated given the real possibility that gangs can have negative effects on the school environment in ways that disrupt learning. However, as we have learned much on gangs in the last 25 years, the realities of gangs may be different from the presumed and/or stereotypical expectations that often surround them.

Importantly, future research will ideally pay close attention not only to the key challenges discussed in this chapter, including the problem of defining gangs and gang crime and the problem of determining causality, but also to key features of gangs and gang membership. This would include the knowledge that gangs and gang membership often occur in "riskier" people and places, yet perhaps paramount is the finding that, for many gang members, the period of active gang membership is often one year or less. Not only is it wise for researchers to contemplate this key finding in terms of research designs, but it would also be sensible for school officials to contemplate this when dealing with students who may be gang members. As noted by Decker et al. (2014, 594), "the goal should be to make it easier, not harder, to leave one's gang; recent research on gang disengagement shows that it is hard enough without law enforcement making it more difficult," to which one could say the same about the potential role of the school system in this process.

References

Arciaga, Michelle, Sakamoto, Wayne, and Jones, Errika Fearbry. 2010. *Responding to Gangs in the School Setting*. Tallahassee, FL: Institute for Intergovernmental Research, National Gang Center.

Beres, Linda S. and Griffith, Thomas D. 2004. "Gangs, Schools and Stereotypes." *Loyola of Los Angeles Law Review* 37, 935–978.

Brunson, Rod K. and Miller, Jody. 2009. "Schools, Neighborhoods, and Adolescent Conflicts: A Situational Examination of Reciprocal Dynamics. *Justice Quarterly* 26, 183–210.

Bureau of Justice Assistance. 1997. *Urban Street Gang Enforcement*. Washington, DC: US Department of Justice.

Carson, Dena C. and Vecchio, J. Michael. 2015. "Leaving the Gang: A Review and Thoughts on Future Research." In *The Handbook of Gangs*, edited by Scott H. Decker and David C. Pyrooz, pp. 257–275. Chichester, UK: Wiley-Blackwell.

Chandler, Kathryn A., Chapman, Christopher D., Rand, Michael R., and Taylor, Bruce M. 1998. *Students' Reports of School Crime: 1989 and 1995*. Washington, DC: US Department of Education, and Bureau of Justice Statistics.

Curry, G. David. 2015. "The Logic of Defining Gangs Revisited." In *The Handbook of Gangs*, edited by Scott H. Decker and David C. Pyrooz, pp. 7–27. Chichester, UK: Wiley-Blackwell.

Curry, G. David, Decker, Scott H., and Pyrooz, David C. 2014. *Confronting Gangs: Crime and Community*. New York: Oxford University Press.

Decker, Scott H., Melde, Chris, and Pyrooz, David C. 2013. "What Do We Know About Gangs and Gang Members and Where Do We Go from Here?" *Justice Quarterly* 30, 369–402.

Decker, Scott H., Pyrooz, David C., Sweeten, Gary, and Moule, Richard K. Jr. 2014. "Validating Self-Nomination in Gang Research: Assessing Differences in Gang Embeddedness across Non-, Current, and Former Gang Members." *Criminology* 30, 577–598.

Decker, Scott H. and Van Winkle, Barrik. 1996. *Life in the Gang: Family, Friends, and Violence*. Cambridge: Cambridge University Press.

Egley, Arlen Jr., Howell, James C., and Harris, Meena. 2014. *Highlights of the 2012 National Youth Gang Survey*. Washington, DC: Office of Juvenile Justice and Delinquency Prevention.

Esbensen, Finn-Aage, Peterson, Dana, Taylor, Terrance J., and Freng, Adrienne. 2010. *Youth Violence: Sex and Race Differences in Offending, Victimization, and Gang Membership*. Philadelphia, PA: Temple University Press.

Esbensen, Finn-Aage, Winfree, L. Thomas, He, Ni, and Taylor, Terrance J. 2001. "Youth Gangs and Definitional Issues: When Is a Gang a Gang and Why Does It Matter?" *Crime & Delinquency* 47, 105–130.

Forber-Pratt, Anjali J., Aragon, Steven R., and Espelage, Dorothy L. 2013. "The Influence of Gang Presence on Victimization in One Middle School Environment." *Psychology of Violence* 4, 8–20.

Gibson, Chris L., Swatt, Marc L., Miller, J. Mitchell, Jennings, Wesley G., and Glover, Angela R. 2012. "The Causal Relationship between Gang Joining and Violent Victimization: A Critical Review and Directions for Future Research." *Journal of Criminal Justice* 40, 490–501.

Gottfredson, Gary D. 2013. "What Can Schools Do to Help Prevent Gang-Joining?" In *Changing Course: Preventing Gang Membership*, edited by Thomas R. Simon, Nancy M. Ritter, and Reshma R. Mahendra, pp. 89–103. Washington, DC: US Department of Justice.

Greene, Judith and Pranis, Kevin. 2007. *Gang Wars: The Failure of Enforcement Tactics and the Need for Effective Public Safety Strategies*. Washington, DC: Justice Policy Institute.

Hill, Karl G., Howell, James C., Hawkins, J. David, and Battin-Pearson, Sara R. 1999. "Childhood Risk Factors for Adolescent Gang Membership: Results from the Seattle Social Development Study." *Journal of Research in Crime & Delinquency* 36, 300–322.

Holmes, Ronald M., Tewksbury, Richard, and Higgins, George E. 2011. *Introduction to Gangs in America*. Boca Raton, FL: CRC Press.

Howell, James C. 2007. "Menacing or Mimicking? Realities of Youth Gangs." *Juvenile and Family Court Journal* 58, 39–50.

Howell, James C. 2010. *Gang Prevention: An Overview of Research and Programs*. Washington, DC: Office of Juvenile Justice and Delinquency Prevention.

Howell, James C. and Egley, Arlen Jr. 2005. "Moving Risk Factors into Developmental Theories of Gang Membership." *Youth Violence and Juvenile Justice* 3, 334–354.

Howell, James C. and Griffiths, Elizabeth. 2016. *Gangs in America's Communities*, 2nd ed. Thousand Oaks, CA: Sage.

Howell, James C. and Lynch, James P. 2000. *Youth Gangs in Schools*. Washington, DC: Office of Justice Programs, US Department of Justice.

Huff, C. Ronald. 1998. *Comparing the Criminal Behavior of Youth Gangs and At-Risk Youths*. Washington, DC: National Institute of Justice, US Department of Justice.

Huff, C. Ronald and Barrows, Julie. 2015. "Documenting Gang Activity: Intelligence Databases." In *The Handbook of Gangs*, edited by Scott H. Decker and David C. Pyrooz, pp. 28–58. Chichester, UK: Wiley-Blackwell.

Hutchinson, Ray and Kyle, Charles. 1993. "Hispanic Street Gangs in Chicago's Public Schools." In *Gangs: The Origins and Impact of Contemporary Youth Gangs in the United States*, edited by Scott Cummings and Daniel J. Monti, pp. 113–136. Albany, NY: SUNY Press.

Joseph, Janice. 2008. "Gangs and Gang Violence in School." *Journal of Gang Research* 16, 33–50.

Katz, Jack and Jackson-Jacobs, Curtis. 2004. "The Criminologists' Gang." In *The Blackwell Companion to Criminology*, edited by Colin Sumner, pp. 91–124. Oxford: Blackwell.

Klein, Malcolm W. 1995. *The American Street Gang: Its Nature, Prevalence, and Control*. New York: Oxford University Press.

Klein, Malcolm W. 2016. *Chasing after Street Gangs: A Forty Year Journey*. New York: Oxford University Press.

Klein, Malcolm W. and Maxson, Cheryl L. 2006. *Street Gang Patterns and Policies.* New York: Oxford University Press.

Krohn, Marvin D. and Thornberry, Terence P. 2008. "Longitudinal Perspectives on Adolescent Street Gangs." In *The Long View of Crime: A Synthesis of Longitudinal Research*, edited by Akiva M. Liberman, pp. 128–160, New York: Springer.

Laub, John H. and Lauritsen, Janet L. 1998. "The Interdependence of School Violence with Neighborhood and Family Conditions." In *Violence in American Schools*, edited by Delbert S. Elliott, Beatrix A. Hamburg, and Kirk R. Williams, pp. 127–155. Cambridge: Cambridge University Press.

Mateu-Gilbert, Pedro and Lune, Howard. 2003. "School Violence: The Bidirectional Conflict Flow between Neighborhoods and School." *City and Community* 2, 353–369.

Matsuda, Kirsty N., Esbensen, Finn-Aage, and Carson, Dena C. 2012. "Putting the 'Gang' in 'Eurograng': Characteristics of Delinquent Youth Groups by Different Definitional Approaches." In *Youth Gangs in International Perspective: Results from the Eurogang Program Research*, edited by Finn-Aage Esbensen and Cheryl L. Maxson, pp. 17–33. New York: Springer.

Maxson, Cheryl L. 1999. "Gang Homicide: A Review and Extension of the Literature." In *Homicide: A Sourcebook of Social Research*, edited by M. Dwayne Smith and Margaret A. Zahn, pp. 239–254. Thousand Oaks, CA: Sage.

Maxson, Cheryl L. and Matsuda, Kristy N. 2011. "Gang Delinquency." In *The Oxford Handbook of Juvenile Crime and Juvenile Justice*, edited by Barry C. Feld and Donna M. Bishop, pp. 246–271. New York: Oxford University Press.

Naber, Patricia A., May, David C., Decker, Scott H., Minor, Kevin I., and Wells, James B. 2006. "Are There Gangs in Schools? It Depends Upon Whom You Ask." *Journal of School Violence* 5, 53–72.

National Gang Intelligence Center. 2013. *2013 National Gang Report.* Washington, DC: National Gang Intelligence Center.

Neiman, Samantha. 2011. *Crime, Violence, Discipline, and Safety in U.S. Public Schools: Findings from the School Survey on Crime and Safety: 2009–10* (NCES 2011-320). Washington, DC: US Department of Education.

Parks, Carolyn P. 1995. "Gang Behavior in the Schools: Reality or Myth?" *Educational Psychology Review* 7, 41–68.

Pyrooz, David C. 2014. "'From Your First Cigarette to Your Last Dyin' Day': The Patterning of Gang Membership in the Life-Course." *Journal of Quantitative Criminology* 30, 349–372.

Pyrooz, David C. and Decker, Scott H. 2011. "Motives and Methods for Leaving the Gang: Understanding the Process of Gang Desistance." *Journal of Criminal Justice* 39, 417–425.

Pyrooz, David C. and Mitchell, Meghan M. 2015. "Little Gang Research, Big Gang Research." In *The Handbook of Gangs*, edited by Scott H. Decker and David C. Pyrooz, pp. 28–58. Chichester, UK: Wiley-Blackwell.

Pyrooz, David C. and Sweeten, Gary. 2015. "Gang Membership between Ages 5 and 17 Years in the United States." *Journal of Adolescent Health* 56, 414–419.

Pyrooz, David C., Sweeten, Gary, and Piquero, Alex R. 2013. "Continuity and Change in Gang Membership and Gang Embeddedness." *Journal of Research in Crime and Delinquency* 50, 239–271.

Pyrooz, David C., Turanovic, Jillian J., Decker, Scott H., and Wu, Jun. 2016. "Taking Stock of the Relationship between Gang Membership and Offending: A Meta-Analysis." *Criminal Justice and Behavior* 43, 365–397.

Ralph, John H., Colopy, Kelley W., McRae, Christine, and Daniel, Bruce. 1995. *Gangs and Victimization at School.* Washington, DC: National Center for Educational Statistics.

Sanders, Bill. 2017. *Gangs: An Introduction.* New York: Oxford University Press.

Shelden, Randall G., Tracy, Sharon K., and Brown, William B. 2013. *Youth Gangs in American Society.* Belmont, CA: Wadsworth.

Sweeten, Gary, Pyrooz, David C., and Piquero, Alex R. 2013. "Disengaging from Gangs and Desistance from Crime." *Justice Quarterly* 30, 469–500.

Taylor, Terrence J. 2008. "The Boulevard Ain't Safe for Your Kids ... Youth Gang Membership and Violent Victimization." *Journal of Contemporary Criminal Justice* 24,125–136.

Thompkins, Douglas E. 2000. "School Violence: Gangs and a Culture of Fear." *Annals of the American Academy of Political and Social Sciences* 567, 54–71.

Thornberry, Terence P., Krohn, Marvin D., Lizotte, Alan J., Smith, Carolyn A., and Tobin, Kimberly. 2003. *Gangs and Delinquency in Developmental Perspective.* Cambridge: Cambridge University Press.

Ward, T.W. 2013. *Gangsters without Borders: An Ethnography of a Salvadoran Street Gang.* New York: Oxford University Press.

Yiu, Ho Lam, and Gottfredson, Gary D. 2014. "Gang Participation." *Crime and Delinquency* 60, 619–642.

Zhang, Anlan, Musu-Gillette, Lauren, and Oudekerk, Barbara A. 2016. *Indicators of School Crime and Safety: 2015* (NCES 2016-079/NCJ 249758). Washington, DC: National Center for Education Statistics, US Department of Education, and Bureau of Justice Statistics, Office of Justice Programs, US Department of Justice.

9

Socio-Ecological Risk and Protective Factors for Youth Gang Involvement

Joey Nuñez Estrada, Jr., Adrian H. Huerta, Edwin Hernandez,
Robert A. Hernandez, and Steve W. Kim

Introduction

Thousands of students walk to school each day navigating the dangers of gangs and violence in their communities. For some students, arriving at school each morning requires tremendous strength and skills to overcome a matrix of strenuous barriers and challenges. Consider the experience of Reyes,[1] a 13-year-old Latino male who lives in an impoverished community saturated with drugs, gangs, and violence. "I was tired of getting beat up everyday so I joined the gang. My homeboy and I walk to school together now. We got each other's back." Reyes encountered numerous instances of bullying and physical assaults on his way to school. He had little parental support and supervision, and was left to navigate life on his own. "I was invisible." It was in eighth grade that he was jumped into the local gang and when asked what that day felt like, he responded, "To be honest, it felt like I was on top of the world. I felt love from my homeboys." This new inclusivity and acceptance among Reyes's peers provided protection while walking to school and the formation of an identity during a critical developmental stage in his life. He went from nobody to somebody instantaneously and found a community who received him. He became visible.

Joining a gang is not a simple decision. Most individuals are aware of the social repercussions and stigmas of gang embeddedness and the possibility of incarceration or certain death because of their gang involvement (Calabrese and Noboa 1995; Thornberry et al. 2003; Vigil 1988). However, gangs often provide youth an opportunity to feel a part of a community of peers who can share love and support, nurture someone's identity development and sense of validation, and provide a level of emotional fulfillment he or she is not receiving from their home setting (Conchas and Vigil 2012). Gang membership is not a homogeneous process for individuals, but is affected by various internal and external factors related to socioeconomic status, family composition, social networks, and perceptions of marginalization (Curry and Spergel 1992).

---

1 Reyes is a composite of the hundreds of males we have collectively interacted with over the last decade. We are inspired by the use of composite characters in Solorzano and Yosso (2002), and also strive to protect the confidentiality of our relationships with youth.

The Wiley Handbook on Violence in Education: Forms, Factors, and Preventions, First Edition.
Edited by Harvey Shapiro.
© 2018 John Wiley & Sons, Inc. Published 2018 by John Wiley & Sons, Inc.

Reyes's case highlights the complicated position that vulnerable students with limited resources are placed in. This reality is particularly true among youth who are marginalized in multiple settings and feel they are on the outskirts of their schools and communities. Reyes is only one of over one million youth around the United States who are gang involved (Pyrooz and Sweeten 2015). Reyes's feeling of "invisibility" vanished with the acceptance he experienced from a newfound group of peers. However, his new visibility may possibly garner the attention of school personnel and local law enforcement seeking an opportunity to expel or arrest him for his gang involvement and the assumed violence he will perpetrate in school. Yet, empirical data that examine the direct contribution gang involvement may have on school violence behavior are relatively scarce (for recent exceptions, see Estrada et al. 2013, 2014a, 2014b). It is unclear if gang membership contributes to school violence behaviors above and beyond individual, peer, and family factors. Given the complexity of gang and school violence issues, researchers should conceptualize and consider multiple factors inside and outside of the school to determine if and how theoretical awareness and models could be used to address concerns in the community and school environments. Understanding the holistic social context of gang involvement may help to provide a better framework to serve high-risk youth in marginalized schools and communities (Sheldon, Tracy, and Brown 2013; Vigil 1988, 2009).

Theoretical Framework

The School as the Nucleus of a Social-Ecological Model

The goal of this chapter is to examine gang involvement through a socioecological framework deeply inspired by Bronfenbrenner's (1979, 1986) human ecological systems theory and Benbenishty and Astor's (2005) model of social-ecological influences on student victimization, which suggests that schools are entrenched within nested contexts. The socioecological theoretical model depicted in Figure 9.1 places the

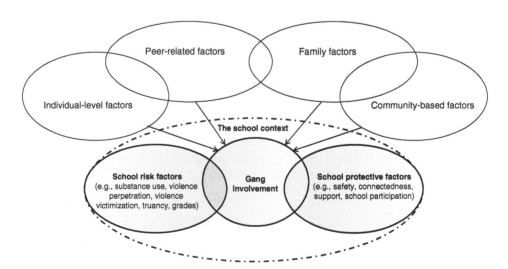

Figure 9.1 A model of individual, peer, family, community, and school influences on gang involvement.

school, rather than the individual, at the center of the model and focuses on how individual, peer, family, community, and school risk and protective factors interact and influence gang involvement and violence in schools. This socioecological model offers a holistic view of gang involvement, and within this framework we will attempt to highlight the systemic failures that push vulnerable, high-risk youth like Reyes to find refuge in gangs.

Addressing Definitional Issues

To determine whether gangs are impacting their schools, educators first need to decide on what comprises a gang, gang member, and gang-related activities. However, given that gangs are a complex phenomenon, defining what constitutes a gang or gang member has been a significant challenge for researchers and practitioners. To date, there "is no single, universally accepted definition of a gang or a gang member" (Howell 2012, 53). In the absence of a definitional consensus, the ability to precisely measure gangs becomes complicated and oftentimes results in the inaccurate over-reporting of the number of gangs, gang members, and what some refer to as "gang-related violence" (Naber et al. 2006). Despite this lack of consensus, a widely accepted legal definition of gangs was developed by the California state legislature in the late 1980s (Klein and Maxson 2006). The legislation known as the Street Terrorism Enforcement and Prevention (S.T.E.P.) Act defines a criminal street gang as:

> any ongoing organization, association, or group of three or more persons, whether formal or informal, having as one of its primary activities the commission of one or more of the criminal acts enumerated in paragraphs (1) to (25), inclusive, or (31) to (33), inclusive, of subdivision (e), having a common name or common identifying sign or symbol, and whose members individually or collectively engage in or have engaged in a pattern of criminal gang activity. (California Penal Code, Section §186.22(f))

This relatively ambiguous and vague legal categorization of a criminal street gang has unfortunately been supported by public officials and adopted by various neighboring states to target, over-police, and prosecute communities of color (Klein and Maxson 2006). This exploitive criminogenic reaction to delinquent youth behavior mainly grew from a "moral panic" that was motivated by racial and ethnic stereotypes. This panic resulted in discriminatory policies, negative perceptions, and the mass incarceration of youth of color (Alexander 2012). The desperately romantic hyper-focus and labeling of gangs demonizes youth of color and distracts researchers from uncovering the underlying root causes of youth violence (Sullivan 2005).

Throughout this chapter, we do not simply focus on the criminal and illegal activities of gangs, but on the more complex human components and the benefits some youth are able to receive from gang involvement. We position the individual student within the different socioecological paradigms of their peers, family, community, and schools to better understand youth gang involvement and school-related violence.

Youth Gang Involvement and Individual Factors

We have briefly provided some of the influences and tensions that led Reyes to join a gang. However, there are other individual factors that play an influential role in his life that either push or pull him toward gang involvement, and these factors continuously evolve in different settings. For example, research has consistently shown that Reyes's race/ethnicity, gender, age, and socioeconomic status are related to a higher likelihood of gang involvement. Klein and Maxson's (2006) comprehensive review of self-report studies concluded that Latino and black youth have at least one-half and often one-third higher gang membership prevalence rates than that of white youth. Additionally, males have one and a half to two times higher gang membership prevalence rates than females (Klein and Maxson 2006). To understand the national context of gang involvement by different individual demographic indicators, see the important work of Pyrooz and Sweeten (2015). At the state level, Table 9.1 represents the individual characteristics of a sample of 606,815 students across California. This table is important in understanding individual-level variables related to gang involvement.

Race/Ethnicity, Gender, Age, Socioeconomic Status and Gang Involvement

Racism and racial tension are well documented throughout the K–12 literature (Laura 2014; Patterson, Hale, and Stessman 2007). It is also well documented that

Table 9.1 Individual sample characteristics of 606,815 students across California.

Variable	All students (n = 606,815) % (n)	Gang members (n = 50,963) % (n)	Non-gang members (n = 555,852) % (n)
Gender			
Male	47.5 (316,269)	59.3 (29,884)	46.4 (255,860)
Female	52.5 (285,744)	40.7 (20,513)	53.6 (295,756)
Ethnicity			
White	27.6 (166,406)	18.7 (9,468)	28.4 (156,938)
Latino	34.6 (208,637)	42.9 (21,754)	33.8 (186,883)
Black	4.4 (26,775)	7.0 (3,549)	4.2 (23,226)
Asian	12.5 (75,193)	8.9 (4,513)	12.8 (70,680)
American Indian	1.2 (7,335)	1.7 (885)	1.2 (6,450)
Multiracial	12.2 (73,575)	12.9 (6,557)	12.1 (67,018)
Other	7.5 (45,135)	7.8 (3,945)	7.5 (41,190)
Grade level			
7th grade	37.6 (228,245)	40.4 (20,578)	37.4 (207,667)
9th grade	34.1 (207,191)	34.9 (17,781)	34.1 (189,410)
11th grade	28.2 (171,379)	24.7 (12,600)	28.6 (158,775)

Source: Adapted from Estrada et al. (2014a). Reproduced with permission of Sage Publications.

students of color are often treated poorly in schools and viewed as problems for educators (Howard 2014; Rios 2011; Vigil 1988). It may be difficult for most educators to acknowledge the presence of racism and racial tensions within their schools and communities and recognize how those pressures contribute to students' perceptions of marginalization. Yet, like Reyes, students of color who feel mistreated and marginalized will challenge educators and not allow themselves to be "punked" by peers or school personnel (Huerta 2016). This unaccommodating school environment that marginalizes youth of color contributes to their street socialization (Vigil 1988, 2002).

Table 9.1 shows that males represent a large percentage of gang members. Different qualitative studies have tried to determine why boys and young men are more likely to join a gang. For Latino and black males, some scholars argue that cultural factors, such as machismo and rites of passage customs, may contribute to gang involvement (Calabrese and Barton 1995; Pinnock 1997). Calabrese and Barton (1995) stressed that Mexican culture and gender dynamics contribute to young men joining gangs. Nevertheless, gender is a complicated aspect because of the multiple social and organizational influences on young men, and also for young girls whose rates of gang involvement are progressively increasing (Connell 1996; Ferguson 2000; Miller and Decker 2001; Thorne 1994).

The age of gang initiation is also important, as this is a critical moment in the life of young people. Studies report that youth join gangs as early as 7 or 8 years old, but their involvement in gangs intensifies at the age of 12 or 13 (Estrada et al. 2014a; Pyrooz and Sweeten 2015; Vigil 2004). Pyrooz and Sweeten (2015) suggest that the average age of gang membership is 13 years old. Estrada and colleagues (2014a) examined gang involvement for California youth and found gang involvement decreased as students moved from seventh to eleventh grade. What is difficult to determine is if the students left the gang as they progressed in school or whether the student left or was pushed out of the school system completely. It is important to note that this transitional period from middle to high school is a significant developmental period for youth. Nakkula and Toshalis (2006) document the multiple physical and psychological stressors adolescents experience on their transition from middle to high school, which include establishing new friendships, navigating relationships with parents, and trying to find their identity in school, whether it is being studious, an athlete, or a gang member. The strain of combining these average physical and psychological pressures to fit into their school and community with a layer of marginalization based on race/ethnic, gender, or socioeconomic status pushes some youth to gangs.

Finally, the role and influence of poverty is a salient and real concern for families. For instance, socioeconomic status impacts how personal resources are accumulated and used by the family in schools and communities to advocate for their children (Lareau 2011). When families live in poverty and have limited social networks to draw resources from to address the various needs of their children, it creates additional challenges (Lareau 2011). Poverty directly affects the type of housing, medical attention, nutrition, and safe spaces available for a child to play (Halpern 1990; Lareau 2011). As a result, low-income families face entirely different demands, threats, expectations, and challenges on a day-to-day basis (Lareau 2011; Ogbu 1985). The social context of the individual may shed light on what influences will push youth to join a gang. These struggles and real challenges for youth like Reyes further prompts the continued urgency to examine socioecological factors that are beyond the micro level of the individual.

Youth Gang Involvement and Peer Influences

The outcome of joining a gang is a group process and youth are provided with both the risk and protective factors that come with the benefits of membership. Through the process of gang involvement the influence of peers is powerful as they fulfill the sense of belonging youth may not receive from their family, community, and school. Therefore, gang peers support one another by providing a sense of security, source of support, and group identification (Estrada, Hernandez, and Kim 2017; Holleran and Waller 2003; Vigil 1988). In addition, the protective features of peer gang involvement grants youth the needed social connections, access to underground information, and resources to thrive in a gang-impacted community (Moule, Decker, and Pyrooz 2013). Gang-involved youth form stronger forms of loyalty with each other through a series of events, which might include partying, drug and alcohol use, street altercations, and other delinquency acts over time (Estrada, Hernandez, and Kim 2017; Vigil 2010a). Ultimately, through this group process youth establish self-identities to individualize their role within the peer group, as they engage in risky behavior to suppress the psychological and traumatic experiences they have encountered in their life (Estrada, Hernandez, and Kim 2017).

At the beginning of the chapter we learned that Reyes was constantly being bullied and physically attacked in his community, which led to his decision to flee to a gang to feel inclusive, accepted, and protected from violence. This was a crucial decision for Reyes. In alignment with his developmental stage, research has shown that many youth make drastic changes in their lives to adapt to daily challenges and risk of violent victimization (Irwin 2004; Taylor et al. 2007). Thus, violence and safety have become a part of the daily realities for many youth across the nation (Marcus 2005), as youth report joining gangs with the expectation that their peers will protect them from potential attackers (Schrek, Fisher, and Miller 2004). Yet, research has shown that youth who are affiliated with risky peers are exposed to greater risks (Hoyt, Ryan, and Cauce 1999; Lauritsen, Laub, and Sampson 1992; Miller and Decker 2001; Schrek, Fisher, and Miller 2004; Schreck, Wright, and Miller 2002; Whitbeck, Hoyt, and Yoder 1999). For example, studies show that involvement in gangs significantly increases youth risk for violence, victimization, and engagement in violent behavior (Barners, Beaver, and Miller 2010; Boxer 2014; Boxer et al. 2015; Dishion, Véronneau, and Myers 2010; Irwin 2004; Taylor et al. 2007). Furthermore, gangs are a multiple-aged peer group, in which young members oftentimes must contend with peers of their own age, but also with those that are older, some in their mid-twenties (Vigil 2004). Those long-term gang members are also considered street elites and often fill the roles of mentors, parents, teachers, and police in the absence of positive socialization from the home and school environments (Katz 1988; Shakur 1994; Vigil 1999; Vigil and Yun 1996). Additionally, older gang members are able to encourage young affiliates to engage in risky behaviors and carry out acts of violence against rival gang members (Vigil 1988). This loyalty is often the driving force of youth being there for the gang and peers regardless of the consequences, which can potentially include incarceration or death (Estrada, Hernandez, and Kim 2017).

Youth Gang Involvement and Family Factors

The family unit plays a critical role in the overall development of young people (Loeber and Farrington 2001). Parents need to be highly invested and involved to ensure their children receive plenty of love and support, are well nourished and healthy, and attain the social, emotional, and academic skills to be successful in life (Vigil 1988). The ability to provide a safe, supportive, healthy home environment is often compromised for impoverished families where the parent(s) may need to dedicate more time to work commitments instead of their children in order to provide adequate shelter and food. Yet, the absence of the overworked parent(s), as well as an array of other situational determinants impacting parenting practices, limits the ability to develop strong family bonds, weakens the overall family structure, and reduces parental supervision, which may prompt gang involvement (Howell and Egley 2005).

Empirical evidence examining family factors has generated inconsistent results (Klein and Maxson 2006). However, some studies have found youth who are at greater risk of gang involvement come from single-parent households, homes struggling with issues of marital discord, homes where there is a prevalence of alcohol and drug abuse, homes with issues of physical and/or sexual abuse, and/or homes that have family members who are gang involved (Hill et al. 1999; Sheldon, Tracy, and Brown 2013; Vigil 1988). As Father Greg Boyle (2015), founder of Homeboy Industries – the nation's largest gang intervention program in the country – states, "No kid is seeking anything when he joins a gang. He's always fleeing something." In the case of Reyes, navigating life on his own was a way to escape the child abuse and domestic violence his dysfunctional alcoholic father imposed on him and his mother. The level and depth of emotional and physical trauma in Reyes's family household will often manifest itself through disruptive and violent behaviors in school or the community (Conchas and Vigil 2012; Zipin 2009).

Youth Gang Involvement and Community Factors

The role of a family's story and experiences in the United States shapes their reception into various communities. The dysfunction and violence in Reyes's home is frequently triggered by the cumulative traumatic incidents his family endures while residing in a fragmented community. Estrada, Hernandez, and Kim (2017) describe a progression model of system-induced traumatization and re-traumatization that may result from historical and structural community failures. They propose that, historically, racially motivated discrimination and legislative policies foster homogeneous ethnic and economic segregation, which results in people of color being pushed into impoverished, clustered enclaves. Although certain ethnic enclaves provide low-income and minority families a buffer against racially discriminatory violence (Vigil 2002), these impoverished neighborhoods often include fragmented social institutions that lack the capacity to sufficiently meet the needs of disenfranchised families.

Research shows that poverty, social disorganization, and the dearth of living wage jobs play a part in the presence of gangs in fragmented communities (Curry and Spergel 1992; Esbensen et al. 2009; Hagedorn 1991; Vigil 1988, 2002). The relegation of being lower class in an economic and social system that disregards the needs of youth in the community produces emotional frustration, forcing youth to satisfy their unmet basic human needs outside of conventional institutions (Estrada, Hernandez, and Kim 2017; Thompkins 2000). Furthermore, racial profiling and discriminatory policies (e.g., gang enhancements, gang injunctions, zero tolerance, etc.) against communities of color are instances of system-induced institutional trauma. This accumulation of community trauma, plus a deprived social status and the continuance of systematic oppression, cultivates multigenerational distress, which manifests itself through violence and street socialization within communities and schools (Estrada, Hernandez, and Kim 2017; Song 2004; Vigil 2010a, 2010b). Howell and Egley (2005) found that in distressed communities there is a higher level of criminal activity, and a larger number of youth engaged in delinquent activities, including the prevalent accessibility and use of illegal drugs and weapons. Sadly, governmental and community-based organizations, churches, and schools in disenfranchised neighborhoods fail to deliver effective gang prevention and intervention services (Howell 2010).

Youth Gang Involvement and School Factors

On average, youth spend nearly seven hours a day in school (National Center for Education Statistics 2007–2008). Therefore, like family and community influences, schools play a critical role in the overall development of youth. For instance, when youth experience a sense of belonging and peer acceptance in school, it can lead to students enjoying school more, being more academically engaged, participating in school activities, and persisting on to complete high school, as well as college (Flores-Gonzales 2005). On the other hand, when students like Reyes experience feelings of exclusion or estrangement they are more likely to disengage academically and act out in class (Calabrese and Noboa 1995). Sadly, some schools will purposely restrict high quality academic curricula, electives, and instructors from students like Reyes, which contributes to their academic disengagement (Flores-Gonzalez 2005). Additionally, schools may restrict access to college and career information because they assume gang-involved youth are not interested or college ready (Huerta 2015). Yet, some gang-involved youth still maintain high aspirations of attending and graduating from college to pursue professional careers (Calabrese and Noboa 1995; Huerta, McDonough, and Allen 2017). However, it is very unfortunate when students like Reyes, who are gang involved, are regularly omitted from certain programs or treated adversely by schools.

Schools are ideal settings for gang recruitment because of the targeted audience of young adolescents, the social group formations that emerge on campus, and it being a place for gangs to foster community between their members (Ayers 2006; Huerta 2015; Rios 2010; Tellez and Estep 1997). Robers et al. (2013) surveyed 12- to 18-year-old students and found that 18% stated there were gangs at their schools. When school administrators and teachers were surveyed, they ranked gangs second only to drugs as the utmost important school safety issue (Stephens 1989; Sullivan and Keeney 2008). Therefore, to promote safety, schools tend to function as a social control agent of student behavior (Vigil 1988). Little effort is made to promote an inclusive and caring academic environment for gang-involved youth (Rios 2011). The majority of school personnel do not receive focused or specialized training on how to engage, support, and redirect gang youth into positive life trajectories (Vigil 1999). Most often, schools depend on the efforts of local police departments or school resource officers who focus on punitive outcomes and the overuse of zero tolerance policies (see Chapters 12 and 13, this volume). This leads to criminal detentions, suspensions, and expulsions of gang youth, and as a result, rival gang members from various communities are being bused to schools outside of their local neighborhood (Parks 1995; Vigil 1999). This criminalization and mistreatment of students by schools tends to ignore the social and economic supportive services needed by students like Reyes (Rios 2011).

When vulnerable high-risk students are pushed out of their schools and forced to attend school with rival gang members, the school climate is impacted and safety and security concerns become an issue (Parks 1995). Unfortunately, this forced interaction in schools could be problematic and may possibly increase the number of rival gang altercations. Consequently, many gang youth may feel unsafe at school, which can potentially increase the likelihood of their bringing a weapon to school for protection (Vigil 1999). This negative unsafe school climate only escalates the situation for the larger school community as it forces others to also carry weapons, and soon many students, including non-gang members, are also "packing" to protect themselves in school (Vigil 1999). Such hostile school environments will oftentimes end the school career of vulnerable high-risk youth and strengthen their commitment to the local gang (Rios 2011; Vigil 1997, 2004).

Research suggests that poorly functioning schools with high levels of student and teacher victimization, large student–teacher ratios, poor academic quality, poor school climates, and high rates of social sanctions (e.g., suspensions, expulsions, and referrals to juvenile court) hold a greater percentage of students who form and join gangs (Howell 2010). Thus, schools can play a major role in a youth's choice of gang involvement and school violence behaviors. Sanchez and Anderson (1990) argue that in-school gang mediation programs can potentially be effective in addressing issues that exist in schools between rival gangs (Parks 1995). Through the efforts of gang mediation, school counselors provide training to representative gang members who become accountable for mediating gang-related issues in school. According to Sanchez and Anderson (1990, 56), "The magic of the mediation process was communication." Schools can either take a punitive approach that criminalizes gang-involved youth, or they can work to improve safety, enhance student connectedness, and increase support from teachers and school personnel so that fewer students will feel the need to resort to gangs and violence (Benbenishty and Astor 2005; Estrada et al. 2013, 2014a, 2014b).

Gang Involvement and School Violence

Most of the literature on gangs and violence has been community based and concentrates largely on the individual, peer, family, and community domains, and almost universally disregards factors in the school context that may be correlated with gang involvement (Klein and Maxson 2006). Studies conducted nearly 20 years ago offer empirical evidence implying that gangs may possibly be the chief explanation for the upswing in school violence within particular schools, and that in those schools, victimization almost doubles if gangs are in the adjacent community (Burnett and Walz 1994; Howell 1998). Intuitively this makes sense. However, empirical studies examining the nexus between gangs and school violence on school grounds is scarce. Nevertheless, theoretically not much is known about how school factors possibly mediate gang involvement and overall school violence incidents within school settings (see Chapter 11, this volume).

Schools have a tendency to focus on gang involvement as the independent, main factor associated with school violence and often fail to consider other possible confounding school factors. In recent studies, Estrada and colleagues (2013, 2014b) examine how school risk (e.g., truancy, school substance use, and risky peer approval) and protective (e.g., connectedness, support and safety) behaviors and attitudes mediate the effects of gang involvement on school violence behaviors. Contrary to intuition and earlier theory, which implied that gangs may well be the source of surges in school violence, Estrada et al (2013, 2014b) found that gang membership alone did not have a direct association with school violence perpetration or victimization. When analyzing mediational relations, the findings indicated that the relations between gang membership and school violence perpetration and victimization were completely mediated by school risk behaviors and attitudes. Therefore, this study suggested that gang involvement alone does not result in school violence; however, when a gang-involved youth participates in school risk factors, such as truancy, substance use, and associating with risky peers, the probability of school perpetration and victimization can increase. Consequently, exactly how and with whom a gang-involved youth associates with in school can directly and indirectly influence the rates of school violence (Estrada et al. 2013, 2014b). Thus, instead of focusing on gang involvement as a distinct independent concern, schools should dedicate more effort to attending to the school risk behaviors of truancy, substance use, and risky peer associations that account for school violence perpetration and victimization. This tactic would be more successful than the punitive suppression methods that tend to be racially motivated and primarily target students of color who are gang involved (Estrada et al. 2013, 2014b).

Implications for Educational Practitioners

The intricacy of comprehending gangs and gang-involved youth has prompted numerous debates about what are the most effective methods to deal with this multifaceted concern. While several efforts to support gang-involved youth have been attempted (Behr, Marston, and Nelson 2014; Howell 2010; Sanchez and Anderson 1990; Vigil 1999, 2010), most intervention programs fail because they only focus attention on a single socioecological domain. However, working with gang-involved youth to heal multiple layers of marginality requires a comprehensive community-based multidimensional approach. A holistic model of prevention and intervention services that address the various systemic and institutional hindrances that gang-involved youth and their families confront regularly needs to be implemented (see Chapter 10, this volume). Such a comprehensive model needs to consider the complex interplay between individuals, peers, families, the community, school, and other societal factors that promote gang violence (Cárdenas 2008).

One such model, the community-based gang intervention model, which was adopted as policy and legislation in 2008 by the City of Los Angeles, is a two-pronged approach that provides hard-core, specialized, street- and detention/prison-based crisis intervention services, as well as the concurrent ongoing gang-responsive specific individual and family redirection services (for a detailed description of the model see Cardenas 2008). What is innovative and noteworthy about this model is that the two-pronged approach utilizes "skilled intervention specialists who have personal knowledge, understanding, and experience of gang life and thereby offer the greatest likelihood for gaining, building, and maintaining trust and confidence among active and former gang members" (Cardenas 2008, 5).

A highlighted program functioning from the community-based gang intervention model is an agency located in the San Fernando Valley of Greater Los Angeles: Communities In Schools (CIS). CIS is a non-profit agency in North Hills, California that offers a wide range of services to gang members and juvenile probationers to help them reduce delinquency and become positive individuals within their community. CIS offers services in an integrative-comprehensive service delivery approach to facilitate change with its constituents through a wide range of services such as educational development, after-school activities, job development, mentoring/tutoring, case management, and individual/family counseling. CIS staff attempt to reduce retaliation by performing street outreach to defuse incidents and motivate gang members away from violence. Drive-by shootings and gang fights on school campuses are a few of the incidents to which staff respond. In addition, the staff utilize peace and rumor control tactics when notified by police or gang members to prevent violence in the community. Staff attempt to intervene before violence is committed. The uniqueness of the program lies with the staff of the program. They bring their own gang experiences to the heart of the program. Almost all of the outreach workers working under CIS are past gang members. They are a group of individuals who have turned their life around and have dedicated themselves to helping the community reduce gang violence. The experience from the street has made rapport building and engagement a significant component in servicing this population. This component has been a barrier for several professional practitioners. The ability to build client rapport is the primary practice skill that makes this program unique. This skill has enabled outreach to become an exclusive intervention for building bridges in the community to curtail violence.

The historic, cultural, community, and school contexts of each individual vary, therefore it is essential to respect the multiple social-ecological systems that may or may not have an impression on gang-involved youth. Starting here would allow for the exploration of the risk and protective factors within each social-ecological domain. When risk and protective factors are acknowledged, efforts to reduce risk factors and advance protective factors are crucial in healing the system-induced traumas that lead many youth to join a gang in the first place (Thompkins 2000). Interventions that are likely to elevate cognitive and behavioral discourses that empower youth to defuse intrinsic and extrinsic strains through recognition of current strengths and accessible resources should be applied (Estrada, Hernandez, and Kim 2017). For example, Behr and associates (2014) evaluated a comprehensive multi-year out-of-school program for high-risk Latino males that provided mentoring, academic tutoring, a life skills course, counseling, information to prepare for postsecondary education or careers, and culturally relevant professional development for teachers. Some of the students were active gang members, embedded in families with one or more gang members, or lived in gang communities. The student outcomes after being involved in the program included an increase in academic grades and ambitions of attending college, and decreases in the likelihood of dropping out and drug and alcohol use.

Given that many educators will likely concentrate on controlling or altering behaviors instead of building a relationship and learning about a youth's life, most will experience defiance from gang-involved youth during early stages of intervention. The utmost fundamental component of a comprehensive intervention model is therefore developing strong rapport and establishing a safe environment of compassion, kinship, and trust (Estrada, Hernandez, and Kim 2017). If educators fail to provide this trusting, safe, supportive space, the youth will abruptly flee back to the street gang that provides an outlet for frustration and anger, often in the form of violence toward others (National Child Traumatic Stress Network 2009). Many marginalized youth believe it is easier to mask their pain behind gang involvement than to discuss their internal trauma with a therapist they do not trust or believe can help (Estrada, Hernandez, and Kim 2017).

Gang intervention models should aim to resolve the system-induced trauma one experiences from multiple marginalities, which may include the negative impact of racial discrimination, poverty, risky peer associations, dysfunctional family unit, poor schooling, and other factors that trigger street socialization among gang-involved youth (Vigil 1988, 2002, 2010a). During each phase of healing, treatment must attend to the biological, psychological, and social components of each socioecological system. An array of services should be offered and could include, for instance, individual and family counseling, social competence training, academic skills, parent–child conflict management training, multi-systemic therapy, and restorative justice practices (Schoenwald, Borduin, and Henggeler 1998). Furthermore, there is a significant need for local communities to unite and advocate to change social systems that are failing marginalized youth (Benda and Turney 2002). Overall, there needs to be a nurturing of social competence to strengthen community kinship and compassion. Through kinship and compassion, "the previously demonized gang member becomes humanized, victims transform into survivors, and hopelessness finds avenues of hope in a life that was once drowned by marginalized inequalities and traumas that became self-fulfilling prophecies" (Estrada, Hernandez, and Kim 2017, 339). Fostering a sense of purpose and a positive outlook in Reyes by providing hope, compassion, and communities of kinship that offer unconditional caring, listening, encouragement, and support can help to remove the mask and make him visible again.

Implications for Educational Researchers

As we have discussed in this chapter, gang involvement is a complicated and multilayered process for youth that requires special attention to advance the research discourse in a more meaningful and interconnected manner. Educational researchers need to take a holistic socioecological approach when investigating the complex phenomena of youth street gangs. The theoretical model in Figure 9.1 offers a holistic view of gang involvement, and researchers need to apply methodology that simultaneously examines how individual, peer, family, community, and school risk and protective factors interact and influence gang involvement and violence in schools.

A particular area of interest for researchers to consider is how complex trauma and systemic marginalization affects social development, student learning, and decisions to engage in school violence behavior. There is an absence of empirical knowledge that examines whether there are significant differences in the level of trauma experienced by gang and non-gang youth. Furthermore, mixed-method evaluations of school resources infused with trauma-informed and restorative interventions are needed to determine if these approaches produce successful outcomes for marginalized and vulnerable high-risk youth. Research that investigates educators' perceptions of gangs and/or gang-affiliated youth, and how this impacts a student's educational trajectory, are also warranted. Research should also be used to inform educators about the impact of placing rival gangs within one school and how this can influence safety, security, and overall school climate. Lastly, research that examines the systemic failures of schools and other institutions is necessary. Empirical evidence that explores different institutional contexts (e.g., traditional vs. alternative school settings), the service and intervention opportunity gap, and the impact of flawed policies that target marginalized youth and exacerbate the youth street gang situation is essential and would enhance our knowledge of socioecological risk and protective factors for youth gang involvement.

References

Alexander, Michelle. 2012. *The New Jim Crow: Mass Incarceration in the Age of Colorblindness*. New York: New Press.

Ayers, William. 2006. "Hearts and Minds: Military Recruitment and the High School Battlefield." *Phi Delta Kappan* 87(8), 594–599.

Barners, J.C., Beaver, Kevin M., and Miller, Mitchell. 2010. "Estimating the Effect of Gang Membership on Nonviolent Delinquency: A Counterfactual Analysis." *Aggressive Behavior* 36, 437–451. DOI: 10.1002/ab.20359.

Behr, Michelle, Marston, Christine, and Nelson, Kyle Anne. 2014. "A Bridge to Graduation for At-risk Latino Males: A Case Study." *Journal of Education for Students Placed At-Risk* 19(3–4), 215–218. DOI: 10.1080/10824669.2014.977104.

Benbenishty, Rami and Astor, Ron Avi. 2005. *School Violence in Context: Cultural, Neighborhood, Family, School,and Gender*. New York: Oxford University Press.

Benda, Brent B. and Turney, Howard M. 2002. "Youthful Violence: Problems and Prospects." *Child and Adolescent Social Work Journal* 19, 5–34. DOI: 10.1023/A:1014051222370.

Boxer, Paul. 2014. "Youth Gangs and Adolescent Development: New Findings, New Challenges, and New Directions: Introduction to the Special Section." *Journal of Research on Adolescent* 24(2), 201–203. DOI: 10.1111/jora.12141.

Boxer, Paul, Veysey, Bonita, Ostermann, Michael, and Kubik, Joanna. 2015. "Measuring Gang Involvement in a Justice-Referred Sample of Youth in Treatment." *Youth Violence and Juvenile Justice* 13, 41–59. DOI: 10.1177/1541204013519828.

Boyle, Greg. 2015. *Opening Plenary Speech*. Los Angeles, CA: The 2nd Annual Gathering of the Global Homeboy Network.

Bronfenbrenner, Urie. 1979. *The Ecology of Human Development: Experiments by Nature and Design*. Cambridge, MA: Harvard University Press.

Bronfenbrenner, Urie. 1986. "Ecology of the Family as a Context for Human Development: Research Perspectives." *Developmental Psychology* 22(6), 723–742.

Burnett, Gary and Walz, Garry. 1994. "Gangs in Schools." *ERIC Digest* 99, 1–4.

Calabrese, Raymond L. and Barton, Angela M. 1995. "Mexican-American Male Students and Anglo Female Teachers: Victims of the Policies of Assimilation." *The High School Journal* 78(3), 115–123.

Calabrese, Raymond L. and Noboa, Julio. 1995. "The Choice for Gang Membership by Mexican-American Adolescents." *The High School Journal* 78(4), 226–235.

Cárdenas, T. 2008. *A Guide for Understanding Effective Community-based Gang Intervention.* Los Angeles, CA: Office of Lost Angeles City Councilmember Tony Cárdenas.

Conchas, Gilberto Q. and Vigil, James Diego. 2012. *Streetsmart Schoolsmart: Urban Poverty and the Education of Adolescent Boys.* New York: Teachers College Press.

Connell, Raewyn W. 1996. "Teaching the Boys: New Research on Masculinity, and Gender Strategies for Schools." *Teachers College Record* 98(2), 206–235.

Curry, G. David. and Spergel, Irving A. 1992. "Gang Involvement and Delinquency among Hispanic and African-American Adolescent Males." *Journal of Research and Delinquency* 29(3), 273–291. DOI: 10.1177/0022427892029003002.

Dishion, Thomas J., Véronneau, Marie-Hélène, and Myers, Michael W. 2010. "Cascading Peer Dynamics Underlying the Progression from Problem Behavior to Violence in Early to Late Adolescence." *Development and Psychopathology* 22, 603–619.

Esbensen, Finn-Aage, Peterson, Dana, Taylor, Terrance J., and Freng, Adrienne. 2009. "Similarities and Differences in Risk Factors for Violent Offending and Gang Membership." *The Australian and New Zealand Journal of Criminology* 42(3), 310–335. DOI: 10.1375/acri.42.3.310.

Estrada, Joey Nuñez, Gilreath, Tamika D., Astor, Ron Avi, and Benbenishty, Rami. 2013. "Gang Membership of California Middle School Students: Behaviors and Attitudes as Mediators of School Violence." *Health Education Research* 28(4), 626–639. DOI: 10.1093/her/cyt037.

Estrada, Joey Nuñez, Gilreath, Tamika D., Astor, Ron Avi, and Benbenishty, Rami. 2014a. "A Statewide Study of Gang Membership in California Secondary Schools." *Youth & Society*, 1–17. E-pub ahead of print April 3, 2014.

Estrada, Joey Nuñez, Gilreath, Tamika D., Astor, Ron Avi, and Benbenishty, Rami. 2014b. "Gang Membership, School Violence, and the Mediating Effects of Risk and Protective Behaviors in California High Schools." *Journal of School Violence* 13(2), 228–251.

Estrada, Joey Nuñez, Hernandez, Robert A., and Kim, Steve W. 2017. "Considering Definitional Issues, Cultural Components, and the Impact of Trauma When Counseling Vulnerable Youth Susceptible to Gang-involvement." In *Handbook of Multicultural Counseling*, 4th ed., edited by J.G. Ponterotto, J.M. Casas, and L.A. Suzuki, pp. 332–340. Thousand Oaks, CA: Sage.

Ferguson, Ann Arnett. 2000. *Bad Boys: Public Schools in the Making of Black Masculinity.* Ann Arbor: University of Michigan Press.

Flores-Gonzales, Nilda. 2005. "Popularity versus Respect: School Structure, Peer Groups and Latino Academic Achievement." *International Journal of Qualitative Studies in Education* 18(5), 625–642. DOI: 10.1080/09518390500224945.

Hagedorn, John M. 1991. "Gangs, Neighborhoods, and Public Policy." *Social Problems* 38, 529–542.

Halpern, Robert. 1990. "Poverty and Early Childhood Parenting; Toward a Framework for Intervention." *American Journal of Orthopsychiatry* 60, 6–18.

Hill, Karl G., Howell, James C., Hawkins, J. David, and Battin-Pearson, Sara R. 1999. "Childhood Risk Factors for Adolescent Gang Membership: Results from the Seattle Social Development Project." *Journal of Research in Crime and Delinquency* 36(3), 300–322. DOI: 10.1177/0022427899036003003.

Holleran, Lori K. and Waller, Margaret A. 2003. "Sources of Resilience among Chicano/a Youth: Forging Identities in the Borderlands." *Child and Adolescent Social Work Journal* 20(5), 335–350.

Howard, Tyrone C. 2014. *Black Male (d): Peril and Promise in the Education of African American males*. New York: Teachers College Press.

Howell, James C. 1998. "Youth Gangs: An Overview." Juvenile Justice Bulletin. Washington, DC: Office of Juvenile Justice and Delinquency Prevention.

Howell, James C. 2010. *Gang Prevention: An Overview of Research and Programs*. Washington, DC: US Department of Justice, Office of Juvenile Justice and Delinquency Prevention.

Howell, James C. 2012. *Gangs in America's Communities*. Thousand Oaks, CA: Sage.

Howell, James C. and Egley, Arlen Jr. 2005. "Moving Risk Factors into Developmental Theories of Gang Membership." *Youth Violence and Juvenile Justice* 3(4), 334–354. DOI: 10.1177/1541204005278679.

Hoyt, Dan R., Ryan, Kimberly D., and Cauce, Ana Mari. 1999. "Personal Victimization in a High-risk Environment: Homeless and Runaway adolescents." *Journal of Research in Crime and Delinquency* 36, 371–392. DOI: 10.1177/0022427899036004002.

Huerta, Adrian H. 2015. "'I didn't want my life to be like that': Gangs, College, or the Military for Latino Male High School Students." *Journal of Latino/Latin American Studies* 7(2), 119–132. DOI: 10.18085/1549-9502-7.2.119.

Huerta, Adrian H. 2016. "Gangs and College Knowledge: An Examination of Latino Male Students Attending Alternative Schools." Unpublished dissertation. University of California, Los Angeles.

Huerta, Adrian H., McDonough, Patricia M., and Allen, Walter R. 2017. "Exploring the College Knowledge of Gang Associated Latino Male Youth: A Qualitative Case Study." Paper submitted for publication.

Irwin, Katherine. 2004. "The Violence of Adolescent Life: Experiencing and Managing Everyday Threats." *Youth and Society* 35, 452–79. DOI: 10.1177/0044118X03260759.

Katz, Jack. 1988. *Seductions of Crime*. New York: Basic Books.

Klein, Malcolm W. and Maxson, Cheryl L. 2006. *Gang Structures, Crime Patterns, and Police Responses*. Social Science Research Institute, University of Southern California, Los Angeles, CA.

Lareau, Annette. 2011. *Unequal Childhoods: Class, Race, and Family Life*, 2nd ed. Berkeley: University of California Press.

Laura, Crystal T. 2014. *Being Bad: My Baby Brother and the School-to-Prison Pipeline*. New York: Teachers College Press.

Lauritsen, Janet L., Laub, John H., and Sampson, Robert J. 1992. "Conventional and Delinquent Activities: Implications for the Prevention of Violent Victimization among Adolescents." *Violence and Victims* 7, 91–108.

Loeber, Rolf and Farrington, David P., eds. 2001. *Child Delinquents: Development, Intervention, and Service Needs*. Thousand Oaks, CA: Sage.

Marcus, Robert F. 2005. "Youth Violence in Everyday life." *Journal of Interpersonal Violence* 20, 442–47. DOI: 10.1177/0886260504267550.

Miller, Jody and Decker, Scott H. 2001. "Young Women and Gang Violence: Gender, Street Offending, and Violent Victimization in Gangs." *Justice Quarterly* 18, 115–140. DOI: 10.1080/07418820100094841.

Moule Jr, Richard K., Decker, Scott H., and Pyrooz, David C. 2013. "Social Capital, the Life-course, and Gangs." In *Handbook of Life-Course Criminology: Emerging Trends and Directions for Future Research*, edited by Marvin D. Krohn and Chris L. Gibson, pp. 143–158. New York: Springer.

Naber, Patricia A., May, David C., Decker, Scott H., Minor, Kevin I., and Wells, James B. 2006. "Are There Gangs in Schools? It Depends upon Whom You Ask." *Journal of School Violence* 5(2), 53–72. DOI:10.1300/J202v05n02_05.

Nakkula, Michael J. and Toshalis, Eric. 2006. *Understanding Youth: Adolescent Development for Educators*. Cambridge, MA: Harvard Education Press.

National Center for Education Statistics (2007–2008). *Schools and Staffing Survey (SASS): "Public School Data File"*. Washington, DC: US Department of Education.

National Child Traumatic Stress Network. 2009. "Trauma in the Lives of Gang-involved Youth: Tips for Volunteers and Community Organizations." http://www.nctsn.org/sites/default/files/assets/pdfs/trauma_and_gang_involved_youth.pdf (last accessed October 11, 2017).

Ogbu, John U. 1985. "Research Currents: Cultural-Ecological Influences on Minority School Learning." *Language Arts* 62, 860–869.

Parks, Carolyn P. 1995. "Gang Behavior in the Schools: Reality or Myth?" *Educational Psychology Review* 7, 41–68. DOI: 10.1007/BF02214206.

Patterson, Jean. A., Hale, Dalia, and Stessman, Martin. 2007. "Cultural Contradictions and School Leaving: A Case Study of an Urban High School." *The High School Journal* 91(2), 1–15.

Pinnock, Don. 1997. *Gangs, Rituals and Rites of Passage*. Cape Town: African Sun Press/Institute of Criminology, University of Cape Town.

Pyrooz, David C. and Sweeten, Gary. 2015. "Gang Membership between Ages 5 and 17 in the United States." *Journal of Adolescent Health* 56(4), 414–419.

Rios, Victor M. 2010. "Navigating the Thin Line between Education and Incarceration: An Action Research Case Study on Gang-associated Latino Youth." *Journal of Education for Students Placed at Risk* 15, 200–212. DOI: 10.1080/10824661003635283.

Rios, Victor M. 2011. *Punished: Policing the Lives of Black and Latino boys*. New York: New York University Press.

Robers, Simone, Zhang, Jijun, Truman, Jennifer, and Snyder, Thomas D. 2013. *Indicators of School Crime and Safety: 2012*. Washington, DC. National Center for Education Statistics and Bureau of Justice Studies. http://nces.ed.gov/pubs2013/2013036.pdf (last accessed October 11, 2017).

Sanchez, F. and Anderson, M.L. 1990. "Gang Mediation: A Process That Works." *Principal*, May, 54–56.

Schoenwald, Sonja K., Borduin, Charles M., and Henggeler, Scott W. 1998. "Multisystemic Therapy: Changing the Natural and Service Ecologies of Adolescents and Families." In *Outcomes for Children and Youth with Behavioral and Emotional Disorders and Their Families: Programs and Evaluations Best Practices*, edited by M. Epstein, K. Kutash, and A. Duchnowski, pp. 485–511. Austin, TX: Pro-ed.

Schreck, Christopher J., Fisher, Bonnie S., and Miller, J. Mitchell. 2004. "The Social Context of Violent Victimization: A Study of the Delinquent Peer Effect." *Justice Quarterly* 21(1), 23–47. DOI: 10.1080/07418820400095731.

Schreck, Christopher J., Wright, Richard A., and Miller, J. Mitchell. 2002. "A Study of Individual and Situational Antecedents of Violent Victimization." *Justice Quarterly* 19, 159–180. DOI: 10.1080/07418820200095201.

Shakur, S. 1994. *Monster*. New York: Penguin.

Shelden, Randall G., Tracy, Sharon K., and Brown, William B. 2013. *Youth Gangs in American Society*, 4th ed. Belmont, CA: Wadsworth.

Solorzano, Daniel G. and Yosso, Tara J. 2002. "A Critical Race Methodology: Counterstorytelling as an Analytical Framework for Educational Research." *Qualitative Inquiry* 8(1), 23–44. DOI: 10.1177/107780040200800103.

Song, Miri. 2004. *Choosing Ethnic Identity*. Cambridge: Polity Press.

Stephens, Ronald D. 1989. "Gangs, Guns, and Drugs." *School Safety*, Fall, 16–19.

Sullivan, Elizabeth and Keeney, Elizabeth. 2008. *Teachers Talk: School Culture, Safety and Human Rights*. New York: National Economic & Social Rights Initiative.

Sullivan, Mercer L. 2005. "Maybe We Shouldn't Study 'Gangs': Does Reification Obscure Youth Violence?" *Journal of Contemporary Criminal Justice* 21(2), 170–190. DOI: 10.1177/1043986204272912.

Taylor, Terrance J., Peterson, Dana, Esbensen, Finn-Aage, and Freng, Adrienne. 2007. "Gang Membership as a Risk Factor for Adolescent Violent Victimization." *Journal of Research in Crime and Delinquency* 44(4), 351–380. DOI: 10.1177/0022427807305845.

Tellez, Kip and Estep, Michelle. 1997. "Latino Youth Gangs and the Meaning of School." *The High School Journal* 81(2), 69–81.

Thompkins, Douglas E. 2000. "School Violence: Gangs and a Culture of Fear." *The Annuals of the American Academy of Political and Social Science* 567(1), 54–71. DOI: 10.1177/000271620056700105.

Thornberry, Terence. P., Krohn, Marvin D., Lizotte, Alan J., and Smith, Carolyn A. 2003. *Gangs and Delinquency in Developmental Perspective*. New York: Cambridge University Press.

Thorne, Barrie. 1994. *Gender Play: Girls and Boys in School*. New Brunswick, NJ: Rutgers University Press.

Vigil, James Diego. 1988. *Barrio Gangs: Street Life and Identity in Southern California*. Austin: University of Texas Press.

Vigil, James Diego. 1997. *Personas Mexicanas: Chicano High Schoolers in a Changing Los Angeles*. Fort Worth, TX: Harcourt Brace.

Vigil, James Diego. 1999. "Streets and Schools: How Educators Can Help Chicano Marginalized Gang Youth." *Harvard Educational Review* 69(3), 270–288. DOI: 10.17763/haer.69.3.237k013137x7313x.

Vigil, James Diego. 2002. *A Rainbow of Gangs: Street Cultures in the Mega-city*. Austin: University of Texas Press.

Vigil, James Diego. 2004. "Gangs and Group Membership: Implications for Schooling." In *School Connections: U.S. Mexican Youth, Peers, and School Achievement*, edited by M. Gibson, P. Gandara, and J. P. Koyama, pp. 87–106. New York: Teachers College Press.

Vigil, James Diego. 2009. "Community Dynamics and the Rise of Street Gangs." In *Latinos: Remaking America*, edited by M.M. Suarez-Orozco and M.M. Paez, pp. 97–109. Berkeley: University of California Press.

Vigil, James Diego. 2010a. *Gang Redux: A Balanced Anti-Gang Strategy*. Long Grove, IL: Waveland Press.

Vigil, James Diego. 2010b. *Barrio Gangs: Street Life and Identity in Southern California*. Austin: University of Texas Press.

Vigil, James Diego and Yun, Steve Chong. 1996. "Southern California Gangs: Comparative Ethnicity and Social Control." In *Gangs in America*, 2nd ed., edited by C. Ronald Huff, pp. 139–156). Thousand Oaks, CA: Sage.

Whitbeck, Les B., Hoyt, Dan R., and Yoder, Kevin A. 1999. "Risk-amplification Model of Victimization and Depressive Symptoms among Runaway and Homeless Adolescents." *American Journal of Community Psychology* 27, 273–296. DOI: 10.1023/A:1022891802943.

Zipin, Lew. 2009. "Dark Funds of Knowledge, Deep Funds of Pedagogy: Exploring Boundaries between Life Worlds and School." *Discourse: Studies in Cultural Politics of Education* 30(3), 317–331. DOI: 10.1080/01596300903037044.

10

School of Hard Knocks

Gangs, Schools, and Education in the United States

Kendra J. Clark, David C. Pyrooz, and Ryan Randa

Introduction

The presence of youth gangs in the United States and their wide-ranging consequences for individuals and communities are well established (Curry, Decker, and Pyrooz 2014; Esbensen 2010; Howell and Griffiths 2015; Klein and Maxson 2006; Thornberry 2003). Gang membership influences youth in significant ways, from their peer networks to their attitudes and behaviors (Melde, Berg, and Esbensen 2014; Matsuda et al. 2013; Medina-Ariza et al. 2013; Melde and Esbensen 2011; Sweeten, Pyrooz, and Piquero 2013; Weerman, Lovegrove, and Thornberry 2015). Life in the gang is often thought of as being insular and all-consuming, making it easy to forget that youth gang members are sons and daughters, churchgoers, employees, citizens, and students (Decker and Van Winkle 1996; Miller 2011; Moore 1991; Thrasher 1927). In addition to the gang, members of gangs are embedded within the context of larger social institutions, including families, neighborhoods, the labor market, churches, and – the focus of this chapter – schools.

Education and the school environment intersect with gangs and gang membership in important ways. Since the ages at which youths are most likely to be in gangs are closely associated with the middle and high school years, it should come as no surprise that gangs and gang members are found in schools. Although only a small portion of the population is involved in gangs, it is especially important to understand gangs and gang membership in school settings. This is particularly true in terms of violence, victimization, and fear in and around schools. Indeed, school is a setting where members of multiple gangs are forced to interact with each other for extended periods of time, multiple days a week. Occupying the same space – where school boundaries rarely align with gang territorial boundaries – can have serious implications in terms of violence and victimization in and around schools (Brunson and Miller 2009; Knox, Laske, and Tromanhauser 1992). Keeping in mind that teachers and non-gang-involved students are also exposed to this heightened tension between gang-involved students, it becomes increasingly important for teachers and school administrators to be adequately prepared to ease tensions and foster an environment where all students can learn. Unfortunately, researchers have found that "educators are not well enough informed about gang culture to foster behaviors that result in successful academic performance" (Vigil 1999, 270).

The Wiley Handbook on Violence in Education: Forms, Factors, and Preventions, First Edition.
Edited by Harvey Shapiro.
© 2018 John Wiley & Sons, Inc. Published 2018 by John Wiley & Sons, Inc.

In terms of gang violence, schools that report a presence of gangs also report higher levels of violence and victimization in both frequency and severity (Ralph et al. 1995). However, more recent research suggests that the relationship between gang members and increased violence and victimization within schools is indirect rather than direct, as many researchers previously believed (Estrada et al. 2014). In other words, rather than a student's risk of offending and victimization being a direct product of his involvement in gangs, his risk is actually indirectly influenced by his involvement in school risk behaviors (i.e., truancy, substance use, negative peer association) and the school's protective measures and supports (i.e., school connectedness, safety, and support). Therefore, while an individual's involvement in gangs does not necessarily increase his level of violence or instances of victimization, when a gang member skips school, hangs out with troublesome peers, or uses drugs, his likelihood of violent perpetration and victimization increases. This is particularly true in schools with limited levels of protective measures and supports.

The focus of this chapter will be to outline the ways in which gangs, schools, and violence interact, and how these interactions are related to the life outcomes of youth. In addition, literature concerning the ways the presence of gangs in schools may be affecting both gang and non-gang members will be reviewed. Much concern surrounds how the education of non-gang members suffers as a result of fear of victimization by gangs. However, little attention is focused on the ways that gang members' educational attainment may be impeded by the same culture of fear. It is important to understand which groups are most affected by the presence of gangs in schools, and in what ways, in order to provide administrators with best practice solutions. This chapter will also review state gang-related school legislation gathered by the National Gang Center and provide a synthesis organized by policy, programming, punishment, training, and discretion. Finally, an analysis and critique of selected gang prevention and intervention programs is provided, followed by suggestions for program development and future research.

Gangs and Gang Membership in the United States

According to the National Gang Center, administrator of the National Youth Gang Survey (NYGS) to law enforcement agencies, 850,000 individuals in the United States were identified as gang members in 2012 – less than one-third of 1% of the population (Egley, Howell, and Harris 2014). Despite this low prevalence, the NYGS indicated that 2,363 homicides were gang-related, accounting for a disproportionately high 16% of nationwide homicides that year (Egley, Howell, and Harris 2014). Although many individuals who become involved with gangs are deviant prior to gang membership (Thornberry 2003), an individual's involvement in deviant and criminal behavior increases greatly after joining a gang (Pyrooz et al. 2016). In addition to an increased likelihood of offending once involved in a gang, researchers have also found there to be an increased likelihood of victimization (Gibson et al. 2012; Katz et al. 2011). Decker and Pyrooz (2010) report that gang members face a homicide victimization rate 100 times greater than that of the general population, and others have identified gang membership as a risk factor for untimely mortality (Hagedorn 1998; Levitt and Venkatesh 2001; Loeber and Farrington 2011).

The NYGS states that there are 3,100 jurisdictions in the United States that report a presence of gangs in their communities – about 30% of jurisdictions (Egley, Howell, and Harris 2014). Although these numbers are useful to some extent, self-report data – which are often used by criminologists to gain a more accurate understanding of crime and victimization in the United States – may provide a more inclusive picture of gangs in America for two reasons. First, the accuracy of official report data may be compromised by individual and institutional bias throughout the data collection process (Esbensen and Huizinga 1993; Thornberry and Krohn 2000). Second, official report data do not consider the dark figure of crime – or those crimes that go unreported or undiscovered (Gibbons 1979).

The National Longitudinal Survey of Youth 1997 (NLSY97) is a nationally representative, longitudinal study of youth behavior that contains the largest subsample of youth gang members that have been collected to date. Because of the large gang member subsample size and the nationally representative sample that eliminates the risk of selection bias for gang membership, the NLSY97 provides some of the most inclusive and useful self-report data available for gang-related research. By integrating the prevalence of gang membership from the self-report data in the NLSY97 with the 2010 US Census Bureau, Pyrooz and Sweeten (2015) estimate that there were 1,059,000 *youth* gang members in the United States in 2010. This estimate from self-report data of gang membership is over 1.4 times larger than the 756,000 gang members estimated in the 2010 NYGS, and it is only considering members who are adolescents (Egley, Howell, and Harris 2014). Furthermore, it is estimated that roughly 70% of youth gang members were male and 42% were racial and ethnic minorities, leaving women to represent nearly 30% and white youth to represent about 58% of youth gang members (Pyrooz and Sweeten 2015). The fact that the majority of youth gang members are white and that a significant portion of them are female may come as a surprise to individuals who use popular media or official report data to help them conceptualize gangs in America: while minorities are disproportionately represented in gangs, they are not the majority.

Another interesting aspect of gangs in the United States is that the prevalence of membership has proven to be strongly age-graded (Lacourse et al. 2003; Miller 2011; Pyrooz and Sweeten 2015; Pyrooz 2014b). Results from the NLSY97 indicated that 1 in 12 individuals will self-report having been involved in a gang throughout his/her lifetime and that 1 in 50 youth aged 5–17 will report active gang membership (Pyrooz 2014b; Pyrooz and Sweeten 2015). The Seattle Social Development Project (SSDP) – a longitudinal survey including 808 multiethnic students attending schools in high-crime neighborhoods – found that 15 was the average age adolescents joined gangs and that 19 years of age was the oldest any student reported joining a gang (Gilman, Hill, and Hawkins 2014). The potential consequences of the age-gradedness of gang membership could have serious implications for gang-involved adolescents, the individuals who regularly interact with gang-involved adolescents, and the settings in which these two groups frequently interact. Schools are perhaps the setting most frequented by adolescent gang members, teachers, and other students, creating an environment of necessary interaction between the three. Understanding the ways in which schools, teachers, and gang members interact with one another is imperative for providing a safe learning environment that fosters the learning of every student, regardless of his/her gang membership status.

Gang Membership, Schooling, and Educational Attainment

Gangs are present in schools throughout the United States. Robers et al. (2014) found that 19% of public and 2% of private schools reported a gang presence in 2011. The Educational Longitudinal Study shows that just over 25% of students report gang activity in their schools (https://nces.ed.gov/surveys/els2002/). At the individual level, Gottfredson and Gottfredson (2001) looked at gang membership nationally and found that, on average, 3.6% of female students and 7.1% of male students report gang membership. In addition, multiple studies have gained insight into student gang membership in specific cities and regions. Naber et al. (2006) conducted a study in Ohio, Kentucky, and Indiana public schools and found that the prevalence of gang membership may be as high as 22.2% of schools having a presence of gangs. Esbensen (2010) gathered data concerning gang membership among eighth grade students in 11 cities across the country and found varying levels of gang involvement ranging from 3.8% all the way up to 15.4%. Based on seventh and eighth grade students in the Rochester, New York public school district, Thornberry and Burch (1997) concluded that 30% of students reported gang membership at some point during their secondary education. While these varying results indicate there is heterogeneity between schools and school districts, it is nonetheless evident that gangs are present in schools across the nation.

One implication of gang presence in American schools is the differential levels of academic attainment between gang and non-gang members that has resulted from a lack of inclusion, integration, and motivation of gang-involved students. Being a gang member is enough to influence teachers to interact differently with these students than they do with non-gang-involved students, creating a very different – usually less beneficial – learning environment and experience for youth in gangs (Lee 1999; Miller 2011; Reep 1996). The educational disparities for those who become involved in the gangs and the criminal justice system at an early age have been explored by researchers, and the consequences of these disparities are not only concerning for those individuals, but for schools, neighborhoods, and the labor market at large. Gang membership during adolescence significantly decreases the likelihood of completing important educational milestones (Gilman, Hill, and Hawkins 2014; Pyrooz 2014a), which creates further obstacles to success later in life (Hout 2012). For instance, Gilman and colleagues (2014) found that individuals who joined a gang during adolescence were half as likely to earn a high school diploma than non-gang members with similar life circumstances. Thornberry (2003) found that males who had been involved with a gang for either a short-term (one year or less) or long-term period (more than one year) were 11.6% and 37.9%, respectively, more likely to drop out of high school than their non-gang member counterparts. Thornberry (2003) also reports that females who had become members of gangs were 16.5% more likely to drop out than females who had never been in a gang. Levitt and Venkatesh (2001) suggest that gang members were 25% less likely to graduate from high school than youth who were not involved with gangs. Finally, using nationally representative data, Pyrooz (2014a) found that gang members were 30% less likely to graduate from high school and 58% less likely to earn a four-year college degree than their non-gang-affiliated counterparts.

With lower levels of education, gang-involved youth become limited in the types of jobs they will be able to obtain in post-industrial America (Moore 1991). Whereas blue-collar jobs have traditionally given those with a high school education or less the opportunity to work and make a living, today's job market presents few job opportunities for those with a limited education (Crutchfield and Pitchford 1997). This increased difficulty in obtaining employment leaves those with minimal education without a means to acquire basic necessities for living.

The decision to drop out of school is often driven by a lack of motivation and inability to relate to course material (Lee 1999; Miller 2011). Gang members have reported that their lack of motivation in school is due to low expectations set for them by their teachers (Reep 1996). Students who are involved in gangs often report that teachers perceive them to be violent and unwilling/unable to learn – sometimes even leaving them out of class activities– even if the student's behavior in the classroom does not reflect these assumptions (Lee 1999). When gang-involved students *feel* that their teachers do not expect anything from them – whether they truly do or not – the student may in turn feel that they have little or no incentive to try to be successful in school. Furthermore, the curriculum in most public schools across the nation is based on a culture where upward mobility is both possible and desired. Therefore, for gang members who foresee their entire lives being lived as members of the lower class, the standard curriculum does very little to prepare them for their futures (Miller 2011). This lack of interest in traditional school curricula and minimal positive, adult engagement leaves these individuals to spend their time at school with their own, usually gang-associated, itineraries. Research has found that gang members' primary reason for attending school is for social reasons – seeing friends, fighting with rival gang members, and recruiting (Boyle 1992; Decker and Van Winkle 1996).

Although research has suggested some potential explanations for the reasons gang members struggle to be successful in or complete school, it is important to remember the difficulties gang membership present in the classroom. The fact that gang-involved students often end up spending the school day defying authority makes them very difficult to deal with in the school setting. To maintain order in the classroom, many districts have come up with ways to help teachers and administrators control those students who do not conform to the rules and requirements of the school. One example of such attempts is alternative schools.

Over time, each state board of education has designed and implemented alternative schools as a way to remove these more problematic – typically gang-involved – students from the traditional classroom. Alternative schools are public facilities where students who have been deemed as dangerous or a threat to other students can go to get an education (Garot 2009). In theory, alternative schools would offer at-risk students an environment where they could flourish and learn in a way they were unable to in a traditional classroom; however, researchers have suggested a very different outcome of alternative schools. When every non-conforming student in a district is sent to one school, not only does it create a situation with a concentrated level of rival gang members, but it also eliminates opportunities for prosocial interaction for these students (Gottfredson 2001; Vigil 1999). These concerns about alternative schools suggest that isolating at-risk students may not be the best option for combating schools' gang and violence problems and highlight a need for a more comprehensive, inclusive solution.

Although considerable research focuses on the negative impact of gang membership on educational opportunities, some exceptions have highlighted the trajectories of gang members who have overcome the odds and continued into higher education. After Miller's (2011) findings that school athletics are sometimes the only positive aspect of high school aged at-risk youth's educational experiences, Rojek et al. (2013) studied the presence of gang-involved individuals who made it to college and participated in collegiate athletics. They found that although gang-member collegiate athletes are not sweeping the nation, nearly 13% of collegiate athletic directors and campus police chiefs indicate that there are gang members on their athletic teams – mainly basketball and football (Rojek et al. 2013). Rios (2011) and Durán (2013), are both former gang members who have earned their PhDs and published highly acclaimed books, *Punished: Policing the Lives of Black and Latino Boys* and *Gang Life in Two Cities: An Insider's Journey*, respectively. These works highlight the potential for gang members to be successful in graduate school and beyond. These examples demonstrate that youth who have become involved in gangs have proven it is possible to overcome the barriers they face to achieve academic success and a conventional lifestyle. Although research concerning the lives of gang members who have left the street life is less common, studies that do exist have demonstrated that upward mobility is possible among this population.

Gangs, Violence, and Fear of Victimization in Schools

Gang violence in and around schools closely reflects the trends for gang violence on the street; schools that report a presence of gangs also report higher levels of violence and victimization (Ralph et al. 1995). Robers, Zhang, Morgan, and Musu-Gillette (2015) report that in 2013 students were over twice as likely to be violently victimized while at school than while away from school. Furthermore, students who are male, urban-minority youths who attend public schools experience higher victimization rates than those reported for the general student population. Gottfredson and Gottfredson (2001) found that both male and female gang members reported higher rates of violent threats involving a weapon and were significantly more likely to carry a weapon themselves than non-gang members. Joseph (2008) found that gang members were responsible for a disproportionate level of delinquent acts in schools. Her study showed that gang members were consistently more likely to be responsible for violent offenses than non-gang members (Joseph 2008). Brunson and Miller (2009) completed a study that found that every student in their sample from a St. Louis, Missouri high school had encountered violence as either offenders, victims, or witnesses – 89%, 87%, and 100%, respectively – and that the majority of these violent incidents were gang related. This victim–offender overlap is well established (Berg 2012; Pyrooz, Moule, and Decker 2014), and is of utmost importance as criminologists continue to study violence, victimization, and fear within US schools. Understanding the relationship between those who are committing acts of violence and those who are being victimized will provide insight into the various mechanisms that need to be addressed in order to combat violence at school.

Schools tend to be tense environments for gang members. As previously discussed, schools present settings where members of multiple gangs are brought together at close quarters and are required to maintain this close proximity for sustained periods of time. For gang members, there may be only one environment that is comparable to school in terms of forcing interaction with rivals and limiting the ability to escape such interaction: prison. This heightened level of interaction ultimately increases the likelihood of confrontation and conflict between members of different gangs during school hours (Brunson and Miller 2009; Knox, Laske, and Tromanhauser 1992). Gang members and non-gang members alike are aware of the increased tension between gangs during the school day, which generates a culture of fear within schools. Furthermore, these tensions are escalated as gang members make the transition into high schools because high schools contain more students from a much wider geographical boundary than elementary and middle schools. This transition not only causes an increased number of gang members to be kept together for long durations of time, but it can also require them to travel through rival gang territory to get to and from school each day (Brunson and Miller 2009). Traveling through rival territories forces gang-on-gang interaction and increases the likelihood that students will carry a weapon for protection during their travels – weapons that then end up with them at school.

According to the National Center for Education Statistics, in 1989 3.5% of students reported that they had been victimized at school during the previous six months. Despite this low rate of victimization, 14.7% of students feared being attacked while traveling to or from school and 21.8% of students feared being attacked while at school (National Center for Education Statistics 1995). Students who attended schools where there was a presence of gangs were about twice as fearful of being attacked as those students who attended gang-free schools; however, these data cannot indicate whether increased fear is a product of a previously violent environment or the presence of gangs (National Center for Education Statistics 1995). When looking at temporal trends of fear of violent victimization in schools, we see a gradual decline in the percentage of students reporting being fearful at school between 1995 (11.8%) and 2013 (3.5%) (Robers et al. 2015). However, as Lane and Meeker (2003) point out, there are no data indicating the change in fear of *gang* victimization over time. It is also important to note that a decrease in the overall level of fear among students does not necessarily mean that there had been a decrease in the level of violence and criminality. These changes in temporal trends and comparisons between fear of victimization between schools with and without gangs shine a light on multiple gaps in the literature concerning the fear of gang violence and victimization.

Despite the decades of research on violence, victimization, and fear in schools, it is unclear what the consequences of such fear may be. Some researchers emphasize the negative consequences that a culture of fear may have on US schools (Thompkins 2000), whereas others argue that this culture of fear may be having a more positive impact (Melde, Berg, and Esbensen 2014). Among those who foresee more negative consequences of fear in schools, Thompkins (2000) highlights the importance of recognizing that such a culture of fear is not rational in all American schools. There has been a moral panic, largely caused by the media's disproportionate reporting of violence in schools, that has caused students and teachers nationwide to fear being victimized by gangs while at school (Thompkins 2000). A few violent offenses in schools that took place in the 1990s caused the media to turn its attention to the unprecedented violence that was occurring within schools, much of which was blamed on gang members (Thompkins 2000). Despite the fact that the acts of school violence the media focused on in the 1990s were mostly school shootings in rural/suburban schools – like the ones in Littleton, CO, Edinboro, PA, and Springfield, OR – and completely unrelated to gangs, an increased fear of gang violence swept the nation and school systems' responses have only exacerbated the problem (Thompkins 2000).

Schools all around the nation – urban, rural, and suburban – started cracking down with increased security measures, including installing metal detectors and cameras and hiring security guards (Thompkins 2000). Although this increase in security measures may help deter a small number of violent acts in a small proportion of schools (mainly the urban schools where gangs are more commonly present), the largest effect these security measures have had is an increased, potentially irrational, fear of victimization among students and teachers (Thompkins 2000). According to Thompkins (2000), in the rural and suburban schools, where there is a lower presence of gangs, these increased security measures make students and teachers feel that there is something they need to be protected from and instill a sense of fear that may not be justified. In schools where gangs are present, this increased fear of victimization that students and teachers have adopted in response to the added security measures only gives gang members more power over those who are fearful (Thompkins 2000). Furthermore, research has shown that when students are fearful and feel unsafe in their school environment they may be up to three times more likely to join a gang themselves as a form of protection (Lenzi et al. 2015). These findings suggest that this moral panic of gang violence and victimization not only could cause unnecessary security measures and fear in rural and suburban teachers and students, but may also be influencing an increase in gang membership within schools where gangs are present. These implications highlight the negative consequences of fear within schools and the importance of gaining a full and factual understanding of the ways that gangs, schools, and violence interact before acting upon assumptions and implementing policies that are not evidence based. Whereas some schools are in extreme need of programing and intervention to combat the effects of gang membership on their students, others can be significantly damaged if they respond to problems that are not present in their schools.

While the negative consequences of fear have been studied for many years, researchers have begun to explore the potential positive consequences of fear of violence and victimization. Among the first to empirically study the functional components of fear, Jackson and Gray (2009) found that roughly one-quarter of their sampled residents who were fearful of crime were able to translate that emotion into practicing more precautionary behaviors. These precautionary behaviors left them feeling safer in their neighborhoods and did not impact their quality of life. Melde, Berg, and Esbensen (2014) took this idea of positive/functional consequences of fear one step further and found that increased fear of crime – and the consequences that come with committing crimes – could lead to precautionary behaviors that decrease the overall level of fear *and* decrease the overall likelihood of becoming a violent offender or victim. In other words, whether or not an individual perceives a high risk of victimization, if he is fearful of the consequences of victimization or offending, it will result in risk-averse behaviors that are likely to reduce his overall likelihood of becoming involved in violent encounters – either as a victim or an offender.

When thinking about positive consequences of fear in terms of gang violence in schools, the frameworks of Jackson and Gray (2009) and Melde, Berg, and Esbensen (2014) are important to consider. Using this framework could help shine a light on the positive outcomes of the increased security measures that many American schools experienced in the 1990s as a response to a few isolated, non-gang-related, violent incidents in schools (Thompkins 2000). First, Thompkins (2000) suggests that the added security measures in schools are causing a culture of fear among teachers and students. However, frameworks that focus on the positive consequences of fear would argue that although this fear may be irrational in some schools, it also serves as a protective factor that heightens awareness and encourages risk-averse behaviors that will ultimately make fearful teachers and students feel safer (Jackson and Gray 2009; Melde, Berg, and Esbensen 2014).

Second, increased surveillance (i.e., security officers, metal detectors, security cameras, etc.) could also help deter offending and victimization. As previously discussed, it is well established that the largest predictive factor in determining an individual's likelihood of violent victimization is that individual's own violent behavior. In other words, those who are actively participating in violent offending are also the ones who are most frequently victims of violence themselves (Melde, Berg, and Esbensen 2014). By combining the victim–offender overlap with Melde et al.'s (2014) idea that fear of criminal consequences can serve as a deterrent to violence, the fear that these added security measures are causing may be providing a protective factor not only for non-violent students and teachers but gang members, as well. The added security measures in schools where gang violence is common are likely to not only decrease the likelihood of these members offending – because surveillance increases their likelihood of getting caught – but also decrease the level of violent victimization within schools because of the victim–offender overlap (Melde, Berg, and Esbensen 2014; but see Chapter 13, this volume).

These studies highlight the importance of considering all possible factors and outcomes of fear before policy makers and school administrators attempt to combat gang violence in schools. Although researchers have made empirical and persuasive arguments for both the positive and negative consequences of fear, much more research is needed to determine which of these possible consequences and factors are most salient when considering school violence. In addition, more research is needed that looks specifically at gangs and what portion of students' fear is attributable to gang presence. By gaining a more accurate understanding of how students' and teachers' fears are being developed, researchers, school administrators, and policy makers will be better equipped to design and implement effective school programs aimed at the prevention of and intervention in gang membership within American schools.

Zero Tolerance Policies and Gang Legislation

In addition to added security measures as a response to the increased fear of violence and victimization, many schools and school districts across the country have implemented punishment policies – commonly known as zero tolerance policies – related to gang involvement, violence, and behavior (see Chapter 12, this volume). Although having such policies may be important for protecting students from harm, many of these policies are so ambiguous in nature that they give school administrators considerable discretion in deciding what is "gang related" (see Chapter 11, this volume; Morrison et al. 2001). This discrepancy becomes problematic when school administrators lack the knowledge and training to accurately detect gang involvement and activity among students, potentially creating disproportionately harsh punitive measures for rather minor actions (Skiba and Knesting 2001). Scholars have recognized that when acts of violence threaten the security and stability of a school, administrators are likely to respond with reactive disciplinary procedures in an attempt to address public concern about the school's safety (Morrison et al. 2001). These disciplinary practices are often ineffective in addressing the source of the problem, but because they satisfy public demand for safe schools they have become standard procedure.

One of the main reasons for these policies is a shift toward the tough-on-crime policies of the 1980s and 1990s (American Psychological Association 2006; Cobb 2009). As of 2001, 80% of US schools had at least one element of the typical zero tolerance policy in their disciplinary policies and procedures and they continue to become more common as schools continue to be sites of violence (Skiba and Knesting 2001). In 2006, the American Psychological Association conducted a review to determine the effectiveness of zero tolerance policies' ability to increase safety in schools and found that not only were they ineffective at increasing safety, but they were inconsistently utilized and actually increased delinquency in schools (American Psychological Association 2006).

This inconsistency in application is perhaps one of the most problematic issues with zero tolerance policies, because they can result in disproportionate minority referrals to the juvenile courts (Cobb 2009). School administrators and criminal justice officers are typically white (Gates, Ringel, and Santibanez 2003; Maciag 2015) and much older than the students in their charge. Cultural and generational unfamiliarity has the potential to lead administrators to misinterpret the actions and attitudes of their racial/ethnic minority students. In turn, misinterpretation can lead to unjustified negative perceptions and continued racial stereotyping of these students. Complicating matters is the well-established fact that racial/ethnic minorities are overrepresented in US gangs. This may result in the application of zero tolerance policies to disproportionately target minorities, significantly hindering these already disadvantaged populations. Unfamiliarity between racially, ethnically, and generationally disconnected administrators and students results in zero tolerance policies that ultimately target minority students. These students can be disproportionately suspected to be involved with gangs, which can have the effect of premature involvement in the criminal justice system. Furthermore, the combination of zero tolerance policies and early entry into the criminal justice system fosters low self-efficacy and a limited, negative perception of future life outcomes for these students (Cobb 2009).

One example of ambiguous and inconsistent zero tolerance policies can be found in the Atlanta public school system. Specifically, Atlanta public schools employ a zero tolerance policy concerning gang activity on school property or at school events (Atlanta Public Schools 2015). While this appears to be a well-intentioned policy implemented to protect the students and staff, the list of what qualifies as "gang-related" activity is so vague that any behavior, clothing, action, or conversation could be classified as "gang-related." For example, gang-related behaviors include "the use of certain hand signals or gestures that may, in any way, be linked to a gang or gang-related activity or behavior" (Atlanta Public Schools 2015, 1). Another example of ambiguous zero tolerance policies can be found in one Michigan school district where policy recognizes that "gang activity by its nature is often subtle or covert" and states that "the administration reserves the right to determine which behaviors, dress, or activities are gang related" (Muskegon Public Schools 2015, 1). These examples are only two of the thousands of zero tolerance policies that exist in the United States and they illustrate how much discretion school administrators have to determine what is a gang-related action or behavior. This much discretion risks allowing administrators to punish according to stereotypes, biases, and prejudices.

Figure 10.1 displays which states have formal, state-wide legislation that addresses gangs in and around US schools (National Gang Center 2015). Twenty-seven states have state-mandated legislation regarding gang-related programming, policy, punishment, and training. It is important to understand that while formal legislation may provide guidelines for the school districts in each state, these guidelines are only minimum requirements. In other words, each school and school district has the freedom to enhance its gang-related practices as long as the state-regulated guidelines are satisfied in the process. On that same note, it is equally important to understand that while

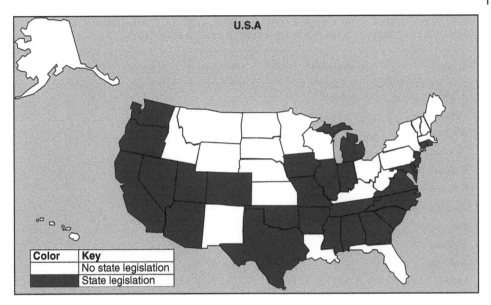

Figure 10.1 Map of United States indicating which states have formal legislation addressing gangs in schools (National Gang Center 2015).

23 states are without formal state legislation concerning gangs in schools, administrators in these states have a great deal of discretion to develop their own gang-related policies, programs, and practices.

Table 10.1 reports what type of gang-related policy/policies – as defined and categorized by the authors of this chapter – have been implemented in each state: programming-based, policy-based, punishment-based, training-based, and discretion-based. Our operational definitions are as follows:[1]

- Programming-based legislation has been defined as any law enforcing schools to fund and/or implement any sort of gang prevention or intervention program in the school.
- Policy-based legislation requires schools to have some sort of gang-related policy – usually concerning gang-associated clothing, colors, symbols, etc. – in their school handbook.
- Punitive-based legislation includes laws with special punitive measures for gang-related activities and behaviors.
- Training-based legislation has been defined as any legislation that requires school administrators, faculty, staff, etc. to receiving training on various gang-related features such as detecting and responding to gang-related behavior and activities.
- Discretion-based legislation refers to legislative language that leaves culpability and punishment to the discretion of school administrators.

---

1 We assessed the inter-rater reliability in recording this legislation classification using two techniques: (i) percent agreement and (ii) Cohen's kappa. Between three raters, there was an 88% agreement in the classifications of each state's gang legislation. A kappa coefficient of .2979 was calculated for the combined agreement of state gang legislation categorization between the three raters – which controls for agreement that can be expected by chance. A kappa coefficient of .2979 is considered to be a fair strength of agreement (Landis and Koch 1977).

Table 10.1 States with gang-related school legislation, by type (National Gang Center 2015). Additional information at: https://www.nationalgangcenter.gov/Legislation/Schools.

State	Programming	Policy	Punishment	Training	Discretion	None
Alabama	X					
Alaska						X
Arizona		X	X		X	
Arkansas		X		X		
California	X	X		X		
Colorado		X				
Connecticut			X			
Delaware				X		
Florida						X
Georgia			X			
Hawaii						X
Idaho						X
Illinois			X			
Indiana	X			X	X	
Iowa		X				
Kansas						X
Kentucky						X
Louisiana						X
Maine						X
Maryland	X	X	X			
Massachusetts						X
Michigan		X				
Minnesota						X
Mississippi	X	X	X			
Missouri		X				
Montana						X
Nebraska						X
Nevada		X				
New Hampshire						X
New Jersey	X			X		
New Mexico						X
New York						X
North Carolina			X			
North Dakota						X
Ohio						X
Oklahoma			X		X	

Table 10.1 (Continued)

State	Programming	Policy	Punishment	Training	Discretion	None
Oregon		X				
Pennsylvania						X
Rhode Island	X					
South Carolina		X				
South Dakota						X
Tennessee		X		X		
Texas		X	X			
Utah	X	X	X	X		
Vermont						X
Virginia	X	X	X			
Washington		X	X			
West Virginia						X
Wisconsin						X
Wyoming						X
Total %	18%	34%	24%	14%	6%	46%

It bears repeating that only state-level legislation is being reported. In other words, this table is not exhaustive, and the number of gang-related policies and practices are expected to vary considerably by school, and from one school district to another within each of these states.

As previously discussed, determining whether a student's behavior should be considered gang related or not can result in major disparities in the severity of the punishment imposed on that student. State legislation that addresses how to handle gang activity in schools varies by state; however, most states consistently punish gang members more harshly than non-gang members. For example, in Arizona a gang-involved student who commits a felony on school property can be sentenced up to five years more than the maximum sentencing for a crime, while a non-gang member can only face one additional year in confinement for committing a felony at school. This increased sentencing is part of a broader trend of enhancement penalties applied to gang members (National Gang Center 2015). This insistence on harsher punishments for gang members not only results in disproportionate racial/ethnic minority contact with punitive institutions – considering these minorities are overrepresented in gangs – but it increases the number of barriers to educational attainment that gang members encounter (see Chapter 9, this volume).

As discussed above, racial/ethnic minorities are overrepresented in the group of students who receive disciplinary action as a result of zero tolerance policies at the school district and state level (Cobb 2009; National Gang Center 2015; Short and Sharp 2005). These same individuals are also those in most desperate need of positive adult guidance and a stable environment. However, zero tolerance policies fail to consider situational influences and respond punitively to actions that may be a cry for help (Cobb 2009; Morrison et al. 2001; Skiba and Noam 2001). Removing such students from the classroom by suspending or expelling them eliminates what little prosocial interaction they had, encourages further delinquent behavior, and forces them to fall behind in coursework (Skiba and Knesting 2001; Morrison et al. 2001).

The lack of empirical support for zero tolerance policies suggests that policy makers and school officials should pursue alternatives that are more likely to foster a positive, safe learning environment. Such alternative policies would primarily feature restorative and rehabilitative focuses that would respond to each student's specific needs with compassion and understanding. Such changes would allow schools to help *all* of their students succeed academically, rather than only those who do not have to worry about how their actions and behaviors are being perceived by those who look differently than themselves (Cobb 2009; Graves and Mirsky 2007).

Prevention and Intervention

Another common response to heightened awareness of violence in schools during the latter portion of the twentieth century was various prevention and intervention programs that were targeted toward violence in schools – often specifically targeting gang violence – created by federal, state, and local governments, as well as various non-profit organizations (Wong et al. 2016). Prevention and intervention programs were attractive to government and community officials because they offered a way to be proactive in addressing gangs (i.e., prevention of gang formation in schools), rather than the reactive responses many schools had traditionally used for addressing gangs (i.e., suppressing the problem, punishing individuals after violence occurs, ignoring small acts of gang crime/violence, etc.) (Thompkins 2000). Although Gottfredson and Gottfredson (2001) reported that there are over 941,000 school-based gang prevention and intervention programs, Wong et al. (2016), based on a recent meta-analytic review of the literature, identified the following as undergoing formal evaluation:

- Gang Resistance Education and Training program (GREAT) (Esbensen et al. 2001);
- Revised Gang Resistance Education and Training program (GREAT II) (Esbensen et al. 2013);
- Gang Prevention Through Targeted Outreach program (GPTTO) (Arbreton and McClanahan 2002);
- National Youth Gang Drug Prevention program (NYGDP) (Cohen et al. 1995);
- Logan Square Prevention project (LSP) (Godley and Velasquez 1998);
- Broader Urban Involvement and Leadership Development program (BUILD) (Thompson and Jason 1988).

Table 10.2 reports the treatment and whether each program increased, decreased, or did not change the level of gang membership.

Although nearly all of the programs revealed that their treatment groups maintained lower rates of gang membership, only the second evaluation of GREAT reported a statistically significant lower likelihood of gang membership between students who completed the GREAT II program and students who did not (Esbensen et al. 2013; Wong et al. 2016). The potential shown by GREAT II is important for school administrators to consider while determining ways to handle gang presence in their schools; therefore, a more in-depth coverage of the program is provided below.

Table 10.2 Summary of results from various gang prevention programs.

Study	Treatment	Change in gang membership
Gang Resistance Education and Training program (GREAT)	Police teach nine weekly lessons to middle school students covering topics such as crime/victim rights, cultural sensitivity/prejudice, conflict resolution, meeting basic needs, dangers of drugs, responsibility, and goal setting	No change
Gang Resistance Education and Training –Revised program (GREAT II)	Police teach 13 weekly lessons to middle school students on topics such as gang violence, community responsibility, goal setting, decision making, communication, listening, body language, peer pressure, anger management, calming others, and conflict resolution	Decrease
Gang Prevention Through Targeted Outreach program (GPTTO)	Promotes activities for hard-to-reach, at-risk youth such as after-school activities, social skills classes, conflict resolution workshops, and education programs	No change
National Youth Gang Drug Prevention program (NYGDP)	Promotes community efforts to prevent youth gang involvement	No change
Logan Square Prevention project (LSP)	Provides activities such as gang prevention seminars, recreational activities, school-based life skills programs, drug abuse treatment, counseling with families, and after-school/summer activities to inner-city youth	No change
Broader Urban Involvement and Leadership Development program (BUILD)	Targets at-risk students during school activities; provides after-school activities, job skills training, and educational programs for at-risk youth	No change

Note: Indicates whether the change in the likelihood of gang membership was statistically different than zero according to the results of Wong et al. (2016).

GREAT II is a nationwide, school-based gang and violence prevention program that was created as a revision to the original design of the GREAT program (Esbensen 2015). The GREAT II program was designed with three goals in mind: (i) to reduce gang membership among students, (ii) to reduce violent and criminal activity in schools, and (iii) to increase positive relationships with local law enforcement officers. The program includes 13 cumulative lessons which are designed to address the three goals listed above and various risk factors that are thought to be linked to these three goals (i.e., "school commitment, school performance, association with conventional and/or delinquent peers, susceptibility to peer influence, involvement in conventional activities, empathy, self-control, perceived guilt, neutralization techniques, and moral disengagement") (Esbensen 2015, 380). GREAT II focuses on these risk factors as a result of the original GREAT research study's finding that the more specific risk factors a student has, the more likely they are to join a gang or become involved in violent situations (Esbensen et al. 2001). As such, the hope was that GREAT II would address these risk factors and be more effective in achieving its goals of lowering gang membership and violence in schools (Esbensen 2015).

A recently completed four-year follow-up on the students who completed GREAT II found that there was a significant difference between those who did complete the GREAT II program and those who did not (Esbensen 2015). Overall, those who completed the program were 24% less likely to have joined a gang. In addition, those who completed the program were also more likely to have positive attitudes toward local police officers. In contrast to these two successes, the four-year follow-up of GREAT II did not show a significant decrease in the amount of violence and delinquency among those who completed the program and those who did not. In terms of risk factors, students who completed GREAT II had more negative attitudes about gangs, were more risk averse, has better control over their anger, used fewer neutralization techniques for violent behavior, used more refusal techniques, and had higher levels of altruism and collective efficacy (Esbensen 2015).

Overall, GREAT II has been found to be the most successful gang membership and violence prevention program thus far (Wong et al. 2016). The program was successful in accomplishing two of the three goals – helping students avoid gang membership and improving attitudes and relationships with local police officers – and was also successful in addressing multiple risk factors students face that may impact their ability to avoid gang membership.

GREAT II has not gone without some criticism. First, some have suggested that the effect sizes produced by the GREAT II program are relatively small. However, Maxson (2013) states that any positive and significant effect size is satisfying as proof that the program has an effect on membership – especially considering the cost effectiveness of the program. A second criticism of GREAT II is that the program was not successful in addressing its third goal – decreasing violence and criminality in schools (Esbensen 2015; Esbensen et al. 2013). This is a particularly salient point, as reducing youth violence and delinquency is arguably the main reason for attempting to decrease gang membership in the first place. Pyrooz (2013) recognized that gang members are not inherently violent; therefore, successfully decreasing the number of people who label themselves as gang members but failing to decrease the number of people who are violent presents some concern. This disconnect leads criminologists to question their understanding of gang membership and violent offending. It is possible that the outcomes of GREAT II support the indirect interaction model presented by Estrada et al. (2014) where an individual's risk of violent offending is indirectly influenced by an individual's school risk behaviors and the school's protective measures, rather than directly related to the individual's involvement in a gang. It is also possible that GREAT II has taught gang members to present their membership covertly, rather than actually decreasing membership – which would help explain why violence was unaffected by the otherwise successful program. One additional possibility is that GREAT II is not approaching/measuring violence and delinquency in a way that would allow a full and factual understanding of the effects of the program on participants. Thus, although GREAT II has proven to be the most effective program in addressing gangs in schools, the program's failure to decrease violence and delinquency indicates a need for continued improvement of the program.

One final critique of the design of GREAT II is that it might target the wrong population. By failing to sample from those adolescents who are at risk of joining gangs, Klein and Maxson (2006) indicate that the vast majority of the sampled students would not have joined a gang even had they gone without GREAT II intervention. This issue with the sampling of GREAT II raises doubt about the validity of the program's ability to decrease gang membership (Klein and Maxson 2006). The shortfalls of this study point to the need for more research investigating the trajectories into gang membership, as well as the relationship between gang membership and violent offending.

Conclusion

This chapter has highlighted many shortcomings in the way that schools and society currently address gangs and has made some suggestions on how to improve upon those shortcomings. Working to address the issue of gangs and violence in schools can result in many improvements; however, more empirical research is needed to determine how to adequately and appropriately handle gangs and violence in schools. The current lack of empirical research focusing on the effects of gang membership on violence – and other risky behaviors such as truancy, substance abuse, and so on – makes it difficult for schools and administrators to effectively identify the true source of the problem. This lack of research has also left schools with few (if any) evidence-based programs and policies that address violence within school settings. The authors of this chapter see an immediate need for empirical work that seeks to understand the association between gang membership and violence, as well as gang membership and other risky behaviors suggested by Estrada et al. (2014). There is also a need for research that will provide a more systematic explanation of the various consequences of fear – both positive and negative – in a school setting. By addressing these two areas of research, much progress may be made in developing evidence-based programs and policies that can address gang membership and violence proactively and productively.

While much more work by researchers is needed, this chapter also points to some necessary changes that can be made by educational practitioners. As indicated by the previous discussion about zero tolerance policies and gang-related state legislation, there is an urgent need for a reform in the policies and practices surrounding gangs and violence in schools. While the authors of this chapter in no way disagree with the clear necessity for rules and guidelines that address violence in schools, they do disagree with the use and ambiguity of zero tolerance policies in practice. Skiba and Knesting (2001) have made some suggestions for how to reduce ambiguity and disparities while disciplining students for gang-related and violent behaviors. These suggestions include:

- Only use zero tolerance-based disciplinary practices for the most severe violent actions and behaviors and have clear definitions of what actions and behaviors are considered the most severe.
- Generate disciplinary procedures that are stratified so that the punishment is proportionate to the action/behavior that was committed, rather than using one-size-fits-all punishments.
- Implement more options for schools when dealing with students who have behaved violently.
- Create preventative measures in schools that can be proactive in addressing violence and that can work to reintegrate students who have been alienated as a result of reactionary punishment.
- Conduct evaluations of school disciplinary practices and policies to ensure only those that are having a positive and productive effect are being maintained.

These suggestions are important starting points for educators who are dealing with violence in their schools. What is especially important is the need for proactive, rather than reactive, policies in schools dealing with violence and gang membership. As indicated by the gang-related state legislation discussed previously, a large number of schools are creating policies and punishments specifically aimed at dealing with gang members in a reactive/punitive way; however, very few states are working to deal with gang-involved students in a proactive way that will decrease their likelihood of remaining involved in a gang or of being violent. Furthermore, it is imperative that schools evaluate their policies and practices to be sure that they are having a positive impact on the students and serving their intended purpose.

As this chapter has highlighted, further research is needed to fully understand the ways that gangs and gang members exist within schools, and how the fear of violence and crime caused by gang members could be helping and/or hindering students at school. Further research is also needed to better understand how and why the third goal of GREAT II – decreasing violence and delinquency in schools – fell short of its objectives. While working with these deviant and oftentimes violent students who are involved in gangs, it is important to remember that they are not a throwaway population. Indeed, the obstacles that youth gang members face are often more significant than the obstacles faced by their non-gang-involved counterparts. They can still overcome the educational and life setbacks they may face during their gang membership years and continue on to higher education and more conventional lifestyles if they are allowed the opportunity to do so.

References

American Psychological Association. 2006. "Zero Tolerance Policies Are Not as Effective as Thought in Reducing Violence and Promoting Learning in School." Press release. http:// www.apa.org/news/press/releases/2006/08/zero-tolerance.aspx (last accessed October 12, 2017).

Arbreton, Amy J. A. and McClanahan, Wendy S. 2002. "Targeted Outreach: Boys & Girls Clubs of America's Approach to Gang Prevention and Intervention." Philadelphia, PA: Public/Private Ventures.

Atlanta Public Schools. 2015. "Gangs (Secret Societies) & Gang-Like Activity." http:// atlantapublicschools.us/page/4767 (last accessed October 12, 2017).

Berg, Mark T. 2012. "The Overlap of Violent Offending and Violent Victimization: Assessing the Evidence and Explanations." In *Violent Offenders: Theory, Research, Policy, and Practice*, edited by Matt DeLisi and Peter J. Conis, pp. 17–38. Burlington, MA: Jones & Bartlett Learning.

Boyle, Kathleen. 1992. "School's a Rough Place: Youth Gangs, Drug Users, and Family Life in Los Angeles." Washington, DC: Department of Education, Office of Educational Research and Improvement, ED 360 435.

Brunson, Rod K. and Miller, Jody. 2009. "Schools, Neighborhoods, and Adolescent Conflicts: A Situational Examination of Reciprocal Dynamics." *Justice Quarterly* 26(2), 183–210. DOI: 10.1080/07418820802245060.

Cobb, Heather. 2009. "Separate and Unequal: The Disparate Impact of School-Based Referrals to Juvenile Court." *Harvard Civil Rights–Civil Liberties Law Review* 44, 581.

Cohen, Marcia, Williams, Katherine, Bekelman, Alan, and Crosse, Scott. 1995. "Evaluation of the National Youth Gang Drug Prevention Program." In *The Modern Gang Reader*, edited by Malcolm W. Klein, Cheryl L. Maxson, and Jody Miller, pp. 266–275. Los Angeles: Roxbury.

Crutchfield, Robert D. and Pitchford, Susan R. 1997. "Work and Crime: The Effects of Labor Stratification." *Social Forces* 76(1), 93–118.

Curry, G. David, Decker, Scott H., and Pyrooz, David. 2014. *Confronting Gangs: Crime and Community*. Oxford: Oxford University Press.

Decker, Scott H. and Pyrooz, David C. 2010. "Gang Violence Worldwide: Context, Culture, and Country." *Small Arms Survey* 5, 129–155.

Decker, Scott H. and Van Winkle, Barrik. 1996. *Life in the Gang: Family, Friends, and Violence*. Cambridge: Cambridge University Press.

Durán, R. 2013. *Gang Life in Two Cities: An Insider's Journey*. New York: Columbia University Press.

Egley, Arlen Jr., Howell, James C., and Harris, Meena. 2014. *Highlights of the 2012 National Youth Gang Survey*. Office of Juvenile Justice and Delinquency Prevention and US Department of Justice.

Esbensen, Finn-Aage. 2010. *Youth Violence: Sex and Race Differences in Offending, Victimization, and Gang Membership*. Philadelphia, PA: Temple University Press.

Esbensen, Finn-Aage. 2015. "The Gang Resistance Education and Training (G.R.E.A.T.) Program." In *The Handbook of Gangs*, edited by Scott H. Decker and David C. Pyrooz, pp. 369–391. John Wiley & Sons, Inc.

Esbensen, Finn-Aage and Huizinga, David. 1993. "Gangs, Drugs, and Delinquency in a Survey of Urban Youth." *Criminology* 31(4), 565–589.

Esbensen, Finn-Aage, Osgood, D. Wayne, Taylor, Terrance J., Peterson, Dana, and Freng, Adrienne. 2001. "How Great Is G.R.E.A.T.? Results for a Longitudinal Quasi-Experimental Design." *Criminology & Public Policy* 1(1), 87–118.

Esbensen, Finn-Aage, Osgood, D. Wayne, Peterson, Dana, Taylor, Terrance J., and Carson, Dena C. 2013. "Short- and Long-Term Outcome Results from a Multisite Evaluation of the G.R.E.A.T. Program." *Criminology & Public Policy* 12(3), 375–411. DOI: 10.1111/1745-9133.12045.

Estrada Jr., Joey Nuñez, Gilreath, Tamika D., Astor, Ron Avi, and Benbenishty, Rami. 2014. "Gang Membership, School Violence, and the Mediating Effects of Risk and Protective Behaviors in California High Schools." *Journal of School Violence* 13(2), 228–251. DOI: 10.1080/15388220.2013.846860.

Garot, Robert. 2009. "The Gang's School: Challenges of Reintegrative Social Control: New Approaches to Social Problems Treatment." In *New Approaches to Social Problems Treatment* (Research in Social Problems and Public Policy, Volume 17), edited by Mark Peyrot and Stacy Lee Burns, pp. 149–176. Bingley, UK: Emerald Group Publishing.

Gates, Susan M., Ringel, Jeanne S., and Santibanez, Lucrecia. 2003. *Who Is Leading Our Schools?: An Overview of School Administrators and Their Careers* (No.1679). Rand Corporation.

Gibbons, Don C. 1979. *The Criminological Enterprise: Theories and Perspectives*. Englewood Cliffs, NJ: Prentice Hall.

Gibson, Chris L., Swatt, Marc L., Miller, Mitchell, Jennings, Wesley G., and Gover, Angela R. 2012. "The Causal Relationship between Gang Joining and Violent Victimization: A Critical Review and Directions for Future Research." *Journal of Criminal Justice* 40(6), 490–501.

Gilman, Amanda B., Hill, Karl G., and Hawkins, J. David. 2014. "Long-Term Consequences of Adolescent Gang Membership for Adult Functioning." *American Journal of Public Health* 104(5), 938–45. DOI: 10.2105/AJPH.2013.301821.

Godley, Mark D. and Velasquez, Rick. 1998. "Effectiveness of the Logan Square Prevention Project: Interim Results." *Drugs & Society* 12(1–2), 87–103. DOI: 10.1300/J023v12n01.

Gottfredson, Denise C. 2001. *Schools and Delinquency*. Cambridge: Cambridge University Press.

Gottfredson, Gary D. and Gottfredson, Denise C. 2001. "Gang Problems and Gang Programs in a National Sample of Schools." Ellicott City, MD: Gottfredson Associates, Inc.

Graves, Doug and Mirsky, Laura. 2007. "American Psychological Association Report Challenges School Zero Tolerance Policies and Recommends Restorative Justice." International Institute for Restorative Practices. https://www.iirp.edu/eforum-archive/4370-american-psychological-association-report-challenges-school-zero-tolerance-policies-and-recommends-restorative-justice (last accessed October 12, 2017).

Hagedorn, John M. 1998. "Gang Violence in the Postindustrial Era." *Crime and Justice* 24, 365–419.

Hout, Michael. 2012. "Social and Economic Returns to College Education in the United States." *Annual Review of Sociology* 38 (August), 379–400. DOI: 10.1146/annurev.soc.012809.102503.

Howell, James C. and Griffiths, Elizabeth. 2015. *Gangs in America's Communities*. Thousand Oaks, CA: Sage.

Jackson, J. and E. Gray. 2009. "Functional Fear and Public Insecurities about Crime." *British Journal of Criminology* 50(1), 1–22. DOI: 10.1093/bjc/azp059.

Joseph, Janice. 2008. "Gangs and Gang Violence in School." *Journal of Gang Research* 16(1), 33–50.

Katz, Charles M., Webb, Vincent J., Fox, Kate, and Shaffer, Jennifer N. 2011. "Understanding the Relationship between Violent Victimization and Gang Membership." *Journal of Criminal Justice* 39(1), 48–59. DOI: 10.1016/j.jcrimjus.2010.10.004.

Klein, Malcolm W. and Maxson, Cheryl L. 2006. "Gang Structures, Crime Patterns, and Police Responses." National Criminal Justice Reference Service. https://www.ncjrs.gov/pdffiles1/nij/grants/188511.pdf (last accessed October 12, 2017).

Knox, George, Laske, David L., and Tromanhauser, Edward D. 1992. *Schools Under Siege*. Dubuque, IA: Kendall/Hunt.

Lacourse, Eric, Nagin, Daniel, Tremblay, Richard E., Vitaro, Frank, and Claes, Michel. 2003. "Developmental Trajectories of Boys' Delinquent Group Membership and Facilitation of Violent Behaviors during Adolescence." *Development and Psychopathology* 15(01), 183–197. DOI: 10.1017.S0954579403000105.

Landis, J. Richard and Koch, Gary G. 1977. "The Measurement of Observer Agreement for Categorical Data." *Biometrics* 33(1), 159–174.

Lane, Jodi and Meeker, James W. 2003. "Fear of Gang Crime: A Look at Three Theoretical Models." *Law & Society Review* 37(2), 425–456. DOI: 10.2307/1555134.

Lee, P.W. 1999. "In Their Own Voices: An Ethnographic Study of Low-Achieving Students within the Context of School Reform." *Urban Education* 34(2), 214–244. DOI: 10.1177/0042085999342005.

Lenzi, Michela, Sharkey, Jill, Vieno, Alessio, Mayworm, Ashley, Dougherty, Danielle, and Nylund-Gibson, Karen. 2015. "Adolescent Gang Involvement: The Role of Individual, Family, Peer, and School Factors in a Multilevel Perspective." *Aggressive Behavior* 41(4), 386–397. DOI: 0.1002/ab.21562.

Levitt, Steven D. and Venkatesh, Sudhir Alladi. 2001. "Growing Up in the Projects: The Economic Lives of a Cohort of Men Who Came of Age in Chicago Public Housing." *American Economic Review* 91(2), 79–84.

Loeber, Rolf and Farrington, David P. 2011. "Young Male Homicide Offenders and Victims: Current Knowledge, Beliefs, and Key Questions." In *Young Homicide Offenders and Victims*. Springer.

Maciag, Mike. 2015. "Diversity on the Force: Where Police Don't Mirror Communities." *Governing*. http://www.governing.com/topics/public-justice-safety/gov-police-department-diversity.html (last accessed October 27, 2017).

Matsuda, Kristy N., Melde, Chris, Taylor, Terrance J., Freng, Adrienne, and Esbensen, Finn-Aage. 2013. "Gang Membership and Adherence to the 'Code of the Street." *Justice Quarterly* 30(3), 440–468. DOI: 10.1080/07418825.2012.684432.

Maxson, Cheryl L. 2013. "Do Not Shoot the Messenger: The Utility of Gang Risk Research in Program Targeting and Content." *Criminology & Public Policy* 12(3), 421–426. DOI: 10.1111/1745-9133.12052.

Medina-Ariza, Juan J., Cebulla, Andreas, Aldridge, Judith, Shute, Jon, and Ross, Andy. 2013. "Proximal Adolescent Outcomes of Gang Membership in England and Wales." *Journal of Research in Crime and Delinquency* 51(2), 168–199.

Melde, Chris, Berg, Mark T., and Esbensen, Finn-Aage. 2014. "Fear, Social Interactions, and Violence Mitigation." *Justice Quarterly* 1–29. DOI: 10.1080/07418825.2014.928348.

Melde, Chris and Esbensen, Finn-Aage. 2011. "Gang Membership as a Turning Point in the Life Course." *Criminology* 49(2), 513–552.

Miller, Walter B. 2011. "City Gangs." http://gangresearch.asu.edu/walter_miller_library/walter-b.-miller-book/city-gangs-book.

Moore, Joan W. 1991. *Going Down to the Barrio: Homeboys and Homegirls in Change.* Philadelphia, PA: Temple University Press.

Morrison, Gale M., Anthony, Suzanne, Storino, Meri H., Cheng, Joanna J., Furlong, Michael J., and Morrison, Richard L.. 2001. "School Expulsion as a Process and an Event: Before and after Effects on Children at Risk for School Discipline." *New Directions for Youth Development* 92, 45–71.

Muskegon Public Schools. 2015. "Gang Policy." http://www.muskegonpublicschools.org/schools/muskegon/Our_School/policiesprocedures/gangpolicy/.

Naber, Patricia A., May, David C., Decker, Scott H., Minor, Kevin I., and Wells, James B. 2006. "Are There Gangs in Schools?" *Journal of School Violence* 5(2), 53–72. DOI: 10.1300/J202v05n02.

National Center for Education Statistics. 1995. "Gangs and Victimization at School." Press release. https://nces.ed.gov/pubs95/95740.pdf (last accessed October 27, 2017).

National Gang Center. 2015. "Gang-Related Legislation – Gangs and Schools." https://www.nationalgangcenter.gov/Legislation/Schools (last accessed October 27, 2017).

Pyrooz, David C. 2013. "Gangs, Criminal Offending, and an Inconvenient Truth: Consideration for Gang Prevention and Intervention in the Lives of Youth." *Criminology & Public Policy* 12(3), 427–436. DOI: 10.1111/1745-9133.12053.

Pyrooz, David C. 2014a. "From Colors and Guns to Caps and Gowns? The Effects of Gang Membership on Educational Attainment." *Journal of Research in Crime and Delinquency* 51(1), 56–87. DOI: 10.1177/0022427813484316.

Pyrooz, David C. 2014b. "'From Your First Cigarette to Your Last Dyin' Day': The Patterning of Gang Membership in the Life-Course." *Journal of Quantitative Criminology* 30(2), 349–372. DOI: 10.1007/s10940-013-9206-1.

Pyrooz, David C., Moule Jr., Richard K., and Decker, Scott H. 2014. "The Contribution of Gang Membership to the Victim–offender Overlap." *Journal of Research in Crime and Delinquency* 51(3), 315–348.

Pyrooz, David C. and Sweeten, Gary. 2015. "Gang Membership Between Ages 5 and 17 Years in the United States." *Journal of Adolescent Health* 56(4), 414–419.

Pyrooz, David C., Turanovic, Jillian J., Decker, Scott H., and Wu, Jun. 2016. "Taking Stock of the Relationship Between Gang Membership and Offending: A Meta-Analysis." *Criminal Justice and Behavior* 43(3), 365–397. DOI: 10.1177/0093854815605528.

Ralph, John H., Colopy, Kelly W., McRae, Christine, and Daniel, Bruce. 1995. "Gangs and Victimization at School." National Center for Education Statistics, US Department of Education, Office of Educational Research and Improvement.

Reep, Beverly B. 1996. "Lessons from the Gang." *School Administrator* 53(2), 26–29.

Rios, Victor M. 2011. *Punished: Policing the Lives of Black and Latino Boys.* New York: NYU Press.

Robers, Simone, Kemp, Jana, Rathbun, Amy, and Morgan, Rachel E. 2014. "Indicators of School Crime and Safety: 2013." National Center for Education Statistics. https://nces. ed.gov/pubs2014/2014042.pdf (last accessed October 12, 2017).

Robers, Simone, Zhang, Anlan, Morgan, Rachel E., and Musu-Gillette, Lauren. 2015. "Indicators of School Crime and Safety: 2014." National Center for Education Statistics. DOI: 10.1037/e541412012-001. https://nces.ed.gov/pubs2015/2015072.pdf (last accessed October 12, 2017).

Rojek, Jeff, Decker, Scott H., Alpert, Geoffrey P., and Hansen, J. Andrew. 2013. "Is the Quarterback a 'Crip'?': The Presence of Gangs in Collegiate Athletics Programs." *Criminal Justice Review.* DOI: 10.1177/0734016813512202.

Short, Jessica and Sharp, Christy. 2005. "Disproportionate Minority Contact Minority Youth in the Juvenile Justice System." Washington, DC: Child Welfare League of America, Inc.

Skiba, Russell J. and Knesting, Kimberly. 2001. "Zero Tolerance, Zero Evidence: An Analysis of School Disciplinary Practice." *New Directions for Youth Development* 92, 17–43.

Skiba, Russell J. and Noam, Gil G. 2001. *Zero Tolerance: Can Suspension and Expulsion Keep Schools Safe?* Jossey-Bass.

Sweeten, Gary, Pyrooz, David C.,and Piquero, Alex R. 2013. "Disengaging from Gangs and Desistance from Crime." *Justice Quarterly* 30(3), 469–500.

Thompkins, Douglas E. 2000. "School Violence: Gangs and a Culture of Fear." *Annals of the American Academy of Political and Social Science* 567(1), 54–71. DOI: 10.1177/0002716200567001005.

Thompson, David W. and Jason, Leonard A. 1988. "Street Gangs and Preventive Interventions." *Criminal Justice and Behavior* 15(3), 323–333. DOI: 0803973233.

Thornberry, Terence P. 2003. *Gangs and Delinquency in Developmental Perspective.* Cambridge: Cambridge University Press.

Thornberry, Terence P. and Burch II, James H. 1997. "Gang Members and Delinquent Behavior." *OJJDP Juvenile Justice Bulletin.* Washington, DC: Department of Justice.

Thornberry, Terence P. and Krohn, Marvin D. 2000. "The Self-Report Method for Measuring Delinquency and Crime." *Criminal Justice* 4(1), 33–83.

Thrasher, Frederic M. 1927. *The Gang: A Study of 1,313 Gangs in Chicago.* Chicago and London: University of Chicago Press.

Vigil, James D. 1999. "Streets and Schools: How Educators Can Help Chicano Marginalized Gang Youth." *Harvard Educational Review* 69(3), 270–288.

Weerman, Frank M., Lovegrove, Peter J., and Thornberry, Terence. 2015. "Gang Membership Transitions and Its Consequences: Exploring Changes Related to Joining and Leaving Gangs in Two Countries." *European Journal of Criminology* 12(1), 70–91. DOI: 10.1177/1477370814539070.

Wong, Jennifer, Gravel, Jason, Bouchard, Martin, Descormiers, Karine, and Morselli, Carlo. 2016. "Promises Kept? A Meta-Analysis of Gang Membership Prevention Programs." *Journal of Criminological Research, Policy, and Practice.* DOI: 10.1108/JCRPP-06-2015-0018.

11

Do School Policies and Programs Improve Outcomes by Reducing Gang Presence in Schools?

Benjamin W. Fisher, F. Chris Curran, F. Alvin Pearman II, and Joseph H. Gardella

The presence of gangs in schools remains a problem that schools are struggling to address. Youth involvement with gangs experienced steady increases between the 1970s and late 1990s (Miller 2001) and is still a significant issue in spite of recent declines in the prevalence of gangs in schools (Robers et al. 2015). In the 2009–2010 school year, for example, 16% of public school administrators reported that gang activity had taken place at their school, and 12% of 12- to 18-year-old students nationwide reported that gangs were present at their school (Robers et al. 2015). Estimates indicate that 35% of gang members nationwide are less than 18 years old (National Gangs Center 2015), suggesting that schools may be institutions that are particularly susceptible to the negative effects of gangs.

Although the presence of gangs in schools affects the lives of many adolescents in grades 9 to 12, research on student outcomes associated with gang presence in schools in the United States is somewhat scarce (Conchas and Vigil 2010; Estrada et al. 2014; Horst and Lomax 2011; Ulloa, Dyson, and Wynes 2012). Available findings suggest that gang presence is associated with increased violence and drug use, lower levels of perceived safety, decreased academic achievement, and other academic problems (Fox 2013; Hill et al. 1999). Although education policy makers are aware of some associations between the presence of gangs in schools and attendant negative outcomes, research often neglects the influence of gangs on school-level outcomes as well as contextual explanations for these effects (Estrada et al. 2014). Consequently, research that examines the role of school-level policies or interventions in the association between gang presence in schools and student outcomes is limited. This chapter uses a nationally representative survey of students and school administrators to examine whether school policies and programs predict lower levels of perceived gang presence in schools as well as fewer school-based problems often associated with gang presence.

The Wiley Handbook on Violence in Education: Forms, Factors, and Preventions, First Edition.
Edited by Harvey Shapiro.
© 2018 John Wiley & Sons, Inc. Published 2018 by John Wiley & Sons, Inc.

Gangs and Violence

One of the outcomes most commonly associated with gangs is violence. For instance, recent research has concluded that the probability of being the victim of a shooting is higher among gang members and those close to gang members than for those not connected with gang members (Estrada et al. 2014; Papachristos, Braga, and Hureau 2012). Moreover, compared with non-gang youth, gang-affiliated youth experienced significantly more violent victimization in school settings (Gover, Jennings, and Tewksbury 2009; Taylor et al. 2007). The link between gangs and victimization appears to also be robust over various stages of gang involvement. An analysis of five waves of data from the Gang Resistance Education and Training (GREAT) program found that gang members were significantly more likely than non-gang members to be victimized before, during, and after gang membership in school settings (Peterson and Esbensen 2004). Gang members were also more likely than non-gang members to carry guns to school and to be threatened with a gun in or around schools (Curry, Decker, and Egley 2002; Decker and Curry 2002; Miller and Decker 2001).

School contextual and personal factors may also influence this relationship between gangs and violence. The mere presence of gang members in schools predicts greater victimization levels at schools for all school members (Wynne and Joo 2011). However, qualitative findings from 440 middle school students indicate that gang presence in schools can influence victimization in two ways: (i) by increasing the likelihood that incidents of violence occur, and (ii) by fostering a school climate conducive to victimization by generating greater imbalances in social power and creating more fear in bystanders who might otherwise intervene (Forber-Pratt, Aragon, and Espelage 2014). In a similar vein, gang presence in schools reflects a latent "school social disorder" construct in a broader model of school safety and disruption (Mayer and Leone 1999). Together, these findings indicate that the presence of gangs in schools may affect overall school climate in such a way that fosters more violence and victimization.

Gangs and Substance Use

There is also a consistent association between gang membership and increased drug use. For example, a study in Denver found that gang members were more likely to use marijuana, cocaine, heroin, and PCP than non-gang members (Esbensen and Huizinga 1993). Results from the Rochester Youth Development Study corroborated this finding; gang members were 53 times more likely to self-report drug use when compared with their non-gang rarely delinquent peers and 28% more likely to self-report drug use when compared with their non-gang delinquent peers (Thornberry 2003). Similarly, findings from the Seattle Social Development Project suggest that gang members were three times as likely to self-report marijuana use than their non-gang-affiliated, non-delinquent peers (Battin et al. 1998). Another study found that students who initiated drug and alcohol use earlier were more likely than their peers to report gang affiliation (Swahn et al. 2010). Yet, the problems associated with substance use amongst gang members may not be limited to gang members themselves, as the presence of gangs in schools may create spillover effects and increase substance use and sales in the general student population (Gatti et al. 2005).

Gangs and Perceptions of Safety

Multiple studies provide evidence to suggest that gang presence in schools predicts decreased feelings of safety among both students and adults in the school. Using nationally representative data, Alvarez and Bachman (1997) showed that gang presence in schools was a predictor of increased fear for students. Likewise, employees in schools with a strong gang presence reported that they felt less safe and were more likely to consider leaving their positions (King 2009). Interestingly, efforts to reduce the negative effect of gang presence in schools on safety-related outcomes may actually exacerbate the issue. The perception of gang presence in and around schools may increase the employment of security measures that themselves may influence perceptions of safety (see Chapter 13, this volume). Researchers speculate that implementation of security measures, in turn, can contribute to cultures of fear via associations perpetuated by media's common coverage of gangs and violence and the need for security measures (Thompkins 2000). Together, these cultures of fear and implicit associations may increase the power of gangs and the appeal of gangs to many students (e.g., schools' increased attention on gangs may serve to lend credibility to gangs and confer an appealing identity of "otherness" on the gangs) thereby contributing to cycles that lead to more fear (Thompkins 2000).

Gang Prevention Policies

Policy responses to gangs in schools have involved multiple levels of government. At the state level, many states have passed legislation that deals either directly or indirectly with gang involvement in school. An examination of data maintained by the National Association of State Boards of Education, which provides a reference list of such state laws, reveals that approximately 40% of states have laws that address gangs in schools (National Association of State Boards of Education 2014). These laws vary in their approach, their severity of response to gangs, and the degree of autonomy they leave to schools and districts to determine policy. For instance, some states explicitly mandate school dress codes that limit gang apparel or require suspension for gang involvement, whereas others only stipulate that a school safety plan or district policy must address gangs (National Association of State Boards of Education 2014). A few states require more restorative approaches to gang involvement, such as Indiana's pilot program aimed at establishing student and parent gang-prevention education programs (National Association of State Boards of Education 2014). Perhaps the most common state-level policies are those that address gangs through dress codes/uniforms, discipline for violence, collaboration with law enforcement, zero tolerance policies, and comprehensive school safety plans (Center for Mental Health in Schools at UCLA 2007).

Although a comparable compilation of local school board policies related to gangs is not available, several studies have explored school board gang policies in limited samples of school districts (Center for Mental Health in Schools at UCLA 2007; Chiprany 2011). These policies generally consist of explicit prohibition of gang involvement and a prominent focus on the prohibition and punishment of outward symbols or actions that suggest gang affiliation (see Chapter 10, this volume). For instance, Wake County Schools prohibit "wearing, possessing, using, distributing, displaying, or selling any clothing, jewelry, emblems, badges, symbols, signs, visible tattoos and body markings, or other items, or being in possession of literature that shows affiliation with a gang, or is evidence of membership or affiliation in any gang or that promotes gang affiliation" (Center for Mental Health in Schools at UCLA 2007).

Near the beginning of the national attention to gang presence in schools, Maloney (1991) suggested a number of different policy approaches to address gang activity. These included limitations on secret organizations, which utilize policies passed in the early half of the twentieth century aimed at limiting fraternal organizations. Also discussed were closed schools, in which access to campus is severely restricted through the use of fences, check-in procedures, and so forth (Maloney 1991). Most prominent among the approaches considered, however, were dress codes, which aim to limit the visible presence of gangs, and would go on to be one of the most widely utilized anti-gang policy approaches implemented during subsequent decades. The data available in the current study allow for an examination of the relationship between school uniform/dress code policies and the outcomes of interest, but lack measures for other policies that have been linked to gang activity. Consequently, we review the literature on dress code and uniform policies.

School Dress Code and Uniform Policies

The promise of school uniforms and dress codes to improve student outcomes gained national attention after the district-wide adoption of a school uniform policy by the Long Beach School District was followed by reported decreases in fighting, vandalism, and suspensions, among other outcomes (Lopez 2003). These findings led President Clinton to call for school uniforms in his 1996 State of the Union address. While subsequent research on the Long Beach implementation of school uniforms found evidence suggesting positive effects on student behavior, the methodological approaches in this research did not allow for causal statements due to the potential for confounding factors (Stanley 2006).

Further research has provided mixed evidence on the relationship between school uniforms and student outcomes. Some studies have found uniforms to be predictive of increased achievement and attendance (Gregory 1998) while others have found a positive relationship between uniform use and school climate (Murray 1997). In contrast, a study utilizing nationally representative data found no relationship between uniforms and attendance, behavior, or academic achievement (Brunsma and Rockquemore 1998). Several recent studies have improved on the earlier evidence by employing longitudinal data with a variety of student and school fixed effects to control for confounding factors. For instance, Yeung (2009) utilized a value-added framework and nationally representative data from the Early Childhood Longitudinal Study, finding no significant relationship between uniforms and achievement. Gentile and Imberman (2012) utilized student and school fixed effects with administrative data and identified improvement in attendance but no impact on discipline or achievement.

The evidence on the use of school dress code policies to mitigate gang activity is largely correlational; however, it does suggest that such policies may have positive impacts on perceptions of gangs in schools. Using data from middle schools in an urban setting, Wade and Stafford (2003) examined the association between school uniform policies and student and teacher perceptions of gang activity. They found that in middle schools with stricter uniform policies, teachers were more likely to report lower rates of gang activity; however, students reported no difference in gang activity. Furthermore, in schools with uniform policies, students reported lower feelings of self-esteem than in those without such policies. In another study, Han (2010) utilized data from the School Survey on Crime and Safety, finding that uniforms were predictive of lower perceptions of problem behaviors and lower perceptions of gang problems. The use of cross-sectional data and correlational analysis in both of these studies, however, precludes any conclusion of a causal relationship between uniforms and gang activity.

Gang Prevention Programs

Although schools have utilized nearly 800,000 different programs, activities, and approaches for dealing with youth gangs (Gottfredson and Gottfredson 2001), the bulk of prevention programs generally take one of two forms (Arciaga, Sakamato, and Jones 2010). First, interventions can be *individually based*, aiming not only to discourage particular students from ongoing gang activity, but also to provide these same students opportunities to learn normative forms of social engagement. Individually based gang intervention programs seek to equip students with skills and mind-sets that allow them to distance themselves from active gang involvement, with the ultimate goal of complete withdrawal from gang-related affairs (e.g., Farrington and Welsh 2007; Welsh and Farrington 2007). This approach might be implemented as a pull-out program, taking the place of scheduled classwork; a lunchtime program; after-school or weekend program; or in-school suspension program. However implemented, the aim is to provide students with the requisite connections, understandings, and tools to detach themselves from gang life.

Second, interventions can take a *whole-school approach*, which focuses on strict behavioral standards involving all students in the school, including but not limited to those currently involved in gang activity (e.g., Solis, Schwartz, and Hinton 2003; Williams, Curry, and Cohen 2002). This approach is based on the idea that by creating a structure and environment less conducive to the expression of gang-related behaviors, associated violence and potential involvement will subside. This approach generally works best with a prescriptive re-entry program for conduct offenders and may also include mental health services, counseling services, and parental classes for guardians of gang-involved youth.

It bears mentioning that researchers have rigorously evaluated very few gang prevention programs (Howell 2000; Klein and Maxson 2006) and little is known, empirically, about precisely what motivates gang behavior and how best to prevent its growth, both in school and beyond. Nevertheless, a small cadre of effective programs has been identified – programs that both *prevent* youth from active involvement with gangs and *intervene with* youth who are already involved in gangs. Of note, only a handful of gang intervention programs have been subject to randomized controlled trials, and even fewer that are school – as opposed to community – based.

Gang Resistance Education and Training (GREAT) is one such program, which provides a cognitive-based curriculum taught by law enforcement personnel that aims to (i) equip students with the necessary skills to avoid gang membership, (ii) prevent criminal and violent acts, and (iii) develop healthy relationships between students and local law enforcement (Gang Resistance Education and Training, n.d.). A multisite randomized control trial of GREAT found that the program reduced gang involvement by nearly 40% for youth involved in the program, but found no statistically significant difference between treatment and control groups in terms of delinquent and violent acts at the one-year follow-up (Esbensen et al. 2012). The program did appear to foster prosocial attitudes toward law enforcement personnel and improved students' refusal skills as well as their ability to withstand peer pressure. Students also became less likely to exhibit positive attitudes toward gangs than students not exposed to the curriculum. Taken together, GREAT appears to be a promising program for addressing gang problems in school.

Another school-related program that has received a fair amount of empirical attention is the Broader Urban Involvement and Leadership Development detention program, or Project Build (Project Build n.d.), a violence prevention program that aims to help youth navigate the challenges they face in their communities, including gangs and gang-related problems. Importantly, the schools in which this program has been evaluated have largely been alternative schools or those located within juvenile delinquency centers. One evaluation of Project Build found that youth who participated in the program were less likely than non-participating peers to reoffend (Lurigio, Flexon, and Greenleaf 2000), although these evaluations were conducted prior to Project Build's curriculum expansion, which now includes a focus on social emotional learning and principles of restorative justice.

Although previous studies have examined the relationship between gang prevention policies and programs and both student outcomes and gang-related outcomes separately, we are unaware of research to date that has examined these constructs simultaneously. Therefore, in the current study, we hypothesize and test a model relating these three constructs to each other. Specifically, we examine whether the use of gang prevention policies and programs in schools is associated with improved safety outcomes, and the extent to which this relationship may be explained by a reduction in the presence or activity of gangs in school. To examine this, we include three measures of the use of gang policies and programs and three different outcomes, including perceptions of safety, exposure to fighting, and exposure to drugs. Additionally, we conduct analyses separately on data that have come from student responses and school administrator responses to gauge whether the findings differ by respondent. The hypotheses we test in the current study are as follows:

Hypothesis 1: The use of gang prevention programs and policies is associated with lower levels of fighting and drugs and increased perceptions of safety at school.

Hypothesis 2: This relationship can be partially explained by the reduction of the presence or activity of gangs in school.

Method

Data

This study used data from the Education Longitudinal Study of 2002 (ELS). The ELS is a nationally representative, longitudinal survey of students followed from high school through early adulthood. The ELS included surveys of students, parents, teachers, and school administrators that asked about a variety of characteristics of the students' school and home experiences. For the purposes of our study, we utilize data from the base year, which can be treated as a cross-sectional data set representative of tenth graders in 2002. The ELS data were collected through a clustered design with oversampling of select groups. Consequently, all analyses utilize appropriate weights to adjust for the complex survey design.

The initial ELS sample contained over 15,000 students; however, we limited our sample to students that could be matched to schools and those with available data on our key independent and dependent variables. The outcome variables were missing data on approximately 10% of observations each. The key independent variables (dress codes, uniforms, and gang prevention programs) were missing data on 12–15% of observations while the gang presence variable was missing data on approximately 11% of observations. As would be expected, the analytic sample differed from those observations dropped due to missing data on key independent and dependent variables. As shown in Table 11.1, the analytic sample contained more advantaged schools (i.e., less urban schools, fewer students receiving free or reduced lunch, and a greater proportion of white students).

Observations with missing values on other covariates were retained through the use of multiple imputation. We utilized 30 imputed data sets in accordance with recommendations from the literature (Allison 2009; Graham, Olchowski, and Gilreath 2007). Imputation was conducted using the multivariate normal approach in Stata (Schafer 1997; StataCorp 2011). After imputation, our analytic sample contained 11,933 students and 586 administrators from the students' schools.

Measures

Independent Variables

The first independent variable of interest represented programs designed to reduce gang presence/activity in schools. The ELS is unique in that it is one of the few publicly available data sets that specifically asks about gang prevention programs. School administrators reported whether or not their school had a gang prevention program, and if so, what percentage of students took part in the prevention program. From these items, we constructed two measures. The first was a binary indicator for whether the school had a gang prevention program, and the second was a continuous measure representing the percentage of students in a gang prevention program. The latter of these two variables served as our key independent variable of interest for gang prevention programs. The binary indicator of the presence of the program functioned as a control variable in all models.

In addition to the gang prevention program variable, we also explored two independent variables that measure policies aimed at reducing gang presence/activity. The literature suggests that strict dress codes and school uniforms are two of the most common policy approaches to reducing gangs in schools. The ELS provides binary indicators from the school administrator survey indicating whether the school enforced a strict dress code and whether or not students were required to wear uniforms. We included each of these binary indicators as key independent variables representing policy approaches to gang prevention in schools.

Table 11.1 Comparison of analytic sample and observations missing data on key independent and dependent variables.

	Analytic Sample		Cases Deleted from Sample		Columns 1 & 3 statistically different
	Mean	S.D.	Mean	S.D.	
	(1)	(2)	(3)	(4)	(5)
Neighborhood crime (1-4 scale)	2.056	(0.646)	2.112	(0.666)	*
Limited English percentage (%)	3.832	(8.259)	5.250	(8.837)	*
Certified teacher (%)	79.722	(36.438)	82.363	(34.460)	*
Students below proficient (%)	25.937	(21.848)	26.150	(21.842)	
Poor school buildings (1-4)	1.542	(0.799)	1.534	(0.748)	
Urban	0.311	(0.463)	0.415	(0.493)	*
Rural	0.196	(0.397)	0.144	(0.351)	*
Suburban	0.493	(0.500)	0.441	(0.497)	*
Northeast	0.182	(0.386)	0.185	(0.388)	
Midwest	0.266	(0.442)	0.202	(0.402)	*
South	0.363	(0.481)	0.363	(0.481)	
West	0.189	(0.391)	0.250	(0.433)	*
Free or reduced lunch (%)	22.542	(23.654)	26.518	(25.706)	*
Enrollment	381.518	(220.126)	372.288	(198.633)	*
Teachers (#)	48.392	(16.188)	52.154	(14.221)	*
Student female	0.501	(0.500)	0.510	(0.500)	
Student white	0.599	(0.490)	0.462	(0.499)	*
Student Native American/ Alaskan	0.009	(0.093)	0.008	(0.087)	
Student Asian Pacific Islander	0.088	(0.284)	0.123	(0.328)	*
Student black	0.119	(0.324)	0.182	(0.386)	*
Student Hispanic	0.137	(0.344)	0.175	(0.380)	*
Student multiracial	0.047	(0.213)	0.051	(0.220)	
Parental input on rules	0.554	(0.497)	0.580	(0.494)	*
Program training parents	0.367	(0.482)	0.371	(0.483)	
Security guards	0.474	(0.499)	0.596	(0.491)	*
Metal detectors	0.051	(0.219)	0.106	(0.308)	*
Security cameras	0.276	(0.447)	0.304	(0.460)	*
Fenced campus	0.249	(0.432)	0.301	(0.459)	*
Sign in for visitors	0.659	(0.474)	0.749	(0.433)	*

Note: Analyses run on non-imputed data. Sample size varies on each variable.
*Statistically significant at 0.05 level.

Dependent Variables

The first student-level outcome we analyzed was a student report of feeling unsafe at school. This measure ranged from 1 (*strongly agree*) to 4 (*strongly disagree*). To facilitate analysis and interpretation, we dichotomized this scale such that responses of 1 and 2 represent feeling unsafe at school while responses of 3 and 4 represent feeling safe. At the student level, we also utilized measures of the frequency of physical altercations and drug presence as perceived by students. Students responded to a question asking how many times they (a) got into a physical fight, or (b) were offered drugs at school during the first semester of the school year. Responses were on a 1–3 scale of *Never, Once or twice,* and *More than twice.* We dichotomized both of these scales by combining the *Once or twice* and *More than twice* categories. These dichotomized variables, therefore, represent *ever* getting into a fight or *ever* being offered drugs. School principals answered similar questions. In particular, principals reported how often physical conflicts among students occur and how often the sale of drugs on the way to or from school or on school grounds occurs. Responses were on a 1–5 scale ranging from *Never happens* to *Happens daily*, although responses in categories 1 and 5 were infrequent. We again dichotomized these variables' categories by coding response options 1 and 2 as 0 and response options 3 to 5 as 1, creating a binary indicator representing frequent versus infrequent occurrences. Although all of the analytic models included dichotomized versions of these variables, we found similar results when treating them as continuous variables; we are unaware of parallel commands that allow them to be treated as ordinal variables.

Gang Presence and Activity

The measures of gang presence and activity served as mediators in our final models, again drawing on responses by both students and administrators. Students responded to a Likert-type item in which they rated their agreement with the statement "There are gangs in school" from strongly disagree (1) to strongly agree (4). We recoded this item into a binary indicator of agree or disagree and used it as a student-reported measure of gang presence. In addition to the student measure, the school administrator responded to a question asking how often gang activity is a problem at school. Responses were categorical on a 1–5 scale ranging from *Never* to *Daily*. As with the principal responses to drugs and fighting, we recoded this variable by combining categories 1 and 2 and then categories 3 to 5. We utilized this binary variable as our measure of "gang activity."

Control Variables

In addition to our key independent and dependent variables, we also included in our models a number of covariates for the purpose of reducing potential endogeneity in our analyses. We controlled for school characteristics including the urbanicity of the school, the region of the country, the condition of buildings, the percentage of students eligible for free and reduced price lunch, and the percentage of students with limited English proficiency. A full list of control variables is provided in Table 11.2.

Table 11.2 Independent, mediating, and control variable means and standard errors.

	Full student sample M	S.E.	Administrator sample M	S.E.
Programs				
Gang prevention program (% enrolled)	6.33	(0.83)	6.89	(1.65)
Gang prevention program present	0.29	(0.02)	0.20	(0.02)
Policies				
Dress code	0.50	(0.02)	0.57	(0.03)
Uniforms	0.09	(0.01)	0.17	(0.02)
Gang measure				
Gang presence (1–4)	0.31	(0.83)		
Gang activity (1–5)			0.22	(0.02)
Controls				
Neighborhood crime (1–4 scale)	2.04	(0.02)	2.03	(0.03)
Limited English percentage (%)	4.49	(0.38)	2.23	(0.40)
Certified teacher (%)	86.00	(1.17)	73.09	(3.37)
Students below proficient (%)	26.56	(0.88)	22.62	(2.09)
Poor school buildings (1–4)	1.61	(0.04)	1.48	(0.05)
Urban	0.28	(0.01)	0.19	(0.02)
Rural	0.21	(0.01)	0.37	(0.03)
Suburban	0.52	(0.51)	0.44	(0.02)
Northeast	0.18	(0.01)	0.17	(0.01)
Midwest	0.25	(0.01)	0.27	(0.02)
South	0.34	(0.01)	0.36	(0.02)
West	0.23	(0.01)	0.20	(0.02)
Free or reduced lunch (%)	24.52	(0.90)	22.68	(1.76)
Enrollment	318.24	(6.69)	505.45	(14.30)
Teachers (#)	51.89	(0.49)	34.75	(1.34)
Student female	0.50	(0.01)	–	
Student white	0.64	(0.01)	–	
Student Native American/ Alaskan	0.01	(0.002)	–	
Student Asian Pacific Islander	0.04	(0.003)	–	
Student black	0.13	(0.007)	–	
Student Hispanic	0.15	(0.009)	–	
Student multiracial	0.04	(0.002)	–	
Parental input on rules	0.60	(0.02)	0.57	(0.03)
Program training parents	0.38	(0.02)	0.31	(0.03)

Table 11.2 (Continued)

	Full student sample M	S.E.	Administrator sample M	S.E.
Security guards	0.52	(0.02)	0.25	(0.02)
Metal detectors	0.06	(0.01)	0.03	(0.008)
Security cameras	0.29	(0.01)	0.17	(0.02)
Fenced campus	0.25	(0.01)	0.17	(0.02)
Sign in for visitors	0.70	(0.02)	0.56	(0.03)
n	11,933		586	

Note: Means from the imputed data set. All means are weighted to account for sampling design.

Data Analysis

We posit a series of path models in which policies and programs influence the outcomes of interest through gang presence/activity. For example, we suggest that a policy such as school uniforms will reduce students' perceptions of gang presence in schools and that, in turn, will increase their feelings of safety. Figure 11.1 displays the path model. Our approach generally followed the three steps outlined by Baron and Kenny (1986). In the first step, the direct relationship between the independent and dependent variable was modeled as follows:

$$\text{Outcome}_i = \beta_{10} + \beta_{11}\text{Policy/Program}_i + \beta_{12}\text{Controls}_i + e \tag{1}$$

where Outcome_i represents the outcome of interest for student i, Policy/Program_i represents the gang prevention policy or program of interest, and Controls_i represents a vector of control variables. In each of these models, we also control for the other policies/programs of interest. In other words, when the primary variable of interest is the presence of school uniforms, we also control for the percentage of students in a gang prevention program. In the second step, the mediator was regressed on the independent variable as shown in Equation 2:

$$\text{GangPresence}_i = \beta_{20} + \beta_{21}\text{Policy/Program}_i + \beta_{22}\text{Controls}_i + e \tag{2}$$

where GangPresence_i represents the measure of gang presence in the school and the other measures are the same as those in Equation 1. Finally, the third step regressed the dependent variable on both the mediator and independent variable, as shown in Equation 3:

$$\text{Outcome}_i = \beta_{30} + \beta_{31}\text{Policy/Program}_i + \beta_{32}\text{GangPresence}_i + \beta_{33}\text{Controls}_i + e \tag{3}$$

In this approach, the paths in the model (Figure 11.1) are stipulated as follows: β_{32} represents path b, β_{31} represents path c', β_{21} represents path a, and β_{11} represents path c. The coefficients of interest then are β_{32} and β_{21} which when multiplied represent the indirect effect of the policy or program on the outcome through gang presence. These models were conducted in Stata 13 using a modified version of the binary_mediation

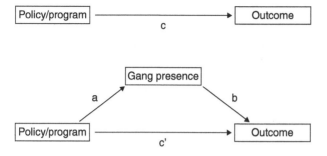

Figure 11.1 Unmediated total effect model and model predicting outcome from policy/programs with an indirect effect through gang presence.

command. Consistent with Preacher and Hayes (2004), a bootstrapping technique was utilized to estimate confidence intervals for the direct and indirect effects.[1]

The primary threat to validity in this study is that of omitted variable bias. In particular, it is possible that schools with gang prevention programs or schools that use strict dress codes or uniforms are the type of schools that, on average, have higher levels of gang presence and higher levels of undesirable outcomes. Such endogeneity could bias results such that the presence of these policies or programs appears to increase gang presence and increase negative outcomes. We address this concern through the use of a robust set of student, school, and neighborhood control measures. To the extent that these controls address the concern of omitted variable bias, the resulting estimates can be interpreted as the relationship between the independent variable of interest and the outcomes of interest, adjusting for included covariates.

Results

In our analytic sample, we find that gang activity is a commonly reported occurrence in schools but that policies and prevention programs aimed at addressing gangs are also nearly as commonplace. Table 11.2 provides descriptive statistics on the independent, mediating, and control variables utilized in the analysis. As shown, nearly one in three students in the sample and nearly one in four administrators report high levels of gang presence or activity. A similar percentage of students, however, attend schools with a gang prevention program present. In general, the gang prevention programs appear to be targeted, serving less than 10% of students in a school on average. The prevalence of strict dress codes and school uniforms diverges, with the former being present in schools that approximately half of the sampled students attend while the latter applies to less than 10% of students.

Table 11.3 provides descriptive statistics on the prevalence of each of the key dependent variables conditional on the presence of a strict dress code, the presence of a uniform policy, and the presence of a gang prevention program. As shown, schools with strict dress codes or uniforms tend to have slightly lower reports of drugs and fights while

---

1 For a discussion of potential issues inherent in deriving bootstrapped confidence intervals from multiply imputed data sets, see Wu and Jia (2013).

Table 11.3 Means and standard deviations of student-level outcome variables for full sample and by dress code, uniform, and gang prevention subgroups.

	Full sample	Strict dress code	Not strict dress code	Uniforms	No uniforms	Gang prev. program	No gang prev. program
Student feels unsafe	0.09	0.09	0.09	0.07	0.09	0.12	0.08
	(0.28)	(0.28)	(0.29)	(0.26)	(0.29)	(0.32)	(0.27)
Offered drugs	0.18	0.17	0.20	0.12	0.19	0.20	0.18
	(0.38)	(0.37)	(0.40)	(0.33)	(0.39)	(0.40)	(0.38)
Fights	0.14	0.13	0.15	0.12	0.14	0.15	0.14
	(0.35)	(0.34)	(0.36)	(0.32)	(0.35)	(0.35)	(0.35)
n	11,933	6,821	5,112	1,943	9,990	3,173	8,760

schools with uniform policies also have students who report feeling safer. Students in schools with a gang prevention program report feeling less safe and report slightly more fights and instances of being offered drugs. These conditional means, however, may be confounded by other systematic differences in schools with or without each policy or practice. As a result, we turn next to models that control for potential confounders while also incorporating gang presence as a mediating variable.

Columns 1 through 3 of Table 11.4 display the point estimates and confidence intervals of the relation between dress code and the three student-reported outcome variables, mediated by students' perceptions of gang presence at school. None of the total effects were statistically significant, indicating that there was no evidence of an association between schools' dress code policies and students' perceptions of safety, fighting, or being offered drugs. After incorporating the mediator, none of these models yielded a statistically significant direct or indirect effect. The only statistically significant parameters were the coefficients for various control variables, which indicated that if students reported having gangs in their schools, they were 25% more likely to feel unsafe ($b = 0.25$, $p < .001$, 95% CI [0.21, 0.29]), involved in fights 15% more frequently ($b = 0.15$, $p < .001$, 95% CI [0.12, 0.21]), and were offered drugs 21% more frequently ($b = 0.21$, $p < .001$, 95% CI [0.18, 0.24]). These coefficients are consistent across all three of the sets of models because the relations between perceived gang presence and the student outcomes were held constant across models.

The results of the models regressing student outcomes on school uniform policies mediated by students' perceptions of gang presence are presented in columns 4 through 6 of Table 11.4. The only model that yielded a significant total effect was the model predicting students being offered drugs ($b = -0.04$, $p = .019$, 95% CI [−0.09, −0.00]), which indicated that students who attended schools with uniform policies were 4% less likely to have been offered drugs at school. All three of the models indicated significant *a*-path coefficients, *b*-path coefficients (as described above), and indirect effects. The *a*-path coefficients – which use school-level variables and thus are expected to be identical across models – indicated that students in schools with uniform policies were

Table 11.4 Regression coefficients from models predicting student outcomes from dress code, uniforms, and gang prevention programs mediated by student perceptions of gang presence.

	Dress code			Uniforms			% in Gang prevention program		
	Student feels unsafe	Fights	Offered drugs	Student feels unsafe	Fights	Offered drugs	Student feels unsafe	Fights	Offered drugs
	(1)	(2)	(3)	(4)	(5)	(6)	(7)	(8)	(9)
a-path coefficient[a]	0.02	0.02	0.02	−0.08**	−0.08**	−0.08**	−0.03†	−0.03†	−0.03†
b-path coefficient[b]	0.25*	0.15**	0.21**	0.25**	0.15**	0.21**	0.25**	0.15**	0.21**
Indirect effect	0.00	0.00	0.00	−0.02**	−0.01**	−0.02**	−0.01†	−0.01†	−0.01†
Direct effect	−0.03	−0.03	−0.02	−0.00	−0.02	−0.03	0.02	−0.00	0.01
Total effect	−0.03	−0.02	−0.02	−0.02	−0.03	−0.04**	0.01	−0.01	0.00
n	11,993	11,993	11,993	11,993	11,993	11,993	11,993	11,993	11,993

Note:

* Statistically significant at 0.05 level.

** Statistically significant at 0.01 level.

† Statistically significant at 0.10 level.

[a] Path from policy/program to students' perceptions of gang presence.

[b] Path from students' perceptions of gang presence to the outcome of interest. Estimates weighted to account for sampling strategy. All models controlled for the full set of control variables listed in Table 11.1.

8% less likely to report gang presence in school ($b = -0.08, p < .001$, 95% CI [-0.12, -0.04]). The significant indirect effects suggested that a reduction in gang presence may be one mechanism that explains the relation between school uniform policies and students' feelings of safety ($b = -0.02, p < .001$, 95% CI [-0.03, -0.01]), fighting ($b = -0.01, p = .001$, 95% CI [-0.02, -0.01]), and experiences of being offered drugs ($b = -0.01, p < .001$, 95% CI [-0.02, -0.01]). It is worth noting, however, that the effect sizes of these indirect effects are quite small; they were only associated with a 1–2% change in the outcome variables. Still, these indirect effects explained between about 87% of the total effect on students feeling unsafe, 39% of the total effect on fighting, and 39% of the total effect on being offered drugs.

Columns 6 through 9 in Table 11.4 provide the estimated parameters of the models regressing each of the student outcomes on the percentage of students in a gang prevention program mediated by students' perceptions of gang presence in schools. None of these models indicated statistically significant total effects, indicating that there was no association between the percentage of students in a gang prevention program and any of the three outcomes of interest. After adding the mediator into the model, only the b-path coefficients were statistically significant (as described above). Thus, these models did not provide evidence that the percentage of students in gang prevention programs was associated with any changes in either students' outcomes related to their perceptions of safety, fighting, or being offered drugs, or students' perceptions of the presence of gangs at school.

Table 11.5 displays the findings from the models predicting administrators' perceptions of student fights and drug availability. Columns 1 and 2 display the model parameters from the models that used the presence of dress code policies as the main exogenous independent variable and administrator perceptions of gang activity as the mediator. Columns 3 and 4 provide the results from the models using school uniform policies as the independent variable, and columns 5 and 6 provide the results from the models using the percentage of students in gang prevention programs as the independent variable. Across all of these models, there were no statistically significant total effects, indicating that none of the policies or programs were associated with administrators' perceptions of students' fighting or drug sales at school. Adding the mediator resulted in statistically significant b-path coefficients across all of the models, with higher perceived gang activity associated with a 24% increase in the perceived frequency of student fights ($b = 0.24, p = .004$, 95% CI [0.06, 0.41]), and 31% increase in perceived drug sales ($b = 0.31, p = .005$, 95% CI [0.07, 0.54]). However, none of the a-path coefficients were statistically significant, nor were the indirect effects. Together, these findings suggest that dress code policies, school uniform policies, and the percentage of students in a gang prevention program were not associated with administrators' perceptions of the frequency of student fights, drug sales, or gang activity.

Discussion

The purpose of this study was to determine if the use of gang prevention policies and programs improve student outcomes and if this association might be explained to some degree by a reduction in gang-related activity at school. There are three main conclusions we can draw from our analysis. First, we found evidence that the presence of gangs

Table 11.5 Regression coefficients from models predicting principal outcomes from dress code, uniforms, and gang prevention programs mediated by principal perceptions of gang activity.

	Dress code		Uniforms		% in Gang prevention program	
	Fights	Offered drugs	Fights	Offered drugs	Fights	Offered drugs
	(1)	(2)	(3)	(4)	(5)	(6)
a coefficient[a]	−0.07	−0.07	−0.10	−0.10	−0.15	−0.15
b coefficient[b]	0.24*	0.31*	0.23*	0.30*	0.24*	0.31*
Indirect effect	−0.02	−0.02	−0.02	−0.03	−0.04	−0.05
Direct effect	−0.05	0.04	−0.09	−0.22	−0.05	−0.05
Total effect	−0.06	0.02	−0.12	−0.25†	−0.08	−0.09
n	586	586	586	586	586	586

Note:
* Statistically significant at 0.05 level.
† Statistically significant at 0.10 level.
[a] Path from policy/program to principal perceptions of gang activity.
[b] Path from principal perceptions of gang activity to the outcome of interest.
Estimates weighted to account for sampling strategy. All models controlled for the full set of control variables listed in Table 11.1.

in schools was negatively associated with several dimensions of student well-being. Both students' perceptions of gang presence and administrators' perceptions of gang activity were associated with decreased perceptions of safety among students and an increase in the likelihood both that students are involved in physical altercations and that students are offered drugs at school. This largely confirms findings from previous studies that indicate that the presence of gangs in schools tends to increase the chances that students experience negative incidents and feel less safe on campus during the school year (Battin et al. 1998; Estrada et al. 2014; Rufino et al. 2013).

Second, we found evidence that school uniform policies appear to be a promising alternative for decreasing students' perceptions of gangs in the school, with the presence of a school uniform policy associated with an 8% reduction in the likelihood that students reported gang presence at their school. Third, school uniform policies were associated with reductions in several negative consequences of exposure to gang presence in schools. In this sample, school uniform policies were associated with an increased likelihood that students felt safe at school, and decreased chances that students reported they had engaged in a physical altercation or had been offered drugs in the preceding semester. While these findings were largely consistent with our primary hypothesis, it is noteworthy that the positive association these programs and policies had with respect to the student outcomes of interest operated largely through reduced perceptions of gang presence. It is worth noting the peculiarity of this pattern. If there is no evidence that a gang-related policy/program is related to a student-level outcome, it may not be intuitive that this lack of a relationship can be explained by an indirect effect through another variable – in this case, perceptions of gang presence. This issue gains some clarity when one considers that a total effect is but the sum of multiple paths of influence, some of which may or may not be included in the specified model (Hayes 2009). It is possible, therefore, that two or more indirect paths may operate in opposite directions, thus canceling each other and producing a total effect that is itself non-significant. Interpretations of models no longer require the existence of a significant total effect before probing indirect effects (Rucker et al. 2011); therefore, gang presence can be understood as one indirect effect among multiple indirect effects relating school uniforms to the three student outcomes. For a further discussion of the differences between indirect effects and mediation, see Mathieu and Taylor (2006).

Limitations

There are several shortcomings in this study that should be considered. First, because of the nature of the data, the measures of gang policies and programs were very general, and we were unable to model variations in the wording of the policies, the degree of enforcement of the policies, the types of programs, and several other dimensions. In our sample of nearly 12,000 students, it is reasonable to suspect a significant range in terms of the focus and effectiveness of these programs. This absence of nuance with respect to gang prevention programs and policies may have prompted our non-significant findings for dress code policies and gang prevention programs. It is possible, for example, that only dress code policies that are strictly enforced are associated with improved school and student outcomes. Similarly, perhaps only some gang prevention programs produce the desired results. Because we were unable to explore this variability with the ELS, we leave it to future researchers to examine the differential effects of various instantiations of school policies and programs on perceptions of gang presence.

A second key limitation is the lack of longitudinal data. Although the ELS is a longitudinal data set, our analyses focused on a single, cross-sectional wave of the data. The restriction to a single wave of data was made because key independent and dependent variables, including the percentage of students in a gang prevention program, the presence of a uniform or strict dress code policy, and perceptions of safety were only included on the tenth grade instruments. Had these questions been included in later time points, we could have pursued other analytic approaches available to longitudinal analysis and would have been better able to establish time order between variables of interest.

Although the findings from this study indicate that school uniforms may be one promising way of reducing the perceived presence of gangs in schools as well as the concomitant problems associated with gang presence, there are ethical considerations to make when implementing school uniform policies. The use of dress code and uniform policies to regulate gang activities within schools raises concerns with the protection of students' rights to freely express themselves. In the landmark 1969 case, *Tinker v Des Moines Independent Community School District*, the United States Supreme Court concluded that the wearing of armbands, a form of dress, constituted free speech protected by the First Amendment and that the school district had failed to show that such dress disrupted the educational process to an extent warranting the restriction of this right (Lane and Richardson 1992). Though later court decisions have confirmed a school's right to place certain limitations on student dress, schools must consider the extent to which such a policy conflicts with legal standards for protected speech.

Conclusion

Although gang presence has been a problem for schools for decades, there has been little research examining school-level policies that may reduce (i) the presence of gangs in school, or (ii) the problems associated with gangs in school. The current study investigated whether dress codes, uniforms, and gang prevention programs are associated with reduced gang-related problems, and whether these relationships might be explained by a reduction in the presence of gangs in schools. Although the findings were mixed, the overall pattern indicates that some school-level strategies may mitigate the problems associated with gangs in schools. In particular, student responses indicated that school uniforms may be a particularly effective strategy for reducing the presence of gangs in school as well as fighting, drug availability, and feeling unsafe at school. Schools that have problems with gangs may consider implementing uniform policies that seek to reduce the opportunity for gang members to distinguish themselves at school by wearing certain colors or styles of clothing. Additionally, we found consistent evidence across a series of models that when students and administrators perceived lower levels of gang presence in their schools, they were also more likely to report lower levels of school problems often associated with gangs, including fighting, drug availability, and perceived safety. This suggests that if there are other policies or interventions that reduce the presence of gangs in schools, there will likely be a secondary effect of reducing other gang-related problems.

As efforts continue to mount to make schools safer along a variety of dimensions, it is important to consider school-level contextual factors that promote reduced crime and violence in schools as well as increased perceptions of safety. Although this study examined a handful of school-level policies and programs intended to improve school safety, this field of study is still emerging and very few best practices have emerged. Therefore, more research is needed examining the multiple intersecting spheres of influence that operate within schools. Studies should examine how individually targeted interventions work in tandem with or opposition to whole-school approaches. Moreover, understanding how these effects differ across school contexts and student characteristics is a critical undertaking for researchers. Because the literature on gangs and schools is largely still being developed, educational practitioners may find it particularly useful to adopt policies and practices based on their particular needs and circumstances rather than attempting to import a one-size-fits-all strategy (see Chapter 9, this volume). Contextually informed interventions provide schools the flexibility to meet the needs of their students and personnel while being able to adapt the interventions as needed. Dress codes, uniforms, and gang prevention programs may be part of a larger initiative toward reducing gang presence and school-based problems associated with gangs, but should not be viewed as a cure-all for school safety concerns.

References

Allison, Paul D. 2009. "Missing Data." In *The Sage Handbook of Quantitative Methods in Psychology*, edited by Roger E. Millsap and Alberty Maydeu-Olivares, pp. 72–89. Thousand Oaks, CA: Sage.

Alvarez, Alex and Bachman, Ronet. 1997. "Predicting the Fear of Assault at School and While Going to and from School in an Adolescent Population." *Violence and Victims* 12, 69–86.

Arciaga, Michelle, Sakamato, Wayne, and Jones, Errika F. 2010. "Responding to Gangs in the School Setting." *National Gang Center Bulletin* 5, 1–15.

Baron, Reuben M. and Kenny, David A. 1986. "The Moderator–Mediator Variable Distinction in Social Psychological Research: Conceptual, Strategic, and Statistical Considerations." *Journal of Personality and Social Psychology* 51, 1173–1182. DOI: 10.1037/0022-3514.51.6.1173.

Battin, Sara R., Hill, Karl G., Abbott, Robert D., Catalano, Richard F., and Hawkins, J. David. 1998. "The Contribution of Gang Membership to Delinquency Beyond Delinquent Friends." *Criminology* 36. 93–116. DOI: 10.1111/j.1745-9125.1998.tb01241.x.

Brunsma, David L. and Rockquemore, Kerry A. 1998. "Effects of Student Uniforms on Attendance, Behavior Problems, Substance Use, and Academic Achievement." *The Journal of Educational Research* 92, 53–62. DOI: 10.1080/00220679809597575.

Center for Mental Health in Schools at UCLA. 2007. *Youth Gangs and Schools*. Los Angeles, CA.

Chiprany, David T. 2011. "A Critical Analysis of the Effectiveness of Administrative Rules for Gang-Related Activities in Middle and High Schools." PhD dissertation. University of Southern Mississippi, Hattiesburg, Mississippi.

Conchas, Gilberty Q. and Vigil, James D. 2010. "Multiple Marginality and Urban Education: Community and School Socialization Among Low-Income Mexican-Descent Youth." *Journal of Education for Students Placed at Risk* 15, 51–65. DOI: 10.1080/10824661003634963.

Curry, G. David, Decker, Scott H., and Egley Jr., Arlen. 2002. "Gang Involvement and Delinquency in a Middle School Population." *Justice Quarterly* 19, 275–292. DOI: 10.1080/07418820200095241.

Decker, Scott H. and Curry, G. David. 2002. "Gangs, Gang Homicides, and Gang Loyalty: Organized Crimes or Disorganized Criminals." *Journal of Criminal Justice* 30, 343–352. DOI: 10.1016/S0047-2352(02)00134-4.

Esbensen, Finn-Aage and Huizinga, David. 1993. "Gangs, Drugs, and Delinquency in a Survey of Urban Youth." *Criminology* 31, 565–589. DOI: 10.1111/j.1745-9125.1993.tb01142.x.

Esbensen, Finn-Aage, Peterson, Dana, Taylor, Terrance J., and Osgood, D. Wayne. 2012. "Results from a Multi-Site Evaluation of the GREAT Program." *Justice Quarterly* 29, 125–151. DOI: 10.1080/07418825.2011.585995.

Estrada, Joey N., Gilreath, Tamika D., Astor, Ron A., and Benbenishty, Rami. 2014. "Gang Membership, School Violence, and the Mediating Effects of Risk and Protective Behaviors in California High Schools." *Journal of School Violence* 13, 228–251. DOI: 10.1080/15388220.2013.846860.

Farrington, David P. and Welsh, Brandon C. 2007. *Saving Children from a Life of Crime: Early Risk Factors and Effective Interventions*. New York: Oxford University Press.

Forber-Pratt, Anjali J., Aragon, Steven R., and Espelage, Dorothy L. 2014. "The Influence of Gang Presence on Victimization in One Middle School Environment." *Psychology of Violence* 4, 8–20. DOI: 10.1037/a0031835.

Fox, Kathleen A. 2013. "New Developments and Implications for Understanding the Victimization of Gang Members." *Violence and Victims* 28, 1015–1040.

Gang Resistance Education and Training. n.d. https://www.great-online.org/GREAT-Home (last accessed October 12, 2017).

Gatti, Umberto, Tremblay, Richard E., Vitaro, Frank, and McDuff, Pierre. 2005. "Youth Gangs, Delinquency and Drug Use: A Test of the Selection, Facilitation, and Enhancement Hypotheses." *Journal of Child Psychology and Psychiatry* 46, 1178–1190. DOI: 10.1111/j.1469-7610.2005.00423.x.

Gentile, Elisabetta and Imberman, Scott A. 2012. "Dressed for Success? The Effect of School Uniforms on Student Achievement and Behavior." *Journal of Urban Economics* 71, 1–17. DOI: 10.1016/j.jue.2011.10.002.

Gottfredson, Gary D. and Gottfredson, Denise C. 2001. "What Schools do to Prevent Problem Behavior and Promote Safe Environments." *Journal of Educational and Psychological Consultation* 12, 313–344. DOI: 10.1207/S1532768XJEPC1204_02.

Gover, Angela R., Jennings, Wesley G., and Tewksbury, Richard. 2009. "Adolescent Male and Female Gang Members' Experiences with Violent Victimization, Dating Violence, and Sexual Assault." *American Journal of Criminal Justice* 34, 103–115. DOI: 10.1007/s12103-008-9053-z.

Graham, John W., Olchowski, Allison E., and Gilreath, Tamika D. 2007. "How Many Imputations are Really Needed? Some Practical Clarifications of Multiple Imputation Theory." *Prevention Science* 8, 206–213. DOI:10.1007/s11121-007-0070-9.

Gregory, Nancy B. 1998. "Effects of School Uniforms on Self-Esteem, Academic Achievement, and Attendance." PhD dissertation. South Carolina State University, Orangeburg, South Carolina.

Han, Seunghee. 2010. "A Mandatory Uniform Policy in Urban Schools: Findings from the School Survey on Crime and Safety: 2003–04." *International Journal of Education Policy and Leadership* 5, 1–13.

Hayes, Andrew F. 2009. "Beyond Baron and Kenny: Statistical Mediation Analysis in the New Millennium." *Communication Monographs* 76, 408–420. DOI: 10.1080/03637750903310360.

Hill, Karl G., Howell, James C., Hawkins, J. David, and Battin-Pearson, Sara R. 1999. "Childhood Risk Factors for Adolescent Gang Membership: Results from the Seattle Social Development Project." *Journal of Research in Crime and Delinquency* 36, 300–322. DOI: 10.1177/0022427899036003003.

Horst, A.V. and Lomax, R.G. 2011. "Youth Gangs: Examining Youth Connectedness to Family and Academics as Mediating Factors." Paper presented at American Educational Research Association Annual Meeting, New Orleans, LA.

Howell, James C. 2000. "Youth Gangs Programs and Strategies." Washington, DC: US Department of Justice, Office of Juvenile Justice and Delinquency Prevention. DOI: 10.1037/e379762004-001.

King, Suzanne. 2009. "Teachers' Reaction to Gangs and School Violence and the Mediating Effects of Security Measures on Intention to Leave Teaching." PhD dissertation. Lynn University, Boca Raton, Florida.

Klein, Malcolm W. and Maxson, Cheryl L. 2006. *Street Gang Patterns and Policies*. New York: Oxford University Press.

Lane, Kenneth E. and Richardson, Michael D. 1992. "School Dress Code Law in the 90s: Tinkering with Fashion and Gangs." Paper presented at the Annual Meeting of the National Organization on Legal problems of Education, Scottsdale, AZ.

Lopez, Rebecca A. 2003. "The Long Beach Unified School District Uniform Initiative: A Prevention–Intervention Strategy for Urban Schools." *Journal of Negro Education* 72, 396–405. DOI: 10.2307/3211191.

Lurigio, Arthur J., Flexon, Jamie L., and Greenleaf, Richard G. 2000. "Predicting Fear of Gangs Among High School Students in Chicago." *Journal of Gang Research* 19, 1–12.

Maloney, James A. 1991. "Constitutional Problems Surrounding the Implementation of 'Anti-Gang' Regulations in the Public Schools." *Marquette Law Review* 75, 179–205.

Mathieu, John E. and Taylor, Scott R. 2006. "Clarifying Conditions and Decision Points for Mediational Type Inferences in Organizational Behavior." *Journal of Organizational Behavior* 27, 1031–1056. DOI: 10.1002/job.406.

Mayer, Matthew J. and Leone, Peter E. 1999. "A Structural Analysis of School Violence and Disruption: Implications for Creating Safer Schools." *Education and Treatment of Children* 22, 333–356.

Miller, Jody and Decker, Scott H. 2001. "Young Women and Gang Violence: Gender, Street Offending, and Violent Victimization in Gangs." *Justice Quarterly* 18, 115–140. DOI: 10.1080/07418820100094841.

Miller, Walter B. 2001. "The Growth of Youth Gang Problems in the United States: 1970–98." US Department of Justice. Office of Justice Programs. Office of Juvenile Justice and Delinquency Prevention. https://www.ncjrs.gov/pdffiles1/ojjdp/181868-1.pdf (last accessed October 26, 2017)

Murray, Richard K. 1997. "The Impact of School Uniforms on School Climate." *NASSP Bulletin* 81, 106–112. DOI: 10.1177/019263659708159314.

National Association of State Boards of Education. 2014. "State School Healthy Policy Database." http://www.nasbe.org/healthy_schools/hs/bytopics.php?topicid=3130 (last accessed October 12, 2017).

National Gangs Center. 2015. "National Youth Gang Survey Analysis." http://www.nationalgangcenter.gov/Survey-Analysis/Demographics (last accessed October 12, 2017).

Papachristos, Andrew V., Braga, Anthony A., and Hureau, David M. 2012. "Social Networks and the Risk of Gunshot Injury." *Journal of Urban Health* 89, 992–1003. DOI: 10.1007/s11524-012-9703-9.

Peterson, Dana and Esbensen, Finn-Aage. 2004. "The Outlook is G.R.E.A.T.: What Educators Say about School-based Prevention and the Gang Resistance Education and Training (G.R.E.A.T.) Program." *Evaluation Review* 28, 218–245. DOI: 10.1177/0193841X03262598.

Preacher, Kristopher J. and Hayes, Andrew F. 2004. "SPSS and SAS Procedures for Estimating Indirect Effects in Simple Mediation Models." *Behavior Research Methods, Instruments, & Computers* 36, 717–731. DOI: 10.3758/BF03206553.

Project Build (Building Uplifting and Impacting Lives in Durham). n.d. http://projectbuild.4hdurham.org/ (accessed June 9, 2016).

Robers, Simone, Zhang, Anlan, Morgan, Rachel E., and Musu-Gillette, Lauren. 2015. "Indicators of School Crime and Safety: 2014." Washington, DC.: US Department of Education, National Center for Education Statistics, and Bureau of Justice Statistics, Office of Justice Programs, US Department of Justice.

Rucker, Derek D., Preacher, Kristopher J., Tormala, Zakary L., and Petty, Richard E. 2011. "Mediation Analysis in Social Psychology: Current Practices and

New Recommendations." *Social and Personality Psychology Compass* 5, 359–371. DOI: 10.1111/j.1751-9004.2011.00355.x.

Rufino, Katrina A., Fox, Kathleen A., Cramer, Robert J., and Kercher, Glen A. 2013. "The Gang–Victimization Link: Considering the Effects of Ethnicity and Protective Behaviors Among Prison Inmates." *Deviant Behavior* 34, 25–37. DOI: 10.1080/01639625.2012.679898.

Schafer, Joseph L. 1997. *Analysis of Incomplete Multivariate Data*. Boca Raton, FL: Chapman & Hall/CRC.

Solis, Angelica, Schwartz, Wendy, and Hinton, Tamika. 2003. "Gang Resistance Is Paramount (GRIP) Program Evaluation: Final Report." Los Angeles: University of Southern California, USC Center for Economic Development.

Stanley, M. Sue. 2006. "School Uniforms and Safety." *Education and Urban Society* 28, 424–435. DOI: 10.1177/0013124596028004003.

StataCorp. 2011. *Stata 12 Multiple-Imputation Reference Manual*. College Station, TX: Stata Press.

Swahn, Monica H., Bossarte, Robert M., West, Bethany, and Topalli, Volkan. 2010. "Alcohol and Drug Use Among Gang Members: Experiences of Adolescents Who Attend School." *Journal of School Health* 80, 353–360. DOI: 10.1111/j.1746-1561.2010.00513.x.

Taylor, Terrance J., Peterson, Dana, Esbensen, Finn-Aage, and Freng, Adrienne. 2007. "Gang Membership as a Risk Factor for Adolescent Violent Victimization." *Journal of Research in Crime and Delinquency* 44, 351–380. DOI: 10.1177/0022427807305845.

Thompkins, Douglas E. 2000. "School Violence: Gangs and a Culture of Fear." *Annals of the American Academy of Political and Social Science* 567, 54–71. DOI: 10.1177/0002716200567001005.

Thornberry, Terrence P. 2003. *Gangs and Delinquency in Developmental Perspective*. New York: Cambridge University Press.

Ulloa, Emilio C., Dyson, Rachel B., and Wynes, Danita D. 2012. "Inter-Partner Violence in the Context of Gangs: A Review." *Aggression and Violent Behavior* 17, 397–404. DOI: 10.1016/j.avb.2012.05.001.

Wade, Kathleen K. and Stafford, Mary E. 2003. "Public School Uniforms Effect on Perceptions of Gang Presence, School Climate, and Student Self-Perceptions." *Education and Urban Society* 35, 399–420. DOI: 10.1177/0013124503255002.

Welsh, Brandon C. and Farrington, David P. 2007. "Save Children from a Life of Crime." *Criminology and Public Policy* 6, 871–879. DOI: 10.1111/j.1745-9133.2007.00465.x.

Williams, Katherine, G. Curry, David, and Cohen, Marcia I. 2002. "Gang Prevention Programs for Female Adolescents: An Evaluation." In *Responding to Gangs: Evaluation and Research*, edited by Winifred L. Reed and Scott H. Decker, pp. 225–263. Washington, DC: US Department of Justice, National Institute of Justice.

Wu, Wei and Jia, Fan. 2013. "A New Procedure to Test Mediation with Missing Data through Nonparametric Bootstrapping and Multiple Imputation." *Multivariate Behavioral Research* 48, 663–691. DOI: 10.1080/00273171.2013.816235.

Wynne, Susan L. and Hee-Jong Joo. 2011. "Predictors of School Victimization: Individual, Familial, and School Factors." *Crime and Delinquency* 57, 458–488. DOI: 10.1177/0011128710389586.

Yeung, Ryan. 2009. "Are School Uniforms a Good Fit? Results from the ECLS-K and the NELS." *Educational Policy* 23, 847–874. DOI: 10.1177/0895904808330170.

12

An Historical Account of the Discursive Construction of Zero Tolerance in Print Media

Jessica Nina Lester and Katherine Evans

Introduction

Research on zero tolerance (ZT) policies overwhelmingly demonstrates the ineffectiveness of mandatory suspensions and expulsions in changing student behavior. While many schools are beginning to soften their stances on such policies (Brown-Dianis 2011; Winton 2013), other schools remain committed to "get tough" approaches that jeopardize students' academic success, unfairly target certain groups of students, and, in many cases, exacerbate student misbehavior (American Psychological Association 2008; Jones 2013; Skiba 2013). The discourses surrounding ZT in public schools can be found across a variety of contexts, from talk shows to YouTube videos; some scholars have suggested that media sources have the potential to create meanings, ideas, and attitudes that ultimately facilitate changes in institutions (Coyne and Leeson 2009). To date, however, few studies have examined the ways in which ZT policies are positioned and talked about within media sources, such as newspapers. Thus, in this study, we considered how ZT policies have been historically positioned within the public discourse, particularly since the passing of the Gun-Free Schools Act of 1994. We trace the public discourse, as presented in the *New York Times*, from 1994 to 2014, examining the ways in which media sources worked up particular versions and stories about the use of ZT policies within educational contexts. The research question that framed our study was: How has zero tolerance been discursively constructed in print media over time?

Review of Literature

The Gun-Free Schools Act of 1994 (GFSA) mandated that states impose a one-year expulsion for any student caught with a weapon on school grounds. Failure to comply with the law jeopardized a school's right to receive federal funding. Prior to the passage of the GFSA, use of the term "zero tolerance" or "ZT" was a fairly widespread phenomenon in law enforcement, referring to policies that were intended to "get tough on crime" (Fries and DeMitchell 2007; Giroux 2003). Upon passage of the

The Wiley Handbook on Violence in Education: Forms, Factors, and Preventions, First Edition.
Edited by Harvey Shapiro.

GFSA, the language of ZT was brought into schools as a way to get tough on discipline for students who were often described as dangerous, out of control, and in need of strict discipline in order to be forced to behave correctly (Nguyen 2013; Skiba and Noam 2001).

The National Center for Education Statistics (NCES) defined a ZT policy as "a school or district policy that mandates predetermined consequences or punishments for specific offenses" (US Department of Education 1998). The American Psychological Association (2008) appointed a task force to determine the effectiveness of ZT, defining it as a "philosophy or policy that mandates the application of predetermined consequences, most often severe and punitive in nature, that are intended to be applied regardless of the gravity of behavior, mitigating circumstances, or situational context" (825).

While initially applied solely to weapons possession on school campuses, ZT policies soon "morphed into a broad, sweeping set of harsh disciplinary practices that exclude children from learning for a range of misbehaviors" (Brown-Dianis 2011, 25), in what some have referred to as "absurd" and "illogical" extremes (Advancement Project/Civil Rights Project 2000; Martinez 2009; Skiba and Peterson 1999). In some states, this "zero-tolerance frenzy" has impacted younger and younger children, with reports of kindergarteners receiving one-year suspensions (Anderson 2004, 1199).

The scholarly research related to ZT is extensive and comes out of a variety of disciplines including education (Caton 2012; Lewis 2006; Nguyen 2013), social work (Dupper, Theriot, and Craun 2009; Peebles-Wilkins 2005), psychology (American Psychological Association 2008; Booker and Mitchell 2011), psychiatry (Mongan and Walker 2012; Teske 2011), pediatrics (American Academy of Pediatrics 2003), criminology (Grona 2000), law (Fries and DeMitchell 2007; Meek 2009), and juvenile justice (Anderson 2004; Jones 2013). The cross-disciplinary nature of the research surrounding ZT highlights the importance of this topic in multiple domains related to youth development.

According to some researchers, ZT policies were introduced into the public discourse as a response to images of juveniles who had spun out of control, were beyond rehabilitation, and in need of punishment (Brown-Dianis 2011; Kennedy-Lewis 2013). The 1980s and 1990s saw the emergence of stereotypes around gang-involved youth, particularly youth of color, as "superpredators" who were "relentlessly violent" (Castillo 2014, 45). Although most school shootings occur in rural or suburban schools, primarily by white males, the rise of gang-related activities in the 1990s was often cited as a rationale for implementing ZT policies (Triplett, Allen, and Lewis 2014).

Contrary to some of the literature (see, for example, Grona 2000; Peebles-Wikins 2005), ZT did not emerge in response to school shootings, such as Columbine; nevertheless, media coverage of school shootings often reinforced these types of images of youth as unruly (Mongan and Walker 2012). Vavrus and Cole (2002), however, found that in the discursive moments between students and teachers, ZT suspensions were rarely precipitated by a violent act, but rather were due to students violating the social norms of the classroom. In addition, many researchers have concluded that ZT policies serve to punish students, rather than educate them (Verdugo 2002), and may deprive schools of the opportunity to devise creative solutions to meeting students' needs (Cassidy and Jackson 2005; Suarez 2010).

Negative Consequences of ZT Policies

Much of the research critiques ZT policies as being overly punitive, disproportionately applied, and as failing to create the safe schools they were intended to create (Advancement Project 2010; Casella 2003; Skiba 2013). For example, the American Psychological Association (2008) claims that ZT policies "appear to run counter to our best knowledge of child development" (860). There is some evidence that ZT policies may have an adverse effect on students' mental health and their potential for cognitive and emotional development (Teske 2011). Gregory and Cornell (2009) suggested that ZT policies are developmentally inappropriate and recommended that schools instead apply discipline practices that uphold both structure and support. Further, Mongan and Walker (2012) examined the theoretical and legal foundations of ZT policies and found them to be unsupported empirically, unsound theoretically, and in contradiction to accepted practices regarding punishment.

Other research related to ZT has examined the impact such policies have had on school climate. Following the passage of the GFSA, the percentage of students being suspended increased by staggering rates (Skiba 2013). For example, in one analysis, school suspension rates increased from 3.7% of students to almost 7% of students across the nation since the implementation of ZT policies (Hirschfield 2008). However, despite the increase in suspensions, many researchers have concluded that the application of ZT policies has failed to produce safer schools (American Psychological Association 2008).

According to some research, ZT policies have resulted in a greater number of school-related arrests (Browne-Dianis 2011) and have contributed to the "school-to-prison pipeline" (Fowler 2011; Jones 2013; Wald and Losen 2003). These findings are consistent with other research that has found that when students are absent from school due to suspensions and expulsions, those students are at an increased risk for being arrested during their suspension; and that this risk increases for students who do not have a history of delinquency (Monahan et al. 2014). Ginwright (2006) and Skiba (2013) have thus argued that ZT policies have not only been ineffective at preventing violence in schools, but that they have actually exacerbated violence, particularly among minority youth (see also Hoffman 2014; Jones 2013).

Although predetermined consequences might be assumed to be effective at doling out punishments at consistent rates, research has consistently shown that ZT policies have perpetuated racial and ethnic disproportionality in school discipline practices (Advancement Project 2010; Caton 2012; Fenning and Rose 2007; Skiba, Arrendondo, and Rausch 2014). An examination of 294 public schools found that schools with predominantly black students were found to be more punitive and more likely to implement ZT policies than schools with fewer black students, even when controlling for social and economic factors (Welch and Payne 2010).

Booker and Mitchell (2011) found that when placement in an alternative school was up to the discretion of administrators, as opposed to a mandatory consequence, that African American students were placed at the alternative school at higher rates than Caucasian students. Some research suggests that teachers are making these types of decisions on a daily basis. In focus group interviews with pre-service and experienced teachers, Fries and DeMitchell (2007) found that teachers will often use their own discretion to decide when to enforce ZT policies and when to handle discipline problems themselves.

In addition, students with certain disability labels are also impacted disproportionally (Kaplan and Cornell 2005; Soodak 2003). Rivkin (2008) noted that schools often "expel, suspend, or otherwise push out" students who demonstrate behaviors that deviate from the norm (267). According to Rivkin, when students with social, emotional, or behavioral disabilities exhibit behaviors symptomatic of those challenges, schools often perceive those behaviors as threatening and respond with punitive rather than supportive responses. Losen and Martinez (2013) found that students with disabilities were suspended at rates twice that of their non-identified peers, even when controlling for racial differences. When race and disability were both factored in, they found that nearly 75% of black males with disabilities had been suspended from school during their middle school years.

Some research has found that school characteristics contribute to more punitive environments and increase the likelihood that ZT policies will be enacted. Examining school characteristics of 161 middle schools in Kentucky, Christle, Nelson, and Jolivette (2004) found that high rates of suspensions correlated with low socioeconomic status, racial diversity, high dropout rates, and low academic achievement. Other research has found that punitive discipline is more likely to be implemented in schools with higher concentrations of students who are minorities or who are economically disadvantaged (Caton 2012; Noguera 2003; Verdugo 2002).

Legal analysts have challenged ZT policies as violating students' Fourteenth Amendment rights, suggesting that although a public education is not a guaranteed right, the Fourteenth Amendment does require that education cannot be deprived without due process (Brady 2002; Meek 2009). Because most states' ZT policies do not require that schools provide for the education of suspended students (Jones 2013; Tobin and Sprague 2000), some research has demonstrated the increased number of students who have been deprived of educational opportunities due to ZT policies (Caton 2012; Suarez 2010). Kennedy-Lewis (2013) found that only 30 states even mentioned alternative education in their ZT policies and only 10 states required that educational opportunities be provided for expelled students. In many cases, even when alternative educational placements are provided, they are substandard or inadequate to provide for students' academic, emotional, or social needs (Brown 2007). Only eight states' ZT policies mention such services (i.e., mental health screenings, drug treatment, anger management) that may be provided for students who are suspended or expelled from school (Kennedy-Lewis 2013).

Some districts are recognizing the detrimental impact of suspensions and are either overturning their ZT policies or significantly curtailing their application (Brown-Dianis 2011; Winton 2013). Others are beginning to implement a variety of alternatives to such exclusionary discipline, such as in-school suspensions (Suarez 2010), mentoring programs (Rollin et al. 2003; Winton 2013), and restorative justice (Evans and Lester 2012; Gonzalez 2012; Hantzopoulos 2013; Sumner, Silverman, and Frampton 2010). Many states, however, continue to enforce ZT policies, claiming they are necessary to send a message to misbehaving students and ensure that schools are safe from dangerous and violent students (Ginwright 2006; Nguyen 2013).

The Discourse of ZT Policies

With two notable exceptions, there has been minimal research examining ZT through a discursive lens. Using critical policy analysis, Kennedy-Lewis (2013) examined specific ZT policies from each of the 50 states. She found that within legislation, competing discourses of safety and equity often led to contradictory messages: on one hand, the policies cried for equity, recognizing the needs of students to be treated holistically, and asserted that ZT ensured that every student was treated fairly; on the other hand, the policies demanded safety by "prioritizing the needs of the group over the needs of individuals" and "advocates for punishments severe enough to deter potential perpetrators" (170). Likewise, Rice (2009) examined the competing messages of schools regarding tolerance: on the one hand, policies insist that there is to be ZT for deviation from normative behavior patterns, while on the other hand, schools are expected to promote tolerance for diverse student populations. The way in which these discussions are positioned discursively, both in policy and in practice, has implications for how ZT has been enacted.

As an historical account, while these policies were gaining traction in schools, popular media sources, such as the *New York Times*, generated a multitude of texts around school discipline practices in relation to ZT policies. To date, however, no studies have systematically examined the ways in which public discourses have served to generate particular storylines around ZT policies in schools.

Theoretical Framework

Epistemologically, we situated this study within a critical social constructionist perspective (Jorgensen and Phillips 2002), a perspective through which we presumed that the interpretation we proffer is one amongst many possibilities and that the social world is socially and culturally bound. The "critical" component of this framework is one in which we did not seek to make sense of only the negatives or "dichotomous explanations" (Wodak 1999). Rather, we sought to complicate and layer our understandings. More specifically, we oriented to discourse as encompassing all objects and actions situated within a system of meaning (Laclau and Mouffe 1985), with meanings being produced within a structure of rules and differences (Foucault 1971). Within this perspective of discourse, then, we oriented to language as action oriented (Potter and Wetherell 1987), thereby presuming that each written word functioned to *do* something consequential (intended or not). These theoretical understandings guided how we analytically made sense of the newspaper texts, shaping the interpretations we proffered.

Methodology

We took a discourse analysis approach to the analysis of newspaper texts, drawing upon poststructural understandings of discourse (Laclau and Mouffe 1985) as well as aspects of conversation analysis (Sacks 1992) and discursive psychology (Potter and Wetherell 1987). We approached this analysis as "methodological bricoleurs" and therefore "refrained from developing an all-purpose technique for discourse analysis," as we assumed that a "totalizing master methodology would serve only to repress new and alternative forms of analysis" (Torfing 1999, 292). Specifically, we took an approach to discourse analysis that was a "theoretical position (locatable as poststructuralist, social constructionist, orientated to process and concerned with material conditions) as well as a declaration of methodology" (Cherrington and Breheny 2005, 91). From this perspective, we viewed one place of knowledge construction as being the interactional work occurring within and through newspaper texts; that is, we assumed that the language produced via newspaper texts generates particular realities of the world. As such, this theoretically grounded methodological orientation shaped both our data collection and analysis process.

Data Sources and Collection

Desiring to analyze media sources with a wide readership, we focused our analysis around articles published in the *New York Times*, which consistently ranks as one of the top five newspapers in the United States. Using the keywords "zero tolerance," "schools," and "discipline," we completed a search for articles published within the selected newspaper, last searching in March of 2014. We did not set limits on the date, as we sought to determine whether discussion around ZT had occurred both after and before the passing of the GFSA. We identified 58 articles published between 1994 and 2014.

Data Analysis

Each article (n = 58) was uploaded into a shared file for analysis. We then engaged in an emergent, four-step analysis process: (1) repeated readings of the texts, making theoretical and analytical memos; (2) selection, organization, and identification of discursive patterns and storylines that spoke to the shifting ways in which the story of ZT was told; (3) generation of explanations; and (4) transparent documentation of claims. We used ATLAS.ti™, a qualitative software package, to organize, annotate, and "code" the data set. Further, we constructed a table (see Appendix A) noting the publication dates, author(s), and stance of the article (for, against, or mixed orientations) to implementation of ZT.

During our initial readings of the articles, we familiarized ourselves with the major arguments, the discursive features employed, and the relationships within and across the data set. We then reread each article in its entirety, writing memos that chronicled our theoretical and analytical hunches, questions, and potential directions. After sharing these memos and discussing a more micro-level analysis of the data, we organized the data using a series of codes (e.g., knowledge sources, lexical choices). These "codes" were emergent and shifted as we continued to interact with the data set, as well as with one another. We isolated patterns of interest in order to carry out a closer analysis. This analysis process eventually led to the production of patterns, set against the backdrop of an overarching storyline. Further, through this process, we created an analytic map (Anfara, Brown, and Mangione 2002) documenting how we moved across multiple levels of data analysis.

We position this study, like many discourse studies, as a reflexive product, as we are a part of the discourse we critique. We acknowledge that our interpretation is situated, positional, and only one of many possibilities. As such, throughout our analysis process, we engaged in particular practices to make explicit our research process. For instance, by maintaining analytic and theoretical memos and recording/storing them electronically, we sought to leave an audit trail that made our decision-making process visible (Creswell and Miller 2000). We also aimed to report our interpretations with enough evidence to illustrate how the *New York Times* constructed a particular and shifting story about ZT policies in schools. Finally, we also sought to transparently chronicle our analytical process, thereby allowing the reader to make sense of how we came to our conclusions. To this end, we include representative excerpts throughout the findings section, along with a line-by-line analysis (Wood and Kroger 2000), and invite the reader to engage with each excerpt and with our interpretations.

Overview of Findings

The historical progression of ZT policies in the *New York Times* represents one of shifting discourses and discursive positioning. Beginning in 1994, the first publications called for, and even demanded, that ZT policies be implemented as a way to ensure school safety. Followed by a decade of published articles that highlight the contested nature of ZT policies, the past six years run parallel to the shift in public perception of policy and a move to replace ZT policies with alternative, less exclusionary, approaches to school discipline.

Specifically, through our analysis, we generated a historical, discursive mapping of the ways in which the language surrounding ZT changed within the *New York Times* across time. Our initial analysis illustrated shifts in the ways that ZT was positioned in the *New York Times* since the first article appeared in 1994. Figure 12.1 highlights the three, overarching discursive moments we noted across the data: demanding zero tolerance; debating zero tolerance; and deconstructing zero tolerance.

Related to these discursive historical moments, as we analyzed each article we paid particular attention to, among other things, how the author oriented to ZT and the stance that they made explicit. In coding for the stance of each article, we found that earlier articles either took a positive stance toward ZT or a mixed stance. Articles were coded as "mixed stance" when the author represented both positive and negative stances toward ZT. Aside from the earliest published articles, where articles were primarily supportive of ZT, the bulk of the articles, at least until 2009, were mixed in their stance toward ZT. In fact, it was not until 1998 (i.e., four years after the first ZT article appeared) that an article was published with a purely opposing stance. Of the 28 articles that were published from 1998 to 2008, seven were coded as "in favor," six were coded as "opposed" and 15 were coded as "mixed," reflecting the public debate surrounding ZT. Between 2008 and 2014, there was only one article in the *New York Times* that took a positive stance toward ZT and one article that took a mixed stance, as opposed to 21 that took a negative stance.

In the next section, we go into greater detail about these three historic eras or discursive shifts. As we do so, we include representative extracts drawn directly from the articles included within the data set.

Figure 12.1 Discursive historical moments in *New York Times* articles.

Demanding Zero Tolerance: Staking Epistemic Claims in a Discourse of Protection

As noted above, the story(ies) told about ZT policies varied from year to year and even, at times, within the same year. Yet, in the early years, we noted a predominant production of discourses demanding ZT policies, with much of the language produced functioning to justify the need for ZT policies and position teachers and other school staff as victims in need of governmental policies that protect them *from* the students they teach.

The first article that appeared in the *New York Times* specifically mentioning ZT in education was in 1994, where the American Federation of Teachers called for such policies as a way to keep "schools safe." Extract 1 illustrates how these early discourses around ZT emerged:

> **Extract 1**
> The American Federation of Teachers today urged the nationwide adoption of a policy of expelling teen-agers who take drugs or weapons to school or assault someone there. "There has to be a message we are not going to tolerate certain behaviors," John Cole, president of the Texas Federation of Teachers, said at the national group's convention here. The policy endorsed by the convention, called "zero-tolerance," is already used in several school districts in Texas and includes establishing alternative schools for students who are expelled. ("Teacher's Union Wants to Expel Students Who Carry Guns," 1995)

Extract 1 begins by positioning the "American Federation of Teachers" as calling for ZT policies and functioned to evoke a sense of authority related to who found ZT justifiable and even necessary. In other words, the American Federation of Teachers has the epistemic right to comment on such things and therefore discursively this functions to bolster the claim that ZT is needed. An epistemic right refers to an individual's right or obligation to know something in a particular area, with this "knowing" and right being variable across domains/topics, time, and interactions (Heritage 2012). Beyond this, the move to quote the president of the federation, John Cole, serves to further bolster the claim that ZT is needed. Quoting John Cole functioned much like reported speech or telling someone what someone else said (e.g., "I heard that ..."). Such speech often functions to increase the veracity of one's claim, while also leaving open the possibility that there is an alternative version of the event in question. Here, also, students are constructed as the problem, being described as bringing "drugs" and "weapons" to school. This type of framing of students as dangerous was used throughout initial articles in support of ZT.

The extract concludes by highlighting that the policy is already endorsed and in "several" schools in Texas, thereby normalizing ZT practices as something that is already in place and even "endorsed" (albeit only within the context of Texas). In general, across the articles published in the early years, there was an emphasis on reporting who endorsed ZT policies, with such emphasis serving to support the claim that ZT was needed.

Further, we noted that the ZT policies were initially positioned as being a "necessary" response to unsafe school conditions (e.g., "no response for school, for the teacher, for the rights of others," 1994). Teachers and school personnel were often cast as "fighters" in a battle against disrespectful and potentially dangerous students. Extract 2 illustrates this well:

> **Extract 2**
> In a 1993 survey by Metropolitan Life, more than 1 in 10 teachers and nearly 1 in 4 students reported that they had been victims of violence in or near their schools. Thirteen percent of the students said they had taken a weapon to school at least once. "There's a climate in which there is no respect for school, for the teacher, for the rights of others," Mr. Cole said. In many schools educators are fighting back with locker searches and metal detectors. In addition, the National Association of Secondary School Principals is asking students to sign a pledge that they will not take weapons to school. ("Teacher's Union Wants to Expel Students Who Carry Guns," 1995)

The primary way that the early articles functioned to justify the demand for ZT was through the positioning of teachers as "victims of violence," which is evident in Extract 2. This was a particularly effective argumentative move; who would argue against protecting vulnerable teachers? In the extract above, "Mr. Cole" is quoted again, with his words functioning to construct schools as unsafe spaces where students show "no respect for school, for the teacher, for the rights of others." This serves to cast students as the primary problem – a problem that can presumably only be solved by "fighting back with locker searchers and metal detectors." Similar to other articles published in 1995–1996, Extract 2 ends with a move to further justify the demand for ZT by referencing an authoritative body – the "National Association of Secondary School Principals" – which presumably has the epistemic rights to be knowledgeable on such matters.

In addition to referencing authoritative bodies, many of the early articles also cited the official legislation to support the implementation of ZT policies, as seen in Extract 3:

> **Extract 3**
> The 1994 statute says school districts must mandate the yearlong expulsion of any student found carrying a firearm to school, an approach known as "zero tolerance." If a state does not adopt a mandatory one-year expulsion policy by Oct. 20, it will lose Federal education money. *("Measure on Guns in Schools Contradicts Disability Law," 1995)*

In Extract 3, ZT is constructed as a "mandate" that entails a "must." In this case, the "must" is a "yearlong expulsion" for all students who carry "a firearm to school." ZT is linked with this "must," with states cast as being *required* to adopt this policy. We noted that across the early articles there were often references to what would happen if states did not adopt ZT policies, which typically involved loss of funding or support from the federal government. In this way, the authors positioned schools as at once needing ZT policies to protect their staff and having to implement them even if they did not need them in order to protect their funding stream.

Debating Zero Tolerance: Asserting Protections and Offering Warnings

The initial storyline surrounding ZT policies was one in which the school was positioned as morally justified in fighting against presumably "unsafe students," despite the lack of clarity and inconsistent implementation of the policy at a national level. However, even though this initial storyline was noted in the first publication in 1994, the public discourse surrounding ZT policies quickly turned to one grounded in critiques and warnings, particularly as concerns regarding racialized and ability-based discriminations became coupled with disciplinary practices. Debates, then, surrounding the justifiable use of ZT emerged, with more recent publications, particularly those since 2009, proffering an urgent call to address what some were constructing as unjust practices targeting youth of color and children with disabilities in particular. The debate began to center around the idea that the very policy described as protecting students may actually function to serve as an affront to their identities and ability to safely learn.

This debate began with early critiques that the expanding coverage of the ZT policies may be standing in contrast to other educational policies, as illustrated in Extract 4:

> **Extract 4**
> But as states and school districts rush to adopt the expulsion measures, zero tolerance is clashing with the educational policies of "zero rejection," which protect disabled students from long-term expulsions. ("Measure on Guns in Schools Contradicts Disability Law," 1995)

Extract 4 begins by making relevant the "rush" to take up measures that perpetuated "expulsion"; school districts were then faced with a contradictory practice. With schools positioned by states as needing to be inclusive of all learners, ZT policies were constructed here as being contradictory to this stance. The use of the word "clashing" highlights the degree to which ZT policies were constructed as being in contradiction to baseline school beliefs/policies. The ZT policies did not simply contradict, they "clashed," evoking an image of deep division and disconnection.

Relatedly, as ZT policies were debated in the media, there was a continual focus on the ways in which the expansive application of ZT policies was being unfairly applied. Extract 5 highlights this element of the debate well:

> **Extract 5**
> In Indianapolis, Jenna Fribley, a 15-year-old honor student, was expelled for carrying a Swiss Army knife, which violated a zero-tolerance policy on weapons. While some educators criticize such cases as ridiculous overreactions, others say the benefit of zero-tolerance policies in raising a school's overall standard of conduct outweighs the harm done to any child who inadvertently breaks a rule. ("School Codes Without Mercy Snare Pupils Without Malice," 1997)

The above extract provides an example of how a "weapon" could be interpreted in different ways, allowing for a broad or narrow application of ZT policies. In this case, the expulsion of a student who brought a "Swiss Army knife" to school was cast as an example of "harm" being done to a student with no (presumed) personal intention to harm others. "Some educators" were positioned as criticizing these practices, viewing them as "ridiculous overreactions," while others saw a "benefit" to ZT policies, viewing them as necessary in "raising a school's overall standard of conduct." This positioning constructed a contrast between those against ZT and those educators in favor of ZT, with such a contrast producing a divide. Those educators described as being against

ZT policies were often reported as pointing to the negative impact on student learning and youth of color. Those educators described as being in favor of ZT policies were often reported as citing incidences of school violence that were so shocking and concerning that it would be impossible, even dangerous, not to support ZT policies. For example, in Extract 6, "Columbine" and "Virginia Tech" shootings were cited:

Extract 6
Spurred in part by the Columbine and Virginia Tech shootings, many school districts around the country adopted zero-tolerance policies on the possession of weapons on school grounds. More recently, there has been growing debate over whether the policies have gone too far. ("It's a Fork, It's a Spoon, It's a Weapon? School Suspends Boy, 6," 2009)

Here, ZT policies were constructed as aligning with the horrendous Columbine and Virginia Tech shootings, even though their initial inception was not directly connected to these events. Yet, discursively, aligning ZT policies with such events was rhetorically useful, as it is difficult for a concerned citizen to argue against policies that are positioned as being in direct response to such tragedies. Even in Extract 6, the possibility that things have gone "too far" was made relevant, bringing into question the purpose and scope of ZT policies.

Relatedly, across the articles that centered on debating ZT policies, there was a gradual focus on the negative consequences of ZT policies:

Extract 7
Schools suspend or expel students for trivial infractions even though we know that a child who has been suspended is far more likely to fall behind in school, drop out, commit a crime or become incarcerated. ("Harsh School Discipline," 2009)

In Extract 7, the use of the word "trivial" is quite significant, as it stands in contrast to those newspaper publications that position teachers as being "at risk" or "in danger." In this instance, the "child" was positioned as being subjected to falling "behind in school" due to "trivial infractions." As such, the individual placed at risk within the school context was no longer the teacher but the student. Further, the risk was not just academic, but also could lead to a "crime," evoking the image of the school-to-prison pipeline. Such strong critiques slowly evolved into a discursive shift toward a deconstruction of ZT policies, which we explore next.

Deconstructing Zero Tolerance: Undoing its Usefulness

In the most recent publications surrounding ZT policies, those published since 2008, there have been virtually no arguments about the problems and negative consequence of ZT policies. In fact, the majority of the publications highlight the well-documented targeting of "African-American boys." Extract 8 illustrates this focus:

Extract 8
On March 8, the education secretary, Arne Duncan, lamented "schools that seem to suspend and discipline only young African-American boys" as he pledged

stronger efforts to ensure racial equality in schooling. A growing body of research, scholars say, suggests that heavy use of suspensions does less to pacify schools than to push already troubled students toward academic failure and dropping out – and sometimes into what critics have called the "school-to-prison pipeline." ("School Suspensions Lead to Questions and Legal Challenge," 2010)

In Extract 8, the disproportionate impact of ZT policies is cited, implicitly justifying the need to deconstruct ZT policies. Arne Duncan, the United States' Secretary of Education is directly quoted as lamenting how ZT-informed disciplinary practices have targeted "African American boys." As previously noted, quoting the speech of another is a powerful discursive strategy, as it functions to increase the veracity of one's claims. In this case, the identity of the speaker is also important, as a Secretary of Education is typically presumed to possess a significant level of authority when making a claim. Thus, in this extract, we noted that Duncan's quote functioned to build a case against ZT on the grounds of disproportional application of ZT policies. Further, in this extract, reference to a "growing body of research" further justified the implicit criticism of ZT policies, implicating them in the perpetuation of the "school-to-prison-pipeline." Through citing "research" and "scholars," the author justifies why/how ZT policies might be questioned.

Another way by which authors began deconstructing ZT policies was by following a critique of ZT policies with a description of alternative disciplinary practices. In this way, ZT policies were deconstructed with presumably better, more just practices being touted as "more effective." Extract 9 illustrates this well:

Extract 9

A rising number of districts are already reversing course and trying new approaches, including behavioral counseling and mediation, to reduce conflict and create safer, quieter schools while ejecting only the worst offenders. ("School Suspensions Lead to Questions and Legal Challenge," 2010)

Extract 9 begins by referencing the "rising number of districts" that are overturning ZT policies and "trying new approaches." A reference to the "rising number of districts" discursively functions to position the practice of overturning ZT and/or using alternative disciplinary approaches as reasonable and even popular. Further, the authors highlight new approaches to discipline as creating "safer" schools, implying that these new disciplinary practices are more effective than ZT policy-based practices. Extract 10 provides an additional example of this move to call for a "reversal" of all ZT policies in schools:

Extract 10

We are pleased to note the gradual reversal of zero tolerance policies in schools – something the American Psychological Association eight years ago evaluated as ineffective and harmful to children. Zero tolerance policies have failed to curb violence, drug abuse and, more recently, bullying, because they don't address the underlying causes of behavior, of which there are many. What does make a visible dent, though, is teaching students emotional skills. ("School Discipline: What Works Best?" 2014)

Here, the "reversal" of ZT policies is aligned with the "American Psychological Association," an authoritative body of scholars and practitioners, that claimed ZT policies are not only "ineffective" but also "harmful to children." Discursively, the move to align the call for reversing ZT policies with an entity as established and powerful as the American Psychological Association serves to further justify the call to deconstruct and overturn ZT. The use of the phrase "pleased to note" at the beginning of the excerpt aligned the authors with a position that was opposed to ZT. The call for a reversal, then, was not simply reported in a neutral tone; rather, this call was positioned as something the authors were "pleased to note." To further justify their claims, the authors highlight how ZT policies "failed" to decrease the behaviors they are presumed to address.

Discussion and Conclusion

Ideas in education take shape and run their course through mediums of public discourse. Examining those trends highlights how public discourse orients to such ideas, potentially influencing public perceptions and responses (Coyne and Leeson 2009). Further, research that examines school-based issues at the level of discourse enables us to explore questions on the role of media in shaping everyday perceptions, particularly with people who are often inexperienced with a particular topic.

The stories told about ZT point to a shift in public discourse about the way students are treated in schools. We see this shift taking place in print media and, to some degree, in public policy (e.g., Colorado and Michigan have recently reversed their stance on ZT policies). Although there is a great deal of evidence that ZT policies are ineffective at changing school climate (American Psychological Association 2008; Skiba, Arrendondo, and Rausch 2014), the rhetoric about school safety and the use of extreme case formulation continue to function to justify ZT at the local level.

The discursive analysis approach used in this study brings to light issues of rhetoric, policy, and practice, raising questions about which comes first. There appears to be an uneven degree of change across these different mediums of rhetoric. The public discourse on ZT has indeed shifted within print media, from one of acceptance to one of concern. This study provides a means by which to tease out what has been rhetorically coupled and used to make a strong case for ZT policies from what is, in reality, disconnected. For example, the coupling of Columbine and school safety are often rhetorically linked to the passage of the Gun-Free Schools Act. Yet, in reality, the GFSA was passed two years prior to the Columbine tragedy; however, at the level of discourse, these two events have been coupled to build a storyline that justifies what other research deems inequitable and damaging to the very educational process (i.e., ZT policies).

In light of these findings, we suggest that educators and educational researchers work to raise awareness about the myriad ways in which rhetorical devices are employed to support various policy decisions including, but not limited to, ZT policies. Discourse analysis and similar methodologies provide empirical opportunities to disrupt narratives that perpetuate injustice and reify negative images of youth. These analyses are warranted, particularly in the current educational climate and the ever-increasing availability of media and other forms of public discourse.

Additionally, these findings suggest the need to generate alternative storylines about youth, particularly youth of color. In a recent study, a teacher researcher engaged with gang-affiliated youth placed in a remedial English I class, utilizing literature and assignments designed to promote "discussion and interpersonal relationship" in addition to academic content. The findings of that study suggested that while such pedagogical choices might not reduce students' gang activity, they were able to "carve out at least one classroom where they felt successful, included, and knowledgeable" (Gass and Laughter 2015, 343). Research, as well as relational interactions with gang-affiliated youth, creates opportunities for these types of alternative narratives.

Indeed, this study was limited in scope given it did not consider how the public consumed or made sense of public texts related to ZT; however, this may be a point of future study. Further, given our study did not examine multiple media sources, the findings we shared are limited in their reach and perhaps fail to take into account broader variability in how ZT policies are represented. Nevertheless, this limitation too points to a need for further study, wherein additional media publication outlets are included as possible sites of data. More broadly, we call for an ongoing evaluation of the rhetorical devices used to generate particular stories around school safety and discipline, particularly those that function to sustain institutional practices and discourses that perpetuate approaches deemed questionable and even detrimental to students. By considering the historical telling of the birth and evolution of ZT policies, we are able to examine those discourses of our times that shape everyday disciplinary practices and, at times, conflict with local policy.

Appendix A: Articles Included within the Data Set

Article	Date	Author	Stance	Year
1	January 16, 2014	Editorial Desk/Letters to the Editor	Opposed	2014
2	January 9, 2014	Motoko Rich	Opposed	2014
3	January 6, 2014	Editorial Board	Opposed	2014
4	December 9, 2013	Editorial Desk	Opposed	2013
5	December 3, 2013	Lizette Alvarez	Opposed	2013
6	April 4, 2013	Patricia Leigh Brown	Opposed	2013
7	December 9, 2012	Donna Lieberman	Opposed	2012
8	March 7, 2012	Editor's Desk	Opposed	2012
9	March 6, 2012	Tamar Lewin	Opposed	2012
10	May 1, 2011	R. Barker Bausell	In favor	2011
11	January 28, 2011	Fernanda Santos	Opposed	2011
12	December 25, 2010	Editor's Desk	Opposed	2010
13	October 9, 2010	Erik Eckholm	Opposed	2010
14	September 14, 2010	Sam Dillon	Opposed	2010
15	March 19, 2010	Erik Eckholm	Opposed	2010
16	November 23, 2009	Editorial – Donna Lieberman	Opposed	2009
17	October 17, 2009	Letter to the editor – by ACLU of Delaware	Opposed	2009
18	October 15, 2009	Iam Urbina	Opposed	2009

Article	Date	Author	Stance	Year
19	October 13, 2009	Editorial	Opposed	2009
20	October 12, 2009	Iam Urbina	Opposed	2009
21	June 26, 2009	Adam Liptak	Mixed	2009
22	March 24, 2009	Adam Liptak	Opposed	2009
23	January 5, 2009	Editorial	Opposed	2009
24	March 22, 2007	Susan Saulny	In favor	2007
25	April 14, 2006	David M. Herszenhorn	Mixed	2006
26	March 30, 2005	Greg Winter	Mixed	2005
27	January 4, 2004	Sara Rimer	Mixed	2004
28	December 23, 2003	David M. Herszenhorn	Mixed	2003
29	November 16, 2003	Jane Gordan	Mixed	2003
30	September 17, 2003	John O'Neil	Mixed	2003
31	May 20, 2003	David M. Herszenhorn	In favor	2003
32	October 27, 2002	Merri Rosenberg	In favor	2002
33	May 17, 2001	Kate Zernike	Opposed	2001
34	April 8, 2001	John Leland	Mixed	2001
35	March 25, 2001	Mark Schone	Opposed	2001
36	February 4, 2001	Jeffrey Rosen	Mixed	2001
37	January 10, 2001	Richard Rothstein	In favor	2001
38	September 3, 2000	Debra Nussbaum	Opposed	2000
39	September 3, 2000	Debra Nussbaum	Opposed	2000
40	April 29, 2000	Excerpts Gore speech about education	In favor	2000
41	January 12, 2000	Dirk Johnson	Mixed	2000
42	January 3, 2000	Dirk Johnson	Mixed	2000
43	December 2, 1999	Editorial by Maria Hrabowski	Opposed	1999
44	December 1, 1999	Dirk Johnson	Mixed	1999
45	November 17, 1999	Dirk Johnson	Mixed	1999
46	September 23, 1999	Diana Jean Schemo	In favor	1999
47	June 6, 1999	Richard Weizel	In favor	1999
48	September 20, 1998	Linda Saslow	Opposed	1998
49	August 30, 1998	Richard Weizel	Mixed	1998
50	July 5, 1998	Alex Kotlowitz	Mixed	1998
51	February 6, 1998	Tamar Lewin	Mixed	1998
52	March 20, 1997	Somini Sengupta	Mixed	1997
53	March 12, 1997	Tamar Lewin	Mixed	1997
54	April 21, 1996	Meryl Spiegel	Mixed	1996
55	October 27, 1995	Maria Newman	Mixed	1995
56	May 10, 1995	Sarah Kershaw	Mixed	1995
57	March 15, 1995	William Celis	In favor	1995
58	July 19, 1994	Associated Press	Mixed	1994

References

Advancement Project/Civil Rights Project. 2000. *Opportunities Suspended: The Devastating Consequences of Zero Tolerance and School Discipline.* Cambridge, MA: Advancement Project/Civil Rights Project.

Advancement Project. 2010. *Test, Punish, and Push Out: How "Zero Tolerance" and High-Stakes Testing Funnel Youth into the School-to-Prison Pipeline*. Washington, DC: Advancement Project.

American Academy of Pediatrics, Committee on School Health. 2003. "Out-of-school Suspension and Expulsion: Policy Statement." *Pediatrics* 112(5), 1206–1220.

American Psychological Association 2008. "Are Zero Tolerance Policies Effective in the Schools? An Evidentiary Review and Recommendations." *American Psychologist* 63(9), 852–862.

Anderson, C.L. 2004. "Double Jeopardy: The Modern Dilemma for Juvenile Justice." *University of Pennsylvania Law Review* 152(3), 1181–1219.

Anfara, V.A., Brown, K.M., and Mangione, T.L. 2002. "Qualitative Analysis on Stage: Making the Research Process More Public." *Educational Researcher* 31(7), 28–38.

Booker, K. and Mitchell, A. 2011. "Patterns in Recidivism and Discretionary Placement in Disciplinary Alternative Education: The Impact of Gender, Ethnicity, Age, and Special Education Status." *Education and Treatment of Children* 34(2), 193–208.

Brady, K.P. 2002. "Zero Tolerance or (In)tolerance Policies? Weaponless School Violence, Due Process, and the Law of Student Suspensions and Expulsions: An Examination of Fuller v. Decatur Public School Board of Education School District." *B.Y.U. Education and Law Journal* 2002, 159–209.

Brown, T.M. 2007. "Lost and Turned Out: Academic, Social and Emotional Experiences of Students Excluded from School." *Urban Education* 42(5), 432–455.

Browne-Dianis, J. 2011. "Stepping Back from Zero Tolerance." *Educational Leadership* 69(1).

Casella, R. 2003. "Zero Tolerance Policy in Schools: Rationale, Consequences, and Alternatives." *Teachers College Record* 105(5), 872–892.

Cassidy, W. and Jackson, M. 2005. "The Need for Equality in Education: An Intersectionality Examination of Labeling and Zero Tolerance Practices." *McGill Journal of Education* 40(3), 445–466.

Castillo, J. 2014. "Tolerance in Schools for Latino Students: Dismantling the School-to-Prison Pipeline. *Harvard Journal of Hispanic Policy* 26, 43–58.

Caton, M.T. 2012. "Black Male Perspectives on Their Educational Experiences in High School." *Urban Education* 47(6), 1055–1085. DOI: 10.1177/0042085912454442.

Cherrington, J. and Breheny, M. 2005. "Politicizing Dominant Discursive Constructions about Teenage Pregnancy: Re-locating the Subject as Social." *Health: An Interdisciplinary Journal for the Social Study of Health, Illness and Medicine* 9(1), 89–111.

Christle, C. Nelson, C.M., and Jolivette, K. 2004. "School Characteristics Related to the Use of Suspension." *Education and Treatment of Children* 27(4), 509–526.

Coyne, C. and Leeson, P. 2009. "Media as Mechanism of Institutional Change and Reinforcement." *Kyklos* 62(1), 1–14.

Creswell, J.W. and Miller, D.L. 2000. "Determining Validity in Qualitative Inquiry." *Theory into Practice* 39, 124–130.

Dupper, D.R. Theriot, M.T., and Craun, S.W. 2009. "Reducing Out-of-school Suspensions: Practice Guidelines for School Social Workers." *Children & Schools* 31(1), 6–14.

Evans, K.R. and Lester, J.N. 2012. "Zero Tolerance: Moving the Conversation Forward. *Intervention in School and Clinic* 48(2), 108–114.

Fenning, P. and Rose, J. 2007. "Overrepresentation of African American Students in Exclusionary Discipline: The Role of School Policy." *Urban Education* 42(6), 536–559.

Foucault, M. 1971. "Orders of Discourse." *Social Science Information* 10(2), 7–30.

Fowler, D. 2011. "School Discipline Feeds the 'Pipeline to Prison." *Phi Delta Kappan* 93(2), 14–19.

Fries, K. and DeMitchell, T.A. 2007. "Zero Tolerance and the Paradox of Fairness: Viewpoints from the Classroom." *Journal of Law & Education* 36(2), 211.

Gass, K.M. and Laughter, J.C. 2015. "'Can I Make Any Difference?' Gang Affiliation, the School-to-Prison Pipeline, and Implications for Teachers." *The Journal of Negro Education* 84(3), 333–347.

Ginwright, S. 2006. "Racial Justice through Resistance: Important Dimensions of Youth Development for African Americans." *National Civic Review* 91(1), 41–46.

Giroux, H. 2003. "Racial Injustice and Disposable Youth in the Age of Zero Tolerance." *Qualitative Studies in Education* 16(4), 553–565.

Gonzalez, T. 2012. "Keeping Kids in Schools: Restorative Justice, Punitive Discipline, and the School to Prison Pipeline." *Journal of Law and Education* 41(2). https://ssrn.com/abstract=2658513 (last accessed October 13, 2017).

Gregory, A. and Cornell, D. 2009. "'Tolerating' Adolescent Needs: Moving beyond Zero Tolerance Policies in High School." *Theory into Practice* 48(2), 106–113.

Grona, B. 2000. "School Discipline: What Process Is Due? What Process Is Deserved?" *American Journal of Criminal Law* 27(2), 233.

Gun Free Schools Act of 1994. 20 U.S.C. Chapter 70, Sec. 8921.

Hantzopoulos, M. 2011. "Deepening Democracy: How One School's Fairness Committee Offers an Alternative to 'Discipline." *Schools: Studies in Education* 1, 112. DOI: 10.1086/659440.

Heritage, J. 2012. "Epistemics in Action: Action Formation and Territories of Knowledge." *Research on Language and Social Interaction* 45(1), 1–29.

Hirschfield, P.J. 2008. "Preparing for Prison: The Criminalization of School Discipline in the USA." *Theoretical Criminology* 12(1), 79–101.

Hoffman, S. 2014. "Zero Benefit: Estimating the Effect of Zero Tolerance Discipline Polices on Racial Disparities in School Discipline." *Educational Policy* 28(1), 69–95. DOI: 10.1177/0895904812453999.

Jones, K. 2013. "#zerotolerance #KeepingupwiththeTimes: How Federal Zero Tolerance Policies Failed to Promote Educational Success, Deter Juvenile Legal Consequences, and Confront New Social Media Concerns in Public Schools." *Journal of Law & Education* 42(4), 739–749.

Jorgensen, M. and Phillips, L. 2002. *Discourse Analysis as Theory and Method*. London: Sage.

Kaplan, S. and Cornell, D. 2005. "Threats of Violence by Students in Special Education." *Behavioral Disorders* 31(1), 107–119.

Kennedy-Lewis, B. 2013. "Using Critical Policy Analysis to Examine Competing Discourses in Zero Tolerance Legislation: Do We Really Want to Leave No Child Behind?" *Journal of Education Policy* 29(2), 165–194.

Laclau, E. and Mouffe, C. 1985. *Hegemony and Socialist Strategy*. London: Verso.

Lewis, T.E. 2006. "The School as an Exceptional Space: Rethinking Education from the Perspective of the Biopedagogical." *Educational Theory* 56(2), 159–176. DOI: 10.1111/j.1741-5446.2006.00009.x.

Losen, D.J. and Martinez, T.E. 2013. *Out of School & Off Track: The Overuse of Suspensions in American Middle and High Schools*. Los Angeles, CA: The UCLA Center for Civil Rights Remedies at The Civil Rights Project.

Martinez, S. 2009. "A System Gone Berserk: How are Zero-tolerance Policies Really Affecting Schools?" *Preventing School Failure* 53(3), 153–157.

Meek, A.P. 2009. "School Discipline "as part of the teaching process": Alternative and Compensatory Education Required by the State's Interest in Keeping Children in School." *Yale Law & Policy Review* 28, 155–185.

Monahan, K.C., Vanderhei, S., Bechtold, J., and Cauffman, E. 2014. "From the School Yard to the Squad Car: School Discipline, Truancy, and Arrest." *Journal of Youth and Adolescence* 43(7), 1110–1122.

Mongan, P. and Walker, R. 2012. "'The road to hell is paved with good intentions': A Historical, Theoretical, and Legal Analysis of Zero-tolerance Weapons Policies in American Schools." *Preventing School Failure* 56(4), 232–240. DOI: 10.1080/1045988X.2011.654366.

Nguyen, N. 2013. "Scripting 'Safe' Schools: Mapping Urban Education and Zero Tolerance during the Long War." *Review of Education, Pedagogy & Cultural Studies* 35(4), 277–297. DOI: 10.1080/10714413.2013.819725.

Noguera, P. 2003. "Schools, Prisons, and Social Implications of Punishment: Rethinking Disciplinary Practices. *Theory into Practice* 42(4), 341–350.

Peebles-Wilkins, W. 2005. "Zero Tolerance in Educational Settings." *Children & Schools* 27(1), 3–3.

Potter, J. and Wetherell, M. 1987. *Discourse and Social Psychology*. London: Sage.

Rice, S. 2009. "Education for Toleration in an Era of Zero Tolerance School Policies: A Deweyan Analysis." *Educational Studies* 45(6), 556–571. DOI: 10.1080/00131940903338308.

Rivkin, D.H. 2008. "Legal Advocacy and Education Reform: Litigating School Exclusion." *Tennessee Law Review* 75, 265–284.

Rollin, S., Kaiser-Ulrey, C., Potts, I., and Creason, A. 2003. "A School-based Violence Prevention Model for At-Risk Eighth Grade Youth." *Psychology in the Schools* 40(4), 403–416.

Sacks, H. 1992. *Lectures on Conversation*. Oxford: Blackwell.

Skiba, R.J. 2013. "Reaching a Critical Juncture for Our Kids: The Need to Reassess School-Justice Practices." *Family Court Review* 51(3), 380–387. DOI: 10.1111/fcre.12034.

Skiba, R.J., Arrendondo, M.I., and Rausch, M.K. 2014. *New and Developing Research on Disparities in Discipline*. Bloomington, IN: The Equity Project, Center for Evaluation and Education Policy.

Skiba, R.J. and Noam, G.G., eds. 2001. *Zero Tolerance: Can Suspension and Expulsion Keep Schools Safe?* San Francisco: Jossey-Bass.

Skiba, R.J. and Peterson, R.L. 1999. "The Dark Side of Zero Tolerance: Can Punishment Lead to Safe Schools?" *Phi Delta Kappan* 80(5), 372–382.

Soodak, L. 2003. "Classroom Management in Inclusive Settings." *Theory into Practice* 42(4), 327–333.

Suarez, C. 2010. "School Discipline in New Haven: Law, Norms, and Beating the Game." *Journal of Law & Education* 39(4), 503–540.

Sumner, M.D., Silverman, C.J., and Frampton, M.L. 2010. *School-based Restorative Justice as an Alternative to Zero Tolerance Policies: Lessons from West Oakland*. Thelton E. Henderson Center for Social Justice. Berkeley, CA: University of California, Berkeley, School of Law.

Teske, S.C. 2011. "A Study of Zero Tolerance Policies in Public Schools: A Multi-integrated Systems Approach to Improve Outcomes for Adolescents." *Journal of Child & Adolescent Psychiatric Nursing* 24(2), 88–97. DOI: 10.1111/j.1744-6171.2011.00273.x.

Tobin, T. and Sprague, J. 2000. "Alternative Education Strategies: Reducing Violence in School and the Community." *Journal of Emotional and Behavioral Disorders* 8(3), 177–186.

Torfing, J. 1999. *New Theories of Discourses: Laclau, Mouffe and Zizek.* Oxford: Blackwell.

Triplett, N.P., Allen, A., and Lewis, C.W. 2014. "Zero Tolerance, School Shootings, and the Post-Brown Quest for Equity in Discipline Policy: An Examination of How Urban Minorities Are Punished for White Suburban Violence." *The Journal of Negro Education* 83(3), 352–370.

US Department of Education. 1998. *Annual Report on School Safety: 1998.* http://www2. ed.gov/PDFDocs/schoolsafety.pdf (last accessed October 13, 2017).

Vavrus, F. and Cole, K. 2002. "'I didn't do nothin'": The Discursive Construction of School Suspension." *The Urban Review* 34(2), 87–111.

Verdugo, R.R. [b1] (analytic). 2002. "Race-ethnicity, Social Class, and Zero-Tolerance Policies: The Cultural and Structural Wars." ("Race-Ethnicité, Classe Sociale, et Politiques de La Tolérance-Zéro : Les Guerres Structurelles et Culturelles") *Education and Urban Society* 35(1), 50–75.

Wald, J. and Losen, D.J. 2003. *New Directions for Youth Development: Deconstructing the School-to-Prison Pipeline.* San Francisco: Jossey-Bass.

Welch, K. and Payne, A.A. 2010. "Racial Threat and Punitive School Discipline." *Social Problems* 57, 25–48.

Winton, S. 2013. "From Zero Tolerance to Student Success in Ontario, Canada." *Educational Policy* 27(3), 467–498. DOI: 10.1177/0895904812453994.

Wodak, R. 1999. "Critical Discourse Analysis at the End of the 20th Century." *Research on Language and Social Interaction* 32(1&2), 185–193.

Wood, L.A. and Kroger, R.O. 2000. *Doing Discourse Analysis: Methods for Studying Action in Talk and Text.* Thousand Oaks, CA: Sage.

13

School Surveillance and Gang Violence

Deterrent, Criminalizing, or Context-Specific Effects

Lynn A. Addington and Emily E. Tanner-Smith

The problem of gangs in schools is one that concerns educators, policy makers, and parents. The presence of gangs can contribute to a negative school climate characterized by increased fear among students as well as a poor learning environment (Howell and Lynch 2000; Laub and Lauritsen 1999; Mayer and Leone 1999). The presence of gangs also tends to co-occur with overall rates of school violence: schools where gangs are present also tend to be schools where violence occurs (DeVoe and Bauer 2011; Howell and Lynch 2000). Despite the observed correlation of gang activity and school violence, as well as conventional beliefs in a causal relationship, the actual amount of violence and rate of school crime attributable to gangs has not been well established (Estrada et al. 2014a). Although the causal direction between gang activity and school violence is still uncertain, many administrators seek ways to address actual and perceived problems with gangs in order to promote their schools as safe and supportive learning environments for all students (see Chapter 11, this volume).

School administrators have employed different tactics to address the issue of gangs. One set of approaches aims to prevent or reduce membership in gangs. These programs include both gang-specific programming and targets, such as the Gang Resistance Education and Training (GREAT) program (Esbensen et al. 2012; Peterson et al. 2009), as well as more general programs aimed at improving youth development overall through mentoring programs (Medina, Ralphs, and Aldridge 2012). In contrast to this orientation to reduce the number of gang members, an alternative approach seeks to reduce the criminal activity of gang members. These policies capitalize on the current trend toward an increased use of school security, especially surveillance measures such as security cameras, metal detectors, police officers, and other forms of security personnel. Relatively scant empirical research has been devoted to examining the relationship between the use of school security, gang activity, and violence in schools. This chapter explores the use of school security and surveillance policies – particularly the use of police and other security personnel for maintaining order at school – as a response to gang violence in schools.

The Wiley Handbook on Violence in Education: Forms, Factors, and Preventions, First Edition.
Edited by Harvey Shapiro.
© 2018 John Wiley & Sons, Inc. Published 2018 by John Wiley & Sons, Inc.

Background

Established and growing bodies of research focus on the issues of youth gangs (Estrada et al. 2014a; Pyrooz 2014; Pyrooz, Sweeten, and Piquero 2013) and security as a response to school violence (Brady, Balmer, and Phenix 2007; Fisher and Tanner-Smith 2016; Mayer and Leone 1999; Na and Gottfredson 2013). While these two areas of study have garnered significant research attention, to date the intersection between them has not been considered. Our study will therefore focus on this intersection, examining the associations between school security and surveillance policies and gang activity at school. To provide context for our study, the following sections review the existing research in the areas of youth gangs and school security measures, highlighting the need for more systematic examination of whether these policies are associated with gang activities in schools.

The Role of Youth Gangs in School Violence

In the area of youth gang research,[1] much attention has focused on gang activities in the community rather than in schools (Estrada et al. 2014a; Howell 2015). School-oriented studies tend to focus only tangentially on gangs, as a predictor of school climate or as an attribute of schools where violence occurs (e.g., DeVoe and Bauer 2011; Schreck and Miller 2003; Tillyer, Fisher, and Wilcox 2011). Despite the conventional wisdom that gangs are associated with school violence, surprisingly little empirical research actually has examined the frequency or incidence of gang-related crime at school, or the role of youth gangs in school violence. One challenge to this work is how best to define gangs in schools: the prevalence of gangs in schools can vary widely depending on measurement methods and definitions (Howell 2015; Naber et al. 2006).

An additional – and likely related – challenge is the lack of national data that include information on gang-related crime in schools. Student-level data include sources such as that collected by the National Crime Victimization Survey's School Crime Supplement (SCS). These data do gather details about school climate, including the presence of gangs as well as students' experiences with various forms of violence. The SCS is limited by its inability to aggregate to the school level. As such, researchers have had to collect their own data to explore gang-related crime at school. Using statewide data from middle and high school students in California, Estrada and colleagues (2014a) found that approximately 8% of students self-identified as a gang member, and that gang membership was relatively consistent across schools and regions. Using the same statewide data source from the California Health Kids Survey, Estrada and colleagues (2014b) also found no direct association between gang membership and school violence. Rather, the effect of gang membership on school violence was partially mediated by other risk and protective behaviors, including perceptions of school safety. This research highlights the need to investigate the relationship between school security measures and gang-related school violence, especially the extent to which security measures are related to students' feelings of safety.

---

1 A larger body of research has focused on gangs more generally, but not youth gangs specifically. Because our study focuses on school-related violence and adolescent gang involvement, this body of work is not reviewed here.

School Security and Surveillance as a Means of Addressing Gang Violence

A growing body of literature has examined the changes in the use and types of school security and surveillance since the shootings at Columbine High School (Addington 2009; Muschert and Peguero 2010). Since the 1970s, school security and surveillance measures (such as security cameras, metal detectors, police officers, drug-sniffing dogs, contraband sweeps) were most prevalent in disadvantaged urban schools battling crime and other problems, including gangs (Lawrence 2007). More recently, the use of school security has expanded to schools located in rural and suburban areas, ones not identified as violence prone, and elementary and middle schools (Addington 2014; Steinka-Fry, Fisher, and Tanner-Smith 2016). The most frequently used types of security are security cameras and police officers or other "security personnel," which are defined broadly here as including sworn law enforcement officials, security guards, or school resource officers (SROs) (Addington 2009, 2014). A primary reason for the increase in police and security personnel in schools is likely attributable to federal funding programs such as Cops in Schools (Addington 2009; James and McCallion 2013; The White House 2013).

In addition to their increased use over the past dozen years, security personnel comprise a unique form of school security. Unlike cameras or metal detectors, security personnel are not static surveillance measures but can be deployed in different ways.[2] These roles range widely from those aligned with traditional law enforcement to mentorship and teaching roles (particularly for programs such as GREAT), and they can include a mix of these responsibilities (Finn et al. 2005; James and McCallion 2013). This flexibility makes security personnel an important consideration for studying the relationship between school security and gang violence.

Although a growing body of work is examining the role of security personnel in schools (Brady, Balmer, and Phenix 2007; Fisher and Tanner-Smith 2016; Tanner-Smith et al. 2016; Theriot 2009; Tillyer, Fisher, and Wilcox 2011), we are not aware of any prior studies that have specifically addressed the association between security personnel and gang-related crime in schools. As a result, we are limited for our study to borrowing from this work and the relationship between security personnel and school crime generally. For example, prior studies have found an association between the use of security personnel in schools and increased reporting of less serious school crime (Na and Gottfredson 2013). These studies have also noted that the relationship between the use of security personnel and school crime is a complex one (Na and Gottfredson 2013). In addition, security personnel may have differential effects in schools with high proportions of minority students, or socioeconomically disadvantaged or female students, groups who tend to report less favorable attitudes toward police (Hurst and Frank 2000; Theriot 2009). The effect of school security and security personnel on gang violence is also likely to vary depending on the use of other school violence prevention programming (Gottfredson 2001). As such, we would anticipate a nuanced relationship between security personnel and gang-related crime as well as one that varies across school contexts including the use of prevention policies.

---

2 The different security personnel designations vary with regard to their affiliation with local law enforcement (police and SROs typically are sworn law enforcement officers) and their assignment (SROs and security guards typically are assigned specifically to the school). This discussion focuses on the variation of roles that security personnel can play rather than their particular employment status.

Research Questions

No previous research has examined whether or how the association between school security and gang-related crime varies across different types of schools. We seek to address some of the gaps in the existing literature regarding the prevalence of gang-related crime in school and whether school security is associated with gang-related crime in schools. Our present study explores the following three research questions. First, what is the relationship between school security and gang-related crime at school? For descriptive and comparative purposes, when addressing this first research question we also examine how these relationships compare with total crime and serious violent crime rates at school. Second, among schools that employ security personnel, what is the relationship between activities engaged in by school security personnel and gang-related crime at school? Again, to provide context, we examine how these relationships compare with total crime and serious violent crime rates at school. The third, and final, question examined is whether any school policy, or school contextual factors, moderate the relationships between security and school crime.

Methods

Sample

To address the research questions posed, we used restricted data from the School Survey on Crime and Safety (SSOCS). The SSOCS is a cross-sectional survey of principals and administrators of US schools that uses a stratified sampling design based on the Common Core of Data file to stratify on school level, locale, and enrollment size (Ruddy et al. 2010). The SSOCS data have been collected in several iterations. We used the SSOCS survey collected in 2009–2010 as it constitutes the most recent data available to researchers.

Measures

School Crime Incidence
We examined three types of administrator-reported crime at school: number of gang-related crime incidents (excluding gang-related hate crime[3]), total crime incidents, and serious violent crime incidents at school. The SSOCS survey defined a gang as "an ongoing loosely organized association of three or more persons, whether formal or informal, that has a common name, signs, symbols, or colors, whose members engage, either individually or collectively, in violent or other forms of illegal behavior" (Ruddy et al. 2010, 88 [F-3]). Gang-related crime incidents were based on the school administrator respondent counting the number of total crimes that were gang related in the past year. Total crime incidents were based on the school administrator respondent counting the number of total crimes in the past year. Serious violent crime incidents were based on total crime reports but were limited to rape, sexual battery, robbery with

---

3 The SSOCS collected gang-related hate crime as a separate measure from overall gang-related crime. Given the extremely low incidence of gang-related hate crime, and the potential unique factors associated with hate crime, our analysis only focused on non-hate gang-related crimes.

a weapon, assault with a weapon, and threat of assault with a weapon (Ruddy et al. 2010, 88 [F-3]). School administrators reported counts of crime incidents, but all of our analyses are presented as crime incidence rates (per 1,000 students) to adjust for differences in counts across schools of varying sizes.

School Security Measures

We examined six different school security measures. Administrators reported whether their schools used the following security measures in their school during the past year ($0 = No$; $1 = Yes$): metal detectors (daily use or random checks), contraband sweeps (excluding dog sniffs), security cameras, security guards, school resource officers, or sworn law enforcement officers.

Security Personnel Activities

We examined seven measures of the types of activities performed by school security personnel, which could include security guards, school resource officers, sworn law enforcement officers. School administrators reported whether the security personnel in their school routinely did the following ($0 = No$; $1 = Yes$): carried a firearm, participated in security enforcement and patrol, maintained school discipline, coordinated with local police and emergency teams, identified problems in the school and proactively sought solutions to those problems, trained teachers and staff in school safety or crime prevention, or mentored students.

School Policies and Procedures

We examined 13 measures of school programs used to prevent or reduce school violence. School administrators reported whether their school used any of the following formal programs in the past school year ($0 = No$; $1 = Yes$): prevention curriculum, instruction or training for students; behavior modification intervention for students; counseling, social work, psychological, or therapeutic activity; individual attention, mentoring, tutoring, or coaching by other students; individual attention, mentoring, tutoring, or coaching by adults; recreational, enrichment, or leisure activities; student involvement in resolving student conduct problems; programs to promote a sense of community/social integration among students; formal process for obtaining parental input on policies related to school crime and discipline; provision of training or technical assistance to parents in dealing with student problem behavior; programs that involve parents at school helping to maintain school discipline; parent groups involved in school prevention efforts; community involvement in school prevention efforts; and teacher training.

School Contextual Factors

We examined three other school contextual factors as potential moderators of the relationship between school security measures and school crime: percentage of white students (range 0–100), enrollment size (range 10–4,350), urbanicity ($0 = No$; $1 = Yes$), and whether students in the school resided in high crime neighborhoods ($0 = No$; $1 = Yes$).

Other School Characteristics

All analyses were adjusted for five other characteristics of schools: highest grade in school (range 1–12), regular public school ($0 = No$; $1 = Yes$), percentage of students eligible for free/reduced price lunch (FRPL) (range 0–100), percentage of students scoring below the 15th percentile on standardized tests (range 0–100), and percentage of students likely to attend college after high school (range 0–100).

Data Analysis Procedures

Negative binomial regression models were used to predict crime incidence, given that all outcomes were overdispersed, non-negative count variables. All models were estimated in Stata 14.0 using a mean parameterization of dispersion. To account for differences in count outcomes across schools of varying size, school enrollment size was used as an exposure variable, such that all regression models predicted incidence rates.

We first estimated a series of main effects models to examine the relationship between school security measures and school crime incidence rates. We next estimated a series of regression models that examined the relationship between security personnel activities and school crime rates, on the subset of schools that employed security personnel. Finally, multiplicative interaction terms were used to examine whether other school policies/procedures or school contextual factors moderated the effect of school security measures on school crime incidence rates.

All analyses used jackknife variance estimates to adjust for the complex survey design of the SSOCS. Statistical significance was assessed at $\alpha = .05$ level for all main effects in the regression models. Given the large number of significance tests used to explore interactions, all interaction effects were assessed at $\alpha = .01$ level. There were no missing data on the key variables of interest, as the US Department of Education used a hot-deck imputation method for imputing missing data (Ruddy et al. 2010).

Results

Descriptive Statistics

Table 13.1 presents descriptive statistics for the 2,650 schools in the sample.[4] Schools were comprised of 60% white students, with an average enrollment size of 572 students ($SD = 601$), and 26% located in urban areas. Almost all schools (90%) were regular public schools, with an average of 52% free/reduced price lunch (FRPL) eligible students, 12% of students scoring below the 15th percentile on standardized tests, 59% likely to attend college after high school, and 7% residing in high crime neighborhoods.

On average, schools reported 39 total crime incidents per 1,000 students in the past year, only 0.35 of which were gang-related crimes, and 1.17 of which were for serious violent crimes. Thus, on average, gang-related crime was quite rare in schools and less common than serious violent crime at school. Gang-related crime rates at school did vary across the schools in the sample. Although most schools reported few if any gang-related crime incidents, the school with the most gang-related crime reported 128 gang-related crime incidents per 1,000 students in the past year.

The most commonly reported school security measures were security cameras (61%), followed by school resource officers (31%), security guards (22%), contraband sweeps

---

4 Note that all sample sizes are rounded to the nearest 10, per requirements in our restricted use data license agreements with the Institute of Education Sciences.

Table 13.1 Descriptive statistics for the characteristics of the schools in the sample (n = 2,650).

	M or %	SD	Range
School characteristics			
Percent white students	59.74	32.54	0–100
Enrollment size	572	601	10–4350
Urban	0.26		0–1
Highest grade in school	7.30	2.81	1–12
Regular public school	0.90		0–1
Percent free/reduced price lunch (FRPL) eligible	51.76	26.96	0–100
Percent below 15th percentile	11.95	13.39	0–100
Percent likely to attend college	59.39	24.53	0–100
Students live in high crime area	0.07		0–1
Crime incidence rates (per 1,000 students)			
Total crime	39.31	58.19	0–634.09
Gang-related crime	0.35	4.43	0–128.76
Serious violent crime	1.17	5.74	0–100.76
School security measures			
Metal detectors	5.56		0–1
Contraband sweeps	12.05		0–1
Security cameras	61.05		0–1
Security guards	21.67		0–1
School resource officers	31.10		0–1
Sworn law enforcement officers	8.27		0–1
Security personnel activities			
(among n = 1,680 schools with security personnel)			
Carry a firearm	76.90		0–1
Security enforcement and patrol	89.55		0–1
Maintain school discipline	77.55		0–1
Coordinate with local police and emergency teams	88.84		0–1
Identify problems and seek solutions to problems	86.15		0–1
Train teachers and staff	55.28		0–1
Mentor students	70.21		0–1
School policies and procedures			
Prevention curriculum	87.12		0–1
Behavioral modification	91.88		0–1
Counseling, psychological, therapeutic activity	93.20		0–1
Mentoring/tutoring by adults	90.82		0–1
Recreation/enrichment activities	84.59		0–1

(Continued)

Table 13.1 (Continued)

	M or %	SD	Range
Student involvement in resolving conduct problems	47.81		0–1
Programs to promote sense of community	82.32		0–1
Process for obtaining parental input	54.49		0–1
Training assistance for parents	55.39		0–1
Parent involvement at school	20.42		0–1
Community involvement in parent groups	67.09		0–1
Community involvement in school prevention efforts	88.29		0–1
Teacher training discipline policies	61.94		0–1

(12%), sworn law enforcement officers (8%), and metal detectors (6%). Among the schools that used security personnel (security guards, school resource officers, or sworn law enforcement officers; $n = 1,680$), most security personnel carried a firearm, provided security patrol and reinforcement, coordinated with local police, and identified problems in the schools. Fewer schools reported that security personnel trained teachers or staff in school safety or crime prevention (55%) or provided mentoring to students (70%).

The vast majority of schools (85% or more) reported using prevention curricula, behavioral modification, and student counseling, mentoring, and enrichment activities in an effort to prevent or reduce school violence. The least frequently used school prevention efforts were parent involvement at school (20%), student involvement in problem solving (48%), and formal processes for obtaining parental input on policies related to school crime and discipline (54%).

School Security Measures and School Crime

Types of School Security Measures

To address our first research question, we estimated negative binomial regression models predicting the association between types of school security measures and the incidence of gang-related crime, total crime, and serious violent crime in schools. Table 13.2 presents the unstandardized coefficients and 95% confidence intervals from these models, all of which accounted for exposure via school enrollment sizes, and included school security measures and school contextual factors as covariates.

As shown in the left section of Table 13.2, none of the school security measures were associated with gang-related crime incidence after adjusting for the other school characteristics. Gang-related crime incidence was significantly higher in schools with fewer white students ($b = -0.03$, 95% CI [-0.04, -0.01]), schools with older students, that is, higher grade levels ($b = 0.34$, 95% CI [0.21, 0.47]), and regular public schools ($b = 1.23$, 95% CI [0.14, 2.32]). After adjusting for a range of school characteristics, we found no evidence that schools' use of metal detectors, contraband sweeps, surveillance cameras, or security personnel were associated with higher or lower rates of gang-related crime.

As shown in the middle section of Table 13.2, the use of contraband sweeps in schools was associated with higher incident rates of total crime at schools, even after adjusting

Table 13.2 Results from negative binomial models predicting crime incidence (n = 2,650).

	Gang-related crime		Total crime		Serious violent crime	
	b	95% CI	b	95% CI	b	95% CI
Metal detectors	−0.27	[−1.74, 1.21]	−0.11	[−0.45, 0.24]	0.97	[−0.81, 2.74]
Contraband sweeps	0.48	[−0.56, 1.51]	0.32*	[0.08, 0.55]	0.29	[−0.46, 1.03]
Surveillance cameras	0.36	[−0.54, 1.27]	0.02	[−0.17, 0.20]	−0.22	[−0.69, 0.25]
Security guards	−0.22	[−1.03, 0.59]	0.12	[−0.10, 0.34]	−0.04	[−0.76, 0.67]
School resource officers	0.37	[−0.47, 1.21]	0.15	[−0.02, 0.32]	0.04	[−0.49, 0.57]
Sworn law enforcement	0.43	[−0.85, 1.71]	0.09	[−0.08, 0.26]	0.22	[−0.31, 0.75]
Percent white students	−0.03*	[−0.04, −0.01]	0.00	[−0.00, 0.01]	0.00	[−0.01, 0.02]
Urban	0.54	[−0.09, 1.18]	0.08	[−0.11, 0.28]	−0.39	[−0.99, 0.22]
Highest grade in school	0.34*	[0.21, 0.47]	0.09*	[0.06, 0.13]	0.06	[−0.03, 0.15]
Regular public school	1.23*	[0.14, 2.32]	0.00	[−0.35, 0.36]	0.40	[−0.13, 0.94]
Percent FRPL	0.01	[−0.02, 0.03]	0.01*	[0.00, 0.01]	0.02*	[0.00, 0.04]
Percent below 15th percentile	0.02	[−0.00, 0.03]	0.01*	[0.00, 0.02]	0.01	[−0.01, 0.03]
Percent likely to attend college	−0.00	[−0.04, 0.02]	−0.01*	[−0.01, −0.00]	0.01	[−0.01, 0.02]
Students live in high crime area	0.25	[−0.96, 1.46]	0.08	[−0.21, 0.37]	0.31	[−0.50, 1.12]
F		13.54*		15.68*		1.86

Notes: Results are unstandardized coefficients and 95% confidence intervals based on jackknife standard errors, estimated from negative binomial regression models that account for exposure via school enrollment size.
* $p < .05$.

for the other school characteristics ($b = 0.32$, 95% CI [0.08, 0.55]). For instance, the predicted average number of total crime incidents was 21.05 for schools that did not use contraband sweeps, versus 52.05 for schools that did use contraband sweeps. Total crime incidence was also significantly higher in schools with older students ($b = 0.09$, 95% CI [0.06, 0.13]), a greater proportion of students eligible for FRPL ($b = 0.01$, 95% CI [0.00, 0.01]), lower school-level achievement ($b = 0.01$, 95% CI [0.00, 0.02]), and lower expectations of postsecondary enrollment ($b = -0.01$, 95% CI [-0.01, -0.00]). Although no school security measures were associated with gang-related crime incidence, we did find that contraband sweeps were associated with higher rates of total crime at schools.

Finally, the right section of Table 13.2 provided no evidence that the school security measures were associated with serious violent crime incidents. Serious violent crime incidence was significantly higher in schools with a greater proportion of students eligible for FRPL ($b = 0.02$, 95% CI [0.00, 0.04]), but none of the other school security or school characteristics were associated with serious violent crime incidence. In sum, school security measures were not consistently associated with gang-related crime rates at school, but they also had minimal associations with total crime or serious violent crime rates at school. The only exception was that total crime rates were significantly higher in those schools using contraband sweeps.

Security Personnel Activities

To address our second research question, we next estimated negative binomial regression models predicting the association between specific security personnel activities and school crime incidence, among the 1,680 schools that employed security personnel (i.e., security guards, school resource officers, sworn law enforcement officers). Table 13.3 presents results from these models.

As shown in the left section of Table 13.3, minimal evidence suggested that security personnel activities were associated with gang-crime incidence rates. Gang-related crime was higher in schools with security personnel when those security personnel were involved in training teachers and staff in school safety or crime prevention efforts ($b = 0.95$, 95% CI [0.02, 1.87]). For instance, the predicted number of gang-related crime incidents was 1.11 (per 1,000 students) for schools where security personnel were involved in training teachers and staff in crime prevention efforts, versus only 0.40 in schools where security personnel were not involved in such training. Although the simple presence/absence of security personnel was not associated with higher rates of gang-related crime in schools, gang-related crime was higher in those schools where security personnel were involved in training teachers and staff. Otherwise gang-related crime rates were not associated with security personnel's carrying of firearms, security enforcement, maintenance of school discipline, coordination with police, identifying school problems, or mentoring students.

The middle and right sections of Table 13.3 indicate that security personnel activities have more associations with total crime rates and serious violent crime rates at school. Namely, total crime and serious violent crime incidence was higher in schools with

Table 13.3 Results from negative binomial models predicting crime incidence by security personnel activities (n = 1,680).

	Gang-related crime		Total crime		Serious violent crime	
	b	95% CI	b	95% CI	b	95% CI
Carry a firearm	0.27	[−0.82, 1.36]	0.31*	[0.02, 0.59]	−0.76	[−1.77, 0.24]
Security enforcement and patrol	1.04	[−0.48, 2.55]	−0.29	[−0.68, 0.11]	−0.60	[−1.62, 0.42]
Maintain school discipline	0.61	[−0.52, 1.75]	0.28*	[0.05, 0.52]	0.58*	[0.01, 1.15]
Coordinate with local police	−1.15	[−2.90, 0.60]	−0.07	[−0.34, 0.21]	0.45	[−1.39, 2.29]
Identify problems and seek solutions	−0.24	[−1.95, 1.48]	0.14	[−0.18, 0.46]	0.11	[−0.81, 1.03]
Train teachers and staff	0.95*	[0.02, 1.87]	−0.14	[−0.31, 0.02]	−0.29	[−1.13, 0.55]
Mentor students	−0.09	[−0.72, 0.54]	0.22	[−0.05, 0.49]	0.48	[−0.27, 1.23]

Notes: Results are unstandardized coefficients and 95% confidence intervals based on jackknife standard errors, estimated from separate bivariate negative binomial regression models that account for exposure via school enrollment size and adjust for all variables shown in Table 13.2.
* $p < .05$.

security personnel when those security personnel were involved in maintaining school discipline ($b = 0.28$, 95% CI [0.05, 0.52]; ($b = 0.58$, 95% CI [0.01, 1.15]). For instance, the predicted number of total crime incidents was 47.75 for schools where security personnel were involved in maintaining school discipline, versus 18.56 in schools where security personnel were not involved in maintaining discipline. Further, total crime incidence was higher in schools with security personnel when those personnel carried a firearm ($b = 0.31$, 95% CI [0.02, 0.59]). Although total crime rates were higher in schools where security personnel maintained school discipline and carried firearms, these security personnel activities were not associated with gang-related crime at school.

Moderators of the School Security–School Crime Relationships

To address our third research question, we extended the regression models shown in Table 13.2 by adding multiplicative interaction terms between each school security type and the school policies/procedures and contextual moderators described in the methods section. Given the large number of significance tests used to explore these moderators, all interaction effects were assessed for significance at the $\alpha = .01$ level and we only focus on the significant interactions here.

Overall, little evidence suggested that the association between school security measures and school crime incidence varied across different types of schools, and across schools using different violence prevention policies and procedures. There was evidence, however, that gang-related crime incidence rates were significantly higher in certain school contexts. First, and as shown in the top panel of Figure 13.1, although gang-related crime was generally higher in schools that used behavioral modification interventions for preventing school violence, this was magnified in schools that also used contraband sweeps (interaction $b = 3.94$, 95% CI [2.59, 5.29]). For instance, among schools using contraband sweeps, the predicted average number of gang-related crime incidents was 0.01 for schools that did not use behavioral modification interventions, versus 0.99 for schools that did use behavioral modification programs.

There was also evidence that although gang-related crime incidence rates were generally higher in schools with security guards, they were highest in schools with security guards that did not provide training or technical assistance to parents in dealing with student problem behavior (interaction $b = -1.84$, 95% CI [-3.13, -0.55]; see Figure 13.1). Among schools using security guards, the predicted average number of gang-related crime incidents was 1.35 for schools that did not provide parent assistance, versus 0.69 for schools that did provide training or technical assistance.

As shown in the bottom panel of Figure 13.1, there was also evidence that gang-related crime incidence rates were highest in schools with security guards that also had community involvement in school prevention efforts (interaction $b = -5.26$, 95% CI [-6.57, -3.95]; see Figure 13.1). Among schools using security guards, the predicted average number of gang-related crime incidents was 0.97 for schools where communities were involved, versus 0.28 for schools without community involvement in prevention efforts.

In the models predicting total crime and serious violent crime incidence rates, only one statistically significant interaction term emerged. As shown in Figure 13.2, serious violent crime rates at school were significantly higher in schools where sworn law enforcement officers were present and where the school was located in a high crime neighborhood (interaction $b = 2.44$, 95% CI [0.73, 4.15]). Otherwise, no evidence supported that the association between school security and school crime rates varied across school contexts.

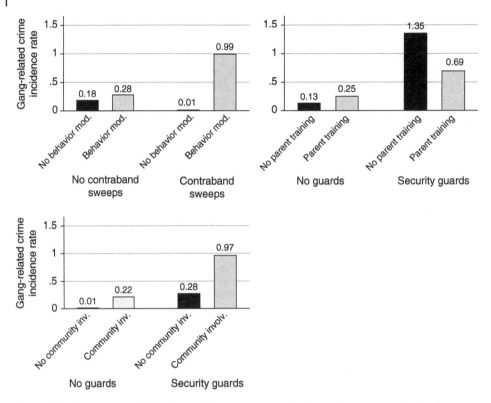

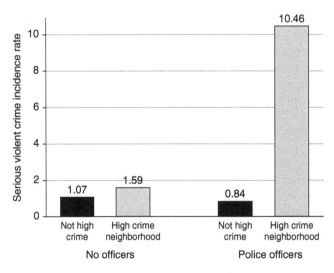

Figure 13.1 Mean gang-related crime incidence rates, by school security type and school policy type.

Figure 13.2 Mean serious violent crime incidence rates, by school security type and neighborhood crime levels.

Discussion

Before returning to our initial research questions, a few of the descriptive findings are important to highlight. One concerns the gang-related crime rates and seeing how these compare with school crime rates overall. As noted previously, relatively little is known about these school-level crime rates. Using national data from the United States, we found that overall school crime rates on average were less than 40 crimes per 1,000 students. For serious violent crime, these average rates drop to 1.17 per 1,000 students. Gang-related crime only accounted for 0.35 incidents on average per 1,000 students. The results also indicated that security cameras were the most common form of security measures that schools use. Security personnel (including security guards, sworn law enforcement officers, and SROs), though, were the second most common form, with SROs comprising the majority of security personnel used by schools. These findings are consistent with prior studies (e.g., Addington 2009). With regard to the roles played by school security personnel, the most common concerned those associated with more traditional law enforcement (security enforcement and patrol and coordinating with local police) as well as community policing oriented work (identifying and seeking solutions to problems). These findings also are consistent with prior research (James and McCallion 2013).

Our initial research question concerned examining the relationship between school security and gang-related crime. For context, we compared the relationship with total school crime and serious violent crime. The results indicated few relationships between security measures and crime rates in schools. Indeed, no relationships were observed between any school security measure and gang-related or serious violent school crime.

We offer a few explanations for this result. One is that security measures are not associated with these more serious forms of school crime. We conducted additional post hoc exploratory analyses to examine whether school security measures were associated with an alternative measure of school crime seriousness, specifically the frequency in the use of removing students from the educational environment through suspensions, expulsions, and transfers. The results from those analyses (not reported here, available upon request) suggested that these exclusionary school discipline rates were significantly higher in schools with SROs. This finding suggests that having security personnel might lower the amount of school crime, but the crime that does occur is addressed via more serious forms of discipline. A second possible explanation for our results is that security measures might reduce school crime, but the cross-sectional data used in this study precluded our ability to examine changes within schools over time. A third possible explanation is that school security measures might have a preventative effect to limit serious forms of school crime including gang-related crime, with unintended crime diffusion effects beyond the school. Namely, this diffusion effect might encourage gang members to conduct offending outside of school and into the surrounding communities and neighborhoods in which they are embedded.

For total school crime, we did find that schools employing contraband sweeps reported higher crime incident rates. The predicted average total crime incidence rate for schools employing sweeps was approximately 52 as compared to 21 in schools that did not use these sweeps. One reason for this finding is likely attributable to the inherent net-widening effect of contraband sweeps. If schools look for contraband in the form of drugs or weapons, they are likely to find it. On a similar note, other contraband might be found during these sweeps, such as stolen items. To the extent these sweeps result in fairly minor violations, the result would produce an increase in total crime rates (rather than serious violent crime rates).

Our second research question focused on those schools employing security personnel. Given the range of roles security personnel can play, we wanted to examine the relationship between these specific activities and gang-related crime. Again, to provide context, we explored the nature of these security personnel roles with total crime and serious violent crime. With regard to gang-related crime, we found higher rates of crime reported by schools where security personnel train teachers and staff in school safety or crime prevention efforts. This finding translates into gang-related crime rates of 1.11 for schools where security personnel engaged in training as compared to rates of 0.40 for schools that did not have this training. One explanation for this finding is again a net-widening effect. Our research was unable to discern the specific form of in-school safety or crime prevention training that security personnel actually provided. Given the fact that training teachers and staff did not have a statistically significant relationship with total or serious crime rates, though, one possibility is that this training could be related to gang awareness or gang issues. To the extent that teachers and staff are trained in identifying gangs or associating gangs with school crime, this information may increase reporting of gangs in school as well as crimes associated with gang members. It is also possible that schools experiencing problems with gangs might engage in more training exercises with teachers and staff. Our study was unable to discern the causal direction of this relationship, which we discuss below regarding the limitations of our study.

In comparison, the security personnel activity of maintaining school discipline resulted in higher rates of overall crime and serious violent crime. This finding might also be attributable to net widening whereby the maintenance of discipline increases the number of school crime incidents that are counted. As discussed above, it may also be that schools with disruption and crime problems initially are the ones where security personnel must be engaged in maintaining discipline, but again, we are unable to identify the causal direction of this relationship.

Our third question considered whether any school policy or contextual factors moderated the effect of security on gang-related crime or other types of school crime. Here we focused on possible interactive effects of school policies and security on crime rates. One significant relationship of interest arose in situations where schools employed security guards (as a specific form of security personnel) and engaged in training assistance for parents. This co-occurrence resulted in lower gang crime incidence rates than ones where guards were employed but no parent training was offered. We can draw limited conclusions from this finding as we do not have information on the training given to parents or whether guards were the ones providing the training. One speculated explanation is that this training might make parents more aware of issues related to the school and may make them more proactive at home to address crime and gang problems.

Limitations

The SSOCS data set has many strengths for the purposes of our study as it provides details not available from other sources such as student-based surveys (such as the School Crime Supplement to the National Crime Victimization Survey or the Youth Risk

Behavior Survey). The SSOCS allows for the computation of school crime rates as well as security measures, school programming, and other school-level demographics. That being said, the data do have limitations that affect our study and the conclusions we can draw. These include the definition of a gang, the identification of gang-related crimes, and the cross-sectional nature of the data.

One limitation is the definition of a gang, which can affect the amount of gang activity captured by our study (e.g., Howell 2015; Naber et al. 2006). The SSOCS definition is fairly narrow as it defines gang as groups "whose members engage, either individually or collectively, in violent or other forms of illegal behavior" (Ruddy et al. 2010, 88 [F-3]). This paradigm of violent activity narrows the scope as compared to other definitions that use delinquency and broader views of criminal activity (Howell 2015). In addition, it is possible that the gang members may no longer be in school, given the requirement that the behavior is illegal.

A related limitation is how gang-related crimes are counted. The SSOCS relies on the school administrator counting the number of total crimes that occurred at the school. A separate question collects the number of these total crimes that are gang related. It is unclear how administrators determined whether a crime was gang related. It could be to further underlying gang activity or a crime that involves a student who is determined to be a gang member. This measurement issue is comparable to those faced by police departments and can lead to an over- or undercounting of gang-related crimes. In addition, given how the SSOCS measures gang-related crime, we were unable to discern specific crimes attributed to gangs at school. For example, it is possible gang-related crimes might account for a smaller number of crimes, but these crimes might be more serious or violent. The SSOCS data do not permit this type of disaggregation.

Finally, we only used one cross-sectional year of data from the SSOCS. This cross-sectional approach limits our ability to draw causal inferences regarding the associations (or lack thereof) between school security measures and school crime rates. Indeed, we cannot determine whether security measures lowered gang-related crime or other forms of school crime, or if those associations are due to other confounding factors. Given the paucity of research in this field, clearly there is a need for more rigorous longitudinal studies to collect school-level data on security measures and rates of violence and crime in schools.

Conclusion

The presence of gangs in schools is an ongoing concern for educators and parents given conventional wisdom that gangs increase school violence and have an overall negative effect on school climate. In response, administrators and policy makers have used tactics to address the problem of gangs (see Chapter 10, this volume). We considered one such approach to confronting gang violence: the use of surveillance measures of school security. We found no evidence that any particular type of security measure was associated with gang-related crime at school. In addition, we did not find any relationship between security measures and total school crime and violent crime at school. Given the frequency with which schools employ security personnel and the various roles that security personnel can play, we investigated possible relationships between particular security personnel roles and gang-related crime at school. We found that schools whose security personnel trained teachers and staff did report higher levels of gang-related crime at school. No other security personnel activities were associated with changes in gang-related crime.

Given the lack of previous research attention to this issue, our study provides an important foundation and identifies the need for additional work in this area. Specifically, future studies can confirm the small contribution of gangs to school violence, but expand this finding to ascertain the types of school crime typically attributed to gang members. The possible net-widening effect of security measures also needs to be further explored. One example is the connection between school security and exclusionary disciplinary measures such as out-of-school suspensions and expulsions. This relationship needs to be fleshed out regarding the likelihood of gang members being removed from school as compared to non-gang members, and the long-term detrimental effects that such exclusionary discipline can have on students' educational and occupational success (as noted by Estrada and colleagues, this volume).

Conclusive policy recommendations cannot be drawn from our exploratory study alone, but certain potential policy implications can be identified and should be explored in future work. One overall implication is that schools are relatively safe places, especially with regard to serious violent crime and gang-related crime. School officials should carefully consider their particular situation before adding security measures. If security measures are being considered, our findings provide initial indications that partnerships between security personnel and teachers as well as security guards and parents may be an important link in combatting gang-related crime. In particular, partnerships that incorporate security personnel-led training seem particularly relevant. One speculation is that training that incorporates ways to identify problem behavior is useful for teachers and parents and is readily transferable to address gang-related issues. Again, it is important to emphasize that these are only provisional suggestions and that they require stronger research support. Overall, though, our findings, coupled with additional work, have the potential to inform school policy in the utility of security measures as a means to address issues of crime and violence at school.

Acknowledgments

All analyses reported in this chapter were conducted under NCES/IES License Number #10050038 for the restricted use SSOCS data. Preliminary findings from this chapter were presented at the 2015 annual meeting of the American Society of Criminology.

References

Addington, Lynn A. 2009. "Cops and Cameras Public School Security as a Policy Response to Columbine." *American Behavioral Scientist* 52, 1426–1446. DOI: 10.1177/0002764209332556.

Addington, Lynn A. 2014. "Surveillance and Security Approaches across Public School Levels." In *Responding to School Violence: Confronting the Columbine Effect*, edited by Glenn W. Muschert, Stuart Henry, Nicole L. Bracy, and Anthony A. Peguero, pp. 71–88. Boulder, CO: Lynne Rienner.

Brady, Kevin P., Balmer, Sharon, and Phenix, Deinya. 2007. "School–Police Partnership Effectiveness in Urban Schools: An Analysis of New York City's Impact Schools Initiative." *Education and Urban Society* 39, 455–478. DOI: 10.1177/0013124507302396.

DeVoe, Jill F. and Bauer, Lynn. 2011. *Student Victimization in U.S. Schools: Results from the 2009 School Crime Supplement to the National Crime Victimization Survey* (NCES 2012-314). US Department of Education, National Center for Education Statistics. http://nces.ed.gov/pubs2012/2012314.pdf (last accessed October 13, 2017).

Esbensen, Finn-Aage, Peterson, Dana, Taylor, Terrance J., and Osgood, D. Wayne. 2012. *Is G.R.E.A.T. Effective? Does the Program Prevent Gang Joining? Results from the National Evaluation of G.R.E.A.T.* St. Louis, MO: University of Missouri-St. Louis.

Estrada, Joey Nuñez, Gilreath, Tamika D., Astor, Ron A., and Benbenishty, Rami. 2014a. "A Statewide Study of Gang Membership in California Secondary Schools." *Youth & Society*. Online. DOI: 10.1177/0044118X14528957.

Estrada, Joey Nuñez, Gilreath, Tamika D., Astor, Ron A., and Benbenishty, Rami. 2014b. "Gang Membership, School Violence, and the Mediating Effects of Risk and Protective Behaviors in California High Schools." *Journal of School Violence* 13, 228–251. DOI: 10.1080/15388220.2013.846860.

Finn, Peter, Shively, Michael, McDevitt, Jack, Lassiter, William, and Rich, Tom. 2005. *Comparison of Program Activities and Lessons Learned among 19 School Resource Officer (SRO) programs.* Document Number 209272. National Institute of Justice.

Fisher, Benjamin W. and Tanner-Smith, Emily E. 2016. "Examining School Security Measures as Moderators of the Association between Homophobic Victimization and School Avoidance." *Journal of School Violence* 15, 234–257. DOI: 10.1080/15388220.2014.983644.

Gottfredson, Denise C. 2001. *Schools and Delinquency.* Cambridge: Cambridge University Press.

Howell, James C. 2015. "Gang Trends, Trajectories, and Solutions." In *Handbook of Juvenile Delinquency and Juvenile Justice*, edited by Marvin D. Krohn and Jodi Lane, pp. 517–535. Malden, MA: Wiley Blackwell.

Howell, James C. and. Lynch, James P. 2000. *Youth Gangs in Schools.* OJJDP Juvenile Justice Bulletin.

Hurst, Yolander G. and Frank, James. 2000. "How Kids View Cops: The Nature of Juvenile Attitudes toward the Police." *Journal of Criminal Justice* 28, 189–202. DOI: 10.1016/S0047-2352(00)00035-0.

James, Nathan and McCallion, Gail. 2013. *School Resource Officers: Law Enforcement Officers in Schools.* Washington, DC: Congressional Research Service Report for Congress (7-5700, R43126).

Laub, John H. and Lauritsen, Janet L. 1999. "The Interdependence of School Violence with Neighborhood and Family Conditions." In *Violence in American Schools*, edited by Delbert S. Elliott, Beatrix A. Hamburg, and Kirk R. Williams, pp. 127–158. Cambridge: Cambridge University Press.

Lawrence, Richard. 2007. *School Crime and Juvenile Justice*, 2nd ed. New York: Oxford University Press.

Mayer, Matthew J. and Leone, Peter E. 1999. "A Structural Analysis of School Violence and Disruption: Implications for Creating Safer Schools." *Education and Treatment of Children* 22, 333–356.

Medina, Juanjo, Ralphs, Robert, and Aldridge, Judith. 2012. "Mentoring Siblings of Gang Members: A Template for Reaching Families of Gang Members?" *Children & Society* 26, 14–24. DOI: 10.1111/j.1099-0860.2010.00307.x.

Muschert, Glenn W. and Peguero, Anthony A. 2010. "The Columbine Effect and School Anti-violence Policy." *Research in Social Problems and Public Policy* 17, 117–148. DOI: 10.1108/S0196-1152(2010)0000017007.

Na, Chongmin and Gottfredson, Denise C. 2013. "Police Officers in Schools: Effects on School Crime and the Processing of Offending Behaviors." *Justice Quarterly* 30. 619–650. DOI: 10.1080/07418825.2011.615754.

Naber, Patricia A., May, David C., Decker, Scott H., Minor, Kevin I., and Wells, James B. 2006. "Are there Gangs in Schools? It Depends Upon Whom You Ask." *Journal of School Violence* 5, 53–72. DOI: 10.1300/J202v05n02_05.

Peterson, Dana, Panfi, Venessa R., Esbensen, Finn-Aage, and Taylor, Terrance J. 2009. *National Evaluation of the Gang Resistance Education and Training (G.R.E.A.T.) Program: School Personnel Survey Report.* St. Louis, MO: University of Missouri-St. Louis.

Pyrooz, David C. 2014. "From Colors and Guns to Caps and Gowns? The Effects of Gang Membership on Educational Attainment." *Journal of Research in Crime and Delinquency* 51, 56–87.

Pyrooz, David C., Sweeten, Gary, and Piquero, Alex R. 2013. "Continuity and Change in Gang Membership and Gang Embeddedness." *Journal of Research in Crime and Delinquency* 50, 239–271.

Ruddy, Sally A., Neiman, Samantha, Hryczaniuk, Cassie A., Thomas, Teresa L., and Parmer, Randall J. 2010. *2007–08 School Survey on Crime and Safety (SSOCS) Survey Documentation for Public-Use Data File Users (NCES 2010-307).* Washington, DC: National Center for Education Statistics, Institute of Education Sciences, US Department of Education.

Schreck, Christopher J. and Miller, Mitchell. 2003. "Sources of Fear of Crime at School: What Is the Relative Contribution of Disorder, Individual Characteristics, and School Security?" *Journal of School Violence* 2, 57–79. DOI: 10.1300/J202v02n04_04.

Steinka-Fry, Katarzyna T., Fisher, Benjamin W., and Tanner-Smith, Emily E. 2016. "Visible School Security Measures across Diverse Middle and High School Settings: Typologies and Predictors." *Journal of Applied Security Research* 11, 1–14. DOI: 10.1080/19361610.2016.1210482.

Tanner-Smith, Emily E., Fisher, Benjamin W., Addington, Lynn A., and Gardella, Joseph H. 2016. "Adding Security, but Subtracting Safety? Exploring Schools' Use of Multiple Visible Security Measures." *American Journal of Criminal Justice.* DOI: 10.1007/s12103-017-9409-3.

The White House. 2013. *Now is the Time*, 1–15. Washington, DC: The White House. https://obamawhitehouse.archives.gov/node/193271 (last accessed October 30, 2017).

Tillyer, Marie S., Fisher, Bonnie S., and Wilcox, Pamela. 2011. "Effects of School Crime Prevention on Students' Violent Victimization, Risk Perception, and Fear of Crime: A Multilevel Opportunity Perspective." *Justice Quarterly* 28, 249–277. DOI: 10.1080/07418825.2010.493526.

Theriot, Matthew T. 2009. "School Resource Officers and the Criminalization of Student Behavior." *Journal of Criminal Justice* 37, 280–287. DOI: 10.1016/j.jcrimjus.2009.04.008.

14

When Gangs Are in Schools

Expectations for Administration and Challenges for Youth

Lisa De La Rue and Anjali J. Forber-Pratt

The presence of gangs in schools permeates multiple aspects of the educational process and has a significant influence on school climate. Dealing with gangs in schools, or in nearby neighborhoods, requires specific attention from teachers and administrators to ensure the safety and well-being of all students, while also challenging the school's mandate to be inclusive to all students on their campuses. Frequently the response to gang activity, or perceived threats of gang violence, includes swift and expansive disciplinary action, often in the form of zero tolerance policies or law enforcement intervention (Mallett 2016; Triplett, Allen, and Lewis 2014). Too often these responses lead to removing students from the school by way of either suspension or expulsion. While discipline has frequently been the first response, there is a growing expectation that school administrators improve their efforts to address these behaviors in a manner that allows the young person to correct their behavior and remain in the school. Indeed, there is a growing recognition that schools should strive to be less punitive in their responses, and should move toward supportive interventions (Gottfredson and Gottfredson 2001; Sharkey, Stifel, and Mayworm 2015). This, of course, is balanced with the importance of ensuring safety in schools.

Nationally, 16% of public schools report gang activity (Robers, Zhang, and Morgan 2015), and, when students are asked, 45% percent of high school students and 35% of middle school students say there are gangs in their schools, or students who consider themselves to be part of a gang (Arciaga, Sakamoto and Jones 2010). While these numbers suggest high gang activity across the nation, the reality is that a gang presence in schools is not as pervasive as some might be led to believe. While high-profile reports in the media suggest otherwise, relatively few young people join gangs, even in highly impacted areas. Indeed, rates of youth gang participation rarely exceed 10% (Burnett and Walz 1994), and in a nationwide survey of students in grades 6–12 regarding self-reported gang involvement, 7.6% of males and 3.8% of females stated they belonged to a gang (Gottfredson and Gottfredson 2001). Furthermore, the perception that much of the violence or criminal activities occurring in schools can be attributed to youth gang activity is often overstated. It has been reported that less than 2% of all juvenile crime is gang related (Burnett and Walz 1994).

The Wiley Handbook on Violence in Education: Forms, Factors, and Preventions, First Edition.
Edited by Harvey Shapiro.

While the number of youth actively involved in gangs rarely exceeds double-digit percentages, it is also important to recognize that students may be connected to gangs in other ways that are not reflected in officially reported statistics. Adolescents tend to have a diverse collection of friends, and consequently some students may be peripherally involved with gangs, or have friends who are affiliated with gangs. Thus, some youth who do not claim gang membership may nonetheless be adjacent to gangs if they have friends who are actively involved in gangs (Curry, Decker, and Egley 2002). As such, schools are challenged to address and support not only students who are actively involved in gangs, but also those students who are exposed to many of the same concerns that gang affiliation brings.

Given the complex and sometimes fluid nature of adolescent peer relationships, it can be difficult for schools to identify students who are gang involved, and often this determination is made hastily and based on superficial attributes. The common stereotype of gang members is that they are young boys and men from racial/ethnic minority groups living in deteriorating urban areas (Esbensen and Carson 2012). Too often teachers, school administrators, and the general public make assumptions about young people based on their racial or ethnic background, and/or on the way they dress. Young people are not oblivious to these underlying attitudes, and in fact these beliefs infiltrate multiple aspects of the educational process, which can make it unwelcoming for some students. For example, Rios's (2010) ethnographic research has shown that some gang-involved youth believed they were racially targeted by school officials and felt stigmatized by school teachers and administrators.

Of additional concern is that these stereotypes persist despite the fact that research has consistently shown that gang members reflect the communities in which they live – in other words, both boys and girls are gang involved – and gang membership is not unique to racial/ethnic minority or immigrant groups (Esbensen and Carson 2012). Furthermore, nationwide surveys indicate law enforcement officers identify a much higher percentage of youth of color as being gang involved, but on youth self-report surveys white students report roughly the same amount of gang membership as black and Latino youth (Boyd 2009). Taken together, it is evident that too often schools, and the general public, are making assumptions about young people, in particular in relation to gang involvement. These assumptions not only influence how schools interact with youth but also how youth feel about their school. This is problematic because when school officials fear their students because of the way they dress, where they come from, or where they live, there is little room left to educate these young people, and instead there tends to be an overreliance on discipline as a system to manage students (Rios and Galicia 2013). Especially in schools that are dealing with gang violence, rule-breaking students are more likely to be defined as criminals, both symbolically and legally, and are treated as such in policy and practice (Hirschfield 2008).

Discipline in Schools

While it is undeniable that some schools need to respond to gang presence – particularly in response to disruptive and sometimes dangerous situations – overwhelmingly the response has been shortsighted. Too often the scenario for youth who are actually, or perceived to be, involved with gangs is to respond with punitive disciplinary policies and procedures that remove the young person from the classroom or often from the entire educational system. These policies and procedures are omnipresent in US schools, and have done little to address youth gang involvement.

Zero Tolerance Policies

Zero tolerance disciplinary policies represent a philosophy that mandates the application of predetermined consequences, most often severe and punitive in nature, that are intended to be applied regardless of the seriousness of the behavior, mitigating circumstances, or any situational contexts (American Psychological Association Zero Tolerance Task Force 2008). These policies are touted as providing the same consequence, regardless of the student, for identified behaviors, with the overarching goal of creating a safe school environment. However, when one chronicles the development of these policies and the associated outcomes, it is evident that the policies are not applied equally to all students and often do more harm than good. In fact, zero tolerance policies often threaten students' potential for academic success and unfairly target certain groups of students (see Chapter 12, this volume).

Many of the current discipline policies in schools are a reflection of larger social and political climates, which are in turn largely influenced by media stereotypes. When considering gangs in particular, politicians, practitioners, and the general public often rely on media-generated stereotypical impressions of gangs (Esbensen and Carson 2012). For example, in the 1980s and 1990s media reports were touting horrific crimes that were being committed by minority youth as part of gang violence, reports that were completely disproportionate to the reality of youth violence at this time (Walker, Spohn, and DeLone 2012). Yet these stories infiltrated the minds of the general public, and the resulting narrative was that people should be wary of minority youth since they were likely in gangs that were causing the violence and aggression in our communities. Despite evidence that these reports were exaggerated and inaccurate, the narrative remains, and indeed continues to be propagated in the media today. (For a more detailed account of the discourse of zero tolerance policies, see Chapter 12, this volume.)

Media reports that youth gang violence was overtaking communities coincided with federal "get tough on crime" efforts that attempted to suppress crime and violence with severe punishments (Esbensen and Carson 2012). The logic was that by not tolerating *any* illegal behaviors there would be sweeping reductions in violence and crime. We would soon see this mind-set creep into our educational system with the rise of zero tolerance policies. The reality is that zero tolerance policies are a reflection of law enforcement crime suppression policies; they just take place in schools.

The influence of the media and the corresponding societal conjectures would continue to demand a response to ensure students were safe in schools, even if the unintended consequences of such policies would only serve to hurt young people. These demands would manifest in policies like the 1994 Gun-Free Schools Act, which was enacted as a response to school shootings and deaths (Gass and Laughter 2015). The Gun-Free Schools Act not only specifically addressed firearms and weapons in schools, but also signified a seal of approval for zero tolerance policies; it paved the way for enhanced school security and expectations of quick disciplinary responses as the primary method of dealing with student behavioral concerns (Mallett 2016). These sweeping, and often oppressive, policies were touted as a way to ensure students were safe in schools, and were maintained partly on the misconceptions perpetuated by media that youth gangs were overwhelming our communities and schools.

It should not be surprising that these initial policies quickly expanded, and were subsequently used to address all types of offenses that occurred in schools, including truancy, the use of obscene language, alcohol and substance use, and fighting. The expansion of these policies also facilitated the criminalization of student discipline. The Gun Free Schools Act, in conjunction with the Safe Schools Act, paved the way for discipline in schools to be implemented by the use of law enforcement officers. Specifically, the Gun-Free Schools Act sanctioned the expansion of police officers in schools (Gass and Laughter 2015). The result was a criminalization of the discipline processes in schools, and often the behaviors targeted by these policies are ones that are strongly associated with gang affiliation (Gass and Laughter 2015).

School Resource Officers

It is increasingly common for schools to partner with law enforcement agencies, again under the guise of increasing school safety. School resource officers (SROs) are sworn law enforcement officers assigned full time to patrol schools (Theriot 2009), and can be found in around 35% of schools across the United States (Weiler and Cray 2011). The 1994 Safe Schools Act, initiated as a response to school shootings and deaths, facilitated the school and police force collaboration and contributed to the perception that it is the norm for police officers to be present in schools (Mallett 2016). Consequently, there has been significant growth in the number of schools that employ SROs, which has been supported by increased federal funding. The Department of Justice has awarded in excess of $765 million in funding to hire SROs nationwide (Na and Gottfredson 2013), funds that have been augmented by additional state grants to increase the money available to put officers in schools (Kupchik and Monahan 2006). This increase is in spite of a lack of research that would indicate such a strategy is actually helpful. Indeed, research has found little evidence suggesting that SROs contribute to school safety (Na and Gottfredson 2013). A 2013 Congressional report noted that research has not found a direct link between SROs and increased safeguards against gun violence in schools (James and McCallion 2013), and in fact the Justice Policy Institute (Petteruti 2011) recently reported that having SROs and other police in schools actually causes more harm than good.

Given that research generally does not support the claim that SROs increase safety in schools, it would seem reasonable that schools would pause and reflect on these current policies, especially when also considering how the presence of officers in schools may contribute to the criminalization of their students. For example, when schools employ law enforcement officers, the all too frequent result is that students, particularly students of color, are criminalized for minor incidents that would normally have been handled by school personnel (Advancement Project 2010). Some argue that the mainstreaming of law enforcement in schools has become a way to compensate for a lack of thoughtful discipline strategies, including restorative approaches, and the unintended consequence is an educational system that underwrites the incarceration of students (Rios and Galicia 2013). That is, the presence of law enforcement in schools has redefined disciplinary issues as criminal justice issues, rather than social, psychological, or academic issues, and the result is an increased likelihood that students are arrested at school (Na and Gottfredson 2013) and become a part of the growing US criminal justice system.

The presence of officers in schools has increased the number of students who are arrested on school grounds by 300–500% annually, and most often these arrests are for non-serious offenses, including unruly behaviors, disobedience, or status offenses (Mallett 2016). The impact of these policies, again, disproportionately hurts students of color. For instance, black students are more likely than white students to have one of the nearly 20,000 SROs working in their schools (Mills 2016). This is problematic given that students in schools with SROs are more likely to be arrested or referred to law enforcement for disorderly conduct and other minor offenses than students in schools without SROs (Mills 2016). Whereas black students comprise 16% of school enrollment in the United States and represent 31% of all school-related arrests, white students represent 51% of the enrolled school population but only 39% of all school-related arrests (Mills 2016). These disproportionate rates mirror systematic problems and injustices seen across society. In the United States an average of 600 youth are arrested each day, and every black boy born in 2001 will have a one-in-three chance of going to prison, and every Latino boy born in the same year will have a one-in-six chance of the same fate (Children's Defense Fund 2007).

Increased Surveillance

The policies and procedures implemented in our schools, with the intended purpose of increasing safety and managing student behavioral concerns, have also had the consequence of increasing surveillance of students. (For a more in-depth discussion of school surveillance in relation to gangs, see Chapter 13, this volume.) SROs provide one form of surveillance, but schools often employ additional means of surveillance including metal detectors, video recordings, ID cards, transparent lockers and backpacks, electronic gates, and more. The dominant rationale for these systems is to increase safety and prevent violence, including violent shootings like those at Columbine High School (Kupchik and Monahan 2006). However, the irony of this rationale is striking given that video surveillance and armed security guards were present at Columbine, and yet these did not (and could not) prevent the shootings (Kupchik and Monahan 2006). Instead, the presence of high tech security measures and other surveillance methods serves to create a prison-like environment in schools, which has the effect of habituating traditionally marginalized populations, including low-income and ethnic and minority youth, to the treatment that would be seen in prison (Wacquant 2001). Furthermore, adding metal detectors, increasing surveillance, or adding more SROs can actually make schools feel unsafe, and when schools appear to be unsafe, this can increase the presence of violence and gang activity in schools. When students feel their school is not safe, and they are not offered a pathway to academic success, it is more likely that they will engage in risky behaviors (Gass and Laughter 2015). These surveillance practices ignore the importance of school climate and serve to create distance between students and school staff.

This increased surveillance presents another disparate impact on students of color. This hyper-surveillance itself is a known correlate of youth contact with the juvenile justice system (Goddard 2014), as they are more likely to be noticed by law enforcement. Law enforcement officers are often directly plugged into surveillance systems, allowing them access to video recordings that can then be a source of evidence for prosecuting students who commit crimes or who violate increasingly restrictive school policies (Kupchik and Monahan 2006). These surveillance practices also make youth feel less connected to school, and too often reflect the same entrance practices that are in place when individuals enter into jails and prisons. A school's daily process of checking students and passing metal detectors across their bodies embodies the same process of entering into a correctional system. When members of school communities are required to enter the building in this manner, this criminalizes the very act of going to school and contributes to a school culture where fear and uncertainty run rampant. Ironically, these surveillance practices aimed at reducing crime may actually contribute to higher rates of youth involvement in disruptive behaviors, including gang activity.

Gangs and School Pushout

Scholars have highlighted how school disciplinary policies interact with the larger shift in education toward school accountability, a force that encourages schools to remove poorly performing and infrequently attending students from their rolls (Hirschfield 2008) in an effort to maintain higher overall test scores. Zero tolerance policies and SROs effectively increase school averages on standardized tests scores and reduce truancy rates by removing students who are engaged in concerning behaviors from the pool of students for whom schools are held accountable (Na and Gottfredson 2013). This not only has immediate impacts for schools and students, but also has long-term implications. As young people lose more days of school due to suspensions or expulsions, promotion to the next grade becomes less likely and consequently graduating becomes less likely (Na and Gottfredson 2013). These policies thus directly and indirectly cause students to exit from the educational system.

School pushout refers to the written and unwritten policies and practices within a school that lead to student dropout (Cope, Korsmo, and Wilkens 2013). While it is true that students drop out of school for a multitude of reasons, school pushout encompasses intentional procedures, like harsh disciplinary practices and frequent use of suspensions, which can then lead to students dropping out of school. These harsh practices include zero tolerance policies and the use of SROs as a first response to violence (including perceived gang activity) in schools. Reflecting patterns of the criminal justice system, school pushout reflects a lack of focus on supporting young people in overcoming obstacles, and instead favors swift action that serves to control students as a way to manage concerning behaviors. As indicated previously, part of this reflects an othering process where some students, including gang-involved youth, are perceived to have poor prospects and therefore punitive disciplinary processes are seen as an acceptable solution for this *other* group of students. This othering is perpetuated by media stories and societal stereotypes, and is often reflected in research examining youth gang members as *others*.

Much of the research on gangs has centered on the *who* instead of the *why*, which results in gang members being identified because of their race/ethnicity, age, and/or socioeconomic status rather than as youth who are responding to social systems that conceptualize them from deficit paradigms (Gass and Laughter 2015). Gangs are often conceptualized as groups that are separate from their communities, and the result is programs that attempt to remove gangs from the communities (Leap 2013). When the focus remains on *who*, the natural result is categories that the *who* can fit into, and less attention is given to context.

The focus on *who* takes schools away from viewing their students within a context, and instead encourages administrators to make judgments based heavily on stereotypes and assumptions. It also requires that schools engage in actions to remove the students *who* are disrupting the educational process away from the *other*, non-disruptive students. These practices contribute to pushing students out of the educational system, given the mandate for quick and significant disciplinary responses and the lack of critical attention to the possible reasons for why the young person is engaged in the behavior. In essence, the response is to address a specific behavior, with less attention given to addressing why the behavior may be manifesting. This mind-set focuses on *who* perpetrated the behavior, removing that *who* from the larger school environment and social context.

Expanding on the consequences of this mind-set, some students choose to drop out prior to being removed from the school environment by administrators. There is a growing awareness that student dropout is not an individual student problem, but that schools also exert important organizational influences on a young person's decision to drop out or stay in school (Lee and Burkam 2003). Some gang-involved youth attribute their detachment from school and their subsequent decision to leave school to the negative treatment they received from school personnel and law enforcement officers (Rios 2010). For these youth, the process of othering makes for an unwelcoming school experience and gives the impression that they are not welcome there. It should not be a surprise that youth who have these experiences may leave school and not return.

School-to-Prison Pipeline

The devastating end result of punitive discipline policies and school pushout is a "school-to-prison pipeline," in which large numbers of students throughout the United States are treated as disposable, and are routinely being pushed out of school toward the juvenile justice system (Advancement Project 2010). While school districts and juvenile courts were never intended to operate in collaboration, the unfortunate reality is that now a partnership between these systems has developed (Mallett 2016). This partnership is being strengthened by information-sharing agreements between education and justice agencies, setting the stage for laws that would allow schools to expel students for legal issues that did not even take place in schools (Hirschfield 2008), thus further blurring the line between education and incarceration. As Giroux (2012) describes, there has been a growing tendency to turn away from helping young people, especially youth of color, and instead move toward criminalizing and arresting students.

Unfortunately for many gang-involved youth, federal legislation continues to provide multiple "on ramps" for schools to place students on the path to incarceration. For example, the Gang Abatement and Prevention Act (GAPA) broadened the definition of gang and gang crime and created a wider net with which to identify "gang-related behavior" (Boyd 2009). As a result, more youth, including those not in gangs, can be penalized for gang-related behavior and the accompanying sanctions (Boyd 2009). Similar to concerns with zero tolerance policies, there are now predetermined and harsh consequences for gang-related behavior that do not give consideration to context or individual circumstances. GAPA has broadened the class of activities that would constitute gang activities and imposes harsh and mandatory sentences for youth who fall under the broadly defined universe of gang or gang-related crimes (Boyd 2009). As a result, there are more options to penalize youth, but less focus on how to support youth.

Shifting Disciplinary Policies to Treatment Policies

Zero tolerance policies and the presence of SROs exacerbate educational inequalities, which highlights the reality that minority students are disproportionately affected by school discipline practices. It has been well documented that disproportionality in discipline is a problem in schools (Boyd 2009; Cope, Korsmo, and Wilkens 2013), with rates of punishment among youth of color far surpassing those of their white counterparts. For example, studies show that black and African American students are subject to disciplinary actions more often than white students, and for less severe infractions (Boyd 2009). In 2014, Secretary of Education Arne Duncan and Attorney General Eric Holder urged schools to abandon zero tolerance policies, recognizing that these policies do not promote democratic principles of educational opportunity and have continued to punish minority students more harshly than their white counterparts (Triplett, Allen, and Lewis 2014). Furthermore, punitive approaches, including suspensions and expulsions, represent short-term solutions that show little evidence of effectiveness, and which may actually be iatrogenic for individuals and schools (Osher et al. 2010).

Schools should thus consider alternative options for addressing concerning student behaviors. For example, although youth wearing gang clothing or other identifiers should not be tolerated in schools, there are a number of responses from administration that do not include suspensions and/or expulsions (Arciaga, Sakamoto, and Jones 2010). Schools may maintain clothes closets (Nash and Bhattacharya 2009) that allow students to change when they wear prohibited items, thus demonstrating to the young person the administration would like them to remain at school. However, schools must also take care to ensure these alternative clothing options do not stigmatize or single out youth (Rios 2010). Other options include scheduling meetings with caregivers to discuss the expectations of clothing and dress at school and have students agree to what items will not be worn at school (Rios 2010). Schools may also choose to implement a school uniform policy, which has been shown to lower perceptions of gang activity and negative consequences of such activity (Chapter 11, this volume). It is also imperative that schools make efforts to support students who are engaged in concerning behaviors, and strive to understand why students may be motivated to join gangs.

Treatment before Punishment

Youth who are involved in gangs have a greater history of trauma and adverse experiences in their lives (Maschi and Bradley 2008; Paton, Crouch, and Camic 2009). Many youth involved in gangs have experienced significant victimization and fractured social relationships, and thus it is imperative that adults in a position to help act in a way that builds positive relationships rather than creates additional ruptures (De La Rue and Espelage 2014). One effective solution may be the use of counseling to help youth respond to trauma and process adverse experiences (Buss, Warren, and Horton 2015). As such, it is crucial that any efforts to address gang concerns in schools include opportunities for students to access treatment, including counseling.

Achieving this aim will require a shift in how schools, communities, and governmental agencies view the best course of action for addressing gang problems. Currently, in most districts the ratio of SROs to school counselors is in favor of officers, and this is especially pronounced in schools that serve traditionally marginalized populations (Petteruti 2011). As the Century Foundation (2016) highlights, there is a tendency toward over-policing and less access to school counselors in high-poverty schools. As discussed above, this highlights how many schools view a disciplinary response as the best course of action. These priorities are reflected in who is employed in the school and who is assumed to be responsible for addressing concerning behaviors. If schools were invested in addressing situational contexts that contribute to gang activity, this would require that they shift support, and funds, to employ more counselors and mental health professionals. Schools could also shift their policies and procedures so that students speak to school counselors first, rather than an administrator or school resource officer (Maddox 2015), which would provide space for students and the adult to explore the situational factors and other concerns that might be affecting the student. This type of process can support efforts to curb gang involvement, and also has the potential to support student engagement in school. When schools create a space that helps students cope with the challenges they may be facing, students are more engaged in school and more likely to attend school (Bryant et al. 2013).

Treatments that are implemented in schools to support gang-involved youth must be multifaceted. Research that has specifically examined the interaction between gang membership and school violence indicates that school administrators should not solely target students who are gang members, but instead should focus their attention on reducing risky behaviors like truancy, substance use, and risky peer interactions (Estrada et al. 2014). This is because school violence reflects a complex set of risky behaviors that are occurring within the school and community environment, and are less a direct reflection of a young person being involved in a gang (Estrada et al. 2014). For example, the US Department of Justice reports (Esbensen 2000) that delinquency generally precedes gang membership, suggesting that treatment and intervention programs should address the possible reasons for delinquency engagement before gang intervention or suppression efforts are attempted. Furthermore, targeting the entire student population may also be helpful in reducing youth gang involvement, with specific attention given to those identified as at risk of gang involvement. Arciaga and colleagues (2010) report that providing students with knowledge, skills, and abilities to help them avoid gang involvement is paramount to preventing student gang involvement.

When implementing any treatment intervention effort, it is also important to note that even well-intentioned policies that seek to identify youth who are *at risk* can have unintended consequences. These risk-oriented policies have been found to marginalize, and even criminalize and demonize, "at-risk" populations, particularly Indigenous, black, and Latino youth (Goddard 2014). Schools would be better served by making efforts to improve the overall school climate, as opposed to looking at specific groups of students. Fostering a positive school climate requires building positive relationships between students and adults in the school, so that schools learn which students may be in need of additional support. This is another reason why more counselors are needed in schools, so that students have adults who are in a position to provide emotional support, and with whom they can develop supportive relationships.

Fortunately, many existing school- and community-based youth programs demonstrate promise in redirecting youth from gangs and thereby preventing gang affiliation in the first place (Charles Hamilton Houston Institute for Race and Justice 2008). However, a common thread with all of these programs is that they include a web of support that includes families, schools, and communities (Osher et al. 2003). Therefore, schools would also benefit from being proactive in building relationships with families and other community supports. Indeed, to address a multitude of concerns, schools should be fully invested in community efforts, and this includes being a part of comprehensive community strategies that aim to address gang violence (Gebo and Sullivan 2014). Schools can also make efforts to engage with community groups, individuals, and institutions like colleges and universities to respond to the needs of youth and their families through case management, family services, mentoring, academic coaching, or other activities. Additionally, counseling supports should be expanded to include the families of gang-involved students. Doing so helps to expand the network of support for gang-involved students and helps broaden the team of people who are actively supporting a young person. Overall, schools would benefit from identifying multiple ways to support the overall well-being of their students, whether with in-school counseling or connecting with community agencies that can provide these services. Research shows that when schools are more empathetic and provide services like counseling and mentoring, violence and gang membership decreases (Rios and Galicia 2013).

An important caveat is that treatment should be voluntary. When situations arise where treatment is chosen over traditional disciplinary consequences because it is a way to avoid punishment, this complicates matters and may actually be no different than a punitive disciplinary response (Ortega et al. 2016). For example, an increasingly popular technique is to use restorative circles that facilitate dialogue to process conflict, with the goal of identifying the root causes of the issues. However, restorative circles work best when they are enacted independent of the discipline system, not as part of it (Evans and Lester 2013; Ortega et al. 2016).

Implications for Teachers and Administrators

The adults in a school play a large role in shaping the school's culture, and the reality is that some teachers and administrators fear a gang presence, or simply do not know how to intervene. A high gang presence in a school can infiltrate various aspects of the educational process, and it is reasonable for adults to have concerns for the safety of students and other school staff. One of the initial steps for teachers and administrators is therefore to ensure schools feel safe. Indeed, students' perception of feeling safe at school has a direct association with gang participation, whereby students who feel safe at school have lower odds of gang participation (Yiu and Gottfredson 2014). One way to ensure a safe environment is to establish a school climate that views intimidation or harm to others as deviations from expected norms (Yiu and Gottfredson 2014). In essence, adults need to establish an environment where it is expected that students and school staff treat each other with kindness and respect.

Establishing a safe school environment also requires that teachers and administrators feel comfortable addressing concerns. For example, there is evidence that when schools have a high gang presence, teachers and administrators are less likely to intervene when they see bullying, which perpetuates these problems (Forber-Pratt, Aragon, and Espelage 2014) and gives the message that school is not a safe place. It is thus imperative that adults in schools be actively engaged in the school culture, and work as a collective to ensure everyone responds to concerns when they arise.

One way to support teachers' and administrators' abilities to intervene is for them know their students on a personal level. Meaningful relationships can make a significant difference for young people, and in many cases these relationships can not only address gang involvement, but also foster a young person's greater connection to school. For example, students are less likely to attend school when they feel school is a place where they will be rejected or excluded. School administrators and teachers can consciously alter how they interact with students, to show that they care about the students as individuals and do not see them as bad people or criminals. The importance of this is undeniable given the clear evidence that students are more likely to stay in school when there are positive social relationships with adults (Lee and Burkam 2003). When young people build positive interactions and relationships with schools, it changes their self-perceptions, and they are more likely to believe that they can overcome obstacles and be successful because there is someone in the institution that cares for them (Rios 2010).

A crucial component of making students feel connected and welcome in school is listening to students as they share their personal pains and triumphs (Bryant et al. 2013). Providing a safe space for students to process these experiences helps to validate the feelings they may be having and equips students with the ability to talk about their past and to plan for their future. Listening to students also requires that administrators take into consideration student feedback and suggestions. When school administrators respond to students' concerns, this validates the students' perspectives and has the potential to improve relationships between students and staff (Bryant et al. 2013).

Teachers can also make a difference if they get to know their students, and are willing to engage with them as people with valuable knowledge (Gass and Laughter 2015). For example, teachers might create a space where students can feel like experts and experience triumphs. Other strategies might involve providing opportunities for success and helping young people connect these successes to future aspirations. When students feel engaged in learning and feel supported in being able to achieve, they are more invested in their own learning and their future planning. Adults in the school should promote positive future aspirations, including attending college, and they should do this for young people in gangs (Sharkey, Stifel, and Mayworm 2015). It is imperative that *all* youth be encouraged to see how education can contribute to later life goals.

Building positive relationships also requires an examination of the context, moving away from the sole focus on *who* to also focus on how systematic elements impact individual students. For example, to address racial biases and the disproportionate impact of harsh discipline policies, schools and school districts must engage in dialogue around the issues of privilege within the context of our nation's history (Cope, Korsmo, and Wilkens 2013). Teachers and administrators could benefit from professional and personal development activities that raise awareness of implicit bias and institutional racism, with the goal of fostering critical reflection about one's own ethnic identity and deficit theories of minority students (Triplett, Allen, and Lewis 2014). Such self-reflection processes can highlight how societal stereotypes infiltrate everyone's implicit assumptions, and it is imperative that we recognize these biases so that they do not manifest in how we treat students.

Finally, positive interactions between adults and students should extend beyond normal school hours. It is imperative that young people have safe places to hang out in their neighborhoods, and there is growing evidence that having a safe place can contribute to gang desistance (Sharkey, Stifel, and Mayworm 2015). Providing young people with after-school activities that provide more opportunities for positive interactions with caring adults and also include academic support and development (Arciaga, Sakamoto, and Jones 2010) can increase students' feelings of connection and provide them opportunities to experience successes. Another option is for schools to implement after-school activities that provide youth with opportunities to become involved with positive groups. Effective after-school programs provide youth with structured and skills-based programming during critical times when many may be unsupervised (Arciaga, Sakamoto, and Jones 2010). These spaces can also provide important opportunities to increase interactions with positive role models.

Conclusions

Schools have a lot of power, both positive and negative, to impact their students. They have the power to educate them and to socialize them to be engaged citizens, but on the other hand, they also have the power to mark students with a discipline record, force students out of school, and catapult them into the correctional system (Rios and Galicia 2013). For many gang-involved, or gang-adjacent youth, schools are not a welcoming space, and many schools miss opportunities to support gang-involved youth by relying solely on discipline as a way to curb gang behaviors in schools. This is especially true for students from traditionally disenfranchised groups.

To truly move toward comprehensive strategies that can support gang-involved youth, it will be important to examine how the intersection of multiple identities influences how schools interact with gang-involved youth. For instance, the US Department of Education (2014) reports that students with disabilities are more than twice as likely to be punished with out-of-school suspension than students without disabilities. People with disabilities are also overrepresented among those arrested and incarcerated (Vallas 2016). Disability interacts with other identities including race, class, and gender, the latter of which have been frequently addressed within the gang literature. However, despite these intersections, and the overrepresentation of students with disability who are part of disciplinary procedures and in our correctional facilities, there is little to no research examining gang-involved youth who may also have a disability. It will be important to increase attention and research in this area to ensure all students are supported in our schools.

There is also a need for more research that looks at the intersection between gang violence in schools and experiences of trauma. There is a paucity of empirical research that examines gang activity in schools, especially research that considers the role trauma exposure may play in a young person's decision to engage in gang activity. Young people involved in gangs experience a disproportionate amount of trauma as compared to youth who are not involved in gangs (De La Rue and Espelage 2014), highlighting the importance of considering contextual factors that may be playing a role in a young person's behavior. Any efforts to curb gang involvement require an exploration of how to support students' emotional well-being, which includes examining how treatment and counseling services may serve as a strategy to reduce gang activity.

Furthermore, it is imperative that school officials who have previously criminalized youth make efforts to establish positive relationships with them (Rios 2010). Schools must bear the responsibility of welcoming all students into their educational spaces, and simultaneously remove the burden from youth having to prove they belong in school.

To be sure, there are times when schools are not equipped to provide everything a student needs to remain in school, and attention must be paid to the collective group. As a result, some young people will need to move to other schools that might better support their needs, or in extreme cases be removed from the educational system altogether. However, it is imperative that schools increase their efforts to support *all* students, and to make strides to ensure as many young people as possible can remain in the educational system. Given the transient nature of gang membership, this is especially important for youth who are gang involved, or who are affiliated with peers who are gang involved.

While traditional notions of risk factors are not without their problems, schools can build on these efforts in a thoughtful way in an effort to support their students. While many schools may be inclined to react with harsh discipline practices or zero tolerance policies, these are unlikely to be the most effective approaches. There is increased evidence that having a relational approach to discipline can decrease student defiance, but this requires the initial process of schools working to build trusting relationships between teachers, administrators, and students (Sharkey, Stifel, and Mayworm 2015). Finally, it is imperative that schools look at ways to address students' behaviors that do not focus solely on disciplinary responses. Schools would benefit from an increased focus on treatment/counseling before punishment, as these efforts would be better suited to addressing the underlying contextual factors influencing gang involvement. Overall, our educational institutions need to be more proactive in welcoming *all* students into these spaces, and resist the tendency to push students out of schools.

References

Advancement Project. 2010. *Test, Punish, and Push Out: How "Zero Tolerance" and High-stakes Testing Funnel Youth into the School-to-Prison Pipeline.* https://b.3cdn.net/advancement/d05cb2181a4545db07_r2im6caqe.pdf (last accessed October 16, 2017).

American Psychological Association Zero Tolerance Task Force. 2008. "Are Zero Tolerance Policies Effective in the Schools?: An Evidentiary Review and Recommendations." *The American Psychologist* 63, 852. DOI: 10.1037/0003-066X.63.9.852.

Arciaga, Michelle, Sakamoto, Wayne, and Jones, Errika Fearbry. 2010. "Responding to Gangs in the School Setting." US Department of Justice, Bureau of Justice Assistance and Office of Juvenile Justice and Delinquency Prevention. *National Gang Center Bulletin*, November. https://www.nationalgangcenter.gov/Content/Documents/Bulletin-5.pdf (last accessed October 16, 2017).

Boyd, Tona M. 2009. "Confronting Racial Disparity: Legislative Responses to the School-to-Prison Pipeline." *Harvard Civil Rights – Civil Liberties Law Review* 44, 571–580.

Bryant, Virletta C., Shdaimah, Corey, Sander, Rebecca L., and Cornelius, Llewellyn J. 2013. "School as Haven: Transforming School Environments into Welcoming Learning Communities." *Children and Youth Services Review* 35, 848–855. DOI: 10.1016/j.childyouth.2013.02.001.

Burnett, Gary and Walz, Garry. 1994. "Gangs in the Schools." *ERIC Digest* 99, 1–4. http://files.eric.ed.gov/fulltext/ED372175.pdf (last accessed October 16, 2017).

Buss, Kristen E., Warren, Jeffrey M., and Horton, Evette. 2015. "Trauma and Treatment in Early Childhood: A Review of the Historical and Emerging Literature for Counselors." *The Professional Counselor* 5, 225. DOI: 10.15241/keb.5.2.225.

Century Foundation. 2016. "Is School Policing Racially Discriminatory?" https://tcf.org/content/commentary/school-policing-racially-discriminatory/ (last accessed October 16, 2017).

Charles Hamilton Houston Institute for Race and Justice. 2008. *No More Children Left Behind Bars: A Briefing on Youth Gang Violence and Juvenile Crime Prevention.* Cambridge, MA: Harvard Law School. http://www.ywcamadison.org/atf/cf/%7B2487BD0F-90C7-49BC-858D-CC50637ECE23%7D/SchooltoPrison_No_More_Children_Left_Behind.pdf (last accessed October 16, 2017).

Children's Defense Fund. 2007. *America's Cradle to Prison Pipeline.* http://www.childrensdefense.org/library/data/cradle-prison-pipeline-report-2007-full-lowres.pdf (last accessed October 16, 2017).

Cope, Heather, Korsmo, Chris, and Wilkens, Maggie. 2013. "Paving a Path to Best Practices in Washington State: How Changing School Discipline Policies Can Curb Disproportionality and close the Achievement Gap." *Journal of Educational Controversy* 7, 13.

Curry, G. David, Decker, Scott H., and Egley Jr., Arlen. 2002. "Gang Involvement and Delinquency in a Middle School Population." *Justice Quarterly* 19, 275–292. DOI: 10.1080/07418820200095241.

De La Rue, Lisa and Espelage, Dorothy L. 2014. "Family and Abuse Characteristics of Gang-involved, Pressured-to-join, and Non–gang-involved Girls." *Psychology of Violence* 4, 253–265. DOI: 10.1037/a0035492.

Esbensen, Finn-Aage. 2000. "Preventing Adolescent Gang Involvement." *Juvenile Justice Bulletin*, September. https://cops.usdoj.gov/html/cd_rom/solution_gang_crime/pubs/preventingadolescentganginvolvement.pdf (last accessed October 16, 2017).

Esbensen, Finn-Aage and Carson. Dena C. 2012. "Who Are the Gangsters? An Examination of the Age, Race/Ethnicity, Sex, and Immigration Status of Self-Reported Gang Members in a Seven-City Study of American Youth." *Journal of Contemporary Criminal Justice* 28, 465–481. DOI: 1043986212458192.

Estrada Jr, Joey Nuñez, Gilreath, Tamika D., Astor, Ron Avi, and Benbenishty, Rami. 2014. "Gang Membership, School Violence, and the Mediating Effects of Risk and Protective Behaviors in California High Schools." *Journal of School Violence* 13, 228–251. DOI: 10.1080/15388220.2013.846860.

Evans, Katherine R. and Lester, Jessica N. 2013. "Restorative Justice in Education: What We Know So Far." *Middle School Journal* 44, 57–63. DOI:10.1080/00940771.2013.11461873.

Forber-Pratt, Anjali J., Aragon, Steven R., and Espelage, Dorothy L. 2014. "The Influence of Gang Presence on victimization in One Middle School Environment." *Psychology of Violence* 4, 8–20. DOI: 10.1037/a0031835.

Gass, Kayla M. and Laughter, Judson C. 2015. "'Can I Make Any Difference?' Gang Affiliation, the School-to-Prison Pipeline, and Implications for Teachers." *The Journal of Negro Education* 84, 333–347. DOI: 10.7709/jnegroeducation.84.3.0333.

Gebo, Erika and Sullivan, Christopher J. 2014. "A Statewide Comparison of Gang and Non-gang Youth in Public High Schools." *Youth Violence and Juvenile Justice* 12, 191–208. DOI: 10.1177/1541204013495900.

Giroux, Henry A. 2012. *Disposable Youth: Racialized Memories, and the Culture of Cruelty*: New York: Routledge.

Goddard, Tim. 2014. "The indeterminacy of the Risk Factor Prevention Paradigm: A Case Study of Community Partnerships Implementing Youth and Gang Violence Prevention Policy." *Youth Justice* 14, 3–21. DOI: 10.1177/1473225413520275.

Gottfredson, Gary D. and Gottfredson, Denise C. 2001. "Gang Problems and Gang Programs in a National Sample of Schools." Department of Justice. http://files.eric. ed.gov/fulltext/ED459408.pdf (last accessed October 16, 2017).

Hirschfield, Paul J. 2008. "Preparing for Prison? The Criminalization of School Discipline in the USA." *Theoretical Criminology* 12, 79–101. DOI: 10.1177/1362480607085795.

James, Nathan and McCallion, Gail. 2013. *School Resource Officers: Law Enforcement Officers in Schools.* Congressional Research Service. http://sde.idaho.gov/student-engagement/sdfs/files/program-guides/School-Resource-Officers-Law-Enforcement-in-Schools.pdf (last accessed October 16, 2017).

Kupchik, Aaron and Monahan, Torin. 2006. "The New American School: Preparation for Post-industrial Discipline." *British Journal of Sociology of Education* 27, 617–631. DOI: 10.1080/01425690600958816.

Leap, Jorja. 2013. "What Should Be Done in the Community to Prevent Gang-Joining?" In *Changing Course: Preventing Gang Membership*, edited by Thomas R. Simon, Nancy M. Ritter, and Reshma R. Mahendra, p. 105. National Institute of Justice. http://www. iacpyouth.org/Portals/0/Resources/Changing_Course_Full_Report.pdf#page=106 (last accessed October 16, 2017).

Lee, Valerie E. and Burkam, David T. 2003. "Dropping out of High School: The Role of School Organization and Structure." *American Educational Research Journal* 40, 353–393. DOI: 10.3102/00028312040002353.

Maddox, Lauren A. 2015. "His Wrists Were Too Small: School Resource Officers and the Over-criminalization of America's Students." *University of Miami Race & Social Justice Law Review* 6, 193–215.

Mallett, Christopher A. 2016. "The School-to-Prison Pipeline: A Critical Review of the Punitive Paradigm Shift." *Child and Adolescent Social Work Journal* 33, 15–24. DOI: 10.1007/s10560-015-0397-1.

Maschi, Tina and Bradley, Carolyn. 2008. "Exploring the Moderating Influence of Delinquent Peers on the Link Between Trauma, Anger, and Violence among Male Youth: Implications for Social Work Practice." *Child and Adolescent Social Work Journal* 25, 125–138.

Mills, Jerrad M. 2016. "From the Principal's Office to Prison: How America's School Discipline System Defies Brown." *University of San Francisco Law Review* 50, 529.

Na, Chongmin and Gottfredson, Denise C. 2013. "Police Officers in Schools: Effects on School Crime and the Processing of Offending Behaviors." *Justice Quarterly* 30, 619–650. DOI: 10.1080/07418825.2011.615754.

Nash, N. and Bhattacharya, Kakali. 2009. "Urban Middle School Principals' Perceptions of a School Uniform Policy." *Research and Practice in Social Sciences* 4, 46–64.

Ortega, Lilyana, Lyubansky, Mikhail, Nettles, Saundra, and Espelage, Dorothy L. 2016. "Outcomes of a Restorative Circles Program in a High School Setting." *Psychology of Violence* 6, 459–468. DOI: 10.1037/vio0000048.

Osher, David, Bear, George G., Sprague, Jeffrey R., and Doyle, Walter. 2010. "How Can We Improve School Discipline?" *Educational Researcher* 39, 48–58. DOI: 10.3102/ 0013189X09357618.

Osher, David, Quinn, Mary Magee, Poirer, Jeffery M., and Rutherford, Robert B. 2003. "Deconstructing the Pipeline: Using Efficacy and Effectiveness Data and Cost–Benefit Analyses to Reduce Minority Youth Incarceration." *New Directions in Youth Development* 99, 91–120.

Paton, Joni, Crouch, William, and Camic, Paul. 2009. "Young Offenders' Experiences of Traumatic Life Events: A Qualitative Investigation." *Clinical Child Psychology and Psychiatry* 14, 43–62.

Petteruti, Amanda. 2011. *Education under Arrest: The Case Against Police in Schools.* Washington, DC: Justice Policy Institute.

Rios, Victor M. 2010. "Navigating the Thin Line between Education and Incarceration: An Action Research Case Study on Gang-Associated Latino Youth." *Journal of Education for Students Placed at Risk* 15, 200–212. DOI: 10.1080/10824661003635283.

Rios, Victor M. and Galicia, Mario G. 2013. "Smoking Guns or Smoke & Mirrors?: Schools and the Policing of Latino Boys." *Association of Mexican American Educators Journal* 7, 54–66.

Robers, Simone, Zhang, Anlan, and Morgan, Rachel E. 2015. *Indicators of School Crime and Safety: 2014.* NCES 2015-072/NCJ 248036. National Center for Education Statistics. http://files.eric.ed.gov/fulltext/ED557756.pdf (last accessed October 16, 2017).

Sharkey, Jill D., Stifel, Skye, and Mayworm, Ashley M. 2015. "How to Help Me Get Out of a Gang: Youth Recommendations to Family, School, Community, and Law Enforcement Systems." *Journal of Juvenile Justice* 4, 64–83.

Theriot, Matthew T. 2009. "School Resource Officers and the Criminalization of Student Behavior." *Journal of Criminal Justice* 37, 280–287. DOI: 10.1016/j.jcrimjus.2009.04.008.

Triplett, Nicholas P., Allen, Ayana, and Lewis, Chance W. 2014. "Zero Tolerance, School Shootings, and the Post-Brown Quest for Equity in Discipline Policy: An Examination of How Urban Minorities Are Punished for White Suburban Violence." *The Journal of Negro Education* 83, 352–370. DOI: 10.7709/jnegroeducation.83.3.0352.

US Department of Education Office for Civil Rights. 2014. "Civil Rights Data Collection Data Snapshots. School Discipline." Issue Brief No. 1, March. http://ocrdata.ed.gov/Downloads/CRDC-School-Discipline-Snapshot.pdf (last accessed October 16, 2017).

Vallas, Rebecca. 2016. *Disabled Behind Bars: The Mass Incarceration of People with Disabilities in American's Jails and Prisons.* Center for American Progress. https://cdn.americanprogress.org/wp-content/uploads/2016/07/18000151/2CriminalJusticeDisability-report.pdf (last accessed October 16, 2017).

Wacquant, Loic. 2001. "Deadly Symbiosis When Ghetto and Prison Meet and Mesh." *Punishment & Society* 3, 95–133.

Walker, Samuel, Spohn, Cassia, and DeLone, Miriam. 2012. *The Color of Justice: Race, Ethnicity, and Crime in America.* Cengage Learning.

Weiler, Spencer C. and Cray, Martha. 2011. "Police at School: A Brief History and Current Status of School Resource Officers." *The Clearing House: A Journal of Educational Strategies, Issues and Ideas* 84, 160–163. DOI: 10.1080/00098655.2011.564986.

Yiu, Ho Lam Eva and Gottfredson, Gary D. 2014. "Gang Participation." *Crime & Delinquency* 60, 619–642. DOI: 10.1177/0011128713510078.

15

Short School-based Interventions to Reduce Violence

A Review

Nadine M. Connell, Richard Riner, Richard Hernandez, Jordan Riddell, and Justine Medrano

Introduction

In recent years there has been growing interest in examining the efficacy of short school-based intervention programs. These are programs designed to motivate students to improve their behavior and tend to be short in duration and cost effective for schools. In general, brief interventions target high-risk behaviors such as substance abuse, violence, academic disengagement, and gang involvement, primarily through focusing on good decision-making and coping skills. However, there is limited research on the scope of the implementation of such programs and their actual effectiveness (Dembo et al. 2011). To date, many such programs have been implemented without evaluation or without a comprehensive prevention goal; additionally, existing evaluations appear to provide conflicting results and are mired with methodological issues. Nevertheless, school-based brief interventions are worth investigating due to the potential of these cost-effective curricular additions that can target high-risk behaviors among students.

Given the importance of the role of school in the socialization of students (Gottfredson and Gottfredson 2002), and the additional benefit of being able to provide services to a large number of students with relative ease, school-based brief interventions are worth examining as an efficient tool for educators. Here we present the history of the use of brief and short intervention programs and summarize the literature on shorter school-based interventions, with a special emphasis on violence prevention. We include select short interventions (8–17 weeks) that would not fall into the category of "brief" interventions per se, but were deemed as worth noting due to the fact that they are commonly implemented and readily available for schools. Additionally, they are short enough to allow administrators to fit programmatic elements into already stressed curricular restraints. Finally, we offer suggestions for choosing appropriate programs. While the literature does offer conflicting evidence as to the most effective brief intervention programs, we will present a guideline for practitioners to select the most empirically sound intervention practices available. Furthermore, we offer a cost–benefit analysis to highlight the fiscal and social potential of short interventions. We argue that when used appropriately as a general and primary form of prevention, such

The Wiley Handbook on Violence in Education: Forms, Factors, and Preventions, First Edition.
Edited by Harvey Shapiro.
© 2018 John Wiley & Sons, Inc. Published 2018 by John Wiley & Sons, Inc.

programs can offer benefits to schools with little cost, allowing more resources to be diverted to those students who need more targeted interventions in order to succeed (Small et al. 2005). Finally, we will also address methodological and programmatic directions for the future.

In order to address definitional issues, we also narrow our scope to those types of programs that can truly be identified as short. Consensus generally considers brief interventions those which last only a few hours and are usually utilized in emergency medical situations, such as acute substance use situations. Schools, by their very nature, have more flexibility when implementing short programs, so in order to highlight this, we include those programs that consist of 15 or fewer sessions over the course of a period no longer than a semester. This allows for a broad range of interventions while also recognizing that these are not the type of programs designed to be part of a systemic prevention model but rather to be incorporated into existing school curricula to bolster existing efforts.

History of Brief and Select Short Interventions

The effectiveness of brief and short interventions outside of the school setting may provide researchers and practitioners with clues about how to effectively develop and implement successful short interventions within institutions. The existing literature on brief interventions outside of the school setting for a host of problem behaviors does not present definitive solutions, but it does offer insight into how and why such programs could be beneficial. Especially useful are recent systematic reviews and meta-analyses that offer comprehensive overviews of effective elements in these intervention programs.

Brief intervention programs, especially those that are very short in nature (i.e., one to two hours) originated in medical settings but have since expanded their reach into community- and school-based programs. In their review on the efficacy of interventions to reduce alcohol consumption, Platt et al. (2016) examined the outcomes for interventions based in medical settings, including emergency services, hospital inpatient services, and clinical settings, as well as in community-based and university settings. They found that participants who received these interventions, regardless of setting, reported a small, if consistent and significant, decline in the quantity of alcohol consumed. In general, the majority of program components such as setting and content did not substantially affect outcomes, although programs delivered by nurses were deemed most effective. In a different study, assault-injured youth recruited from emergency departments and paired with a supportive mentor for six community-based problem-solving sessions reported increased self-efficacy and lower self-reported levels of aggression (Cheng et al. 2008). This speaks to the potential utility of short interventions in a wide variety of settings to motivate behavioral change.

Emergency departments and trauma centers have long been popular locations for the implementation of brief interventions, especially concerning violence prevention. In their integrative review of the literature, Mikhail and Nemeth (2016) examined the role of both case management models and brief intervention programs to reduce negative outcomes. Brief intervention often consisted of short-term access to case managers or short-term motivational interviews, allowing for care after an emergency situation may have brought an individual into a program. Both of these types of interventions showed evidence of promise for violence reduction; brief interventions strategies in particular were associated with lower levels of self-reported aggression and alcohol use.

A review of brief interventions to reduce alcohol use among adolescents (aged 11 to 18) and young adults (aged 19 to 30) yielded two interesting findings. Tanner-Smith and Lipsey (2015) found that programs with five or fewer hours of contact time with adolescents and young adults were still successful in reducing participants' alcohol consumption and alcohol-related problems. These effects lasted up to one year after implementation and did not vary by demographic characteristics, although some treatment modalities showed more promise than others. For instance, motivational interviewing and goal-setting exercises were associated with larger effects (Tanner-Smith and Lipsey 2015). In a similar review, also focused on brief alcohol interventions, Hennessy and Tanner-Smith (2015) found that treatment modality mattered, with individually delivered interventions showing more promise in reducing alcohol use than group-based delivery of treatment. While definitive conclusions still remain elusive, evidence is mounting that short school-based approaches have merit, at least with regard to alcohol reduction.

In one such example of the potential utility of a brief motivational interviewing approach, the SafERteens program implemented a harm reduction model targeted at young teens, aged 14 to 18, who visited local emergency room departments and had been screened as being at risk for violence and alcohol use (Walton et al. 2010). The program targeted alcohol use and violent behavior using techniques to increase the participants' problem recognition capability, motivation, and self-efficacy. Youth were randomly assigned to one of two conditions: a therapist-led intervention or participation in an interactive computer program. The interactive computer program focused on an animated character guide leading participants through various role-play scenarios that covered the intervention material (Walton et al. 2010). A three-month follow-up found that participants who had engaged in therapist-led interventions experienced a reduction in peer violence, while a six-month follow-up suggested that both youth who engaged with therapist-led sessions and those that received the computerized intervention experienced a reduction in negative consequences from alcohol (Walton et al. 2010).

Other programs have examined the results of broadening the setting from emergency or hospital settings to more community-based interventions. After recruiting participants in an emergency department setting, Cheng et al. (2008) found that there was a reduction in injuries for youth that participated in a subsequent violence prevention program at their home or in their community. Youth (aged 10 to 15) and mentors met for six sessions to discuss conflict management, problem solving, weapon safety, decision making, and goal-setting techniques. These different topics were taught with interactive activities and role-playing scenarios that helped youth learn how to remain non-violent during conflicts with others. Follow-up at six and 12 months suggested that the intervention reduced self-reported aggression and other problem behavior in participants; however, there was no significant impact on the arrest rate for participating youths (Cheng et al. 2008).

While the majority of our knowledge of the efficacy of brief interventions for youth comes from settings outside the school, a concentrated effort has been made to implement programs with similar techniques inside of schools. Shorter interventions in schools did not become prevalent in the United States until the early 1990s. In 1990, one psychologist noted the lack of in-depth research on school-based programs even though the Department of Education and the National Mental Health Association's Commission on the Prevention of Mental-Emotional Disabilities had both emphasized the need for prevention programs (Weissberg 1990). Some of the most familiar ones were designed in the wake of these calls for action. For instance, the Drug Abuse Resistance Education (DARE) program was developed in 1983 (Zagumny and Thompson 1997), the Gang Resistance Education and Training (GREAT) program in 1991, and Hansen's All Stars programs originated in 1993, with GREAT beginning its expansion to the national level in 1992. These programs paved the way for integrating intervention programs into school curricula, and while we would not consider them brief by typical standards, they are relatively short in contact hours, often lasting between 10 and 15 hours spread out over several weeks or months. These types of programs have proliferated, and other short and brief programs have also been developed as additional tools. We discuss these in the following section.

School-based Brief Interventions to Reduce Violence

Brief intervention programs have the potential to prevent future deviant and delinquent behavior, or at the very least reduce their occurrence and frequency in school settings. The school venue is ideal to implement a large-scale intervention that can reach several students at once, especially if such programs are designed to take into consideration the limitations inherent in working in an educational setting, specifically with regard to time. In an era where schools are constantly juggling time constraints, brief interventions can offer meaningful services without taking time away from pedagogical goals. To date, the majority of brief interventions that have been implemented have focused on adults, with efforts only recently focusing on youth (see above for a description of trauma-related brief interventions). In an effort to ensure parsimony and keep the focus on those interventions that could best benefit a juvenile population, we narrow our scope to those programs with a history of implementation in educational settings.

A 1996 study of brief nurse consultations with sixth through eighth grade students in a Florida middle school examined the effectiveness of the Start Taking Alcohol Risks Seriously (STARS) program. The STARS program follows the Multi-Component Motivational Stages (McMOS) prevention model and is based on social learning theory, behavioral self-control theory, and the health belief model. The main goal of the STARS program was to teach students how to avoid the acquisition and use of alcohol. Participants of the STARS program received a brief health consultation followed by six weeks of consultations (Werch et al. 1996). The STARS program focused on informing students of the risk factors that are associated with alcohol use by having nurses educate students on effective methods that would help them make healthier choices. Nurses had students discuss the healthy behaviors they engaged in to help them understand actions they can take to avoid alcohol. The six sessions covered environment and situation, behavioral capability and self-efficacy, risk factors expectations, perceived susceptibility and self-efficacy, emotional coping methods, and self-monitoring and evaluation. All of these topics were explored under the McMOS prevention model and the consultations had clearly defined objectives and exercises designed to build resistance skills. Students who participated in the STARS program were less likely to engage in heavy drinking than the students in the control group; however, there were no significant differences between the groups on other measures of alcohol use such as negative consequences due to drinking (Werch et al. 1996).

In another investigation into school-based short intervention programs, Zagumny and Thompson (1997) examined the effectiveness of the DARE program in a rural Tennessee high school. Police officers were responsible for teaching the DARE curriculum one hour a week, for a period of up to 17 weeks, instructing students on ways to resist using drugs or alcohol. Results showed that the DARE program did not significantly delay a participant's initial drug or alcohol use; this was not the first study to come to this conclusion (see Kochis 1995). Since their analysis found the DARE program to be ineffective, Zagumny and Thompson (1997) suggested more thorough evaluations of the types of problems occurring in specific locations and assessments of the interventions designed to prevent those problems from occurring. Today, DARE offers curricula for elementary, middle, and high school students. The program emphasizes the REAL (Refuse, Explain, Avoid, Leave) strategy for drug resistance (www.dare.com). The elementary and middle school programs consist of 10 one-hour lessons that focus on teaching responsibility and decision-making skills for situations involving peer pressure to use drugs. The high school level features four modules, with each module containing five lessons. Two modules teach the basic prevention techniques, and there are specialized modules for student athletes and for safe celebrations. Police officers are the instructors and they utilize a web-assisted approach to teach two lessons and have students complete the remaining three lessons online (www.dare.com.).

Around the same time, a team of researchers led by Esbensen (Esbensen et al. 2001) began a large-scale evaluation of GREAT, a program that is designed to prevent future gang involvement. The GREAT curriculum is delivered by police officers to middle school students in eight lessons, once a week, for a nine-week period (Howell 2013). Esbensen et al. (2001) found that GREAT had a positive impact for participants over a four-year period, although initial results suggested that it took some time for positive outcomes to become evident. Even over a four-year period, there was little evidence to suggest that GREAT prevented students from joining gangs (Esbensen et al. 2001), although other positive outcomes did emerge. Esbensen et al. (2012) evaluated the revised version of the GREAT program and found a 39% reduction in the odds of a youth joining a gang after a one-year follow-up and lower levels of support for neutralizations of violent behavior. The revised program was administered to sixth and seventh grade students across the country in Albuquerque, Chicago, Dallas-Fort Worth, Greeley, Nashville, Philadelphia, and Portland. The curriculum maintained the same three goals as before: help youth avoid gang membership, reduce violence and criminal behavior, and develop positive relations between police and students (Esbensen et al. 2012). GREAT was expanded to 13 lessons for middle school students that focus on developing skills, problem-solving strategies, and cooperative learning (Esbensen et al. 2013). These lessons cover beliefs about gangs, the relationship between gangs and violence, responsibility and roles in society, goal setting, decision making, communication skills, refusal skills, anger management, and conflict management. The elementary school program is designed for fourth and fifth graders and covers decision making, violence prevention, communication skills, anger management, and respect for others (www.great-online.org).

Another violence prevention program, Hansen's All Star program, was developed to reduce drug use, sexual behavior, and violence in youths (Hansen 1996). The overall theme of the program has been to help students identify their desired lifestyle and then influence them to perceive drug use, sex, and violence as interfering with the lifestyle. Instructors had middle school students make personal commitments to avoid the three behaviors and the one-year follow-up found the program to have short lasting positive effects (Harrington et al. 2001). There is little evidence to suggest that the All Stars program can help prevent violence. Gottfredson et al. (2010) compared the effects of the All Stars program for violence prevention to traditional after-school programs for middle school students and found that the All Stars program was not more effective at reducing violence nor improving prosocial attitudes. At the time of the evaluation, the curriculum sought to build awareness of lifestyle incongruence, clarify beliefs about the prevalence of risky behaviors by peers, have students publicly commit to abstain from drug use, and promote bonds with schools and parental communication (Gottfredson et al. 2010). Currently, the All Stars Core (central program) curriculum is designed for sixth and seventh grade students and can be delivered in 13 45-minute sessions with the option for eight supplemental sessions. The program seeks to prevent bullying and fighting by building belief in the future, establishing positive norms and personal commitments to avoiding risky behaviors, promoting school bonds, and by parental interaction (www.allstarsprevention.com).

Alcohol and drug use prevention has been a popular topic for curricula brief intervention programs. Myers and Kelly (2006) analyzed one such brief intervention, Project Ex, a program aimed at smoking cessation and implemented in a continuation high school. Continuation high schools serve high-risk students that are behind on the completion of their high school credits. The high school students that participated in Project Ex underwent eight different sessions over a six-week period. These sessions focused on the reason for students' tobacco use, the negative effects of tobacco use, methods for breaking tobacco addiction, and maintaining a lifestyle without the use of tobacco. Results showed that a higher percentage of those who had participated in the intervention were more likely to report having quit smoking than those who did not participate. The success of Project Ex suggests that programs should consider targeting other types of drug use.

Brief intervention programs have also been utilized outside of the United States. In Australia, an applied theater prevention program, named "Choices," was implemented in a high school. For 50 minutes, volunteer students attempted to demonstrate the dangers that present themselves at "Schoolies" to graduating students. "Schoolies" are a string of end-of-year parties where students typically engage in binge drinking, drug use, and a host of problem behaviors associated with increased health risks (Quek et al. 2012). After the theater demonstration, graduating students were given 20 minutes to engage in a discussion with the students who performed Choices in order to clarify any questions. The theoretical perspective behind Choices suggested that the presentations would decrease the likelihood of students participating in problem behaviors or illegal drug use; however, results did not suggest that there was a significant reduction in binge drinking (Quek et al. 2012).

In Table 15.1, we offer a brief glimpse of the most common – and as a result, most evaluated – kinds of school-based brief interventions that have been implemented in recent years. These programs, many described above, are included due to the specific

Table 15.1 Results of school-based intervention programs.

First author	Year	Journal	N	Study design	Ages	Setting	Type of intervention	Length of intervention	Follow-up	Behavior	Results
Werch	1996	*Journal of School Health*	138	Longitudinal quasi-experimental with control group	Mean of 12.2	School	STARS program	Initial consult: 6 weekly consults	3 months	Alcohol use	Reduction in heavy alcohol use, but not overall use of alcohol
Esbensen	2001	*Criminology and Public Policy*	3568	Longitudinal quasi-experimental with control group	7th graders	School	GREAT	Once a week for 9 weeks	4 years	Gang involvement	Consistent positive yet modest results
Zagumny	1997	*Journal of Alcohol and Drug Education*	253	Longitudinal quasi-experimental with control group	7th graders	School	DARE	1 hour a week for 6 weeks	3, 4 years	Drug and alcohol use	No significant differences between control and treatment groups
Marsden	2006	*Society for the Study of Addiction*	342	Randomized control trial	16–22	Greater London and SE	Motivational presentation	45–60 minutes	Avg. 28.9 weeks	MDMA cocaine use	Negligible effects
Myers	2006	*Alcohol Research and Health*	28	Randomized control trial	14–18	Clinic	Motivational presentation	Not specified	3, 6 months	Smoking	Significant reduction in smoking among those who received treatment
Quek	2012	*Drug and Alcohol Review*	352	Cross-sectional single group	Mean of 17.14	School	Choices	50 minutes	Less than 30 days	Alcohol and/or drug use	Significant decrease in drug use, but not alcohol consumption
Rudzinski	2012	*Contemporary Drug Problems*	77	Qualitative	18-28	University campuses	Oral and written	30 minutes	3 months	Cannabis	69.4% believed they had undergone positive changes
Esbensen	2013	*Criminology and Public Policy*	3820	Experimental longitudinal Panel design	6th & 7th graders	School	GREAT program	Once a week for 13 weeks	4 years	Gang involvement	Reduced the odds of gang joining among racially/ethnically diverse groups by 24%

intent to evaluate their efficacy as well as the fact that researchers described the components of the interventions in sufficient detail for replication and/or implementation at the school level. Additionally, those that have been evaluated using the most advanced methods, as described below, are denoted. This list, while not exhaustive due to the fact that many programs that may be in use have not made their way into the evaluation literature, can at least offer guidance when determining how best to meet an individual school's needs. Additionally, below we discuss the criteria by which an interested reader can determine if the claims made about program efficacy are worthy.

Criteria to Determine Best Practices

When making the choice to implement a school-based brief intervention, it is important to realize that not all programs are equal in their effectiveness and not all programs have been evaluated using equally stringent standards; thus caution may be warranted when deciding which components are most worthwhile for a specific situation. Therefore, it is imperative that schools put in place criteria for how to choose programs before the selection process begins.

There are multiple possibilities when selecting criteria for evaluating the results of a program evaluation based on the methodology employed by the researchers (Farrington 2003). Gibbs (1989) devised a scale for evaluating studies comprised of 14 factors, each with a specific point value that, when added up, would produce a score from 0 to 100. In the United Kingdom, the Centre for Reviews and Dissemination (Khan et al. 2001) provided a guide for evaluations in the form of a hierarchy of study design. Results produced by randomized controlled double- blind trials are to be given the most credence, and expert opinion the least. David Farrington (2003) suggested an evaluation criterion based on eliminating threats to the various types of validity (internal, descriptive, statistical conclusion, construct, and external). One of the most widespread and influential guides for evaluating studies that test programs currently in use within the scientific community is the Maryland Scientific Methodology Scale (SMS).

The SMS was devised to be simple in its application, making it appropriate for policy makers and academics alike to use when evaluating the results of a study that purports to accurately evaluate the effectiveness of a program or intervention. Instead of a score ranging from 0 to 100 like other evaluation scales, the SMS assigns each study to a particular level, ranging from 1 to 5, with level 3 being the minimum level for drawing conclusions regarding the effectiveness of a program or intervention. The levels and the characteristics are listed below (Sherman 1997). We include them in order for school administrators and decision makers to have tools to make informed decisions about those programs which come across their desk with claims of merit but which may not have been evaluated by the independent scientific community. See Table 15.2 for a concise overview.

Level 1: Studies that fall under the level 1 category are those that look for a correlation between a program and a measure of the outcome of interest, in this case behaviors that students might display that adversely influence academic achievement or violence and aggression. In this type of cross-sectional design, there is no temporal order established, so there is no way to distinguish whether

Table 15.2 Maryland Scientific Methodology Scale (SMS).

Level	Design description	Causal order?	Deemed appropriate for policy evaluation?
1	Cross-sectional single group	No	No
2	Longitudinal single group design	Yes	No
3	Longitudinal quasi-experimental with control group	Yes	Yes – minimum
4	Longitudinal quasi-experimental with multiple control and treatment groups	Yes	Yes
5	Longitudinal randomized control trials	Yes	Yes

the program is responsible for any behavioral or attitudinal change. Additionally, many threats to the validity of the results are not accounted for in studies with this type of design.

Level 2: In these types of studies, the researchers examine a measure of the behavior of interest before and after the intervention (i.e., a pre-experimental, or single group pretest–posttest design). This longitudinal design does invoke a temporal order, such that the intervention is implemented before the measurement of the final outcomes. However, such uncontrolled studies fail to account for factors outside of the intervention that might account for any change that is measured, such as concurrent available programming, family-related factors, or other variables that may impact behavior.

Level 3: Studies that fall into the category of level 3 are those that not only measure the behaviors of interest before and after the intervention, but also then compare those results to a group that did not receive the intervention. This longitudinal design with a comparison group is considered to be the minimum for drawing conclusions regarding the effectiveness of an intervention. Study designs at this level account for many factors that might adversely affect the validity of the results reported by a study, such as outside variables like family and/or personality characteristics. Level 3 studies, however, do not address any potential issues with how individuals were selected into treatment and control groups (i.e., those that did receive the intervention and those that did not), which has the potential to impact outcomes and results if not done correctly.

Level 4: Studies at this level measure behaviors of interest before and after the intervention, using multiple experimental groups and multiple control groups, while also controlling for other factors that might influence the results (age of the students, urban versus rural schools, racial makeup of the student body, socioeconomic situation of the student, etc.). This level accounts for more factors that could possibly influence the results of a study, thus policy makers and administrators can place more confidence in the idea that the results of the study regarding the effectiveness of the intervention are accurate.

Level 5: At the highest level are studies that employ random assignment of students to multiple experimental and control groups as well as the measurement of behaviors of interest before and after the intervention. These studies are often denoted by the fact that they are randomized controlled trials (RCTs). While popular in medical research, RCTs are often less likely to be employed by social scientists. Due to the reliance on randomization, studies utilizing this type of design are able to address potential issues with selection of the sample, such as students that come from diverse backgrounds, as well as the many factors that might threaten the validity of the results regarding the effectiveness of an intervention. While administrators and policy makers can be the most confident in the results produced by these types of studies, they are somewhat rare due to the high cost and logistical difficulty associated with conducting studies of this kind.

The SMS is a widely used guide for evaluating how confident school officials should be when reviewing the results of studies that evaluate intervention programs, but it is not without its weaknesses or critics. First, there are researchers that feel that the hierarchy of design does not take into account the research question being asked, and therefore cannot accurately determine appropriateness (Tugwell and Knottnerus 2015). Also, there are other study designs employed by researchers that evaluate programs that are not included in the SMS. Cluster randomized controlled trials and time series studies, for example, are both used to determine the effectiveness of a policy or intervention and yet are not included in the SMS. Single interrupted time series studies and multiple interrupted time series with control groups are considered to be not just appropriate study designs but in some ways superior designs to those listed in the SMS, in that they can account for the deterioration of the effects attributed to the intervention over time.

While we have chosen to utilize the SMS as our guide, we realize no criteria regarding reviewing studies that evaluate intervention programs will be perfect, and that others have created legitimate criteria as well. These include the Canadian Institutes of Health Research Critical Appraisal Criteria (Ciliska n.d.), the Cochrane Risk of Bias Tool (Higgins, Altman, and Sterne n.d.), the National Heart, Lung and Blood Institute Study Quality Assessment Tools (National Heart, Lung and Blood Institute n.d.), Substance Abuse and Mental Health Administration Program Review Criteria (Substance Abuse and Mental Health Administration n.d.), and The National Institute of Justice methodology for reviewing and rating programs, "How We Review and Rate a Program from Start to Finish" (National Institute of Justice n.d.). Some are more complete and quite complex in their application and others are simpler to use, but we felt using the SMS was appropriate in this instance.

Cost–Benefit Analysis

Implementing brief interventions does cost money but it is important to consider the potential returns from these programs. We argue that when used appropriately as a general and primary form of prevention, such programs can offer benefits to schools at little to no cost, allowing more resources to be diverted to those students who may need more targeted interventions in order to succeed (Small et al. 2005). High school graduation has been found to provide substantial returns to individuals and society (Heckman, Humphries, and Veramendi 2016), which in itself is a benefit to schools when considering implementation. Programs that improve behavior such that graduation rates are positively impacted are worthy of investment. It would make sense that other programs that reduce problem behaviors associated with high school dropout could provide long-term benefits. Heckman (2000) suggests that schools should invest in programs that improve and create human capital in students to increase skills and abilities for the future. Indeed, research on the cost–benefit evaluation of programs that focused on enhancing early life skills bears out the promise of the return on investment for early intervention (Garcia et al 2016). For example, the 35-year follow-up of the Carolina Abecedarian Project (ABC) and the Carolina Approach to Responsive Education (CARE) resulted in real returns of $3 for every $1 spent for the participants of the program at the time the participants were in their thirties. In extrapolating from these data, an estimation of the value of dollars spent when participants are in their fifties suggests returns of $6.30 for every $1 spent. This cost–benefit analysis considered the initial cost of the program ($18,514) and the benefits of reduced health care costs, increased parental incomes (because children were held for 9 hours a day, five days a week for almost the whole year), and reductions in arrests, victimizations, and incarceration (Garcia et al. 2016). Such findings, while not directly measuring the benefit of school-based brief interventions, nonetheless show the potential for a high return on investment with regard to initial investment. Additionally, such analysis also points to the importance of a wide range of positive behavioral outcomes and the long-term impact of small changes.

A 2004 report conducted by the Washington State Institute for Public Policy synthesized cost–benefit analyses for many prevention programs (Aos et al. 2004). Results suggested that DARE cost taxpayers approximately $99 per student with no net positive financial benefits to individuals or society, with a similar reduction of $99 spent in services for every student served. Additionally, the STARS program resulted in an $18 per taxpayer cost with no appreciable return on investment. Conversely, the All Stars violence prevention program had a net return on investment of $3.43 for every dollar spent through the program, and the Strengthening Families Program for Parents and Youth had a net benefit of $7.82 for every dollar spent (Aos et al. 2004; see also Molgaard, Spoth, and Redmond 2000). A similar report completed for the Department of Health and Human Services in 2008 showed returns of $11 for every $1 spent on Strengthening Families Programs, a $34 return on investment for every $1 spent on the All Stars program, and a return of $4 for every $1 spent on the STARS program (Miller and Hendrie 2008).

These types of analyses can guide administrators when making decisions about appropriate programs, since the information can be used to best determine where to invest resources. Some programs, like the Strengthening Families Program for Parents and Youth, require greater investment in terms of both time and resources in order to see long-term results, which may not be beneficial if a school needs to implement interventions with more immediate benefits. In those situations, shorter programs with lower start-up costs may be ideal. Additional considerations beyond start-up costs include program continuation. Some programs require a large initial investment but reduce costs over time. Other programs have more consistent costs over time. Budgetary concerns require that school administrators consider both initial and long-term investment and how those needs match up against expected benefits.

Methodological and Programmatic Directions for the Future

Although there are studies that have evaluated some school-based brief intervention programs, researchers have grappled with methodological issues. We highlight three main concerns. First, inconsistent findings can be related to the varying methodologies used in individual studies; this is a problem that faces the evaluation of many intervention programs, as methodological rigor is often directly related to efficacy outcomes (Mulvey, Arthur, and Reppucci 1993). There is also an issue of differing definitions between studies regarding what constitutes a brief intervention, and differentiating key terms such as delinquency, bullying, etc. thus making it difficult to determine those circumstances under which brief intervention programs will be the most effective (Mulvey, Arthur, and Reppucci 1993). Finally, the issue of follow-up time between the initial intervention and evaluation makes it difficult to quantify the effects of such programs, making it unclear whether programs are preventing behaviors or delaying onset.

The first methodological difference that can cause issues has to do with the definition of key terms, such as "brief intervention" or "prevention." As alluded to in the introduction, there has yet to be a disciplinary consensus as to what criteria an intervention must meet to be classified as a brief intervention. As mentioned earlier, we have determined that a program must meet on 10 or fewer occasions to be included in this review. We fully accept the fact that assigning that value is completely arbitrary. However, in order for a consensus to be reached, we must assign a starting point for the number of meetings for the discussion to begin.

The term "prevention" is another term that, depending on how it is defined, has a profound impact on how we interpret the results of a study; this is especially important as researchers grapple with the ability to collect data over a long enough period of time to determine if a behavior was indeed prevented or merely delayed. For example, Walton et al. (2014) concluded that the program *prevented* marijuana use after a follow-up period of only three months. Other studies with follow-up over a longer period of time may define the decrease in the behavior of interest at three months a delayed onset, giving voice to the fact that the effects of an intervention can dissipate over time (Conrod, Castellanos, and Mackie 2008). As such, it is imperative for those implementing such programs to be wary of any program offering a one-size-fits-all approach or claiming effects that seem too good to be true.

The second methodological difference between studies of school-based brief interventions is the age of the target audience. While studies targeting early childhood are focused on a narrow age range (Mann and Reynolds 2006; Zigler, Taussig, and Black 1992), school-based intervention programs may have a much broader target age range. Prior studies have examined the effect of programs on children as young as 12 (Walton et al. 2014) or as old as 28 (Rudzinski et al. 2012). One way in which the wide age range can possibly pose a challenge in the interpretation of results goes back to the issue of defining what behaviors are to be defined as delinquent. How should researchers handle behaviors that are delinquent for 12-year-olds, but not necessarily problematic (from a criminal justice system perspective) for 18-year-olds, like smoking? Indeed, from a delinquency perspective, many of the behaviors that intervention programs seek to impact, such as alcohol and tobacco use, become normative or at least non-criminal, in adulthood. And while an argument can be made for the importance of harm-reduction strategies in order to reduce health-care-related costs for such behaviors, the question remains as to how such behaviors related to violence and aggression should be operationalized by age.

The third methodological issue in comparing results across studies is the variation across evaluation studies with regard to follow-up times. While following study participants longitudinally involves a great deal of time, effort, and often expense, we see that shorter follow-up times can affect the way we interpret results. Often, we see that encouraging initial effects begin to diminish and attenuate over time (Tanner-Smith and Lipsey 2015). For example, in their smoking cessation study, Myers and Kelly (2006) found that after three months, student outcomes were encouraging, but those effects began to diminish at the six-month mark. In another study, Walton and colleagues (2014) found that a program that had prevented marijuana use at a three-month follow-up no longer affected marijuana use at six- and twelve-month follow-ups, suggesting a delay instead of a prevention effect. Other studies do not include follow-up information (see Quek et al. 2012), leaving room for interpretation of the true efficacy of results. The inconsistencies point to the importance of longer follow-up periods whenever possible, in order to assess for long-term and possibly delayed program effects (Esbensen et al. 2001, 2012, 2013).

It has been shown that the most effective intervention programs are those that take place in early childhood or the preschool years (Mann and Reynolds 2006; Zigler, Taussig, and Black 1992). The studies that examine the effects of those programs are often longitudinal in design. They also employ the parents as primary sources of behavioral data of the children involved in the program. With school-based intervention programs, however, researchers are dependent upon students, who are more often than not minors, to report engaging in behaviors that are possibly illegal. These facts make conducting research on school-based interventions difficult, and there are several obstacles to overcome in order to successfully conduct research in schools. Concerns about the content of the survey instrument, parental consent, and taking valuable class time to administer surveys all contribute to the relatively high difficulty level of conducting research in schools, and may account for many of the methodological differences we see across studies. Even so, it is important that we continue to push toward doing the most complete, methodologically sound research that the schools will allow.

Conclusions

Here we have provided a summary of short intervention programs, from their start in the medical intervention literature to their current use in schools, with an emphasis on those shorter school-based interventions that have some evidence of efficacy. While not all programs had long-lasting effects, an argument can be made for the benefit of delayed onset of certain behaviors, especially with regard to aggression and violence. And while here we focus on violence in general, it is important to note that several shorter interventions are designed for specific types of violence: GREAT targets gang violence and shows promise in several school-based settings (Esbensen et al. 2013; see also discussion in Chapter 10, this volume).

We have come to know that these types of short interventions are popular due to their cost effectiveness, generalizability, and short durations. However, we have outlined here the methodological issues that must be considered when evaluating such interventions for efficacy. We encourage school administrators and other practitioners to think critically about those programs that would best fit their needs and to make decisions based on available research instead of flashy testimonials. In this same light, it is important to remember that short interventions can have positive effects beyond targeted behaviors; programs that reduce aggression, for example, can increase academic engagement and achievement (Hansen 1996). And violence and aggression can be targeted in indirect ways. In their discussion of the social-ecological model, Estrada et al. (Chapter 9, this volume) point to the ways that school protective factors can decrease gang involvement, which can decrease violence in general. Short-term interventions also have the potential to increase these protective factors and help increase connectedness and social support. One benefit to the use of shorter term and brief interventions is that they can be cost effective, giving schools the ability to target several domains at once, offering more holistic solutions (Chapters 9 and 10, this volume).

The utility of shorter intervention programs in school settings is based on the fact that these types of approaches can be more cost effective and can offer school administrators more creativity in serving the needs of their students and their communities. The ones described here are not exhaustive of those available to schools, but due to the fact that many intervention programs have still not been rigorously evaluated, we recommend that administrators are critical when making investment decisions. To that end, we offer ways in which administrators can make educated decisions when determining which programs best fit their needs and their resources.

References

Aos, Steve, Lieb, Roxanne, Mayfield, Jim, Miller, Marna, and Pennucci, Annie. 2004. "Benefits and Costs of Prevention and Early Intervention Programs for Youth." Washington State Institute for Public Policy.

Cheng, Tina L., Haynie, Denise, Brenner, Ruth, Wright, Joseph. L., Chung, Shang-en, and Simons-Morton, Bruce. 2008. "Effectiveness of a Mentor-Implemented Violence Prevention Intervention for Assault-Injured Youth Presenting to the Emergency Department: Results of a Randomized Trial." *Pediatrics* 122(5), 938–946. DOI: 10.1542/peds.2007-2096.

Ciliska, Donna. n.d. "Critical Appraisal of Intervention Studies." Canadian Institutes of Health Research. http://www.cihr-irsc.gc.ca/e/45235.html (last accessed October 16, 2017).

Conrod, Patricia J., Castellanos, Natalie, and Mackie, Clare. 2008. "Personality-Targeted Interventions Delay the Growth of Adolescent Drinking and Binge Drinking." *Journal of Child Psychology and Psychiatry* 49(2), 181–190. DOI: 10.1111/j.1469-7610.2007.01826.x.

Dembo, Richard, Gulledge, Laura, Briones-Robinson, Rhissa, and Winters, Ken C. 2011. "Enrolling and Engaging High-Risk Youths and Families in Community-Based, Brief Intervention Services." *Journal of Child and Adolescent Substance Abuse* 20(4), 330–350. DOI: 10.1080/1067828X.2011.598837.

Esbensen, Finn-Aage, Osgood, Wayne D., Taylor, Terrence J., Peterson, Dana, and Freng, Adrienne. 2001. "How Great Is G.R.E.A.T.? Results from a Longitudinal

Quasi-Experimental Design." *Criminology and Public Policy* 1: 87–118. DOI: 10.1111/j.1745-9133.2001.tb00078.x.

Esbensen, Finn Aage, Peterson, Dana, Taylor, Terrance J., and Osgood, D. Wayne. 2012. "Results from a Multi-Site Evaluation of the G.R.E.A.T. Program." *Justice Quarterly* 29, 125–151. DOI: 10.1080/07418825.2011.585995.

Esbensen, Finn Aage, Osgood, Wayne D., Peterson, Dana, Taylor, Terrence J., and Carson, Dena C. 2013. "Short-and Long-Term Outcome Results from a Multisite Evaluation of the GREAT Program." *Criminology and Public Policy* 12(3), 375–411. DOI: 10.1111/1745-9133.12048.

Farrington, David P. 2003. "Methodological Quality Standards for Evaluation Research." *The Annals of the American Academy of Political and Social Science* 587(1), 49–68. DOI: 10.1177/0002716202250789.

García, Jorge L., Heckman, James J., Leaf, Duncan E., and Prados, María J. 2016. "The Life-cycle Benefits of an Influential Early Childhood Program." *Human Capital and Economic Opportunity Working Paper Series.* National Bureau of Economic Research.

Gibbs, Leonard E. 1989. "Quality of Study Rating Form: An Instrument for Synthesizing Evaluation Studies." *Journal of Social Work Education* 25(1), 55–67. DOI: 10.1080/10437797.1989.10671270.

Gottfredson, Denise C. and Gottfredson, Gary. 2002. "Quality of School-Based Prevention Programs: Results from a National Survey." *Journal of Research in Crime and Delinquency* 39(1), 3–35. DOI: 10.1177/002242780203900101.

Gottfredson, Denise, C., Cross, Amanda, Wilson, Denise, Rorie, Melissa, and Connell, Nadine. 2010. "An Experimental Evaluation of the All Start Prevention Curriculum in an After School Setting." *Prevention Science* 11, 142–154. DOI: 10.1007/s11121-009-0156.

Hansen, William. 1996. "Pilot Test Results Comparing the All Stars Prevention Program with Seventh Grade D.A.R.E.: Program Integrity and Mediating Variable Analysis." *Substance Use and Misuse* 31, 1359–1377. DOI: 10.3109/10826089609063981.

Harrington, Nancy G., Giles, Steven M., Hoyle, Rick H., Feeney, Greg J., and Yungbluth, Stephen C. 2001. "Evaluation of the All Stars Character Education and Problem Behavior Prevention Program: Effects on Mediator and Outcome Variables." *Health Education & Behavior* 28, 533–546.

Heckman, James J. 2000. "Policies to Foster Human Capital." *Research in Economics* 54, 3–56. DOI: 10.1006/reec.1999.0225.

Heckman, James J., Humphries, John Eric, and Veramendi, Gregory. 2016. "Returns to Education: The Causal Effects of Education on Earnings, Health, and Smoking." National Bureau of Economic Research. http://www.nber.org/data-appendix/w22291/HHV_jpe_Web-App_2016-03-06a_jld.pdf (last accessed October 16, 2017).

Hennessy, Emily A. and Tanner-Smith, Emily E. 2015. "Effectiveness of Brief School-Based Interventions for Adolescents: A Meta-Analysis of Alcohol Use Prevention Programs." *Prevention Science* 16, 463–474. DOI: 10.1007/s11121-014-0512.

Higgins, Julian P.T., Altman, Douglas G., and Sterne, Jonathan A.C. n.d. "Assessing Risk of Bias in Included Studies." Cochrane. http://methods.cochrane.org/bias/assessing-risk-bias-included-studies (last accessed October 16, 2017).

Howell, James C. 2013. "GREAT Results." *Criminology and Public Policy* 12(3), 413–420. DOI: 10.1111/1745-9133.12051.

Khan, Khalid S., Ter Riet, Gerben, Glanville, Julie, Sowden, Amanda J., and Kleijnen, Jos. 2001. *Undertaking Systematic Reviews of Research on Effectiveness: CRD's Guidance for*

Carrying Out or Commissioning Reviews (No. 4 (2n)). York, UK: NHS Centre for Reviews and Dissemination.

Kochis, Donna S. 1995. "The Effectiveness of Project DARE: Does It Work?" *Journal of Alcohol and Drug Education* 40(2), 40–47.

Mann, Emily A. and Reynolds, Arthur J. 2006. "Early Intervention and Juvenile Delinquency Prevention: Evidence from the Chicago Longitudinal Study." *Social Work Research* 30(3), 153–167. DOI: 10.1093/swr/30.3.153.

Marsden, John, Stillwell, Gary, Barlow, Helen, Boys, Annabelle, Taylor, Colin, Hunt, Neil, and Farrell, Michael. 2006. "An Evaluation of a Brief Motivational Intervention among Young Ecstasy and Cocaine Users: No Effect on Substance and Alcohol Use Outcomes." *Addiction* 101, 1014–1026. DOI: 10.1111/j.1360-0443.2006.01290.x.

Mikhail, Judy Nanette and Nemeth, Lynne Sheri. 2016. "Trauma Center Based Youth Violence Prevention Programs: An Integrative Review." *Trauma, Violence, and Abuse* 17(5), 500–519. DOI: 10.1177/1524838015584373.

Miller, Ted R. and Hendrie, Debra. 2008. "Substance Abuse Prevention Dollars and Cents: A Cost-Benefit Analysis." US Department of Health and Human Services, Substance Abuse and Mental Health Services Administration, Center for Substance Abuse Prevention, no. 07-4298.

Molgaard, Virginia K., Spoth, Richard L., and Redmond, Cleve. 2000. "Competency Training The Strengthening Families Program: For Parents and Youth 10–14." Juvenile Justice Bulletin. https://www.ncjrs.gov/App/Publications/abstract.aspx?ID=182208 (last accessed October 16, 2017).

Mulvey, Edward P., Arthur, Michael W., and Reppucci, N. Dickon. 1993. "The Prevention and Treatment of Juvenile Delinquency: A Review of the Research." *Clinical Psychology Review* 13, 133–167. DOI: 10.1016/0272-7358(93)90038-N.

Myers, Mark G. and Kelly, John F. 2006. "Cigarette Smoking Among Adolescents with Alcohol and Other Drug Use Problems." *Alcohol Research and Health* 29(3), 221–227. https://www.ncbi.nlm.nih.gov/pmc/articles/PMC1931414/ (last accessed October 16, 2017).

National Heart, Lung and Blood Institute. n.d. "Study Quality Assessment Tools." https://www.nhlbi.nih.gov/health-pro/guidelines/in-develop/cardiovascular-risk-reduction/tools (last accessed October 16, 2017).

National Institute of Justice. n.d. "How We Review and Rate a Program From Start to Finish." Crimesolutions.gov. https://www.crimesolutions.gov/about_starttofinish.aspx (accessed October 16, 2017).

Platt, Lucy, Melendez-Torres, G.J., O'Donnell, Amy, Bradley, Jennifer, Newbury-Birch, Dorothy, Kaner, Eileen, and Ashton, Charlotte. 2016. "How Effective Are Brief Interventions in Reducing Alcohol Consumption: Do the Setting, Practitioner Group and Content Matter? Findings from a Systematic Review and Metaregression Analysis." *BMJ Open.* DOI: 10.1136/bmjopen-2016-011473.

Quek, Lake-Hui, White, Angela, Low, Christine, Brown, Judith, Dalton, Nigel, Dow, Debbie, and Connor, Jason P. 2012. "Good Choices, Great Future: An Applied Theatre Prevention Program to Reduce Alcohol-Related Risky Behaviors During Schoolies." *Drug and Alcohol Review* 31(7), 897–902. DOI: 10.1111/j.1465-3362.2012.00453.x.

Rudzinski, Katherine, McGuire, Fraser, Dawe, Meghan, Shuper, Paul, Bilsker, Dan, Capler, Rielle, Rehm, Jürgen, and Fischer, Benedikt. 2012. "Brief Intervention Experiences of Young High-Frequency Cannabis Users in a Canadian Setting." *Contemporary Drug Problems* 39, 49–72.

Sherman, Lawrence W., Gottfredson, Denise, MacKenzie, Doris, Eck, John, Reuter, Peter, and Bushway, Shawn. 1997. *Preventing Crime: What Works, What Doesn't, and What's Promising?* A Report to the United States Congress. Washington, DC: National Institute of Justice. https://eric.ed.gov/?id=ED423321 (last accessed October 16, 2017).

Small, Stephen A., Reynolds, Arthur J., O'Connor, Caitlin, and Cooney, Siobhan M. 2005. "What Works, Wisconsin: What Science Tells Us about Cost-Effective Programs for Juvenile Delinquency Prevention." *Madison, WI: University of Wisconsin–Madison.* https://www.ncjrs.gov/app/abstractdb/AbstractDBDetails.aspx?id=234019 (last accessed October 16, 2017).

Substance Abuse and Mental Health Administration. n.d. "Program Review Criteria." http://nrepp.samhsa.gov/04e_reviews_program.aspx (last accessed October 7, 2017).

Tanner-Smith, Emily E. and Lipsey, Mark W. 2015. "Brief Alcohol Interventions for Adolescents and Young Adults: A Systematic Review and Meta-Analysis." *Journal of Substance Abuse Treatment* 51, 1–18. DOI: 10.1016/j.jsat.2014.09.001.

Tugwell, Peter and Knottnerus, Andre J. 2015. "Is the 'Evidence-Pyramid' now dead?" *Journal of Cilinical Epidemiology* 68(11), 1247–1250. DOI: 10.1016/j.jclinepi.2015. 10.001.

Walton, Maureen A., Chermack, Stephen T., Shope, Jean T., Bingham, C. Raymond, Zimmerman, Marc A., Blow, Frederic C., and Cunningham, Rebecca M. 2010. "Effects of a Brief Intervention for Reducing Violence and Alcohol Misuse Among Adolescents: A Randomized Controlled Trial." *American Medical Association* 304(5), 527–535. DOI: 10.1001/jama.2010.1066.

Walton, Maureen A., Resko, Stella, Barry, Kristen L., Chermack, Stephen T., Zucker, Robert A., Zimmerman, Marc A., Booth, Brenda M., and Blow, Frederic C. 2014. "A Randomized Controlled Trial Testing the Efficacy of a Brief Cannabis Universal Prevention Program Among Adolescents in Primary Care." *Addiction* 109(5), 786–797. DOI: 10.1111/add.12469.

Weissberg, Roger P. 1990. "Support for School-Based Social Competence Promotion." *American Psychologist* 986–987.

Werch, Chudley E., Carlson, Joan M., Pappas, Deborah M., and DiClemente, Carlo C. 1996. "Brief Nurse Consultations for Preventing Alcohol Use among Urban School Youth." *Journal of School Health* 66(9), 335–338. DOI: 10.1111/j.1746-1561.1996.tb03414.x.

Zagumny, Matthew J. and Thompson, Michael K. 1997. "Does D.A.R.E. Work? An Evaluation in Rural Tennessee." *Journal of Alcohol and Drug Education* 42(2), 32–41.

Zigler, Edward, Taussig, Cara, and Black, Kathryn. 1992. "Early Childhood Intervention: A Promising Preventative for Juvenile Delinquency." *American Psychologist* 47(8), 997–1006.

Section 3

Bullying, Sexual Violence, and Suicide in Education
Section Editor: Dorothy L. Espelage

Section 3 Introduction

Bullying, Sexual Violence, and Suicide in Education

Dorothy L. Espelage

Bullying and sexual violence are both increasingly being recognized as public health concerns (Basile et al. 2016; Robers, Zhang, and Morgan 2015) in the United States. Bullying is a pervasive issue today, with approximately 21% of public school students who reported being bullied in 2013 (Robers Zhang, and Morgan 2015). Bullying perpetration is a multifaceted phenomenon that is characterized as the intentional, unsolicited, and repeated use of physical (e.g., hitting, kicking, pushing, shoving), verbal (e.g., name-calling, teasing), and/or social (e.g., spreading rumors, social exclusion) aggression toward one's peers to inflict physical, psychological, social, or educational harm (Gladden et al. 2014; Olweus 1997). The relationship between perpetrators and victims is often characterized by an imbalance of strength and power, used to coerce a person of lesser strength or status (Olweus 1993). If not prevented early, children are at risk of developing psychopathology in adulthood (Bender and Lösel 2011; Copeland et al. 2013).

Sexual violence (SV) is non-consensual completed or attempted penetration (vaginal, oral, or anal), unwanted touching (e.g., groping or fondling), or non-contact acts such as exposing oneself or verbal sexual harassment, committed by any perpetrator (Basile and Saltzman 2002; Basile et al. 2005). Sexual harassment, a subset of the larger SV construct, is defined as unwanted sexual comments, sexual rumor spreading, or groping (Espelage, Basile, and Hamburger 2012; Espelage et al. 2015). The 2011 Youth Risk Behavior Survey, a national survey of students in grades 9–12, found a lifetime reported prevalence for unwanted physically forced sexual intercourse of 11.8% for girls and 4.5% for boys (Basile et al. 2016). In addition, physical or verbal sexual harassment is extremely common in schools among adolescents; 40% of males and 56% of females in seventh through twelfth grade reported experiencing sexual harassment during the 2010–2011 school year (American Association of University Women 2011).

Although the research base on bullying has grown exponentially over the last 10 years, prevention and intervention programs have met with limited success (Ttofi and Farrington 2011). In relation to sexual violence among adolescents and young adults, research progress has been relatively slow and fewer programs have been evaluated for sexual violence in comparison to bullying prevention. Thus, much more basic, applied, and intervention research is needed in order to prevent bullying and sexual violence. This book section is an attempt to review the extant literature on bullying and sexual violence in order to establish future research agendas.

In Chapter 16, Amanda Nickerson, Danielle Guttman, and Samantha VanHout provide a comprehensive review of the extant research on prevalence, trends, definitions, current legislation, and national initiatives on bullying and cyberbullying in the school system. The authors explore multiple risk and protective factors for bullying and cyberbullying which are centered on associations of individual, peer, school, family, and societal factors with corresponding levels of victimization. Some of the challenges for a complete understanding of bullying and cyberbullying given in the chapter include issues with special populations, use of inconsistent definitions, and varying measurement tools to assess bullying. The chapter concludes with recommendations for policies and interventions to reduce bullying and cyberbullying which include greater collaboration between and among researchers, practitioners and policy makers, a focus on social-emotional skills development, and school-wide positive behavioral intervention supports for students. In the following chapter, Jun Sung Hong, Dorothy Espelage, and Jeoung Min Lee review the extant research on the association between bullying and school climate and argue that bullying prevention should consider the larger school context beyond individuals and classrooms. School climate components reviewed in this chapter include physical safety as well as emotional safety and feeling connected. The chapter highlights the modest reductions in bullying and peer victimization that have been reported with current school-wide prevention programs. The chapter concludes with recommendations for building effective programs by encouraging the collaboration of parents, teachers, administrators, and students equally to improve school climate and safety.

As bullying is often correlated with sexual violence, the next chapter, by Anjali Forber-Pratt and Dorothy Espelage, provides a nice review of what we know about sexual harassment and sexual violence in K–12 settings. Special attention is given to the types of sexual harassment as well as the specific areas of the school where sexual harassment takes place. The chapter explores the sociodemographic characteristics of those involved, as well as how social connectedness and homophobic teasing can be related to sexual harassment. Additional concerns about school policies and procedures are discussed, as well as recommendations for effective prevention and intervention efforts. Among the recommendations for schools, special attention is given to monitoring and consistency in the enforcement of the different policies to reduce sexual harassment.

In Chapter 19, Elizabeth Payne and Melissa Smith evaluate the shortcomings of current lesbian, gay, bisexual, and transgender (LGBT) bullying prevention programs to eliminate the marginalization of these students. The authors argue that the school programs in place to reduce the bullying of LGBT students are based in the cultural privilege of heterosexual gender norms. To overcome the issue, the authors recommend a broader perspective that critically evaluates cultural and social patterns of aggression, norms of sexuality, and gender expression built into the prevention programs currently available. Bullying is discussed as a way of maintaining the status quo of privileged heterosexual gender binary worldviews. Effective programs would need to deconstruct and redefine the concept of bullying underlying the marginalization of LGBT students by using more inclusive concepts and programs.

In the following chapter, Sheila Katz and Laura McGuire offer an overview on the topic of intimate partner violence (IPV). They identify gaps in the research on IPV in higher education, exploring the specific obstacles that college students may face to form and maintain healthy relationships. An emotional experience of IPV is told in the personal story of Mercedes, a college student who was experiencing physical harm in an intimate relationship but struggled to leave the relationship. The chapter reviews the history and the federal regulatory policies against IPV in higher education and identifies the shortcomings these policies have faced during their implementation on campuses. Suggestions for prevention are provided and include annual workshops, courses, centralized resources, and faculty training programs to send a unified message of support for survivors of IPV.

Sexual violence is a global public health concern. Thus, Chapter 21, by Relebohile Moletsane and Claudia Mitchell, is critical to our understanding of sexual violence across the world. The chapter explores the difficulties of conducting research on gender violence with girls and women in South Africa and discusses ethical and cultural limitations for the participation of South African girls in research involving sexual violence. The authors outline the challenges of using participatory visual methods such as photovoice, digital storytelling, asset mapping, participatory video, and cellphilming (i.e., filming using a cell phone) with the "girl-method", an innovative feminist-oriented research methodology conducted "for girls, by girls, and about girls" (Mitchell 2011). Focusing on the project "Networks for Change," the chapter identifies community taboo issues surrounding teenage sex and sexuality as obstacles to disclosing information to researchers about their experiences of sexual violence. The authors conclude that although visual participatory methods could be extended to the study of sexual violence in school-based and community-based interventions globally, the results could lead to manifestations of the same cultural norms that helped to marginalize the groups without doing much to change their status of oppression.

In the final chapter in this section, Melissa Holt, Chelsey Bowman, Anastasia Alexis, and Alyssa Murphy review the literature on bullying and suicide. These authors analyze the associations between bullying victimization and suicidality and describe several suicide prevention programs for schools. An analysis of individual, familial, and environmental characteristics that could become risk or protective factors for bullying are contrasted with similar characteristics for suicidality. After exploring the associations between bullying and suicide, the chapter recommends empirically based interventions that could target both bullying and suicide jointly in school settings.

Conclusion

Taken together, the content of these chapters represents a comprehensive examination of bullying and sexual violence among adolescents in community, public school, and higher education settings. Bullying and sexual violence continue to be public health concerns that have deleterious outcomes for all involved, including victims, perpetrators, and witnesses. Each chapter has reviewed the most current literature and has focused on what we know about each topic, but has also provided excellent discussions about how best to prevent these phenomena and to intervene when victims are identified. Each chapter also offers researchers and practitioners ideas for future research and intervention directions.

References

American Association of University Women. 2011. *Crossing the Line: Sexual Harassment at School.* Washington, DC: American Association of University Women. Retrieved from http://www.aauw.org/resource/crossing-the-line-sexual-harassment-at-school-executive-summary/.

Basile, K.C., DeGue, S., Jones, K., Freire, K., Dills, J., Smith, S.G., et al. 2016. *STOP SV: A Technical Package to Prevent Sexual Violence.* Atlanta, GA: National Center for Injury Prevention and Control, Centers for Disease Control and Prevention.

Basile, K.C., Lang, K.S., Bartenfeld, T.A., and Clinton-Sherrod, M. 2005. "Report from the CDC: Evaluability Assessment of the Rape Prevention and Education Program: Summary of findings and recommendations." *Journal of Women's Health* 14(3), 201–207.

Basile, K.C. and Saltzman, L.E. 2002. *Sexual Violence Surveillance: Uniform Definitions and Recommended Data Elements Version 1.0.* Atlanta: Centers for Disease Control and Prevention, National Center for Injury Prevention and Control. www.cdc.gov/ncipc/pub-res/sv_surveillance/sv.htm.

Bender, D. and Lösel, F. 2011. "Bullying at School as a Predictor of Delinquency, Violence and Other Anti-social Behaviour in Adulthood." *Criminal Behaviour and Mental Health* 21(2), 99–106.

Copeland, W.E., Wolke, D., Angold, A., and Costello, E.J. 2013. "Adult Psychiatric Outcomes of Bullying and Being Bullied by Peers in Childhood and Adolescence". *JAMA Psychiatry* 70(4), 419–426.

Espelage, D.L., Basile, K.C., and Hamburger, M.E. 2012. "Bullying Perpetration and Subsequent Sexual Violence Perpetration among Middle School Students. *Journal of Adolescent Health* 50, 60–65. DOI: 10.1016/j.jadohealth.2011.07.015.

Espelage, D.L., Basile, K.C., De La Rue, L., and Hamburger, M.E. 2015. "Longitudinal Associations among Bully, Homophobic Teasing, and Sexual Violence Perpetration among Middle School Students." *Journal of Interpersonal Violence* 30, 2541–2561. DOI: 10.1177/0886260514553113.

Gladden, R.M., Vivolo-Kantor, A.M., Hamburger, M.E., and Lumpkin, C.D. 2014. *Bullying Surveillance among Youths: Uniform Definitions for Public Health and Recommended Data Elements.* Atlanta: National Center for Injury Prevention and Control, Centers for Disease Control and Prevention.

Mitchell, C. 2011. "What's Participation Got to Do with It? Visual Methodologies in 'Girl-Method' to Address Gender-based Violence in the Time of AIDS." *Global Studies of Childhood* 1(1), 51–59. DOI: 10.2304/gsch.2011.1.1.51.

Olweus, D. 1993. *Bullying at School.* Oxford: Blackwell.

Olweus, D. 1997. "Bully/victim Problems in School: Facts and Intervention." *European Journal of Psychology of Education* 7, 495–510.

Robers, S., Zhang, A., and Morgan, R.E. 2015. "Indicators of School Crime and Safety: 2014." NCES 2015-072/NCJ 248036. National Center for Education Statistics. US Department of Education, US Department of Justice Office of Justice Programs. https://nces.ed.gov/pubs2015/2015072.pdf (last accessed October 17, 2017).

Ttofi, M.M. and Farrington, D.P. 2011. "Effectiveness of School-based Programs to Reduce Bullying: A Systematic and Meta-analytic Review." *Journal of Experimental Criminology* 7(1), 27–56. DOI: 10.1007/s11292-010-9109-1.

16

Bullying and Cyberbullying Prevalence as a Form of Violence in Education

Amanda Nickerson, Danielle Guttman, and Samantha VanHout

Bullying has received public attention as an issue facing our nation's schoolchildren. In order to place bullying and cyberbullying within the context of a form of violence in education, it is important to take a historical perspective. Although bullying has been a problem in the United States for decades, there was a relative lack of attention on bullying as compared to other countries, especially European countries and Japan, before 1999 (Koo 2007). The Columbine High School shooting in 1999 led bullying to became a focus of national attention based on the perpetrators' publicly and widely available Internet posts, many of which mentioned being bullied and rejected by peers (Larkin 2009). This attention can be exemplified in terms of the research literature, legislation, and national initiatives focused on bullying and cyberbullying. This chapter reviews these trends, and introduces the definition and distinguishing features of bullying and cyberbullying. The prevalence and impact of this form of violence are then reviewed. Risk and protective factors are highlighted, concluding with a discussion of the challenges that remain in understanding and addressing bullying and cyberbullying.

Research Trends

To examine trends in research across the decades, we conducted a PsycInfo search using keywords: bullying and school; aggression and school; cyberbullying; and cyberbullying and school. As shown in Figure 16.1, there was a gradual increase in the number of peer-reviewed articles published regarding school bullying and aggression between 1926 and 1985; then, from 1986 through 2015, the number of publications tripled each decade. As Figure 16.2 shows, research on cyberbullying is even more recent, with the first publication appearing in 2006, followed by a sharp increase in the number of peer-reviewed articles published regarding cyberbullying in schools from 2006 to 2015.

The Wiley Handbook on Violence in Education: Forms, Factors, and Preventions, First Edition.
Edited by Harvey Shapiro.
© 2018 John Wiley & Sons, Inc. Published 2018 by John Wiley & Sons, Inc.

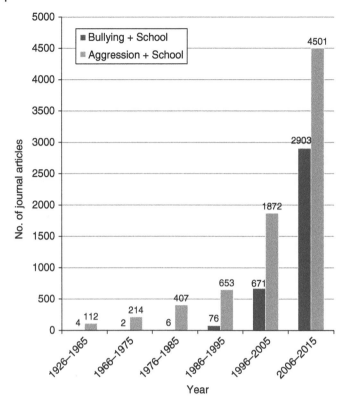

Figure 16.1 Number of peer-reviewed journal articles on bullying and aggression in schools: 1926–2015.

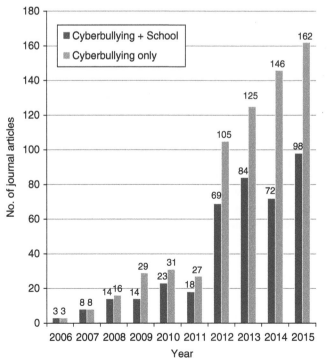

Figure 16.2 Number of peer-reviewed journal articles on cyberbullying: 2006–2015.

Legislation

According to an analysis by the United States Department of Education (DOE; Stuart-Cassel, Bell, and Springer 2011), since the Columbine High School shootings in 1999, 49 of the 50 states have passed legislation to address bullying in schools. Despite the DOE's identification of 16 components of state legislation, this investigation found wide variability in the legislative components mandated across states (Stuart-Cassel, Bell, and Springer 2011). Although there is no federal anti-bullying law, there are relevant antidiscrimination laws that can be applied to bullying in certain situations. The United States Department of Education's Office for Civil Rights (OCR) issued a "Dear Colleague" letter (2010) advising schools that many forms of bullying grounded in disability status, race or ethnicity, or gender constitute violations of federal antidiscrimination laws, for which schools must take prompt and effective steps to prevent and eliminate harassment. Follow-up "Dear Colleague" letters from the DOE's Office of Special Education and Rehabilitative Services (2013) and the OCR (2014) asserted that bullying of a student with a disability also may deny a meaningful education; therefore, a new Individualized Education Program (IEP) or 504 plan must be tailored for the student being bullied (or doing the bullying) to ensure the provision of a "free and appropriate public education."

There are very few studies assessing the effectiveness of anti-bullying legislation in the United States, although existing empirical studies show some modest correlational support between legislative mandates and compliance with reduced bullying and other related outcomes (Cosgrove and Nickerson 2015; Hatzenbuehler et al. 2015). Hatzenbuehler and colleagues (2015) found that students from states that had bullying policies with at least one of the DOE legislative components had 24% and 20% reduced odds of bullying and cyberbullying, respectively, compared to states with no legislative components. Furthermore, three legislative components were consistently associated with lower probabilities of student reports of being bullied or cyberbullied (statement of scope, description of prohibited behaviors, and requirement of local policies developed and implemented by school districts), yet there was no particular combination of components that appeared to work best. Cosgrove and Nickerson (2015) conducted a cross-sectional analysis of a matched sample of New York state educators before and after implementation of the state's anti-bullying and harassment legislation, the Dignity for All Students Act (DASA). Alignment with the DASA mandates predicted educator perceptions of less severe bullying and harassment, positive school climate, and less need for improvement in school anti-bullying practices. However, the associations did not differ before and after the DASA, suggesting that implementing practices aligned with the legislation was associated with positive outcomes, although the relations may not be due to the mandate itself.

National Initiatives

Several large, nationally representative samples and census surveys are conducted annually or biennially to assess the frequency of violent and disruptive incidents as reported by students or teachers. In the 1970s, the DOE funded the Safe Schools Study to assess the quality of safety in our nation's school systems by surveying principals, teachers, and students (National Center for Education Statistics [NCES] 2000). The School Survey on Crime and Safety (SSOCS) was developed in 1999 as an expansion of the original Safe Schools Study to gather current information on crime, violence, and disorder, as well as school policies, disciplinary actions, and school violence prevention programs and practices in America's public schools. Bullying has been assessed in the SSOCS since it was first administered in 1999, and cyberbullying was added to the 2009–2010 revision (National Center for Education Statistics 2010). The Youth Risk Behavior Surveillance System (YRBSS) was developed in 1990 and first administered in 1991 (Centers for Disease Control and Prevention 2015). Bullying on school property was included, from the 2009 revision of the YRBSS questionnaire onward, for both high school and middle school students, with a "yes" or "no" response (Centers for Disease Control and Prevention 2009a, 2009b). Cyberbullying was added to the YRBSS in the 2011 revision (Centers for Disease Control and Prevention 2011a, 2011b).

In 2008, the Federal Partners in Bullying Prevention Steering Committee was originated to provide guidance on bullying. In 2010, the first Federal Partners in Bullying Prevention Summit was held with over 150 leaders, researchers, practitioners, parents, and children to pinpoint the challenges experienced in bullying prevention endeavors. Also as a result of the Bullying Prevention Steering Committee, Stopbullying.gov was launched on March 10, 2011, at the White House Conference on Bullying Prevention, with the goal of providing information to the public on bullying, risk factors, and warning signs (The White House 2011).

Definition and Distinguishing Features

Dan Olweus (1978) initially defined bullying as physical bullying or verbal taunting by the bully or bullies directly to the victim. As the research expanded in the 1990s, indirect aggression or relational aggression was increasingly recognized as an important issue (Bjorkqvist, Lagerspetz, and Kaukiainen 1992; Crick and Grotpeter 1995, 1996; Galen and Underwood 1997). In 1999, Olweus revised his definition, indicating that bullying is an action that is aggressive with the intent to cause harm, caused by an imbalance of power, and carried out repeatedly and over time. Although these components of bullying have been widely recognized, there is great variability in bullying definitions and measurement, which likely contributes to the wide variation in prevalence rates (Swearer, Siebecker, et al. 2010).

To address the Federal Partners in Bullying Prevention Summit's recommendations, the DOE and CDC provided funding to convene an expert panel of 12 researchers and practitioners tasked with developing a uniform definition of bullying to gather comparable data across contexts. After incorporating feedback from external experts and federal partners, the final definition was released:

> Bullying is any *unwanted aggressive behavior(s)* by another youth or group of youths who are not siblings or current dating partners that involves *an observed or perceived power imbalance and is repeated multiple times or is highly likely to be repeated.* Bullying may inflict harm or distress on the targeted youth including physical, psychological, social, or educational *harm.* (Gladden et al. 2014, 7; emphasis in original)

The definition applies to school-aged youth aged 5 to 18 years, and goes on to describe two modes of bullying (direct and indirect), and four types of bullying (physical, verbal, relational, and damage to property). It was also noted that bullying occurs in many contexts, including electronically (e.g., cyberbullying). Researchers have reinforced the idea that bullying definitions should always include reference to repetition, imbalance of power, and intent of harm (Law, Shapka, Hymel et al. 2012). Together, the three components of bullying (intent, repetition, and power imbalance) make it distinct from related concepts of aggression, conflict, violence, abuse, and harassment (Cook et al. 2010; Felix et al. 2011; Gladden et al. 2014).

Cyberbullying has been an elusive construct, partly because of the different labels (e.g., internet bullying, online bullying, internet aggression/violence, and electronic bullying), and the wide range of definitions used. Most definitions of cyberbullying characterize it as the repetitive and willful (purposeful) harm through the use of technology (Patchin and Hinduja 2006; Tokunaga 2010). As shown in Table 16.1, there are numerous forms of

Table 16.1 Forms of cyberbullying.

Form of cyberbullying	Definition
Flaming	The exchange of insults, and/or the sending or posting of angry, hostile, vulgar, or annoying messages with the aim of provoking the target's emotions.
Online harassment	The repeated sending of insulting or offensive messages to a person.
Cyberstalking	The use of electronic messages to harass an individual by repeatedly threatening harm or significantly intimidating or annoying them.
Online physical threats	Actual threats directed at an individual's physical safety that are either posted on social media or sent in a message.
Denigration (put-downs)	The dissemination of harmful, untrue, or derogatory information about an individual to other people.
Tagging and untagging	The linking of a target to a photo, video, statement, or link that the target doesn't want to be associated with due to its negative, embarrassing, or cruel nature (e.g., tagging the target in a picture of a person with Down syndrome and writing "this reminds me of @Sarah.Hill").
Impersonation	An individual pretending to be someone else and sending or posting negative, unkind, or inappropriate information as if it were coming from the targeted individual, which in turn portrays the target in a negative light or places them in possible danger. *Catfishing* is a type of impersonation that involves creating a fake profile in an attempt to lure someone into a deceitful romantic relationship.
Outing and trickery	The sending or posting of private or sensitive information (e.g., home address, phone number, sexual orientation, etc.) or photos or videos of an individual. This also includes participating in "tricks" to get hold of humiliating information that is then shared with others or the public.
Exclusion	Acts that purposely omit a person from an online group (e.g., being removed from a buddy list or password protected online environments).

Source: Adapted from N. Willard, *Educator's Guide to Cyberbullying: Addressing the Harm Caused by Online Social Cruelty*, 2004, retrieved from http://cyberbully.org; S. Hinduja and J.W. Patchin, *Bullying Beyond the Schoolyard: Preventing and Responding to Cyberbullying* (2nd ed.), Thousand Oaks, CA: Corwin, 2015; and R.M. Kowalski, S.P. Limber, and P.W. Agatston, *Cyber Bullying: Bullying in the Digital Age*, Malden, MA: Blackwell Publishing, 2008.

cyberbullying, as well as various labels for these forms, including flaming, online harassment, online physical threats, cyberstalking, denigration/rumor spreading, tagging and untagging, impersonation/masquerade, outing/information spreading, or exclusion/ostracism (Hinduja and Patchin 2015; Kowalski, Limber, and Agatston 2008; Willard 2004).

Distinctions between cyberbullying and traditional bullying include the anonymity, repetition, wide reach, and the conceptualization of power (Li 2008). The ability to quickly reach a wide audience is a concerning aspect of cyberbullying (Kowalski and Limber 2007). Some argue that the repetition criterion is fulfilled in all instances of cyberbullying due to the number of times one individual and/or new individuals can view the message(s) (Langos 2012). The power differential does not focus on the perpetrator's power per se but on the victim's inability to control or escape the bullying (Dooley, Pyzalski, and Cross 2009; Langos 2012). The power of the person cyberbullying may relate to being technologically savvy, having more experience, and considering oneself an online expert (Dooley, Pyzalski, and Cross 2009). Another difference between cyberbullying and traditional bullying is that, in cyberbullying, individuals identify more with the method used (e.g., posting embarrassing photos, sending mean messages, developing hostile websites) than the role they had in the bullying (e.g., bullying, victim, witness; Law, Shapka, Domene, and Gagne 2012). In addition, youths involved in cyberbullying tend to be involved both as perpetrators and victims (Mishna et al. 2012).

Prevalence

There is a wide divergence in prevalence rates, likely due to the use of different measurement tools and definitions of bullying and the quality of the definitions used across studies (Vivolo-Kantor et al. 2014). A recent meta-analysis of 80 studies found that the prevalence of traditional bullying is more than two times that of cyberbullying, and the two forms of bullying are highly correlated (Modecki et al. 2014). Specifically, 34.5% were perpetrators of traditional bullying and 36% were victims of traditional bullying, whereas only 15.5% were the perpetrators of cyberbullying and 15.2% were the victims of cyberbullying (Modecki et al. 2014). Prevalence rates also vary across the different forms of bullying. For example, the highest rates of bullying occur for verbal and relational bullying, with lower rates found for physical and cyberbullying (Wang, Iannotti, and Nansel 2009; Williams and Guerra, 2007). Contrary to public opinion, there is no evidence to suggest that bullying is increasing; in fact, there has been a slow decrease over time (Centers for Disease Control and Prevention 2010, 2012, 2014; Currie et al. 2012; Perlus et al. 2014).

Some subgroups of students are at increased risk of bullying involvement, either due to individual characteristics (e.g., disability status) or a deviation from traditionally accepted norms within a given social environment (Farmer et al. 2015; Poteat and Russell 2013; Rose, Monda-Amaya, and Espelage 2011; Tynes et al. 2015). Despite variable results across studies, a generally consistent finding is that students with disabilities are at increased risk for being involved in bullying as victims, perpetrators, and bully-victims than their peers without disabilities (Blake et al. 2012; Estell et al. 2009; Rose, Espelage, and Monda-Amaya 2009; Rose, Monda-Amaya, and Espelage 2011). Children who identify as lesbian, gay, bisexual, transgender, and questioning (LGBTQ) report higher rates of bullying victimization (59–84%) than their heterosexual peers

(D'Augelli, Pilkington, and Hershberger 2002; Kosciw et al. 2010; McGuire et al. 2010). Bullying of the LGBTQ population typically involves the use of homophobic epithets (Poteat, O'Dwyer, and Mereish 2012), which serve as a way to marginalize this population and which contribute to a hostile school environment (Kosciw, Greytak, and Diaz 2009; Swearer et al. 2008).

Bullying is most pervasive from fourth to eighth grade (Dinkes et al. 2009; Rivers et al. 2009; Tokunaga 2010), with middle school students being at highest risk for being involved in bullying (Bradshaw, Sawyer, and O'Brennan 2009; Goldweber, Waasdorp, and Bradshaw 2013). Research findings regarding gender and cyberbullying are mixed. Some studies have found girls to be more involved in cyberbullying (Hoff and Mitchell 2008; Mishna et al. 2012; Nickerson et al, 2014; Rivers and Noret 2010), whereas others have found boys to be more involved (Erdur-Baker 2010; Slonje and Smith 2008), and still others have shown no gender differences in the prevalence of cyberbullying (Tokunaga 2010). The interaction between age and gender remains unclear, with some research finding larger gender gaps in victimization with age and others finding smaller gender gaps with age (Astor, Guerra, and Van Acker 2010).

Impact

A rapidly growing body of literature has identified bullying and cyberbullying as problems that have both concurrent and lasting impacts on various physical, psychological, academic, social, and behavioral outcomes (e.g., Copeland et al. 2013; Nickerson and Orrange-Torchia 2015). Victims of bullying report significantly higher levels of somatic complaints (Beckman, Hagquist, and Hellström 2012; Gini and Pozzoli 2009) and additional visits to medical professionals (Greco, Freeman, and Dufton 2010) than their non-involved peers. Victims of traditional bullying also experience higher levels of internalizing problems, including anxiety and depression (Hugh-Jones and Smith 1999; Kochenderfer and Ladd 1996), and symptoms such as sadness, loneliness, withdrawal (Kochenderfer and Ladd 1996; van Oort et al. 2011), low self-worth (Hugh-Jones and Smith 1999), and self-blame (Graham and Juvonen 1998) compared to their non-bullied peers. Youth bullied by their peers also tend to have other social difficulties such as low social status, rejection, and lack of acceptance (Ivarsson et al. 2005; Salmivalli et al. 1996). Victims of both traditional bullying and cyberbullying are also more likely to experience depression (Ttofi et al. 2011), suicidal ideation, and suicide attempts than their peers (Hinduja and Patchin 2010; Klomek et al. 2007; Meltzer et al. 2011; Nickerson and Slater 2009).

Bullying victimization is also associated with poor school outcomes, including lack of connectedness, feeling unsafe (Glew et al. 2005), and withdrawing from or avoiding school altogether (Kochenderfer and Ladd 1996). These youth may also be less successful academically (Brown and Taylor 2008; Glew et al. 2005) when considering grade point average and performance on achievement tests (Schwartz et al. 2005), especially in math (Konishi et al. 2010). Bullying victims who have a lower grade point average are more likely to report a negative school climate (Wang et al. 2014). Furthermore, youths who experience Internet harassment are at a higher risk for bringing a weapon to school than their peers (Ybarra, Diener-West, and Leaf 2007), which can also increase the chances of receiving disciplinary action.

The negative impact can be long lasting, as victims of childhood bullying are at an increased risk for stress symptomology (Newman, Holden, and Delville 2004), depressive symptoms (Carlyle and Steinman 2007; Ttofi et al. 2011), and anxiety disorders in adulthood (Copeland et al. 2013; Sourander et al. 2007). Women who were bullied as children were more likely to report suicidal behaviors than non-involved individuals, even after controlling for depressive symptoms (Klomek et al. 2009; Meltzer et al. 2011). Victims of bullying have also been found to earn less and have higher rates of job changes and termination as adults (Brown and Taylor 2008) compared to their non-victimized peers (Sansone, Leung, and Wiederman 2013). Emerging neurobiological research suggests that victimization experiences may significantly affect the way stress hormones are produced during victimization and beyond, with early and more frequent instances resulting in more negative outcomes than later and isolated incidents (McDougall and Vaillancourt 2015).

Perpetrators of bullying are more likely than their peers to engage in other high-risk behaviors, such as carrying weapons (Dukes, Stein, and Zane 2010) and abusing substances (Carlyle and Steinman 2007; Kaltiala-Heino et al. 2000; Kim et al. 2011). Bullying others is also associated with depression, suicidal ideation, and suicide attempts (Espelage and Holt 2013; Klomek et al. 2007; Nickerson and Slater 2009). Students who bully have also been found to have poorer school adjustment and less school success (e.g., difficulty completing homework) than both victims and non-involved peers (Brown and Taylor 2008; Nansel, Haynie, and Simons-Morton 2003). In addition, perpetrators are more likely to feel sad and unsafe in school than their peers (Glew et al. 2005).

Longitudinal research has indicated ongoing difficulties for individuals who bully, including a greater likelihood of engaging in aggressive behavior such as sexually harassing others (Espelage, Basile, and Hamburger 2012) and engaging in spousal abuse (Kim et al. 2011). Bullying is also related to subsequent violent crime (Farrington and Ttofi 2011; Lösel and Bender 2011), later criminal convictions (Renda, Vassallo, and Edwards 2011; Sourander et al. 2011), and increased risk for diagnosis of antisocial personality disorder (Copeland et al. 2013). Males who bullied others frequently at age 8 were at increased risk for suicidality at age 25 compared to their non-involved peers (Klomek et al. 2009).

Youths who both bully others and are victimized by their peers (i.e., bully-victims) tend to exhibit more problem behaviors (e.g., drinking, smoking, rule violations, theft, property damage), depressive symptoms, and lower social competence than peers who are either bullied or who bully others (Haynie et al. 2001; Veenstra et al. 2005). Bully-victims have also been found to have greater difficulties associated with school, such as poor academic achievement, lack a sense of connectedness, and lower perceptions of school safety and less school involvement than their peers (Cunningham 2007; Glew et al. 2005; O'Brennan, Bradshaw, and Sawyer 2009). In addition, increased rates of bulimia have been found among male bully-victims; both male and female bully-victims have increased rates of anorexia (Kaltiala-Heino et al. 2000). Bully-victims have been found to have the highest rates of suicidality of any of the bullying groups, with rates as high as 60% for ideation and 44% for suicidal behaviors (Espelage and Holt 2013). Some research has suggested that cyber bully-victims have the most negative mental and physical health and impaired educational performance (Kowalski and Limber 2013).

The impact of bullying is experienced not only by perpetrators, victims, and bully-victims, but also by peers that witness bullying (i.e., bystanders). Witnesses of bullying have been shown to suffer mental health consequences similar to children who witness domestic violence and other types of trauma or abuse (Rivers 2011). Individuals who witness bullying may feel as though they want to help but do not know the best way to provide support, which leads them to feel uncomfortable. Bystanders report the ambivalence of the experience to be an emotionally isolating experience (Hutchinson 2012). Empirical studies find that bystanders report increased anxiety, depression, hostility, and paranoia (Nishina and Juvonen 2005; Rivers et al. 2009). In fact, when college students were asked to recall observing bullying incidents, their levels of trauma symptomatology were similar to those of survivors of natural disasters and mass shootings (Janson and Hazler 2004). Bystanders who have also been victimized report more social maladjustment (i.e., problems interacting with others) than those who have not been victimized (Werth et al. 2015).

Risk and Protective Factors

As detailed in the previous sections on prevalence and impact, there are many individual, peer, school, family, and larger societal issues that are associated with bullying perpetration and/or victimization for youths that may be considered risk factors. As mentioned in the prevalence section of this chapter, students with disabilities and youths who identify as or are perceived by peers as LGBTQ are at higher risk for being bullied. According to teacher and student report, children with higher body mass indexes, and in particular, obese children, are at risk for both victimization and perpetration of bullying (Jansen et al. 2014). Children with chronic medical illnesses are also bullied at higher rates (Faith et al. 2015).

There are also individual factors that serve as risk and protective factors for bullying. A meta-analysis conducted by Cook and colleagues (2010) found that externalizing and also internalizing symptoms predicted bullying victimization and perpetration. Individual variables that protect bully perpetrators from negative outcomes in later life include being intelligent, having social skills and coping skills, and exhibiting prosocial behavior (Ttofi et al. 2014). Lacking social skills is also an individual risk factor for bullying victimization (Cook et al. 2010). History of physical and sexual abuse, mental health issues, running away from home, self-injurious behavior, and increased negative emotionality were significant risk factors for suicidality among victims of bullying (Borowsky, Taliaferro, and McMorris 2013).

Cognitions and attitudes can also increase risk or serve as protective influences. For example, a predictor of bullying is holding negative thoughts and attitudes about the self, others, and the school climate (Cook et al. 2010). Individuals with stronger antibullying attitudes are less likely to engage in bullying (Boulton et al. 1999). For perpetrators of bullying, having more prosocial attitudes is a protective factor that decreases the risk of exhibiting externalizing problems in adulthood (Ttofi et al. 2014). In terms of victimization, students who perceive themselves to be victims of bullying have poorer psychosocial adjustment than students who do not believe they have been victimized (Juvonen, Nishina, and Graham 2000). In addition, Graham et al. (2009) found that characterological self-blame mediated the relationship between peer victimization and maladjustment for Latinos and African Americans in schools where they were the majority ethnic group. Therefore, it appears that perceptions and attitudes about bullying, prosocial behavior, and the victimization experience itself may influence involvement with and outcomes from bullying.

Peers can also serve as a risk or protective factor for bullying. Negative peer influences predict bullying perpetration (Cook et al. 2010; Espelage and Swearer 2009), and bullying itself may shape peer norms, leading to increased bullying and acceptance of it in the peer group (Rodkin, Espelage, and Hanish 2015; Swearer, Espelage, et al. 2010). In contrast, having caring, prosocial friends buffers the negative outcomes for all youths involved in bullying as perpetrators, victims, or both (Borowsky, Taliaferro, and McMorris 2013; Ttofi et al. 2014). It is well known that victims of bullying are often visibly excluded and isolated by their peers (Cook et al. 2010). Victimized students who feel isolated by peers report elevated levels of stress (Newman, Holden, and Delville 2004). Interestingly, students who were harassed themselves but did not witness other students being harassed were found to report higher levels of humiliation and anger compared to those who had been both a victim and a witness in the same day (Nishina and Juvonen 2005). This suggests that if students see others being targeted, they may feel a sense of affiliation. Bullied students who are defended by a peer have better psychosocial adjustment and social standing (Sainio et al. 2010). Support seeking from friends is linked to reduced depressive symptoms (Machmutow et al. 2012), and support from classmates has been found to moderate the relationship between victimization and internalizing distress for boys (Davidson and Demaray 2007). Together, these findings indicate that isolation can exacerbate the negative impact, whereas social support is a protective factor.

There are several school and classroom contextual factors related to bullying and outcomes. School transitions, such as moving from elementary to middle school, and being a lower classman is associated with increased bullying (Bradshaw, Waasdorp, and Johnson 2015; Espelage, Hong, et al. 2015). Students who experience an increase in bullying in the transition to middle school also report lower sense of school belonging and less satisfaction with their teachers. Some research has found a greater risk of bullying is also associated with schools with high student–teacher ratios, high suspension rates, more poverty, and larger numbers of students with behavioral concerns (Bradshaw, Waasdorp, and Johnson 2015; Khoury-Kassabri et al. 2004), although the most recent data from NCES did not find measurable differences in the percentage of students who reported being bullied by school characteristics (Zhang, Musu-Gillette, and Oudekerk 2016). Both traditional bullying and cyberbullying are increased when there is a pervasively negative school climate without peer support, and where bullying is deemed acceptable (i.e., perceiving adults' prevention and intervention efforts as ineffective; Goldweber, Waasdorp, and Bradshaw 2013; Williams and Guerra 2007), and in schools that lack positively framed behavioral expectations enacted and posted around the school (Bradshaw, Waasdorp, and Johnson 2015). A protective factor for bullying involvement is feeling safe and having a sense of belonging or connectedness in school (Goldweber et al. 2013).

Family factors also play a role in bullying and its effects. Individuals involved in bullying report less caring parent–child relationships (Espelage and Swearer 2009). A risk factor for becoming a bully is a poor family environment where there is significant conflict and inadequate supervision, and undesirable community factors (Cook et al. 2010). Feeling attached to parents and having caring, prosocial friends and/or siblings were found to be protective factors that buffer the negative outcomes for all youth involved in bullying as perpetrators, victims, or both (Borowsky, Taliaferro, and McMorris 2013; Ttofi et al. 2014). Furthermore, parental support moderates the relationship between victimization and internalizing distress for girls (Davidson and Demaray 2007). Seeking support from family relates to reduced depressive symptoms (Machmutow et al. 2012). Students who have families that are stable (undisrupted), emotionally supportive, and that teach them coping skills, as well as those who consistently dine together (e.g., ≥ four nights a week), are more likely to adjust positively to being involved in bullying (Elgar et al. 2014; Ttofi et al. 2014). Parental supervision is also a protective factor for bullies (Ttofi et al. 2014). Clearly, there is a range of risk and protective factors for bullying involvement, all of which may inform prevention and intervention efforts.

Challenges in Understanding and Addressing Bullying and Cyberbullying

Despite the advances in the field, several challenges face researchers and practitioners in understanding and ultimately preventing and intervening with bullying and cyberbullying. First, definitional and measurement issues remain, and variation exists depending on the source and method of information gathered. Second, and related to both conceptualization of bullying and its effective prevention, are issues related to special populations. Third, issues surrounding cyberbullying, such as conceptualization, technological challenges, and legal considerations particular to this form of bullying as a form of violence in education continue. Finally, how to best prevent and intervene with bullying remains elusive.

Definitional and Measurement Issues

As mentioned previously, creating a uniform definition of bullying was identified as a priority from the Federal Partners in Bullying Prevention Summit. Although the definition has been created, challenges remain in measuring bullying. For example, although the definition of bullying includes three main components (i.e., intent to harm, power imbalance, repetition; Gladden et al. 2014), there is great variation in the extent to which repetition and power imbalance are specified in various measurement approaches (Cascardi et al. 2014; Felix et al. 2011). Studies that consider bullying to be a single or infrequent occurrence yield higher prevalence rates (Bear et al. 2015; Blake et al. 2012; Swearer et al. 2012) than those using more conservative recommendations (e.g., two or more times per month; Felix et al. 2011; Solberg and Olweus 2003). Also, studies that ask one question about bullying victimization yield lower prevalence than when the measure is comprised of several items measuring bullying specific behaviors (Bear at el. 2015). In self-reports, youths report less bullying when the term *bully* is used and when a definition is provided than when the term and definition are not used (Kert et al. 2010; Vaillancourt et al. 2008). The criterion of power imbalance is quite complex from both a conceptual and measurement standpoint (Rose, Nickerson, and Stormont 2015). Ybarra et al. (2012) found that adding a specific follow-up about differential power leads to a more accurate classification of bullying from peer nominations.

The source and collection of information is also important. Students are reluctant to report bullying and it usually goes undetected by teachers and other school personnel (Unnever and Cornell 2004). Not surprisingly, school staff members underestimate the number of students involved in frequent bullying when compared to student reports about bullying (Bradshaw, Sawyer, and O'Brennan 2007; Demaray et al. 2013; Stockdale et al. 2002). In assessing elementary student and teacher reports of bullies and their victims, Ahn, Rodkin, and Gest (2013) found an average of agreement on only 8% of bully–victim dyads. Although less research has been conducted with parents, existing studies show that parents also tend to report less victimization than children (Demaray et al. 2013; Stockdale et al. 2002), but agreement between parents and children is better than among teachers and students (Demaray et al. 2013). Because of issues with youth self-reports and reports by adults, peer nominations have been used and recommended as a method of assessing children's bullying involvement as they provide a collective agreement of bullying involvement from a student perspective, thereby reducing the risk of an individual's response bias (Cornell, Sheras, and Cole 2006; Goossens, Olthof, and Dekker 2006; Paul, Smith, and Blumberg 2013).

In a recent review of measurement issues related to bullying involvement, Casper, Meter, and Card (2015) made several important points about psychometric considerations. First, they stressed the importance of establishing not only reliability, but also validity and measurement equivalence across contexts and intervention conditions when assessing bullying perpetration and victimization in each sample. They also discussed the issues with using multiple reporters of bullying behavior, and the importance of matching informants to specific research goals. Using multitrait-multimethod analyses to form constructs that account for variance shared across reporters is an alternative. Finally, they emphasize the importance of assessing multiple participant roles in bullying as well as using developmentally appropriate measures. There are many issues and challenges that researchers and practitioners face with regard to the definition and assessment of bullying, although progress is being made in having greater uniformity in definitions and precision in measurement.

Special Populations

Race and ethnicity have a complex relation to bullying. Some scholars have suggested that African American students experience higher levels of victimization (Goldweber, Waasdorp, and Bradshaw 2013), whereas others suggest that these students are less likely to be victimized (Graham and Juvonen 2002) when compared to their white peers. Vervoort, Scholte, and Overbeek (2010) found that victimization was more prominent in heterogeneous classrooms, and students from ethnic minorities engaged in higher rates of bullying in more diverse classrooms.

Even if youths of color do not directly experience high levels of traditional forms of bullying, a majority report experiencing some level of racial discrimination (Niwa, Way, and Hughes 2014). It is also possible that youths of color experience transgressions that may not constitute bullying, but rather micro-aggressions, or "brief and commonplace daily, verbal, behavioral, and environmental indignities, whether intentional or unintentional, that communicate hostile, derogatory, or negative racial slights and insults to the target person or group" (Sue et al. 2007, 273). Adults' reported experiences of racial micro-aggressions are correlated with mental health problems (Nadal et al. 2015), and preliminary research suggests that the consequences in terms of psychological and social maladjustment may be similar to those experienced by victims of bullying (Niwa, Way, and Hughes 2014). In addition, Peguero and Williams (2013) found that stereotypes about socioeconomic status, academic performance, and sports participation moderated the effects of race and ethnicity on bullying victimization in a diverse sample. It is possible that statistics that show limited impact of bullying within communities of color may fail to examine stereotyping and micro-aggressions as related issues.

Socioeconomic status (SES) is another factor that has been explored as it relates to bullying. In a meta-analysis by Tippett and Wolke (2014), 28 studies were analyzed that explored the relationship between bullying and SES. Results indicated a weak relationship between SES and bullying, although there was some evidence that low SES increased the likelihood of being a victim or bully-victim. Other research has found suburban schools to be associated with higher rates of bullying (Bradshaw et al. 2009). Clearly, bullying is a pervasive problem that cuts across environments, although it may manifest itself differently, which may have implications for prevention and intervention.

Cyberbullying: Conceptualization and Impact, Technological, and Legal Considerations

There is mixed evidence about the impact of traditional bullying compared to cyberbullying. Some findings comparing the impacts of traditional bullying and cyberbullying found that the effects of traditional bullying lead to more negative outcomes (i.e., psychological arm) over and above the effect of cyberbullying (Campbell et al. 2012; Hase et al. 2015). However, it has also been found that public ridicule by an anonymous perpetrator is the most damaging form of harassment (Sticca and Perren 2013). In one study, experience with cyberbullying both as a perpetrator or a victim contributed to the presence of depressive symptoms and suicidal thoughts significantly more than the effect of traditional bullying (Bonanno and Hymel 2013).

There is an emerging research base on cyberbullying programs. Mishna et al.'s (2009) systematic review found that i-Safe, the Missing Program, and Help, Assert Yourself, Humor, Avoid, Self-talk, Own it (HAHASO) increased knowledge about Internet safety but did not impact risky online behavior. More recently, Della Cioppa, O'Neil, and Craig's (2015) systematic review of cyberbullying programs found that few are rigorously investigated and only three of these programs showed maintenance over time: i-Safe Digital Learning program in the United States (Chibnall et al. 2006), the KiVa Anti-Bullying Program in Finland (Salmivalli, Kärnä, and Poskiparta 2011), and ConRed cyberbullying program in Spain (Ortega-Ruiz, Del Rey, and Casas 2012). These programs offered continued trainer support to schools. Overall, this analysis demonstrated that few programs were sensitive to developmental needs of children, little is known about what actually works, and many programs only focus on peers and teachers but not other adults or contexts in the child's life (i.e., home or extracurricular activities). Van Cleempt and colleagues (2014) conducted a meta-analysis of a wide range of cyberbullying programs, finding modest reductions in cyberbullying across programs. The authors noted that most cyberbullying programs included a curriculum and one other element (e.g., teacher training), in contrast to traditional bullying prevention programs that often contain multiple elements at the school-wide level.

It has been suggested schools need to promote ethical online behavior rather than focusing on reactive approaches to cyberbullying (Couvillon and Ilieva 2011). Adults can promote digital citizenship by establishing clear guidelines for acceptable and unacceptable behavior online to address existing and changing technologies both within and outside of the school. For example, spending more time on the computer and sharing passwords with friends is associated with higher risk of involvement in cyberbullying (Mishna et al. 2012; Smith et al. 2008), so educating students about these facts may help them to make better choices. It is also generally recommended that offensive cyberbullying content should be saved and shared with adults who can further investigate to identify the perpetrator(s) (Diamanduros, Downs, and Jenkins 2008; Snakenborg, Van Acker, and Gable 2011).

A number of websites offer specific strategies, resources, and curriculum activities for educators to address in the school setting and to provide to families for continued discussion at home. NetSmartz (www.netsmartz.org) is an educational website sponsored by the National Center for Missing and Exploited Children (2016), which provides information and training materials for law enforcement, students, families, and educators on being safer online. Common Sense Education (2016) (https://www.commonsensemedia.org/educators/digital-citizenship) provides materials for families, games for students, in addition to training materials for educators. Digital Citizenship: Using Technology Appropriately (http://digitalcitizenship.net/) offers classroom activities to discuss cyber issues and a sample contract promoting appropriate behaviors for being a good digital citizen (Ribble 2016). The Cyberbullying Research Center (http://cyberbullying.org/) provides factsheets for easy distribution, and links to webinar presentations and scholarly publications (Hinduja and Patchin 2016).

Given the new applications and websites that emerge almost daily, schools should take a proactive, multifaceted approach that includes addressing cyberbullying from a technological perspective (see Table 16.2). For example, there are proactive strategies used by social media sites to curtail bullying, such as having mechanisms for users to report abusive content, and providing tools and resources to empower individuals to find help and advocate for themselves, such as removing inappropriate content (Cohen et al. 2014). In addition, schools should have policies that clearly explain the acceptable use of technology, the circumstances in which devices will be confiscated, and the procedure for parental pickup (Snakenborg, Van Acker, and Gable 2011).

Schools must also consider legal issues with cyberbullying. Typically, the controversy lies in balancing avoiding appearing indifferent to the victim's experience of harassment while not overstepping boundaries set forth by the First Amendment guaranteeing free speech. Legal precedent from numerous federal court decisions imply three important factors when considering whether or not the school can forcibly intervene in cases of cyberbullying. Schools can only discipline students if the potential cyber act (i) interferes with the learning or educational processes at school (i.e., if an individual's learning is negatively affected or school cannot proceed); (ii) has occurred with technology owned by the school or on school grounds; and/or (iii) specifically violates the civil rights of other student(s) (for further information and reviews of relevant cases, see Chiquillo 2015; Hinduja and Patchin 2009, 2015; Kowalski, Limber, and Agatston 2008).

Table 16.2 Proactive solutions to reduce cyberbullying on social media.

Strategy	Description	Examples of social media sites
Build automatic filters.	Create a machine algorithm to search text and identify messages that are overtly hostile and contain key words.	Does not exist as an option in most sites.
Have an option for positive and negative feedback (as in a "dislike" and "like" button).	Program the social network site to automatically monitor posts that accrue a specific amount of negative feedback.	Most social media sites offer the opportunity to "like" posts but few offer the option to "dislike."
Ensure messages identified as potentially harmful are flagged and removed from public view.	These messages are removed from public view but remain available for investigations if necessary.	Facebook, Instagram, and Snapchat all have policies for removing from public view messages deemed offensive.
Create a filter for incoming messages like a spam filter.	The filter would identify key words or language that is negative or abusive as well as information about the sender to send to third party (e.g., parent/guardian) who may be able to read them and take the necessary action (e.g., identifying them as false positives, taking actions like contacting the police if necessary).	Most social media sights offer the option to block specific users but do not provide a filter.
Have a mechanism to report content that is abusive and targets a particular individual.	Once an offensive comment is identified, that particular post is frozen and is no longer able to be viewed or edited by the author or others. Law enforcement should have access to these posts to take necessary steps.	Facebook and Instagram allow anyone to report content that may be abusive. Snapchat only allows an individual user and/or their parent or guardian to report specific offensive content.
Provide resources for users of social media for bullying prevention.	Offer users specific strategies and resources if they feel they have been targeted.	Facebook offers a "Bullying Prevention Hub" with specific strategies and resources.

Prevention and Intervention Approaches to Bullying

Meta-analyses have generally revealed that although bullying prevention programs can increase awareness, knowledge, and teacher reports of increased ability to intervene, they do not necessarily produce substantial reductions in bullying behaviors and victimization (Merrell et al. 2008; Smith et al. 2004). Ttofi and Farrington's (2011) meta-analysis of international bullying prevention programs has revealed more promising results. Comprehensive, multicomponent programs (consistent with the Olweus Bullying Prevention Program) demonstrated the largest effect sizes. Programs with more intensive efforts (e.g., intensive training for teachers, more education for students) had a greater impact on both bullying and victimization than briefer programs. The most important program elements in reducing bullying were meetings and training efforts for parents and close playground supervision. Firm disciplinary sanctions for students engaged in bullying such as serious talks, principal referrals, and loss of privileges were also associated with reduced bullying. It should be noted that bullying prevention programs were more effective in Europe and less effective in the United States.

Swearer, Espelage, et al. (2010) cited five possible reasons that whole-school approaches to bullying prevention have been largely ineffective: (i) reliance on self-report of bullying and victimization may not be sufficient in detecting behavioral change; (ii) most programs are not guided by theory; (iii) most programs neglect the social ecology (e.g., peers and families) as targets of intervention; (iv) many programs do not incorporate race, disability, and sexual orientation; and (v) schoolwide programs do not usually include direct interventions for perpetrators.

There is also increasing evidence to suggest that developmental issues play an important role in bullying prevention and intervention approaches. A recent meta-analysis found that although bullying prevention programs showed some effectiveness for youths in grades 7 and below, these results were nullified in grade 8, and were even harmful in grades 9–12 (Yeager et al. 2015). Garandeau, Poskiparta, and Salmivalli (2014) assessed the effectiveness of confronting (e.g., "Bullying behavior is wrong and should stop immediately") and non-confronting (e.g., share concern for victim, ask for suggestions for improvement) approaches to bullying. Although both were found both to be effective (with victims reporting that bullying stopped in 78% of cases), results varied by grade level. The confronting approach was more effective than the non-confronting approach in grades 7–9 and in cases of short-term victimization (e.g., one month or less), but not in grades 1–6 or in cases of long-term victimization, suggesting that younger children who have less developed moral reasoning and perspective-taking skills may benefit from non-confrontational strategies that raise awareness of the victim's suffering (Garandeau et al. 2014). In contrast, a more confrontational approach may be necessary for aggressive adolescents who exhibit advanced moral competence (i.e., know right from wrong), but have low levels of empathy and compassion (Gini, Pozzoli, and Hauser 2011).

Instead of targeting bullying specifically, another approach to preventing bullying and related behaviors is social-emotional learning (SEL), or explicitly teaching skills that may include recognizing and managing emotions, caring and showing concern for others, developing positive relationships, making responsible decisions, and handling challenging situations constructively (Elias et al. 1997). SEL programs have been shown to lead to improved academic functioning and social competence, better school attendance, less disruptive classroom behavior, reduced need for discipline, and lower rates of suspensions (Collaborative for Academic, Social, and Emotional Learning 2012; Durlak et al. 2011). Espelage and colleagues have conducted an ongoing randomized controlled trial of Second Step: Student Success Through Prevention program (Committee for Children 2008), and found that after one year (15 lessons) of implementation, students in schools receiving Second Step were less likely to report engaging in physical fights compared with students in the control schools (Espelage et al. 2013). Two years of implementation resulted in reduced victimization through homophobic name-calling, lower sexual harassment perpetration (Espelage, Low, and Jimerson 2014), and reduced bullying perpetration for students with disabilities (Espelage, Rose, and Polanin 2015) in the Second Step schools compared with youths in the control schools. After three years, there were no direct effects of Second Step on reduced bullying and related aggressive behaviors, but there were significant reductions in delinquency in the first two years which in turn related to significant changes in bullying, cyberbullying, and homophobic name-calling from year 1 to year 3 (Espelage et al. 2015).

Positive Behavioral Interventions and Supports (PBIS) is another comprehensive approach for preventing and intervening with problematic behaviors (Sugai and Horner 2006). Bradshaw and colleagues conducted large-scale randomized controlled trials of PBIS across the state of Maryland, finding that schools using PBIS had reductions in teacher-reported bullying and rejection (Waasdorp, Bradshaw, and Leaf 2012), decreased discipline problems (Bradshaw, Mitchell, and Leaf 2010), and improved school climate (Bradshaw et al. 2009).

There is also some evidence to suggest that targeting the social ecology of the peer group and bystanders may be central to bullying prevention efforts. Polanin, Espelage, and Pigott's (2012) meta-analysis of school-based programs that emphasized changing bystander intervention behavior revealed that samples with high school students only showed greater treatment effects compared to elementary schools only. In addition, the KiVa school-wide bullying prevention program and intervention program, developed in Finland and found to be effective, focuses largely on building "allies" for victims by increasing self-efficacy among bystanders (Williford et al. 2012).

Taken together, these findings suggest that perhaps a narrower focus on bullying is not the best approach, but rather prevention efforts that focus on social-emotional skills, positive behavioral interventions, and the social ecology (role of peers) in bullying may have more promise. Of course, this does not suggest that working with youth who already engage in bullying or who are victims is not important, but from a prevention standpoint it may be that focusing on skills that generalize across healthy behaviors may have promise. Indeed, having sustained, coordinated prevention program efforts is less likely to overwhelm already taxed school systems and lead to better implementation fidelity (Bradshaw 2015).

Conclusion

Bullying has received unprecedented attention in the past two decades, evidenced by legislation, research, and national attention to this issue. Advancements have been made in understanding how bullying is distinct from other aggressive behavior, and who is at risk, with prevalence data highlighting the susceptibility of students with disabilities and those who identify as LGBTQ. From a social-ecological perspective, there are a number of individual and contextual (family, peers, school) factors that can serve as risk or protective factors for bullying involvement. Despite the advancements in the field, challenges remain regarding the best sources and methodologies to obtain precise measurement of bullying according to its definition. There is also more work needed to understand bullying for different populations – for example, the extent to which discrimination, bias, and microaggressions experienced by members of racial and ethnic minority groups are part of the construct of bullying. Cyberbullying, a more recent form of bullying, continues to challenge researchers and practitioners in terms of its conceptualization, the technological advances and outlets for this behavior, and specific legal considerations. Although strides have been made in prevention and intervention, reducing this form of violence, particularly with regard to perpetration, continues to be an area where greater collaboration and focus on social-emotional skill development, positive behavioral interventions, and interventions with the social ecology (e.g., peer group) is needed.

Acknowledgment

We gratefully acknowledge Michelle Crandall and Sebastian Cheong for their contributions.

References

Ahn, H., Rodkin, P.C., and Gest, S. 2013. "Teacher–Student Agreement on "Bullies and Kids They Pick on" in Elementary School Classrooms: Gender and Grade Differences." *Theory Into Practice* 52, 257–263. DOI: 10.1080/00405841.2013.829728.

Astor, R.A., Guerra, N., and Van Acker, R. 2010. "How Can We Improve School Safety Research?" *Educational Researcher* 39, 69–78. DOI: 10.3102/0013189X09357619.

Bear, G.G., Mantz, L.S., Glutting, J.J., Yang, C., and Boyer, D.E. 2015. "Differences in Bullying Victimization Between Students With and Without Disabilities." *School Psychology Review* 44, 98–116. DOI: 10.17105/SPR44-1.98-116.

Beckman, L.l., Hagquist, C., and Hellström, L. 2012. "Does the Association with Psychosomatic Health Problems Differ between Cyberbullying and Traditional Bullying?" *Emotional & Behavioural Difficulties* 17, 421–434. DOI: 10.1080/13632752. 2012.704228.

Bjorkqvist, K., Lagerspetz, K.M.J., and Kaukiainen, A. 1992. "Do Girls Manipulate and Boys Fight? Developmental Trends in Regard to Direct and Indirect Aggression." *Aggressive Behavior* 18, 117–127. DOI: 10.1002/1098-2337(1992)18:2<117::AID-AB2480180205> 3.0.CO;2-3.

Blake, J.J., Lund, E.M., Zhou, Q., Kwok, O.M., and Benz, M.R. 2012. "National Prevalence Rates of Bully Victimization among Students with Disabilities in the United States." *School Psychology Quarterly* 27, 210–222. DOI: 10.1037/spq0000008.

Bonanno, R.A. and Hymel, S. 2013. "Cyber Bullying and Internalizing Difficulties: Above and beyond the Impact of Traditional Forms of Bullying." *Journal of Youth and Adolescence* 42, 685–697. DOI: 10.1007/s10964-013-9937-1.

Borowsky, I.W., Taliaferro, L.A., and McMorris, B.J. 2013. "Suicidal Thinking and Behavior among Youth Involved in Verbal and Social Bullying: Risk and Protective Factors." *Journal of Adolescent Health* 53(1), S4–S12. DOI: 10.1016/j.jadohealth.2012.10.280.

Boulton, M.J., Trueman, M., Chau, C.A.M., Whitehand, C., and Amatya, K. 1999. "Concurrent and Longitudinal Links between Friendship and Peer Victimization: Implications for Befriending Interventions." *Journal of Adolescence* 22, 461–466. DOI: http://dx.doi.org/10.1006/jado.1999.0240.

Bradshaw, C.P. 2015. Translating research to practice in bullying prevention. *American Psychologist*, 70, 322–332. DOI: 10.1037/a0039114.

Bradshaw, C.P., Koth, C.W., Thornton, L.A., and Leaf, P.J. 2009. "Altering School Climate through School-Wide Positive Behavioral Interventions and Supports: Findings from a Group-Randomized Effectiveness Trial." *Prevention Science* 10, 100–115. DOI: 10.1007/ s11121-008-0114-9.

Bradshaw, C.P., Mitchell, M.M., and Leaf, P.J. 2010. "Examining the Effects of School-wide Positive Behavioral Interventions and Supports on Student Outcomes: Results From a Randomized Controlled Effectiveness Trial in Elementary Schools." *Journal of Positive Behavior Interventions* 12, 133–148. DOI: 10.1177/1098300709334798.

Bradshaw, C.P., Sawyer, A.L., and O'Brennan, L.M. 2007. "Bullying and Peer Victimization at School: Perceptual Differences between Students and School Staff." *School Psychology Review* 36, 361–382.

Bradshaw, C.P., Sawyer, A.L., and O'Brennan, L.M. 2009. "A Social Disorganization Perspective on Bullying-Related Attitudes and Behaviors: The Influence of School Context." *American Journal of Community Psychology* 43, 204–220.

Bradshaw, C.P., Waasdorp, T.E., and Johnson, S.L. 2015. "Overlapping Verbal, Relational, Physical, and Electronic Forms of Bullying in Adolescence: Influence of School Context." *Journal of Clinical Child and Adolescent Psychology* 44, 494–508. DOI: 10.1080/15374416.2014.893516.

Brown, S. and Taylor, K. 2008. "Bullying, Education, and Earnings: Evidence from the National Child Development Study." *Economics of Education Review* 27, 387–401. DOI: 10.1016/j.econedurev.2007.03.003.

Campbell, M.M., Spears, B., Slee, P., Butler, D., and Kift, S. 2012. "Victims' Perceptions of Traditional and Cyberbullying, and the Psychosocial Correlates of Their Victimisation." *Emotional & Behavioural Difficulties* 17(3/4), 389–401. DOI: 10.1080/13632752.2012.704316.

Carlyle, K.E. and Steinman, K.J. 2007. "Demographic Differences in the Prevalence, Co-Occurrence, and Correlates of Adolescent Bullying at School." *Journal of School Health* 9, 623–629. DOI: 10.1111/j.1746-1561.2007.00242.x.

Cascardi, M., Brown, C., Iannarone, M., and Cardona, N. 2014. "The Problem with Overly Broad Definitions of Bullying: Implications for the Schoolhouse, the Statehouse, and the Ivory Tower." *Journal of School Violence* 13, 253–276. DOI: 10.1080/15388220.2013.846861.

Casper, D.M., Meter, D.J., and Card, N.A. 2015. "Addressing Measurement Issues Related to Bullying Involvement." *School Psychology Review* 44, 353–371.

Centers for Disease Control and Prevention. 2009a. "2009 High School Youth Risk Behavior Survey." Retrieved from ftp://ftp.cdc.gov/pub/data/yrbs/2009/2009_hs_questionnaire.pdf.

Centers for Disease Control and Prevention. 2009b. "2009 Middle School Youth Risk Behavior Survey." Retrieved from ftp://ftp.cdc.gov/pub/data/yrbs/2009/2009_ms_questionnaire.pdf.

Centers for Disease Control and Prevention. 2010. "Youth Risk Behavior Surveillance – United States, 2009." Retrieved from http://www.cdc.gov/mmwr/pdf/ss/ss5905.pdf.

Centers for Disease Control and Prevention. 2011a. "2011 High School Youth Risk Behavior Survey." Retrieved from ftp://ftp.cdc.gov/pub/data/yrbs/2011/2011_hs_questionnaire.pdf.

Centers for Disease Control and Prevention. 2011b. "2011 Middle School Youth Risk Behavior Survey." Retrieved from ftp://ftp.cdc.gov/pub/data/yrbs/2011/2011_ms_questionnaire.pdf.

Centers for Disease Control and Prevention. 2012. "Youth Risk Behavior Surveillance – United States, 2011." Retrieved from http://www.cdc.gov/mmwr/pdf/ss/ss6104.pdf.

Centers for Disease Control and Prevention. 2014. "Youth Risk Behavior Surveillance – United States, 2013." Retrieved from http://www.cdc.gov/mmwr/pdf/ss/ss6304.pdf.

Centers for Disease Control and Prevention. 2015. "Youth Risk Behavior Surveillance System YRBSS) overview." Retrieved from http://www.cdc.gov/healthyyouth/data/yrbs/overview.htm.

Chibnall, S., Wallace, M., Leicht, C., and Lunghofer L. 2006. "I-safe Evaluation." DOJ Document No. 213715. Washington, DC: National Criminal Justice Reference Service. http://www.ncjrs.gov/pdffiles1/nij/grants/213715.pdf (last accessed October 17, 2017).

Chiquillo, J. 2015. "Four Cases That Test Reach of Student Free-Speech Rights in Age of Cyberbullying." *The Dallas Morning News*, April 27.

Cohen, R., Lam, D.Y., Agarwal, N., Cormier, M., Jagdev, J., Jin, T., Kukreti, M., ... Wexler, M. 2014. "Using Computer Technology to Address the Problem of Cyberbullying." *SIGCAS Computers & Society* 44, 52–61. DOI: 10.1145/2656870.2656876.

Collaborative for Academic, Social, and Emotional Learning. 2012. *Effective Social and Emotional Learning Programs: Preschool and Elementary School Edition*. Chicago: Collaborative for Academic, Social, and Emotional Learning. www.casel.org/guide/.

Committee for Children. 2008. *Second step: Student Success through Prevention Program*. Seattle, WA: Committee for Children.

Common Sense Education. 2016. "Common Sense Education: Digital Citizenship." https://www.commonsensemedia.org/educators/digital-citizenship (last accessed October 17, 2017).

Cook, C.R., Williams, K.R., Guerra, N.G., Kim, T.E., and Sadek, S. 2010. "Predictors of Bullying and Victimization in Childhood and Adolescence: A Meta-analytic Investigation." *School Psychology Quarterly* 25, 65–83. DOI: 10.1037/a0020149.

Copeland, W.E., Wolke, D., Angold, A., and Costello, E.J. 2013. "Adult Psychiatric Outcomes of Bullying and Being Bullied by Peers in Childhood and Adolescence." *JAMA Psychiatry* 70(4), 419–426. DOI: 10.1001/jamapsychiatry.2013.504.

Cornell, D., Sheras, P., and Cole, J. 2006. "Assessment of Bullying." In *The Handbook of School Violence and School Safety: From Research to Practice*, edited by S.R. Jimerson and M.J. Furlong, pp. 191–210. Mahwah, NJ: Lawrence Erlbaum.

Cosgrove, H. and Nickerson, A.B. 2017. "Anti-bullying/harassment Legislation and Educator Perceptions of Severity, Effectiveness, and School Climate: A Cross-Sectional Analysis." *Educational Policy* 31(4), 518–545.

Couvillon, M.A. and Ilieva, V. 2011. "Recommended Practices: A Review of Schoolwide Preventative Programs and Strategies on Cyberbullying." *Preventing School Failure* 55, 96–101. DOI: 10.1080/1045988X.2011.539461.

Crick, N.R. and Grotpeter, J.K. 1995. "Relational Aggression, Gender, and Social-Psychological Adjustment." *Child Development* 66, 710–722. DOI: 10.1111/j.1467-8624.1995.tb00900.x.

Crick, N.R. and Grotpeter, J.K. 1996. "Children's Mistreatment by Peers: Victims of Relational and Overt Aggression." *Development and Psychopathology* 8, 367–380. DOI: 10.1017/S0954579400007148.

Cunningham, N.J. 2007. "Level of Bonding to School and Perception of the School Environment by Bullies, Victims, and Bully Victims." *Journal of Early Adolescence* 27, 457–478. DOI: 10.1177/0272431607302940.

Currie, C., Zanotti, C., Morgan, A., Currie, D., DeLooze, M., Roberts, C., Samdal, O., Smith, O.R.F., and Barnekow, V. 2012. "Social Determinants of Health and Well-being among Young People." *Health Behaviour in School-aged Children (HBSC) Study: International Report from the 2009/2010 Survey*. Copenhagen, WHO Regional Office for Europe, 2012 (Health Policy for Children and Adolescents, No. 6).

D'Augelli, A.R., Pilkington, N.W., and Hershberger, S.L. 2002. "Incidence and Mental Health Impact of Sexual Orientation Victimization of Lesbian, Gay, and Bisexual Youths in High School." *School Psychology Quarterly* 17, 148–167. DOI: 10.1521/scpq.17.2.148.20854.

Davidson, L.M. and Demaray, M.K. 2007. "Social Support as a Moderator between Victimization and Internalizing/Externalizing Behaviors from Bullying." *School Psychology Review* 36, 383–405.

Della Cioppa, V., O'Neil, A., and Craig, W. 2015. "Learning from Traditional Bullying Interventions: A Review of Research on Cyberbullying and Best Practice." *Aggression and Violent Behavior* 23, 61–68. DOI: 10.1016/j.avb.2015.05.009.

Demaray, M.K., Malecki, C.K., Secord, S.M., and Lyell, K.M. 2013. "Agreement among Students', Teachers' and Parents' Perceptions of Victimization by Bullying." *Children and Youth Services Review* 35, 2091–2100. DOI: 10.1016/j.childyouth.2013.10.018.

Diamanduros, T., Downs, E., and Jenkins, S.J. 2008. "The Role of School Psychologists in the Assessment, Prevention, and Intervention of Cyberbullying." *Psychology in the Schools* 45(8), 693–704. DOI: 10.1002/pits.20335.

Dinkes, R., Kemp, J., Baum, K., and Snyder, T.D. 2009. *Indicators of School Crime and Safety: 2009* (NCES 2010–012/ NCJ 228478). National Center for Education Statistics, Institute of Education Sciences, US Department of Education, and Bureau of Justice Statistics, Office of Justice Programs, US Department of Justice. Washington, DC.

Dooley, J.J., Pyzalski, J., and Cross, D. 2009. "Cyberbullying versus Face-to-Face Bullying: A Theoretical and Conceptual Review." *Journal of Psychology* 217(4), 182–188. DOI: 10.1027/0044-3409.217.4.182.

Dukes, R.L., Stein, J.A., and Zane, J.I. 2010. "Gender Differences in the Relative Impact of Physical and Relational Bullying on Adolescent Injury and Weapon Carrying." *Journal of School Psychology* 48(6), 511–532. DOI: 10.1016/j.jsp.2010.08.001.

Durlak, J.A., Weissberg, R.P., Dymnicki, A.B., Taylor, R.D., and Schellinger, K.B. 2011. "The Impact of Enhancing Students' Social and Emotional Learning: A Meta-Analysis of School-based Universal Interventions." *Child Development* 82(1), 405–432. DOI: 10.1111/j.14678624.2010.01564.x.

Elgar, F.J., Napoletano, A., Saul, G., Dirks, M.A., Craig, W., Poteat, V.P., Holt, M., and Koenig, B.W. 2014). "Cyberbullying Victimization and Mental Health in Adolescents and the Moderating Role of Family Dinners." *JAMA Pediatrics* 168(11), 1015–1022. DOI: 10.1001/jamapediatrics.2014.1223.

Elias, M.J., Zins, J.E., Weissberg, R.P., Frey, K.S., Greenberg, M.T., Haynes, N.M., … Shriver, T.P. 1997. *Promoting Social and Emotional Learning: Guidelines for Educators.* Alexandria, VA: Association for Supervision and Curriculum Development.

Erdur-Baker, Ö. 2010. "Cyberbullying and Its Correlation to Traditional Bullying, Gender and Frequent and Risky Usage of Internet-Mediated Communication Tools." *New Media and Society* 12, 109–125. DOI: 10.1177/1461444809341260.

Espelage, D.L., Basile, K.C., and Hamburger, M.E. 2012. "Bullying Perpetration and Subsequent Sexual Violence Perpetration among Middle School Students." *Journal of Adolescent Health* 50, 60–65. DOI: 10.1016/j.jadohealth.2011.07.015.

Espelage, D.L. and Holt, M.K. 2013. "Suicidal Ideation and School Bullying Experiences after Controlling for Depression and Delinquency." *Journal of Adolescent Health* 53, S27–S31. DOI: 10.1016/j.jadohealth.2012.09.017.

Espelage, D.L., Hong, J.S., Rao, M.A., and Thornberg, R. 2015. "Understanding Ecological Factors Associated with Bullying across the Elementary to Middle School Transition in the United States." *Violence and* Victims 30, 470–487. DOI: 10.1891/0886-6708. VV-D-14-00046.

Espelage, D.L., Low, S., and Jimerson, S. 2014. "Understanding School Climate, Aggression, Peer Victimization, and Bully Perpetration: Contemporary Science, Practice, and Policy." *School Psychology Quarterly* 29, 233–237. DOI: 10.1037/spq0000090.

Espelage, D.L., Low, S., Polanin, J., and Brown, E. 2013. "The Impact of a Middle-School Program to Reduce Aggression, Victimization, and Sexual Violence." *Journal of Adolescent Health* 53, 180–186. DOI: 10.1016/j.jadohealth.2013.02.021.

Espelage, D.L., Low, S., Van Ryzin, M.J., and Polanin, J.R. 2015. "Clinical Trial of Second Step Middle School Program: Impact on Bullying, Cyberbullying, Homophobic Teasing, and Sexual Harassment Perpetration." *School Psychology Review* 44, 464–479.

Espelage, D.L., Rose, C.A., and Polanin, J.R. 2015. "Social-Emotional Learning Program to Reduce Bullying, Fighting, and Victimization among Middle School Students with Disabilities." *Remedial and Special Education* 36, 299–311. DOI: 10.1177/0741932514564564.

Espelage, D.L. and Swearer, S.M. 2009. "Contributions of Three Social Theories to Understanding Bullying Perpetration and Victimization among School-Aged Youth." In *Bullying, Rejection, and Peer Victimization: A Social Cognitive Neuroscience Perspective*, edited by M.J. Harris, pp. 151–170. New York: Springer.

Estell, D.B., Farmer, T.W., Irvin, M.J., Crowther, A., Akos, P., and Boudah, D.J. 2009. "Students with Exceptionalities and the Peer Group Context of Bullying and Victimization in Late Elementary School." *Journal of Child and Family Studies* 18, 136–150. DOI: 10.1007/s10826-008-9214-1.

Faith, M.A., Reed, G., Heppner, C.E., Hamill, L.C., Tarkenton T.R., and Donewar, C.W. 2015. "Bullying in Medically Fragile Youth: A Review of Risks, Protective Factors, and Recommendations for Medical Providers." *Journal of Developmental & Behavioral Pediatrics* 36, 285–301. DOI: 10.1097/DBP.0000000000000155.

Farmer, T., Wike, T.L., Alexander, Q.R., Rodkin, P.C., and Mehtaji, M. 2015. "Students with Disabilities and Involvement in Peer Victimization: Theory, Research, and Considerations for the Future." *Remedial and Special Education* 36, 263–274. DOI: 10.1177/0741932515572911.

Farrington, D.P. and Ttofi, M.M. 2011. "Bullying as a Predictor of Offending, Violence and Later Life Outcomes." *Criminal Behaviour and Mental Health* 21(2), 90–98. DOI: 10.1002/cbm.801.

Felix, E.D., Sharkey, J.D., Green, J.G., Furlong, M.J., and Tanigawa, D. 2011. "Getting Precise and Pragmatic about the Assessment of Bullying: The Development of the California Bullying Victimization Scale." *Aggressive Behavior* 37, 234–247. DOI: 10.1002/ab.20389.

Galen, B.R. and Underwood, M.K. 1997. "A Developmental Investigation of Social Aggression among Children." *Developmental Psychology* 33, 589–600. DOI: 10.1037/0012-1649.33.4.589.

Garandeau, C.F., Poskiparta, E., and Salmivalli, C. 2014. "Tackling Acute Cases of School Bullying in the Kiva Anti-Bullying Program: A Comparison of Two Approaches." *Journal of Abnormal Child Psychology* 42, 981–991. DOI: 10.1007/s10802-014-9861-1.

Gini, G. and Pozzoli, T. 2009. "Association between Bullying and Psychosomatic Problems: A Meta-analysis." *Pediatrics* 123, 1059–1065. DOI: 10.1542/peds.2008-1215.

Gini, G., Pozzoli, T., and Hauser, M. 2011. "Bullies Have Enhanced Moral Competence to Judge Relative to Victims, But Lack Moral Compassion." *Personality and Individual Differences* 50(5), 603–608. DOI: 10.1016/j.paid.2010.12.002.

Gladden, R.M., Vivolo-Kantor, A.M., Hamburger, M.E., and Lumpkin, C.D. 2014. *Bullying Surveillance among Youth: Uniform Definitions for Public Health and Recommended Data Elements, Version 1.0.* Atlanta, GA: National Center for Injury Prevention and Control, Centers for Disease Control and Prevention and US Department of Education.

Glew, G.M., Fan, M., Katon, W.J., Rivara, F.P., and Kernic, M.A. 2005. "Bullying, Psychosocial Adjustment, and Academic Performance in Elementary School." *Archives of Pediatric and Adolescent Medicine* 159, 1026–1031. DOI: 10.1001/archpedi.159.11.1026.

Goldweber, A., Waasdorp, T.E., and Bradshaw, C.P. 2013. "Examining the Link between Forms of Bullying Behaviors and Perceptions of Safety and Belonging among Secondary School Students." *Journal of School Psychology* 51(4), 469–485. DOI: 10.1016/j.jsp.2013.04.004.

Goossens, F.A., Olthof, T., and Dekker, P.H. 2006. "New Participant Role Scales: Comparison between Various Criteria for Assigning Roles and Indications for Their Validity." *Aggressive Behavior* 32, 343–357. DOI: 10.1002/ab.20133.

Graham, S., Bellmore, A., Nishina, A., and Juvonen, J. 2009. "'It must be me': Ethnic Diversity and Attributions for Peer Victimization in Middle School." *Journal of Youth and Adolescence* 38, 487–499. DOI: 10.1007/s10964-008-9386-4.

Graham, S. and Juvonen, J. 1998. "Self-blame and Peer Victimization in Middle School: An Attributional Analysis." *Developmental Psychology* 34, 587–599. DOI: 10.1037/0012-1649.34.3.587.

Graham, S. and Juvonen, J. 2002. "Ethnicity, Peer Harassment, and Adjustment in Middle School: An Exploratory Study." *Journal of Early Adolescence* 22, 173–199. DOI: 10.1177/0272431602022002003.

Greco, L.A., Freeman, K.E., and Dufton, L. 2010. "Overt and Relational Victimization among Children with Frequent Abdominal Pain: Links to Social Skills, Academic Functioning, and Health Service Use." *Journal of Pediatric Psychology* 32, 319–329. DOI: 10.1093/jpepsy/jsl016.

Hase, C.N., Goldberg, S.B., Smith, D., Stuck, A., and Campain, J. 2015. "Impacts of Traditional Bullying and Cyberbullying on the Mental Health of Middle School and High School Students." *Psychology in the Schools* 52, 607–617. DOI: 10.1002/pits.21841.

Hatzenbuehler, M.L., Schwab-Reese, L., Ranapurwala, S.I., Hertz, M.F., and Ramirez, M.R. 2015. "Associations between Antibullying Policies and Bullying in 25 States." *JAMA Pediatrics* 169(10): e152411. DOI: 10.1001/jamapediatrics.2015.2411.

Haynie, D.L., Nansel, T., Eitel, P., Crump, A.D., Saylor, K., Yu, K., and Simons-Morton, B. 2001. "Bullies, Victims, and Bully/Victims: Distinct Groups of At-Risk Youth." *Journal of Early Adolescence* 21, 29–49. DOI: 10.1177/0272431601021001002.

Hinduja, S. and Patchin, J.W. 2009. *Bullying beyond the Schoolyard: Preventing and Responding to Cyberbullying.* Thousand Oaks, CA: Corwin Press.

Hinduja, S. and Patchin, J.W. 2010. "Bullying, Cyberbullying, and Suicide." *Archives of Suicide Research* 14, 206–221. DOI: 10.1080/13811118.2010.494133.

Hinduja, S. and Patchin, J.W. 2015. *Bullying beyond the Schoolyard: Preventing and Responding to Cyberbullying,* 2nd ed. Thousand Oaks, CA: Corwin Press.

Hinduja, S. and Patchin, J.W. 2016. *The Cyberbullying Research Center.* Retrieved from http://cyberbullying.org/.

Hoff, D.L. and Mitchell, S.N. 2008. "Cyberbullying: Causes, Effects, and Remedies." *Journal of Educational Administration* 47, 652–665. DOI: 10.1108/09578230910981107.

Hugh-Jones, S. and Smith, P.K. 1999. "Self-reports of Short- and Long-Term Effects of Bullying on Children Who Stammer." *British Journal of Educational Psychology* 69, 141–158. DOI: 10.1348/000709999157626.

Hutchinson, M. 2012. "Exploring the Impact of Bullying on Young Bystanders." *Educational Psychology in Practice* 28, 425–442. DOI: 10.1080/02667363.2012.727785.

Ivarsson, T., Broberg, A.G., Arvidsson, T., and Gillberg, C. 2005. "Bullying in Adolescence: Psychiatric Problems in Victims and Bullies as Measured by the Youth Self Report (YSR) and the Depression Self-Rating Scale (DSRS)." *Nordic Journal of Psychiatry* 59, 365–373. DOI: 10.1080/08039480500227816.

Jansen, P.W., Verlinden, M., Berkel, A.D., Mieloo, C.L., Raat, H., Hofman, A., ... and Tiemeier, H. 2014. "Teacher and Peer Reports of Overweight and Bullying among Young Primary School Children." *Pediatrics* 134(3), 473–480. DOI: 10.1542/peds.2013-3274.

Janson, G.R. and Hazler, R.J. 2004. "Trauma Reactions of Bystanders and Victims to Repetitive Abuse Experiences. *Violence and Victims* 19, 239–255. DOI: 10.1891/vivi.19.2.239.64102.

Juvonen, J., Nishina, A., and Graham, S. 2000. "Peer Harassment, Psychological Adjustment, and School Functioning in Early Adolescence." *Journal of Educational Psychology* 92, 349–359. DOI: 10.1037/0022-0663.92.2.349.

Kaltiala-Heino, R., Rimpelä, M., Rantanen, P., and Rimpelä, A. 2000. "Bullying at School— An Indicator of Adolescents at Risk for Mental Disorders." *Journal of Adolescence* 23, 661–674. DOI: 10.1006/jado.2000.0351.

Kert, A.S., Codding, R.S., Tryon, G.S., and Shiyko, M. 2010. "Impact of the Word 'Bully' on the Reported Rate of Bullying Behavior." *Psychology in the Schools* 47, 193–204. DOI: 10.1002/pits.20464.

Khoury-Kassabri, M., Benbenishty, R., Astor, R.A., and Zeira, A. 2004. "The Contributions of Community, Family, and School Variables to Student Victimization." *American Journal of Community Psychology* 34, 187–204. DOI: 10.1007/s10464-004-7414-4.

Kim, M.J., Catalano, R.F., Haggerty, K.P., and Abbott, R.D. 2011. "Bullying at Elementary School and Problem Behaviour in Young Adulthood: A Study of Bullying, Violence and Substance Use from Age 11 to Age 21." *Criminal Behaviour and Mental Health* 21, 136–144. DOI: 10.1002/cbm.804.

Klomek, A.B., Marrocco, F., Kleinman, M., Schonfeld, I.S., and Gould, M.S. 2007. "Bullying, Depression, and Suicidality in Adolescents." *Journal of the American Academy of Child and Adolescent Psychiatry* 46, 40–49. DOI: 10.1097/01.chi.0000242237.84925.18.

Klomek, A.B., Sourander, A., Niemelä, S., Kumpulainen, K., Piha, J., Tamminen, T., and ... Gould, M.S. 2009. "Childhood Bullying Behaviors as a Risk for Suicide Attempts and Completed Suicides: A Population-based Birth Cohort Study." *Journal of the American Academy of Child & Adolescent Psychiatry* 48, 254–261. DOI: 10.1097/CHI.0b013e318196b91f.

Kochenderfer, B.J. and Ladd, G.W. 1996. "Peer Victimization: Cause or Consequence of School Maladjustment?" *Child Development* 67, 1305–1317. DOI: 10.1111/j.1467-8624.1996.tb01797.x.

Konishi, C., Hymel, S., Zumbo, B.D., and Li, Z. 2010. "Do School Bullying and Student–Teacher Elations Matter for Academic Achievement?: A Multilevel Analysis." *Canadian Journal of School Psychology* 25, 19–39. DOI: 10.1177/0829573509357550.

Koo, H. 2007. "A Timeline of the Evolution of School Bullying In Differing Social Contexts." *Asia Pacific Education Review* 8(1), 107–116. DOI: 10.1007/BF03025837.

Kosciw, J.G., Greytak, E.A., and Diaz, E.M. 2009. "Who, What, When, Where, and Why: Demographic and Ecological Factors Contributing to Hostile School Climate for Lesbian, Gay, Bisexual, and Transgender Youth." *Journal of Youth and Adolescence* 38, 976–988. DOI: 10.1007/s10964-009-9412-1.

Kosciw, J.G., Greytak, E.A., Diaz, E.M., and Bartkiewicz, M.J. 2010. *The 2009 National School Climate Survey: The Experiences of Lesbian, Gay, Bisexual, and Transgender Youth in Our Nation's Schools.* New York: GLSEN.

Kowalski, R.M. and Limber, S.P. 2007. "Electronic Bullying among Middle School Students." *Journal of Adolescent Health* 41, S22–S30. DOI: 10.1016/j.jadohealth.2007. 08.017.

Kowalski, R.M. and Limber, S.P. 2013. "Psychological, Physical, and Academic Correlates of Cyberbullying and Traditional Bullying." *Journal of Adolescent Health* 53, S13–S20. DOI: 10.1016/j.jadohealth.2012.09.018.

Kowalski, R.M., Limber, S.P., and Agatston, P.W. 2008. *Cyberbullying: Bullying in the Digital Age.* Malden, MA: Blackwell.

Langos, C. 2012. "Cyberbullying: The Challenge to Define." *Cyberpsychology, Behavior, and Social Networking* 15(6), 285–289. DOI: 10.1089/cyber.2011.0588.

Larkin, R.W. 2009. "The Columbine Legacy: Rampage Shootings as Political Acts." *American Behavioral Scientist* 52, 1309–1326. DOI: 10.1177/0002764209332548.

Law, D.M., Shapka, J.D., Domene, J.F., and Gagne, M.H. 2012. "Are Cyberbullies Really Bullies? An Investigation of Reactive and Proactive Online Aggression." *Computers in Human Behavior* 28, 664–672. DOI: 10.1016/j.chb.2011.11.013.

Law, D.M., Shapka, J.D., Hymel, S., Olson, B.F., and Waterhouse, T. 2012. "The Changing Face of Bullying: An Empirical Comparison between Traditional and Internet Bullying and Victimization." *Computers in Human Behavior* 28, 226–232. DOI: 10.1016/j. chb.2011.09.004.

Li, Q. 2008. "A Cross-cultural Comparison of Adolescents' Experience Related to Cyberbullying." *Educational Research* 50(3), 223–234. DOI: 10.1080/00131880802309333.

Lösel, F. and Bender, D. 2011. "Emotional and Antisocial Outcomes of Bullying and Victimization at School: A Follow-up from Childhood to Adolescence." *Journal of Aggression, Conflict and Peace Research* 3, 89–96.

Machmutow, K., Perren, S.P., Sticca, F., and Alsaker, F.D. 2012. "Peer Victimisation and Depressive Symptoms: Can Specific Coping Strategies Buffer the Negative Impact of Cybervictimisation?" *Emotional and Behavioural Difficulties* 17, 403–420. DOI:10.1080/ 13632752.2012.704310.

McDougall, P. and Vaillancourt, T. 2015. "Long-term Adult Outcomes of Peer Victimization in Childhood and Adolescence: Pathways to Adjustment and Maladjustment." *American Psychologist* 70, 300–310. DOI: 10.1037/a0039174.

McGuire, J.K., Anderson, C.R., Toomey, R.B., and Russell, S.T. 2010. "School Climate for Transgender Youth: A Mixed Method Investigation of Student Experiences and School Responses." *Journal of Youth and Adolescence* 39, 1175–1188. DOI: 10.1007/ s10964-010-9540-7.

Meltzer, H., Vostanis, P., Ford, T., Bebbington, P., and Dennis, M.S. 2011. "Victims of Bullying in Childhood and Suicide Attempts in Adulthood." *European Psychiatry* 26, 49–8503. DOI: 10.1016/j.eurpsy.2010.11.006.

Merrell, K.W., Gueldner, B.A., Ross, S.W., and Isava, D.M. 2008. "How Effective Are School Bullying Intervention Programs? A Meta-Analysis of Intervention Research." *School Psychology Quarterly* 23, 26–42. DOI: 10.1037/1045-3830.23.1.26.

Mishna, F., Cook, C., Saini, M., Wu, M.-J., and MacFadden, R. 2009. "Interventions for Children, Youth, and Parents to Prevent and Reduce Cyber Abuse." *Campbell Systematic Reviews* 2, 1–54.

Mishna, F., Khoury-Kassabri, M., Gadalla, T., and Daciuk, J. 2012. "Risk Factors for Involvement in Cyberbullying: Victims, Bullies and Bully–Victims." *Children and Youth Services Review* 34, 63–70. DOI: 10.1016/j.childyouth.2011.08.032.

Modecki, K.L., Minchin, J.M., Harbaugh, A.G., Guerra, N.G., and Runions, K.C. 2014. "Bullying Prevalence across Contexts: A Meta-Analysis Measuring Cyber and Traditional Bullying." *Journal of Adolescent Health* 55, 602–611. DOI: 10.1016/j.jadohealth.2014.06.007.

Nadal, K.L., Wong, Y., Sriken, J., Griffin, K., and Fujii-Doe, W. 2015. "Racial Microaggressions and Asian Americans: An Exploratory Study on Within-Group Differences and Mental Health." *Asian American Journal of Psychology* 6, 136–144. DOI: 10.1037/a0038058.

Nansel, T.R., Haynie, D.L., and Simons-Morton, B.G. 2003. "The Association of Bullying and Victimization with Middle School Adjustment." *Journal of Applied School Psychology* 19, 45–61. DOI: 10.1300/J008v19n02_04.

National Center for Education Statistics 2000. "School Survey on Crime and Safety." https://nces.ed.gov/surveys/ssocs/pdf/SSOCS_2000_Questionnaire.pdf (last accessed October 17, 2017).

National Center for Education Statistics 2010. "School Survey on Crime and Safety." https://nces.ed.gov/surveys/ssocs/pdf/SSOCS_2010_Questionnaire.pdf (last accessed October 17, 2017).

National Center for Missing and Exploited Children 2016. *Netsmartz Workshop: A Program of The National Center for Missing and Exploited Children.* Retrieved from www.netsmartz.org.

Newman, M.L., Holden, G.W., and Delville, Y. 2004. "Isolation and the Stress of Being Bullied." *Journal of Adolescence* 28, 343–357. DOI: 10.1016/j.adolescence.2004.08.002.

Nickerson, A.B. and Orrange-Torchia, T. 2015. "The Mental Health Impact of Bullying." In *The Challenges of Youth Bullying and Suicide*, edited by P. Goldblum, D. Espelage, J. Chu, and B. Bongar, pp. 39–49. New York: Oxford University Press.

Nickerson, A.B., Singleton, D., Schnurr, B., and Collen, M. 2014. "Perceptions of School Climate as a Function of Bullying Involvement." *Journal of Applied School Psychology* 30, 157–181. DOI: 10.1080/15377903.2014.888530.

Nickerson, A.B. and Slater, E.D. 2009. "School and Community Violence and Victimization as Predictors of Adolescent Suicidal Behavior." *School Psychology Review* 38, 218–232.

Nishina, A. and Juvonen, J. 2005. "Daily Reports of Witnessing and Experiencing Peer Harassment in Middle School." *Child Development* 76, 435–450. DOI: 10.1111/j.1467-8624.2005.00855.x.

Niwa, E.Y., Way, N., and Hughes, D.L. 2014. "Trajectories of Ethnic-Racial Discrimination among Ethnically Diverse Early Adolescents: Associations with Psychological and Social Adjustment." *Child Development* 85, 2339–2354. DOI: 10.1111/cdev.12310.

O'Brennan, L.M., Bradshaw, C.P. and Sawyer, A.L. 2009. "Examining Developmental Differences in the Social-Emotional Problems among Frequent Bullies, Victims, and Bully/Victims." *Psychology in the Schools* 46, 100–115. DOI: 10.1002/pits.20357.

Olweus, D. 1978. *Aggression in the Schools: Bullies and Whipping Boys.* Washington, DC: Hemisphere Press (Wiley).

Olweus, D. 1999. "Sweden." In *The nature of school bullying: A cross-national perspective*, edited by P.K. Smith, Y. Morita, J. Junger-Tas, D. Olweus, R. Catalano, and P. Slee, pp. 7–27. New York: Routledge.

Ortega-Ruiz, R., Del Rey, R., and Casas, J.A. 2012. "Knowing, Building and Living Together on Internet and Social Networks: The Conred Cyberbullying Prevention Program." *International Journal of Conflict and Violence* 6, 303–312.

Patchin, J. and Hinduja, S. 2006. "Bullies Move beyond the School Yard: A Preliminary Look at Cyberbullying." *Youth Violence and Juvenile Justice* 4, 148–169. DOI: 10.1177/154120400628628.

Paul, S., Smith, P.K., and Blumberg, H.H. 2013. "Surveying Bullying Using Peer Nomination Methods." *Pediatrics Today* 9, 102–111. DOI: 10.5457/p2005-114.67.

Peguero, A.A. and Williams, L.M. 2013. "Racial and Ethnic Stereotypes and Bullying Victimization." *Youth & Society* 45(4), 545–564. DOI: 10.1177/0044118X11424757.

Perlus, J.G., Brooks-Russell, A., Wang, J., and Iannotti, R.J. 2014. "Trends in Bullying, Physical Fighting, and Weapon Carrying among 6th- through 10th-Grade Students from 1998 to 2010: Findings from a national Study." *American Journal of Public Health* 104, 1100–1106. DOI: 10.2105/AJPH.2013.301761.

Polanin, J.R., Espelage, D.L., and Pigott, T.D. 2012. "A meta-analysis of School-based Bulling Prevention Programs' Effects on Bystander Intervention Behavior." *School Psychology Review* 41, 47–65.

Poteat, V.P., O' Dwyer, L.M., and Mereish, E.H. 2012. "Changes in How Students Use and Are Called Homophobic Epithets over Time: Patterns Predicted by Gender, Bullying and Victimization Status." *Journal of Educational Psychology* 104, 393–406. DOI: 10.1037/a0026437.

Poteat, V.P. and Russell, S.T. 2013. "Understanding Homophobic Behavior and Its Implications for Policy and Practice." *Theory Into Practice* 52, 264–271. DOI: 10.1080/00405841.2013.829729.

Renda, J., Vassallo, S., and Edwards, B. 2011. "Bullying in Early Adolescence and Its Association with Anti-social Behaviour, Criminality and Violence 6 and 10 Years Later." *Criminal Behaviour and Mental Health* 21, 117–127. DOI: 10.1002/cbm.805.

Ribble, M. 2016. "Digital Citizenship: Using Technology Appropriately." Retrieved from http://digitalcitizenship.net/.

Rivers, I. 2011. "Morbidity among Bystanders of Bullying Behaviors at School: Concepts, Concerns, and Clinical/Research Issues." *International Journal of Adolescent Medicine and Health* 24, 11–16. DOI: 10.1515/ijamh.2012.003.

Rivers, I. and Noret, N. 2010. "'I h8 u': Findings from a Five-Year Study of Text and Email Bullying." *British Educational Research Journal* 36, 643–671. DOI: 10.1080/01411920903071918.

Rivers, I., Poteat, V.P., Noret, N., and Ashurst, N. 2009. "Observing Bullying at School: The Mental Health Implications of Witness Status." *School Psychology Quarterly* 24, 211–223. DOI: 10.1037/a0018164.

Rodkin, P.C., Espelage, D.L., and Hanish, L.D. 2015. "A Relational Framework for Understanding Bullying: Developmental Antecedents and Outcomes." *American Psychologist* 70, 311–321.

Rose, C.A., Espelage, D.L., and Monda-Amaya, L.E. 2009. "Bullying and Victimization Rates among Students in General and Special Education: A Comparative Analysis." *Educational Psychology* 29, 761–776. DOI: 10.1080/01443410903254864.

Rose, C.A., Monda-Amaya, L.E., and Espelage, D.L. 2011. "Bullying Perpetration and Victimization in Special Education: A Review of the Literature." *Remedial and Special Education* 32, 114–130. DOI: 10.1177/0741932510361247.

Rose, C.A., Nickerson, A.B., and Stormont, M. 2015. "Advancing Bullying Research from a Social-Ecological Lens: An Introduction to the Special Issue." *School Psychology Review* 44, 339–352.

Sainio, M., Veenstra, R., Huitsing, G., and Salmivalli, C. 2010. "Victims and Their Defenders: A Dyadic Approach." *International Journal of Behavioural Development* 35, 144–151. DOI: 10.1177/0165025410378068.

Salmivalli, C., Kärnä, A., and Poskiparta, E. 2011. "Counteracting Bullying in Finland: The KiVa Program and Its Effects on Different Forms of Being Bullied." *International Journal of Behavioral Development* 35, 405–411. DOI: 10.1177/0165025411407457.

Salmivalli, C., Lagerspetz, K., Björkqvist, K., Österman, K., and Kaukiainen, A. 1996. "Bullying as a Group Process: Participant Roles and Their Relations to Social Status within the Group." *Aggressive Behavior* 22, 1–15. DOI: 10.1002/(SICI)1098-2337(1996)22:1<1::AID-AB1>3.0.CO;2-T.

Sansone, R.A., Leung, J.S., and Wiederman, M.W. 2013. "Self-reported Bullying in Childhood: Relationships with Employment in Adulthood." *International Journal of Psychiatry in Clinical Practice* 17, 64–68. DOI: 10.3109/13651501.2012.709867.

Schwartz, D., Gorman, A.H., Nakamoto, J., and Toblin, R.L. 2005. "Victimization in the Peer Group and Children's Academic Functioning." *Journal of Educational Psychology* 97, 425–435. DOI: 10.1037/0022-0663.97.3.425.

Slonje, R. and Smith, P.K. 2008. "Cyberbullying: Another Main Type of Bullying?" *Scandinavian Journal of Psychology* 49, 147–154. DOI: 10.1111/j.1467-9450.2007.00611.x.

Smith, J.D., Schneider, B.H., Smith, P.K., and Ananiadou, K. 2004. "The Effectiveness of Whole-School Antibullying Programs: A Synthesis of Evaluation Research." *School Psychology Review* 33, 54–560.

Smith, P.K., Mahdavi, J., Carvalho, M., Fisher, S., Russell, S., and Tippett, N. 2008. "Cyberbullying: Its Nature and Impact in Secondary School Pupils." *Journal of Child Psychology and Psychiatry* 49, 376–385. DOI: 10.1111/j.1469-7610.2007.01846.x.

Snakenborg, J., Van Acker, R., and Gable, R.A. 2011. "Cyberbullying: Prevention and Intervention to Protect Our Children and Youth." *Preventing School Failure* 55, 88–95. DOI: 10.1080/1045988X.2011.539454.

Solberg, M. and Olweus, D. 2003. "Prevalence Estimation of School Bullying with the Olweus/Bully Victim Questionnaire." *Aggressive Behavior* 29, 239–268. DOI: http://dx.doi.org/10.1002/ab.10047.

Sourander, A., Jensen, P., Rönning, J.A., Niemelä, S., Helenius, H., Sillanmäki, L., and … Almqvist, F. 2007. "What Is the Early Adulthood Outcome of Boys Who Bully or Are Bullied in Childhood? The Finnish 'From a Boy to a Man' Study." *Pediatrics* 120, 397–404. DOI: 10.1542/peds.2006-2704.

Sourander, A., Klomek, A.B., Kumpulainen, K., Puustjärvi, A., Elonheimo, H., Ristkari, T., and … Ronning, J.A. 2011. "Bullying at Age Eight and Criminality in Adulthood: Findings from the Finnish Nationwide 1981 Birth Cohort Study." *Social Psychiatry and Psychiatric Epidemiology* 46, 1211–1219. DOI: 10.1007/s00127-010-0292-1.

Sticca, F. and Perren, S. 2013. "Is Cyberbullying Worse than Traditional Bullying? Examining the Differential Roles of Medium, Publicity, and Anonymity for the Perceived Severity of Bullying." *Journal of Youth Adolescence* 42, 739–750. DOI: 10.1007/s10964-012-9867-3.

Stockdale, M.S., Hangaduambo, S., Duys, D., Larson, K., and Sarvela, P.D. 2002. "Rural Elementary Students', Parents', and Teachers' Perceptions of Bullying." *American Journal of Health Behavior* 26, 266–277.

Stuart-Cassel, V., Bell, A., and Springer, J.F. 2011. *Analysis of State Bullying Laws and Policies*. Folsom, CA: EMT Associates.

Sue, D.W., Capodilupo, C.M., Torino, G.C., Bucceri, J.M., Holder, A.B., Nadal, K.L., and Esquilin, M. 2007. "Racial Microaggressions in Everyday Life: Implications for Clinical Practice." *American Psychologist* 62, 271–286. DOI: 10.1037/0003-066X.62.4.271.

Sugai, G. and Horner, R. 2006. "A Promising Approach for Expanding and Sustaining School-wide Positive Behavior Support." *School Psychology Review* 35, 245–259.

Swearer, S.M., Espelage, D.L., Vaillancourt, T., and Hymel, S. 2010. "What Can Be Done about School Bullying? Linking Research to Educational Practice." *Educational Researcher* 39, 38–47. DOI: 10.3102/0013189X09357622.

Swearer, S.M., Siebecker, A.B., Johnsen-Frerichs, L.A., and Wang, C. 2010. "Assessment of Bullying/Victimization: The Problem of Comparability across Studies and across Methodologies." In *Handbook of Bullying in Schools: An International Perspective*, edited by S.R. Jimerson, S.B. Swearer, and D.L. Espelage, pp. 305–327. New York: Routledge.

Swearer, S.M., Turner, R.K., Givens, J.E., and Pollack, W.S. 2008. "'You're so gay!': Do Different Forms of Bullying Matter for Adolescent Males? *School Psychology Review* 37, 160–173.

Swearer, S.M., Wang, C., Maag, J.W., Siebecker, A.B., and Frerichs, L.J. 2012. "Understanding the Bullying Dynamic among Students in Special and General Education." *Journal of School Psychology* 50, 503–520. DOI: 10.1016/j.jsp.2012.04.001.

The White House. 2011, March 10. "President and First Lady Call for a United Effort to Address Bullying." https://www.whitehouse.gov/the-press-office/2011/03/10/president-and-first-lady-call-united-effort-address-bullying (last accessed October 17, 2017).

Tippett, N. and Wolke, D. 2014. "Socioeconomic Status and Bullying: A Meta-analysis." *American Journal of Public Health* 104, e48–e59. DOI: 10.2105/AJPH.2014.301960.

Tokunaga, R.S. 2010. "Following You Home from School: A Critical Review and Synthesis of Research on Cyberbullying Victimization." *Computers in Human Behavior* 26, 277–287. DOI: 10.1016/j.chb.2009.11.014.

Ttofi, M.M., Bowes, L., Farrington, D.P., and Lösel, F. 2014. "Protective Factors Interrupting the Continuity from School Bullying to Later Internalizing and Externalizing Problems: A Systematic Review of Prospective Longitudinal Studies." *Journal of School Violence* 13, 5–38. DOI: 10.1080/15388220.2013.857345.

Ttofi, M.M. and Farrington, D.P. 2011. "Effectiveness of School-based Programs to Reduce Bullying: A Systematic and Meta-analytic Review." *Journal of Experimental Criminology* 7(1), 27–56. DOI: 10.1007/s11292-010-9109-1.

Ttofi, M.M., Farrington, D.P., Lösel, F., and Loeber, R. 2011. "Do the Victims of School Bullies Tend to Become Depressed Later in Life? A Systematic Review and Meta-analysis of Longitudinal Studies." *Journal of Aggression, Conflict and Peace Research* 3, 63–73.

Tynes, B.M., Hiss, S., Ryan, A., and Rose, C.A. 2015. "Discrimination in School vs. Online Contexts, Mental Health and Motivation among Diverse Adolescents in the US." In *The Social Psychology of the Classroom International Handbook*, edited by C. Davies, pp. 112–121. New York: Routledge.

United States Department of Education Office for Civil Rights. 2010. "Dear Colleague Letter on Harassment and Bullying." http://www.ed.gov/ocr/letters/colleague-201010. pdf (last accessed October 17, 2017).

United States Department of Education Office for Civil Rights. 2014. "Dear Colleague Letter: Responding to Bullying of Students with Disabilities." http://www2.ed.gov/about/ offices/list/ocr/letters/colleague-bullying-201410.pdf (last accessed October 17, 2017).

United States Department of Education Office of Special Education and Rehabilitative Services. 2013. "Dear Colleague Letter on Bullying of Students with Disabilities." http:// www.ed.gov/policy/speced/guid/idea/memosdcltrs/bullyingdcl-8-20-13.doc (last accessed October 17, 2017).

Unnever, J.D. and Cornell, D.G. 2004. "Middle School Victims of Bullying: Who Reports Being Bullied?" *Aggressive Behavior* 30, 373–388. DOI: 10.1002/ab.20030.

Vaillancourt, T., McDougall, P., Hymel, S., Krygsman, A., Miller, J., Stiver, K., and Davis, C. 2008. "Bullying: Are Researchers and Children/Youth Talking about the Same Thing?" *Journal of Behavioral Development* 32, 486–495. DOI: 10.1177/0165025408095553.

Van Cleemput, K., Vandebosch, H., Bastiaensens, S., Poels, K., DeSmet, A., and De Bourdeaudhuij, I. 2014, February. "A Systematic Review of Studies Evaluating Anticyberbullying Programs." Paper presented at Etmaal van de Communicatiewetenschap, Wageningen, Netherlands.

van Oort, F.A., Greaves-Lord, K., Ormel, J., Verhulst, F.C., and Huizink, A.C. 2011. "Risk Indicators of Anxiety throughout Adolescence: The TRAILS Study." *Depression and Anxiety* 28, 485–494. DOI: 10.1002/da.20818.

Veenstra, R., Lindenberg, S., Oldehinkel, A.J., De Winter, A.F., Verhulst, F.C., and Ormel, J. 2005. "Bullying and Victimization in Elementary Schools: A Comparison of Bullies, Victims, Bully/Victims, and Uninvolved Preadolescents." *Developmental Psychology* 41, 672–682. DOI: 10.1037/0012-1649.41.4.672.

Vervoort, M.H.M., Scholte, R.H.J., and Overbeek, G. 2010. "Bullying and Victimization among Adolescents: The Role of Ethnicity and Ethnic Composition of Social Class." *Journal of Youth and Adolescence* 39, 1–11. DOI: 10.1007/s10964-008-9355-y.

Vivolo-Kantor, A.M., Martell, B.N., Holland, K.M., and Westby, R. 2014. "A Systematic Review and Content Analysis of Bullying and Cyber-Bullying Measurement Strategies." *Aggression and Violent Behavior* 19, 423–434. DOI: 10.1016/j.avb.2014.06.008.

Waasdorp, T.E., Bradshaw, C.P., and Leaf, P.J. 2012. "The Impact of Schoolwide Positive Behavioral Interventions and Supports on Bullying and Peer Rejection: A Randomized Controlled Effectiveness Trial." *Archives of Pediatrics & Adolescent Medicine* 166, 149–156. DOI: 10.1001/archpediatrics.2011.755.

Wang, J., Iannotti, R.J., and Nansel, T.R. 2009. "School Bullying among Adolescents in the United States: Physical, Verbal, Relational, and Cyber." *Journal of Adolescent Health* 45, 368–375. DOI: 10.1016/j.jadohealth.2009.03.021.

Wang, W., Vaillancourt, T., Brittain, H.L., McDougall, P., Krygsman, A., Smith, D., and … Hymel, S. 2014. "School Climate, Peer Victimization, and Academic Achievement: Results from a Multi-Informant Study." *School Psychology Quarterly* 29, 360–377. DOI: 10.1037/spq0000084.

Werth, J.M., Nickerson, A.B., Aloe, A.M., and Swearer, S.M. 2015. "Bullying Victimization and the Social and Emotional Maladjustment of Bystanders: A Propensity Score Analysis." *Journal of School Psychology* 53, 295–308. DOI: 10.1016/j.jsp.2015.05.004.

Willard, N. 2004. *Educator's Guide to Cyberbullying: Addressing the Harm Caused by Online Social Cruelty.* http://cyberbully.org.

Williams, K.R. and Guerra, N.G. 2007. "Prevalence and Predictors of Internet Bullying." *Journal of Adolescent Health* 41, S14–S21. DOI: 10.1016/j.jadohealth.2007.08.018.

Williford, A., Boulton, A., Noland, B., Little, T.D., Kärnä, A., and Salmivalli, C. 2012. "Effects of the KiVa Anti-bullying Program on Adolescents' Depression, Anxiety, and Perception of Peers." *Journal of Abnormal Child Psychology* 40, 289–300. DOI: 10.1007/s10802-011-9562-y.

Ybarra, M.L., Boyd, D., Korchmaros, J.D., and Oppenheim, J. 2012. "Defining and Measuring Cyberbullying within the Larger Context of Bullying Victimization." *Journal of Adolescent Health* 51, 53–58. DOI: 10.1016/j.jadohealth.2011.12.031.

Ybarra, M.L., Diener-West, M., and Leaf, P.J. 2007. "Examining the Overlap in Internet Harassment and School Bullying: Implications for School Intervention." *Journal of Adolescent Health* 41, S42–S50. DOI: 10.1016/j.jadohealth.2007.09.004.

Yeager, D.S., Fong, C.J., Lee, H.Y., and Espelage, D.L. 2015. "Declines in Efficacy of Anti-Bullying Programs among Older Adolescents: Theory and a Three-level Meta-analysis." *Journal of Applied Developmental Psychology* 37, 36–51. DOI: 10.1016/j.appdev.2014.11.005.

Zhang, A., Musu-Gillette, L., and Oudekerk, B.A. 2016. *Indicators of School Crime and Safety: 2015.* (NCES Publication No. 2016-079/NCJ 249758. Washington, DC: National Center for Education Statistics, US Department of Education, and Bureau of Justice Statistics, Office of Justice Programs, US. Department of Justice.

17

School Climate and Bullying Prevention Programs

Jun Sung Hong, Dorothy L. Espelage, and Jeoung Min Lee

Schools are primary institutions where students' social activities and learning takes place, and, not surprisingly, the majority of bullying incidents occur on school grounds in the absence of an adult figure. School hallways, classrooms, cafeterias, and buses are potential areas where students witness or experience bullying (Astor, Meyer, and Behre, 1999; Hong et al. 2015). Given that bullying occurs in various school areas, educators and researchers have emphasized the importance of creating schools that prevent bullying and provide safe and supportive environments for students (Thapa et al. 2013). *School climate* is defined as the quality and character of the school's environment, based on patterns of individuals' experiences of school life, and involves interactions among many individuals. School climate reflects the norms, goals, values, interpersonal relationships, teaching and learning practices, and school structures (Cohen et al. 2009; Thapa et al., 2013). A positive school climate enhances students' feelings of social, emotional, and physical safety; effectively addresses violence and aggression; and provides comfortable physical environments (National School Climate Center 2016; Thapa et al. 2013) –all of which contribute to prosocial behavior, healthy socialization, and high level of academic performance. On the other hand, a school climate that is supportive of aggressive behavior and other forms of misbehavior can elevate students' risk of bullying involvement and peer victimization (Klein, Cornell, and Konold 2012). In other words, school climate is relevant in students' involvement in bullying and risk of peer victimization.

Prevalence, Types, and Characteristics of Bullying and Peer Victimization

According to the National Center for Education Statistics (NCES) of the Bureau of Justice Statistics, public schools reported bullying to be the most common disciplinary problem during the 2013–2014 school year (Zhang, Musu-Gillette, and Oudekerk 2016). According to the NCES, 17% of public high schools, 25% of public middle schools, and 12% of public elementary schools reported that bullying among students (12 to 18 years of age) occurred at least once a week, and 22% of the students reported being bullied during the school year (Zhang, Musu-Gillette, and Oudekerk 2016). Also, schools located in towns reported the highest rate of school bullying (24%), followed by schools in suburban (13%), urban (15%), and rural (15%) areas (Zhang, Musu-Gillette, and Oudekerk 2016).

Students report experiencing both direct (e.g., physical) and indirect (e.g., spreading malicious rumors and gossip or cyberbullying) forms of bullying (Craig, Pepler, and Blais 2007). From a nationally representative sample of 7,182 students in sixth to tenth grade, Wang, Iannotti, and Nansel (2009) found that within the past two months, 20.8% were physically bullied, 53.6% were verbally bullied, 51.4% were socially excluded, and 13.6% were cyberbullied. Also according to NCES, 14% of public school students (age 12–18 years) reported being made fun of, called names, or insulted (direct bullying); 13% reported being subjects of rumors (indirect forms); and 1% reported being pushed, shoved, tripped, or spat on (direct bullying; Zhang, Musu-Gillette, and Oudekerk 2016).

Prevalence of bullying varies when sociodemographic characteristics, such as race/ethnicity and sex, are considered. In terms of race/ethnicity, white students were more likely than their peers of other races to be victimized by their peers. However, research findings indicate that African American students showed a higher rate of bullying and a lower rate of victimization than their peers of other racial and ethnic groups (Spriggs et al. 2007; Wang, Iannotti, and Nansel 2009). With regard to sex differences, there appear to be inconsistent findings. Some studies reported that males were more involved in bullying than females (e.g., Varjas, Henrich, and Meyers 2009) while other studies suggest no sex differences (Espelage, Polanin, and Low 2014; Zhang, Musu-Gillette, and Oudekerk 2016). On the other hand, Wang and colleagues (2009) found that boys were more frequently involved in direct bullying (e.g., physical and verbal), whereas girls were more involved in indirect bullying (e.g., spreading rumor, socially excluding someone).

Components of the School Climate

As previously mentioned, students spend a great deal of time in school where they develop socialization skills. Thus, it is important that schools provide a climate where students feel safe, are connected and engaged with their school, and feel comfortable in their physical environment. These components are also essential for effectively addressing and reducing school bullying and peer victimization (Bandyopadhyay, Cornell, and Konold 2009; Cohen et al. 2015; Espelage, Polanin, and Low 2014; Gage, Prykanowski, and Larson 2014; Klein, Cornell, and Konold 2012; Thapa et al. 2013).

Feeling Safe

School officials need to ensure a safe school climate because students' perception of school safety is necessary for their learning and healthy psychosocial development (Cohen et al. 2009; Orpinas and Horne 2009; Thapa et al. 2013). However, involvement in bullying and experiences in peer victimization can seriously undermine students' feelings of school safety, which can negatively affect their learning and healthy development (Devine and Cohen 2007; Varjas, Henrich, and Meyers 2009). Among a sample of 427 middle school students, Varjas and colleagues (2009) found that males and older students reported feeling safer at their school than younger students. Bullying peaks during middle school years and declines as students get older" (Espelage, Van Ryzin, and Holt 2017; Pepler et al. 2008; Smith, Madsen, and Moody 1999). In addition, studies report that relational aggression, a type of bullying that refers to intentionally damaging peer relationships, is significantly associated with adolescents' psychosocial adjustment (Crick and Grotpeter 1995; Prinstein, Boergers, and Vernberg 2001), which can undermine their sense of school safety. One study examined the effects of relational aggression on perceptions of school safety among 1,335 African American and white adolescents in grades 7 through 12 (Goldstein, Young, and Boyd 2008). The study found that adolescents who experienced high levels of relational aggression perceived their school climate as less safe and less satisfactory. Moreover, the study also found that boys who are victims of relational aggression report carrying a weapon to their school.

For students of certain sociodemographics, bullying is a frequent experience, making school an unsafe experience. Studies document that sexual minority youth are at an elevated risk of peer victimization (Birkett, Espelage, and Koenig 2009; Espelage, Merrin, and Hatchel, in press; Evans and Chapman 2014; Toomey, McGuire, and Russell 2012). According to Toomey and colleagues' (2012) study, 84% of students identified as lesbian, gay, bisexual, transgender, and queer (LGBTQ) reported being harassed and bullied which are reinforced in a heteronormative school climate (Toomey, McGuire, and Russell 2012). Consequently, a significant percentage of sexual minority students report perceiving their school climate as unsafe. According to the National School Climate Survey, 55.5% of lesbian, gay, bisexual, and transgender students reported feeling unsafe in their school because of their sexual orientation (Kosciw et al. 2014). Also, 30.3% of sexual minority students reported missing a day of school during the past month because they were fearful of being victimized. The National School Climate Survey also reported that sexual minority students feel unsafe in particular school areas, such as bathrooms and locker rooms (Kosciw et al. 2014).

Connectedness and Engagement

A school climate that is characterized as being well structured, having fair disciplinary practice, having supportive student–teacher relationships, having active classroom participation, and having a strong sense of school connectedness can foster students' engagement. School engagement in turn can contribute to higher academic performance and less bullying (Bond et al. 2007; Kochenderfer-Ladd and Pelletier 2008; Konishi et al. 2010; McNeely and Falci 2004; Webb 2009). *School connectedness* refers to students' sense of belonging, attachment, and bonding. Students with a strong sense of school connectedness are those who receive adequate social support from their peers and teachers, which increases their academic engagement and decreases their risk of behavior problems, such as bullying. Similarly, students who exhibit behavior problems such as bullying and experience peer victimization are at an increased risk of school disengagement (Eisenberg, Neumark-Sztainer, and Perry 2003; Fonagy et al. 2005).

Supportive and caring teachers especially play an important role in fostering students' school engagement (Midgley et al. 2000). Students spend a great deal of time with their schoolteacher, an important adult figure who plays a significant role in their academic and social development. A supportive teacher with a well-structured classroom (e.g., small group learning) can engage students in active participation and collaboration in the classroom (Webb 2009), and positive teacher–student relations is an essential component of a positive school climate (Slaughter-Defoe and Carlson 1996). Teacher support can also decrease students' risk of bullying and peer victimization (Gage, Prykanowski, and Larson 2014). Schools that are characterized as highly structured and highly supportive, that provide fair discipline and reinforce respect for school authority, are more willing to support students, which can contribute to less bullying (Gregory et al. 2010). If students who are frequently bullied seek help and support from a teacher, they are more likely to be engaged in their school and less likely to become involved in risky behaviors (Klein, Cornell, and Konold 2012). On the other hand, when students perceive that teachers are uninvolved or do not intervene in bullying situations, bullying may be encouraged (Espelage, Polanin, and Low 2014; Milsom and Gallo 2006; Unnever and Cornell 2003). Recognizing the important role of teachers in bullying prevention efforts, a number of bullying intervention programs have considered teacher training (Astor, Guerra, and Van Acker 2010; Astor et al. 2005).

Physical Environment

School climate includes not only social but also physical aspects of the school (Zullig et al. 2010), which is an important component of bullying prevention and school safety efforts. Earlier scholars have argued that undefined public space is an important concept in understanding school violence (Newman 1995; Newman and Franck 1982). Undefined public spaces are physical areas that might not be perceived as anyone's responsibility to consistently monitor and maintain (Astor et al. 2006). However, an effective school must ensure that the physical environment of the school is safe (Hernandez and Seem 2004), and that students, parents, and school officials are actively contributing to the operation of the school and the monitoring of its physical environment (Cohen et al. 2009). Physically safe school environments require students, parents, teachers, and school officials to all work together to develop and contribute to a shared vision (Cohen et al. 2009). According to Cohen and colleagues (2009), dimensions of the safe physical environment includes, for example, a crisis plan, clearly communicated rules and regulations including anti-bullying rules and policies (see Astor et al. 2005; Milsom and Gallo 2006), and a clear and consistent response to misbehavior and violence.

Developing and maintaining a safe physical environment can be an insurmountable task for schools with a sizable number of students (e.g., 1,000 or more students). Students in schools with large student populations may feel more unsafe and report higher incidents of bullying than students in schools with smaller populations (Zhang, Musu-Gillette, and Oudekerk 2016). A longitudinal study using a nationally representative sample found that school size was a significant predictor of peer victimization (Bowes et al. 2009). A high teacher–student ratio can make it difficult for teachers to monitor and manage students' behavior in class and to effectively intervene in bullying situations. As a result, students may have more opportunities to engage in and observe bullying in their classroom, which can undermine their sense of school safety (Bradshaw, Sawyer, and O'Brennan 2009; Koth, Bradshaw, and Leaf 2008).

Bullying Prevention Programs and the School Climate

Many bullying prevention and intervention programs have been developed and implemented in US schools in response to adverse outcomes for students involved in bullying. Most anti-bullying programs include strategies to change bullying behaviors by providing activities to heighten children's concerns for bullying victims, putting classroom rules and school policies in place, and implementing skills training or conflict resolution strategies (Stevens, Van Oost, and Bourdeaudhuij 2000). It is uncertain whether these programs have been effective, as many of them have not been systematically evaluated (Ferguson et al. 2007). Although an increasing number of schools have invested in anti-bullying programs, the impact of these programs on bullying has been found to be modest (Bradshaw 2015).

Scholars and practitioners have argued that bullying not only affects the students involved but also the entire school climate (Black and Jackson 2007) and the community environment. There has been a movement toward an adoption of school-wide programs to prevent bullying by promoting a positive school climate (Bradshaw and Waasdorp 2009; Cohen et al. 2015). Scholars have called for assessing and targeting school climate in bullying prevention efforts by establishing a common set of behavioral expectations across school contexts and involving all relevant stakeholders in prevention (Waasdorp, Bradshaw, and Leaf 2012). The Olweus Bullying Prevention Program, KiVa, Positive Behavioral Interventions and Supports (PBIS), Creating a Peaceful School Learning Environment (CAPSLE), and Second Step are just some examples of programs that have considered the school climate in bullying prevention.

Olweus Bullying Prevention Program

The Olweus Bullying Prevention Program (OBPP) was developed by the pioneering researcher Dan Olweus in the early 1980s in response to three boys who committed suicide as a result of persistent bullying victimization. These incidents led to a nation-wide campaign against school bullying by the Norwegian Ministry of Education (Kallestad and Olweus 2003). It was first implemented as the First Bergin Project Against Bullying and involved approximately 2,500 Norwegian schoolchildren between 1983 and 1985 (Limber 2011). The aim of the OBPP is to reduce bullying in school, prevent the development of bullying, and promote students' prosocial behaviors (Olweus 1993; Olweus et al. 2007; Olweus, Limber, and Mihalic 1999). The OBPP consists of several components at the individual, classroom, school, and community levels:

- *individual level*: supervise students' activities, ensure that all staff intervene on the spot when bullying is observed, meet with students involved in bullying, and meet with parents of the students involved in bullying;
- *classroom level*: enforce school-wide anti-bullying rules, hold regular class meetings to discuss bullying and other relevant topics, and hold class-level meetings with the parents of the students;
- *school level*: launch a Bullying Prevention Coordinating Committee (BPCC), provide trainings for BPCC and all relevant staff members, administer the Olweus Bullying Questionnaire, hold staff group meetings, introduce anti-bullying school rules, review

or refine school's supervisory system, hold a school-wide kick-off event to launch the OBPP, and involve parents;
- *community level*: involve community members on BPCC, develop school–community partnerships, and help disseminate anti-bullying messages and practice in the community (Limber et al. 2015, 205).

The outcomes of the program were generally positive outside of the United States: there were significant decreases in students' reports of bullying and school violence, decreases in students' antisocial behaviors, significant improvements in school climate, and more positive attitudes toward school work (Olweus 2005). Olweus (2005) conducted a study in which three consecutive cohorts of students ($n = 21,000$) in Norway completed the Olweus Bully/Victim Questionnaire eight months before and after students participated in the OBPP intervention. The results indicated substantial reductions in peer victimization: by 32% to 49%. Another study evaluated a nationwide anti-bullying program in Irish schools, which was based on the OBPP in 1996 (O'Moore and Minton 2005). Professionals (11 teachers) were trained to coordinate the OBPP in the school. Other activities involved teacher and parent training sessions in three to five schools. Students and teachers from 22 of the schools completed the Olweus Bully/Victim Questionnaire prior to and after the implementation of the training program. Results indicated significant reductions in bullying and peer victimization in school.

Although the OBPP has demonstrated effectiveness in several European school districts, findings have been somewhat inconsistent in US schools. Several studies evaluating the effectiveness of the OBPP in US schools have reported a significant drop in bullying incidents (Bowllan 2011; Kallestad and Olweus 2003; Limber 2004). A systematic evaluation of the OBPP conducted in 18 middle schools in South Carolina found that, one year after the implementation, there were significant decreases in students' reports of bullying, peer victimization, and social isolation (Limber 2004). Kallestad and Olweus (2003) examined the effectiveness of the OBPP in US schools from a sample of 37 schools and 89 teachers who utilized the OBPP in their classrooms. They found that certain components of the OBPP were put into practice by most of the teachers, and the majority of the teachers reported satisfaction with the program outcomes. Another study, which evaluated the OBPP in 12 elementary schools in Philadelphia, revealed that schools that utilized the program reported significant reductions in students' and adults' reports of bullying in school (Black 2003). On the other hand, Bauer, Lozano, and Rivara (2007), who tested the effectiveness of the OBPP in US public middle schools utilizing a randomized controlled trial with students, found that the program had mixed positive outcomes, which varied by sex, race/ethnicity, and grade levels, but no overall effect. Relational and physical victimization decreased among European American students relative to those in the comparison groups, but no similar effect was found for racial/ethnic minority students by sex or by grade levels.

KiVa Anti-Bullying Program

KiVa Anti-Bullying Program is an evidence-based, whole-school bullying prevention program targeted at various age ranges. KiVa is based on the premise that bullying is a group phenomenon, and children who are uninvolved in bullying react and behave when they witness bullying, and their actions (or lack thereof) can influence the maintenance of bullying or put an end to it (Salmivalli, Kärnä, and Poskiparta 2011).

Developed at the University of Turku with funding support by the Finnish Ministry of Education and Culture, KiVa was developed from decades of research conducted in Finland and in other countries. The aims of KiVa include putting an end to persistent bullying, preventing the emergence of bullying, and minimizing the consequences of peer victimization (Salmivalli and Poskiparta 2012). KiVa contains two main components: *universal* and *indicated actions*. Universal actions focus primarily on preventing bullying and include student lessons (primary school) and themes containing several lessons (secondary school). These lessons are accompanied by virtual learning environments (e.g., computer game, Internet forum) that are closely connected to their contents, motivating participants and enhancing their learning process (Salmivalli and Poskiparta 2012). Activities include group discussions, role-play exercises, and short films related to bullying. Contents of the lessons proceed from general topics (e.g., emotions, respecting others, group pressure) to bullying and its consequences (Salmivalli and Poskiparta 2012). Indicated actions, on the other hand, are designed to address bullying by having discussions with both bullies and victims, as well as with selected classmates who play a role in supporting the victim. The KiVa teams of teachers or other school personnel, along with the classroom teachers, organize a meeting with the supporter of victims, individual or small group discussions with bullies and victims, and follow-up meetings (Salmivalli, Kärnä, and Poskiparta 2011).

The effectiveness of KiVa has been evaluated in numerous studies in Finland and in a few other countries. One study, which evaluated KiVa in a large randomized control trial (117 intervention schools and 117 control schools), showed a significant reduction of both self- and peer-reported bullying and victimization, along with a reduction in anxiety and depressive symptoms (Kärnä et al. 2011). Remarkably, a significant majority of the victims in the intervention school reported that their situation had improved. Other studies also report the positive effects of KiVa on students' connectedness to their school, academic motivation, and academic performance (Kärnä et al. 2011; Salmivalli, Garandeau, and Veenstra 2012). Using two samples of students, one of grades 1–3 ($n = 6,927$) and the other of grades 7–9 ($n = 16,503$) who were randomly assigned to intervention and control groups, Kärnä and colleagues (2011) reported that the KiVa program was effective in reducing bullying and peer victimization in grades 1–3. Hutchings and Clarkson (2015), who led a pilot study of KiVa in 14 UK schools, also revealed a significant reduction in bullying and peer victimization, as indicated in their pretest/posttest results.

Positive Behavioral Interventions and Supports

Positive Behavioral Interventions and Supports (PBIS) is a non-curricular, universal intervention that is aimed at enhancing students' academic achievement and social behaviors. Although established to promote evidence-based interventions for students with behavioral problems, the shift focused on school-wide behavior support for all students. PBIS is a framework that enhances the adoption and implementation of a continuum of evidence-based interventions to achieve students' positive academic and behavioral outcomes (Sugai et al. 2000). PBIS utilizes a three-tiered system of effective behavioral supports at the primary, secondary, and tertiary prevention levels (Walker et al. 1996). Primary prevention is a universal approach, which is aimed at addressing the entire school to maximize achievement, intervening in behavior problems, and increasing positive student interactions with peers and adults. Secondary prevention targets students or subgroups with behavior problems who are unresponsive to the universal prevention. Tertiary prevention targets the remaining 1–5% of the students with behaviors related to emotional behavioral disorder or mental illness. These interventions are designed to reduce students' maladaptive behaviors and provide them with prosocial behaviors that can replace maladaptive ones (Muscott et al. 2004).

PBIS is implemented by following six steps:

- forming a PBIS team (six to ten staff members) who provide leadership, attend annual training, and develop an action plan;
- designating an external behavior support coach who provides on-site consultation and technical assistance;
- defining and disseminating expectations for positive student behaviors to students and staff;
- teaching defined behavioral expectations to the students through lesson plans;
- establishing a school-wide system; and
- creating an agreed-upon system to respond to violations of behavioral expectations. (Bradshaw, Mitchell, and Leaf 2010)

Research findings emphasize the importance of school-wide prevention programs that provide positive behavior support, establish a consistently enforced set of expectations for positive behaviors across the school context, and involve all school staff in prevention activities (Bradshaw, Waasdorp, and Leaf 2012; Ross and Horner 2009). The continued data collection efforts of PBIS can help identify where, when, and for whom bullying is occurring (Bradshaw, Waasdorp, and Leaf 2012). Data collected on bullying incidents from anonymous surveys can also inform the supervision and intervention process (Bradshaw, Waasdorp, and Leaf 2012). Moreover, through sustained efforts, PBIS can provide a school-wide context for teaching, practicing, and reinforcing skills throughout the school day (Bradshaw et al. 2009). Results from two recent studies have shown positive effects of PBIS in decreasing bullying and peer victimization. Using a randomized controlled effectiveness trial, Waasdorp and colleagues (2012) explored the effects of PBIS on students bullying and peer rejection during early adolescence. Thirty-seven Maryland public schools with 12,344 students were recruited for the study and were followed longitudinally across four school years. The study found that children in intervention schools exhibited significantly lower rates of bullying and peer rejection compared to their peers in control schools. A more recent pilot study evaluated the association between the implementation of Bully Prevention in PBIS and students' attitudes related to bullying, harassment, and school safety from a sample of third to fifth graders in three school districts (Ross and Horner 2014). The study results indicated a significant improvement in the participants' assertiveness, bystander support, and the use of a "stop" signal to prevent bullying.

Creating a Peaceful School Learning Environment

Creating a Peaceful School Learning Environment (CAPSLE), is a manualized, psychodynamic social systems approach to addressing the relationships among bully perpetrators, victims, and bystanders (Twemlow, Fonagy, and Sacco 2004; Twemlow, Sacco, and Williams 1996). CAPSLE purports that all members of the school community (students, teachers, staff members) have a role in bullying. The goal of CAPSLE is to improve the capacity of school members to help students resist the urge to bully others through a mentalized power dynamics perspective (i.e., interpreting both one's own and others' behavior; Fonagy et al. 2009). The components of CAPSLE are as follows:

- *Positive climate campaign*, which is led by a counselor, involves discussions, posters, magnets, bookmarks, and other methods to promote a change in the language and thinking of the school.
- *Classroom management*, which assists teachers' efforts in discipline by pinpointing underlying problems instead of punishing or criticizing students' misbehavior.
- *Peer and adult mentorship*, in which the goal is to get the entire school to understand violent interactions and to see if school members can collaboratively resolve problems without placing blame.
- *The Gentle Warrior Physical Education Program*, which utilizes a combination of role-playing, relaxation, and defensive martial arts to assist children to protect themselves and others through non-aggressive physical and cognitive strategies.
- *Reflection time*, which promotes mentalizing among students and teachers. (Twemlow, Fonagy, and Sacco 2005)

Positive outcomes of CAPSLE, in relation to bullying and other forms of student mis-behaviors, have been documented in research findings. Twemlow and colleagues (2001) examined the impact of CAPSLE on the learning environment in elementary schools over four years. The study consisted of an intervention school, which was based on zero tolerance for bullying, and a control school, which received only regular psychiatric con-sultation. Students in the intervention school were found to display significant reduc-tions in disciplinary referrals and increases in academic achievement. Fonagy and colleagues' (2009) controlled trial study compared the effects of manualized school psychiatric consultation (SPC) and CAPSLE in reducing aggressive behavior in 1,345 third to fifth graders in nine elementary school districts. The researchers observed a significant behavior change in CAPSLE participants whereas no behavior change was observed among SPC participants. CAPSLE also produced a significant reduction in students' off-task and disruptive classroom behaviors. A more recent study, which implemented and evaluated the effectiveness of CAPSLE on violent and prejudiced behaviors in Jamaican schools with low-income children (grades 7–9), reported a sig-nificant improvement in academic performance and helpful behavior (especially in boys) as well as a reduction in victimization (Twemlow et al. 2011). More specifically, the study found that the frequency of physical peer victimization (i.e., hitting, kicking, pushing, being grabbed, and being held or touched) declined significantly in the first year of the program implementation and more moderately in the second year.

Second Step: Student Success Through Prevention (SS-SSTP) Middle School Program

The Second Step© is designed for sixth through eighth graders and covers similar social emotional targets (e.g., empathy, communication skills, problem solving, bully preven-tion, friendship skills, harassment, emotion regulation, alcohol and drug prevention) across the grades (Committee for Children 2008). However, the context increases in complexity from one grade level to the next. Second Step is used in conjunction with school-based efforts to address bullying, including school climate assessments, teacher training, and policy changes. Fifteen lessons are delivered in sixth grade, and 13 lessons are delivered at the seventh and eighth grade levels. Each lesson is designed to take one 50-minute session or two 25-minute sessions. Prior to implementation, teachers in the intervention condition completed a four-hour training that covered several areas. First, research on bully prevention and social emotional learning is reviewed in order to help the teachers understand the rationale for the project. Second, teachers are given the intervention kits and the trainer takes them through several lessons in order to demonstrate that they could be successful in implementing the program. Finally, teachers are given specific implementation strategies to maximize fidelity. Lessons include direct lessons in risk and protective factors linked to aggression and violence, such as empathy training, emotion regulation, communication skills, and problem-solving strategies. Drawing on Bandura's (1973) social learning theory, lessons are skills based and students receive cueing, coaching, and suggestions for improvement on their performance. Lessons are supplemented by homework that reinforces the instruction, extension activities, academic integration lessons, and videos, which are practices that are associated with greater skill acquisition. The use of group and collaborative work also leads to increased skill acquisition by allowing students to practice new skills in an environment of positive peer support. Again, a recent meta-analysis supports this practice of using a direct approach to address barriers to helping others, and implement and teach role-playing strategies to encourage bystanders' involvement (Polanin, Espelage, and Pigott 2012). Also in the seventh grade curriculum, students learn their school's sexual harassment policy, how sexual harassment differs from simple flirting, and assertive skills to rebuff sexual harassment. The SS-SSTP lessons are scripted and highly interactive, incorporating small group discussions and activities, class discussions, dyadic exercises, whole class instruction, and individual work. Lessons are supported through an accompanying DVD, which contains media-rich content including topic-focused interviews with students and video demonstrations of skills. Indeed, video has been found to be one important element of efficacious programs (Ttofi and Farrington 2011). In a large randomized clinical trial of over 3,600 students across 36 middle school students, reductions in fighting were found after the sixth grade curriculum (Espelage et al. 2013). Also, sexual harassment and homophobic name-calling was reduced after two years of implementation (Espelage, Low et al. 2015), and bullying, homophobic name-calling, and cyberbullying was reduced after three years of implementation (Espelage, Van Ryzin et al. 2015). Bully perpetration was also reduced for students with disabilities in the Second Step condition compared to students with disabilities in the control condition (Espelage, Rose, and Polanin 2015). Furthermore, when teachers spent more time prepping the lesson and prepared the lesson as a group, reductions were found in a global statistic of aggression, including bullying (Polanin and Espelage 2014).

Conclusion

Over the past four decades, researchers and practitioners have worked together to address school-based bullying. However, much more work needs to be done. In reality, school-based bullying prevention programs have yielded modest reductions in bullying and peer victimization. Increasingly, classroom curricula are being used in conjunction with school-wide initiatives to address the larger school climate that might be reinforcing bullying behavior. School climate improvement processes involve all stakeholders (teachers, parents, administrators, students) working together to promote school safety, positive adult–student relationships, and academic engaging environments. It is evident that school climate is an important aspect of bullying intervention efforts, and effectively preventing and deterring bullying requires an assessment and intervention targeting the entire school community rather than only students who are involved in bullying.

References

Astor, R.A., Benbenishty, R., Marachi, R., and Meyer, H.A. 2006. "The Social Context of Schools: Monitoring and Mapping Student Victimization in Schools." In *Handbook of School Violence and School Safety: From Research to Practice*, edited by S.R. Jimerson and M.J. Furlong, pp. 221–233. Mahwah, NJ: Lawrence Erlbaum.

Astor, R.A., Meyer, H.A., and Behre, W.J. 1999. "Unowned Places and Times: Maps and Interviews about Violence in High Schools." *American Educational Research Journal* 36, 3–42.

Astor, R.A., Meyer, H.A., Benbenishty, R., Marachi, R., and Rosemond, M. 2005. "School Safety Interventions: Best Practices and Programs." *Children and Schools* 27, 17–32.

Astor, R.A., Guerra, N., and Van Acker, R. 2010. "How Can We Improve School Safety Research?" *Educational Researcher* 39, 69–78.

Bandura, A. 1973. *Aggression: A Social Learning Analysis.* Oxford: Prentice Hall.

Bandyopadhyay, S., Cornell, D.G., and Konold, T.R. 2009. "Validity of Three School Climate Scales to Assess Bullying, Aggressive Attitudes, and Help Seeking." *School Psychology Review* 38, 338–355.

Bauer, N., Lozano, P., and Rivara, F. 2007. "The Effectiveness of the Olweus Bullying Prevention Program in Public Middle Schools: A Controlled Trial." *Journal of Adolescent Health* 40, 266–274.

Birkett, M., Espelage, D.L., and Koenig, B. 2009. "LGB and Questioning Students in Schools: The Moderating Effects of Homophobic Bullying and School Climate on Negative Outcomes." *Journal of Youth and Adolescence* 38, 989–1000.

Black, S. 2003. "An Ongoing Evaluation of the Bullying Prevention Program in Philadelphia Schools: Student Survey and Student Observation Data." Paper presented at the Centers for Disease Control's Safety in Numbers Conference, Atlanta, GA.

Black, S.A. and Jackson, E. 2007. "Using Bullying Incident Density to Evaluate the Olweus Bullying Prevention Program." *School Psychology International* 28, 623–638.

Bond, L., Butler, H., Thomas, L., Carlin, J., Glover, S., Bowes, G., and Patton, G. 2007. "Social and School Connectedness in Early Secondary School as Predictors of Late Teenage Substance Use, Mental Health, and Academic Outcomes." *Journal of Adolescent Health* 40, 357.e9–357.e18.

Bowes, L., Arseneault, L., Maughan, B., Taylor, A., Caspi, A., and Moffitt, T.E. 2009. "School, Neighborhood, and Family Factors Are Associated with Children's Bullying Involvement: A Nationally Representative Longitudinal Study." *Journal of the American Academy of Child & Adolescent Psychiatry* 48, 545–553.

Bowllan, N.M. 2011. "Implementation and Evaluation of a Comprehensive School-wide Bullying Prevention Program in an Urban/Suburban Middle School." *Journal of School Health* 81, 167–173.

Bradshaw, C.P. 2015. "Translating Research to Practice in Bullying Prevention." *American Psychologist* 70(4), 322–332.

Bradshaw, C.P., Koth, C.W., Thorton, L.A., and Leaf, P.J. 2009. "Altering School Climate through School-wide Positive Behavioral Interventions and Supports: Findings from a Group-Randomized Effectiveness Trial." *Prevention Science* 10, 100–115.

Bradshaw, C.P., Mitchell, M.M., and Leaf, P.J. 2010. "Examining the Effects of Schoolwide Positive Behavioral Interventions and Supports on Student Outcomes: Results from a Randomized Controlled Effectiveness Trial in Elementary Schools." *Journal of Positive Behavior Interventions* 12, 133–148.

Bradshaw, C.P., Sawyer, A.L., and O'Brennan, L.M. 2009. "A Social Disorganization Perspective on Bullying-related Attitudes and Behaviors: The Influence of School Context. *American Journal of Community Psychology* 43, 204–220.

Bradshaw, C.P. and Waasdorp, T.E. 2009. "Measuring and Changing a 'Culture of Bullying.'" *School Psychology Review* 38, 356–361.

Bradshaw, C.P., Waasdorp, T.E., and Leaf, P. 2012. "Effects of School-wide Positive Behavioral Interventions and Supports on Child Behavior Problems." *Pediatrics* 130(5), e1136–e1145.

Cohen, J., Espelage, D.L., Berkowitz, M., Twemlow, S., and Comer, J. 2015. "Rethinking Effective Bully and Violence Prevention Efforts: Promoting Healthy School Climates, Positive Youth Development, and Preventing Bully-Victim-Bystander Behavior." *International Journal of Violence and Schools* 15, 2–40.

Cohen, J., McCabe, L., Michelli, N.M., and Pickeral, T. 2009. "School Climate: Research, Policy, Practice, and Teacher Education." *Teachers College Record* 111, 180–213.

Committee for Children. 2008. *Second Step: Student Success Through Prevention Program.* Seattle, WA: Committee for Children.

Craig, W., Pepler, D., and Blais, J. 2007. "Responding to Bullying: What Works?" *School Psychology International* 28, 465–477.

Crick, N.R. and Grotpeter, J.K. 1995. "Relational Aggression, Gender, and Social-psychological Adjustment." *Child Development* 66(3), 710–722.

Devine, J.F. and Cohen, J. 2007. *Making Your School Safe: Strategies to Protect Children and Promote Learning.* New York: Teachers College Press.

Eisenberg, M.E., Neumark-Sztainer, D., and Perry, C.L. 2003. "Peer Harassment, School Connectedness, and Academic Achievement." *Journal of School Health* 73, 311–316.

Espelage, D.L., Low, S., Polanin, J., and Brown, E. 2013. "The Impact of a Middle-School Program to Reduce Aggression, Victimization, and Sexual Violence." *Journal of Adolescent Health* 53(2), 180–186. DOI: 10.1016/j.jadohealth.2013.02.021.

Espelage, D.L., Low, S., Polanin, J., and Brown, E. 2015. "Clinical Trial of Second Step© Middle-School Program: Impact on Aggression and Victimization." *Journal of Applied Developmental Psychology* 37, 52–63.

Espelage, D.L., Merrin, G.J., and Hatchel, T. in press. "Peer Victimization and Dating Violence among LGBTQ Youth: The Impact of School Violence and Crime on Mental Health Outcomes." *Youth Violence and Juvenile Justice.* DOI: 10.1177/1541204016680408.

Espelage, D.L., Polanin, J.R., and Low, S.K. 2014. "Teacher and Staff Perceptions of School Environment as Predictors of Student Aggression, Victimization, and Willingness to Intervene in Bullying Situations." *School Psychology Quarterly* 29, 287–05.

Espelage, D.L., Rose, C.A., and Polanin, J.R. 2015. "Social-emotional Learning Program to Reduce Bullying, Fighting, and Victimization among Middle School Students with Disabilities." *Remedial and Special Education* 36(5), 299–311.

Espelage, D.L., Van Ryzin, M., and Holt, M. 2017. "Trajectories of Bully Perpetration across Early Adolescence: Static Risk Factors, Dynamic Covariates and Longitudinal Outcomes." *Psychology of Violence*. Advance online publication. DOI: 10.1037/vio0000095.

Espelage, D.L., Van Ryzin, M., Low, S., and Polanin, J. 2015. "Clinical Trial of Second Step© Middle-School Program: Impact on Bullying, Cyberbullying, Homophobic Teasing and Sexual Harassment Perpetration." *School Psychology Review* 44 (4), 464–479.

Evans, C.B. and Chapman, M.V. 2014. "Bullied Youth: The Impact of Bullying through Lesbian, Gay, and Bisexual Name Calling." *American Journal of Orthopsychiatry* 84, 644–652.

Ferguson, C.J., Miguel, C.S., Kilburn, J.C., and Sanchez, P. 2007. "The Effectiveness of School-based Anti-bullying Programs: A Meta-Analytic Review." *Criminal Justice Review* 32, 401–414.

Fonagy, P., Twemlow, S.W., Vernberg, E.M., Nelson, J.M., Dill, E.J., Little, T.D., and Sargent, J.A. 2009. "A Cluster Randomized Control Trial of Child-focused Psychiatric Consultation and a School Systems-focused Intervention to Reduce Aggression." *Journal of Child Psychology and Psychiatry* 50, 607–616.

Fonagy, P., Twemlow, S.W., Vernberg, E., Sacco, F.C., and Little, T.D. 2005. "Creating a Peaceful School Learning Environment: The Impact of an Antibullying Program on Educational Attainment in Elementary Schools." *Medical Science Monitor* 11, CR317–CR325.

Gage, N.A., Prykanowski, D.A., and Larson, A. 2014. "School Climate and Bullying Victimization: A Latent Class Growth Model Analysis." *School Psychology Quarterly* 29, 256–271.

Goldstein, S.E., Young, A., and Boyd, C. 2008. "Relational Aggression at School: Associations with School Safety and Social Climate." *Journal of Youth and Adolescence* 37, 641–654.

Gregory, A., Cornell, D., Fan, X., Sheras, P., Shih, T.H., and Huang, F. 2010. "Authoritative School Discipline: High School Practices Associated with Lower Bullying and Victimization." *Journal of Educational Psychology* 102, 483–496.

Hernandez, T.J. and Seem, S.R. 2004. "A Safe School Climate: A Systemic Approach and the School Counselor." *Professional School Counseling* 7, 256–262.

Hong, J.S., Day, A., Lee, J.M., and Crosby, S. 2015. *Report Summary: Adolescents' Reporting of Bullying and Peer Victimization in School: What Do They Report and How Can We Respond?* Final Report to the School Community Health Alliance of Michigan.

Hutchings, J. and Clarkson, S. 2015. "Introducing and Piloting the KiVa Bullying Prevention Programme in the UK." *Educational & Child Psychology* 32, 49–61.

Kallestad, J.H. and Olweus, D. 2003. "Predicting Teachers' and Schools' Implementation of the Olweus Bullying Prevention Program: A Multilevel Study." *Prevention & Treatment* 6. DOI: http://dx.doi.org/10.1037/1522-3736.6.1.621a.

Kärnä, A., Voeten, M., Little, T., Poskiparta, E., Kalijonen, A., and Salmivalli, C. 2011. "A Large Scale Evaluation of the Kiva Antibullying Program." *Child Development* 82, 311–330.

Klein, J., Cornell, D., and Konold, T. 2012. "Relationships between Bullying, School Climate, and Student Risk Behaviors." *School Psychology Quarterly* 27, 154–169.

Kochenderfer-Ladd, B. and Pelletier, M.E. 2008. "Teachers' Views and Beliefs about Bullying: Influences on Classroom Management Strategies and Students' Coping with Peer Victimization." *Journal of School Psychology* 46, 431–453.

Konishi, C., Hymel, S., Zumbo, B.D., and Li, Z. 2010. "Do School Bullying and Student–Teacher Relationships Matter for Academic Achievement? A Multilevel Analysis." *Canadian Journal of School Psychology* 25, 19–39.

Kosciw, J.G., Greytak, E.A., Palmer, N.A., and Boesen, M.J. 2014. *The 2013 National School Climate Survey: The Experiences of Lesbian, Gay, Bisexual and Transgender Youth in Our Nation's Schools*. New York: Gay, Lesbian and Straight Education Network.

Koth, C.W., Bradshaw, C.P., and Leaf, P.J. 2008. "A Multilevel Study of Predictors of Student Perceptions of School Climate: The Effect of Classroom-level Factors." *Journal of Educational Psychology* 100, 96–104.

Limber, S.P. 2004. "Implementation of the Olweus Bullying Prevention Program: Lessons Learned from the Field." In *Bullying in American Schools: A Social-Ecological Perspective on Prevention and Intervention*, edited by D.L. Espelage and S.M. Swearer, pp. 351–363. Mahwah, NJ: Lawrence Erlbaum.

Limber, S.P. 2011. "Development, Evaluation, and Future Directions of the Olweus Bullying Prevention Program." *Journal of School Violence* 10, 71–87.

Limber, S.P., Riese, J., Snyder, M.J., and Olweus, D. 2015. "The Olweus Bullying Prevention Program: Efforts to Address Risks Associated with Suicide and Suicide-related Behaviors." In *Youth Suicide and Bullying: Challenges and Strategies for Prevention and Intervention*, edited by P. Golblum, D.L. Espelage, J. Chu, and B. Bongar, pp. 203–215. Oxford and New York: Oxford University Press.

McNeely, C. and Falci, C. 2004. "School Connectedness and the Transition into and out of Health-risk Behavior among Adolescents: A Comparison of Social Belonging and Teacher Support." *Journal of School Health* 74, 284–292.

Midgley, C., Maehr, M.L., Hruda, L.Z., Anderman, E., Anderman, L., Freeman, K.E., and Urdan, T. 2000. *Manual for the Patterns of Adaptive Learning Scales*. Ann Arbor: University of Michigan Press. http://www.umich.edu/~pals/PALS%202000_V12Word97.pdf (last accessed October 18, 2017).

Milsom, A. and Gallo, L.L. 2006. "Bullying in Middle Schools: Prevention and Intervention." *Middle School Journal* 37, 12–19.

Muscott, H.S., Mann, E., Benjamin, T.B., Gateley, S., Bell, K.E., and Muscott, A. J. 2004. "Positive Behavioral Interventions and Supports in New Hampshire: Preliminary Results of a Statewide System for Implementing Schoolwide Discipline Practices." *Education and Treatment of Children* 27, 453–475.

National School Climate Center. 2016. "School Climate." National School Climate Center. www.schoolclimate.org/climate/ (last accessed October 18, 2017).

Newman, O. 1995. "Defensible Space: A New Physical Planning Tool for Urban Revitalization." *Journal of the American Planning Association* 61, 149–155.

Newman, O. and Franck, K.A. 1982. "The Effect of Building Size on Personal Crime and Fear of Crime." *Population and Environment* 5, 203–220.

Olweus, D. 1993. *Bullying at School: What We Know and What We Can Do*. Oxford: Blackwell.

Olweus, D. 2005. "A Useful Evaluation Design, and Effects of the Olweus Bullying Prevention Program." *Psychology, Crime & Law* 11, 389–402.

Olweus, D., Limber, S.P., Flerx, V., Mullin, N., Riese, J., and Snyder, M. 2007. *Olweus Bullying Prevention Program: Schoolwide Guide*. Center City, MN: Hazelden.

Olweus, D., Limber, S., and Mihalic, S. 1999. *Blueprints for Violence Prevention: Volume 9. The Bullying Prevention Program*. Boulder, CO: Institute of Behavioral Science, University of Colorado.

O'Moore, A.M. and Minton, S.J. 2005. "Evaluation of the Effectiveness of an Anti-bullying Programme in Primary School." *Aggressive Behavior* 31, 609–622.

Orpinas, P. and Horne, A. 2009. "Creating a Positive School Climate and Developing Social Competence." In *Handbook of Bullying in Schools: An International Perspective*, edited by S.R. Jimerson, S.M. Swearer, and D.L. Espelage, pp. 49–59. New York and London: Routledge.

Pepler, D., Jiang, D., Craig, W., and Connolly, J. 2008. "Developmental Trajectories of Bullying and Associated Factors." *Child Development* 79, 325–338.

Polanin, J. and Espelage, D.L. 2014. "Using a Meta-analytic Technique to Assess the Impact of Treatment Intensity Measures in a Multi-site Cluster-randomized Trial." *Journal of Behavioral Education.* Online first September 2014.

Polanin, J., Espelage, D.L., and Pigott, T.D. 2012. "A Meta-analysis of School-Based Bullying Prevention Programs' Effects on Bystander Intervention Behavior and Empathy Attitude." *School Psychology Review* 41(1), 47–65.

Prinstein, M.J., Boergers, J., and Vernberg, E.M. 2001. "Overt and Relational Aggression in Adolescents: Social-Psychological Adjustment of Aggressors and Victims." *Journal of Clinical Child Psychology* 30, 479–491.

Ross, S.W. and Horner, R.H. 2009. "Bully Prevention in Positive Behavior Support." *Journal of Applied Behavior Analysis* 42, 747–759.

Ross, S. W. and Horner, R. H. 2014. "Bully Prevention in Positive Behavior Support: Preliminary Evaluation of Third-, Fourth-, and Fifth-Grade Attitudes toward Bullying." *Journal of Emotional and Behavioral Disorders* 22, 225–236.

Salmivalli, C., Garandeau, C., and Veenstra, R. 2012. "KiVa Antibullying Program: Implications for School Adjustment." In *Peer Relationships and Adjustment at School*, edited by G. Ladd and A. Ryan, pp. 279–307. Charlotte, NC: Information Age Publishing.

Salmivalli, C., Kärnä, A., and Poskiparta, E. 2011. "Counteracting Bullying in Finland: The KiVa Program and Its Effects on Different Forms of Being Bullied." *International Journal of Behavioral Development* 35, 405–411.

Salmivalli, C. and Poskiparta, E. 2012. "Making Bullying Prevention a Priority in Finnish Schools: The KiVa Antibullying Program." *New Directions for Youth Development* 133, 41–53.

Slaughter-Defoe, D.T. and Carlson, K.G. 1996. "Young African American and Latino Children in High-Poverty Urban Schools: How They Perceive School Climate." *Journal of Negro Education* 65, 60–70.

Smith, P.K., Madsen, K.C., and Moody, J.C. 1999. "What Causes the Age Decline in Reports of Being Bullied at School? Towards a Developmental Analysis of Risks of Being Bullied." *Educational Research* 41, 267–285.

Spriggs, A.L., Iannotti, R.J., Nansel, T.R., and Haynie, D.L. 2007. "Adolescent Bullying Involvement and Perceived Family, Peer and School Relations: Commonalities and Differences across Race/Ethnicity." *Journal of Adolescent Health* 41, 283–293.

Stevens, V., Van Oost, P., and Bourdeaudhuij, I.D. 2000. "The Effects of an Anti-bullying Intervention Programme on Peers' Attitudes and Behaviour." *Journal of Adolescence* 23, 21–34.

Sugai, G., Horner, R.H., Dunlap, G. Hieneman, M., Lewis, T.J., Nelson, C.M., Scott, T. …, and Wilcox, B. 2000. "Applying Positive Behavioral Support and Functional Behavioral Assessment in Schools." *Journal of Positive Behavioral Interventions* 2, 131–143.

Thapa, A., Cohen, J., Guffey, S., and Higgins-D'Alessandro, A. 2013. "A Review of School Climate Research." *Review of Educational Research* 83, 357–385.

Toomey, R.B., McGuire, J.K., and Russell, S.T. 2012. "Heteronormativity, School Climates, and Perceived Safety for Gender Nonconforming Peers." *Journal of Adolescence* 35, 187–196.

Ttofi, M.M. and Farrington, D.P. 2011. "Effectiveness of school-based programs to reduce bullying: A systematic and meta-analytic review." *Journal of Experimental Criminology* 7, 27–56. DOI: 10. 1007/s11292-010-9109-1.

Twemlow, S.W., Fonagy, P., and Sacco, F.C. 2004. "The Role of Bystander in Social Architecture of Bullying and Violence in Schools and Communities." *Annals of the New York Academy of Sciences* 1036, 215–232.

Twemlow, S.W., Fonagy, P., and Sacco, F.C. 2005. "A Developmental Approach to Mentalizing Communities: II. The Peaceful Schools Experiment." *Bulletin of the Menninger Clinic* 69, 282–304.

Twemlow, S.W., Fonagy, P., Sacco, F.C., Gies, M.L., Evans, R., and Ewbank, R. 2001. "Creating a Peaceful School learning environment: A Controlled Study of an Elementary School Intervention to Reduce Violence." *The American Journal of Psychiatry* 158, 808–810.

Twemlow, S.W., Fonagy, P., Sacco, F.C., Vernberg, E., and Malcolm, J.M. 2011. "Reducing Violence and Prejudice in a Jamaican All Age School Using Attachment and Mentalization Theory." *Psychoanalytic Psychology* 28, 497–511.

Twemlow, S., Sacco, F., and Williams, P. 1996. "A Clinical and Interactionist Perspective on the Bully/Victim/Bystander Relationship." *Bulletin of the Menninger Clinic* 60, 296–313.

Unnever, J.D. and Cornell, D.G. 2003. "The Culture of Bullying in Middle School." *Journal of School Violence* 2, 5–27.

Varjas, K., Henrich, C.C., and Meyers, J. 2009. "Urban Middle School Students' Perceptions of Bullying, Cyberbullying, and School Safety." *Journal of School Violence* 8, 159–176.

Waasdorp, T.E., Bradshaw, C.P., and Leaf, P.J. 2012. "The Impact of Schoolwide Positive Behavioral Interventions and Supports on Bullying and Peer Rejection: A Randomized Control Effectiveness Trial." *Archives of Pediatric & Adolescent Medicine* 166, 149–156.

Walker, H.M., Horner, R.H., Sugai, G., Bullis, M., Sprague, J.R., Bricker, D., and Kauffman, J.M. 1996. "Integrated Approaches to Preventing Antisocial Behavior Patterns among School-age Children and Youth." *Journal of Emotional and Behavioral Disorders* 4, 193–256.

Wang, J., Iannotti, R.J., and Nansel, T.R. 2009. "School Bullying among Adolescents in the United States: Physical, Verbal, Relational, and Cyber." *Journal of Adolescent Health* 45, 368–375.

Webb, N.M. 2009. "The Teacher's Role in Promoting Collaborative Dialogue in the Classroom." *British Journal of Educational Psychology* 79, 1–28.

Zhang, A., Musu-Gillette, L., and Oudekerk, B.A. 2016. *Indicators of School Crime and Safety: 2015.* NCES 2016-079/NCJ 249758. National Center for Education Statistics, Department of Education and Bureau of Justice Statistics, Office of Justice Programs, US Department of Justice, Washington, DC. https://nces.ed.gov/pubs2016/2016079.pdf (last accessed October 28, 2017).

Zullig, K.J., Koopman, T.M., Patton, J M., and Ubbes, V.A. 2010. "School Climate: Historical Review, Instrument Development, and School Assessment." *Journal of Psychoeducational Assessment* 28, 139–152.

18

Sexual Violence in K–12 Settings

Anjali J. Forber-Pratt and Dorothy L. Espelage

In the school, context, sexual harassment, a subset of the larger sexual violence construct, is defined as unwanted sexual conduct – unwelcome verbal, non-verbal, and physical behaviors – that interferes with an individual's right to receive an equal education (American Association of University Women [AAUW] 2011; US Department of Education, Office for Civil Rights 2001). Sexual violence is defined as non-consensual completed or attempted penetration (vaginal, oral, or anal), unwanted touching (e.g., groping or fondling), or non-contact acts such as exposing oneself or verbal sexual harassment, committed by any perpetrator (Basile and Saltzman, 2002; Basile et al. 2005).

Sexual violence is common, consequential, and a priority for prevention. The Centers for Disease Control (CDC) report that nearly 1 in 5 women and 1 in 59 men experience rape at some point in their lives, inclusive of completed and attempted forced penetration or alcohol/drug facilitated penetration (Breiding et al. 2014). Additionally, an estimated 2 in 5 women and 1 in 5 men will experience other forms of sexual violence including being forced to penetrate someone else, sexual coercion, unwanted sexual contact and non-contact unwanted sexual experiences (Breiding et al. 2014). According to the Colorado Bureau of Investigation (CBI; 2014), there were 2,961 reported rapes in Colorado in 2014, up from 2,903 in 2013 (2014 Crime in Colorado Report). It is a public health priority to prevent sexual violence and is a Healthy People 2020 objective (www.healthypeople.gov).

Sexual harassment is prohibited in schools by Title IX (US Department of Education, Office for Civil Rights 2001) and is a form of sex discrimination. The US public health sphere increasingly recognizes sexual harassment during adolescence as a concern (Centers for Disease Control and Prevention 2012). Title IX of the Office of Civil Rights in the US Department of Education has mandated that schools protect their students from sexual harassment (US Department of Education, Office of Civil Rights 2001, 2010) due to the prevalence of sexual harassment in schools and adverse outcomes for victims. With this legal mandate in place, understanding the pervasiveness of sexual harassment in adolescence is important. Adolescence marks a period of time when cross-sex social contacts become more prominent (Pellegrini 2001), which provides not only opportunities for cross-sex friendships and intimate relationships, but also for sexual victimization, such as sexual harassment (Shute, Owens, and Slee 2008). Research

The Wiley Handbook on Violence in Education: Forms, Factors, and Preventions, First Edition.
Edited by Harvey Shapiro.
© 2018 John Wiley & Sons, Inc. Published 2018 by John Wiley & Sons, Inc.

on sexual harassment in educational settings has largely focused on high school students and emerging adults, though given that middle school is a developmental time when sexual exploration occurs, research ought to also explore this phenomenon at earlier middle school ages (Browning, Leventhal, and Brooks-Gunn 2005). A limited number of studies report that sexual harassment is a common occurrence in middle schools (Espelage, Basile, and Hamburger 2012; Gruber and Fineran 2007), which also has important implications for experiences of victimization.

Sexual Harassment during Early Adolescence

Adolescents go through major biological and developmental changes between sixth and eighth grade, and this time period also marks increased prevalence of sexual harassment (Peterson and Hyde 2009). Sexual harassment is relatively common among middle and high school youth, and is deemed a form of gendered harassment that acts to reinforce sexism and homophobia, which then highlights existing patriarchal power structures (Connell 1987; Kimmel and Mahler 2003; Meyer 2008; Shute, Owens, and Slee 2016). The cumulative impact of sexual harassment and power structures on educational engagement must also be considered. Students' abilities to participate in or benefit from their education experiences can be greatly affected by instances of sexual harassment. Furthermore, the educational environment can be perceived as hostile or abusive based on severity, persistence, or pervasiveness of sexual harassment (Espelage and De La Rue 2013; De La Rue and Espelage 2014).

Physical or verbal sexual harassment is extremely common in schools among adolescents. The extant literature indicates a wide range of estimated prevalence rates of sexual harassment in schools, from between 23% and 87% (Clear et al. 2014). The AAUW found that during the 2010–2011 school year, about 48% of US students nationwide in grades 7–12 reported experiencing some form of sexual harassment while in school (Hill and Kearl 2011), which is similar to other study findings. For example, one study in Sweden (Witkowska and Menckel 2005) found that 49% of the respondents identified that sexual harassment was a serious problem in school. Moreover, approximately 12% of girls and 5% of boys reported the incident to an adult authority in school (Hill and Kearl 2011). A short-term longitudinal study also found that that 32% of middle school boys and 22% of middle school girls in the United States reported making unwanted sexual comments to other students in school (Espelage, Basile, and Hamburger 2012). This same AAUW study found 81% of students experienced some form of physical or non-physical sexual harassment at some point during their lives (American Association of University Women 2011). The most common form experienced was unwanted sexual comments, jokes, gestures, or looks (66%), followed by being touched, grabbed, or pinched in a sexual way (49%) (American Association of University Women 2001).

Most of the literature suggests that males are overwhelmingly the perpetrators of physically forced forms of sexual violence (e.g., rape, etc.) (Black et al. 2011; Tjaden and Thoennes 2006). Males also report sexual harassment perpetration more often, even though girls engage in this behavior as well (American Association of University Women 2011; Fineran and Bennett 1999).

Despite these prevalence rates, a nationally representative survey of 1,965 US students in grades 7–12 found that as many as 49% of students (47% girls and 51% boys) who had experienced sexual harassment reported that they would ignore the incident (Hill and Kearl 2011). Additionally, 22% of boys and slightly over 10% of girls said they tried to turn the incident into a joke (Hill and Kearl 2011). From a nationally representative sample of US high school students, Hand and Sanchez (2000) also found that girls are far more likely to perceive sexual harassment to be harmful than boys.

Many scholars have also argued that behaviors that are indicative of sexual harassment come in many forms (Schnoll et al. 2015). Three common expressions of sexual harassment, as proposed by the tripartite model, are gender-based harassment, sexual coercion, and unwanted sexual attention (Fitzgerald, Gelfand, and Drasgow 1995; Fitzgerald and Hesson-McInnis 1989 – as cited in Schnoll et al. 2015). Initially, the model was applied to adults in the workplace; it has been extended to adolescent populations and research has confirmed the validity of these domains in middle and high school student populations (Felix and McMahon 2006; Omerod, Collinsworth, and Perry 2008). Research indicates that bullying is a precursor to the use of homophobic epithets in middle school (e.g., *fag, gay*; Espelage, Basile, and Hamburger 2012), and some youth resort to sexually harassing other students in order to exert their heterosexuality (Meyer 2008), a behavior that peaks in middle school (Espelage et al. 2017). This will be discussed further in a later section.

Types of Sexual Harassment in K–12 Settings

It is important to understand the types of sexual harassment middle school youth experience because it is representative of the larger school environment where staff, teachers, and students are often dismissive of sexual harassment (Jamal et al. 2015; Kimmel and Mahler 2003; Meyer 2008; Rinehart and Espelage 2016; Stein 1995). In the United States, existing research on sexual harassment among middle school students has focused on its prevalence and its intersection with other forms of aggression, such as bullying (Espelage, Basile, and Hamburger 2012; Fineran, McDonald, and Constable 2008; Gruber and Fineran 2007, 2008; Jamal et al. 2015; Pellegrini 2001). Broadly defined, the types of sexual harassment seen in schools include making sexual comments, jokes, gestures or looks; displaying or handing out sexual pictures, photographs, illustrations, messages, or notes; writing sexually explicit messages on bathroom/locker room walls; spreading sexual rumors; accusing someone of being gay; grabbing, pinching, pulling at clothes, or brushing against someone in a sexual way; pulling clothing off/down ("pantsing"); cornering someone in a sexual way; and coercing someone into kissing you or doing something sexual other than kissing (Johnson and Lennon 1997, 21). Additionally, anti-gay insults such as "gay" or "fag" and terms such as "slut" or "whore" are recognized as sexual harassment (Hill and Kearl 2011).

As children and adolescents learn to develop intimate relationships, it is not uncommon for them to tease each other as the designation between teasing and sexual harassment is not always clear (Johnson and Lennon 1997). In a recent exploration of the types of sexual harassment experienced by 878 middle school youth, verbal sexual harassment was more frequent than physical sexual harassment and sexual assault, and being the target of homophobic slurs (e.g., gay, fag) was quite prevalent (Espelage et al. 2016). Specifically, approximately 43% of the sample reported experiencing unwanted sexual commentary, such as comments, jokes, and/or gestures and 14% were targets of sexual rumors, 11% reported that someone showed them sexually graphic pictures, 9% indicated that someone had written sexual messages/graffiti on bathroom walls or in locker rooms, 21% reported being touched, grabbed, or pinched in a sexual way, 18% were brushed up against in a sexual way; and 7% were blocked in a sexual way.

Locations of Sexual Harassment in K-12 Settings

Youth are more likely to experience harassment and violence in certain locations in schools than others (Astor, Meyer, and Pitner 2001). In order to better enable school officials to be able to monitor locations where sexual harassment is most likely to occur, we must first identify the locations where sexual harassment takes place. Keeping these locations in mind, we can also begin to explore the social dynamics and interactions that are happening within schools (Astor, Meyer, and Behre 1999). Therefore, some prevention programs employ a technique called a "hot spot" analysis to identify where youth experience bullying, sexual harassment, and teen dating violence in order to home in on the location where these incidents occur (e.g., Astor, Meyer, and Pitner 2001; Taylor et al. 2013). Studies explicitly focused on sexual harassment, however, are less common. In a 2001 survey of US public school districts, it was found that sexual harassment occurred most frequently in the hallway (71%), followed by classrooms (61%), gymnasium/playing field/pool areas (45%), and outside the school on school ground (41%) (Harris Interactive 2001). On the contrary, a study by Harris Interactive (2001) that looked at sexual harassment of 2,808 14- and 15-year-old students by teachers and by peers in 22 Dutch secondary schools found that sexual harassment by peers occurs in public places – classrooms (41%), followed by corridors (16%), cafeterias (6%), and gyms (3%) (Timmerman 2003). In the United States, a recent study on the locations of sexual harassment incidents in schools found that the most frequent location was in hallways, followed by classrooms, gym locker rooms, gym class, lunch room, and outside of the school (Espelage et al. 2016).

Race, Sex, Disability, and Grade Differences in Sexual Harassment Victimization Experiences

Race

Important aspects of sexual harassment among US adolescents include sociodemographic characteristics including race, sex, and disability. Research that specifically examined racial differences in sexual harassment in adolescence is limited. Although the sample sizes for racial/ethnic minority students are relatively small, extant findings suggest that racial and ethnic minority students may be affected more than white students. According to the AAUW, racial/ethnic minority students in US schools were more likely than their white peers to stop doing an activity, report difficulty in concentrating on their school work, change their route to/from school, and transfer to another school in response to sexual harassment (Hill and Kearl 2011). Other studies on sexual harassment of racial/ethnic minority adolescents have produced inconsistent findings. Goldstein et al. (2007) found in a sample of 872 African American and white adolescents (mean age = 14.2 years) that females and African Americans reported more frequent peer sexual harassment victimization than males and white students. On the other hand, in their examination of the association between bullying subtypes, sexual harassment, and dating violence experienced by 684 US middle and high school students, Espelage and Holt (2007) found that African American students did not report higher rates of peer sexual harassment than white students. There appears to be a serious lack of research attention paid to racial and ethnic differences in sexual harassment in adolescents, as a bulk of the studies is based on non-representative samples of middle-class, white female students (Zeira, Astor, and Benbenishty 2002).

Sex and Grade

Existing school-based studies report significant sex differences in terms of frequency and types of peer-to-peer sexual harassment (Hand and Sanchez 2000). Other studies report that female students experience sexual harassment victimization and perpetration more than male students in the United States (Fineran and Bennett 1999; Goldstein et al. 2007; Hill and Kearl 2011), Brazil (DeSouza and Ribeiro 2005), and Australia (Shute, Owens, and Slee 2008). In schools where hegemonic heterosexual masculinities are reinforced, females are particularly targeted for sexualized forms of violence and harassment (Duncan 1999).

Interestingly, in another study of US adolescents in grades 5–9 about longitudinal trends in sexual harassment, boys reported sexual harassment victimization more frequently than girls at each grade level (Peterson and Hyde 2009). Furthermore, this study found that boys experienced more same-sex sexual harassment victimization than girls, even though sex differences were not found in cross-sex sexual harassment. For adolescents identifying as heterosexual, cross-sex sexual harassment might result in sexual advances, possibly motivated by romantic or sexual interest (McMaster et al. 2002). On the other hand, for same-sex sexual harassment, it is more likely an expression of verbal aggression, which might entail homophobic epithets, jokes, and name-calling (McMaster et al. 2002). Another study (Fineran and Bennett 1999), comprising a sample of 342 urban high school students in the United States, also reported that female students experienced more overt forms of sexual harassment while male students perpetrated sexually harassing behaviors more frequently. Sex differences in sexual harassment are related to how these behaviors are perceived and interpreted by adolescents. From the findings of a study consisting of 73 third to fifth grade US students who were presented with eight scenarios related to peer sexual harassment, Murnen and Smolak (2000) concluded that meanings and interpretations of sexual harassment differed for boys and girls.

In the adult literature, more has been studied about these interpretations and sex differences. Some researchers have examined gender differences in appraisals. For example, compared to men, women considered sexual harassment vignettes to be more anxiety-producing (Berdahl, Magley, and Waldo 1996) and were more likely to rate their personal experiences of sexual harassment as bothersome (de Haas, Timmerman, and Höing 2009). In a 2011 study (Settles et al. 2011) with 6,304 adults, perceptions of sexual harassment and sex differences were explored. Settles and colleagues found that sexual harassment may have become so commonplace for women that they have built up resistance to harassing behavior they considered bothersome, but were not reporting distress. For women, sexual harassment was distressing when they saw it as frightening but not when they saw it as bothersome, whereas for men, sexual harassment was distressing when they saw it as either frightening or bothersome (Settles et al. 2011). With adults in schools serving as role models and on the frontlines to intervene when sexual violence incidents occur, these adult perceptions are important to consider as youth are facing these incidents. These findings suggest this is an important phenomenon to explore further in student populations.

Taken together, extant findings in the United States appear to be similar to those reported in other countries, which suggest that sexual harassment is a prevalent problem among adolescents. In addition, findings are consistent from studies conducted using middle school samples with those using high school samples. For example, findings from one study indicated that female high school students were more likely than male students to report sexual harassment, and perpetration was correlated with gender and racial/ethnic minority status, which is similar to findings from research on middle school students (Clear et al. 2014). However, most of the aforementioned studies in the United States and in other countries did not specifically focus on middle school students, as many have combined middle and high school student samples. As such, questions arise as to whether school-based violence prevention programs, which are inclusive of sexual harassment, are developmentally and culturally appropriate for racially diverse middle school students, many of whom are transitioning from childhood to early adolescence.

Disability

Research studies that specifically examine the role of disability status and sexual harassment in adolescence in schools is limited (Linn and Rousso 2001). However, outside of school environments, research indicates that individuals with disabilities may be at an even greater risk for sexual harassment, in the role of both victim and perpetrator (Sobsey 1994). In a 2012 meta-analysis (Jones et al. 2012) about violence against children with disabilities, 15 studies were found related to sexual violence in children with disabilities, though the location of these incidents was not reported. The pooled prevalence rate across these studies was 14%, including a total of 1,455 sexual violence incidents in 14,675 children with disabilities (Jones et al. 2012). These results confirm that children with disabilities are more likely to be victims of violence, including sexual violence, than are their peers who are not disabled. It is possible this increased risk, in part, is due to difficulties with peer interaction and inability to detect the intentions of others (Fisher, Moskowitz, and Hodapp 2013; Jawaid et al. 2012).

In the context of schools, Young and colleagues (2008) investigated the perceptions of 129 special education teachers about the prevalence and characteristics of sexual harassment among students identified with disabilities. While this study did not include student data, special education teachers reported on observed incidents of sexual harassment, which provides insight on this understudied population. In general, special educators who worked with students with mild to moderate and combined disabilities reported significantly more verbal sexual harassment than special educators who worked with students with more severe disabilities (Young et al. 2008). This finding is corroborated by work specifically about individuals with intellectual disability (Lumley and Miltenberger 1997; Reiter, Bryen, and Shachar 2007). On the contrary, regardless of the severity of disability, participants reported incidents of physical sexual harassment in similar proportions (Young et al. 2008). In terms of gender differences, in this study, females were as likely to be the target of sexual harassment as were males (Young et al 2008). The scarcity of literature in this area indicates that more research is needed to better understand the intricacies of disability with race and sex differences pertaining to sexual harassment in schools.

Social Connectedness

Links between social connectedness and sexual violence (SV) perpetration have also been demonstrated. Connectedness with friends and adults in the community has also been found to decrease the likelihood of sexually violent behavior (Basile et al. 2009; Borowsky, Hogan, and Ireland 1997). Further, when youth report a strong support system, this was associated with decreased likelihood of same-sex peer SV perpetration (Basile et al. 2013). Further, the presence of gender-based harassment in schools leads to the greater likelihood of isolation. Poteat and Espelage (2007), for example, found that homophobic slurs, compared with other types of comments, resulted in increased anxiety and depression, and greater alienation from school among middle school children. Along the same lines, Swearer et al. (2008) discovered that, among boys, being called gay was associated with greater depression and anxiety and less favorable perceptions of school climate. In a recent study of high school students, Gruber and Fineran (2016) found that sexual harassment victimization was associated with lower school engagement and student alienation from teachers. These studies point to the potential significance of preventing sexual violence in schools through promoting positive connections between students and faculty, and attending to the school climate.

Related to climate, peer and school norms and social connectedness must also be considered. Unfortunately, these aspects have been overlooked as major drivers of bullying and gender-based harassment and violence by prevention programs. The prevalence and outcomes associated with gender-based violence, including sexual violence, suggest that their public health costs are enormous and thus there is a need for effective, broad-based prevention programs. In one study, 20% of sixth to seventh graders perpetrated dating violence, and close to 50% perpetrated sexual harassment, with boys 1.2 times more likely to report sexual harassment and violence perpetration (Taylor et al. 2013). Another study of fifth to seventh graders indicated that 34% of boys and 20% of girls engaged in high rates of homophobic teasing (Espelage, Basile, and Hamburger 2012). Similarly, 50% of students in grades 7–12 have experienced sexual harassment in the past academic year (Hill and Kearl 2011). Sexual harassment is associated with serious mental health consequences (Gruber and Fineran 2008) and lower academic achievement, quitting activities, and changing friends during adolescence (Gruber and Fineran 2007). Based on 28 school-based studies of randomly selected youth, Friedman et al. (2011) found that 43% of gay and 50% of bisexual teenage males reported physical assault by a peer at school (prior year). These rates far exceeded those of heterosexual youth. However, adolescents attending schools with support groups (e.g., Gay–Straight Alliances, or GSAs) report lower rates of victimization at school and suicide attempts (Goodenow, Szalacha, and Westheimer 2006; Heck, Flentje, and Cochran 2011), suggesting that peer and school norms are malleable targets for prevention. Further, there is less homophobic perpetration and sexual harassment perpetration reported by youth in schools where teachers and staff are intolerant of sexual harassment and have policies in place to protect all youth (Rinehart and Espelage 2016).

Homophobic Teasing

Homophobic teasing is a particular form of gender-based victimization. Homophobia, the underlying attitude that informs this form of teasing, is the product of negative beliefs, attitudes, stereotypes, and behaviors directed toward gay, lesbian, and bisexual people or gender non-conforming individuals (Wright, Adams, and Bernat 1999). Examples of homophobic teasing include epithets that imply or otherwise expose the victim as homosexual, threats of physical violence, and social isolation. Homophobic teasing, while less studied, is a commonly reported experience, particularly by students who identify as lesbian, gay, bisexual, or transgender (LGBT). In a recent longitudinal investigation of US middle school youth, those who were more likely to be dismissive of sexual harassment displayed higher levels of homophobic name-calling, a form of gendered harassment (Espelage et al. 2017).

Rivers (2001) reported that gay and lesbian students frequently experienced incidents of name-calling (82%) and being teased (58%), and reported incidents of assaults (60%). These students also experienced rumor spreading (59%) and social isolation (27%). But homophobic teasing is not only directed at sexual minority students. In California, a large-scale survey of students in grades 7–11 found that 7.5% reported being bullied at school because of their actual *or perceived* sexual orientation, with two-thirds of those students who identified as lesbian, gay, bisexual, or transgender reporting victimization (California Safe Schools Coalition and 4-H Center for Youth Development 2004). Converging evidence documents moderate to high rates of SV against youth. The 2011 Youth Risk Behavior Survey, a national survey of students in grades 9–12, found a lifetime reported prevalence for unwanted physically forced sexual intercourse of 11.8% for girls and 4.5% for boys (Centers for Disease Control and Prevention 2012).

Considerations for Implementing Prevention Programs

Oftentimes, prevention programs focus on singular types of violence instead of shared risk and protective factors. Bullying, homophobic name-calling, and sexual harassment are each associated with deficits in emotional regulatory and interpersonal skills; peer and school norms supporting violence; and unique family dynamics and certain masculine ideologies (Espelage 2012; Foshee and Matthew 2007; Kimmel and Mahler 2003; Poteat 2007; Poteat, O'Dwyer, and Mereish 2012). Most school-based anti-violence programs have homed in on individual types of aggression, typically physical aggression occurring among youth (Leff et al. 2001). Concentration on singular types of violence may be ineffective, because, poly-victimization is highly prevalent, and youth who experience multiple types of victimization experience the worst health outcomes (Finkelhor, Ormrod, and Turner 2007; Finkelhor et al. 2009; Hamby and Grych 2013). Therefore, these findings suggest that programs targeting multiple types of victimization and perpetration will be more effective in decreasing school-based violence and may have a synergistic impact on health outcomes. Evidence is increasing suggesting that many mental health and drug abuse prevention programs delivered across childhood and adolescence have "crossover" effects (i.e., unanticipated beneficial effects) (Reider and Sims 2016) on other health behavior problems, including HIV risk behaviors and suicidal behavior, which adds further motivation to simultaneously identify preventive interventions that reduce multiple forms of interpersonal violence.

When considered more broadly, bias-based harassment carries magnified effects beyond those attributable to general bullying. In 600,000+ students in 16,185 schools, nearly 40% of those who experienced victimization (past year) considered at least some of it to be based on their sexual orientation, gender, race or ethnicity, or religion (Russell et al. 2012). Although sexual minorities face more victimization than heterosexual youth, heterosexual youth are often targets of gender-based harassment. Youth use homophobic language or engage in other forms of gender-based harassment as a way to enforce gender norms (Kimmel and Mahler 2003; Poteat, Kimmel, and Wilchins 2011). Boys, whether sexual minority or heterosexual, who engage in gender non-conforming behavior often are targets of homophobic bullying (Poteat et al. 2011; Pascoe 2007, 2013). Recent findings indicate that the frequency of experiencing homophobic victimization increases for boys from grades 7 to 12 (Poteat et al. 2011).

Implementing effective sexual violence prevention programs in middle schools requires the efforts of faculty, staff, school administrators, practitioners (e.g., counseling psychologists, school psychologists, school counselors), and students. Teachers, school officials, and staff members need to accept that sexual harassment happens in middle school, as many of them do not even acknowledge this (Charmaraman et al. 2013). Once they understand that then they need to recognize that sexual harassment comes in various forms, from physical (e.g., "pantsed," being forced to do something sexual) to non-physical (e.g., homophobic verbal harassment, target of sexual commentary). Oftentimes, school administrators, teachers, school officials, and staff members in the building only think about physical sexual behavior when describing sexual violence in schools. Furthermore, as research shows, girls are more likely than boys to report experiencing sexual harassment in various places, such as bathrooms and locker rooms; therefore practitioners in collaboration with school staff and officials need to work together to monitor areas where sexual harassment and assault are likely to take place.

Practitioners need to recognize that sexual harassment is experienced differently across students, with sex, race, and age playing a factor, and likely disability too, though further research is needed in this area to substantiate this. Counseling techniques and interventions for students affected by sexual harassment must consider these sociodemographic differences. It is important that practitioners identify programs that not only demonstrate efficacy but also are culturally valid. Prevention programs also need to address relevant factors that contribute to sexual harassment (Kopels and Dupper 1999) in racially diverse student populations. One such program is the Expect Respect Elementary School Project. The Expect Respect Project is a whole-school approach, which consists of training staff members, educating students in the classroom, educating parents, and assisting with policy and social support development. Six public schools in Austin, Texas that implemented the Expect Respect program reported a significant increase in identifying sexual harassment, having greater awareness of school policies on sexual harassment, and being willing to intervene on behalf of a student who is sexually harassed (Sanchez et al. 2001). Also, the social-emotional learning program Second Step (Committee for Children 2008) has yielded significant reductions in sexual harassment in large-scale randomized trials (Espelage, Low, Polanin, and Brown 2015; Espelage, Low, Van Ryzin, and Polanin 2015). These programs have been found to be effective among racially and ethnically diverse student populations and for middle school students with disabilities (Espelage, Rose, and Polanin 2015). All programs being implemented should include provisions to ensure cultural sensitivity and accessibility for students with disabilities. For example, students with intellectual disabilities may need additional supports to learn about sexual violence, including a school's sexual violence education and prevention programs, what constitutes sexual violence, and how students can report incidents of sexual violence.

School Policies, Procedures, and Guidelines

It is also important that school districts have a consistently enforced policy, such as Title IX, that clearly defines sexual harassment and regulations against engaging in such behaviors. Parents, teachers, and school administrators are often unaware that Title IX regulations also apply to primary and secondary education, and are often unsure of what should happen after a sexual violence incident has been reported to authorities. For example, students may end up still attending classes with their perpetrator because no one has removed the attacker from their classrooms. Important to note, when students with disabilities experience sexual violence, federal civil rights laws other than Title IX may also be relevant.

The US Department of Education (2014) issued guidance further explaining details about what schools should do in cases of student-to-student sexual harassment or assault and also has specific provisions and recommendations when students with disabilities and/or undocumented students are involved. The school should ensure an alleged victim and their accused perpetrator do not come in contact with each other, and any ongoing bullying or retaliation related to an allegation of assault should be stopped too (US Department of Education 2010). Even if a criminal investigation is ongoing, a school must still conduct its own Title IX investigation and discipline a student as it deems necessary, which may include suspension or expulsion (US Department of Education 2014).

Furthermore, school officials need to provide guidelines about how school staff members should deal with incidents of sexual harassment, and what to do when a student reports being sexually harassed by someone. It is also important to recognize that teachers, counselors, and administrators may also serve as community or family members of students, which can create additional challenges related to confidentiality, and may also discourage students from disclosing the abuse. Such guidelines must be able to inform decision makers if an incident occurs between students, as the school has to make a decision regarding the rights to education of the students involved, whether that decision is expulsion or something else. The Office of Civil Rights issued guidance that explicitly states that in cases involving allegations of sexual assault, mediation is not appropriate even on a voluntary basis (US Department of Education 2011). It is recommended that schools further clarify in their grievance procedures that mediation will not be used to resolve sexual harassment complaints.

Conclusion

This chapter presents key findings indicating that sexual violence is a frequent and multifaceted problem in US schools. We must critically consider the types of sexual harassment students face and the location of these incidents, as these are paramount for effective prevention and intervention efforts. It is important that future work in this area includes a continued focus on sociodemographic differences in order to better understand what is happening for specific subgroups of students. We must also be intentional about our school policies and procedures. Effective prevention and intervention efforts require ongoing assessment and monitoring as well as a sexual harassment policy that is consistently enforced.

References

American Association of University Women Educational Foundation. 2001. *Hostile Hallways: Bullying, Teasing, and Sexual Harassment in School.* Washington, DC: Author. http://www.aauw.org/resource/hostile-hallways-bullying-teasing-and-sexual-harassment-in-school/ (last accessed October 19, 2017).

American Association of University Women. 2011. *Crossing the Line: Sexual Harassment at School.* Washington, DC: Author. http://www.aauw.org/resource/crossing-the-line-sexual-harassment-at-school-executive-summary/ (last accessed October 19, 2017).

Astor, R.A., Meyer, H.A., and Behre, W.J. 1999. "Unowned Places and Times: Maps and Interviews about Violence in High Schools." *American Educational Research Journal* 36, 3–42. DOI: 10.3102/00028312036001003.

Astor, R.A., Meyer, H.A., and Pitner, R.O. 2001. "Elementary and Middle School Students' Perceptions of Violence-prone School Subcontexts." *The Elementary School Journal* 101, 511–528.

Basile, K.C., Espelage, D.L., Rivers, I., McMahon, P.M., and Simon, T. 2009. "The Theoretical and Empirical Links between Bullying Behavior and Male Sexual Violence Perpetration." *Aggression and Violent Behavior* 14, 336–347. DOI: 10.1016/j.avb.2009.06.001.

Basile, K.C., Hamburger, M.E., Swahn, M.H., and Choi, C. 2013. "Sexual Violence Perpetration by Adolescents in Dating versus Same-sex Peer Relationships: Differences in Associated Risk and Protective Factors." *Western Journal of Emergency Medicine* 14(4), 329.

Basile, K.C., Lang, K.S., Bartenfeld, T.A., and Clinton-Sherrod, M. 2005. "Report from the CDC: Evaluability Assessment of the Rape Prevention and Education Program: Summary of Findings and Recommendations." *Journal of Women's Health* 14(3), 201–207.

Basile, K.C. and Saltzman, L.E. 2002. *Sexual Violence Surveillance: Uniform Definitions and Recommended Data Elements, Version 1.0.* Atlanta: Centers for Disease Control and Prevention, National Center for Injury Prevention and Control. www.cdc.gov/violenceprevention/pdf/sv_surveillance_definitionsl-2009-a.pdf (last accessed November 2, 2017).

Berdahl, J.L., Magley, V.J., and Waldo, C.R. 1996. "The Sexual Harassment of Men?" *Psychology of Women Quarterly* 20(4), 527–547.

Black, M.C., Basile, K.C., Breiding, M.J., Smith, S.G., Walters, M.L., Merrick, M.T., … Stevens, M.R. 2011. *The National Intimate Partner and Sexual Violence Survey*

(NISVS): 2010 Summary Report. Atlanta, GA: National Center for Injury Prevention and Control, Centers for Disease Control and Prevention.

Borowsky, I.W., Hogan, M., and Ireland, M. 1997. "Adolescent Sexual Aggression: Risk and Protective Factors." *Pediatrics* 100, e7.

Breiding, M.J., Smith, S.G., Basile, K.C., Walter, M.L., Chen, J., and Merrick, M.T. 2014. "Prevalence and Characteristics of Sexual Violence, Stalking and Intimate Partner Violence Victimization – National Intimate Partner and Sexual Violence Survey, United States, 2011. *MMWR Surveillance Summary* 63(8), 1–18.

Browning, C.R., Leventhal, T., and Brooks-Gunn, J. 2005. "Sexual Initiation in Early Adolescence: The Nexus of Parental and Community Control." *American Sociological Review* 70, 758–788. DOI: 10.1177/000312240507000502.

California Safe Schools Coalition and 4-H Center for Youth Development, University of California, Davis. 2004. *Consequences of Harassment Based on Actual or Perceived Sexual Orientation and Gender Non-conformity and Steps to Making Schools Safer*. Davis, CA: Authors.

Centers for Disease Control and Prevention. 2012. "Sexual Violence." http://www.cdc.gov/ViolencePrevention/sexualviolence/ (last accessed October 19, 2017).

Charmaraman, L., Jones, A.E., Stein, N., and Espelage, D.L. 2013. "Is It Bullying or Sexual Harassment? Knowledge, Attitudes, and Professional Development Experiences of Middle School Staff." *Journal of School Health* 83, 438–444. DOI: 10.1111/josh.12048.

Clear, E.R., Coker, A.L., Cook-Craig, P.G., Bush, H.M., Garcia, L.S., Williams, C.M., Lewis, A.M., and Fisher, B.S. 2014. "Sexual Harassment Victimization and Perpetration among High School Students." *Violence Against Women* 20, 1203–1219. DOI: 10.1177/1077801214551287.

Colorado Bureau of Investigation. 2014. "Crime in Colorado 2014." http://crimeinco.cbi.state.co.us/cic2k14/index.html (accessed October 18, 2017).

Committee for Children. 2008. *Second Step: Student Success through Prevention Program*. Seattle, WA: Committee for Children.

Connell, R.W. 1987. *Gender and Power: Society, the Person and Sexual Politics*. Cambridge: Polity Press.

de Haas, S., Timmerman, G., and Höing, M. 2009. "Sexual Harassment and Health among Male and Female Police Officers." *Journal of Occupational Health Psychology* 14, 390–401. DOI: 10.1037/a0017046.

De La Rue, L. and Espelage, D.L. 2014. "Family and Abuse Characteristics of Gang-involved, Pressured-to-join, and Non-gang-involved Girls." *Psychology of Violence* 4(3), 253–265. DOI: 10.1037/a0035492.

DeSouza, E.R.,and Ribeiro, J. 2005. "Bullying and Sexual Harassment among Brazilian High School Students." *Journal of Interpersonal Violence* 20, 1018–1038. DOI: 10.1177/0886260505277731.

Duncan, N. 1999. *Sexual Bullying: Gender Conflict and Pupil Culture in Secondary Schools*. London: Routledge.

Espelage, D.L. 2012. "Bullying Prevention: A Research Dialogue with Dorothy Espelage." *Prevention Researcher* 19(3), 17–19.

Espelage, D.L., Basile, K.C., and Hamburger, M.E. 2012. "Bullying Perpetration and Subsequent Sexual Violence Perpetration among Middle School Students." *Journal of Adolescent Health* 50, 60–65. DOI: 10.1016/j.jadohealth.2011.07.015.

Espelage, D.L. and De La Rue, L. 2013. "Examining Predictors of Bullying and Sexual Violence Perpetration among Middle School Female Students." In *Perceptions of Female Offenders: How Stereotypes and Social Norms Affect Criminal Justice Responses*, edited by B. Russell, pp. 25–46. New York: Springer.

Espelage, D.L. and Holt, M.K. 2007. "Dating Violence and Sexual Harassment across the Bully-Victim Continuum among Middle and High School Students." *Journal of Youth and Adolescence* 36, 799–811. DOI: 10.1007/s10964-006-9109-7.

Espelage, D.L., Hong, S.J., Merrin, G.J., Davis, J.P., Rose, C.A., and Little, T.D. 2017. "A Longitudinal Examination of Homophobic Name-Calling in Middle School: Bullying, Traditional Masculinity, and Sexual Harassment as Predictors." *Psychology of Violence.* Advance online publication. DOI: 10.1037/vio0000083.

Espelage, D.L., Hong, J.S., Rinehart, S., and Doshi, N. 2016. "Understanding Types, Locations, and Perpetrators of Peer-to-Peer Sexual Harassment in US Middle Schools: A Focus on Sex, Racial, and Grade Differences." *Children and Youth Services Review* 71, 174–183.

Espelage, D.L., Low, S., Polanin, J., and Brown, E. 2015. "Clinical Trial of Second Step© Middle-School Program: Impact on Aggression and Victimization." *Journal of Applied Developmental Psychology* 37, 52–63.

Espelage, D.L., Low, S., Van Ryzin, M.J., and Polanin, J. 2015. "Clinical Trial of Second Step© Middle-School Program: Impact on Bullying, Cyberbullying, Homophobic Teasing and Sexual Harassment Perpetration." *School Psychology Review* 44(4), 464–479.

Espelage, D.L., Rose, C.A., and Polanin, J.R. 2015. "Social-emotional Learning Program to Reduce Bullying, Fighting, and Victimization among Middle School Students with Disabilities." *Remedial and Special Education* 36(5), 299–311.

Felix, E.D. and McMahon, S.D. 2006. "Gender and Multiple Forms of Peer Victimization: How Do They Influence Adolescent Psychosocial Adjustment?" *Violence and Victims* 21, 707–724. DOI: 10.1891/0886-6708.21.6.707.

Fineran, S. and Bennett, L. 1999. "Gender and Power Issues of Peer Sexual Harassment among Teenagers." *Journal of Interpersonal Violence* 14, 626–641. DOI: 10.1177/088626 099014006004.

Fineran, S., McDonald, S., and Constable, R. 2008. "Bullying and Peer Sexual Harassment in Schools: Pathways to Assessment." In *School Social Work: Practice, Policy, and Research*, 7th ed., edited by R. Constable, C.R. Massat, S. McDonald, and J.P. Flynn, pp. 713–727. Chicago, IL: Lyceum Books.

Finkelhor, D., Ormrod, R.K., and Turner, H.A. 2007. "Poly-victimization: A Neglected Component in Child Victimization." *Child Abuse & Neglect* 31(1), 7–26.

Finkelhor, D., Ormrod, R., Turner, H., and Holt, M. 2009. "Pathways to Poly-victimization." *Child Maltreatment* 14(4), 316–329.

Fisher, M.H., Moskowitz, A.L., and Hodapp, R.M. 2013." Differences in Social Vulnerability among Individuals with Autism Spectrum Disorder, Williams Syndrome, and Down Syndrome." *Research in Autism Spectrum Disorders* 7(8), 931–937.

Fitzgerald, L.F., Gelfand, M.J., and Drasgow, F. 1995. "Measuring Sexual Harassment: Theoretical and Psychometric Advances." *Basic and Applied Social Psychology* 17, 425–445. DOI: 10.1207/s15324834basp1704_2.

Fitzgerald, L.F. and Hesson-McInnis, M. 1989. "The Dimensions of Sexual Harassment: A Structural Analysis." *Journal of Vocational Behavior* 35, 309–326. DOI: 10.1016/0001-8791(89)90032-8.

Foshee, V.A. and Matthew, R.A. 2007. "Adolescent Dating Abuse Perpetration: A Review of Findings, Methodological Limitations and Suggestions for Future Research." In *The Cambridge Handbook of Violent Behavior and Aggression*, edited by D. Flannery, A. Vazonsyi, and I. Waldman, pp. 431–449. New York: Cambridge University Press.

Friedman, M.S., Marshal, M.P., Guadamuz, T.E., Wei, C., Wong, C.F., Saewyc, E.M., and Stall, R. 2011. "A Meta-analysis of Disparities in Childhood Sexual Abuse, Parental Physical Abuse, and Peer Victimization among Sexual Minority and Sexual Nonminority Individuals." *American Journal of Public Health* 101(8), 1481–1494.

Goldstein, S.E., Malanchuk, O., Davis-Kean, P.E., and Eccles, J.S. 2007. "Risk Factors of Sexual Harassment by Peers: A Longitudinal Investigation of African American and European American Adolescents." *Journal of Research on Adolescence* 17, 285–300.

Goodenow, C., Szalacha, L., and Westheimer, K. 2006. "School Support Groups, Other School Factors, and the Safety of Sexual Minority Adolescents." *Psychology in the Schools* 43(5), 573–589.

Gruber, J.E. and Fineran, S. 2007. "The Impact of Bullying and Sexual Harassment on Middle and High School Girls." *Violence Against Women* 13, 627–643. DOI: 10.1177/1077801207301557.

Gruber, J.E., and Fineran, S. 2008. "Comparing the Impact of Bullying and Sexual Harassment Victimization on the Mental and Physical Health of Adolescents." *Sex Roles: A Journal of Research* 59, 1–13. DOI: 10.1007/s11199-008-9431-5.

Gruber, J.E. and Fineran, S. 2016. "Sexual Harassment, Bullying, and School Outcomes for High School Girls and Boys." *Journal of Violence Against Women* 22(1), 568–583. DOI: 10.1177/1077801215599079.

Hamby, S. and Grych, J.H. 2013. *The Web of Violence: Exploring Connections among Different Forms of Interpersonal Violence and Abuse*. New York: Springer.

Hand, J.Z. and Sanchez, L. 2000. "Badgering or Bantering? Gender Differences in Experience of, and Reactions to, Sexual Harassment among U.S. High School Students." *Gender & Society* 14, 718–746. DOI: 10.1177/089124300014006002.

Harris Interactive. 2001. *Hostile Hallways: Bullying, Teasing, and Sexual Harassment in School*. Washington, DC: American Association of University Women Educational Foundation. http://www.aauw.org/files/2013/02/hostile-hallways-bullying-teasing-and-sexual-harassment-in-school.pdf (last accessed October 19, 2017).

Heck, N.C., Flentje, A., and Cochran, B.N. 2011. "Offsetting risks: High School Gay–Straight Alliances and Lesbian, Gay, Bisexual, and Transgender (LGBT) Youth." *School Psychology Quarterly* 26(2), 161.

Hill, C. and Kearl, H. 2011. *Crossing the Line: Sexual Harassment at School*. Washington, DC: American Association of University Women. http://www.aauw.org/files/2013/02/Crossing-the-Line-Sexual-Harassment-at-School.pdf (last accessed October 19, 2017).

Jamal, F., Bonell, C., Harden, A., and Lorenc, T. 2015. "The Social Ecology of Girls' Bullying Practices: Exploratory Research in Two London Schools." *Sociology of Health & Illness* 37, 731–744. DOI: 10.1111/1467-9566.12231.

Jawaid, A., Riby, D.M., Owens, J., White, S.W., Tarar, T., and Schulz, P.E. 2012. "'Too withdrawn' or 'too friendly': Considering Social Vulnerability in Two Neuro-developmental Disorders. *Journal of Intellectual Disability Research* 56(4), 335–350. DOI: 10.1111/j.1365-2788.2011.01452.x

Johnson, K.K.P. and Lennon, S.J. 1997. "Sexual Harassment in the Schools: Strategies for Prevention." *Journal of Family and Consumer Sciences* 89, 20–24.

Jones, L., Bellis, M.A., Wood, S., Hughes, K., McCoy, E., Eckley, L., … and Officer, A. 2012. "Prevalence and Risk of Violence against Children with Disabilities: A Systematic Review and Meta-Analysis of Observational Studies." *The Lancet* 380(9845), 899–907. DOI: 10.1016/S0140-6736(12)60692-8.

Kimmel, M.S. and Mahler, M. 2003. "Adolescent Masculinity, Homophobia, and Violence: Random School Shootings, 1982–2001." *American Behavioral Scientist* 46, 1439–1458. DOI: 10.1177/ 0002764203046010010.

Kopels, S. and Dupper, D.R. 1999. "School-based Peer Sexual Harassment." *Child Welfare* 78, 435–460.

Leff, S., Power, T.J., Manz, P.H., Costigan, T.E., and Nabors, L.A. 2001. "School-based Aggression Prevention Program for Young Children: Current Status and Implications For Violence Prevention." *School Psychology Review* 30(3), 344–362.

Linn, E. and Rousso, H. 2001. "Stopping Sexual Harassment in Schools." In *Double Jeopardy: Addressing Gender Equity in Special Education*, edited by H. Rousso and M.L. Wehmeyer. New York: SUNY Press.

Lumley, V. and Miltenberger, R. 1997. "Sexual Abuse Prevention for Persons with Mental Retardation." *American Journal on Mental Retardation* 101, 459–472.

McMaster, L.E., Connolly, J., Pepler, D., and Craig, W.M. 2002. "Peer to Peer Sexual Harassment in Early Adolescence: A Developmental Perspective." *Development and Psychopathology* 14, 91–105.

Meyer, E.J. 2008. "Gendered Harassment in Secondary Schools: Understanding Teachers' (Non.) Interventions." *Gender and Education* 20, 555–570. DOI: 10.1080/ 09540250802213115.

Murnen, S.K. and Smolak, L. 2000. "The Experience of Sexual Harassment among Grade-School Students: Early Socialization of Female Subordination?" *Sex Roles* 43, 1–17. DOI: 10.1023/A:1007007727370.

Omerod, A.J., Collinsworth, L.L., and Perry, L.A. 2008. "Critical Climate: Relations among Sexual Harassment, Climate, and Outcomes for High School Girls and Boys." *Psychology of Women's Quarterly* 32, 113–125. DOI: 10.1111/j.1471-6402.2008.00417.x.

Pascoe, C.J. 2007. *Dude, You're a Fag: Masculinity and Sexuality in High School*. Los Angeles: University of California Press.

Pascoe, C.J. 2013. "Notes on a Sociology of Bullying: Young Men's Homophobia as Gender Socialization." *QED: A Journal in GLBTQ Worldmaking* (inaugural issue), 1, 87–104.

Pellegrini, A.D. 2001. "A Longitudinal Study of Heterosexual Relationships, Aggression and Sexual Harassment during the Transition from Primary School through Middle School." *Journal of Applied Developmental Psychology* 22, 119–133. DOI: 10.1016/S0193-3973(01)00072-7.

Peterson, J.L. and Hyde, J.S. 2009. "A Longitudinal Investigation of Peer Sexual Harassment Victimization in Adolescence." *Journal of Adolescence* 32, 1173–1188. DOI: 10.1016/j. adolescence.2009.01.011.

Poteat, V.P. 2007. Peer group socialization of homophobic attitudes and behaviors during adolescence. *Child Development*, 78, 1830–1842. DOI: 10.1111/j.1467-8624.2007. 01101.x

Poteat, V.P. and Espelage, D.L. 2007. "Predicting Psychosocial Consequences of Homophobic Victimization in Middle School Students." *Journal of Early Adolescence* 27, 175–191. DOI: 10.1177/0272431606294839.

Poteat, V.P., Kimmel, M.S., and Wilchins, R. 2011. "The Moderating Effects of Support for Violence Beliefs on Masculine Norms, Aggression, and Homophobic Behavior during Adolescence." *Journal of Research on Adolescence* 21(2), 434–447.

Poteat, V.P., Mereish, E.H., DiGiovanni, C.D., and Koenig, B.W. 2011. "The Effects of General and Homophobic Victimization on Adolescents' Psychosocial and Educational Concerns: The Importance of Intersecting Identities and Parent Support." *Journal of Counseling Psychology* 58(4), 597–609. DOI: 10.1037/a0025095.

Poteat, V.P., O'Dwyer, L.M., and Mereish, E.H. 2012. "Changes in How Students Use and Are Called Homophobic Epithets over Time: Patterns Predicted by Gender, Bullying, and Victimization Status." *Journal of Educational Psychology* 104(2), 393–406. DOI: 10.1037/a0026437.

Reider, E.E. and Sims, B.E. 2016. "Family-based Preventive Interventions: Can the Onset of Suicidal Ideation and Behavior Be Prevented?" *Suicide and Life-Threatening Behavior* 46(S1), S3–S7. DOI: 10.1111/sltb.12252.

Reiter, S., Bryen, D.N., and Shachar, I. 2007. "Adolescents with Intellectual Disabilities as Victims of Abuse." *Journal of Intellectual Disabilities* 11(4), 371–387.

Rinehart, S.J. and Espelage, D.L. 2016. "School Level Predictors of Homophobic Name-Calling and Sexual Harassment Victimization/Perpetration among Middle School Youth." *Psychology of Violence* 6, 213–222.

Rivers, I. 2001. "The Bullying of Sexual Minorities at School: Its Nature and Long-term Correlates." *Educational and Child Psychology* 18, 32–46.

Russell, S.T., Sinclair, K.O., Poteat, V.P., and Koenig, B.W. 2012. "Adolescent Health and Harassment Based on Discriminatory Bias." *American Journal of Public Health* 102(3), 493–495.

Sanchez, E., Robertson, T.R., Lewis, C.M., Rosenbluth, B., Bohman, T., and Casey, D.M. 2001. "Preventing Bullying and Sexual Harassment in Elementary Schools: The Expect Respect Model." *Journal of Emotional Abuse* 2, 157–180. DOI: 10.1300/J135v02n02_10.

Schnoll, J.S., Connolly, J., Josephson, W.J., Pepler, D., and Simkins-Strong, E. 2015. "Same- and Cross-gender Sexual Harassment Victimization in Middle School: A Developmental-contextual Perspective." *Journal of School Violence* 14, 196–216. DOI: 10.1080/15388220.2014.906311.

Settles, I.H., Harrell, Z.A., Buchanan, N.T., and Yap, S.C. 2011. "Frightened or Bothered: Two Types of Sexual Harassment Appraisals." *Social Psychological and Personality Science* 2(6), 600–608. DOI: 10.1177/1948550611402520.

Shute, R., Owens, L., and Slee, P. 2008. "Everyday Victimization of Adolescent Girls by Boys: Sexual Harassment, Bullying or Aggression?" *Sex Roles* 58, 477–489. DOI: 10.1007/s11199-007-9363-5.

Shute, R., Owens, L., and Slee, P. 2016. "High School Girls' Experience of Victimization by Boys: Where Sexual Harassment Meets Aggression." *Journal of Aggression, Maltreatment & Trauma* 25(3), 269–285. DOI: 10.1080/10926771.2015.1129656.

Sobsey, D. 1994. *Violence and Abuse in the Lives of People with Disabilities: The End of Silent Acceptance?* Baltimore, MD: Paul H. Brookes Publishing.

Stein, N. 1995. "Sexual Harassment in School: The Public Performance of Gendered Violence." *Harvard Educational Review* 65, 145–162.

Swearer, S.M., Turner, R.K., Givens, J.E., and Pollack, W.S. 2008. "'You're so gay!': Do Different Forms of Bullying Matter for Adolescent Males?" *School Psychology Review* 37(2), 160.

Taylor, B.G., Stein, N.D., Mumford, E.A., and Woods, D. 2013. "Shifting Boundaries: An Experimental Evaluation of a Dating Violence Prevention Program in Middle Schools." *Prevention Science* 14, 64–76. DOI: 10.1007/s11121-012-0293-2.

Timmerman, G. 2003. "Sexual Harassment of Adolescents Perpetrated by Teachers and by Peers: An Exploration of the Dynamics of Power, Culture, and Gender in Secondary Schools." *Sex Roles* 48, 231–244. DOI: 10.1023/A:1022821320739.

Tjaden, P. and Thoennes, N. 2006. *Extent, Nature, and Consequences of Rape Victimization: Findings from the National Violence against Women Survey* (NCJ 210346). National Institute of Justice. https://www.ncjrs.gov/pdffiles1/nij/210346.pdf (last accessed October 19, 2017).

US Department of Education, Office for Civil Rights. 2001. "Revised Sexual Harassment Guidance: Harassment of Students by School Employees, Other Students, or Third Parties: Title IX." http://www2.ed.gov/about/offices/list/ocr/docs/shguide.html (last accessed October 19, 2017).

US Department of Education, Office for Civil Rights. 2011. "Dear Colleague Letter: Sexual Violence," April 4. http://www2.ed.gov/about/offices/list/ocr/letters/colleague-201104.pdf (last accessed October 19, 2017).

US Department of Education, Office for Civil Rights. 2014. "Questions and Answers on Title IX and Sexual Violence." http://www2.ed.gov/about/offices/list/ocr/docs/qa-201404-title-ix.pdf (last accessed October 19, 2017).

US Department of Education, Office for Civil Rights. 2010. "Dear Colleague Letter: Harassment and Bullying," October 26. http://www2.Ed.gov/about/offices/list/ocr/letters/colleague-201010.html (last accessed October 19, 2017).

Witkowska, E. and Menckel, E. 2005. "Perceptions of Sexual Harassment in Swedish High Schools: Experiences and School-Environment Problems." *European Journal of Public Health* 15, 78–85. DOI: 10.1093/eurpub/cki119.

Wright, L.W., Adams, H.E., and Bernat, J. 1999. "Development and Validation of the Homophobia Scale." *Journal of Psychopathology and Behavioral Assessment* 21, 337–347. DOI: 10.1023/A:1022172816258.

Young, E.L., Heath, M.A., Ashbaker, B.Y., and Smith, B. 2008. "Sexual Harassment among Students with Educational Disabilities Perspectives of Special Educators." *Remedial and Special Education* 29(4), 208–221. DOI: 10.1177/0741932507311635.

Zeira, A., Astor, R.A., and Benbenishty, R. 2002. "Sexual Harassment in Jewish and Arab Public Schools in Israel." *Child Abuse & Neglect* 26, 149–166.

19

Violence against LGBTQ Students

Punishing and Marginalizing Difference*

Elizabethe Payne and Melissa J. Smith

In recent years, bullying as a social phenomenon has become part of public conscious-ness as a problem demanding immediate attention. Books on LGBTQ (lesbian, gay, bisexual, transgender, queer) bullying now proliferate, and anti-bullying laws have been enacted around the country. The US Department of Education has hosted bul-lying summits, further lending credence to particular ways of understanding the problem of in-schools bullying, including the experiences of LGBTQ students. These conversations typically focus on LGBTQ students as "victims"; the correlation between victimization and negative psychological, social, and educational outcomes; and the responsibility of schools to protect vulnerable students from aggressive, anti-social peers. These public dialogues around in-school harassment and the marginali-zation of LGBTQ youth reduce the complexities of peer-to-peer aggression to "anti-social behaviour where one student wields power over [a victim]," (Walton 2011, 131) and conceptualize "the problem of bullying in terms of individual or family pathology" of a singular aggressive student (Bansel et al. 2009, 59). This definition of "the problem" reproduces bullying discourses, which "are now so accepted … in schools that they have gained hegemonic status" (Ringrose and Renold 2010, 590). It has become practically impossible to understand in-school violence and school responses to it outside "the binary logic of protection (for 'victims') and vilification (i.e. pathologising the aggressor)" (574). LGBTQ youth are perpetually painted as victims, bullies as "bad kids," and schools as negligent due to their ineffective methods of intervention.

This dominant narrative depends on inaccurate premises: It assumes schools to be neutral sites where students of all genders and sexualities have equal opportunities to succeed and that barriers to success only appear when individuals' injurious behavior or attitudes create a "negative" school climate where student safety and belonging are

---

* A version of this chapter was previously published as: Payne, E. and Smith, M. (2013). "LGBTQ Kids, School Safety, and Missing the Big Picture: How the Dominant Bullying Discourse Prevents School Professionals from Thinking about Systemic Marginalization or … Why We Need to Rethink LGBTQ Bullying." *QED: A Journal of GLBTQ World Making* 1(1), 1–36.

The Wiley Handbook on Violence in Education: Forms, Factors, and Preventions, First Edition.
Edited by Harvey Shapiro.
© 2018 John Wiley & Sons, Inc. Published 2018 by John Wiley & Sons, Inc.

threatened. However, as Walton (2010) argues, "framing the notion of bullying in a generic manner by focusing on the individual behavior and relational power rather than on the specific constructs of difference that underlie incidents of bullying, operates to perpetuate practices that are fostered within the grid of social regularities" (142). Simply, the dominant understanding of bullying fails to acknowledge heteronormative social systems of power that support acts of bullying targeted at LGBTQ and gender non-conforming students. Overt acts of violence against LGBTQ youth (or those who are perceived to be) are only the surface-level explicit effects of heteronormative school cultures that celebrate idealized (hetero) genders and create social benefits for peer-to-peer policing of non-normative sexualities and gender expressions (Payne 2007). We must come to understand the problem of LGBTQ student bullying differently if we are to have different outcomes in our intervention efforts.

In this chapter, we will briefly review the limitations of the dominant bullying and school climate discourses and illustrate the ways typical bullying intervention efforts constrain educators' abilities to understand the range of aggressions targeting LGBTQ students and to enact change. Throughout the chapter, we will use data from QuERI (Queering Education Research Institute) research projects to illustrate how the dominant bullying discourse manifests in educators' approaches to the problem of aggression targeting LGBTQ youth. We challenge the taken-for-granted conceptualization of LGBTQ youths' school experiences of violence and argue for a broader worldview that encompasses cultural systems of power – particularly along the lines of gender and sexuality – that persistently privilege specific groups of youth while marginalizing others. Shifting the definition of "the problem" in this way demands a different understanding of peer-to-peer aggression than that underlying the dominant bullying discourse. It requires recognition of how aggression functions in processes of social positioning and how patterns of youth aggression are reflective of cultural norms for sexuality and gender expression. Bullying is a tool for preservation of the status quo, the privileging of heterosexuality, and adherence to the gender binary. It "reflects, reproduces, and prepares young people to accept inequalities embedded in larger social structures" (Pascoe 2013, 95).

Methods

The data excerpts presented in this chapter are all drawn from QuERI research on our professional development model, the Reduction of Stigma in Schools© (RSIS). RSIS is a research-based professional development program providing educators with tools and knowledge for creating more affirming school environments for LGBTQ youth. The larger data set consisted of workshop evaluations, semi-structured interviews, and questionnaires completed by past participants of RSIS workshops. Complete descriptions of the research methods are available in the program design and evaluation papers (Payne and Smith 2010, 2011). Though the educators in this study were interviewed to gain insight into their experiences participating in the RSIS program, all participants also devoted significant interview time to the "state of things" regarding LGBTQ student experiences and bullying in their respective school contexts.

Breaking Down the Bullying Discourse

The Construction of "Bullying"

Both the popular discourse and the dominant research on bullying reflect cultural myths about who bullies are, what they look like, and whom they target. Bansel et al. (2009) argue, "The predominant trend in bullying research, and current interventions arising from that research, tend to conceptualize the problem of bullying in terms of individual or family pathology" (59). Research on bullying often aims to identify factors that increase students' risk for engaging in bullying behaviors, and interventions designed in light of this research typically involve managing the aggressive behavior and changing the attitudes of students who are identified as bullies (see Dupper and Meyer-Adams 2002; Espelage and Swearer 2010; Orpinas and Horne 2010; Swearer et al. 2010). This body of work is predominantly shaped by a bully/victim binary in which "power is conceptualized mostly as the capacity of an individual student for abusing another who is perceived by the bully as being weaker or deficient in some way" (Walton 2005, 102). Olweus (2010) defines bullying as a specific type of aggressive behavior characterized by intent, repetition, and an imbalance of power between bully and victim. His definition is frequently used in bullying scholarship and often in survey instruments (see Frey et al. 2009; Smith and Brain 2000; Swearer et al. 2010; Waasdorp, Bradshaw, and Duong 2011). Other researchers have added to this baseline definition: Students who bully are also understood as individuals who exhibit antisocial behavior (Alsaker and Gutzwiller-Helfenfinger 2010), report low levels of empathy (Hymel et al. 2010), and/or have been affected by adults (e.g., family members) and other environmental factors (e.g., a violent home) that have inadvertently supported the development of aggressive behavior (Espelage and Swearer 2010; Green et al. 2011; Johnson et al. 2011; Nickerson, Mele, and Osborne-Oliver 2010). These conceptualizations of bullying assume an individual-to-individual relationship between bully and victim and define power in terms of an individual bully's capacity to abuse and intimidate a victim.

This binary construction of bullying carries implications for possible interventions: bullies need rehabilitation, victims need protection, and schools define the problem as individual students who learn aggressive, antisocial behaviors from family, community, and cultural influences. Intervention efforts are designed to correct dysfunctional behaviors that are assumed to be learned outside school, but they are unlikely to account for how systems of oppression shape social hierarchies and how identity differences – such as gender and sexuality – are relevant to students' positions in the social hierarchy and their experiences of bullying and other forms of violence.

When QuERI research participants describe the LGBTQ targeting that happens in their schools, they reproduce the dominant bullying discourse by deflecting the root causes of individual students' in-school aggression to cultural forces outside the school. They argue that students learn aggressive behavior and biased attitudes from family and mainstream media, and these influences are so powerful that the school will never be able to stop their effects on social interactions inside school. The data excerpts below are from two different school professionals:

> I think that, no matter what programs you have instilled, you are going to have kids in a school environment that come from homes that are, um, racist, um, that are prejudiced against types of differences.

> And I think it's the same way with all this other stuff about attitudes of tolerance and, you know, of anything, that it comes from somewhere out here in society and I think that our kids pick up on that real easily and depending on how your family is and how, you know, people are viewed in your family, you know, what's talked about and are people, you know, is there a joke that's been made in your family, and people laugh about some gay/lesbian joke or whatever, or racist joke or whatever it is. You know, I think kids pick up on that attitude and then they live it. And … I think our school has some problems with that.

Both participants claim that students learn bias from their families, which places schools in the difficult position of fighting cultural and familial values in the interest of greater tolerance between youth. Neither educator acknowledges the possibility that school culture could be reproducing and reinforcing those same biases. Interpreting LGBTQ bullying in this way limits the possibilities for successful intervention because all attention is focused on correcting bad behaviors that individual students learn elsewhere and bring into the school environment rather than critically examining what exactly the *school* is teaching students about difference and identity, who belongs and who does not.

LGBTQ-specific Bullying and Victimization

Research on LGBTQ youths' school experiences comes largely from educational psychology and positions this group of students as victims within the bully/victim binary. The central questions unifying this scholarship are: In what ways are LGBTQ students "at risk," and what are the environmental factors that have the potential to alleviate/reduce that risk? Building from this starting point, these studies seek to identify individual and environmental variables that (i) predict negative psychosocial consequences, and (ii) either mediate these negative effects or eliminate them altogether.

It has been long established that there is a correlation between victimization and higher incidence of health and sexual risk for LGBTQ-identified youth. Researchers have examined the relationships between homophobic victimization and LGBTQ students' mental health outcomes, sense of school belonging, likelihood to engage in disruptive behavior, academic outcomes, truancy, suicidality, and drug use (Birkett, Espelage, and Koening 2009; Murdock and Bolch 2005; Poteat and Espelage 2007). More recently, this line of questioning has extended to compare the risk data for heterosexual and LGBTQ-identified youth who reported similar victimization experiences (Robinson and Espelage 2013; Robinson, Espelage, and Rivers 2013). Results indicate that LGBTQ-identified respondents experience higher rates of risk (Robinson and Espelage 2013) and higher levels of long-term emotional distress (Robinson, Espelage, and Rivers 2013) than their heterosexual peers who had similar victimization experiences. A significant implication of this line of research is that bullying and harassment do not fully account for risk discrepancies between heterosexual and LGBTQ-identified youth; there is a clear need within educational psychology research for a more complex understanding of how LGBTQ-identified youth experience stigma beyond peer victimization.

Much of the educational psychology research focused on LGBTQ youth has prioritized identifying environmental factors that have a positive impact on LGBTQ students' health and academic outcomes. Scholars have pursued questions about correlations between LGBTQ students' reports of suicidality, depression, or victimization and supportive factors such as perceived school safety or positive school climate, presence of a Gay–Straight Alliance and supportive teachers, LGBTQ-inclusive school policies, and family support (Goodenow, Szalacha, and Westheimer 2006; Espelage et al. 2008). These supportive factors have also been connected to increased academic achievement (Kosciw et al. 2013). In particular, having supportive educators is "one of the stronger predictors of a less hostile school climate and of greater self-esteem for LGBT students" (Kosciw et al. 2013, 58).

Recently, educational psychology scholars have paid additional attention to teacher attitudes toward LGBTQ students (Dragowski, McCabe, and Rubinson 2016); their awareness of the amount and type of peer-to-peer aggression that occurs in school (Dragowski, McCabe, and Rubinson 2016; Espelage, Polanin, and Low 2014; Perez, Schanding, and Dao 2013); intention to intervene when they witness LGBTQ bullying (Dragowski, McCabe, and Rubinson 2016; Perez, Schanding, and Dao 2013); and their perceptions of school-wide support for LGBTQ students (Rinehart and Espelage 2016). Collectively, this research positions teachers as a powerful factor within whole-school anti-bullying efforts. These scholars argue that in order for LGBTQ safety and inclusion efforts to be successful, the adults throughout a school building need to receive explicit messages from leaders that intervening in LGBTQ bullying and harassment is expected and supported.

Teachers who have participated in QuERI research projects provide additional insight to how educators interpret the quality of school environments and the work that needs to be done in their schools to better support LGBTQ students. Their comments predominantly focused on the observable behavior they felt conveyed "intolerant" attitudes. Teachers expressed concern that hearing homophobic language throughout the school put LGBTQ students at risk for emotional or psychological distress and increased their risk for absenteeism, social isolation, drug and alcohol use, and suicide. They believed teachers should play an active role in reducing this risk by consistently intervening when they observe homophobic language, because doing so teaches students that verbal expressions of bias – even when it is careless or unintentional – can cause significant harm to a LGBTQ peer. One teacher described how convincing the entire faculty to commit to this work had been a struggle in her school:

> I think, pretty much, people do kind of see it [homophobic language] as a normalized, you know, behavior. That, I don't know if anybody's ears go (*makes a surprised sound*). You know what I mean? Like profanity, they would. You know? Umm, and not [to] say that they like it or accept it or say that that's okay, but I just don't know if people would go out of their way to go over to somebody that they don't know [and correct them]. Now if they know the kid, they might say something to 'em, but, you know, would they turn around in the hall to a kid they don't know? I would (*laughs*). And, umm, you know, just say something. I just don't know if they [other teachers] would.

This teacher attributes her school's inconsistency in addressing homophobic language to lack of understanding about the injurious effects of homophobic language. Normalization of this language means that teachers perceive it to be neutral or "no big deal." This teacher believes the potential harm is significant enough to "go out of [her] way" to stop students from saying things like "that's so gay" or "no homo." She, and many other teachers in our research, sees interrupting anti-gay speech as an important risk reduction strategy for LGBTQ students and is deeply committed to gaining cooperation from fellow teachers in these intervention efforts. Though they acknowledged the impossibility of achieving this goal, many participants believed that eradication of such language would significantly improve the school climate if not completely solve the problem. DePalma and Jennett (2010) caution against this common understanding of "the problem" of LGBTQ student marginalization primarily in terms of homophobic and transphobic language. They argue that it "reflects a shallow understanding of the social processes underpinning these phenomena" (16).

The problem of LGBTQ students' negative school experiences has been shaped by a discourse of bullying that neglects research that examines "the situational and socio-cultural dimensions of power" along the lines of gender, and sexuality (Ringrose 2008, 510) as well as the dynamics of the social "hierarchies that young people must some-how manage" (512). Reducing "risk" through intervening in anti-LGBTQ targeting is indeed critical for the well-being of LGBTQ students, but that does not address the problem of diminished social capital for those who do not conform to normative expectations for gender and sexuality. It is that reduced social capital and marginalized position within the school that puts these students at risk for targeting and its conse-quences. To be positioned as a "victim" is to be additionally marked out as "deviant" within the normative contexts of school. In the following section, we will examine the limitations of the bullying discourse as they appear in three common LGBTQ bullying interventions.

Addressing Bullying and Harassment In Schools

Anti-Bullying Interventions

Given that anti-bullying initiatives are common responses to the problem of gender-based targeting, identifying the goals, processes, and assumptions of these programs provides insight to how school leaders, policy makers, and educators understand the problem of violence toward LGBTQ youth. Most anti-bullying programs contain four components: (i) assessment of how much bullying is happening, quantifying the prob-lem; (ii) direct responses to active bullies and targets; (iii) whole-school education for educators, parents, and students; and (iv) a system of monitoring where all members of the community are expected to report possible bullying activity (Jacobson 2013). The bullies are imagined as students who are attracted to aggressive behaviors or lack the ability to empathize with others' feelings (Hymel et al. 2010) or fail to accept peers from diverse backgrounds (Bandyopadhyay, Cornell, and Konold 2009), thus solutions focus on changing how individual students interact with their peers and behave in the school environment.

Throughout the United States, schools are often attracted to "whole school" programs that promise to decrease bullying and improve school climate. There are countless anti-bullying models available, but the Olweus Bullying Prevention Program (OBPP) is argu-ably the most famous and widely used anti-bullying program in the United States and Europe. It is particularly significant because its designers hold an authoritative position in the academic conversation about what bullying is and successful strategies for decreasing bullying behaviors (Swearer et al. 2010). OBPP asks schools to implement new policies and procedures at the student, classroom, institutional, and community levels in order to establish consistent messaging and buy-in from all stakeholders for the mission of eliminating bullying. The intent is for all members of the community to raise their awareness of bullying, have a shared understanding of what bullying is, learn how to have more positive interactions that reflect acceptance and empathy, and to make a collective effort to report and intervene (Olweus and Limber 2010). Evaluations of OBPP (many executed by Dan Olweus and his team) have measured its effectiveness according to students' self-reported experiences of bullying or being bullied. External evaluators have been more cautious than the Olweus team in their endorsement of the Olweus model. Smith, Schneider, Smith, and Ananiadou's (2004) review of studies evaluating OBPP concluded, "It is clear that the whole school approach has led to important reductions in bullying ... but the results are simply too inconsistent to justify adoption of these particular procedures to the exclusion of others" (557). Swearer, Espelage, Vaillancourt, and Hymel (2010) question the validity of reliance on "self-reported data about bullying and victimization" (42) and call attention to the failure to account for factors such as race, disability, or sexual orientation in how they define the problem of *bullying*.

The success of school interventions is typically evaluated by measuring the frequency of reported bullying behaviors or student perceptions of safety. However, "reduction [of bullying] is a measurable outcome ... [that] merely *contains, regulates, and manages* violence rather than *addresses* it" (Walton 2005, 112). When the absence of reported bullying functions as *the* indicator of a safe or inclusive school for LGBTQ students, we fail to account for both the social processes underpinning homophobic bullying and "the subtle ways in which schools are complicit in sustaining them" (DePalma and Jennett 2010, 16). Further, anti-bullying programs' focus on "statistics, characteristics, psychological profiles, and measurable events" (Walton 2010, 113) fails to question why the same groups of students are targeted decade after decade. Anti-bullying programs are more often pushing violent behavior underground than they are calling systemic privileging and marginalization into question. They do not get to the "root" of the problem.

Just Be Nice: Character Education

Embedded within anti-bullying programs are narratives about the value of civility, kindness, and decency; *who* such programs think a bully is; and the kinds of school environments that allow bullying to take place. According to Rigby (2010), "Probably the most common way of responding to bullying in schools is to assert the importance of certain values or ideals that should govern interpersonal relationships between students" (547). Anti-bullying programs often address this issue by including "character education" components in their behavior management systems. *Character* is "the complex set of psychological characteristics that enable an individual to act as a moral agent" (Berkowitz and Bier 2004, 73), and character education aims to "help children learn the character attributes that enable them to become caring and responsible adults" (Leming 2000, 414). Students who do not act morally – who do not express care and responsibility – are considered to lack "sociomoral competency" (Berkowitz and

Bier 2004, 73) and are in need of specific instruction in order to "develop a structured system of values, ethics and morals" (Leming 2000, 414). Bullying programs that include character education components are, therefore, attempting to compensate for the deficiencies in students' values and belief systems that are leading them to act aggressively or impose power over their peers. The Olweus Bullying Prevention Program includes activities intended "to help build empathy and perspective-taking skills" (Olweus and Limber 2010, 382). The Steps to Respect program asks students to take a pledge to resist bullying – asking them to make the morally "right" decision to keep one's promise (Frey et al. 2009). Bully-Proofing Your School aims to develop a "caring community," where social power is held by the "caring majority" (Porter et al. 2010). The Bully Busters program "is predicated on the assumption that aggression and bullying are behaviors borne of social skills deficits, lack of skills for taking others' perspective or a failure to empathically relate with others, and a moral or value system that denigrates others" (Horne et al. 2010, 508). Although these programs do not take identical approaches to bullying, they *do* share similar assumptions about the relationship between student aggression and individual students' values, beliefs, and morals. In short, students who have "good" character will express respect, tolerance, and empathy toward their peers, not aggression. This focus on psychosocial deficiencies in individual students neglects both educational institutions' role in supporting bullying behaviors and the underlying value system that allows some students to be targeted based on difference.

Donna, a high school teacher, demonstrates this idea in her discussion of attempts to convince students to stop using homophobic language:

> I mean, I can sit and try to tell kids how it is, you know, and like, say, you know, "suicide rates higher" and all that kind of stuff, but I think the general kid is like, "Oh well. Too bad." You know what I mean? Like, they don't understand and they don't, they don't have that empathy and I think that probably, that empathy would be important to our kids.

Donna's definition of "the problem" and vision for solving it reflect messages within the bullying discourse that claim that students who engage in aggressive behavior do so because of individual negative attitudes or poor social skills learned from family and other cultural sources (Espelage and Swearer 2010). Her reasoning for encouraging kids to be more empathetic is suicide risk reduction. Further, her claim that an absence of empathy is to blame reflects a belief that problems of bias and violence in schools only have effects on the feelings and self-worth of individual victims who may be personally injured – either by being directly targeted or by hearing the language circulating in their environment. This interpretation fails to acknowledge the constant reproduction of heterosexuality and hegemonic gender norms occurring through the "normal" usage of biased speech. Homophobic speech used in reference to something students deem abnormal or unpleasant implicitly cites heteronormative discourse – which defines heterosexuality and stereotypical gender roles as normal and other genders and sexualities as deviant (Ngo 2003). She believes that if kids are just "nicer" to one another, the problem will be solved. Niceness cannot erase stigma – it merely asks students in the dominant majority not to be unkind to those they deem deviant.

Safety, Safe Spaces, and GSAs

When discussing bullying and anti-bullying efforts for LGBTQ students, educators often rely heavily on the language of "safety." LGBTQ students need to be "safe" in school and they need designated "safe spaces" in which to "be themselves" – where it is "safe" to be openly LGBTQ free from violence. In our experience, teachers' thinking about "safe spaces" is closely aligned with Stengel's (2010) argument that "educators take for granted the need to protect [marginalized] students ... from apparently threatening social circumstances" (524). Further, "safe space" is code for the argument that it is an educator's responsibility to "create positive conditions for learning and growth" (524) and – therefore – separate students from the possibility of harassment. So, while our research participants believe in the power and necessity of such spaces (as do the authors), most described visible "safe spaces" as signs of success for their schools without considering how the safety rhetoric paints LGBTQ students as victims in need of protection (Hackford-Peer 2010) and fails to "elevate the status of LGBT[Q] people from a protected class to a valued group in the school community" (Hirschfeld 2001, 611). As Youdell (2011) explains:

> [S]ubtle or implicit hierarchies and everyday injustices [in school] often have their origins in institutional and educator judgments about "who" students are. These judgments inform practice both explicitly and implicitly as they are taken up by educational institutions and educators to predict and explain what students can or cannot do, how they will or will not behave, the futures that are or are not open to them. This "who" is drawn on by educators as they forge different relationships with differently positioned students and as they explain and constrain the relationships that these differently positioned students can and cannot make and sustain. These everyday judgments have massive implications for students' experiences of education, shaping and constraining how students understand themselves and the opportunities, relationships and futures they see as being open to them. (9)

The LGBTQ student "who" that is institutionally created and recreated through the pervasive safety rhetoric is synonymous with "victim" and vulnerable "at risk" student.

In our data, "safety" was most often represented as a designated time or space, marked by a scheduled meeting or a Safe Space sticker. Having safe spaces where students feel that they can have a temporary reprieve from harassment is important, and many students have spent significant portions of their high school days in the library or a supportive teacher's classroom seeking that reprieve (Payne 2007; Mahan et al. 2007). However, the establishment of these spaces, rather than being an answer to the problem, should only make the problem more apparent. The real problem is that students do not experience the entirety of their school as safe and therefore require these zones.

QuERI research participants have been nearly unanimous in their belief that LGBTQ students need a place to *go* where they can escape the possibility of hostility in the school environment. Donna explained her understanding of what posting a Safe Space sticker symbolizes:

> I think ... that it just means in my classroom, you're safe here, and nobody's going to pick on you, say something, and if somebody does say something that's, you know, derogatory, judgmental, or whatever, that I'm gonna say something about

it. You know, I'm not gonna tolerate that. So you're safe in my room. ... If they're having a, you know, if they see the sticker and they want to say something to you [about their sexuality] then yeah, you're there to support them and help them in some way that you can.

Donna's description is representative of the teacher interpretations of "Safe Space" that occur throughout our data: educators who display these stickers are promising that homophobic language will not occur in their classrooms or offices, but if it does it will be addressed immediately. Further, the stickers are meant to show kids where they could safely tell a teacher about their LGBTQ identity or seek help if they are experiencing any kind of distress in relation to their gender or sexual identity. Research participants understood the need for Gay–Straight Alliances and similar student groups in much the same way, with the addition that they saw a need for LGBTQ students to have a formalized time and space to share experiences with their peers. However, some were concerned that such student groups gained a reputation as the "gay club" which could contribute to continued marginalization. The stigmatization of LGBTQ identities also limited student participation in the group:

> But I think there are people who, I don't know, I'd like to be able to have kids have the experience that can come with the Acceptance Coalition meetings and not feel like that's where the gay kids go, and, so if you are with them [the gay kids], you are one of them [gay] and if you are one of them [gay], that's bad, you know? I wish there was a more open, um, environment.

This club advisor is noting that some students assume that anyone who attends the Acceptance Coalition meeting is LGBTQ, "one of them," and that being "one of them" is "bad." Although the club has successfully provided a "safe space" for students to connect with peers and adults, the group itself is marginalized, stigmatized, and isolated in the school environment – and this stigma likely prevents many kids who are seeking support from attending meetings. So, while the participating students may feel a greater sense of connection and belonging in their school and have a brief scheduled time designated free from harassment, the larger social hierarchy continues to marginalize queer kids in the school and the act of attending a meeting potentially produces more marginalization.

Despite the increasing numbers of character education and anti-bullying programs, schools are still experienced as hostile environments by LGBTQ students and families (Hirschfeld 2001). Addressing this problem by focusing on safety issues is comfortable for most staff, and even for most communities, as safety practices reflect the "moral self-image that most people have of themselves" (7). Like anti-bullying programs, the establishment of Safe Spaces is vital to the school success of LGBTQ students; however, it fails to address the heteronormative system that privileges heterosexuality and hegemonic gender. Research indicates that "gay," "fag," and "dyke" are considered by youth to be among the worst of possible pejoratives (Thurlow 2001) and that to be "called 'gay' by others was among the most psychologically disturbing forms of sexual harassment" to students (Mahan et al. 2007). Safe Space initiatives are attuned to the injurious effects of this language, but they do not expose or challenge the value system that positions "gay" as such a horrible way to be or that provides popularity and prestige to the harasser (Mahan et al. 2007). They fail to address how and why students are systematically excluded through "apparently mundane and everyday practices inside school" (Youdell 2006, 5). Anti-bullying programs, Safe Space stickers, Gay–Straight Alliances, and other such interventions fail to be disruptive, and LGBTQ and gender non-conforming students' position in the social hierarchy remains largely marginalized and unchanged and the systems of power that put them there remain intact (Payne and Smith 2012a).

Rethinking LGBTQ Bullying and Interventions

Bullying as Regulation of Gender Difference

The majority of bullying research has been "gender blind" (Ringrose and Renold 2010, 576) – failing to look at the sociocultural context of bullying and the ways many bullying behaviors are rooted in reinforcing the rules for "appropriate" gender behavior and sexuality. The scant bullying research that has attended to gender comes largely from the field of developmental psychology and has served to reinforce gendered stereotypes and "essentialised" norms of masculinity and femininity rather than exploring the policing of gender boundaries as a primary social function of bullying behavior (Ringrose and Renold 2010, 577). We propose (as have others) that bullying behaviors are not antisocial but rather highly social acts deeply entrenched in the perpetuation of cultural norms and values. Significantly, those norms require a fixed relationship between (hetero) gender, sex and sexuality, and the maintaining of "gender coherence" (Ringrose and Renold 2010) through this "constellation" (Youdell 2005).

Students' speech, behavior, and dress are regulated by cultural rules related to the "right" way to exist in the school environment, and youths' everyday gender policing practices often fail to draw adults' attention because these behaviors largely align with the institutional values of school. Young people's attitudes about difference are partially formed in a school-based social scene that rewards conformity. Children learn "'their place' in the U.S. political and social order through their public school experiences" (Lugg 2006, 49), and school is a primary cultural site where young people learn the rules about who men and women are expected to be. Youth regularly regulate and discipline the boundaries between "normal" and "different" along the lines of sex, gender, and sexuality (and their intersections with race, class, ability), and this process is a mechanism for acquiring and increasing social status.

These patterns of aggression occur constantly throughout the school, producing and reproducing systems of value based on gender conformity, and they often occur *within* friendship groups (Ringrose 2008), making it all the more difficult to see and to intervene. Boys' misogynistic teasing and sexual harassment of girls, girls' verbal policing of one another's appearance and sexual reputations, and boys' homophobic teasing of one another are examples of verbal aggression that constantly circulate within peer groups and police the boundaries of acceptable gender, but fall outside dominant discourses of bullying (Duncan 2004; Payne 2007, 2010; Payne and Smith 2012a; Youdell 2005). In addition, some forms of aggression are considered "normal" based on cultural expectations for gendered behavior – for example, "for boys to be heroically and 'playfully' violent and for girls to be repressively and secretly 'mean'" (Ringrose and Renold 2010, 591). Youth operate within these acceptable dynamics of aggression to battle for position in social hierarchies without (much) adult scrutiny, reproducing gender norms including those for "relational aggression" (586) along the way. Students who are socially powerful are those who successfully perform normative gender and heterosexuality, and great importance is placed on youths' success in the "heterosexual marketplace" (Eckert 1994) through acquiring (heterosexual) dating opportunities and demonstrating attractiveness to the "opposite" sex. Those who most successfully conform to gender expectations are "celebrated" (Lugg 2006, 49) in their peer groups and in school culture.

Young people who are viewed as having inadequate gender characteristics or a gender identity not normatively associated with their biological sex are more violently and publicly "marked" (Payne 2007, 64) and denied access to social power and popularity. The further youth fall from idealized forms of masculinity and femininity, the more vulnerable they are to these patterns of heightened policing as well as more severe forms of violence. LGBTQ youth are often the most vulnerable in this system. Through "the continual, vocal branding of [the] Other" (Thurlow 2001, 26), students not only fight for power and establish their own positions within the social hierarchy by marking others' positions as higher or lower than their own (Pascoe 2007), but they (re)establish who they cannot "be." Biased speech and other verbal aggressions and micro-aggressions (Solorzano, Ceja, and Yosso 2000) should be understood as "citational practices" – "drawing on and repeating past articulations and perceptions" (Ngo 2003, 116). Homophobic language does not need to be explained in the moment, which signifies that it is citing and reproducing cultural and historical understandings about this kind of speech, and these cultural norms are reproduced each time kids use this language to regulate one another. Hate speech acts – "faggot," "dyke," "homo," "slut" – "injure" individuals *and* the larger group of queer and non-conforming students by repeatedly placing them in "subordinate position[s]" in the social hierarchy and publicly reaffirming the associated gender transgressions as deviant (McInnes and Couch 2004). However, it is only the students who are overtly, publicly, repeatedly targeted who are framed within dominant bullying discourses as the victims of bullying.

Because these escalated verbal acts of aggression draw from the same cultural system of meaning and practice as everyday gender policing – a normalized part of social life – they are not viewed as abnormal by youth. It is, therefore, possible that those who "bully" do so because they are making an "extreme investment" in a cultural system that allows them to access power through the "normative regulation of others" (Bansel et al. 2009, 67). In other words, the violence termed "bullying" is the heightened and visible form of aggression that circulates every day in schools and in the larger culture – aggression that targets appearance, personal interests and hobbies, academic engagement, bodily comportment, physical size and shape, and sexual behavior in ways that continuously reassert the "right" way to be a gendered person and affirm the expected alignment of sex, gender, and sexuality.

Connelly (2012) notes that high school is "one of the most intensely and often violently anti-gay sites in our culture" (254). Each time a LGBTQ student is harassed, it communicates the message that "a central element of the gay student's identity is deficient, shameful, and worthy of ridicule" (Wallace 2011, 748). "Student [and adult] discourses of 'normal' gender and sexuality make the school feel unsafe for [LGBTQ] students" (Ngo 2003, 118), so it is imperative that anti-bullying work focus on gaining a deeper understanding of the subtle ways that privileging of heteronormative gender in appearance and behaviors constantly influences how students negotiate their school environments. Targeting others for their failure to "do" gender "right" is a learned mechanism for improving or affirming one's *own* social status as well as reaffirming the "rightness" of the gender "rules," and schools are participants in both teaching youth to use these tools and in privileging some groups of (conforming) students over others. It is, therefore, important to examine the various ways in which schools institutionalize heterosexuality and silence and marginalize gender and sexual difference, thus support- ing social positioning practices that privilege idealized heterosexual performance – from social rituals like prom, to elections of school queens and kings, to awards for "cutest couple," to the heterocentric curriculum, to school dress codes that affirm the gender binary. Heterosexuality and gender conformity are rewarded with a position at the top of the school's social hierarchy – visibly reaffirming the school ideal (Payne and Smith 2012a) – often through the awarding of crowns.

Attending to Climate and Culture

A high incidence of bullying is often assumed to be the cause of a negative school cli- mate, not the iteration of the values and beliefs of the larger school culture. Climate research is "the most frequently studied school characteristic linked to bullying" (Gendron, Williams, and Guerra 2011, 151) and it intends to identify "the mediating variables between the structural features of the school and the outcomes for pupils and teachers" (Van Houtte 2005, 71). Climate assessment tools measure student and faculty perceptions of factors such as school attachment, school involvement, clarity and fairness of school rules, parental involvement, safety, respect between students and staff, strength of leadership, student and staff morale, and clarity of educational mission (Gottfredson et al. 2005; Stewart 2003; Welsh 2000).

A major tension in the climate research is the uncomfortable relationship between *climate* and *behavior*. Connecting the two means identifying concrete, measurable ele- ments that are indicative of the overall quality (whether positive or negative) of an organization's environment and linking these (often implicitly) to student and staff behavior. This research evaluates climate through school community members' collec- tive perception of the quality of the environment. For example, Welsh (2000) utilized a climate assessment that asked for perceptions of school safety, clarity of rules, fairness of rules, respect for students, student influence on school affairs, and planning and action. Stewart's (2003) research on the relationship between "school-level characteris- tics" and misbehavior collected data addressing students' perceptions of school attachment, school involvement, belief in school rules, association with positive peers, and parental school involvement, and compared schools according to size, "school social problems," and "school cohesion" (576). Gottfredson et al. (2005) measured school climate using student perceptions of fairness and clarity of rules, and teachers' perceptions of "organizational focus," "morale," school-wide strategies for problem solv- ing, and "administrative leadership" (423–424). Such measurements (e.g., "fairness," "morale") establish a normative standard for what the school environment should be, and they ask participants for their general perception of how the school measures against these standards while implicitly assuming that all respondents hold the same standard for concepts such as "fair" or "not fair" and thus are able to usefully report. The implication is that if there are deficiencies, the structural features of the school will need to be altered in some way to "fix" the climate. It is, therefore, unsurprising that anti-bullying and school climate interventions often go hand in hand, as many school safety studies argue a causal relationship between decreases in violent behavior and a more positive school climate.

Some of this climate research has focused specifically on the experiences of LGBTQ students. For example, Toomey, McGuire, and Russell (2012) conducted research to assess "students' perceptions of the school climate as safe for gender nonconformity" and "how the visibility of safe school strategies … may be associated with greater perceptions of safety" (189). This study discussed a relationship between heteronormativity and school climate, but ultimately their conclusions were focused on correlating specific interventions – inclusive anti-harassment policies, GSAs, professional development – with students' feelings of safety rather than with indicators of strict heteronormative values. Kosciw, Palmer, Kull, and Greytak (2013) "examined simultaneously the effect of school climate on achievement and the role that school-based supports for LGBT students may have in offsetting this effect" (48). Like Toomey, McGuire, and Russell, they reported that the presence of in-school supports such as GSAs and supportive educators were indicators for a less hostile climate and fewer incidences of victimization. Research studies such as these are attractive to political and educational leaders because they support the assumption that climate is a measurable phenomenon and, therefore, it is possible to prove the effectiveness (or lack thereof) of specific interventions.

Notably, these studies and others (Birkett, Espelage, and Koenig 2009; Goodenow, Szalacha, and Westheimer 2006; Murdock and Bolch 2005) measure school climate with student reports of *feelings of safety* and *incidents of victimization*. In other words, climate is either positive or negative, depending on the presence or absence of reported violence. This body of research is attempting to identify specific structural elements that when addressed will help LGBTQ students feel safer, but these interventions are primarily focused on raising awareness of LGBTQ bullying and providing spaces in the school where students do not feel the threat of victimization. These interventions are undoubtedly important, but they do not address *school culture*: the institutional value systems that privilege gender conformity and heterosexuality.

This link between climate and anti-bullying divorces climate from culture, continues the limited focus on visible signs of a deeper cultural problem, and eliminates the possibility to gain understanding of how students use social norms as tools to battle for position in the social hierarchy. Culture and climate are both prevalent concepts in discussions about institutional beliefs, values, and attitudes, and they are often conflated in educational discourse, collapsed under the umbrella of *school climate* (Anderson 1982; Hoy 1990; Van Houtte 2005; Welsh 2000). However, "researchers concentrating on *culture* maintain that culture may offer a more profound insight into an organization, because ultimately climate is nothing more than 'a surface manifestation of culture'" (Van Houtte 2005, 78 citing Schein 1990, 91). In other words, culture represents the system of values and beliefs that give an organization identity and shape how it (and the people in it) function, and climate is created through individuals' interactions within that organization based upon those values and beliefs (Hoy 1990; Maxwell and Thomas 1991; Van Houtte 2005). In terms of students' school experiences, one can conceptualize climate "as the way school culture affects a child's sense of safety and acceptance, and consequently is a critical determinant of their ability to focus on the task of learning" (Dessel

2010, 414), whereas culture encompasses the systems of knowledge and belief that are available within a given context for people to use in making meaning of their experiences of marginalization. The impetus to target students with harassment based upon their gender or sexual difference lies in the values and belief system of the school and larger culture. Marginalized students' interpretations of what this targeting "means" about them as people and members of that school community draws from the same value system. Moving forward, "we must take into consideration how bullying is influenced by a patriarchal macrosystem" (Carrera, DePalma, and Lameiras 2011, 490) and how the behaviors associated with bullying, "as well as the everyday practices of oppression that are normalized and naturalized in institutional school settings, demonstrate a strong gendered component" (493). Research on school culture and heteronormativity should ask questions about institutional beliefs and values, school rituals that elevate the status of heterosexuality and gender conformity, and policies and practices that reinforce the gender binary. These are questions that will provide insight to how school culture is contributing to the ways students police one another's identities, expressions, and behaviors.

Rethinking Violence against LGBTQ Students

The literature reviewed here and the data excerpts from some of our own research represent the dominant narrative about US schools' responsibilities to LGBTQ students. The "problem" of LGBTQ students' negative school experiences has been shaped by a discourse where "overly individualized and psychologized analyses ... distort larger issues of inequality" (Pascoe 2007, 17) and that neglects research examining youths' negotiations of the social hierarchies in their peer groups (Ringrose 2008). A "lack of theorizing the power of social difference" perpetuates the dominant discourse on bullying (Walton 2011) and its narrow focus on the bully/victim binary. "Anti-bullying" responses to this understanding of "the problem" include a need to protect individual victims and overlook "the role that schools play in the reproduction of social relations along axes of class, gender, race and ... sexuality" (Youdell 2005, 250) that privilege some and marginalize others. LGBTQ sexuality and non-normative genders appear in the school environment only as sites of risk and vulnerability, calling for surveillance and intervention by adults, and LGBTQ youth are only acknowledged and supported as victims, or potential victims, in need of protection and care (Fields 2013). When educators understand "the problem" in this way, the cultural, systemic privileging of heterosexuality and gender normativity is never called into question, the marginalization of LGBTQ youth is reproduced and re-entrenched in new ways, and schools avoid claiming responsibility for their complicity in the aggression targeting LGBTQ and gender non-conforming youth.

The bullying discourse is rarely questioned because it aligns with the cultural mythology of the K–12 school experience. This mythology has a socially unifying force – anyone who has been educated in US public schools can provide a recognizable narrative of "the bully," and while there is a collective desire for the bully to be eliminated, there is also an acceptance of the bully's presence as a rite of passage or a "normal" part of the K–12 schooling experience. The problem of pervasive and persistent targeting and harassment of LGBTQ students fits easily into this collective memory of schooling.

However, this meaning making of LGBTQ harassment fails to address why LGBTQ students have historically been hyper-visible figures of "deviance" in the school environment (and thus the targets), and why for decades homophobic epithets like "fag" have served as such powerful tools for marking any student who falls outside social norms (Smith and Smith 1998). Bullying is not an individual "pathology" but "a form of gender socialization and a mechanism by which gender privilege is reproduced" (Pascoe 2013, 87). Traditional bullying discourses do not account for the social norms that dictate who students are "allowed" to be in the school environment, or who has access to power and prestige in the social environment of school (Payne 2007). What is needed is an understanding of bullying as more than "autonomous acts, free-floating from their histories and contexts that can be accounted for through the character of one faulty individual" (Bansel et al. 2009, 66). "Generic" anti-bullying policies – though "masquerading as providing protection for all" – do not address the "specific ways that particular children, and not others, are continual targets of peer violence" (Walton 2011, 137). Violence targeting LGBTQ students is embedded in and reproduces "normative power structures [which] discursively organize ideals of masculinity and femininity" (Ringrose 2008, 512). Thus, acts of LGBTQ harassment are "reiterations of the dominant order" (Bansel et al. 2009, 66) that normalize the marginalization of students who do not conform or meet the standards of hegemonic gender in some way. Bullying LGBTQ students is an act of social violence not only against an individual, but against gender and sexual difference. And in that way, bullying is a political act.

The educators we cite here from our research data are interpreting their LGBTQ students' experiences and their school climates through a lens that allows them to "see" overt acts of sexist and homophobic violence but not the ways in which "schools play a part in structuring adolescent selves ... including relations of power, labor, emotion, and symbolism" (Pascoe 2007, 18). Although the participants recognize the presence of homophobia in their schools, they lack insight on how social stigma and marginalization work "in the most mundane moments everyday inside schools" (Youdell 2006, 13), or "how school processes act unwittingly to exclude particular students from the educational endeavour" (1). Furthermore, as Ringrose and Renold (2010) argue, "the dominant 'bully discourses' employed to make sense of and address [peer-to-peer] conflict offer few resources or practical tools for addressing and coping with everyday, normative aggression and violence in schools" (575). These "normative cruelties" are "exclusionary and injurious practices" (575) that are taken for granted as normal gendered behavior. Our research participants' perspectives on peer-to-peer aggression reflect this argument that social interactions such as girls' gossiping, boys' roughhousing, or "playful" exchanges of insults like "slut" and "fag" are rarely considered to be overtly aggressive behavior. Therefore, such low-level aggressions – which actively reproduce normative expectations for gender and sexuality – are rarely noticed, let alone monitored. Prevention and intervention methods as well as professional development designed for teachers should highlight the relationships between "normative cruelties" (Ringrose and Renold 2010), sexual harassment, and the acts currently termed "bullying" and include a thorough education on the "constructed nature of gender, making gender boundaries more flexible, and valuing sexual diversity in the classroom" (Carrera, DePalma, and Lameiras 2011, 494).

We propose a new definition of bullying that aims to address the issues described above and that will provide a more useful framework for (i) understanding the social nature of the aggression that occurs between peers, and (ii) designing interventions that will address the cultural roots of peer-to-peer aggression. Further, we wanted to develop a definition that challenges the bullying discourse and draws attention to the daily violence that often fades into the landscape of "normal" adolescent behavior. We argue that it is imperative to keep this subtle aggression in the foreground because it reflects the cultural norms embedded in a given context – like a school or community – and is the mechanism through which youth regulate the boundaries between "normal" and "other." Finally, we take the position that a majority of peer-to-peer aggression in US public schools is some form of *gender policing* and we believe bullying must be redefined to account for relationships between peer targeting and structural inequalities:

> Bullying is overt verbal, physical, or technology-based ("cyber," text messaging, etc.) aggression that is persistently focused on targeted person(s) over time. This behavior is visible aggression that has escalated from a larger system of low-level or covert normalized aggression that polices the boundaries between "normal" and "different" in a specific social context. Targeted person(s) are victimized because they are perceived to be outside the boundaries of "normal" as culturally defined within a peer group. This aggression is a tool for acquiring higher social status in a peer group because by targeting others as "different," the aggressor claims a higher position in the social hierarchy and reinforces the social "rules" of acceptability. Peer-to-peer aggression typically replicates structural inequality, and therefore patterns of targeting are likely to reflect systemic marginalization along lines of gender, sex, sexuality, race, (dis)ability, and class. Bullying frequently reinforces gender norms – ideas about "correct" and "normal" masculinity and femininity. Students who are viewed as having non-normative gender (and by extension, sexuality) are frequent targets. Not all aggressive behaviors between students can be termed "bullying" – some are the result of individual conflict or personality differences.

By redefining bullying in this way, we hope to disrupt the cultural mythology of bullying as a taken-for-granted, coming-of-age experience in US K–12 schools. This definition is meant to create emphasis on the cultural roots of "the problem" of peer-to-peer aggression, which will ultimately drive interventions that focus on shifting cultural norms.

"The hegemony and ultimate stranglehold of the bully and anti-bully discourses over educational research, policy and practice is in much need of a critical overhaul" (Ringrose and Renold 2010, 591). Moving forward, research on and a re-envisioning of in-school aggression must address the sociocultural dimensions of bullying and aggression (Ringrose 2008) and the "intense" social competition (Ringrose and Renold 2010) and gendered expectations central to what it means to be a gendered subject within school contexts. We are looking for ways to achieve sustainable change, and for any change to be sustainable, school interventions must take on the task of cultural change alongside violence intervention. The anti-bullying paradigm does not offer the tools to accomplish this goal because, "[b]y using vague terms such as bullying and name calling, [it] avoid[s] examining the underlying power dynamics that such behaviors build and reinforce, [which] effectively reinforce[s] the status quo" (Meyer 2008, 44). Additionally, the increased surveillance and reporting that often accompanies anti-bullying programs disproportionately impacts already marginalized youth including LGBTQ youth and students of color (Smith and Payne 2013).

What is needed are interventions that see schooling "as being shaped by the ongoing deployment of available discursive strategies" and believe "the school is also a material location" (Youdell 2006, 58). It is important to understand schools on a macro- and micro-sociological level, accounting for both the lived experience of the students and the cultural processes of elevating hegemonic gender performance and heterosexuality to a position of prestige in the school environment. Bullying is not antisocial behavior, but rather is both intensely social and functional behavior rooted in the school and larger cultural value systems. It serves a "social purpose by reinforcing hierarchies of power and privilege" and is "a reflection of broader social inequity and prejudice" (Walton 2011, 140). "It is a barometer of collective social, cultural, and political anxieties" and routinely "marginalize[s]" and "villifie[s] those who are seen as 'different'" (140). A primary area of difference marked and targeted is gender (and by extension, sexuality) and schools are still complicit "in the everyday cruelties of the enforcement of hetero-sexist/homophobic hegemony" (Smith and Smith 1998, 309). The power at play in acts of bullying needs to be reconceptualized in both research and policy, moving away from the limited notion of one more powerful individual acting against another who is weaker and toward an account of "the situational and sociocultural aspects of power and identity and their dimensions in terms of gender and sexuality" (Carrera, DePalma, and Lameiras 2011, 488). Ultimately, this lens provides a richer understanding of how students are stigmatized in school – and this understanding is imperative for designing interventions that have any hope of creating sustainable change.

About QuERI

Queering Education Research Institute© (QuERI) is an independent think tank, qualitative research and education center dedicated to bridging the gap between research and practice to improve the school experiences of LGBTQ students and families. QuERI began in 2006 with the Reduction of Stigma in Schools (RSIS) program – a research-based professional development program for K–12 educators, and expanded in 2008 to become a research, training, and policy institute. QuERI was founded by Dr. Elizabethe Payne and housed in the Syracuse University School of Education from 2006 to 2014. QuERI is located at the LGBT Social Science and Public Policy Center, Roosevelt House Public Policy Institute, Hunter College, City University of New York, through 2018. For more information about the research and applied work of QuERI, see the website www.queeringeducation.org. QuERI can also be found on Huffington Post, Facebook, Twitter, and on Academia.edu.

References

Alsaker, Francoise D. and Gutzwiller-Helfenfinger, Eveline. 2010. "Social Behavior and Peer Relationships of Victims, Bully-Victims, and Bullies in Kindergarten." In *Handbook of Bullying in Schools: An International Perspective*, edited by Shane R. Jimerson, Susan M. Swearer, and Dorothy L. Espelage, pp. 87–99. New York: Routledge.

Anderson, Carolyn S. 1982. "The Search for School Climate: A Review of the Research." *Review of Educational Research* 52, 368–420.

Bandyopadhyay, Sharmilla, Cornell, Dewey G., and Konold, Timothy R. 2009. "Validity of Three School Climate Scales to Assess Bullying, Aggressive Attitudes, and Help Seeking." *School Psychology Review* 38, 338–355.

Bansel, Peter, Davies, Bronwyn, Laws, Cath, and Linnell, Sheridan. 2009. "Bullies, Bullying and Power in the Contexts of Schooling." *British Journal of Sociology of Education* 30, 59–69.

Berkowitz, Marvin W. and Bier, Melinda C. 2004. "Research-Based Character Education." *Annals of the American Academy of Political and Social Science* 591, 72–85.

Birkett, Michelle, Espelage, Dorothy L., and Koenig, Brian. 2009. "LGB and Questioning Students in Schools: The Moderating Effects of Homophobic Bullying and School Climate on Negative Outcomes." *Journal of Youth and Adolescence* 38, 989–1000.

Carrera, María Victoria, DePalma, Renée, and Lameiras, María. 2011. "Toward a More Comprehensive Understanding of Bullying in School Settings." *Educational Psychology Review* 23, 479–499.

Connelly, Lisa C. 2012. "Anti-Gay Bullying in Schools: Are Anti-Bullying Statutes the Solution?" *New York University Law Review* 87, 248–283.

DePalma, Renee and Jennett, Mark. 2010. "Homophobia, Transphobia and Culture: Deconstructing Heteronormativity in English Primary Schools." *Intercultural Education* 21, 15–26.

Dessel, Adrienne. 2010. "Prejudice in Schools: Promotion of an Inclusive Culture and Climate." *Education and Urban Society* 42, 407–429.

Dragowski, Eliza A., McCabe, Paul C., and Rubinson, Florence. 2016. "Educators' Reports on Incidence of Harassment and Advocacy Toward LGBTQ Students." *Psychology in the Schools* 53, 127–142.

Duncan, Neil. 2004. "It's Important to Be Nice, but It's Nicer to Be Important: Girls, Popularity and Sexual Competition." *Sex Education* 4, 137–152.

Dupper, David R. and Meyer-Adams, Nancy. 2002. "Low-Level Violence: A Neglected Aspect of School Culture." *Urban Education* 37, 350–364.

Eckert, Penelope. 1994. "Entering the Heterosexual Marketplace: Identities of Subordination as a Developmental Imperative." *Working Papers on Learning and Identity, Stanford*. Palo Alto, CA: Institute for Research on Learning.

Espelage, Dorothy L., Aragon, Steven R., Birkett, Michelle, and Koenig, Brian W. 2008. "Homophobic Teasing, Psychological Outcomes, and Sexual Orientation among High School Students: What Influence Do Parents and Schools Have?" *School Psychology Review* 37, 202–216.

Espelage, Dorothy L., Polanin, Joshua R., and Low, Sabina K. 2014. "Teacher and Staff Perceptions of School Environment as Predictors of Student Aggression, Victimization, and Willingness to Intervene in Bullying Situations." *School Psychology Quarterly* 29, 287–305.

Espelage, Dorothy L. and Swearer, Susan M. 2010. "A Social-Ecological Model for Bullying Prevention and Intervention." In *Handbook of Bullying in Schools: An International Perspective*, edited by Shane R. Jimerson, Susan M. Swearer, and Dorothy L. Espelage, pp. 61–72. New York: Routledge.

Fields, Jessica. 2013. "A Different Story: LGBTQ Sexuality and the Limited Promise of Anti-Bullying Efforts." Paper presented at the Annual Meeting of the American Education Research Association, San Francisco, CA.

Frey, Karin S., Hirschstein, Miriam K., Edstrom, Leihua V., and Snell, Jennie L. 2009. "Observed Reductions in School Bullying, Nonbullying Aggression, and Destructive

Bystander Behavior: A Longitudinal Evaluation." *Journal of Educational Psychology* 101, 466–481.

Gendron, Brian P., Williams, Kirk R., and Guerra, Nancy G. 2011. "An Analysis of Bullying among Students within Schools: Estimating the Effects of Individual Normative Beliefs, Self-Esteem, and School Climate." *Journal of School Violence* 10, 150–164.

Goodenow, Carol, Szalacha, Laura, and Westheimer, Kim. 2006. "School Support Groups, Other School Factors, and the Safety of Sexual Minority Adolescents." *Psychology in the Schools* 43, 573–589.

Gottfredson, Gary D., Gottfredson, Denise C., Payne, Allison Ann, and Gottfredson, Nisha C. 2005. "School Climate Predictors of School Disorder: Results from a National Study of Delinquency Prevention in Schools." *Journal of Research in Crime and Delinquency* 42, 412–444.

Green, Jennifer Greif, Dunn, Erin C., Johnson, Renee M., and Molnar, Beth E. 2011. "A Multilevel Investigation of the Association between School Context and Adolescent Nonphysical Bullying." *Journal of School Violence* 10, 133–149.

Hackford-Peer, Kim. 2010. "In the Name of Safety: Discursive Positionings of Queer Youth." *Studies in Philosophy and Education* 29, 541–556.

Hirschfeld, Scott. 2001. "Moving Beyond the Safety Zone: A Staff Development Approach to Anti-Heterosexist Education." *Fordham Urban Law Journal* 29, 611.

Horne, Arthur M., Swearer, Susan M., Givens, Jami, and Meints, Christina. 2010. "Bully Busters: Reducing Bullying by Changing Teacher and Student Behavior," in *Handbook of Bullying in Schools: An International Perspective*, edited by Shane R. Jimerson, Susan M. Swearer, and Dorothy L. Espelage, pp. 507–516. New York: Routledge.

Hoy, Wayne K. 1990. "Organizational Climate and Culture: A Conceptual Analysis of the School Workplace." *Journal of Educational and Psychological Consultation* 1, 149–168.

Hymel, Shelley, Schonert-Reichl, Kimberly A., Bonnano, R.A., Vaillancourt, Tracy, and Henderson, N. Rocke. 2010. "Bullying and Morality." In *Handbook of Bullying in Schools: An International Perspective*, edited by Shane R. Jimerson, Susan M. Swearer, and Dorothy L. Espelage, pp. 101–118. New York: Routledge.

Jacobson, Ronald B. 2013. *Rethinking School Bullying: Dominance, Identity, and School Culture*. New York: Routledge.

Johnson, Renee M., Kidd, Jeremy D., Dunn, Erin C., Green, Jennifer Greif, Corliss, Heather L., and Bowen, Deborah. 2011. "Associations between Caregiver Support, Bullying, and Depressive Symptomatology among Sexual Minority and Heterosexual Girls: Results from the 2008 Boston Youth Survey." *Journal of School Violence* 10, 185–200.

Kosciw, Joseph G., Palmer, Neal A., Kull, Ryan M., and Greytak, Emily A. 2013. "The Effect of Negative School Climate on Academic Outcomes for LGBT Youth and the Role of In-School Supports." *Journal of School Violence* 12, 45–63.

Leming, James S. 2000. "Tell Me a Story: An Evaluation of a Literature-based Character Education Programme." *Journal of Moral Education* 29, 413–427.

Lugg, Catherine A. 2006. "Thinking about Sodomy: Public Schools, Legal Panopticons, and Queers." *Educational Policy* 20, 35–58.

Mahan, Will C., Varjas, Kris, Dew, Brian J., Meyers, Joel, Singh, Anneliese A., Marshall, Megan L., and Graybill, Emily C. 2007. "School and Community Service Providers' Perspectives on Gay, Lesbian and Questioning Bullying." *Journal of LGBT Issues in Counseling* 1, 45–66.

Maxwell, T.W. Maxwell and Thomas, A. Ross. 1991. "School Climate and School Culture." *Journal of Educational Administration* 29, 72–82.

McInnes, David and Couch, Murray. 2004. "Quiet Please! There's a Lady on the Stage – Boys, Gender and Sexuality Non-Conformity and Class." *Discourse* 25, 435–436.

Meyer, Elizabeth J. 2008. "A Feminist Reframing of Bullying and Harassment: Transforming Schools through Critical Pedagogy." *McGill Journal of Education/Revue des sciences de l'éducation de McGill* 43, 33–48.

Murdock, Tamera B. and Bolch, Megan B. 2005. "Risk and Protective Factors for Poor School Adjustment in Lesbian, Gay, and Bisexual (LGB) High School Youth: Variable and Person-Centered Analyses." *Psychology in the Schools* 42, 159–172.

Ngo, Bic. 2003. "Citing Discourses: Making Sense of Homophobia and Heteronormativity at Dynamic High School." *Equity and Excellence in Education* 36, 115–124.

Nickerson, Amanda B., Mele, Danielle, and Osborne-Oliver, Kristina M. 2010. "Parent–Child Relationships and Bullying." In *Handbook of Bullying in Schools: An International Perspective*, edited by Shane R. Jimerson, Susan M. Swearer, and Dorothy L. Espelage, pp. 187–197. New York: Routledge.

Olweus, Dan. 2010. "Understanding and Researching Bullying." In *Handbook of Bullying in Schools: An International Perspective*, edited by Shane R. Jimerson, Susan M. Swearer, and Dorothy L. Espelage, pp. 9–34. New York: Routledge.

Olweus, Dan and Limber, Susan P. 2010. "The Olweus Bullying Prevention Program: Implementation and Evaluation over Two Decades." In *Handbook of Bullying in Schools: An International Perspective*, edited by Shane R. Jimerson, Susan M. Swearer, and Dorothy L. Espelage, pp. 377–402. New York: Routledge.

Orpinas, Pamela and Horne, Arthur. 2010. "Creating a Positive School Climate and Developing Social Competence." In *Handbook of Bullying in Schools: An International Perspective*, edited by Shane R. Jimerson, Susan M. Swearer and Dorothy L. Espelage, pp. 49–59. New York: Routledge.

Pascoe, C.J. 2007. *Dude, You're a Fag: Masculinity and Sexuality in Adolescence.* Berkeley: University of California Press.

Pascoe, C.J. 2013. "Notes on a Sociology of Bullying: Young Men's Homophobia as Gender Socialization." *QED: A Journal in GLBTQ Worldmaking* 1, 87–103.

Payne, Elizabethe. 2007. "Heterosexism, Perfection, and Popularity: Young Lesbians' Experiences of the High School Social Scene." *Educational Studies* 41, 60–79.

Payne, Elizabethe. 2010. "Sluts: Heteronormative Policing in the Stories of Lesbian Youth." *Educational Studies* 46, 317–336.

Payne, Elizabethe and Smith, Melissa J. 2010. "Reduction of Stigma in Schools: An Evaluation of the First Three Years." *Issues in Teacher Education* 19, 11–36.

Payne, Elizabethe and Smith, Melissa J. 2011. "The Reduction of Stigma in Schools: A New Professional Development Model for Empowering Educators to Support LGBTQ Students." *Journal of LGBT Youth* 8, 174–200.

Payne, Elizabethe and Melissa Smith. 2012a. "Rethinking Safe Schools Approaches for LGBTQ Students: Changing the Questions We Ask." *Multicultural Perspectives* 14, 187–193.

Payne, Elizabethe and Smith, Melissa J. 2012b. "Safety, Celebration, and Risk: Educator Responses to LGBTQ Professional Development." *Teaching Education* 23, 265–285.

Perez, Evelyn R., Schanding Jr, G. Thomas, and Dao, Tam K. 2013. "Educators' Perceptions in Addressing Bullying of LGBTQ/Gender Nonconforming Youth." *Journal of School Violence* 12, 64–79.

Porter, William, Plog, Amy, Jens, Kathryn, Garrity, Carla, and Sager, Nancy. 2010. "Bully-Proofing Your Elementary School." In *Handbook of Bullying in Schools: An International Perspective*, edited by Shane R. Jimerson, Susan M. Swearer, and Dorothy L. Espelage, pp. 431–440. New York: Routledge.

Poteat, Paul V. and Espelage, Dorothy L. 2007. "Predicting Psychosocial Consequences of Homophobic Victimization in Middle School Students." *Journal of Early Adolescence* 27, 175–191.

Rigby, Ken. 2010. "School Bullying and the Case for the Method of Shared Concern." In *Handbook of Bullying in Schools: An International Perspective*, edited by Shane R. Jimerson, Susan M. Swearer, and Dorothy L. Espelage, pp. 547–558. New York: Routledge.

Rinehart, Sarah J. and Espelage, Dorothy L. 2016. "A Multilevel Analysis of School Climate, Homophobic Name-calling, and Sexual Harassment Victimization/Perpetration Among Middle School Youth." *Psychology of Violence* 6, 213–222.

Ringrose, Jessica. 2008. "'Just be Friends': Exposing the Limits of Educational Bully Discourses for Understanding Teen Girls' Heterosexualized Friendships and Conflicts." *British Journal of Sociology of Education* 29, 509–522.

Ringrose, Jessica and Renold, Emma. 2010. "Normative Cruelties and Gender Deviants: The Performative Effects of Bully Discourses for Girls and Boys in School." *British Educational Research Journal* 36, 590.

Robinson, Joseph P. and Espelage, Dorothy L. 2013. "Peer Victimization and Sexual Risk Differences between Lesbian, Gay, Bisexual, Transgender, or Questioning and Nontransgender Heterosexual Youths in Grades 7–12." *American Journal of Public Health* 103, 1810–1819.

Robinson, Joseph P., Espelage, Dorothy L., and Rivers, Ian. 2013. "Developmental Trends in Peer Victimization and Emotional Distress in LGB and Heterosexual Youth." *Pediatrics* 131, 423–430.

Smith, David J., Schneider, Barry H., Smith, Peter K., and Ananiadou, Katerina. 2004. "The Effectiveness of Whole-School Antibullying Programs: A Synthesis of Evaluation Research." *School Psychology Review* 33, 547–560.

Smith, George W. and Smith. Dorothy E. 1998. "The Ideology of 'Fag.'" *Sociological Quarterly* 39, 309–335.

Smith, Melissa and Payne, Elizabethe. 2013. "Position Statement on Zero Tolerance Policies." https://www.academia.edu/5393470/Smith_M._and_Payne_E._Fall_2013._QuERI_Position_Statement_Zero_Tolerance_Discipline_Policies (last accessed October 19, 2017).

Smith, Peter K. and Brain, Paul. 2000. "Bullying in Schools: Lessons from Two." *Aggressive Behavior* 26, 1–9.

Solorzano, Daniel, Ceja, Miguel, and Yosso, Tara. 2000. "Critical Race Theory, Racial Microaggressions, and Campus Racial Climate: The Experiences of African American College Students." *Journal of Negro Education* 69(1/2), 60–73.

Stengel, Barbara. 2010. "The Complex Case of Fear and Safe Space." *Studies in Philosophy and Education* 29, 523–540.

Stewart, Eric A. 2003. "School Social Bonds, School Climate, and School Misbehavior: A Multilevel Analysis." *Justice Quarterly* 20, 575–604.

Swearer, Susan M., Espelage, Dorothy L., Vaillancourt, Tracy, and Hymel, Shelley. 2010. "What Can be Done about School Bullying? Linking Research to Educational Practice." *Educational Researcher* 39, 38–47.

Thurlow, Crispin. 2001. "Naming the 'Outsider Within': Homophobic Pejoratives and the Verbal Abuse of Lesbian, Gay and Bisexual High-School Pupils." *Journal of Adolescence* 24, 25–38.

Toomey, Russell B., McGuire, Jenifer K., and Russell, Stephen T. 2012. "Heteronormativity, School Climates, and Perceived Safety for Gender Nonconforming Peers." *Journal of Adolescence* 35, 187–196.

Van Houtte, Mieke. 2005. "Climate or Culture? A Plea for Conceptual Clarity in School Effectiveness Research." *School Effectiveness and School Improvement* 16, 71–89.

Waasdorp, Tracy Evian, Bradshaw, Catherine P., and Duong, Jeffrey. 2011. "The Link between Parents' Perceptions of the School and Their Responses to School Bullying: Variation by Child Characteristics and the Forms of Victimization." *Journal of Educational Psychology* 103, 324–335.

Wallace, Jason A. 2011. "Bullycide in American Schools: Forging a Comprehensive Legislative Solution." *Indiana Law Journal* 86, 748.

Walton, Gerald. 2005. "Bullying Widespread: A Critical Analysis of Research and Public Discourse on Bullying." *Journal of School Violence* 4, 91–118.

Walton, Gerald. 2010. "The Problem Trap: Implications of Policy Archaeology Methodology for Anti-Bullying Policies." *Journal of Education Policy* 25, 135–150.

Walton, Gerald. 2011. "Spinning our Wheels: Reconceptualizing Bullying beyond Behaviour-focused Approaches." *Discourse: Studies in the Cultural Politics of Education* 32, 131–144.

Welsh, Wayne N. 2000. "The Effects of School Climate on School Disorder." *Annals of the American Academy of Political and Social Science* 567, 88–107.

Youdell, Deborah. 2005. "Sex–Gender–Sexuality: How Sex, Gender and Sexuality Constellations Are Constituted in Secondary Schools." *Gender and Education* 17, 249–270.

Youdell, Deborah. 2006. *Impossible Bodies, Impossible Selves: Exclusions and Student Subjectivities*. Dordrecht: Springer.

Youdell, Deborah. 2011. *School Trouble: Identity, Power and Politics in Education*. New York: Routledge.

20

Intimate Partner Violence in Higher Education

Integrated Approaches for Reducing Domestic Violence and Sexual Assault on Campus

Sheila M. Katz and Laura J. McGuire

Domestic violence, sexual assault, stalking, rape, and battering are all considered forms of intimate partner violence (IPV) by the Centers for Disease Control and Prevention (CDC). Recently, renewed attention to Title IX and sexual assault on university campuses has brought light to this area, but a broader conversation about various forms of IPV and how they affect institutions of higher education is needed. In this chapter, we examine intimate partner violence within institutions of higher education. This chapter uses a feminist sociological perspective to address the issue of domestic violence and IPV. Our main purpose is to explore ways that institutions of higher education can contribute to prevention and survival measures. We ask: Why focus on the issue of domestic violence and IPV in the context of higher education? What form does this type of violence take in the context of higher education? What are the factors that contribute to it? What factors perpetuate it in the context of higher education? What preventions can we take to change it?

To accomplish this, we consider how federal legislation like Title IX addresses it within the context of gender discrimination. We discuss the strengths and shortcomings of federal legislation and programs such as Title IX and the Clery Act, as applied broadly to the issue of domestic violence and IPV. Federal efforts have failed to adequately address the complete scope of the issue of IPV on campus. Therefore, we suggest best practices for institutions of higher education to consider in order to address and reduce IPV on campus. In the last section, we tackle institutional assumptions in higher education, campus climate issues including patriarchy and rape culture, and the ability of higher educational actors to cope with domestic violence. Campus communities can make institutional changes to decrease the occurrence and influence of IPV. Faculty, staff, and students can take steps to be more aware of the issue of domestic violence/IPV and more able to cope with it. The chapter concludes with suggestions on how to create a campus climate where healthier relationships are a priority to help reduce IPV, sexual assault, and overall rape culture on campus.

The Wiley Handbook on Violence in Education: Forms, Factors, and Preventions, First Edition.
Edited by Harvey Shapiro.

Understanding IPV and Domestic Violence

The CDC defines intimate partner violence as violence between people that "includes physical violence, sexual violence, stalking and psychological aggression (including coercive tactics) by a current or former intimate partner (i.e., spouse, boyfriend/ girlfriend, dating partner, or ongoing sexual partner)" (Breiding et al. 2015, 11). The National Coalition Against Domestic Violence defines it as "the willful intimidation, physical assault, battery, sexual assault, and/or other abusive behavior as part of a systematic pattern of power and control perpetrated by one intimate partner against another. It includes physical violence, sexual violence, psychological violence, and emotional abuse" (National Coalition Against Domestic Violence 2017). Domestic violence has five central forms: physical, sexual, verbal, emotional, and financial. Further, feminists connect the issues of control present in domestic violence and IPV to broader issues of gender inequality, patriarchy, and systems of oppression. Therefore, intimate partner violence is not just between individuals who know each other or are in a relationship, but is a form of control or violence that is embedded in systems of power and privilege that positions power of certain groups over others – such as men over women, whites over non-whites, higher socioeconomic classes above lower ones, and so on.

Research finds that approximately half of women in the United States experience some type of domestic or sexual violence at some point in their lives (Breidling, Chen, and Black 2014). For college students, research estimates between 10% and 50% experience dating violence (Kaukinen 2014). IPV happens to students from all backgrounds regardless of socioeconomic status, race/ethnicity, religion, or sexual orientation (Roberts 2002). IPV and domestic violence is usually thought of through a heteronormative frame; in other words, men abusing women. However, IPV and unhealthy relationships can occur in both heterosexual and same-gender relationships. Research finds that "LGBT students are at a greater risk of all types of dating violence as compared to heterosexual students" (Kaukinen 2014, 291). Further, research is clear that IPV and unhealthy relationships have numerous "negative consequences on health and well-being, including physical injury, depression, low self-esteem, and anxiety disorders" (Kaukinen 2014, 284). The CDC reports that IPV survivors report more health problems such as headaches, poor physical and mental health, trouble sleeping, and increased chronic pain than those who have never experienced IPV (Black et al. 2011). After leaving abusive relationships, people can experience multiple mental health problems including PTSD (post-traumatic stress disorder), depression, low self-esteem, or increased anxiety (Brewster 2002).

IPV is also considered a form of gendered violence and connecting it to issues of gender inequality can help us better understand and address IPV. Theories of domestic violence include how the "power differential in the patriarchal structure" can contribute to or encourage IPV, but also, the issue of control in relationships is important factor (Brewster 2002, 30). Changes in gender roles or conflict about gender role expectations increase chances for IPV. One person, who typically has power or control in a relationship or generally in society, may feel threatened by the person who is presumed to have less power or control in the situation or in society, and may respond in abusive ways.

IPV and Domestic Violence in Higher Education

Consequently, when we consider IPV in institutions of higher education, we also need to consider how economics, forms of privilege, and other power and control dynamics are present in relationships and society. Institutions of higher education are "charged spaces" for the ramifications of IPV or dating violence (Lee 2008). From first-time freshmen through older students, many challenges exist for students dealing with IPV. For example, older students may have experienced IPV before coming to college and have different needs than freshmen living on campus and away from their families for the first time (Lee 2008). The demographics of the undergraduate population are shifting and more non-traditional students are enrolling in bachelor's degree programs. For example, during the Great Recession (2008), the nationwide population of under-graduates who were non-traditional and had children increased by about 900,000 (Gault, Reichlin, and Reynolds 2014; Miller, Gault, and Thorman 2011). These students come to college from diverse backgrounds and life experiences, some of them IPV survivors. Further, faculty and staff may also have experience with IPV. Balancing professional obligations with their own current or past personal IPV experiences can be difficult when working with students surviving IPV or within institutions that are not designed to handle effects of IPV. Academic demands and stress can exacerbate the negative consequences of IPV for students and faculty/staff. Given the negative health consequences of IPV, students who have experienced IPV may have a difficult time focusing on academic work, dealing with stress and demands of rigorous courses, meeting deadlines, attending classes or meetings, being consistent in their work, or avoiding triggering situations. The same is true for faculty or staff. IPV in higher education needs to be addressed in similar ways to how IPV in the workplace is researched. However, in both settings, not nearly enough is being done to help survivors cope and rebuild their lives.

Institutions of higher education are often thought of as "ivory towers" where the demands and pressures of the larger society are more distant. However, we all know that is a debilitating myth. Instead, institutions of higher education are complex structures of society that contain diverse sites, purposes, and elements. The multiple missions of higher education converge to create a complex institution. The university is an educational setting, a work setting, a residential setting, a community-gathering place, a research facility, host of sports, arts, and recreational events, and so on. All of these sites are fraught with their own risks for IPV, sexual assault, sexual harassment, etc. Therefore, when considering the forms of IPV on campuses, we must understand that each site contributes to the risks of IPV or sexual assault, can exacerbate its trauma, or delay recovery from it.

Further, economic status and financial dependence make it more difficult for people, but especially women, to leave abusive relationships (Davis 1999). Students are often financially constrained by having to balance the costs of living and the costs of higher education. Escaping IPV or coping with the effects of it is often very expensive: costs such as moving, leaving the relationship, starting over, and dealing with health or mental health effects add up quickly. Women often need financial assistance to leave abusive relationships, and turn to their families, shelters or other advocacy groups, or the welfare system to provide the emotional and financial support to leave (Davis 1999). Domestic violence is one of the most commonly mentioned barriers to higher education and employment among low-income women (Katz 2008, Katz forthcoming). Domestic violence is frequently exacerbated when mothers seek education, training, or work (Tolman and Raphael 2000). For example, women on welfare experienced an increase in domestic violence when they tried to get a job or attend higher education as a way to change their economic situation (Lyon 2000). IPV/domestic violence can have drastic implications for the physical, emotional, and economic well-being of low-income women and their children. In terms of health, higher rates of depression and PTSD are found among mothers on welfare who have experienced abuse than those who have not (Lyon 2000). Additionally, mothers on welfare who have experienced domestic violence are almost twice as likely to report a "physical limitation" or rate their health as "poor" as those who have never been abused (Allard, Tolman, and Rosen 2003).

Domestic violence or IPV can derail a woman's efforts to obtain self-sufficient employment and move off welfare or out of poverty. Batterers often sabotage women's efforts to work or study by making threats, inflicting injuries before tests or interviews, preventing women from sleeping or studying, stalking on campus or at work, or refusing at the last minute to provide promised childcare that women need to work or attend school (Beechey and Payne 2002; Davis 1999; Raphael 1999). A 1999 study of women on welfare in Wisconsin found that 63% were fired or forced to quit their jobs due to domestic violence (Moore and Selkowe 1999). Furthermore, a 1999 study of Colorado welfare women found that 44% were prevented from working by abusive ex-partners (Pearson, Theonnes, and Griswold 1999). Even when women are able to secure employment, domestic violence makes sustained employment more difficult and greatly affects the employment options, quality of the employment, and earnings potential for domestic violence victims with children in the welfare system (Davis 1999; Lyon 2000).

Experiences of IPV on Campus

Katz's research explores the experiences of women on welfare who completed higher education (2008 and forthcoming). Domestic violence while in college was often discussed by participants who were on welfare, mothering, and pursuing a higher education. The following vignette illustrates several of these points. Mercedes, a 38-year-old mother of four and recent graduate with a bachelor's degree, was a first-generation Latina American. She experienced ongoing domestic violence while she was in community college and after she transferred to a four-year university. Her boyfriend was the father of her two youngest children, and she had an on/off relationship with him. The abuse and fighting would escalate, she would leave him, then the "honeymoon" phase would occur, he would convince her to come back, and the situation would improve, until it escalated again in a violent incident. She grappled with her feelings for him. She remained emotionally conflicted about him even after he was deported, as she related in the incident below, which happened just before her college graduation. Her response is to my request to tell me about her college graduation day:

> Umm it was happy, I was really happy and excited, but I was kind of sad though. Because right, a week before graduation, her dad [indicated to her daughter in her lap] and I had a fight, an awful fight. I was inside the car and he punched the window. He said he was punching the window, regardless, the glass broke and it cut my

eye. So I was, just like, really crazy. I was in the hospital, got stitches here and here [indicating her face and head]. My mom saw everything, which is what I didn't want. She knew we had troubles, but I didn't want her to see that. And he ran. It was just really crazy. That was a whole week before graduation, because up until that time, he was going to be there. So, it was kind of weird for me. Everyone was, well my mom was there and important people … but he was the one person that wasn't there. Deep down, I mean, this is the weird part of the whole domestic violence stuff, but deep down, I wanted him to be there, but I knew he couldn't because I had pressed charges. I had this scar on my face; it just wasn't the right thing.

Mercedes struggled with her happiness at completing her degree and graduating from college, and the pain of the continued abuse from her partner. She eventually reported the abuse, which added to her partner's ongoing immigration issues with INS. Eventually he was jailed and then deported after the charges were filed against him after this incident. I asked her in this interview who she turned to or who helped her cope with the domestic violence, or helped her consider her options to leave. Could she confide in anyone – maybe a faculty member, an advisor, a counselor? Was there a women's resource center available for students dealing with domestic violence? She said there was nothing that helped, no resources she used. She knew of a few, but she felt the waiting lists were not worth the assistance. A trusted academic advisor knew the ongoing issues, but there weren't comprehensive resources available at her campus to help her with her trouble. Her experience is not unusual. Although IPV, domestic violence, and rape are common experiences in higher education, most campuses do not have comprehensive resources, training, or education about IPV or domestic violence. Even fewer have the vision to challenge the rape culture that perpetuates IPV and help IPV survivors overcome multiple recovery obstacles and succeed in higher education. Most institutions of higher education are simply doing the minimum that is federally required by Title IX and the Clery Act. There may be interest at institutions to do more, but the drive and resources to accomplish it are lacking.

Federal Policy and IPV on Campus

Domestic violence and IPV are often grouped in the legal breadth of what is considered sexual misconduct. Evidence for this can be found in numerous higher education sexual misconduct policies (Northwestern University 2016; Yale University 2016). Sexual violence and domestic violence are interrelated in social and cultural paradigms that are part of the construct known as "rape culture" (Flood and Pease 2009; Herman 1988; Walker 1999). In 1987, in one of the first national studies addressing sexual violence on campuses, Koss and colleagues explored the vast and compounding ways in which women were mistreated in higher education and their experiences with IPV on university campuses. The study examined the dehumanizing experiences, such as rampant sexual harassment, stalking, and assault, that women were forced to endure for the sake of educational access (Koss, Gidycz, and Wisniewski 1987). Yet, more recent research shows that only a little has changed since Koss' study.

Three pieces of federal policy and legislation currently contribute to the approach that institutions of higher education take toward IPV and sexual assault: Title IX, the

Clery Act, and the 2011 Department of Education "Dear Colleague" letter. The first, Title IX, was passed in 1972. Title IX addresses equal access to education on the basis of sex at institutions that receive federal funding, from kindergarten through graduate school. It considers sex/gender discrimination as a barrier in educational institutions. Originally, Title IX did not directly focus on issues of sexual violence or domestic violence. It was not until the 1990s that attention was paid to the gross failure of universities to address sexual violence on college and university campuses (Faber 1992).

This coincided with the passing of the Clery Act, which was created by the Clery family, whose daughter was raped and murdered in her dorm room during her first semester of college (Clery Center 2016). Two laws then connected the Clery Act and Title IX: the Violence Against Women Act and the Campus SaVE Act. Both of these laws focused on gendered sexual violence, which Clery does not (Clery Center 2016). Today, Title IX not only focuses on these issues, but it is a hallmark in access to athletics for all genders, preventing discrimination for pregnant or parenting students, preventing sexual violence against all genders. Additionally, Title IX is being used in new frontiers such as barriers and prejudice faced by LGBTQ students in seeking educational equity.

In 2011, colleges and universities across the nation were shaken by a "Dear Colleague" letter from the Department of Education's Office for Civil Rights that went out to all federally funded institutions of higher education (National Sexual Violence Resource Center 2016). The letter states: "The sexual harassment of students, including sexual violence, interferes with students' right to receive an education free from discrimination and, in the case of sexual violence, is a crime" (US Department of Education Department of Education 2011). The letter placed new focus and emphasis on higher education's responsibility to prevent and address instances of sexual misconduct that occur on campuses. A number of new requirements were implemented in hundreds of college campuses as a reaction to trying to remain in compliance with the new federal guidelines and to receive federal funding. Many of these changes were poorly planned, directed by individuals with little or no training in these subject areas, and implemented with little forethought or analysis. Five years later, very few universities have made true concerted efforts in partnership with content experts to develop strategies, curricula, and policies that best address the structural issues and inequalities that lead to sexual misconduct and low rates of reporting. More attention needs to be placed on the best evidence-based practices instead of merely covering legal liability or preventing the loss of federal funds.

Shortcomings of Federal Policy Implementation on Campuses

After the Dear Colleague letter came out, universities scrambled to make changes to their sexual assault policies and reporting procedures. Researchers suggested how universities can comply and why these changes were important (Block 2012). Compliance with the federal policies was key. The main point of focus by officials in higher education was a need to introduce the concept of compliance, not prevention, into their new student orientations and through online training modules. However, a "compliance first" focus was not the most effective approach. New guidelines on mandatory reporting for staff and faculty were created (Engle 2015). The idea behind this was that the central issues of Title IX violations were rooted in the problem that survivor reports of sexual misconduct were ignored or erased by university staff. The next sweeping conclusion was that this would be remedied if everything, in all circumstances, was reported to the Title IX coordinator. This went as far as requiring faculty and staff to report things they overheard but were unsure of the context of, "just in case" it was related to sexual misconduct. An investigation could then be triggered, even without the victim's consent. "Investigation" can be considered a term used casually by institutions as these investigations are often not conducted by professionally trained detectives or police officials. Instead, a staff member can be assigned the task by the university, but these staff are not required to have training, guidance, or specific criteria. These investigations can be done by lawyers who work for and within the university and whose positions foster an innate conflict of interest.

Another concern is the training or background of the person who is put in the role of Title IX coordinator. Title IX coordinators are responsible for such sensitive and precarious responsibilities as stated by the US Department of Justice (2017): "The Title IX coordinator has a responsibility to coordinate the recipient's efforts to comply with its obligations under Title IX and the Title IX regulations. These responsibilities include coordinating any investigations of complaints received pursuant to Title IX and the implementing regulations." Yet, Title IX offices and coordinators can be staffed by almost anyone at a university. There is no specific required training, certification, or licensure for the position. Schools have appointed deans, faculty, and other staff who have little or no background in gender-responsive issues or trauma-informed care. The same concern is present regarding sexual prevention educators. While a number of national experts have risen on the national stage in their roles as compliance and education professionals, the job titles of "Title IX coordinator," "Clery Act compliance officer," and "prevention educator" are still often staffed by egregiously unqualified practitioners. The pressure of the 2011 Dear Colleague letter further exacerbated this issue – many campuses scrambled to fill these new requirements with "warm bodies" no matter what their delivery, bias, or experience might be. With no federal or regional curriculum or guidelines for prevention education, this is unlikely to be remedied in the near future.

Staff and faculty pushed back against the new requirements of the "tell us everything or be fired" mentality (Flaherty 2015). In one infamous case, a former residential advisor who was seeking a promotion refused to name a victim – who he was a friend of and had spoken with in confidence – and lost his job as a result (Grasgreen 2013). Staff and faculty who were used to working with autonomous, albeit young, adults were now forced to report as if they were working with minors. They were required to accomplish this without any comprehensive employee training on trauma-informed practices or victim/offender rights. Many student survivors McGuire has worked with have expressed their experiences as compounded trauma at being forced to be investigated by the university, when all they were seeking was to simply find an initial place to share their story or ask for further clarification on options for reporting or therapeutic resources (also see Deamicis 2013). McGuire notes that she has yet to meet a single student who fully understood that even telling a story of sexual harassment that occurred off campus would potentially be mandate reported, triggering contact from lawyers and an investigation.

The issue here is twofold. First of all, it makes the objective of reporting under Title IX to be the gold standard, the only "right" option for a survivor to take. It does not allow for other options to be explored first, much less reprioritized. Legal or police reporting is not the only – and may not even be the best – option for many survivors of sexual violence or domestic violence. In certain circumstances, for both protective measures and trauma-centered healing, not reporting may be the best option. Being forced "for your own good" to undergo an investigation or procedure of any kind without a victim's full consent not only demoralizes the individual but re-victimizes and infantilizes them in the process. If we, as prevention and compliance professionals, are discussing bodily autonomy, consent, and supporting survivors, we must not do what their abuser did to them: take away their ability to choose, be heard, and be trusted in whatever decision they make.

Second, to combat sexual violence and promote gender equity, which laws like Title IX, the Clery Act, and the Violence Against Women Act claim to do, we, as a society, must see the value in addressing the complexities of the alternatives that we desire to move toward. Focusing on compliance is an infantile script of punishment and punitive messaging without reasoning or explanation of the pitfalls or multiple dimensions of moving into a culture of consent. As cute and catchy as the now famous "Consent: It's Simple as Tea" video is (https://www.youtube.com/watch?v= oQbei5JGiT8), it does not explain all the complexities and facets of what the new vision of consent needs to address. On most campuses, in most institutions of higher education, the focus is on compliance with federal policies and laws and not on what is best for victims, survivors, or students. The institution's needs are prioritized over the human needs of the individuals. This compliance first focus is deeply problematic and will serve only as a band aid for the deeper issues of gender discrimination, rape culture, sexual assault, and IPV on campus and in society. However, some colleges and universities understand this problem and are proactively trying to change this dynamic on their campus. A few schools, such as Dartmouth, with its four-year prevention education initiative (Kingkade 2015), have made reasonable, rational, and systemic changes to inform students of policy and guidelines and shift cultural norms and scripting. However, initiatives like Dartmouth's are too few. More campuses need to create systemic changes to establish IPV prevention instead of just compliance with federal policies.

Challenging Rape Culture on Campus

Students enter higher education coming from a rape culture. One of the main factors in IPV on campus is that students, staff, faculty, administrators, and the institutions are embedded in our patriarchal culture and all have experience in rampant rape culture. Most of us have been socialized or conditioned to believe in the sexist, racist, heteronormative, misogynistic frameworks that the media, families, religions, government, or communities have taught. Only through proactive efforts can these normative ideas be challenged. Feminists have worked for decades to bring attention to these issues and the patriarchal power structures that create them. It is naive and foolish, then, to think that a university employee who has little or no interaction with victims, perpetrators, or the feminist theories and paradigms that shape them, can adequately speak on these topics and have an impactful response. McGuire shares an example from working with one university:

one time when I was asked to come on as a content expert at a university, I found out my position had been previously filled by a cobbling together of entry level lawyers in the prevention education role. One lawyer, who fiercely defended her right to be a main prevention educator, confided in me that a student had asked her if, "It was always consensual if a woman was on top?," to which she had no answer. She had no answer, because she had no real comprehension of what consent is beyond a written policy. And yet both she, and the university, continued to use her as a main prevention and compliance educator.

Consent and relationships are extraordinarily complicated and nuanced. Ignoring an issue because it doesn't fit neatly on a policy document or can't be addressed adequately by non-experts at a 30-minute orientation or online video/training is reckless, irresponsible, and unjust to the students the university is purported to serve. IPV and sexual assault prevention is only truly effective when conducted and executed with a focus on shifting social norms and cultural scripts. The structural norms that must be addressed are relationship and dating violence, consent as a cultural mandate, and the destigmatization of victimization for both female and male victims (Manzano 1998). Adverse childhood experiences, sexual violence, and domestic violence are a common and prevalent part of Western culture (Finkelhor et al. 1990; Foege 1998). Despite this prevalence, many faculty and staff have little knowledge of the prevalence, effects, and best practices for supporting survivors. Training in trauma-informed pedagogy and practices will help to mend these gaps in creating a survivor-centered supportive campus climate (Ngo et al. 2008). The training is best conducted by trained professionals, and can be effective in either mixed gender or single gender environments (Edwards 2009). To solidify the messages presented, colleges and universities must also have in place policies that support survivors holistically.

Coordinated Campus Resources Focused on Survivor Needs

In the 1980s and 1990s, cities and advocacy centers began to unravel the systemic issues that prevented survivors of domestic and relationship violence from reporting and seeking services. One of the landmark programs of the period was started in Duluth, Minnesota. Now known as the Duluth Model, it was the first to synchronize and coordinate services for survivors. Legal, emotional, economic, and familial support, which had previously been siloed, were now connected. This allowed survivors to access services in the most synchronized manner possible (Shepard and Pence 1999). Having both served on domestic violence counsels ourselves, we can attest to the hurdles and challenges that agencies face in this coordination effort. The majority of cities and universities continue to lament that their right hand does not know what the left hand is doing. Politics, and the value placed on departments for being known as "the place" on campus to support survivors, have created a hostile and inhospitable environment for university-wide collaboration. Struggles for resources, office space, and political power on campuses can mean that programs, centers, or departments that should work together are in conflict or struggle with one another. In order to remedy this situation, it must be made absolutely clear which department will handle all of the issues concerning sexual and domestic violence, instead of allowing the hodgepodge of support, resources, and conflicting messages that exist in many universities and communities today.

Above all, survivors and evidence-based practices must guide and lead institutional efforts and policies. Research has shown that survivors are excellent at predicting future violence and knowing what services would best service their unique circumstances and situation (Weisz, Tolman, and Saunders 2000). These efforts should range from student education and training at all levels (first-time freshmen through doctoral students), ongoing faculty/staff training and accountability, dedicated resources for victims and survivors including counselors, and institutional resources to respond to specific issues. Even physical elements, such as campus buildings or institutional resources, need to be considered in order to challenge rape culture, respond to victims' needs, and create a safer environment for all involved. Physical campus environments have been included in these discussions with attention to items like lighting in parking lots, emergency phones, and escort services. Other elements could be included, such as the way classrooms are designed. Some spaces can trigger anxiety or exacerbate panic disorders for someone who is coping with IPV or in survival/recovery from it. For example, one semester Katz taught in a basement room that was made of cinder blocks, had a low ceiling, no windows, and was situated next to the elevator shaft – so the mechanical noise of the elevator was ever present. The tiny room was filled to capacity by a completely full course. The room was hot and claustrophobic even for those who did not suffer from anxiety or panic disorders. For Katz, recovering from PTSD and panic attacks from an abusive marriage, the room was almost unmanageable:

> two semesters ago I would not have been able to deal with it. Several students asked me privately to try to get the rooms switched for similar reasons – they also were dealing with anxiety and panic disorders and the small, hot, windowless, loud space felt suffocating. I requested several times for a room change – and my department did all they could to relocate us – but given the course time and day (a popular choice) – no other classroom was available. We coped and managed for the semester, several times propping the door open to just get a bit of light and air into the room. I also had to consciously work harder on my own IPV recovery in order to teach in such a space. Students managed and coped – yet, attendance suffered from students who couldn't learn in such a claustrophobic environment.

However, if institutions considered such elements during space design, then issues like this one would be rarer. This is not the first time we have taught in such spaces at a variety of universities. Room such as this one could be used for other purposes than a classroom, and classrooms can be designed in ways that reduce the anxiety and claustrophobia that is common in many mental health disorders, not just for those students dealing with IPV or trauma recovery. The literature on supporting G.I. Bill students, many of whom are combat veterans, also makes a similar observation about windowless classrooms or offices (for example, see Lighthall 2012).

Finally, strong social support is necessary (Tan et al. 1995). Creating campuses with strong trauma-informed policies that support survivors, coupled with faculty and staff who have at least an entry-level education in sexual and domestic violence and empathic pedagogical practices, would allow survivors access to the avenues needed to not only survive but thrive in higher education. Ideally this would create a communal ripple effect. Students, faculty, and staff would reiterate these messages in their communities and families, further shifting the normalization of violence and working to challenge and eradicate the structural inequalities that cause them. In her work, McGuire often asks parents if they have talked to their children about consent before coming to school; most often they reply that they have warned their daughters to "watch out" for predators and not to have sex while at school, which are futile and rape culture-centered messages. If the students and employees of universities are getting their first messages about consent culture, communication, and bodily autonomy during their time at college, the messages must be formatted to be powerful as life skills and not solely as compliance standards.

Preventions: Social Policies and Institutional Best Practices

Given recent attention to Title IX and campuses that have paid huge settlements to students who are sexual assault survivors, we can also use this moment to broaden the conversation to best practices. Federal social policies need improvement. Further, campuses need an institutional evidence-based best practices plan to effectively deal with issues of IPV. These plans should surpass compliance-based policies to focus on how to teach about healthy relationships, how to reduce rape culture, how to create safe spaces on campus for survivors, how to train faculty and staff to work with students (or other faculty and staff) when they disclose their IPV experiences, and how to consider these issues when designing attendance policies, human resources policies, and into institutional culture.

Generally, articles about IPV or domestic violence end with basic suggestions for social changes to reduce or address the problem. For example, Brewster suggests that "a combination of educational prevention programs, crisis intervention approaches, long-term treatment for victims and batterers, and institutional changes that both reduce intimate partner violence and empower victims to overcome abusive relationships is an appropriate, multifaceted approach to helping battered women" (2002, 44). Further, in studies of IPV survivors' needs, research finds that services are most effective if they are "individualized, comprehensive, and driven by survivors' priorities" (Allen, Bybee, and Sullivan 2004, 1031). In other words, not everyone needs the same thing – and an institutional response needs to account for this.

As previously mentioned, a few institutions of higher education have taken up the task of actually altering campus culture rather than submitting to fearmongering compliance. But generally what students hear is, "Do what you have to to avoid getting into trouble," not "Change the way you have been taught to think about relationships and consent." Colleges and universities push back against this standard by saying they don't have enough time to require all students to have these more complex and multifaceted discussions. Their faculty and staff, who may be very well versed on the topic or know nothing at all about it not, are already over-burdened and there just isn't enough time, they say. However, given the pervasiveness of this issue, institutions need to prioritize it for all members of the campus community.

A few universities have taken on this challenge by requiring all students to take a yearly course on different dimensions of sexual assault and domestic violence for every year they attend. Dartmouth unveiled its cutting-edge four-year program to rave reviews and accolades. Rice University, in Houston, TX, has reportedly followed suit. But other major universities still scoff at the idea of that much time, energy, and expense going toward ending sexual assault and domestic violence.

Best Practice Suggestions

Three major components are key for universities and institutions of higher education to adopt as a minimum attempt at preventing IPV and sexual assault, and challenging rape culture on campus. These measures work to authentically and rationally address systemic change that would decrease instances of IPV, sexual assault, and dating violence on campuses and in communities.

First, universities should require all undergraduate and graduate students to complete in-person annual workshops or courses on sexual and domestic violence. Universities require courses for undergraduate and graduate students in many fields and forms. Common required courses for graduation include writing, math, and study skills. The idea behind a university-wide required course is that it is seen as a cornerstone for successful learning and maturation in student development. Therefore, an annual workshop or course covering a different dimension of rape culture, gender identity, IPV, consent, sexuality, communication, relationships, and perpetrator psychology should be required by all institutions of higher education. If writing and math are necessary for producing scholars that a university can be proud of, no less should it be required that they create scholars who will identify, prevent, and speak up against gendered violence. Additionally, institutions of higher education should train their faculty and staff about these issues as well. Most universities have required annual training for faculty and staff, so IPV needs to be included in these workshops, modules, or training. Research shows that online modules are the least effective training mechanism for sensitive topics so, as best practice, universities should consider conducting in-person workshops and trainings.

Second, universities should have multiple expert sources to discuss reporting options with victims and survivors. At many institutions of higher education, the only options for confidential support for survivors of sexual violence and domestic violence are the health center or the counseling center. While these are key resources, the harsh reality of both of these centers is that often neither counselors nor nurses/physicians are required (in most states) to have training in guiding victims/survivors through the reporting process or the legal implications of each option. Providing students with multiple trained advocates, in multiple areas of the university, gives the survivor the freedom of choice and resource specialists who can thoroughly support and answer their questions.

Third, universities need to prioritize a unified and centralized set of resources – into a center or a central location. Legal, advocacy, and educational resources should be centralized and unified. Too often, multiple departments convey very different messages and perspectives on sexual and domestic violence. Each department has their own agenda, varying levels of training or awareness of the issues, and diverging requirements. Students can feel further confused and bewildered about topics that should be clear and concise. Coordinating resources to have unified messages and a clear chain of command, would aid both survivors and university administrations.

These best practices are just a starting point for institutions of higher education to tackle the massive issue of intimate partner violence and sexual assault on campus. IPV and sexual assault is highly preventable through comprehensive education for all members of a campus community. The first step is for a university to make combating IPV on campus an institutional priority. Then, universities should use their central pillars – research and education – to create a comprehensive plan for their campus community.

References

Allard, S., Tolman, T., and Rosen, D. 2003. "Access to Mental Health and Substance Abuse Services Among Women Receiving Welfare in Detroit." *Urban Affairs Review* 38, 787–807.

Allen, N., Bybee, D., and Sullivan, C. 2004. "Battered Women's Multitude of Needs." *Violence Against Women* 10(9), 1015–1035.

Beechey, S. and Payne, J. 2002. "Surviving Violence and Poverty: A Focus on the Link Between Domestic and Sexual Violence, Women's Poverty, and Welfare." Washington, DC: Legal Momentum.

Black, M.C., Basile, K.C., Breiding, M.J., Smith, S.G., Walters, M.L., Merrick, M.T., Chen, J., and Stevens, M.R. 2011. *The National Intimate Partner and Sexual Violence Survey (NISVS): 2010 Summary Report.* Atlanta, GA: National Center for Injury Prevention and Control, Centers for Disease Control and Prevention.

Block, J.A. 2012. "'Prompt and equitable' explained: How to Craft a Title IX Compliant Sexual Assault Harassment Policy and Why It Matters." *College Student Affairs Journal* 30(2), 61–71.

Breiding, M., Basile, K., Smith, S., Black, M., and Mahendra, R. 2015. *Intimate Partner Violence Surveillance Uniform Definitions and Recommended Data Elements, Version 2.0.* Atlanta, GA: National Center for Injury Prevention and Control, Centers for Disease Control and Prevention.

Breiding, M., Chen, J., and Black, M. 2014. *Intimate Partner Violence in the United States, 2010.* Atlanta, GA: National Center for Injury Prevention and Control, Centers for Disease Control and Prevention.

Brewster, M.P. 2002. "Domestic Violence Theories, Research, and Practice Implications." In *Handbook of Domestic Violence Intervention Strategies: Policies, Programs, and Legal Remedies,* edited by A. Roberts, pp. 23–48. Oxford: Oxford University Press.

Clery Center. 2016. "Our History." http://clerycenter.org/our-history (last accessed October 20, 2017).

Davis, M. 1999. "Economics of Abuse: How Violence Perpetuates Women's Poverty." In *Battered Women, Children, and Welfare Reform,* edited by Ruth A. Brandwein, pp. 17–30. Thousand Oaks, CA: Sage.

Deamicis, C. 2013. "Which Matters More: Reporting Assault or Respecting a Victim's Wishes?" *The Atlantic,* May 20. http://www.theatlantic.com/national/archive/2013/05/which-matters-more-reporting-assault-or-respecting-a-victims-wishes/276042/(last accessed October 20, 2017).

Edwards, K.E. 2009. "Effectiveness of a Social Change Approach to Sexual Assault Prevention." *College Student Affairs Journal* 28(1), 22.

Engle, J.C. 2015. "Mandatory Reporting of Campus Sexual Assault and Domestic Violence: Moving to a Victim-centric Protocol that Comports with Federal Law." *Temple Political & Civil Rights Law Review* 24(401).

Faber, J. 1992. "Expanding Title IX of the Education Amendments of 1972 to Prohibit Student to Student Sexual Harassment." *UCLA Women's Law Journal* 2, 85.

Finkelhor, D., Hotaling, G., Lewis, I., and Smith, C. 1990. "Sexual Abuse in a National Survey of Adult Men and Women: Prevalence, Characteristics, and Risk Factors." *Child Abuse & Neglect* 14(1), 19–28.

Flaherty, C. 2015. "Endangering a Trust." *Inside Higher Ed,* February 4. https://www.insidehighered.com/news/2015/02/04/faculty-members-object-new-policies-making-all-professors-mandatory-reporters-sexual (last accessed October 20, 2017).

Flood, M. and Pease, B. 2009. "Factors Influencing Attitudes to Violence against Women." *Trauma, Violence, & Abuse* 10(2), 125–142.

Foege, W.H. 1998. "Adverse Childhood Experiences: A Public Health Perspective." *American Journal of Preventive Medicine* 14(4), 354–55.

Gault, B., Reichlin, L. and Reynolds, E. 2014. "4.8 Million College Students are Raising Children." Fact Sheet C424. November. Washington, DC: Institute for Women's Policy Research.

Grasgreen, A. 2013. "Mandatory Reporting Perils." *Inside Higher Ed*, August 30. https://www.insidehighered.com/news/2013/08/30/firing-sexual-assault-activist-and-swarthmore-ra-raises-questions-about-mandatory (last accessed October 20, 2017).

Herman, D. 1988. "The Rape Culture." *Culture* 1(10), 45–53.

Katz, S. 2008. "Pursuing a 'Reformed' Dream: CalWORKs Mothers in Higher Education after 'ending welfare as we know it'." Unpublished doctoral dissertation. Vanderbilt University, Nashville, TN.

Katz, S. Forthcoming. *Reformed American Dreams: Welfare Mothers, Higher Education, and Activism*. New Brunswick, NJ: Rutgers University Press.

Kaukinen, C. 2014. "Dating Violence among College Students: The Risk and Protective Factors." *Trauma, Violence, & Abuse* 15(4), 283–296.

Kingkade, T. 2015. "How Dartmouth Is Getting Students to Help Prevent Sexual Assault." *Huffington Post*, September 23. http://www.huffingtonpost.com/entry/dartmouth-sexual-assault_us_5601f7b7e4b00310edf9263a (last accessed October 20, 2017).

Koss, M., Gidycz, C.A., and Wisniewski, N. 1987. "The Scope of Rape: Incidence and Prevalence of Sexual Aggression and Victimization in a National Sample of Higher Education Students." *Journal of Consulting & Clinical Psychology* 55(2), 162–170.

Lee, J. 2008. "Survivors of Gendered Violence in the Feminist Classroom. *Violence Against Women* 14(12), 1451–1464.

Lighthall, A. 2012. "Ten Things You Should Know about Today's Student Veterans." *Thought and Action* Fall, 81–90.

Lyon, E. 2000. *Welfare, Poverty, and Abused women: New Research and Its Implications* Building Comprehensive Solutions to Domestic Violence #10. Harrisburg, PA: Pennsylvania Coalition Against Domestic Violence, National Resource Center on Domestic Violence.

Manzano, L.J. 1998. "Men Raped: Supporting the Male Survivor of Sexual Assault on the College Campus." https://www.uvm.edu/~vtconn/v19/manzano.html (last accessed October 20, 2017).

Miller, K, Gault, B., and Thorman, A. 2011. *Improving Child Care Access to Promote Postsecondary Success Among Low-Income Parents*. Institute for Women's Policy Research. Research Report. March.

Moore, T. and Selkowe, V. 1999. "Domestic Violence Victims in Transition from Welfare to Work: Barriers to Self-Sufficiency and the W-2 Response." Institute for Wisconsin's Future.

National Coalition Against Domestic Violence. http://www.ncadv.org (last accessed January 5, 2017).

National Sexual Violence Resource Center 2016. "Dear Colleague Letter: Sexual Violence." http://www.nsvrc.org/publications/dear-colleague-letter-sexual-violence (last accessed October 20, 2017).

Northwestern University. 2016. "Sexual Misconduct Response and Prevention." http://www.northwestern.edu/sexual-misconduct/sexual-misconduct-and-title-IX/laws-definitions-facts.html (last accessed October 20, 2017).

Ngo, V., Langley, A., Kataoka, S.H., Nadeem, E., Escudero, P., and Stein, B.D. 2008. "Providing Evidence Based Practice to Ethnically Diverse Youth: Examples from the Cognitive Behavioral Intervention for Trauma in Schools (CBITS) Program." *Journal of the American Academy of Child and Adolescent Psychiatry* 47(8), 858.

Pearson, J., Theonnes, N., and Griswold, E.A. 1999. "Child Support and Domestic Violence: The Victims Speak Out." *Violence Against Women* 5, 427–448.

Raphael, Jody. 1999. "Keeping Women Poor: How Domestic Violence Prevents Women from Leaving Welfare and Entering the World of Work." In *Battered Women, Children, and Welfare Reform*, edited by R. Brandwein, pp. 31–43. Thousand Oaks, CA: Sage.

Roberts, A. 2002. "Myths, Facts, and Realities Regarding Battered Women and Their Children: An Overview." In *Handbook of Domestic Violence Intervention Strategies: Policies, Programs, and Legal Remedies*, edited by A. Roberts, pp. 1–22. Oxford: Oxford University Press.

Shepard, M.F. and Pence, E.L., eds. 1999. *Coordinating Community Responses to Domestic Violence: Lessons from Duluth and Beyond, Volume 12*. Thousand Oaks, CA: Sage.

Tan, C., Basta, J., Sullivan, C.M., and Davidson, W.S. 1995. "The Role of Social Support in the Lives of Women Exiting Domestic Violence Shelters an Experimental Study." *Journal of Interpersonal Violence* 10(4), 437–451.

Tolman, R. and Raphael, J. 2000. "A Review of Research on Welfare and Domestic Violence." *Journal of Social Issues* 56, 655–682.

US Department of Education, Office for Civil Rights. 2011. "Dear Colleague Letter from the Assistant Secretary for Civil Rights Russlynn Ali," April 4. Washington, DC: US Department of Education, Office for Civil Rights. https://www2.ed.gov/about/offices/list/ocr/letters/colleague-201104.html (last accessed October 20, 2017).

US Department of Justice. 2017. "Federal Coordination and Compliance Section 152." Accessed January 2017. https://www.justice.gov/crt/federal-coordination-and-compliance-section-152

Walker, L.E. 1999. "Psychology and Domestic Violence around the World." *American Psychologist* 54(1), 21.

Weisz, A.N., Tolman, R.M., and Saunders, D.G. 2000. "Assessing the Risk of Severe Domestic Violence: The Importance of Survivors' Predictions." *Journal of Interpersonal Violence* 15(1), 75–90.

Yale University. 2016. "Yale Sexual Misconduct Policies and Related Definitions." http://smr.yale.edu/sexual-misconduct-policies-and-definitions (last accessed January 5, 2017).

21

Researching Sexual Violence with Girls in Rural South Africa

Some Methodological Challenges in Using Participatory
Visual Methodologies

Relebohile Moletsane and Claudia Mitchell

Introduction

Social scientists have long concluded that for research to effectively address the needs of marginalized groups and communities, it must be largely informed by the voices of the participants themselves. For example, Maclure (1990) asserted that in order to improve the lives of marginal groups, researchers must enlist alternative research paradigms. For Maclure, this meant that "the insights and aptitudes of local people must be enlisted and brought to bear on the research process itself" (Maclure 1990, 2). Similarly, Oakley (1994) challenged scholars to consider the significance of studying "the world from the standpoint of children both as knowers and as actors" (25). However, evidence from various studies suggests that research with marginalized groups in communities is generally fraught with challenges, including methodological and ethical dilemmas. For example, our own work with girls in southern African rural contexts suggests that working with girls – who, based on gender, social class, and age, among other factors, are on the margins in most communities – is especially challenging (Henderson 2003; Moletsane et al. 2008; Treffry-Goatley, Wiebesiek, and Moletsane 2016). In particular, researching gender violence, including sexual violence, with girls and women in these communities has proved difficult.

Reasons for this are varied. As Treffry-Goatley, Wiebesiek, and Moletsane (2016) contend, reasons for this include this group's vulnerability to such violence and the concern by gatekeepers and institutional ethics boards (IEBs) that researchers need to take extra care to protect them from further harm resulting from their participation in such studies. For the authors, it is often these additional procedures that make research with this group particularly difficult. A second factor that contributes to the difficulty of conducting research on sexual violence with girls in these contexts involves negotiating access to communities and institutions for purpose of research. Gatekeepers may deny such access if they feel the project ventures into areas that are culturally forbidden or sanctioned, such as sex, sexuality, and sexual violence. Even when access is granted, the participants, particularly those who belong to less powerful groups based on gender, social class, or age, etc., may be unable or unwilling to discuss such topics because of these taboos.

The Wiley Handbook on Violence in Education: Forms, Factors, and Preventions, First Edition.
Edited by Harvey Shapiro.

To negotiate these barriers and effectively enlist the voices of this group, who are often on the receiving end of violence, including sexual violence, requires adopting alternative research paradigms and methodologies. Such methodologies must aim to democratize the research space (Mitchell and Sommer 2016) so as to facilitate the participation of both the researchers and the participants in understanding the issues, as well as identifying or developing interventions to improve the lives of marginalized people in these communities. This is particularly important in contexts where unequal power relations and cultural taboos, among others, tend to silence participants, particularly those who are less powerful in communities (such as young people, girls, women, sexual minorities, people with disabilities, and others), around the issues that affect them, such as sexuality and sexual violence. As a number of scholars have argued, it is when the perspectives of those who are most impacted by the issues (e.g., sexual violence) inform the design and implementation of the interventions that they are likely to work (Moletsane et al. 2007; Schenk and Williamson 2005). Of particular relevance to the discussion in this chapter is Mitchell's (2011) argument that, while social researchers have agreed that young people's participation in research is key to its influence on social change, when it comes to issues related to sex, childhood or adolescent sexuality, and sexual violence, there is continuing debate about whose voices count, with adults, such as parents, teachers, and researchers, often speaking for and on behalf of young people. As part of addressing this gap, Mitchell makes a case for participatory research methods, and, in particular, for "girl-method" being instrumental to unearthing the voices and perspectives of girls in research.

Thus, this chapter explores the use of participatory methods in doing research on sexual violence with girls in rural KwaZulu-Natal, South Africa. In particular, it examines the methodological benefits and challenges that arise from the use of "girl-method" in the context of unequal gender norms and cultural taboos against discussing sex and sexual violence, particularly between young people and adults (including researchers).

On Girl-Method in Addressing Sexual Violence

Citing her work with Jacqueline Reid-Walsh, Mitchell (2011) defines girl-method as a feminist methodology that involves research *for* girls, *with* girls, and *about* girls. Mitchell and Reid-Walsh (2008), in their earlier writing, highlight that this work is not limited to working with contemporary girls in relation to sources of evidence, and indeed the ideas of feminist memory work about girlhood (women studying their own experiences of girlhood) and a recognition of girlhood-in-history both serve to align this work with feminist research more broadly. For example, Smith Lefebvre's (2016) analysis, which traces Indigenous girlhood in Canada from seventeenth- to nineteenth-century representations through to contemporary representations is a powerful example of girlhood-in-history. At the heart of girl-method are "methodologies (theories and analyses of how research should proceed) and methods (techniques for gathering and analyzing evidence) in girl-centered research that takes on an advocacy role in defending the rights of girls (for girls)" (Smith Lefebvre 2016, 52). Thus, a key feature of fieldwork with girls involves "the unique positioning of contemporary girls as full participants in mapping out the issues in their lives (with girls), and [in making girlhood itself visible] as a critical space (about girls)" (52). Arguing for the significance of a feminist visual culture in relation to ensuring that the issues of girls and young women are highly visible, Mitchell highlights the unique features of participatory visual methods – such as photovoice – which are rooted in the feminist scholarship of Caroline Wang and Brinton Lykes. This work is far from straightforward and is much more than simply giving a girl or woman a camera, as Spence and Solomon (1995) acknowledge in their book *What Can a Woman Do with a Camera?* Visual tools (photovoice, digital storytelling, participatory video, cellphilming, and participatory asset mapping), each with their own conventions and technologies, the gaze of the producers, the types of knowledge explored, and the ownership of the knowing are all aspects of the "critical space" of contesting issues of social justice. When applied to work with girls in relation to sexual violence, participatory visual work as part of girl-method can both complicate and trouble even as it serves to illuminate the issues. It is this aspect of girl-method that we explore in the case studies that follow. It is not our intention in this chapter to dispute the uses of the participatory visual methods in addressing sexual violence, but rather to draw attention to the ways in which the tools and methods themselves become central to the questions under investigation in both school-based and community-based work.

The Project: Networks for Change and Well-being

The project we are reflecting on in this chapter, "Networks for Change and Wellbeing: Girl-led 'From the Ground Up' Policy Making in Addressing sexual Violence in Canada and South Africa" (hereafter referred to as Networks for Change), is part of a six-year, international, and interdisciplinary partnership led by McGill University in Canada and the University of KwaZulu-Natal (UKZN) in South Africa. The partnership is made up of universities in Canada and South Africa, girl-focused organizations in each country, and several key national and international organizations and stakeholders responsible for policy and programing related to girls' lives. It draws on an interdisciplinary "partnership of partnerships" team of co-applicants and collaborators and other partners working across girlhood studies, youth media studies, policy, participatory visual studies, Aboriginal studies, Indigenous knowledge systems, and sexual violence.

As a participatory research project, Networks for Change seeks to understand and address sexual violence against girls and young women in rural South African and in Indigenous communities in Canada. This is framed by the critical need for innovative approaches to policy making and programming in relation to the safety and security of girls and young women and particularly in contexts of high levels of sexual violence. While the two country contexts are different in many ways, what makes them ideal for an interdisciplinary project such as this are the high rates of violence and HIV infections among young women in rural communities, in the case of South Africa, and among Indigenous young women in Canada. South Africa is known to have one of the highest rates of sexual assault in the world, with adolescent girls between the ages of 12 and 17 being particularly at risk. In essence, there is a consistent (and unrelenting) possibility of sexual violence that runs counter to girls' safety and security in schools and communities, and to their reproductive health, particularly in the context of HIV/AIDS (Moletsane, Mitchell, and Lewin 2015). In their guest editorial article titled "The Dual Burden of Gender-based Violence and HIV in Adolescent Girls and Young Women in South Africa," Abdool-Karim and Baxter (2016) argue that "young women aged 15–24 years, who have the least power in society, bear an enormous burden of both intimate partner violence (IPV) and HIV" (1151). To illustrate this link, they cite evidence suggesting that:

- young women between the ages of 15 and 24 years have up to six times more HIV infection than their male peers, and are experiencing the highest death rates;
- men and women who have experienced GBV [gender-based violence] are more likely to have behaviors that increase their risk of acquiring HIV infection; and
- compared with an HIV-negative woman, a woman who discloses her HIV-positive status to a partner of unknown HIV status is more likely to experience physical and emotional abuse (Abdool-Karim and Baxter 2016, 1152).

Similarly, investigations into the lives of girls in Canada reveal that girls, especially those who are marginalized as a result of race and disability, experience many subtle and overt forms of violence, particularly in the context of relational and community violence (Berman and Jiwani 2002; Morrison 2011). Because much of this violence – occurring in schools, the community, in intimate settings, and on the street – can be so pervasive, victimization can easily go unnoticed. Indeed, girls themselves often accept violence or fail to identify it as such when it occurs (Berman and Jiwani 2002; Wolfe and Chiodo 2008). In their review, Collin-Vézina, Dion, and Trocmé (2009) found an estimated 25–50% child sexual abuse prevalence rate in Aboriginal adults surveyed in several communities across Canada over the past 20 years. Aboriginal women continue to face high rates of sexual assault and abuse: they are eight times more likely than non-Aboriginal women to be killed by an intimate partner (Statistics Canada 2006). Amongst NGO (non-governmental organization) workers there is growing awareness of Aboriginal women and children being trafficked in the sex and drug trades within the country and from Canada to the United States (Oxman-Martinez, Hanley, and Lacroix 2008). Across Canada, commercial sexual exploitation of Aboriginal youth and children forms more than 90% of the visible sex trade (Kingsley and Mark 2000). Downe (2008) highlights how Aboriginal girls remain vulnerable to violence because often the racism that is directed at them is sexualized. Aboriginal women confront a constellation of factors that contribute to sexual violence: colonization and its components of patriarchy, racism, and sexism; residential schools; historical trauma; Bill C-31 that determines Indian status and its accompanying band compensation, infrastructure, support, as well as access to their community of origins. Many girls do not report sexual attacks at all because of the complex jurisdictional issues on and near reservations. Similar to the situation of many girls in South Africa, displacement is a concern. Aboriginal girls are pushed into extremely dangerous situations because of policies (e.g., Bill C-31) that force them to move away from their communities; they are isolated in situations of heightened danger stemming from sexualized racism, sexism, poverty, and through criminalization where historical dislocation and devaluation collide. Critically, the shocking statistics about missing and murdered Indigenous women and girls have led to a national inquiry.[1]

What is of concern to the partners in Networks for Change is that the statistics on sexual violence for girls under the age of 18 in both country contexts are shocking and

---

1 The National Inquiry on Missing and Murdered Indigenous Women and Girls was established by the government of Justin Trudeau in 2016. At the time of writing this chapter, we are able to only report that its work is just beginning.
See https://www.aadnc-aandc.gc.ca/eng/1448633299414/1448633350146 (last accessed October 23, 2017).

call for an intensifying of effort in relation to addressing the lived realities of girls who are marginalized and who suffer from persistent insecurity, injustice, and abuse of power at the local level in otherwise democratic states. The partnership aims to influence the ways in which the voices of girls can inform local, national, global, and virtual communities in relation to curbing sexual violence. Thus, to understand the dynamics in the two contexts, the Networks for Change project seeks to study and advance the use of innovative approaches to programming, knowledge production, policy making, and communication in addressing sexual violence amongst girls and young women. While sexual violence is a global issue, the partnership specifically interrogates the ways in which the participation of girls in democratic societies *could be* and indeed *must be* transformative. Working with girl-led initiatives addressing gender violence in two democratic country contexts, Canada and South Africa, the program focuses on "from the ground up" policy making, or what the UN organization Habitat refers to as "youth-led development," through various participatory initiatives, including those involving digital technology. Specifically, the project addresses two key questions:

- What does it mean to study the world through the eyes of adolescent girls both as knowers and as actors?
- What approaches, mechanisms, and structures would make it possible for girls as knowers and actors, especially those who are the most marginalized, to influence social policy and social change in the context of sexual violence?

In South Africa, the research project is organized around three rural school communities in the KwaZulu-Natal, Free State, and Eastern Cape provinces. In Canada, the project is organized around sites in Nova Scotia, Saskatchewan, and British Columbia. This chapter analyzes work done in just one of the field sites in KwaZulu-Natal (KZN).

One Field Site

As one of the most rural provinces in the country, KZN has one of the highest rates of the twin epidemics of HIV and sexual violence. Available research suggests that these twin epidemics are more prevalent in rural districts. For example, Abdool-Karim and Baxter (2016) note that "Four out of the five districts in [South Africa] that have an HIV prevalence of >40% among pregnant women are in KwaZulu-Natal Province. The remaining seven districts in KwaZulu-Natal have HIV prevalence rates ranging between 33.7% and 40.0% among pregnant women, compared with the overall prevalence of 30% in [South Africa]" (1152). In particular, the project is located in the rural district of uThukela and the Okhahlamba municipality, located at the foot of the Drakensberg mountain range, which forms part of the boundary between South Africa and Lesotho. A report by the local municipality suggests that a variety of social issues face the residents in this area, including, among others, high rates of HIV, tuberculosis, poverty, unemployment, gender violence, poor access to social services such as health care, as well as poor infrastructure (Okhahlamba Local Municipality 2015).

While our target population in the project includes girls of school-going age, as a way of facilitating a more girl-friendly environment for our workshops, we decided not to use the school as a venue. Instead, we have collaborated with and use the premises of a local NGO, the Isibani Community Centre. The center provides a variety of services such as food and clothing distribution, home-based health care, HIV counseling and testing, and support to victims of violence (see http://isibanicentre.org/tl/index.php). In our first meeting with staff at Isibani, they reported high levels of gender violence in the area, including sexual violence. The staff assisted us with recruiting girls as well as with identifying local stakeholders and decision makers. They committed to be on standby to provide counseling to our participants when the need arises throughout the six years of the project.

The girls participating in the project were recruited from the local high school in the township (Khethani) with the help of a teacher who introduced to us by Isibani staff.[2] The 13 young people who attended our first information sessions were peer educators in the high school. The group designs and promotes awareness campaigns in the areas of HIV and AIDS, unwanted teenage pregnancy, and sexual violence. The teacher chose this group as she felt they were already providing a service in the school.

Even though we had made it clear that we were recruiting girls to participate in the project, a boy, with the support of the girls in the peer education group, insisted that he wanted to participate. Elsewhere (Treffry-Goatley, Wiebesiek, and Moletsane, 2016), we reflect on the effect the participation of the boy has had on our work, noting, for example, that:

> The boy's desire to be part of the group, supported enthusiastically by his fellow peer educators, forced us to confront our own conceptualization of gender in our work. It [quickly became] clear that this participant is gender-non-conforming and identifies strongly with the girls in the group. While our decision to include [him] in our research may be more ethical and inclusive, it has led to certain complications in our work, since we are not always certain how to frame our questions. If we ask about "youth" safety rather than "girls'" safety, we risk losing our focus on [violence against women], the key issue in this project. Yet, if we continue to ask always about "girls'" safety, we risk excluding our male participant from these discussions, who because of his identity, might face similar violence in the context of traditional gender norms prevailing in this community. (353)

We continue to grapple with these issues as the project unfolds. What this does is to continually remind us that the methodological and ethical choices we make in the project need to be cognizant of and respond to the local gender dynamics among the population group we target.

In the end, seven participants showed up for the first series of workshops, which we have made sure happen during the school holidays, on weekends, and after school. This is to avoid disrupting the academic program at the school as well as to ensure that we have extended periods of time with the participants. As 2016 progressed and, we believe, word got around, more girls registered interest in participating in the project, and after parents or guardians had signed the usual consent forms and the girls themselves had signed their assent forms, they were welcomed into the project. By the end of 2016, a total of 20 girls and the one boy were participating in the project. Their ages range from 15 to 18 years. While we did not ask the girls why they were keen to join the project, during the various activities we have implemented since the project started, various girls

---

2 Elsewhere (Treffry-Goatley, Wiebesiek, and Moletsane 2016), we describe the project and the methodology in more detail.

have cited reasons such as wanting to help other young people, wanting to develop their own facilitation skills, decreasing teenage pregnancy and drug abuse among teenagers, and meeting new people. We suspect, also, that some of the girls joined because the project offered them some form of engagement (something to do) during the school holidays, this in a community where there are very few entertainment opportunities for young people.

Methodology

To address both the methodological and ethical challenges, as described above, the project has adopted "girl-method" as an approach to research with girls. In particular, we have used participatory visual research (research with, by, and for girls, using digital media and other participatory visual methods). In 2016, in addition to other engagements in the community (gaining access, participant recruitment, consultations with community partners, and so on), we held a series of workshops in the community. The first was a one-day broader community engagement workshop at the local health care center, in which we introduced the project and facilitated a brainstorming session about issues related to girls' safety in the community. The workshop also involved a participatory asset mapping session to identify resources available in the community for addressing girls' safety and security. The second and third workshops, lasting three and five days respectively, were participatory visual methodology workshops used to explore sexual violence against girls in the community and the school and possible strategies for addressing it with the participants. Specifically, in the second workshop, which took place over three days during the June school holidays, we engaged the participants using drawing, photovoice, body mapping, and participatory asset mapping. As a participatory research method, drawing involves the participants working around a given prompt to capture their experiences of the phenomenon under discussion – for example, sexual violence – using simple paper, pencil and/or crayon. In a similar vein, using cameras, in photovoice, participants, again working around a prompt, take pictures to capture their experiences and then collaboratively give meaning to the photographs in relation to understanding the issues and developing strategies for addressing them (Wang et al. 2004). In the drawing and photovoice workshops we gave the participants a simple prompt: *Take/draw a picture showing places and instances where you feel safe or unsafe in your community.* Following a visual ethics tutorial, in which the participants were taught about the ethics of taking and using pictures, each participant was asked to take two photographs, one representing "feeling safe," and the second showing "feeling unsafe." We used entry-level Samsung Galaxy Tab 4 tablet computers, which we have purchased for the project. All of the photos were printed out and the participants were then asked to write captions for each of them. These were exhibited on the wall and each participant presented their pictures and answered questions from the group.

The body mapping exercise activity asked participants to draw/trace an outline of their bodies, with the assistance of a facilitator or another group member, and then to use the outline to show the ways in which their safety was ensured or compromised in the community. The prompt for the activity was: *What does it mean to be a girl in my community?* The body maps have become "living" artworks, where in subsequent workshops they are displayed and participants continue to add more information on them.

The final visual activity that the group took part in was the "drawing workshop." In this process, we asked the participants to address four questions:

1) What are the challenges facing you being safe in your community?
2) What things would you change so that you can feel safe in your community?
3) What resources exist in your community already that can support this change?
4) How can we put this change into action?

The activity involved the participants individually using the art materials we provided (pencils and crayons) to explore these issues. Once the drawings were complete, the participants posted them on posters and wrote captions and notes on them to further explain the issues they were exploring.

The third workshop, which took place over five days during the October school holidays, focused on cellphilm making (two days) and digital storytelling (three days). Cellphilms, as Dockney and Tomaselli (2009) define them, are participatory videos made with cell phones (mobile phones) usually with an intention to identify and address community issues. In this project, instead of cell phones, we used the entry-level Samsung Galaxy Tab 4 tablet computers, which have the same functionality as cell phones.

Our cellphilms workshop started with a tutorial on the "no editing required" (NER) approach to participatory video (Moletsane et al. 2009). This allows for the filming of multiple scenes without the use of complicated and largely unavailable editing software. We revisited visual ethics, including the need to ask for permission before filming someone or their property and the potential dangers of filming young children in the community, and looked at strategies that could be used to address some of the ethical concerns (including the use of anonymous photographic ad filming techniques to protect identities).

We then divided the participants into small groups (four or five people) to work on the creation of a narrative using the prompt: *What is it like to be a teenage girl in my community?* First, the participants developed storyboards for their films, and then, with all of them choosing to use melodrama as a genre, they filmed each other acting out/performing the scenes for their cellphilms. By the end of the process, they had created five cellphilms ranging in length from 1 minute and 2 seconds to 3 minutes and 20 seconds, addressing a variety of issues:

1) *Cheeky Girls*: A girl is chased and harassed by two men because she is a lesbian. She responds with angry retorts and then runs off crying to her mother at home.
2) Untitled: A pregnant girl falls asleep in class at school and is rude to her teacher. She is called to the principal's office and thrown out the school. She runs out of the door wailing.
3) Untitled: A girl is raped on her way to the local store. The girl cries from the time that boy drags her off until her mother calls the police and the perpetrator is imprisoned.
4) Untitled: Boys on the road harass a girl because she is fat and is not a virgin. She runs off crying.
5) Untitled: A group of three teenagers pool their money and go to the tavern before school. They arrive late at school drunk and have a physical fight over the money.

The last three days of the week focused on producing digital stories. In this chapter, our analysis focuses specifically on the digital storytelling process and the digital stories the participants produced after the three-day workshop.

What Is Digital Storytelling?

The digital storytelling workshop was part of a series of multimedia workshops[3] that we held in the rural district. For this particular workshop, we used the relatively inexpensive entry-level tablets described above, at a cost of about R2,500 (about US$185). These have the same functionality as smartphones. Cell phones have become ubiquitous in South Africa, with the country hosting more than 59,474,500 cell phones, according to a 2011 Global Systems for Mobile (GSM) Communication Association study. Even though smartphones are less widespread (GSM Association 2011), we believe that, unlike digital and video cameras, most people in the country, including our participants, have access to a cell phone. This addresses, to some extent, the ethical dilemma we have faced in the past using expensive digital technology, which, when the project ends, is often beyond the reach of the participants and leads to poor sustainability of our interventions.

As we write elsewhere (Treffry-Goatley et al. 2017), digital storytelling uses a combination of digital technology (a cell phone or a smartphone or a video camera) and oral storytelling. The method, while still in its infancy in its use in community-based research, has been used in a variety of research and development contexts, including education, health, community engagement, HIV prevention, and advocacy (D'Amico et al. 2016). The method is useful in deepening our understanding of the issues we study from the perspective of those most affected and enhances the participants' sense of agency and creativity (Burgess 2006, 207).

Over three days, we organized structured workshops in which the participants created short video stories which they illustrated with drawings, photographs, written texts, and music. We started the first day by giving the participants a brief tutorial on digital storytelling as advanced by the Center for Digital Storytelling (Lambert 2013). While the method involves individual participants producing individual narratives, in our workshops we adapted this by dividing the participants into smaller groups of four to five. Each group was tasked with developing a digital story around one of the issues the participants had already identified as negatively impacting their lives (sexual violence, drug abuse, or teenage pregnancy). The tutorial was followed by a screening of a number of examples from our previous projects to alert the participants to what they would be expected to create.

On the second day of the workshop, in their small groups, the participants spent time developing their stories, which they presented to the larger group in our feedback session. The next step was for each group to create a storyboard using drawings (mostly stick figures) to plan and illustrate their storyline. After the completion of the drawing activity, we gave a second tutorial on the ways in which drawing and photography can be used in creating digital stories. This was followed by a hands-on demonstration of how to use a free-to-download editing software, WeVideo, that we had pre-installed on the tablet computers. The participants had already learned how to use these to record sound, to take photographs, and to create videos. Armed with these skills, and accompanied by a facilitator, each group found a quiet room or space to record their stories using the WeVideo software. Finally, each group decided on a song, which they sang in the background to their digital story.

The three-day workshop resulted in a total of five digital stories: *Poverty* (about a selfish father who eats all the food while his wife and children starve); *Poverty Leads You to Prostitution* (about an orphaned girl who resorts to prostitution to take care of her younger

---

3 We describe the digital storytelling workshop in more detail elsewhere (Treffry-Goatley et al. 2017).

siblings); *Crime* (about a young motherless girl whose father neglects her and, as a result, she ends up stealing from neighbors, leading to her arrest by the police); *Whatever You Do, You Do It for Yourself* (about a girl who, under peer pressure, neglects her sick mother and goes drinking with friends, and ends up being raped and getting infected with HIV and becoming pregnant); and *The Life of a Teenager* (about a teenager who is influenced by peer pressure to drink and do drugs and ends up being HIV positive and pregnant).

The data collection activities we implement in the Networks for Change broadly, and in this community, are designed to put young women and girls at ease and in control of the information collected. The participatory methods, including digital storytelling, prompt a deliberate process of reflexivity on sexual violence in and around the participants' lives without the requirement of personal discloser. Each project activity is typically conducted in a limited amount of time and with a certain amount of improvisation. This means that individual stories become a co-production in the art-making process. This allows a second level of removal from the personal and a co-construction of knowledge and ideas about violence/gender/sex. As participants discuss their co-productions, topics of discussion and reflections are limited to these and do not require participants to relate personal experiences to a group but instead invite a more general discussion reflecting on issues at a community and/or societal level. Thus, the focus, reiterated throughout the process by the Partnership members and workshop facilitator(s) in the prompts, in the making, and in the discussing, is not on personal disclosure but on social commentary.

The Digital Productions

Here we offer transcripts of two of the five digital stories. In each case the girls themselves narrate the stories:

Transcript 1: *Whatever You Do, You Do It for Yourself*

Thandi, an adolescent, leaves her sick mother and goes to a tavern or local bar with her friends at night. She meets a young man in the tavern and he buys drinks for her and her friends. When it is time to go, he tells Thandi to go with him. When they get to his house, the guy forces himself on Thandi. Thandi goes to the hospital to consult with a doctor and she finds out she is HIV positive and also pregnant. Thandi decides to go to her mother and apologise. However, Thandi's friends turn their backs on her, treat her like she is a monster.

Thandi decides to make a difference in her life. After the baby is born, she decides to go back to school. She passes her Matric (Grade 12) with flying colours. She goes to the university to do Medicine. After graduating and becoming a doctor, she buys a car and a house for her mother. Thandi's friends want to come back to her life because she has succeeded in life.

Transcript 2: *The Life of a Teenager*

I was a very well behaved girl at school, and at home I respected my parents. When I was in Grade 10, I met friends who were involved in wrong things and who introduced me to drugs. One day we went and started drinking and taking drugs. After that I could not remember what happened. After three months I went to the clinic and found out that I was HIV positive and pregnant too. I did not know who the father of my child was. I then told my mother, who was not well at the time, that I was HIV+ and pregnant too. When I told her, she fainted and ended up in hospital. Boom! My mother was dead without me telling her how sorry I was. The death of my mother left me miserable and unwanted, I was all alone. What do I do with my life now? I had to drop out of school to go and work. From then on my life was full of misery.

What do we learn from these digital stories? A close reading of the stories reveals that across all five stories, predictably, issues that affect girls and young women include poverty, sexual violence, physical abuse, HIV/AIDS, and death. Interestingly, almost all the stories end with the main character, a girl, experiencing some form of sexual violence, and as a result, being infected with HIV and getting impregnated by the perpetrator. This is in line with evidence from literature suggesting that "Entrenched economic and gender inequities together are driving a globally expanding, increasingly female, human immunodeficiency virus (HIV)/AIDS epidemic" (Krishnan et al. 2008, 101). From our reading of the transcripts, we highlight two related narratives emerging from the stories: Teenage sex and sexuality as taboo, teenage girls "ask for it," and teenage girls cannot resist peer pressure and the influence of "bad" friends.

Teenage Sex and Sexuality as Taboo

In both narratives, although sex is dominant – albeit in the form of rape, in that both teenage pregnancy and HIV infections result from non-consensual sex – it is never named. In *Whatever You Do, You Do It for Yourself,* "the guy forces himself on Thandi," while in *The Life of a Teenager*, the narrator, a girl, reports: "After that I could not remember what happened. After three months I went to the clinic and found out that I was HIV positive and pregnant too." Available literature suggests that sex and sexuality, particularly among teenagers, remains taboo in many communities. As such, talking about these, particularly in the presence of adults (such as teachers and researchers) remains forbidden (Masinga 2013). This, as Masinga charges, happens in a context where "issues of sexuality for most young people extend beyond deciding whether, when and how to have sex. Instead, [young people] are engaged in an often-perplexing process of coming to terms with what it means to be a sexual being and with the complex emotional and relational aspects of sexuality" (2013, 2).

As both narratives analyzed here warn, for those who transgress, the consequences are often dire. For example, both girls in the two stories are "HIV positive and pregnan." With the stigma attached to both, and the burden of illness related to HIV and AIDS, and of caring for a child as a teenager, as the narrator in *The Life of a Teenager* states, "The death of my mother left me miserable and unwanted, I was all alone. What do I do with my life now? I had to drop out of school to go and work. From then on my life was full of misery." It is not surprising, then, that these narratives, produced by teenagers for adults (researchers), while dealing with sex, would not name it as such.

Girls "Ask for It"

In their article titled "'Diseases Come from Girls': Perspectives of Male Learners in Rural KwaZulu-Natal on HIV Infection and AIDS," Sathiparsad and Taylor (2006) reported that male learners overwhelmingly believed that girls (and women) were responsible for infecting boys and men with HIV in their communities. In their analysis, they state: "These learners attribute the spread of HIV/AIDS to women's careless behavior such as the inability to control themselves, being beautiful and attractive, having multiple sexual partners, and deliberately spreading the virus. By implication then, additional pressure is placed on beautiful women to discipline themselves" (2006, 124).

Citing the work of Jewkes et al. (2009), Moletsane, Mitchell, and Lewin (2015) assert that dominant discourses in communities tend to frame teenage sexuality as a moral issue and often call for "a return to morality" and ethics as a solution. In this context, girls who "fall" pregnant and are infected with HIV are regarded as promiscuous and their sexuality is viewed as problematic and as contributing to, if not causing, sexual violence.

Similarly, the two stories highlighted in this chapter also tend to blame the victim, suggesting that the characters are somehow responsible for their fate. With the exception of poverty, the narratives suggest that the protagonists are somehow responsible for the negative things that happen in their lives. For example, they succumb to peer pressure and make wrong/bad decisions (drink alcohol, take drugs, go out at night, etc.) and do not respect their parents. In *Whatever You Do, You Do It for Yourself*, "Thandi leaves her sick mother and goes to a tavern (a local bar) with her friends at night. She meets a guy in the tavern and the guy buys drinks for her and her friends.". In *The Life of a Teenager*, the narrator consistently points to herself, stating, "When I was in Grade 10, I met friends who were involved in wrong things and who introduced me to drugs. One day we went and started drinking and taking drugs." In both narratives, the victim gets blamed while the perpetrator remains blameless, even when his actions result in unwanted pregnancy, HIV infection, and death. The male character, almost invisible in the story, except during the imagined sexual violence act, seems entitled to these girls' bodies. After all, what were they doing out at night? Why were they drinking? Why were they wearing short skirts? In these communities such as the one where these participants live, unequal gender norms tend to render girls and women powerless, and boys and men as decision makers, including whether or not, when, and how to have sex.

Discussion

Our analysis of the two transcripts above suggests that rather than challenge the unequal gender norms which produce the violence depicted in the two narratives, or even to condemn the violence and its perpetrators, the two digital stories and others tend to mimic and reproduce the dominant discourses on gender and femininity that blame girls and young women for violence perpetrated against them, and absolve the perpetrators (men). Blaming girls and women for sexual violence and HIV and AIDS as these stories depict, places the burden of prevention and addressing the issues on them.

One approach would be to simply leave the digital stories as they are, with an acknowledgment that they represent the voices of the girls. However, as we have seen in other work involving digital production in community-based research, often the productions are really just the first step in a longer process that involves speaking and then, as we have termed it, "speaking back" (Mitchell and de Lange 2013; Mitchell, De Lange, and Moletsane 2017). As we are realizing, it is not enough to use participatory methodologies to uncover the voices of girls in relation to sexual violence and other violations of girls' rights. It is important that we also ensure that, in doing so, we create safe spaces where they can challenge the unequal gender norms and cultural factors that marginalize them and put them at risk of sexual violence, HIV infections, and unwanted pregnancies. In previous participatory visual research with teachers, we have explored the ways in which participants might go back over their productions and interrogate through review and dialogue to create a second story that speaks back to or contests some of the unequal gender norms and cultural factors (Mitchell, De Lange, and Moletsane 2018). In our future work with girls and young women, we envisage implementing a similar process of speaking back, and indeed see it as a dimension of the notion of critical space taken up in girl-method.

Broader Implications of Networks for Change

The various challenges that we have highlighted above draw attention to the types of tensions and concerns that exist. At the same time, the work at just one site points to the rich possibilities. What is apparent is that there is a great deal to be gained when it is the voices of girls and young women that are shaping knowledge about their own lives. There are a number of implications to be considered. First, we are seeing that the time frames for girls and young women are very different from what is typically seen in adult-driven projects. There is urgency, so that participants are typically action oriented; they want to see things happen. We are also seeing that girls and young women are more likely to be *risk takers* in relation to issues that affect their lives in ways that adults might not be, often venturing into topics that adult participants might have shied away from. They are also *innovative*, as we have seen in the vast range of technologies they have been willing to test out and the artistic platforms that they have seized when it has been possible to speak out. At the same time, it is obvious that sexual violence is seldom regarded by those most affected as a single issue. Rather, as is obvious in the examples cited in this chapter, participants often see sexual violence as interacting with and happening together other social challenges in their lives. Further, participants want to talk about their own sense of themselves in their communities, relationships with family, and poverty. One of the most common narratives across a range of field sites, including this one, is pregnancy and concerns about their future. For these reasons, it is challenging to manage a project that is about sexual violence. More than anything, this highlights the responsibilities of researchers and practitioners who take on this work.

Conclusions

While we have located our analysis of work with girls in relation to sexual violence in rural South Africa, there are clearly many implications for addressing sexual violence in school-based and community-based work globally. Participatory visual work through such tools as photovoice, participatory video or cellphilms, and digital storytelling helps to make visible the issues, but, as we have argued here, the absences, the gaps, and the reproduction of many of the very norms and cultural factors that marginalize the girls in the first place should be challenged – by and with the girls and young women themselves. This does not just happen on its own and as researchers we are obliged to find strategies and methods that extend the idea of "with girls." Overall, such strategies will align well with girl-method, and the idea of creating critical spaces where exploring issues of power and positionality, action and activism, and speaking back becomes possible.

Acknowledgments

This work was supported through an International Development Research Centre (IDRC) grant (award number 107777-001) and a Social Sciences and Humanities Research Council of Canada (SSHRC) grant (award number 895-2013-3007). The views expressed in this paper are not necessarily those of the IDRC or SSHRC. The authors would like to acknowledge Lisa Wiebesiek, Astrid Treffry-Goatley, Nokukhanya Ngcobo, and Naydene de Lange for their contribution to the data collection and preliminary analysis discussed in this paper. Most importantly, we would like to thank the participants for sharing their perspectives and stories with us.

References

Abdool-Karim, Q. and Baxter, C. 2016. "The Dual Burden of Gender-based Violence and HIV in Adolescent Girls and Young Women in South Africa." *South African Medical Journal* 106(12), 1151–1153.

Berman, H. and Jiwani, Y. 2002. *In the Best Interests of the Girl Child: Phase II Report*. NP The Alliances of Five Research Centres on Violence. Ottawa: Status of Women Canada.

Burgess, J. 2006. "Hearing Ordinary Voices: Cultural Studies, Vernacular Creativity and Digital Storytelling." *Continuum: Journal of Media & Cultural Studies* 20, 201–214. DOI: 10.1080/10304310600641737.

Collin-Vézina, D., Dion, J., and Trocmé, N. 2009. "Sexual Abuse in Canadian Aboriginal Communities: A Comprehensive Review of Conflicting Evidence." *Pimatisiwin: A Journal of Aboriginal and Indigenous Community Health* 7, 27–47.

D'Amico, M., Denov, M., Khan, F., Linds, W., and Akessone, B. 2016. "Research as Intervention? Exploring the Health and Well-being of Children and Youth Facing Global Adversity through Participatory Visual Methods." *Global Public Health* 11(5–6), 528–545. DOI: 10.1080/17441692.2016.1165719.

Dockney, J. and Tomaselli, K. 2009. "Fit for the Small(er) Screen: Films, Mobile TV and the New Individual Television Experience." *Journal of African Cinema* 1(1), 126–132.

Downe, P. 2008. "La violence exercée contre les filles autochtones: Le probème, sa face caché, les sources d'espour et les interventions possibles." In *Les violences faites aux femmes*, edited by D. Damant, S. Gravel, and E. Harper. Montréal: Presses de L'université du Québec.

GSM Association. 2011. *African Mobile Observatory 2011: Driving Economic and Social Development through Mobile Services*. GSMA. https://www.gsma.com/spectrum/wp-content/uploads/2011/12/Africa-Mobile-Observatory-2011.pdf (last accessed November 3, 2017).

Henderson, P. 2003. *Annotated Bibliography on Childhood with Emphasis on Africa: General Findings and Recommendations*. Dakar: CODESRIA.

Jewkes, R., Skweyiya, Y., Morrell, R., and Dunkel, K. 2009. *Understanding Men's Health and Use of Violence: Interface of Rape and HIV in South Africa*. Pretoria: Medical Research Council.

Kingsley, C. and Mark, M. 2000. *Sacred Lives: Canadian Aboriginal Children and Youth Speak Out about Sexual Exploitation*. National Aboriginal Consultation Project. Vancouver, BC: Save the Children Canada.

Krishnan, S., Dundar, M.S., Minnis, A.M., Medlim, C.A., Gerdts, C.E., and Padian, N.S. 2008. "Poverty, Gender Inequities, and Women's Risk of Human Immunodeficiency Virus/AIDS." *Annals of the New York Academy of Science* 1136, 101–110. DOI: 10.1196/annals.1425.013.

Lambert, J. 2013. *Digital Storytelling: Capturing Lives Creating Community*, 4th ed. Berkeley, CA: Digital Diner Press.

Maclure, R. 1990. "The Challenge of Participatory Research and Its Implications for Funding Agencies." *International Journal of Sociology and Social Policy* 10(3), 1–19.

Masinga, L. 2013. "Journeys to Self-Knowledge: A Participatory Study of Teachers as Sexuality Educators." Unpublished PhD thesis. University of KwaZulu-Natal, South Africa.

Mitchell, C. 2011. "What's Participation Got to Do with It? Visual Methodologies in 'Girl-Method' to Address Gender-Based Violence in the Time of AIDS." *Global Studies of Childhood* 1(1), 51–59. DOI: 10.2304/gsch.2011.1.1.51.

Mitchell, C. and De Lange, N. 2013. "What Can a Teacher Do with a Cellphone? Using Participatory Visual Research to Speak Back in Addressing HIV&AIDS." *South African Journal of Education* 33(4), 1–13.

Mitchell, C., De Lange, N., and Moletsane, R. 2017. *Participatory Visual Methodologies: Social Change through Community and Policy Dialogue*. London: Sage.

Mitchell, C., de Lange, N., and Moletsane, R. 2018. "Addressing Sexual Violence in South Africa: 'Gender activism in the making." In *What Politics? Youth and Political Engagement in Contemporary Africa*, edited by E. Oinas, H. Onodera and L. Suurpaa. Leiden: Brill.

Mitchell, C. and Reid-Walsh. J. 2008. "Girl Method: Placing Girl-centred Research Methodologies on the Map of Girlhood Studies." In *Roadblocks to Equality: Women Challenging Boundaries*, edited by J. Klaehn. Montreal: Black Rose Books.

Mitchell, C. and Sommer, M. 2016. "Participatory Visual Methodologies in Global Public Health." *Global Public Health* 11(5–6), 521–527. DOI: 10.1080/17441692.2016.1170184.

Moletsane, R., de Lange, N., Mitchell, C., Stuart, J., Buthelezi, T., and Taylor, M. 2007. "Photo-Voice as an Analytical and Activist Tool in the Fight Against HIV and AIDS Stigma in a Rural KwaZulu-Natal School." *Journal of Child and Adolescent Mental Health* 19(1), 19–28.

Moletsane, R., Mitchell, C., De Lange, N., Stuart, J., Buthelezi, T., and Taylor, M. 2009. "What Can a Woman Do with a Camera? Turning the Female Gaze on Poverty and HIV and AIDS in Rural South Africa." *International Journal of Qualitative Studies in Education* 22(3), 1–36.

Moletsane, R., Mitchell, C., and Lewin, T. 2015. "Gender Violence, Teenage Pregnancy and Gender Equity Policy in South Africa: Privileging the Voices of Women and Girls through Participatory Visual Methods." In *Gender Violence in Poverty Contexts*, edited by J. Parkes. London and New York: Taylor & Francis.

Moletsane, R., Mitchell, C., Smith, A., and Chisholm, L 2008. *Methodologies for Mapping Southern African Girlhoods in the Era of AIDS*. Rotterdam, New York, and Taipei: Sense Publishers.

Morrison, C. 2011. "Avatars and the Cultural Politics of Representation: Girlhood Identity in Social Networking Spaces." PhD thesis. Memorial University of Newfoundland, Canada.

Oakley, A. 1994. "Women and Children First and Last. Parallels and Differences between Children's and Women's Studies." In *Children's Childhoods Observed and Experienced*, edited by B. Mayall. London: Falmer Press.

Okhahlamba Local Municipality. 2015. *Okhahlamba Local Municipality 2013/2014 Annual Report*. Bergville, KwaZulu-Natal. http://www.okhahlamba.org.za/docs/reports/2015/Okhahlamba%20%202013-2014%20Annual%20Report_12%20January%202015_Edited.pdf (last accessed November 3, 2017).

Oxman-Martinez, J., Hanley, J., and Lacroix, M. 2008. "The Voices of NGOs: Demand and Supply for Protection Services for Victims of Trafficking." In *Violences faites aux femmes*, edited by S. Arcand, D. Damant, E. Harper, and S. Gravel. Québec, Canada: Presses de l'Université du Québec.

Sathiparsad, R. and Taylor, M. 2006. "Diseases come from girls": Perspectives of Male Learners in Rural KwaZulu-Natal on HIV Infection and AIDS. *Journal of Education* 38(1), 17–37.

Schenk, K. and Williamson, J. 2005. *Ethical Approaches to Gathering Information from Children and Adolescents in International Settings: Guidelines and Resources*. Washington, DC: Population Council.

Smith Lefebvre, H. 2016. "Overlapping Time and Place: Early Modern England and Girlhood Discourse and Indigenous Girlhood in the Dominion of Canada (1684–1868)." *Girlhood Studies: An Interdisciplinary Journal* 9, 2.

Spence, J. and Solomon, J. 1995. *What Can a Woman Do with a Camera? Photography for Women*. London: Scarlett Press.

Statistics Canada. 2006. *Measure de la violence faite aux femmes: Tendances statistiques* Ottawa: Centre Canadien de la statistique juridique.

Treffry-Goatley, A.J., Wiebesiek, L., and Moletsane, R. 2016. "Using the Visual to Address Gender-based Violence in Rural South Africa: Ethical Considerations." *LEARNing Landscapes* 10(1), 341–359.

Treffry-Goatley, A., Wiebesiek, L., Moletsane, R., and de Lange, N. 2017. "Technologies of Non-violence? The Ethics of Participatory Visual Research in the Context of Gender Based Violence in South Africa and Canada." *Girlhood Studies Girlhood Studies* 10(2), 45–61 DOI: 10.3167/ghs.2017.100205.

Wang, C.C., Morrel-Samuels, S., Hutchison, P.M., Bell, L., and Perstronk, R.M. 2004. "Flint Photovoice: Community Building among Youths, Adults, and Policymakers." *American Journal of Public Health* 94(6), 911–913.

Wolfe, D.A. and Chiodo, D. 2008. *Sexual Harassment and Related Behaviors Reported among Youth from Grade 9 to Grade 11*. Vancouver, BC. Centre for Addiction and Mental Health.

22

Bullying, Suicide, and Suicide Prevention in Education

Melissa K. Holt, Chelsey Bowman, Anastasia Alexis, and Alyssa Murphy

Bullying and suicide among adolescents are two of the major public health problems facing youth in the United States today (Centers for Disease Control and Prevention 2015; Srabstein and Leventhal 2010). Both affect a considerable number of youth each year (Kann et al. 2014) and, therefore, prevention efforts have been developed to address each. Although approaches attending to multiple levels of the social ecology are recommended for both bullying and suicide (Espelage et al. 2015), given that adolescents spend the majority of their time in schools, school-based prevention programs are particularly well positioned to address these public health concerns. In this chapter, we provide a brief overview of bullying and suicide, consider research evidence on the association between bullying involvement and suicidal ideation and behaviors, and highlight evidence-based suicide prevention programs designed for the school context (for a review of school-based bullying prevention programs, please refer to Chapter 17 in this volume). We conclude by suggesting that, given shared risk and protective factors, selecting prevention efforts in line with these might address both critical public health concerns simultaneously.

Bullying

Prevalence and Disparities

In 2014 the Centers for Disease Control and Prevention released a uniform definition of bullying that states: "Bullying is any unwanted aggressive behavior(s) by another youth or group of youths who are not siblings or current dating partners that involves an observed or perceived power imbalance and is repeated multiple times or is highly likely to be repeated. Bullying may inflict harm or distress on the targeted youth including physical, psychological, social, or educational harm" (Gladden et al. 2014, 7). Notably, most research on bullying from which prevalence rates are derived does not measure bullying in a way that taps into all of these components, and measurement approaches across studies vary. Based in part on measurement approach differences (Furlong et al. 2010), a range of bullying prevalence rates exist.

The Wiley Handbook on Violence in Education: Forms, Factors, and Preventions, First Edition.
Edited by Harvey Shapiro.
© 2018 John Wiley & Sons, Inc. Published 2018 by John Wiley & Sons, Inc.

A nationally representative study of students in grades 6–10 found that 13% of students reported perpetrating bullying, 10.6% indicated being the target of bullying, and 6.3% of students reported that they had both perpetrated and been the target of bullying (Nansel et al. 2001). Similar rates emerged from the 2013 Youth Risk Behavior Survey (YRBS), in which 19.6% of high school students reported being bullied on school property and 14.8% reported being cyberbullied (Kann et al. 2014). The most recent national data support these earlier findings. Specifically, in the School Crime Supplement (SCS) to the National Crime Victimization Survey, which assessed bullying victimization rates among 12- to 18-year-old students, 22% of students reported being bullied at school and 7% of students reported being cyberbullied (Robers et al. 2015). Notably, bullying involvement roles are not static, but rather students' roles demonstrate fluctuation throughout their schooling (Juvonen and Graham 2014).

In terms of developmental patterns, bullying peaks in middle school and declines in high school (Furlong et al. 2010; US Department of Education 2015). A meta-analysis on bullying found that boys are more likely to be victims of bullying than girls, though the effect size for this association is weak (Cook et al. 2010). With respect to forms of bullying, research indicates that boys report more physical and verbal bullying involvement, whereas as they approach late childhood, girls report more relational bullying (Björkqvist, Lagerspetz, and Kaukiainen 1992; Wang, Iannotti, and Nansel 2009; Zimmer-Gembeck, Geiger, and Crick 2005).

There have been calls for increased research on bullying experiences for groups who have traditionally been overlooked in the field (e.g., LGBTQ students, students with disabilities, African American youth) (American Educational Research Association 2013), and for whom extant research suggests higher rates of bullying involvement. For instance, LGBTQ (lesbian, gay, bisexual, transgender, and queer) youth experience more bullying victimization than their heterosexual peers (Berlan et al. 2010; Kann et al. 2011; Robinson and Espelage 2011). Studies on differences by race/ethnicity have yielded mixed findings; some studies have found that African American youth are less likely to be victimized by bullying than white youth (Haynie et al. 2001; Juvonen, Graham, and Schuster 2003; Wang, Iannotti, and Nansel 2009), whereas recent national data found similar rates of bullying victimization for black non-Hispanic and white non-Hispanic youth (Devoe and Murphy 2011). Finally, students with disabilities have an elevated risk for bullying victimization (Rose, Espelage, and Monda-Amaya 2009; Rose, Monda-Amaya, and Espelage 2011).

Correlates

There is extensive empirical evidence documenting that any type of involvement in bullying (i.e., as a perpetrator, target, or bully-victim) is associated with a number of detrimental mental and physical health outcomes as well as poor academic outcomes (Fekkes et al. 2006; Gini and Pozzoli 2013; Holt et al. 2015; Juvonen, Wang, and Espinoza 2011). Further, bullying is also associated with risky behaviors in adolescence, such as substance use and sexual risk taking (Holt et al. 2013; Luk, Wang, and Simons-Morton 2010; Radliff et al. 2012). The deleterious mental health effects of bullying also extend to witnesses of bullying (Rivers et al. 2009). Finally, compromises to mental health can continue into college and later adulthood (Copeland et al. 2013; Holt et al. 2014; Sourander et al. 2016). Moreover, the association between bullying involvement during childhood and negative outcomes in adulthood is strongest for youth who report frequent involvement in bullying (Klomek, Sourander, and Elonheimo 2015).

Risk and Protective Factors

Research has identified a number of risk and protective factors at multiple levels of the social ecology that are associated with involvement in bullying, a few of which are described below; for more comprehensive reviews, please refer to reviews and meta-analyses by Cook et al. (2010), Kljakovic and Hunt (2016), and Rodkin, Espelage, and Hanish (2015).

With respect to individual characteristics, a meta-analysis revealed that involvement in bullying as a bully, victim, or bully-victim is associated with impaired social problem-solving skills (Cook et al. 2010). Compared to their peers, bullies are more likely to report externalizing behaviors (Cook et al. 2010), use violence as a problem-solving strategy (Crick and Dodge 1999), and demonstrate hyperactivity (Gini 2008). A recent meta-analysis of longitudinal studies found that internalizing behaviors predicted victimization (Kljakovic and Hunt 2016). As noted earlier, certain characteristics of youth are associated with increased risk of bullying victimization, including identifying as LGBTQ, having a disability, and being obese (Jankauskiene et al. 2008).

Familial characteristics and the home environment can influence children's risk of bullying involvement, and can also act as protective factors. Individuals who are perpetrators of bullying are more likely to grow up in homes where physical discipline is used (Espelage, Bosworth, and Simon 2000). Also, both bullies and victims report experiencing higher levels of child maltreatment compared to uninvolved youth (Holt, Finkelhor, and Kantor 2007). Maternal mental health influences bullying involvement as well, with research demonstrating that maternal depression is a risk factor for both bullying perpetration and victimization (Georgiou 2008). Finally, higher levels of parental support predict lower involvement in all types of bullying (Wang, Iannotti, and Nansel 2009), although research suggests that parenting style and support are more influential risk and protective factors for bully-victims than victims (Lereya, Samara, and Wolke 2013).

With respect to the social environment, peer groups are quite influential. For example, having friends protects against victimization, but can increase the likelihood of bullying perpetration (Wang, Iannotti, and Nansel 2009). Further, even after controlling for baseline bullying behaviors, involvement in a peer group with higher levels of bullying behaviors is associated with increases in an individual's bullying perpetration over time (Espelage, Holt, and Henkel 2003). Research also has highlighted the importance of friendship quality as a protective factor against bullying. Bollmer and colleagues (2005) found that students with externalizing problems reported less bullying behavior if they also reported having a higher quality best friendship, illuminating the buffering effect of friendship quality.

Suicide

Prevalence and Disparities

In 2014, suicide was the second leading cause of death for youth aged 10 to 25 (Centers for Disease Control and Prevention 2014). In the 2013 YRBS, 17% of high school students reported seriously considering suicide in the last year, 8% reported attempting suicide in the last year, and 2.7% indicated being treated by a doctor or nurse for their suicide attempt (Kann et al. 2014). Among youth who chronically attempt suicide, the first attempt often occurs in late elementary or middle school (Mazza, Catalano, Abbott, and Haggerty 2011).

With respect to demographic differences, adolescent males are more likely to die by suicide than females, in part because males use more lethal means such as hanging and firearms (Beautrais 2003; Bridge, Goldstein, and Brent 2006). In contrast, adolescent females are more likely to report suicidal ideation and suicide attempts (Bridge, Goldstein, and Brent 2006; Kann et al. 2014).

Studies have consistently found that sexual minority youth are at an increased risk for suicidal ideation and behavior (Marshal et al. 2011; Mueller et al. 2015). For instance, a meta-analysis that compared rates of suicidality between sexual minority youth and heterosexual youth found that sexual minority youth were over two times more likely to report indicators of suicide than heterosexual youth (Marshal et al. 2011). There are significant variations in suicidal ideation and behaviors among adolescents of different races and ethnicities. For instance, Native American and Alaska Native youth have the highest risk of suicide (Goldston et al. 2008; Shaughnessy, Doshi, and Jones 2004), with recent data showing that 17.3% of Navajo high school students reported attempting suicide, in the past 12 months (Navajo Nation 2013). In addition, among high school students Hispanic youth report more suicidal ideation and attempts than their black or white peers (Kann et al. 2014). Finally, mirroring the much more comprehensive literature on the association between having a disability and suicide risk among adults (Giannini et al. 2010), research suggests that youth with disabilities are at greater risk for suicide than youth without disabilities (Ludi et al. 2012).

Risk Factors and Protective Factors

Similar to bullying, research has identified a number of risk and protective factors at multiple levels of the social ecology that are associated with youth suicide. Key factors are described below, with an emphasis on those that are similar to those for bullying. For a more comprehensive discussion of risk and protective factors, please refer to reviews by Bridge, Goldstein, and Brent (2006) and Gould and colleagues (2003).

With respect to individual characteristics associated with increased risk of suicide among adolescents, a robust relationship exists between depression and suicide (Evans, Hawton, and Rodham 2004). Previous self-harm, specifically self-cutting, is also associated with suicide risk (Hawton et al. 2012). In addition, alcohol use is related to suicidal behavior, even among adolescents who previously have not reported suicidal ideation (Schilling et al. 2009). Specifically, self-reported heavy episodic drinking (HED) at 13 years of age or younger increases suicide risk by threefold, even after controlling for reported depressive symptoms (Schilling et al. 2009).

Familial history and childhood home environment also have an impact on adolescents' risk of suicide. One study found that relatives of deceased adolescents who had committed suicide were more likely to report suicidal behavior than relatives of adolescents without suicidal behavior, even after controlling for psychopathology (Brent et al. 1996). Similarly, students who engage in suicidal behaviors, in contrast to those who only report suicidal ideation, are significantly more likely to report having a family member or friend who attempted suicide or intentionally hurt themselves, and to believe that suicidal ideation and behaviors are normative in their peer groups (O'Connor et al. 2012). In addition, adolescents with extensive histories of physical and sexual abuse are at increased risk of suicidal ideation and behavior compared to adolescents with no or less extensive abuse histories (Evans, Hawton, and Rodham 2005). Finally, the presence of a gun in the home is a known risk factor for adolescent suicide (Brent et al. 1991). Despite the strong associations among suicide and a host of family risk factors, notably adolescents at greatest risk for suicidal behavior are those who experience multiple risk factors (Brent and Mann 2006)

Social relationships can serve as both a risk and protective factor for adolescent suicide depending on the relationships and psychopathology present in the family. In terms of protective factors, social connectedness, especially family connectedness, is associated with less suicidal ideation and behavior (Stone et al. 2015). Similarly, having friends is a protective factor against suicidal behavior (Hacker et al. 2006). For LGBTQ students in particular, family connectedness, a safe school environment, and a relationship with a caring adult have all been identified as factors that buffer against risk (Eisenberg and Resnick 2006). Conversely, an examination of completed suicide among 10- to 17-year-olds in 16 states found that half of the deceased had non-romantic relationship difficulties (e.g., parent or friend difficulties) prior to suicide (Karch et al. 2013).

Association between Bullying Involvement and Suicide

There is a clear yet complex relationship between bullying and suicide (Centers for Disease Control and Prevention 2014). Despite frequent media reports that bullying leads to suicide attempts, from a research perspective empirical evidence supports an association, but not a causal relationship. A meta-analysis of 23 studies found that bullying involvement of any type, and particularly for bully-victims, was associated with more suicidal ideation and behaviors (Holt et al. 2015). With respect to cyberbullying specifically, there is some evidence that cyberbullying involvement might be more strongly associated with suicidal ideation than school-based bullying involvement, although only three studies were included in this particular analysis (van Geel, Vedder, and Tanilon 2014).

Research suggests there might be different patterns of association between bullying involvement and suicidal ideation/behavior for boys and girls. For example, in a study that followed youth from age 8 through early adulthood, findings indicated that the relation between bullying victimization and suicide was significant for girls regardless of depression or conduct problems at age 8 (Klomek et al. 2009). In contrast, taking depression and conduct problems into account rendered the association no longer significant for boys (Klomek et al. 2009). In addition, a study of high school students found that boys and girls who reported greater involvement in bullying as either a bully or a victim were more likely to report depression, serious suicidal ideation, and suicide attempts compared to their peers who did not report bullying involvement (Klomek et al. 2007). However, when considering the influence of infrequent bullying involvement, there was only a significant association for girls (Klomek et al. 2007).

Recently, studies have taken a more nuanced approach to understanding the link between bullying involvement and suicide. For instance, a study of 10- to 13-year-old students found that victims of bullying and bully-victims reported greater suicidal ideation than their peers, even after controlling for depression and delinquency (Espelage and Holt 2013). Notably, this association was particularly strong for female bully-victims. Another study examining data from the 2009 YRBS found that depression accounted for a significant portion of the association between traditional bullying and cyberbullying victimization and suicide attempts, but did not mediate the relationship between cyberbullying and suicide attempts (Bauman, Toomey, and Walker 2013). Further, a retrospective study of gay males found that bullying mediated the relationship between exhibiting gender-role nonconforming behavior (GRNB) and suicidal ideation and behavior during childhood (Friedman et al. 2006). Finally, for middle and high school youth involved in social or relational bullying, emotional distress and self-harm increased risk for suicidal ideation and behaviors, whereas parent connectedness was a protective factor (Borowsky, Taliaferro, and McMorris 2013). These associations held for victims, perpetrators, and bully-victims. Additional risk and protective factors emerged that were relevant for some, or not all, groups. For instance, for victims and perpetrators only, physical and sexual abuse, mental health concerns, and having run away from home conferred additional risk for suicidal thoughts or attempts.

Suicide Prevention in Schools

Given that adolescents spend much of their time in schools, schools are uniquely positioned to both identify youth who might be at risk for suicide and to implement prevention efforts. In the school context, suicide prevention programs and intervention efforts have been developed at the universal, selected, and indicated levels (Robinson et al. 2013). Schools can engage in activities including gatekeeper training, implementing curricula designed to increase awareness or knowledge, screening youth, training youth to serve as peer leaders, and offering skills building training (Katz et al. 2013). Unfortunately, there are only a handful of school-based programs designated as promising or effective.

Although a thorough review of school-based programs is outside the scope of this chapter, lists and descriptions of evidence-based suicide prevention efforts have been compiled by a number of registries and organizations, including the SAMSHA National Registry of Evidence-based Programs and Practices (NREPP; www.samhsa.gov/nrepp) and the Suicide Prevention Resource Center (SPRC; www.sprc.org). Further, Katz et al. (2013) completed a systematic review of school-based suicide prevention programs. Finally, guidance for schools interested in enhancing suicide prevention efforts exists; for instance, SAMSHA offers a free toolkit (http://store.samhsa.gov/shin/content// SMA12-4669/SMA12-4669.pdf) for high schools that includes factsheets, risk assessment protocols, and programs from NREPP and best practices registries.

The remainder of this section will provide details about three school-based approaches that are among the most promising: Signs of Suicide (SOS), a universal school-based prevention program; Sources of Strength (SOS), also a universal school-based program; and the combination of Counselors Care (C-CARE), a selected screening program, with Coping and Support Training (CAST), a selected skills-building program.

Signs of Suicide

Signs of Suicide (SOS) is an evidence-based universal suicide prevention program developed by Screening for Mental Health Inc. that targets middle and high school students. SOS has two primary components: (i) a curriculum that focuses on raising awareness about suicide and related issues, and (ii) a screening for depression and other factors associated with increased risk of engaging in suicidal behaviors, most notably depression and alcohol use (Aseltine et al. 2007). Through the curriculum adolescents are taught to respond to signs of suicide through the ACT model, which stands for "Acknowledge" signs of suicide and take them seriously; express that you "Care" for the person and that you would like to help; and "Tell" an adult (Aseltine and Demartino 2004).

The SAMSHA National Registry of Evidence-based Programs and Practices (NREPP) classifies SOS as promising, specifically with respect to thoughts and behaviors related to suicide, and mental health attitudes, knowledge, and beliefs (http://nrepp.samhsa.gov/ProgramProfile.aspx?id=85#hide1). A handful of randomized clinical trials have been completed to assess the effectiveness of SOS. Aseltine and colleagues conducted two of the earliest trials (Aseltine and Demartino 2004; Aseltine et al. 2007), both of which examined the short-term effects of the SOS program among high school students. Results from these studies indicated that students in the SOS intervention groups, in comparison to those in the control groups, reported significantly fewer self-reported suicide attempts and demonstrated increased knowledge about depression and suicide at three months post-treatment. However, there were no differences between the treatment and control groups on help-seeking behaviors or suicidal ideation at posttest (Aseltine and Demartino 2004; Aseltine et al. 2007).

Findings from more recent evaluations have also demonstrated the promise of SOS. For instance, in a study of middle school students enrolled in schools with a high percentage of military connected youth, findings indicated that students in the intervention condition reported increased knowledge about suicide and suicide prevention at posttest compared to those in the control condition (Schilling et al. 2014). Moreover, among students with suicidal ideation at baseline, those who were exposed to SOS reported fewer suicidal behaviors at posttest than did students in the control group. Similarly promising results emerged from an evaluation of SOS among high school students, in which ninth grade students who participated in SOS revealed fewer suicide attempts three months after the program than students who did not participate in the program; this finding held after controlling for pretest reports of suicidal behaviors (Schilling, Aseltine, and James 2016). Taken together, results of the randomized control trials for SOS suggest that it is a promising universal suicide prevention approach.

Sources of Strength (SOS)

Sources of Strength (SOS) is a universal school-based suicide prevention program that targets high school students. SOS emphasizes the role of peer leaders, who are advised by adult mentors, and views these leaders as central to creating positive perceptions of help seeking, helping students develop stronger bonds with adult staff, and increasing students' use of coping strategies. The program consists of three phases: (i) preparation (for the school and community), (ii) peer leader training, and (iii) school-wide messaging, which is led by peer leaders. With respect to messaging, peer leaders are trained to deliver messages through social media, school broadcasts, and texts, all of which offer encouragement and emphasize resiliency and strength. Specific sources of strength highlighted by SOS are family support, positive friends, mentors, healthy activities, generosity, spirituality, medical access, and mental health access (Petrova et al. 2015).

The SAMSHA National Registry of Evidence-based Programs and Practices (NREPP), lists SOS as a Legacy Program, given it was reviewed by NREPP prior to September 2015. In a study of adolescents enrolled at 18 schools located in metropolitan and rural areas, results indicated that peer leaders experienced a number of benefits through their training (Wyman et al. 2010). For instance, in contrast to peer leaders who did not participate in training, those who did were more likely to indicate that teachers offer help to students expressing suicidal thoughts and to provide support to peers in distress. Importantly, differences emerged at the school level as well, such that students enrolled in schools with trained leaders were more likely to believe adults would help suicidal peers, and to report more positive norms around help-seeking from adults at school.

In another study that evaluated the peer presentation component of SOS, Petrova and colleagues (2015) compared control group students to students in two program conditions involving peer leader presentations. The first presentation condition consisted of peer leaders discussing their own use of healthy coping strategies and connecting with trusted adults, and the second presentation condition consisted of peer leaders discussing these same experiences *and* asking student audience members to identify trusted adults in their own lives. Results indicated that students in both peer messaging groups demonstrated more positive views of coping strategies and increased perceptions of adult support in comparison to students in the control group (Petrova et al. 2015). Additionally, students in the presentation condition with audience involvement reported more improvements in perceptions of adult support, and for both presentation types, students who had recent suicidal ideation seemed to benefit most.

Taken together, findings from these two studies suggest that SOS is a promising peer-led approach to suicide prevention.

Counselors Care (C-CARE) and Coping and Support Training (CAST)

C-CARE and CAST are often delivered together, given that when combined these two interventions complement each other and show evidence of long-term effectiveness (Thompson et al. 2001). C-CARE pairs a computerized assessment with motivational counseling, and is designed to identify youth at high risk for suicide (Katz et al. 2013). Brief counseling follows the initial assessment, and it emphasizes coping skills and help-seeking behaviors and provides youth with a safe environment in which they feel supported. Although CAST can be delivered at the universal, selected, or indicated levels (Robinson et al. 2013), it often is implemented at the indicated level with youth identified through C-CARE. At this level, CAST consists of 12 sessions and is implemented in small groups in school or community settings (Katz et al. 2013; Thompson et al. 2001). The goal of CAST is to improve social support and life skills. CAST also aims to increase adolescents' feelings of personal control, especially surrounding drug use, and to improve mood management and academic functioning (Thompson et al. 2001).

Based on their systematic review of school-based prevention programs, Katz et al. (2013) rated the combination of C-CARE plus CAST as a "B" for its demonstration of improvements in knowledge and its skills training efficacy (scoring based on the Oxford Centre for Evidence-based Medicine Rubric). With respect to specific research evidence for C-CARE and CAST, a study of youth at risk for high school dropout found that in comparison to adolescents in the control group, those youth who participated in C-CARE or C-CARE plus CAST demonstrated increases in protective factors and decreases in risk factors for suicide such as hopelessness, depression, and anxiety (Thompson et al. 2001). Participation in CAST also was associated with improvements in problem solving and personal control, consistent with the goals of this program. Some results from this evaluation suggested potentially increased effectiveness for females in both experimental conditions, specifically with respect to reductions in anxiety and anger control problems. Two additional studies examining both C-CARE and CAST had analogous results (Eggert et al. 2002; Randell, Eggert, and Pike 2001), supporting the programs' efficacy at reducing risk factors associated with suicide. In one study assessing C-CARE alone that followed youth from high school into early adulthood, findings indicated that youth who had participated in C-CARE continued to maintain reductions in depression, anger, and suicide risk behavior (Hooven, Herting, and Snedker 2010).

Addressing Both Bullying and Suicide in Prevention Efforts

To date, school-based prevention programs have largely focused on either bullying or suicide. However, given the overlap in risk and protective factors, focusing on these factors might benefit youth in both areas. For instance, as articulated by Duong and Bradshaw (Duong and Bradshaw 2015), implementing targeted prevention programs that address early common risk factors has the potential to reduce the likelihood that youth become involved in bullying or experience suicidal ideation or behaviors. Similarly, given documented associations between school climate and bullying, and school climate and suicide, school climate improvements would benefit students in both areas (Birkett, Espelage, and Koenig 2009; Cornell and Huang 2016; Denny et al. 2016). Further, as described previously, there are a number of factors at multiple levels of the social ecology that serve to increase risk or protect youth against involvement in bullying or suicidal behavior (e.g., child maltreatment history, social support); these are factors that, if addressed by schools, would have the potential to positively affect youth in both domains.

To that end, there have been some emerging efforts to develop programs that could reduce bullying involvement and suicidal ideation and behaviors. For instance, Links to Enhancing Teens' Connectedness (LET's CONNECT) is an intervention for youth at risk for suicidal behavior due to problems with bullying or social connectedness (King, Gipson, and Opperman 2015). Although it is not a school-based program, but rather is a community-based mentoring intervention, it nonetheless has the potential to positively affect youth broadly and in the educational context. The trial evaluating LET'S CONNECT is still underway, and thus to date there is no evidence for the program's effectiveness; however, this program reflects a unique approach to addressing two key public health issues for adolescents.

Conclusion

Both bullying and suicide are key public health concerns for youth today, and research has identified a number of risk and protective factors for each. Efforts to address suicide in the school context have yielded some promising results, and streamlined approaches to simultaneously prevent involvement in bullying and suicidal thoughts and behaviors are increasingly being considered and developed. As a primary context for youth development, schools are well positioned to serve as a key location for intervention and prevention program delivery.

References

American Educational Research Association. 2013. *Prevention of Bullying in Schools, Colleges, and Universities: Research Report and Recommendations*. Washington, DC: American Educational Research Association.

Aseltine, R. and Demartino, R. 2004. "An Outcome Evaluation of the SOS Suicide Prevention Program." *American Journal of Public Health* 94(3), 446–451.

Aseltine, R.H., James, A., Schilling, E.A., and Glanovsky, J. 2007. "Evaluating the SOS Suicide Prevention Program: A Replication and Extension." *BMC Public Health* 7, 161. DOI: 10.1186/1471-2458-7-161.

Bauman, S., Toomey, R.B., and Walker, J.L. 2013. "Associations among bullying, Cyberbullying, and Suicide in High School Students." *Journal of Adolescence* 36(2), 341–350. DOI: 10.1016/j.adolescence.2012.12.001.

Beautrais, A. 2003. "Suicide and Serious Suicide Attempts in Youth: A Multiple-group Comparison Study." *American Journal of Psychiatry* 160(6), 1093–1099.

Berlan, E.D., Corliss, H. L., Field, A.E., Goodman, E., and Bryn Austin, S. 2010. "Sexual Orientation and Bullying among Adolescents in the Growing Up Today Study. *Journal of Adolescent Health* 46(4), 366–371. DOI: 10.1016/j.jadohealth.2009.10.015.

Birkett, M., Espelage, D.L., and Koenig, B. 2009. "LGB and Questioning Students in Schools: The Moderating Effects of Homophobic Bullying and School Climate on Negative Outcomes." *Journal of Youth and Adolescence* 38(7), 989–1000. DOI: 10.1007/s10964-008-9389-1.

Björkqvist, K., Lagerspetz, K. M. J., and Kaukiainen, A. 1992. "Do Girls Manipulate and Boys Fight? Developmental Trends in Regard to Direct and Indirect Aggression." *Aggressive Behavior* 18(2), 117–127. DOI: 10.1002/1098-2337(1992)18:2<117::A ID-AB2480180205>3.0.CO;2-3.

Bollmer, J.M., Milich, R., Harris, M.J., and Maras, M.A. 2005. "A friend in Need: The Role if Friendship Quality as a Protective Factor in Peer Victimization and Bullying." *Journal of Interpersonal Violence* 20(6), 701–712. DOI: 10.1177/0886260504272897.

Borowsky, I.W., Taliaferro, L.A., and McMorris, B.J. 2013. "Suicidal Thinking and Behavior among Youth Involved in Verbal and Social Bullying: Risk and Protective Factors." *Journal of Adolescent Health* 53, S4–12.

Brent, D.A., Bridge, J., Johnson, B.A., and Connolly, J. 1996. "Suicidal Behavior Runs in Families. A Controlled Family Study of Adolescent Suicide Victims." *Archives of General Psychiatry* 53(12), 1145–1152.

Brent, D.A. and Mann, J.J. 2006. "Familial Pathways to Suicidal Behavior – Understanding and Preventing Suicide among Adolescents." *The New England Journal of Medicine* 355(26), 2719–2721.

Brent, D.A., Perper, J.A., Allman, C.J., Moritz, G.M., Wartella, M.E., and Zelenak, J.P. 1991. "The Presence and Accessibility of Firearms in the Homes of Adolescent Suicides. A Case-control Study." *JAMA* 266(21), 2989–2995.

Bridge, J.A., Goldstein, T.R., and Brent, D.A. 2006. "Adolescent Suicide and Suicidal Behavior." *Journal of Child Psychology and Psychiatry* 47, 372–394. DOI: 10.1111/j.1469-7610.2006.01615.x.

Centers for Disease Control and Prevention 2014. "Web-based Injury Statistics Query and Reporting System (WISQARS)." http://www.cdc.gov/injury/wisqars/index.html.

Centers for Disease Control and Prevention. 2015. "Youth Risk Behavior Surveillance—United States, 2015." MMWR, Surveillance Summaries 2016;65(SS9). http://www.cdc.gov/mmwr/volumes/65/ss/ss6506a1.htm (last accessed November 5, 2017).

Cook, C. R., Williams, K.R., Guerra, N.G., Kim, T.E., and Sadek, S. 2010. "Predictors of Bullying and Victimization in Childhood and Adolescence: A Meta-analytic Investigation." *School Psychology Quarterly* 25(2), 65–83. DOI: 10.1037/a0020149.

Copeland, W.E., Wolke, D., Angold, A., and Costello, E. 2013. "Adult Psychiatric Outcomes of Bullying and Being Bullied by Peers in Childhood and Adolescence." *JAMA Psychiatry* 70(4), 419–426. DOI: 10.1001/jamapsychiatry.2013.504.

Cornell, D. and Huang, F. 2016. "Authoritative School Climate and High School Student Risk Behavior: A Cross-Sectional Multi-level Analysis of Student Self-Reports." *Journal of Youth and Adolescence* 45(11), 2246–2259. DOI: 10.1007/s10964-016-0424-3.

Crick, N.R. and Dodge, K..1999. "'Superiority' is in the Eye of the Beholder: A Comment on Sutton, Smith, and Swettenham." *Social Development* 8(1), 128–131.

Denny, S., Lucassen, M.F.G., Stuart, J., Fleming, T., Bullen, P., Peiris-John, R., ... Utter, J. 2016. "The Association between supportive High School Environments and Depressive Symptoms and Suicidality among Sexual Minority Students." *Journal of Clinical Child and Adolescent Psychology* 45(3), 248–261. DOI: 10.1080/15374416.2014.958842.

Devoe, J. and Murphy, C. 2011. *Student Reports of Bullying and Cyber-bullying: Results from the 2009 School Crime Supplement to the National Crime Victimization Survey.* Washington, DC: http://nces.ed.gov/pubs2011/2011336.pdf (last accessed October 23, 2017).

Duong, J. and Bradshaw, C.P. 2015. "Bullying and Suicide Prevention: Taking a Balanced Approach That Is Scientifically Informed." In *Youth Suicide and Bullying: Challenges and Strategies for Prevention and Intervention*, edited by P. Goldblum, D.L. Espelage, J. Chu, and B. Bongar. New York: Oxford University Press.

Eggert, L. L., Thompson, E. A., Randell, B. P., and Pike, K. C. 2002. "Preliminary Effects of Brief School-based Prevention Approaches for Reducing Youth Suicide-Risk Behaviors, Depression and Drug Involvement." *Journal of Child and Adolescent Psychiatric Nursing* 15, 48–64.

Eisenberg, M.E. and Resnick, M.D. 2006. "Suicidality among Gay, Lesbian and Bisexual Youth: The Role of Protective Factors." *Journal of Adolescent Health* 39(5), 662–668. DOI: 10.1016/j.jadohealth.2006.04.024.

Espelage, D.L., Bosworth, K., and Simon, T.R. 2000. "Examining the Social Context of Bullying Behaviors in Early Adolescence." *Journal of Counseling and Development* 78(3), 326–333.

Espelage, D.L., Goldblum, P., Chu, J., Bongar, B., Pflum, S., and De La Rue, L. 2015. "Developing an Ecological Approach to Address Challenges of Youth Bullying and Suicide: Recommendations for Practice, Policy, and Training." In *Youth Suicide and Bullying: Challenges and Strategies for Prevention and Intervention*, edited by P. Goldblum, D.L. Espelage, J. Chu, and B. Bongar. New York: Oxford University Press.

Espelage, D.L. and Holt, M.K. 2013. "Suicidal Ideation and School Bullying Experiences after Controlling for Depression and Delinquency." *Journal of Adolescent Health* 53, S27–31.

Espelage, D.L., Holt, M.K., and Henkel, R. R. 2003. "Examination of Peer–group Contextual Effects on Aggression during Early Adolescence." *Child Development* 74(1), 205–220. DOI: 10.1111/1467-8624.00531.

Evans, E., Hawton, K., and Rodham, K. 2004. "Factors Associated with Suicidal Phenomena in Adolescents: A Systematic Review on Population-based Studies." *Clinical Psychology Review* 24(8), 957–979. DOI: 10.1016/j.cpr.2004.04.005.

Evans, E., Hawton, K., and Rodham, K. 2005. "Suicidal Phenomena and Abuse in Adolescents: A Review of Epidemiological Studies." *Child Abuse and Neglect: The International Journal* 29(1), 45–58. DOI: 10.1016/j.chiabu.2004.06.014.

Fekkes, M., Pijpers, F.I.M., Fredriks, A.M., Vogels, T., and Verloove-Vanhorick, S..2006. "Do Bullied Children Get Ill, or Do Ill Children Get Bullied? A Prospective Cohort Study on the Relationship between Bullying and Health-related Symptoms." *Pediatrics* 117(5), 1568–1574. DOI: 10.1542/peds.2005-0187.

Friedman, M.S., Koeske, G.F., Silvestre, A.J., Korr, W.S., and Sites, E.W. 2006. "The Impact of Gender-role Nonconforming Behavior, Bullying, and Social Support on Suicidality among Gay Male Youth." *Journal of Adolescent Health* 38(5), 621–623. DOI: 10.1016/j.jadohealth.2005.04.014.

Furlong, M.J., Sharkey, J.D., Felix, E.D., Tanigawa, D., and Green, J.G. 2010. "Bullying Assessment: A Call for Increased Precision of Self-reporting Procedures." In *Handbook of Bullying in Schools: An International Perspective*, edited by S.R. Jimerson, S.M. Swearer, and D.L. Espelage, pp. 329–345. New York: Routledge.

Georgiou, S.N. 2008. "Bullying and Victimization at School: The Role of Mothers." *British Journal of Educational Psychology* 78(1), 109–125. DOI: 10.1348/000709907X204363.

Giannini, M.J., Bergmark, B., Kreshover, S., Elias, E., Plummer, C., and O'Keefe, E. 2010. "Understanding Suicide and Disability through Three Major Disabling Conditions: Intellectual Disability, Spinal Cord Injury, and Multiple Sclerosis." *Disability and Health Journal* 3(2), 74–78. DOI: 10.1016/j.dhjo.2009.09.001.

Gini, G. 2008. "Associations between Bullying Behaviour, Psychosomatic Complaints, Emotional and Behavioural Problems." *Journal of Paediatrics and Child Health* 44(9), 492–497. DOI: 10.1111/j.1440-1754.2007.01155.x.

Gini, G. and Pozzoli, T. 2013. "Bullied Children and Psychosomatic Problems: A Meta-analysis." *Pediatrics* 132(4), 720–729. DOI: 10.1542/peds.2013-0614.

Gladden, M.R., Vivolo-Kantor, A.M., Hamburger, M.E., and Lumpkin, C.D. 2014. *Bullying Surveillance Among Youth: Uniform Definitions for Public Health and Recommended Data Elements, Version 1.0.* Atlanta, GA.

Goldston, D.B., Molock, S.D., Whitbeck, L. B., Murakami, J.L., Zayas, L.H., and Hall, G.C.N. 2008. "Cultural considerations in Adolescent Suicide Prevention and Psychosocial Treatment." *American Psychologist* 63(1), 14–31. DOI: 10.1037/0003-066X.63.1.14.

Gould, M.S., Greenberg, T., Velting, D.M., and Shaffer, D. 2003. "Youth Suicide Risk and Preventive Interventions: A Review of the Past 10 Years." *Journal of the American Academy of Child & Adolescent Psychiatry* 42(4), 386–405.

Hacker, K.A., Suglia, S.F., Fried, L. E., Rappaport, N., and Cabral, H. 2006. "Developmental Differences in Risk Factors for Suicide Attempts between Ninth and Eleventh Graders." *Suicide and Life-Threatening Behavior* 36(2), 154–166.

Hawton, K., Bergen, H., Kapur, N., Cooper, J., Steeg, S., Ness, J., and Waters, K. 2012. "Repetition of Self-Harm and Suicide Following Self-Harm in Children and Adolescents: Findings from the Multicentre Study of Self-Harm in England." *Journal of Child Psychology and Psychiatry* 53(12), 1212–1219. DOI: 10.1111/j.1469-7610.2012.02559.x.

Haynie, D.L., Nansel, T., Eitel, P., Crump, A.D., Saylor, K., Yu, K., and Simons-Morton, B. 2001. "Bullies, Victims, and Bully/Victims: Distinct Groups of At-risk Youth." *The Journal of Early Adolescence* 21(1), 29–49. DOI: 10.1177/0272431601021001002.

Holt, M.K., Finkelhor, D., and Kantor, G. K. 2007. "Hidden Forms of Victimization in Elementary Students Involved in Bullying." *School Psychology Review* 36(3), 345–360.

Holt, M.K., Green, J.G., Reid, G., DiMeo, A., Espelage, D.L., Felix, E.D., ... Sharkey, J.D. 2014. "Associations between Past Bullying Experiences and Psychosocial and Academic Functioning among College Students." *Journal of American College Health* 62(8), 552–560. DOI: 10.1080/07448481.2014.947990.

Holt, M.K., Matjasko, J.L., Espelage, D., Reid, G., and Koenig, B. 2013. "Sexual Risk Taking and Bullying Among Adolescents." *Pediatrics* 132(6), e1481–1487. DOI: 10.1542/peds.2013-0401.

Holt, M.K., Vivolo-Kantor, A.M., Polanin, J.R., Holland, K.M., Degue, S., Matjasko, J.L., ... Reid, G. 2015. "Bullying and Suicidal Ideation and Behaviors: A Meta-analysis." *Pediatrics* 135(2), e496–509. DOI: 10.1542/peds.2014-1864.

Hooven, C., Herting, J.R., and Snedker, K.A. 2010. "Long-term Outcomes for the Promoting CARE Suicide Prevention Program." *American Journal of Health Behavior* 34(6), 721–736. DOI: 10.5993/AJHB.34.6.8.

Jankauskiene, R., Kardelis, K., Sukys, S., and Kardeliene, L. 2008. "Associations between School Bullying and Psychosocial Factors." *Social Behavior and Personality* 36(2), 145–162. DOI: 10.2224/sbp.2008.36.2.145.

Juvonen, J. and Graham, S. 2014. "Bullying in Schools: The power of Bullies and the Plight of Victims." *Annual Review of Psychology* 65, 159–185.

Juvonen, J., Graham, S., and Schuster, M. A. 2003. "Bullying among Young Adolescents: The Strong, the Weak and the Troubled." *Pediatrics* 112(6), 1231–1237.

Juvonen, J., Wang, Y., and Espinoza, G. 2011. "Bullying Experiences and Compromised Academic Performance across Middle School Grades." *Journal of Early Adolescence* 31(1), 152–173. DOI: 10.1177/0272431610379415.

Kann, L., Kinchen, S., Shanklin, S.L., Flint, K.H., Hawkins, J., Harris, W.A., ... S., Z. 2014. "Youth Risk Behavior Surveillance – United States, 2013." *MMWR* 63, 1–168.

Kann, L., Olsen, E.O., McManus, T., Kinchen, S., Chyen, D., and Harris, W.A. 2011. "Sexual Identity, Sex of Sexual Contacts, and Health-risk Behaviors among Students in Grades 9–12: Youth Risk Behavior, Surveillance, Selected Sites, United States, 2001–2009." *MMWR Surveillance Summaries* 60, 1–133.

Karch, D.L., Logan, J., McDaniel, D.D., Floyd, C.F., and Vagi, K.J. 2013. "Precipitating Circumstances of Suicide among Youth Aged 10–17 Years by Sex: Data from the

National Violent Death Reporting System, 16 States, 2005–2008." *Journal of Adolescent Health* 53, S51–S53.

Katz, C., Bolton, S.-L., Katz, L.Y., Isaak, C., Tilston-Jones, T., and Sareen, J. 2013. "A Systematic Review of School-based Suicide Prevention Programs." *Depression and Anxiety* 30(10), 1030–1045. DOI: 10.1002/da.22114.

King, C.A., Gipson, P.Y., and Opperman, K. 2015. "The LET'S CONNECT Intervention." In *Youth Suicide and Bullying: Challenges and Strategies for Prevention and Intervention*, edited by P. Goldblum, D.L. Espelage, J. Chu, and B. Bongar, pp. 246–259. New York: Oxford University Press.

Kljakovic, M. and Hunt, C. 2016. "A Meta-analysis of Predictors of Bullying and Victimisation in Adolescence." *Journal of Adolescence* 49, 134–145. DOI: 10.1016/j. adolescence.2016.03.002.

Klomek, A B., Marrocco, F., Kleinman, M., Schonfeld, I.S., and Gould, M.S. 2007. "Bullying, Depression, and Suicidality in Adolescents." *Journal of the American Academy of Child & Adolescent Psychiatry* 46(1), 40–49. DOI: 10.1097/01.chi.0000242237.84925.18.

Klomek, A.B., Sourander, A., and Elonheimo, H. 2015. "Bullying by peers in Childhood and Effects on Psychopathology, Suicidality, and Criminality in Adulthood." *The Lancet Psychiatry* 2(10), 930–941. DOI: 10.1016/S2215-0366(15)00223-0.

Klomek, A.B., Sourander, A., Niemelä, S., Kumpulainen, K., Piha, J., Tamminen, T., ...Gould, M.S. 2009. "Childhood Bullying Behaviors as a Risk for Suicide Attempts and Completed Suicides: A Population-based Birth Cohort Study." *Journal of the American Academy of Child & Adolescent Psychiatry* 48(3), 254–261. DOI: 10.1097/CHI.0b013e318196b91f.

Lereya, S.T., Samara, M., and Wolke, D. 2013. "Parenting Behavior and the Risk of Becoming a Victim and a Bully/Victim: A Meta-analysis Study." *Child Abuse & Neglect* 37(12), 1091–1108. DOI: 10.1016/j.chiabu.2013.03.001.

Ludi, E., Ballard, E.D., Greenbaum, R., Pao, M., Bridge, J., Reynolds, W., and Horowitz, L. 2012. "Suicide Risk in Youth with Intellectual Disabilities: The Challenges of Screening." *Journal of Developmental and Behavioral Pediatric*, 33(5), 431–440. DOI: 10.1097/ DBP.0b013e3182599295.

Luk, J.W., Wang, J., and Simons-Morton, B.G. 2010. "Bullying victimization and Substance Use among U.S. Adolescents: Mediation by Depression." *Prevention Science* 11(4), 355–359. DOI: 10.1007/s11121-010-0179-0.

Marshal, M.P., Dietz, L.., Friedman, M.S., Stall, R., Smith, H. A., McGinley, J., ... Brent, D.A. 2011. "Suicidality and depression disparities between sexual minority and heterosexual youth: A meta-analytic review." *Journal of Adolescent Health* 49(2), 115–123. doi:10.1016/j.jadohealth.2011.02.005.

Mazza, J.J., Catalano, R.F., Abbott, R.D., and Haggerty, K.P. 2011. "An Examination of the Validity of Retrospective Measures of Suicide Attempts in Youth." *Journal of Adolescent Health* 49(5), 532–537. DOI: 10.1016/j.jadohealth.2011.04.009.

Mueller, A.S., James, W., Abrutyn, S., and Levin, M.L. 2015. "Suicide Ideation and Bullying among US Adolescents: Examining the Intersections of Sexual Orientation, Gender, and Race/Ethnicity." *American Journal of Public Health* 105(5), 980–985. DOI: 10.2105/ AJPH.2014.302391.

Nansel, T.R., Overpeck, M., Pilla, R.S., Ruan, W.J., Simons-Morton, B., and Scheidt, P. 2001. "Bullying behaviors among US Youth: Prevalence and Association with Psychosocial Adjustment." *JAMA* 285(16), 2094–2100.

Navajo Nation. 2013. *2011 Navajo Nation High School Youth Risk Behavior Survey Report.* http://www.nec.navajo-nsn.gov/Portals/0/Reports/2011%20NYRBS%20HS% 20Report%20-%20Final.pdf (last accessed October 23, 2017).

O'Connor, R.C., Rasmussen, S., and Hawton, K. 2012. "Distinguishing adolescents who think about self-harm from those who engage in self-harm." *The British Journal of Psychiatry* 200, 330–335.

Petrova, M., Wyman, P.A., Schmeelk-Cone, K., and Pisani, A.R. 2015. "Positive-themed Suicide Prevention Messages Delivered by Adolescent Peer Leaders: Proximal Impact on Classmates' Coping Attitudes and Perceptions of Adult Support." *Suicide and Life-Threatening Behavior* 45(6), 651–663.

Radliff, K.M., Wheaton, J.E., Robinson, K., and Morris, J. 2012. "Illuminating the Relationship between Bullying and Substance Use among Middle and High School Youth." *Addictive Behaviors* 37(4), 569–572. DOI: 10.1016/j.addbeh.2012.01.001.

Randell, B.P., Eggert, L.L., and Pike, K.C. 2001. "Immediate Post Intervention Effects of Two Brief Youth Suicide Prevention Interventions." *Suicide and Life-Threatening Behavior* 31(1), 41–61. DOI: 10.1521/suli.31.1.41.21308.

Rivers, I., Poteat, V.P., Noret, N., and Ashurst, N. 2009. "Observing Bullying at School: The Mental Health Implications of Witness Status." *School Psychology Quarterly* 24(4), 211–223. DOI: 10.1037/a0018164.

Robers, S., Zhang, A., Morgan, R.E., and Musu-Gillette, L. 2015. *Indicators of School Crime and Safety: 2014* (NCES 2015-072/NCJ 248036. National Center for Education Statistics, US Department of Education, and Bureau of Justice Statistics, Office of Justice Programs, U.S. Department of Justice. Washington, DC.

Robinson, J., Cox, G., Malone, A., Williamson, M., Baldwin, G., Fletcher, K., and O'brien, M. 2013. "A systematic Review of School-Based Interventions Aimed at Preventing, Treating, and Responding to Suicide-related Behavior in Young People." *Crisis: The Journal of Crisis Intervention and Suicide Prevention*,34(3), 164–182. DOI: 10.1027/0227-5910/a000168.

Robinson, J P. and Espelage, D.L. 2011. "Inequities in Educational and Psychological Outcomes between LGBTQ and Straight Students in Middle and High School." *Educational Researcher* 40(7), 315–330. DOI: 10.3102/0013189X11422112.

Rodkin, P.C., Espelage, D.L., and Hanish, L.D. 2015. "A Relational Framework for Understanding Bullying: Developmental Antecedents and Outcomes." *The American Psychologist* 70(4), 311–321. DOI: doi:10.1037/a0038658.

Rose, C.A., Espelage, D.L., and Monda-Amaya, L.E. 2009. "Bullying and Victimisation Rates among Students in General and Special Education: A Comparative Analysis." *Educational Psychology* 29(7), 761–776. DOI 10.1080/01443410903254864.

Rose, C.A., Monda-Amaya, L.E., and Espelage, D.L. 2011. "Bullying Perpetration and Victimization in Special Education: A Review of the Literature." *Remedial and Special Education* 32(2), 114–130. DOI: 10.1177/0741932510361247.

Schilling, E.A., Aseltine, R.H., Glanovsky, J.L., James, A., and Jacobs, D. 2009. "Adolescent Alcohol Use, Suicidal Ideation, and Suicide Attempts." *Journal of Adolescent Health* 44(4), 335–341. DOI: 10.1016/j.jadohealth.2008.08.006.

Schilling, E.A., Aseltine, R.H., and James, A. 2016. "The SOS Suicide Prevention Program: Further Evidence of Efficacy and Effectiveness." *Prevention Science* 17(2), 157–166. DOI: DOI: 10.1007/s11121-015-0594-3.

Schilling, E.A., Lawless, M., Buchanan, L., and Aseltine, R.H., Jr. 2014. "'Signs of Suicide' shows Promise as a Middle School Suicide Prevention Program." *Suicide and Life-Threatening Behavior* 44(6), 653–667. DOI: 10.1111/sltb.12097.

Shaughnessy, L., Doshi, S.R., and Jones, S.E. 2004. "Attempted Suicide and Associated Health Risk Behaviors among Native American High School Students." *Journal of School Health* 74(5), 177–182. DOI: 10.1111/j.1746-1561.2004.tb08217.x.

Sourander, A., Gyllenberg, D., Brunstein Klomek, A., Sillanmäki, L., Ilola, A.-M., and Kumpulainen, K. 2016. "Association of Bullying Behavior at 8 Years of Age and Use of Specialized Services for Psychiatric Disorders by 29 Years of Age." *JAMA Psychiatry* 73(2), 159–165. DOI: 10.1001/jamapsychiatry.2015.2419.

Srabstein, J.C. and Leventhal, B.L. 2010. "Prevention of Bullying-related Morbidity and Mortality: A Call for Public Health Policies." *Bulletin of the World Health Organization* 88, 403.

Stone, D.M., Luo, F., Lippy, C., and McIntosh, W.L. 2015. "The Role of Social Connectedness and Sexual Orientation in the Prevention of Youth Suicide Ideation and Attempts among Sexually Active Adolescents." *Suicide and Life-Threatening Behavior* 45(4), 415–430. DOI: 10.1111/sltb.12139.

Thompson, E.A., Eggert, L.L., Randell, B.P., and Pike, K. C. 2001. "Evaluation of Indicated Suicide Risk Prevention Approaches for Potential High School Dropouts." *American Journal of Public Health* 91(5), 742–752.

van Geel, M., Vedder, P., and Tanilon, J. 2014. "Relationship between Peer Victimization, Cyberbullying, and Suicide in Children And Adolescents." *JAMA Pediatrics* e1–e8. DOI: 10.1001/jamapediatrics.2013.4143.

US Department of Education 2015. *Student Reports of Bullying and Cyber-bullying: Results from the 2013 School Crime Supplement to the National Crime Victimization Survey.* http://nces.ed.gov/pubs2015/2015056.pdf (last accessed October 23, 2017).

Wang, J., Iannotti, R.J., and Nansel, T.R. 2009. "School Bullying among Adolescents in the United States: Physical, Verbal, Relational, and Cyber." *Journal of Adolescent Health* 45(4), 368–375.

Wyman, P.A., Brown, C.H., LoMurray, M., Schmeelk-Cone, K., Petrova, M., Yu, Q., … Wang, W. 2010. "An Outcome Evaluation of the Sources of Strength Suicide Prevention Program Delivered by Adolescent Peer Leaders in High Schools." *American Journal of Public Health* 100(9), 1653–1661. DOI: 10.2105/AJPH.2009.190025.

Zimmer-Gembeck, M.J., Geiger, T.C., and Crick, N.R. 2005. "Relational and Physical Aggression, Prosocial Behavior, and Peer Relations: Gender Moderation and Bidirectional Associations." *Journal of Early Adolescence* 25(4), 421–452. DOI: 10.1177/0272431605279841.

Section 4

Structural and Symbolic Violence in Education
Section Editor: Harvey Shapiro

Section 4 Introduction

Structures of Violence in Education

Harvey Shapiro

In this section, critical theorists, feminist scholars, ethicists, social activists, and educational philosophers address the other side of the violence equation: Education's ironic position of being the subject, rather than the object, of violence. Though it may be counterintuitive to consider it as violent or excessively coercive, education has long been associated, even in enlightened circles, with what in German is called *Gewalt* – force and/or violence. The European Enlightenment extended this partnership between pedagogy and coercion with arguments that a human being ("man") "is nothing but what education makes of him" (Kant 1904, 107). Indeed, philosophers such as Kant and Hegel claim an essential place for education's use of force. While these two influential icons of modern philosophy approached the issue from very different perspectives regarding the nature of human beings, their assertions about educational force are consistent in certain respects. Let us first hear from Kant: "One of the greatest problems of education is, how one can unite subjection under the rules of law with the ability to use one's own freedom. Because force is necessary! How do I cultivate freedom under the conditions of force?" (1904, 131)? This seemingly oxymoronic notion of "educational-force" remains a perennial challenge, even in societies that believe they are the apotheoses of democracy. As Geulen (2005) puts it, an enduring "tension within education is the problematic status of violent means in the service of pedagogical ends," leading "pedagogical discourse systematically into the contradictions of a circular autopoiesis" (943–944).

Like Kant, Hegel's ethical philosophy provides for "pedagogical coercion" in the state's paradoxical right and duty to liberate students' "free will" (1952, 93). For Hegel, the task of education is to allow the student's free will to respond with equal force to combat the student's unbridled "natural will" – also "implicitly a force" (93). Education, then, must act on this essential duty through "counter-violence" (Geulen 2005, 946). Often, this kind of educational force is unseen in its structural forms.

Structural violence is a well-researched, now well-traveled concept that refers to, among other factors, inequities based on gender, race, socioeconomic class, sexual orientation, and the conditions of racist, sexist, and classist educational oppression. Though elusive and less tangible than some of the other forms of violence discussed in this volume, its manifestations include everyday educational practices: Unfairly limiting financial resources for those schools most in need, lower levels of teacher training, deteriorating infrastructures, low student performance expectations, disproportionate,

The Wiley Handbook on Violence in Education: Forms, Factors, and Preventions, First Edition.
Edited by Harvey Shapiro.

unjust punitive actions, and implicit, as well as explicit racism, classism, sexism, and homophobia, among others.

These are the forms that this section seeks to expose, situating students' physical, verbal, sexual, emotional, and gender violence in the context of pervasive, systemic educational violence. Doing so allows us to step back and ask the difficult and unsavory question of how educational systems themselves might contribute to a violent educational climate. Revealing how structural violence is linguistic, discursive, expression-suppressing, honorific, objectifying, or conflict-producing, this section's contributors offer penetrating analyses and new, ambitious proposals for addressing these systemic, often violent, dimensions of education.

Bryan Warnick, Sang Hyun Kim, and Shannon Robinson's opening chapter provides the keynote for this section in Chapter 23 by asking the fundamental question of why schools, in particular, are places where gun violence occurs. The authors offer three compelling explanations: (i) schools are often places of coercion, hierarchical power, and control, making them ready hosts for violent emulation; (ii) schools are settings in which young people's relationships blossom, presenting a stark contrast with those who are excluded and disconnected from their peers; (iii) the educational aspiration to foster authentic personal expression often is fraught with inequities that can lead to expression in the form of violence. Warnick, Kim, and Robinson then offer proposals for systemic change: increasing the range of opportunities and forms for self-expression, creating a more central place for the fine arts, and reducing "micro-aggressive" testing.

In Chapter 24, Claudia Ruitenberg also considers "a conception of violence that is not restricted to physical violence." She examines the violence in social media, demonstrating how language itself can inflict violence, as she suggests the import of Judith Butler's notions of injurious and insurrectionary speech. Disclosing the violent discursive performance in social media's misogynistic "trolling," Ruitenberg argues that this phenomenon is not only violent in its consequence, but also in its very form: the perpetrator's dominant anonymity against a named, individual woman's body, as the "troll" furtively inflicts public violation. To confront and subvert this form of violence, she presents a "feminist public pedagogy" that "speaks back," in a perduring voice of resistance and dissent in social media, one of popular culture's most powerful pedagogical spaces.

In Chapter 25, Amy Shuffelton considers school shootings in the context of a problematic masculine conception of honor. Explicating the meaning of honor, she provides an understanding of what it means to be *dis*honored, marginalized, to have lost face at the hands of peers and institutions. In the case of school shootings, a certain notion of achieving honor often becomes a perpetrator's motivation. To address this kind of performance of masculine honor, Shuffelton suggests reconstructing our gendered cultural scripts that inform honor's meaning. In particular, she argues for recentering the capacity to listen, to communicate honestly, and to recognize others as equals, in a reconstructed pedagogy of honor.

In Chapter 26, David Ragland discusses the racist dimensions of structural violence: black and brown bodies being placed in a school-to-prison pipeline, suppression of voices, denials of racism, narratives that are unconscionably ignorant of black histories, and the denials of white privilege despite its unwavering hegemony. Drawing on critical race theory, he argues that state-sponsored violence, exemplified in 2014 in Ferguson, Missouri, and which has continued throughout the country, is the physically violent manifestation of embedded structural, systemic oppression. A social activist, and co-director and cofounder of the Truth Telling Project (http://thetruthtellingproject.org), Ragland writes of "specific school-based structural violence" in educational policies and practices: "Public education policies and practices in the United States provide clear examples of structural violence and the importance of truth telling about the intersections of poverty, lack of equitable funding for urban schools, increased policing, arrests of black and brown students for minor infractions, deficit-based teaching, and pedagogies with little regard for student identity, representation, and acknowledgment."

In Chapter 27, Gabriel Keehn and Deron Boyles approach the problem of violence from the standpoint of ethics, first examining the systemic, symbolic violence embedded within many of today's schools: corporate control, poor building conditions, increased police surveillance, and mechanical, scripted teaching. The authors argue that Emmanuel Levinas's ethics of alterity is a necessary response to these coercive, often confrontational practices that constitute a provocative ethos conducive to physical violence. A French-Jewish philosopher, Levinas was a French military officer during World War II and survived a five-year internment in a German prisoner-of-war camp. He devoted his life's work to showing that a prerequisite for confronting and precluding the kinds of violence to which he was witness is rigorously reconceptualizing the ethical relation to the "Other." Keehn and Boyles argue that a reconstructed ethics of alterity would involve recognizing students and educators as irreducible to categories, such as grades and learning tracks, and freeing education from the controlling bondage of corporate interests.

In Chapter 28, Hilary Cremin and Alex Guilherme consider the role of peace education as a form of response and prevention. Emphasizing the concept of "peacebuilding," they draw on their expertise in critical pedagogy and restorative approaches to conflict and violence. They call for an "epistemological shift" in order to cultivate an education that seeks peace as a genuine achievement. Pursuing such an aspiration requires a form of peace education that addresses multiple dimensions of violence – physical, structural, cultural, and psychological – thus recognizing the violence implicitly inflicted by educational institutions and systems themselves. They then argue for transforming the very nature of social, personal, and professional relationships in schools, applying Martin Buber's philosophy of dialogue.

Finally, in Chapter 29, Michalinos Zembylas approaches the structural problem of violence and peace education from the perspective of his own divided society of Cyprus. Arguing for the importance of emotional knowledge, he moves our thinking forward, beyond violence itself, to new conceptions of what it means to educate for non-violence and peace. His argument involves a critical examination of the way emotions are embedded in pervasive community narratives. He also challenges prevalent conceptions of what peace and conflict actually mean when considering the particularities of their contexts. Showing that peace education can, perhaps unwittingly or counterintuitively, perpetuate the kinds of problems it seeks to resolve, Zembylas calls for a *critical* peace education and peacebuilding.

This section, then, explains some of the most significant forms of structural violence. The contributors show the need to consider violence against the background of our quotidian, embedded practices, cultural norms, and sociopolitical relations. This structural perspective suggests that taking a proactive stance against the more visible forms of violence discussed in this volume requires a critical understanding of their sociopolitical landscape.

References

Geulen, E. 2005. "Walter Benjamin after the 20th Century: The Future of a Past: Legislating Education: Kant, Hegel, and Benjamin on 'Pedagogical Violence.'" *Cordozo Law Review* 26.

Kant, I. 1904. *Lecture Notes on Pedagogy*. Edited by E.F. Buchner. London: J.B. Lippincott. First published 1803.

Hegel, G.W.F. 1952. *Philosophy of Right*. Translated by T.M. Knox. Oxford: Clarendon Press. First published 1820.

23

Why Schools? Coercion, Refuge, and Expression as Factors in Gun Violence

Bryan R. Warnick, Sang Hyun Kim, and Shannon Robinson

On February 27, 2012, 17-year-old Thomas "T. J." Lane entered Chardon High School in Chardon, Ohio, with a Ruger MK III .22 caliber handgun. He fired 10 shots at a group of students sitting at a cafeteria table, killing three students. T. J. has never explained why he took a gun to the lunchroom that day. He has never explained why the idea of perpetrating violence in a school intrigued him and tempted him. Whatever the reason, this incident was one of the latest episodes in the tragic history of "targeted school shootings." These are shootings "where the school was deliberately selected as the location for the attack and was not simply a random site of opportunity" (Vossekuil et al. 2002, 9). These shootings involve a student or former student as the shooter, with the target being current students or teachers. Examples include the shootings at West Paducah, Kentucky (1997), Jonesboro, Arkansas (1998), Springfield, Oregon (1998), Littleton, Colorado (1999), Red Lake, Minnesota (2005), Blacksburg, Virginia (2007), Newtown, Connecticut (2012), Marysville, Washington (2014), and, most recently, Umpqua Community College (2015).

In this chapter, we try to better understand the phenomenon of targeted school shootings. We approach this topic with some reluctance. The exaggeration of chaos and school violence is often a vehicle that detractors of public schools use to reinforce their claim that public education or progressive education has failed.[1] For those of us that care about public education, it is wise not to exaggerate or overemphasize school shootings. In reality, overt violence has been declining steadily in schools since the 1990s (Dinkes et al. 2006, 10). Another reason for this reluctance has to do with our doubts about whether a philosophical response to this sort of suffering is appropriate. When the Sandy Hook Elementary School shootings occurred in 2012, we authors were all deeply saddened and troubled. Some of us had children who were six or seven years old, about the age of the children who had died. We felt the urge to "do something," and we turned to philosophy of education because that is what we have been trained to do. But when kids have died – particularly when children have been killed by other children – the abstracting task of philosophy, the making of broad connections and abstract generalizations, seems to do violence to the individuality of each story. The only way we have found to partially alleviate the unease of

---

1 One commentator, for example, overemphasizing the presence of violence in schools, writes, "[t]his retrogression toward anarchy has occurred during the reign of 'progressive' education" (Wolceshyn 1997).

The Wiley Handbook on Violence in Education: Forms, Factors, and Preventions, First Edition.
Edited by Harvey Shapiro.
© 2018 John Wiley & Sons, Inc. Published 2018 by John Wiley & Sons, Inc.

approaching school shootings philosophically is to immerse ourselves in the tragic stories surrounding school shootings – to learn about, and remember, the individual narratives.

As we read about these stories, we found it difficult to find many compelling generalizations. Most of the shooters were white males in rural or suburban contexts, and most were socially troubled in some way. Beyond that, what impressed us at first was how little the perpetrators seemed to have in common. Some of them were bullied, whereas others were bullies. Some came from obviously dysfunctional homes, whereas others had seemingly very concerned and engaged parents. Some had identifiable mental illness, whereas others had no such diagnosis. Some had particular quarrels with certain people within the school, whereas others wanted to make an expressive statement about who they were, not caring much about who they killed. Some of them seemed remorseful after the shooting, shaken by what they had done; others have spent their time in prison as quasi-celebrities, reveling in their fame and status.

This lack of generalizations across the stories is sometimes even apparent within an individual story itself. For example, the state attorney's report on the Sandy Hook shooting is a collection of inconsistent descriptions of the shooter, Adam Lanza. There is no clear vision of who he was, what he had experienced in his life, or why he did what he did. The report concludes:

> The obvious question ... is: "Why did the shooter murder twenty-seven people, including twenty children?" Unfortunately, that question may never be answered conclusively, despite the collection of extensive background information on the shooter through a multitude of interviews and other sources. The evidence clearly shows that the shooter planned his actions, including the taking of his own life, but there is no clear indication why he did so, or why he targeted Sandy Hook Elementary School. (Sedensky 2013, 3)

The same thing could be said about the phenomenon of school shootings in general. The only factors that initially seem to draw these events together are (i) easy access to powerful firearms, and (ii) a troubled student who interprets a school as an appropriate place use them.

While we believe that the most important thing to be done about school shootings is to somehow limit the access that troubled individuals have to deadly weapons, for now we want to focus on the second question of interpretation: Why are *schools* interpreted as appropriate places for violence? One can imagine many venues in which such violence could be possible, many venues in which kids congregate, many venues in which a troubled youth could wreak the desired havoc. Why don't we have a genre of violence targeting youth soccer games, for example, or shopping malls? It is true that students spend a lot of time in schools, but this by itself does not explain why schools are chosen to be places of violence. Our task is to try to explain why schools are specifically chosen for this particular genre of violence.

To answer this question, the "exegetical question of school shootings," we must investigate the meaning of American schooling. In what follows, we first explore how schools as institutions and spaces are understood and imagined in American society. We analyze the social "meaning" of school by using empirical data, everyday observations, films, and poetry. We explore both experiential meanings (the ideas students construct about schools from their lived interaction with schools) as well as aspirational meanings (the ideas that exist in the larger culture about what schools *should* be). We then connect these meanings to the stories of individual school shooters. We argue that there are at least three possible "points of meaning" that contribute to schools being interpreted as places appropriate for violence. First, schools are places of both real and symbolic violence, where force and power often rule the day. Second, schools are places connected to our highest expectations of hope and refuge, friendship and romance, and when these expectations are not met, bitter resentment flows against schools. Third, suburban schools are seen as places of expressive individualism, which, in rare cases, is manifest in terms of "expressive violence" – violence meant to send a message about the identity of the shooter. Together, these points of meaning create a view of schools suggesting to some students that schools are appropriate places to express violent emotions.

Micro-aggression and Symbolic Violence

An initial answer to the exegetical question of school violence was proposed by Warnick, Johnson, and Rocha (2010). There, it was speculated that schools are considered appropriate places for shootings because schools are, in some fundamental sense, already places filled with coercion and force. Bullying is an obvious example. The most recent survey from the National Center for Education Statistics, *Indicators of School Crime and Safety*, reports that 28% of 12- to 18-year-old students indicated being bullied at school during the school year (National Center for Education Statistics 2014). The percentage seems to climb as the children get younger, with 37% of sixth graders indicating that they have been bullied at school. Twenty-three percent of schools reported that bullying occurs in their schools on a daily or weekly basis. The stories linking bullying to some school shootings are well known and need not be rehearsed here. Many school shooters did indeed face intense, humiliating, and heartbreaking bullying. It makes sense that students who are bullied perceive schools as a place of violence. However, it is not simply that students are bullied and then become violently angry at their victimizers. The existence of bullying also changes how all students interpret the meaning of the school environment. Even those that were not bullied themselves can see that bullying occurs and this sends a message that schools are appropriate places for force and intimidation.

There is more contributing to the interpretation of schools as places appropriate for violence. There are the omnipresent "micro-aggressions," which are brief, everyday exchanges that (often unintentionally) send a message of dominance and denigration.[2] Micro-aggression often occurs as teachers and educators use shame and humiliation in the classroom. Paul Zimmer addresses this type of violence in his poem, "Zimmer's Head Thudding against the Blackboard," where basketball is used as a metaphor for the violence:

> At the blackboard I had missed
> Five number problems in a row,
> And was about to foul a sixth,
> When the old, exasperated nun
> Began to pound my head against
> My six mistakes.

---

2 Usually, this term has been invoked in racial contexts, where a dominant culture sends messages of inferiority to a minority group (see Sue 2010).

Zimmer begins to cry, whereupon he is then thrown back into his seat. At that point, he swears to be a poet one day and to "curse her yellow teeth with this [poem]" (Zimmer 1999, 21). Experiences of intentional and unintentional humiliation, shame, and degradation are not uncommon in schools. Educators can exercise power against students in ways that send the message that schools are places dominated by the use of force.

It is important to keep in mind not only the explicit acts of violence, or the humiliation and shame that they cause, but also the violence that can occur in the day-to-day practice of schools. Of course, force and coercion are present in many social contexts. Schools are unique, however, in that attendance is legally compulsory. Schools are also different from other contexts in terms of the overall amount and intensity of coercion. Students are forced to do examinations, test preparation, and classroom exercises. They are forced to sit in certain assigned seats, forced to speak or to remain silent, forced to run or to not run, forced to use the bathroom or to "hold it," depending on the time. Coercion even extends beyond school hours as students are forced to do homework and out-of-class projects. Some trends in educational reform – for example, the increasingly strict surveillance and control advocated by some educational reformers – only serve to increase the presence of coercion. If we define violence as an exertion of force to change the environment, then schools are fundamentally places of violence.[3]

Looking back over the stories of school shootings, it is easy to find ample evidence that school-related coercion and control played a role in the lives of school shooters. Andrew Golden shot five people, partly as a reaction against the disciplining actions of his teachers. Peter Langman claims that "the primary motivation [Golden] had for the attack was his anger at teachers" (Langman 2009, 24). This seems odd because Golden was seen as a well-behaved student who rarely required disciplining (Fast 2008, 43), so the discipline he received must not have been out of the ordinary in frequency or intensity. But when Mitchell Johnson was asked why the two boys attacked the school, he replied, "Andrew was mad at a teacher. He was tired of their crap" (Fast 2008, 47). The "crap" of the teachers in this case seems to be nothing more than the day-to-day practice of schooling in which teachers exercise authority and control over students.

Another possible example of the day-to-day use of force in education contributing to a school shooting incident is the case of Virginia Tech shooter, Seung-Hui Cho. On April 16, 2007, Seung-Hui shot and killed 32 individuals, professors, and students, and wounded 25 others. He was painfully shy, a loner who rarely talked. At 14, he was diagnosed with "selective mutism," which is the consistent inability to speak in selected social situations, particularly school. Those who suffer from selective mutism often have a deep-seated fear of embarrassment. In high school, Seung-Hui was given an exemption from oral presentations as part of an individualized education program (IEP), and with this accommodation he successfully earned his diploma. At Virginia Tech, however, he received no such accommodations. He was repeatedly placed in situations where he was forced to talk in front of others. The situation escalated during the fall of 2005 when he was enrolled in a creative writing course taught by the renowned writer Nikki Giovanni. The report from the Virginia Tech Review Panel states:

---

3 Keehn and Boyles (2015) offer an additional way of thinking about how this violence is expressed in schools, where commercialism in schools reduces student relationships to relations of consumers and commodity.

[Cho] wore reflector glasses and a hat pulled down to obscure his face. Dr. Giovanni reported to the panel that she would have to take time away from teaching at the beginning of each class to ask him to please take off his hat and please take off his glasses. She would have to stand beside his desk until he complied. ... Cho also was uncooperative in presenting and changing the pieces that he wrote. He would read from his desk in a voice that could not be heard. (Virginia Tech Review Panel 2007, 42)

This off-putting behavior, together with some violent writing, prompted Giovanni to demand that Seung-Hui be removed from her class, threatening to resign if he was not removed. Seung-Hui subsequently met with the chair of the English department and another faculty member, where he was asked to withdraw from the class and participate in personal tutoring. He interpreted this (correctly) as being "kicked out" of Giovanni's class. He reluctantly agreed, but after the conversation, he "appeared to be crying" (Virginia Tech Review Panel 2007, 50). In subsequent semesters, Seung-Hui had difficult encounters with other faculty members. The professors would demand that he remove his hat, that he speak up, and that he fully participate in discussions and group projects, or that he withdraw from their courses. Some faculty members reacted to his quiet personality with contempt, one of them claiming that his quietness was an attempt to manipulate his professors in order to get out of coursework (Virginia Tech Review Panel 2007, 50).

There are many examples, therefore, of Seung-Hui being forced to comply with the demands of those in power. He responded with his own show of force and many people were subsequently killed. It is important to point out that nothing that happened to him seems much different from what occurs in schools and universities every day, so it hardly counts as a criticism against the faculty of Virginia Tech. It is clear that educators at all levels have the ability to force students to speak, to demand that they remove hats and sunglasses, and to control what they say and when they say it. Whether they are a necessary evil of education or not, such commands send the message that schools are places dominated by the use of coercion and power. This sort of symbolic violence plays a role in investing the school with certain experiential meanings. Because schools are places of force, power, and imposition, they are places where displays of force and power are deemed as natural and appropriate. Because schools are places of symbolic violence, they are places where real violence can seem to be a logical fit.

Thwarted Expectations

It is too simplistic, however, to say that schools are interpreted as places appropriate for violence because of the day-to-day micro-aggressions and coercion that are experienced in them every day. There are not only these experiential meanings of schools, but also the aspirational meanings. We think the spell that schools sometimes cast over those contemplating violence has as much to do with the highest hopes and ideals we have for schools as it does with the flaws and shortcomings of actual schools. Schools are often experienced as places of force and coercion, to be sure, but they are also seen as places where students hope to find refuge, romance, and friendship. It is not just the disappointments of life that lead to violence, but the fact that those disappointments are framed against a backdrop of much higher ideals. This is a psychological experience that we are probably all familiar with: the pain of a letdown is intensified when expectations are high.

Schools are, first of all, places that we hope are geared toward the protection and nurturing of children and young people. And, in fact, many students do find a sort of refuge in schools. They find friends and mentors, teachers, administrators, and staff who care about them. Consider, for example, Naomi Nye's poem "Rain." In this poem, a teacher contemplates her supposed failure, that the only thing a student remembered from his year in her classroom was that "somebody tutched [him]/on the sholder." The teacher holds this up to the narrator of the poem as an example of her "wasted life" – this touch, after all, was all the third grader would remember! Looking at the words that the child had written, though, the narrator sees the letters as "houses in a landscape" where the child could "go inside" and "be safe," in spite of the rain clouds gathering outside (Nye 1999, 54). In school, the student had found at least one place of compassion and friendship in the face of what the reader imagines is a rather bleak life outside of school. The touch of a caring adult had transformed the school into a type of sanctuary. Of course, not all schools provide these experiences, perhaps even fewer after the dehumanizing educational reform efforts of recent years. Yet, it remains the case that we *want* schools to be these places.

This aspirational vision of schools as refuge creates an expectation: In school, you will find somebody who understands and cares. This is the hope that many bruised and battered children take with them to school. When this expectation is not met, however, what seems to follow is a deep sense of betrayal, a betrayal that turns to animus directed at the school community. School becomes an appropriate place for violence because it is the site of this betrayal of high expectations. The school promised refuge, it produced ostracism; it promised caring relationships, it produced cruelty; it promised the nurturing of individual potential, it produced stifling conformity.

Consider the case of Scott Pennington, a 17-year-old who in 1993 killed his teacher and a janitor, and took his English class hostage for 15 minutes. Pennington's mother was psychotic, his father physically abusive and distant. Pennington was slow to develop physically and talked with a stutter. He was teased mercilessly at school for his skinny body, thick glasses, and strange haircut. He was once seriously beaten when he accidently bumped into a student in a hallway. As an apparent beacon of hope in the story, Pennington was befriended by a caring teacher, Mrs. McDavid, a woman with a reputation for her devotion to her students. She even gave Pennington her unlisted personal telephone number. Here was the teacher, we might have hoped, that would give this battered student refuge. Mrs. McDavid, unfortunately, began to grow increasingly concerned about Scott's tortuous writing and self-loathing, but she did not seek help. Pennington was devastated when Mrs. McDavid later in the year gave him a "C" for his midterm grade, ruining, he thought, his chance for a college scholarship. He begged Mrs. McDavid to change his grade and she refused, sending Pennington into a downward spiral. Mrs. McDavid later became one of the two victims of Pennington's rampage. In this case, at least, it seems to us that it was not just the violence that Pennington endured from his peers; it was that he sensed hope and sanctuary in the school under the watchful eye of a caring teacher, and this hope was thwarted (Fast 2008, 28–30).

Expectations can be thwarted by school systems that do not live up to the idea of being a refuge where caring adults nurture students who are hurting. Schools also set expectations when it comes to peer relationships. They are seen as places to forge meaningful peer connections and friendships, and this expectation can often lead to bitter disappointment. The disappointment of being a social outcast is intensified because the school holds out the possibility of so much more. Schools not only promise friendship, but perhaps even more prominently, they are built up as places of hetero-sexual romance and sex. Think of the portrayals of schools in American television shows and movies, where social events and romance among students are central to the plot. In films like *Porky's* (Clark 1981) and *American Pie* (Weitz and Weitz 1999), young men fervently pursue the opposite sex in the interest of defining their sexuality. The plot of *American Pie* revolves around five friends making a pact to lose their virginity on prom night – and they are all successful. Both *Prom* (Nussbaum 2011) and *Pretty in Pink* (Deutch 1986) portray troubled romantic relationships between two students from different social classes. In each of these films the barriers of class are overcome when the students unite in a dramatic yet happy ending at a school dance. In his sociological analysis of Hollywood films about high school, Robert Bulman writes about the pro-tagonists in *Prom*: "They meet up, dance, and kiss in a stereotypically magical prom moment. As happens often in suburban school films, love conquers all" (Bulman 2004).

A central meaning of American schools, then, is that they are places to find love and sex. Reading the stories of shootings, there are many instances of male shooters who long for female companionship and then feel rejected. Schools hold this promise of romance in a way that shopping malls and soccer fields do not; therefore, schools become the site to express disappointment and bitterness.

In their book *Rampage: The Social Roots of School Shootings*, Katherine Newman and her coauthors describe the factors contributing to the Westside Middle School shooting near Jonesboro, Arkansas. One of the shooters, Mitchell Johnson, was driven by social frustration, anger, and fear. For example, Mitchell was "cut from the basketball team, dumped by his girlfriend" (Newman et al. 2004, 151). Mitchell and his partner, Andrew Golden (discussed previously), sensed that they had failed the school's tests of mascu-linity and were therefore destined to be outsiders in the social life of their small town. In other words, they sensed that they had lost the "status tournament of adolescence" (Newman et al. 2004, 271).

The idea that schools were places of romance resonated with Mitchell. According to Langman, Mitchell "developed two obsessions: girls and gangs" (Langman 2009, 108). Mitchell did well with girls, but his standards were very high. He tended to take his relationships with girls too seriously for his age, even discussing marriage with them. Even though Mitchell later denied it, a student reported that Mitchell had said that he was going to shoot all the girls who had broken up with him. According to a friend of Mitchell's victims, two of the victims were girls who had refused to go out with him. And a third victim, Candace, had broken up with him (Langman 2009, 110). Because school held the promise of romance and peer connection, the school was caught up in the disappointment of thwarted love and friendship, thereby becoming the appropriate place for violence. Newman and her coauthors write, "It is not coincidence that the boys used the school as the outlet for their anger. Schools are both the location of their social failures and the center of community life, not just for students but for everyone in [American] small towns" (Newman et al. 2004, 152).

Perhaps it is Columbine shooter Dylan Klebold who best exemplifies the explosive potential of thwarted expectations. Dylan seems to have clearly felt a sense of social isolation. He wrote in his journal that he must "go to school, be scared and nervous, hoping that people can accept [him]" (Cullen 2009, 174). He often felt that his peers did not accept him, which led to increasing bitterness. Such feelings made Dylan feel, in the words of author David Cullen, "cut off from humanity" (Cullen 2009, 174), as can be seen when Dylan writes in his journal, "My existence is shit" and "I don't fit in here" (Cullen 2009, 174–175). Dylan did not find the friends he wanted. The school offered hopes that people would "accept him" but did not deliver. Dylan also seemed to accept the idea that schools were places to forge romantic connections. Langman claims that Dylan's journal reveals a desperate fear of rejection and an obsession with finding true love, an observation echoed by Cullen (Langman 2009, 52; Cullen 2009, 174–175). Unfortunately, Dylan found success at this task of finding love in school to be elusive. He writes in his journal, "I don't know why I do wrong with people (mainly women) – it's like they are set out to hate and scare me," and "I know I can never have them" (Langman 2009, 53). On April 20, 1999, Dylan saw his school as the appropriate place to show his disappointment with the thwarted social promises of schooling, killing 12 students and a teacher at Columbine High School.

Schools as Stages for Individual Expression

The last piece of the puzzle has to do with specifically middle-class expectations for the role of the school. It surprises some people that many of these targeted shootings occur in otherwise peaceful rural or suburban environments. It is therefore possible to refine the question we are exploring here: What is it about *these* schools that make them seem like acceptable places for violence?

Robert Bulman (2004) makes the argument that high school films express the values of the suburban middle class. The middle class has the resources to access consumer entertainment on a mass scale. Hollywood therefore responds to, and perpetuates, the value structure of the middle class. Bulman notices that the value structure of the high school films he surveys often depends on the setting in which the film is placed. Films set in urban environments express a set of middle-class values that is different from films set in other environments. Urban school films champion what Bulman labels "utilitarian individualism," the view that individuals can get ahead socially and economically if they work hard and play by the rules. In urban school films, middle-class teachers descend on schools to impart suburban values to wild urban youths. Examples of these films include *Stand and Deliver* and *Blackboard Jungle* (Menéndez 1988; Brooks 1955).

Suburban films, in contrast, display a different value structure. Suburban films focus almost exclusively on the students. These films tell stories of suburban youths seeking to find and express themselves in the face of stultifying school rules, oppressive parents, uncaring teachers, and rigid social cliques – think of *The Breakfast Club* (Hughes 1985), *Ferris Bueller's Day Off* (Hughes 1986), or, more recently, *The Perks of Being a Wallflower* (Chbosky 2012). Instead of utilitarian individualism, you see championed the expressive individualism of Henry David Thoreau. High school is a journey about being true to yourself, resisting social pressure, and finding the "real you." The search for expressive individualism amid peer conformity and school authority is how the middle class understands the high school experience.

One particular focus of these high school films is how they engage with the notion of social cliques. The various groups in suburban high schools – jocks, nerds, preppies, druggies, and so forth – often play significant roles in advancing the suburban film narrative. Often students in suburban high school films come to find, construct, or express their own identities by resisting these social groups, or by forming friendships across different groups. This sort of reaction against social cliques frequently seems to play a role in how the shooters understand themselves. In suburban films, the hero students react against cliques and conformity, breaking down social barriers and asserting their individuality.

This same pattern can be seen in many suburban school shootings, where the violence is seen as an act of defiant self-expression (often a specifically masculine type of self-expression) against social groupings. The shooter uses violence to assert his individuality against oppressive cliques, rules, or authority figures. As Jonathan Fast writes, "adopting an *identity* that justifies or even glamorizes extreme violence as a way of righting the wrongs a child has endured offers an ameliorative way of thinking about previous indignities, as well as providing hope for the future" (Fast 2008, 152).[4]

There is an aspect of the shooter's personality that Fast believes can best be expressed in terms of violence. And because schools are then interpreted as appropriate places for individual expression – that is, as sites on which students can unveil a new personality – schools then become the site appropriate for violence. In this way, school shootings operate as existential statements, asserting a self in the middle of suburban conformity. The violence as expressive individualism can be seen in the publicity efforts that some school shooters undertake prior to their actions. For example, the expressive elements are evident in the Columbine shooters' production of their "basement tapes," and with Seung-Hui Cho, who "paused during his shooting in order to ship a press kit with photos, a DVD, and a document explaining his motives, to NBC news" (Fast 2008, 19). These students wanted people to know who they were and why they were going to start shooting.

One of the clearest examples of school violence serving as a stage for expressive individualism can be found in the case of Luke Woodham, who killed two students and wounded seven others on October 1, 1997. Luke was overweight, wore thick glasses, and was often teased. He would retreat into his room to read philosophy and write poetry. He believed himself to be a unique personality, writing in his journal that "no one would think like I did" (Fast 2008, 142). He fell in with a group of friends who were interested in violence and the occult, and who goaded him into committing increasingly serious crimes and acts of aggression, including the torture and murder of his family dog. On the day of his school shooting, he also beat and stabbed his mother, eventually suffocating her to death under a pillow. After her death, he left a sort of "manifesto" to the world. In it he describes his sense of being hated and ridiculed. He describes how his own identity had become constructed around hate: "I am the hate in every man's heart." This identity was about to be enacted on the expressive stage of the school. He urges his readers, "Live by your own rules ... Live your life in a bold new way. For you, dear friend, are a superman." He continues, "I am not insane. I am angry. The world shit on me for the final time. I am not spoiled or lazy, for murder is not weak and slow-witted. Murder is gutsy and daring" (Fast 2008, 156). With the shooting, Luke became the gutsy and

---

4 Fast's language of "adopting" an identity is a useful corrective here. It is not necessarily the case that school shooters have access to a singular, authentic inner identity, an identity that they then outwardly express through violence. It may be that the violence constructs an identity as much as exposes a pre-existing identity. The school, though, remains a stage on which one constructs an identity as much as a venue for expressing an identity.

daring superman that he believed existed inside him but that no one else seemed to recognize. The school became the place where he would show the world who he really was, where he would be true to the identity that he believed was full of hate.

In a school shooting at Heath High School in West Paducah, Kentucky, 14-year-old Michael Carneal killed three students and injured five more on December 1, 1997. Michael came from a family of highly successful people. His father was a high-profile lawyer, his mother was a stay-at-home mom who had some postgraduate education and his sister was valedictorian of her high school class and popular among her peers (Newman et al. 2004, 22). Michael was much less successful in his social journey than the rest of his family. In Michael's story, we see interaction with multiple school groups as he attempts to find his place on the social ladder. He tried hard to fit in with a fringe group (the Goths) by giving them stolen goods and by bringing a gun to school. Although he was teased sometimes at school for his strange antics, it seems that he did not shoot the people who made fun of him, but rather the people he envied. He targeted the socially and academically successful students, later acknowledging that he "envied the popularity of the students in the prayer group whom he shot" (Langman 2009, 150). Afterward, he described his reaction to the shooting, speaking of it as an expressive project: "I was feeling proud, strong, good, and more respected. I had accomplished something. I'm not the kind of kid who accomplishes anything. This is the only adventure I've ever had" (Newman et al. 2004, 6). Newman and her coauthors conclude, "In his mind, [the shooting] refuted the claims that he was weak or gay and provided definitive evidence that he could be every bit the man to the kids who had thrown him into lockers. As Michael put it, 'I thought maybe they would be scared and then no one would mess with Michael'" (152).

Violence as an act of expressive individualism can also be seen in the Columbine shooters, where we see a fixation on social cliques and groups that is characteristic of expressive individualism. Langman reports that, in his journals, Dylan Klebold did not complain about harassment or bullying, but expressed hostility toward the popular students because of their status. He wrote, "I see jocks having fun, friends, women, ALIVE," and "I hated the happiness that they [jocks] have"; he also noted that "others' achievements are tormentations" (Langman 2009, 53–54). During the shooting, Dylan and Eric Harris were said to target the "white hats," or jocks (even though it seems no "jocks" were actually killed).

Thus, in the Columbine shootings, we see the attempt to break free from social cliques and from suburban conformity. We also clearly see the idea that the violence was an attempt at self-expression. Eric and Dylan carefully prepared hours of videotape, explaining to the world why they had done what they had done, reveling in their preparations. In the basement tapes, there is much discussion of the legacy they wanted to leave through their violence. They "assure each other that their murderous rampage will endure in the daydreams and nightmares of the public," and they talk about "being ghosts who haunt the survivors" (Fast 2008, 202). They discuss their actions as moving them to a higher level of existence, their lives becoming "art," their killings a "masterpiece." Sociologist Ralph Larkin writes:

> [Eric Harris] seemed to be enthralled by the notoriety that they would receive. This appeared to be his major concern when talking with a journalist in a chat room about the Oklahoma City bombings. In the basement tapes, Klebold noted

that people would take notice at the time and date of the videotapes they were making. He also considered what movie director could best be trusted with the script of their story; Quentin Tarantino topped their list. They also wanted the story to have a lot of "dramatic irony." (Larkin 2007, 194)

The Columbine shooters' concern with individual expression is best exemplified by Eric, who was particularly bothered by the idea that his life, and his carnage, would be deemed "unoriginal" (Langman 2009, 33). Thus, he tried to distance what he had done from the actions of other school shooters who had preceded him: "Do not think," he says, "we're trying to copy anyone" (Gibbs and Roche 1999, 24). Columbine was to be his *individual* statement.

Eric's journals are filled with reflections about a part of himself buried deep inside that could only be expressed in terms of violence and dominance. He wrote, "My belief is that if I say something, it goes. I am the law, if you don't like it, you die" (Langman 2009, 142). But, as Langman points out, Eric knew that his peers did not perceive him as "the law." His position would have to be asserted by killing those who did not recognize his superiority, including boys who teased him and girls who rejected him. Eric wanted not only the school to know, but also the whole world to know, the true self that was inside. As he wrote in his journal, "HATE! I'm full of hate and I love it ... Yes I hate and I guess I want others to know it" (Larkin 2007, 135). Because suburban schools are deemed places of self-expression, the school became the place were Eric expressed the hate he found within himself.

Conclusion

We have moved toward an admittedly speculative response to the exegetical question of school shootings. We have analyzed the cultural meanings of American schools, using empirical data, everyday observations, films, and poetry, and we have tried to connect this analysis to the individual stories of school shooters. We conclude that schools are interpreted as places appropriate for violence because of the following three points of meaning:

1) Schools are already places of symbolic micro-aggression and coercion where force rules the day. Thus, they are places where the use of force seems natural and appropriate.
2) Schools are places where we invest hope in creating places of refuge, friendship, and romance. When these expectations are not met, resentment flows against schools.
3) Suburban schools are seen as places of "expressive individualism," where students react against social cliques and find out who they really are. For students who see themselves as having a violent identity, schools become appropriate places to express this identity.

Is there anything in this analysis that might provide guidance on how we can respond to school shootings?

With respect to the first meaning involving the prevalence of force, this analysis suggests that we make schools more student centered and less coercive. It suggests that the more tightly we try to *control* schools in order to make them safe, the less safe they may actually become. It may also be that certain educational reforms, such as intensive testing focused on externally imposed standards, intensify messages of coercion and control, therefore contributing to the interpretation of schools as places for violence. The focus on maximizing "instructional time" has led some schools to cut art, music, and physical education programs, and also to cut back on unstructured playtime, such as at recess (Center on Educational Policy 2007). As a result, some schools are lacking many of the activities that once made school intrinsically enjoyable, turning them less into places where students want to be and more into places where they are forced to be. With that, overemphasis on testing within subjects such as math, science, and reading might diminish the intrinsic value of academics for students. Perhaps academics themselves could offer refuge to students if they were not so coercive. One solution, then, might be to reverse some of these trends, reinstating those practices that make school intrinsically desirable places to be.

Metal detectors, video surveillance, and the like also support the message that schools are places of domination, power exertion, and control, amplifying the very message that leads some students to see violence as appropriate for schools. These technologies, while they are designed to increase student safety, by their very presence also signify that the environment is dangerous and insecure. The sense of place is destabilized, leading students to conclude that violent expressions are to be expected and anticipated. This leads to an odd quandary: Sure, we want to implement measures to help schools be safe, but those measures may also contribute to a school climate that encourages violence. There is, perhaps, no easy solution to this dilemma. One possible solution might involve embodying safety and security measures in forms that are less overtly present and controlling. For example, the problem with surveillance cameras is not that they are watchful – we want educators to be watchful, keeping an eye on students and making sure they are safe. The problem with surveillance cameras is that this surveillance and control is their *only* function (Warnick 2007). A watchful teacher might keep an eye on students, to be sure, but she may also smile at students, say hello, congratulate achievements, and share sorrow. The fact that the watchful teacher is not defined by watchfulness *alone* makes all the difference to how the security is experienced. The solution, then, might be to maintain watchfulness, but not in a way that defines the school environment as starkly about control and power.

With respect to the second point of meaning, there are at least two options. First, schools could try to better live up to the expectations that are placed upon them. This would mean that schools redouble their efforts to become places of refuge where troubled students can find caring adults and form authentic human relationships. Particularly promising are efforts to increase the conviviality and humaneness of American schools along the lines endorsed by the "small schools movement," a movement which holds that schools should be communities that are small enough to allow for a sense of connectedness among students and between students and teachers. The better teachers and students know one another, the greater the possibilities of refuge. We would strongly endorse this approach.

At the same time, though, if we redouble efforts to recreate schools as places of refuge, it might also serve to highlight and strengthen the high expectation that leads to bitterness and disappointment. For those students who do not find refuge in schools – and there will always be some, even with increased efforts at conviviality and humaneness – the distance between the now heightened expectation and their lived reality will be all the greater, perhaps contributing to increased rage against the school.

This suggests the second option, which would be to *lower* expectations for schools as places to find refuge and relationships. It is difficult to contemplate what such an approach might mean, and we, at least, would be reluctant to give up the idea that schools should provide refuge, connectedness, and friendship. The strategy of lowering expectations does make some sense, though, when it comes to expectations of romance. Is it really necessary, for example, for American high schools to focus on pairing up heterosexual couples through dances, proms, royal courts, and so forth? The educational rationale for such practices has never been clear, while the downsides have always been apparent to those that were paying attention -- the exclusion of outcasts, the glorification of physical beauty, and the official endorsement of schools as simply another vehicle in the adolescent quest for sex and romance. Such practices set an expectation that no school can live up to, and there is little reason to try. Perhaps the best solution to thwarted expectations, therefore, would be one that takes a mixed approach: redoubling efforts at making schools more caring and convivial, while de-emphasizing schools as places to find true love.

In order to do this, however, we might first need to address the role that American films and television play in perpetuating romantic and social expectations. These media sources elevate the importance of love and friendship for making meaning in schools. With that, the movies generally end happily: the unlikely romance is almost always forged, the uncool kid becomes popular, and the friendships between young people become an important source of fulfillment. While it is unlikely that we can change popular culture, perhaps schools should have a role in facilitating conversations with students regarding the myths perpetuated by the media.

Finally, with respect to the third point of meaning, the implications are perhaps even less clear. For one thing, we are not sure how to change the "cultural meaning" that American schools are stages for individual expression. For another, we are not certain that we should want to try. After all, this would imply that we stop thinking of schools in terms of Thoreauvian ideals, where students can find and express their authentic thoughts and feelings. One does not have to believe in the notion of a presocial, atomistic self to believe that schools should be places where students learn to think and act independently, to live life from the inside rather than have lives foisted upon them by social cliques, domineering educators, or consumer culture.

Rather than moving away from the idea that schools should be places of expressive individualism, perhaps schools should instead multiply alternative avenues for self-formation, giving students expressive tools that can be used in the place of gun violence. This might perhaps involve a renewed emphasis on art, music, and creative writing –precisely those subjects that are de-emphasized when placed in competition with the "tested subjects," like mathematics, science, and reading. Students who have not found acceptance in other dimensions of school life (in sports, proms, or academic work) have sometimes found refuge and expressive voice in these other subjects. Indeed, many of the school shooters have often been somewhat drawn toward the arts – many of them seemed to think of themselves as writers or film producers. More encouragement in this direction might have swayed students in this direction as an alternative to expressive violence.

Schools might also de-emphasize testing and reduce the feelings of coercion often attached to academic study. Not only could this serve to minimize the "micro-aggressive" ethos of schooling, it could also leave room for schools to provide more of the fodder for "expressive individualism." While this opens up more possibilities for students to find outlets to express themselves in healthy ways, it also might help redefine the meaning of schooling to include a more academic focus with less emphasis on unrealistic romantic aspirations. This, coupled with allowing students many different types of opportunities and formats for speaking, writing, and creating, might pull some troubled students back from the brink.

References

Brooks, Richard, dir. 1955. *Blackboard Jungle*. Video. 1:41:00 mins. USA: Metro-Goldwyn-Mayer. Theatre in Video.

Bulman, Robert C. 2004. *Hollywood Goes to High School: Cinema, Schools, and American Culture*. New York: Worth.

Center on Educational Policy. 2007. "Choices, Changes, and Challenges: Curriculum and Instruction in the NCLB Era." file:///C:/Users/user/Downloads/McMurrer_FullReport_CurricAndInstruction_072407.pdf (accessed December 7, 2015).

Chbosky, Stephen, dir. 2012. *The Perks of Being a Wallflower*. Video. 1:42:00 mins. California: Summit. Theatre in Video.

Clark, Bob, dir. 1981. *Porky's*. Video. 1:38:00 mins. California: 20th Century Fox. Theater in Video.

Cullen, David. 2009. *Columbine*. New York: Twelve.

Deutch, Howard, dir. 1986. *Pretty in Pink*. Video. 1:36:00 mins. California: Paramount Pictures. Theater in Video.

Dinkes, Rachel, Cataldi, Emily Forrest, Kena, Grace, and Baum, Katrina. 2006. *Indicators of School Crime and Safety*. Washington, DC: US Government Printing Office and US Departments of Education and Justice.

Fast, Jonathan. 2008. *Ceremonial Violence: A Psychological Explanation of School Shootings*. New York: Overlook Press.

Gibbs, Nancy and Roche, Timothy. 1999. "The Columbine Tapes." *Time International* 154(25), 24–36.

Hughes, John, dir. 1985. *The Breakfast Club*. Video. 97:00 mins. California: Universal. Theatre in Video.

Hughes, John. 1986. *Ferris Bueller's Day Off*. Video. 1:43:00 mins. California: Paramount. Theatre in Video.

Keehan, Gabriel and Boyles, Deron. 2015. "Sense, Nonsense, and Violence: Levinas and the Internal Logic of School Shootings." *Educational Theory* 65(4): 441–458. DOI: 10.1111/edth.12126.

Larkin, Ralph W. 2007. *Comprehending Columbine*. Philadelphia: Temple University Press.

Langman, Peter F. 2009. *Why Kids Kill: Inside the Minds of School Shooters*. New York: Palgrave Macmillan.

Menéndez, Ramón, dir. 1988. *Stand and Deliver. Video. 1:43:00 mins*. Burbank, CA: Warner Brothers. Theatre in Video.

National Center for Education Statistics. 2014. *Indicators of School Crime and Safety, 2013*. June. https://nces.ed.gov/pubs2014/2014042.pdf (last accessed October 24, 2017).

Newman, Katherine S., Fox, Cybelle, Roth, Wendy, Mehta, Jal, and Harding, David. 2004. *Rampage: The Social Roots of School Shootings*. New York: Basic Books.

Nye, Naomi Shihab. 1999. "Rain." In *Learning by Heart*, edited by Maggie Anderson and David Hassler, p. 21. Iowa: University of Iowa Press.

Nussbaum, Joe, dir. 2011. *Prom*. Video. 1:44:00 mins. California: Walt Disney Pictures. Theater in Video.

Sedensky, Stephen J. III. 2013. *Report of the State's Attorney for the Judicial District of Danbury on the Shootings at Sandy Hook Elementary School and 36 Yogananda Street, Newtown, Connecticut on December 14, 2012*. November 25, 2013. http://www.ct.gov/csao/lib/csao/Sandy_Hook_Final_Report.pdf (last accessed October 24, 2017).

Sue, Derald Wing. 2010. *Microaggressions in Everyday Life: Race, Gender, and Sexual Orientation*. Hoboken, NJ: John Wiley & Sons.

Virginia Tech Review Panel. 2007. "Mass Shootings at Virginia Tech, April 16, 2007." http://cdm16064.contentdm.oclc.org/cdm/ref/collection/p266901coll4/id/904 (last accessed October 24, 2017).

Vossekuil, Bryan, Fein, Robert A., Reddy, Marisa, Borum, Randy, and Modzeleski, William. 2002. *The Final Report and Findings of the Safe School Initiative: Implications for the Prevention of School Attacks in the United States*. Washington, DC: US Government Printing Office.

Warnick, Bryan. 2007. "Surveillance Cameras in Schools: An Ethical Analysis." *Harvard Educational Review* 77(3), 317–343.

Warnick, Bryan R., Johnson, Benjamin A., and Rocha, Samuel. 2010. "Tragedy and the Meaning of School Shootings." *Educational Theory* 60(3), 371–390. DOI: 101111/j.1741-5446.2010.00364.x.

Weitz, Chris and Weitz, Paul, dirs. 1999. *American Pie*. Video. 1:35:00. California: Universal. Theater in Video.

Wolceshyn, Glenn. 1997. "Socializing Students for Anarchy." *Los Angeles Times*, February 17. http://articles.latimes.com/1997-02-18/local/me-29990_1_social-harmony (last accessed October 24, 2017).

Zimmer, Paul. 1999. "Zimmer's Head Thudding against the Blackboard." In *Learning by Heart: Contemporary American Poetry about School*, edited by Maggie Anderson and David Hassler, p. 21. Iowa City: University of Iowa Press.

24

"Don't Feed the Trolls"

Violence and Discursive Performativity
Claudia W. Ruitenberg

Introduction

Over the past few years the media have reported on women being subjected to hateful, and specifically misogynistic, comments on social media. In these media reports, such comments are often described as a form of violence. For example, Brigit Katz (2015) writes that "'Taming the Trolls,' a panel at the Women in the World Summit, addressed a more pernicious brand of trolling – a variety that is vicious, violent, and flagrantly sexist" (par. 1). Mary Beard (about whom more later) refers to misogynistic comments made on the now defunct website Don't Start Me Off as "sexual violence" (in Day 2013, par. 22).

Concerns about abusive online comments targeting women have led to policy responses by state and national governments and supranational organizations. In 2015, US Congresswoman Katherine Clark wrote a letter asking "the Department of Justice to prioritize investigations and prosecutions of cyber abuse crimes targeting women" (Clark 2015, par. 1). In India, Bobins Abraham reports that, "taking note of the rise in complaints by women about online trolling, Women and Child Development Minister Maneka Gandhi has said the government is proposing it be considered as violence against women" (2016, par. 1). In addition, the Working Group on Broadband and Gender of the United Nations Broadband Commission for Digital Development released the report *Cyber Violence Against Women and Girls: A World-Wide Wake-Up Call* in September 2015. The report calls for "sensitization, safeguards and sanctions" to eliminate "cyber violence" against women and girls.

In this chapter, I examine the nature of the violence in misogynistic expressions on social media. After some preliminary conceptual clarifications, I discuss the cases of two women, Anita Sarkeesian and Mary Beard, who were subjected to misogynistic, violent comments on social media. I analyze these cases using the framework of injurious and insurrectionary speech offered by Judith Butler in her work on discursive performativity. In particular, I discuss the asymmetry between the singular focus on the woman's body in online violence and the invisibility of the perpetrator's body. Finally, I argue that Sarkeesian, Beard, and others who stand up publicly to misogynistic, violent expressions on social media offer a feminist public pedagogy.

The Wiley Handbook on Violence in Education: Forms, Factors, and Preventions, First Edition.
Edited by Harvey Shapiro.

Violence

The term "violence" has come to be used for everything from large- and small-scale physical violence – such as the wars that some of our students have fled and the school shootings that seem to occur with alarming regularity – to discursive and symbolic violence. Concern has been expressed that the expansion of the concept of violence to encompass less physical and visible forms risks erasing the differences in the kinds of violence that are inflicted and suffered. Catherine Ashcraft (2000) explains this dynamic in relation to the concept of "domestic violence":

> Because feminists attempted to frame oppressive behavior and its effects within this dominant paradigm – where violent forms of behavior are always more devastating than nonviolent forms – their only available rhetorical strategy for highlighting the seriousness of these often ignored behaviors was to define them also as violence. However, when abuse or violence are brandished as the only acceptable or the preferred ways to describe any form of domestic injustice, the terms are in jeopardy of being rendered meaningless. *If everything is violence, then nothing is.* (5, emphasis added)

It makes perfect sense, Ashcraft acknowledges, that feminists wanted to call attention to the serious harms done by controlling relationships, misogynistic language, and other forms of what she calls "domestic injustice," but the unfortunate result of the expansion of the scope of the term "violence" is that it risks trivializing acts that cause serious bodily harm or death by lumping them together with injurious speech acts and oppressive institutional structures.

Willem de Haan (2008) provides a comprehensive discussion of violence as what Walter Gallie (1956) has called an "essentially contested concept" (as cited in de Haan 2008). De Haan discusses the relative advantages and disadvantages of restrictive and inclusive conceptions of violence in particular contexts. He takes a pragmatic approach, focusing especially on what different conceptions of violence make visible or obscure in particular kinds of research: "Instead of trying to conclusively define the concept of violence[,] empirical researchers could consider the *costs and benefits* involved in holding a particular view on violence. This means that various concepts or definitions of violence are best ... evaluated for their suitability for coming to terms with a particular research problem" (2008, 37, emphasis in original).

For the purposes of this essay, which focuses on discursive violence and, in particular, written language about or directed at women in social media, I can use a conception of violence that is restricted to acts committed by human beings and that have effects on other human beings; I do not need to concern myself with questions of violence perpetrated or suffered by non-human animals or other entities. However, I need a conception of violence that is not restricted to physical violence and that accommodates discursive violence, without losing its capacity to distinguish between discursive acts that can be considered forms of violence and those that may be considered merely rude or annoying. For such a framework, I turn to Newton Garver's (1968) expansive conception of violence as any form of violation of the person, which is to say, a violation of the rights connected with being a person, specifically the right to one's body and the right to autonomy. Garver classifies violence into four categories "based on two criteria, whether the violence is personal or institutionalized, and whether the violence is overt or covert and quiet." Violence, then, can be personal and overt, institutionalized and overt, personal and covert, and institutional and covert. He also recognizes that there are "transition cases" that straddle the boundaries of these categories, such as when someone is threatened with, but not in that moment subject to, overt violence.

Joseph Betz (1997) has critiqued Garver's conception of violence, but I find his critique helpful precisely for showing why Garver's conception is reasonable and Betz's too narrow. Betz writes: "There is no psychological or covert violence, I would claim, except by analogy and extension, simply because all violence is necessarily and by conventional definition overt or physical ... Violence is properly and in its paradigm uses a physical and not a psychological notion" (1997, 432). The problem with Betz's critique is that it relies on a strict and untenable separation of mind and body; for Betz, the only thing that seems to matter is the entry point of the act that is under consideration for the label "violence": if the act is received in the mind, even if it has effects on the body, it is not violence; if it is received in the body, even if it has effects on the mind, it is violence:

> That the force involved in violence is physical means that it affects bodies, however subtly. Ridicule can defeat one's aim to be happy, and fraud can violate one's right to hold property; but neither involves forces which impinge on its victim's body, and so neither is violent. Doing "psychological violence" to a person would be something like pushing his soul down the steps: there is a category mistake involved in both ways of speaking. Violence occurs to living bodies which, of course, behave in ways we call psychological and are explained through the notion of the soul; but what affects the psyche directly and not through the body, though it may be wrong, is not violence. (Betz 1997, 345)

Betz does not acknowledge that words can inflict both short-term and long-term trauma that may not be immediately visible in the way that a stab from a knife or a gun shot breaks the skin, but whose symptoms may be just as physical, including a rise in blood pressure, a surge of adrenaline, nausea, and insomnia. That mind and body affect each other is not a "category mistake."

While I want to acknowledge different kinds of violence and do not equate the threat of physical violence with an act of physical violence, I object to the tidy separation of physical and discursive violence evident in the adage "sticks and stones can break my bones but words can never hurt me." As I hope will become clear through this chapter, while words themselves may be immaterial, they have distinctly material effects. I approach the question of the nature of violence of misogynistic online expressions from a poststructuralist perspective of language as discourse, that is, as *a practice that systematically forms the objects of which it speaks* (Foucault 2002, 54). The material effects of discourse accrue over time, through repetition and recirculation. As will be evident in both of the cases I discuss, the violence of which these women speak involved a large volume of comments in which similar words and images were repeated over and over.

Beatrice Hanssen (2000) underscores that it should be understood that the framework of "discursive violence" is a poststructuralist one. Considering the violence that language-conceived-as-discourse can do also entails a critique of the very conception of language-as-neutral-medium that tends to underpin the liberal defense of free speech (2000, 159–160). As I have written elsewhere, "if the concept of performativity is about what words do, it is important to note that words don't just do things, in the sense that they perform actions, but that words do things *to people*, that is, they affect people" (Ruitenberg 2015, 48). As Butler (1997) tries to work through the differences between injurious speech and physical injury, differences that are more nuanced than Betz's simple binary between the psychological and the physical, she writes: "Certain words or certain forms of address not only operate as threats to one's physical well-being, but there is a strong sense in which the body is alternately sustained and threatened through modes of address" (5).

Trollers, Bullies, and Haters

There is no single definition of trolling. Some define it as a particular subset of online communication that is characterized not only by a desire to disrupt, provoke, or offend but also by the person pretending to be, or pretending to want to be, a member of the group. Claire Hardaker (2010), for example, writes: "A troller is a CMC [computer-mediated communication] user who constructs the identity of sincerely wishing to be part of the group in question, including professing, or conveying pseudo-sincere intentions, but whose real intention(s) is/are to cause disruption and/or to trigger or exacerbate conflict for the purposes of their own amusement" (237). Jonathan Bishop (2013) defines trolling more generally as "the posting of messages via a communications network that are intended to be provocative, offensive or menacing" (28) and further specifies the offensive kind of trolling as "flame trolling" (29). Emma Alice Jane (2012) has coined the term "e-bile" to identify the discursive genre of flame trolling as an object of rhetorical study.

In a document prepared for students and parents, Redcliffe State High School in Australia (n.d.) provides a further useful distinction between online bullying and online trolling:

> Trolling is often performed by a person without a clear relationship to their intended recipient. Their goal in posting the offensive material is often to provoke a reaction … Cyber-bullying, on the other hand, will usually involve people that are known to each other although the person bullying may seek to hide their identity. There is also a clear intention to cause harm or intimidate their recipient.

Indeed, as will be clear in the cases I discuss, the people who engaged in misogynistic expressions targeting Sarkeesian and Beard did not know their targets personally.

While the idea that "trolls should not be fed" and phrases such as "don't feed the trolls" are common, some scholars have suggested that the more accurate term for a person who trolls is not a "troll" but a "troller." Hardaker, in her analysis of references to trolls and trolling in nine years of interactions on the unmoderated newsgroup rec. equestrian, "distinguishes between the 'troller' (the person), 'troll' (the message) and 'trolling' (the act)" (2010, 239). Bishop (2013) also refers to those who engage in trolling as "trollers." Those whose engage in particularly hateful kinds of flame trolling and "go out of their way to bully a specific target" (2013, 29) can be referred to as "hater trollers."

In this chapter, I will follow the usage of "troller" for a person who does not know their target personally but engages in trolling in the broader sense as defined by Bishop; I will limit my discussion to hater trollers who target women. Mantilla (2013) argues that "it is worth naming specifically misogynist variants [of flame trolling] as 'gendertrolling'" and lists the following common characteristics: the participation, often coordinated, of numerous people; gender-based insults; vicious language; credible threats; unusual intensity, scope, and longevity of attacks; reaction to women speaking out. Jane (2013) summarizes the key features of gendertrolling or misogynistic "e-bile" as follows: "they target a woman who is, for one reason or another, visible in the public sphere; their authors are anonymous or otherwise difficult to identify; their sexually explicit rhetoric includes homophobic and misogynist epithets; they prescribe coerced sex acts as all-purpose correctives; they pass scathing, appearance-related judgments and they rely on ad hominem invective" (2013, 560)

Citing Injurious Speech

Before I consider each of the cases in turn, I want to speak to the dilemma I faced in recounting the events. On one hand, I wanted to provide as much detail as possible so as not to sugarcoat the discourse that was circulated nor lose its specificity. Jane (2013), for example, argues that misogynist "e-bile" should be quoted verbatim because "a less explicit and more polite way of discussing e-bile may have the unintended consequence of both hiding from view its distinct characteristics and social, political and ethical upshots, and even blinding us to its existence and proliferation" (558). On the other hand, I wanted to be mindful of Butler's (1997) caution that discussions of hate speech, including critical discussions, tend to recirculate that hate speech. About proposals to regulate hate speech, for example, she writes that these "invariably end up citing such speech at length, offering lengthy lists of examples, codifying such speech for regulatory purposes, or rehearsing in a pedagogical mode the injuries that have been delivered through such speech. It seems that the repetition is inevitable, and that the strategic question remains, what best use is to be made of repetition?" (1997, 37).

When it comes to injurious speech, the insistence on the difference between using language and mentioning it, discussed so extensively in analytic philosophy (see, for example, Searle 1969) rings hollow; rehearing or rereading in a different context, such as a media report or scholarly article, words that were injurious in their original context is not equally injurious, but the harm that was done is reawakened, remembered, relived. Mentioning injurious speech by citing it is thus also a form of use, and it has effects beyond simply referring to the original use.

However, in our digital age it has become a common strategy to retweet or otherwise recirculate an offensive message one has received. One of the purposes of doing so is to expose and shame the sender and show exactly what kind of graphic detail one has been subjected to. When the message is recirculated as a screenshot, a second purpose is to archive the message in case the sender deletes it. In the case of specific threats, the archive can also be turned over to the authorities for investigation. Both Sarkeesian and Beard archived and exposed some of the messages they received. In this chapter, I will mostly describe the types of claims and threats made in gendertrolling, with occasional direct quotation of particular messages.

Anita Sarkeesian

The first case is that of Anita Sarkeesian, a Canadian-American media critic, who was also a participant on the panel "Taming the Trolls" I mentioned in my introduction. Sarkeesian became the target of misogynistic abuse in 2011 after proposing and raising funds for a "5-video series ... entitled Tropes vs Women in Video Games, exploring female character stereotypes throughout the history of the gaming industry" (Sarkeesian 2012a). She raised enough funds for this five-video series in 24 hours, and subsequently successfully raised funds for additional videos. However, she also became the subject of an extensive gendertrolling campaign. Sarkeesian (2012b) posted some of the comments she received on her website Feminist Frequency and wrote:

> Here is a very small sample of the harassment I deal with for daring to criticize sexism in video games. Keep in mind that all this is in response to my Kickstarter project for a video series called *Tropes vs. Women in Video Games* (which I have not even made yet) ... In addition to the torrent of misogyny and hate left on my YouTube video ... the intimidation effort has also included repeated vandalizing of the Wikipedia page about me (with porn), organized efforts to flag my YouTube videos as "terrorism," as well as many threatening messages sent through Twitter, Facebook, Kickstarter, email and my own website. These messages and comments have included everything from the typical sandwich and kitchen "jokes" to threats of violence, death, sexual assault and rape.

Sarkeesian did not retreat and continued to speak out against sexist bias in video games, and now against gendertrolling. For example, in December 2012 she gave a TEDxWomen talk in Washington, DC, which by July 2016 had been viewed more than 560,000 times.

In 2014, she became caught up in "Gamergate," named after the Twitter hashtag #gamergate, in which several women active in the video game industry were targeted with misogynistic e-bile. On August 27, 2014, Sarkeesian tweeted via her Twitter handle Feminist Frequency: "I usually don't share the really scary stuff. But it's important for folks to know how bad it gets [TRIGGER WARNING]." The tweet included a screen-shot of a sample of tweets from one particular gendertroller, often sent less than a minute apart. The troller's tweets include explicit rape and death threats.

Sarkeesian has remained a prominent critic of the inadequate response of social media platforms to the abuse they facilitate. Later in the chapter I discuss how, because of her refusal to back down, her exposure of the abusive comments, and her frequent public lectures and participation on panels addressing misogynistic trolling, Sarkeesian's contributions can be regarded as public pedagogy.

Mary Beard

The second case is that of Mary Beard, a British professor of Classics at Cambridge University, who has also worked with BBC Radio and BBC Television on historical documentaries and other broadcasts. After appearing on the BBC's *Question Time* on January 18, 2013 and raising critical questions about whether immigrants really were straining public services in Lincolnshire the way some people claimed they were, she became the target of a torrent of misogynistic online comments. She discussed the experience in a post on her blog *A Don's Life* on January 27, 2013: "My appearance on *Question Time* prompted a web post that has in the last few days discussed my pubic hair (do I brush the floor with it), whether I need rogering (that comment was taken down, as was the speculation about the capaciousness of my vagina, and the plan to plant a d*** in my mouth)" (Beard 2013a). Like Sarkeesian, Beard did not back down; she exposed the comments and spoke frankly about the experience to various media. But beyond that, she has corresponded and met with some of her trollers. Rebecca Mead (2014) reports:

> Beard retweeted a message that she had received from a twenty-year-old university student: "You filthy old slut. I bet your vagina is disgusting." One of Beard's followers offered to inform the student's mother of his online behavior; meanwhile, he apologized. ... The university student, after apologizing online, came to Cambridge and took Beard out to lunch; she has remained in touch with him, and is even writing letters of reference for him. "He is going to find it hard to get a job, because as soon as you Google his name that is what comes up," she said. "And although he was a very silly, injudicious, and at that moment not very pleasant young guy, I don't actually think one tweet should ruin your job prospects."

Both through this direct one-on-one education and through her media engagement more generally, Beard has offered a feminist public pedagogy, an argument I will take up in the final section of this chapter.

Violence and the Body in Gendertrolling

What are the distinctive characteristics of misogynist online discourse that qualify it as violence? One of the characteristics is the anonymity of the hater troller, who typically sends or posts messages under a Twitter handle or other pseudonym. However, the absence of the troller's real name is not, by itself, sufficient for explaining the violence. After all, as Foucault (1984) argued in the context of scholarly and other literature, the name of the author is a way of categorizing text; the author's name does not have to coincide with, and is not reducible to, a person. Writing under a pseudonym, then, is not inherently violent. The target of gendertrollers can refer to and, if she wishes, respond to these trollers via their Twitter handle or pseudonym. More than anonymity is at stake in understanding the violence done.

The second characteristic is that there is often a significant inequality between the overwhelming volume of utterances by multiple hater trollers and the single target. For example, Sarkeesian (2012b) reported receiving more than a hundred comments within a two-hour period of posting the video to launch her Kickstarter fundraising, and thousands of messages and comments overall. Now, consider the difference between the cases I have described above and the hypothetical case of an academic who publishes an article in an academic journal that sparks strong opposition. Multiple critical responses and letters to the editors ensue, and we can imagine even a whole special issue dedicated to discussing why the author is wrong. We would not consider the chorus of opponents "hater trollers." Why not? One of the reasons is that, presumably, the editor of the journal filters out ad hominem attacks. The academic disputes may be fierce, but they should take aim at the arguments, the research methodology, the presuppositions, and other legitimate targets. By contrast, hater trollers by definition take aim at the person. In the case of misogynistic trollers, the aim is often the woman's *body*.

There is, then, a marked contrast between the focus on the body in the discourse of trollers and the absence of a traceable body of the troller himself. The reference to the body persists in these online environments. There is a stark inequality of vulnerability between the embodied victim, whose body is at the center of unwanted attention, and the disembodied troller. It matters not that the troller, as author, uses a pseudonym, but it does matter that this pseudonym hides the embodied person, while the woman is targeted as named and embodied subject.

Misogynistic hater trollers tend to describe in graphic detail the kinds of rape, mutilation, and even murder they would like to, or promise to, inflict on the victim's body. They write about the kinds of objects they will use to rape the woman, about the various orifices they want to penetrate, both before and after murdering the woman, and about the body parts they would like to cut off. So, while those who defend gender-trolling as free speech might argue that they are "only" using words and that words can't do "real" harm, the crux is that these words almost invariably make reference to the body. The hater troller uses the real name of the victim and sometimes the victim's home address or other details of her embodied life, and threatens her physical safety, while remaining anonymous and disembodied.[1]

As I have argued above, this sustained violent discourse *about* the body also has an effect *on* the body. The violence described by the words is not inflicted on the body, and a distinction between, for example, being raped and being threatened with rape must certainly be maintained, but this does not mean that the words themselves do not inflict their own violence. TV critic Maureen Ryan (2014) illustrates this vividly when she describes her body's response to the misogynistic comments she received:

> *This abuse doesn't happen "online."* It happens in the real world, to a person. It happens to a human being's heart and mind and body. The other day I tweeted a screenshot of an email I got from someone who was angry about something I'd written about the TV show "Stalker." In the first few moments after reading that email, my heart raced. Blood pounded in my ears. My mind blanked. I found it hard to focus on what I'd been doing a minute before. I wondered what other thoughts lurked in this person's mind. I wondered what people who can say things like that are capable of doing in the real world. These questions do not stay "online." These doubts and fears take root in your head and your gut, and get between you and the goals you want to accomplish.

---

1 The publicizing of a person's home address is known as "doxxing." Sarkeesian was "doxxed" in August 2014 when a Twitter user using the name Kevin Dobson posted death threats with Sarkeesian's address information. Sarkeesian posted: "I'm safe. Authorities have been notified. Staying with friends tonight. I'm not giving up. But this harassment of women in tech must stop!"

Writing about the comments that targeted Beard, Day (2013) writes that "the experience has had a lasting impact on Beard, who says it left her feeling 'a sense of assault'. She reeled from it as though from 'a punch'" (par. 8).

Butler (1997) writes that linguistic injury is in some ways unlike physical injury, which is why we often use similes or other tropes. Day (2013) uses the phrase "*as though* from a punch," indicating that Beard was not physically punched, and Butler quotes Charles Lawrence III describing how being subjected to racist speech is "*like* receiving a slap in the face" (as cited in Butler 1997, 4, emphasis added). However, there is more than a metaphorical connection between discursive and physical violence. As I have discussed, the repeated reference to the body and the body's vulnerability in misogynist discursive violence also affects the body. Butler recognizes: "that physical metaphors seize upon nearly every occasion to describe linguistic injury suggests that this somatic dimension may be important to the understanding of linguistic pain" (1997, 4–5).

Butler is cautious not to exaggerate the similarity between discursive and physical violence, because she is concerned about the effects it would have on the victim's agency to argue that the words themselves perform linguistic injury. In order to explain this concern, I now turn to the nature of linguistic performance via illocutionary and perlocutionary performative discursive acts.[2]

Violence as Illocutionary and Perlocutionary Effect

Should the violence done by misogynist e-bile be considered an illocutionary or perlocutionary effect? This question echoes Butler's examination of hate speech in her 1997 book *Excitable Speech*. The distinction between illocutionary and perlocutionary utterances was made by J.L. Austin (1962); Butler's uptake of the distinction shows the political significance of the distinction. As I have explained elsewhere, "illocution refers to the performance of an act *in* saying something; and perlocution refers to the performance of an act *by* saying something. For example: *in* saying 'I'm getting married!' the girl announced her engagement (illocution); *by* saying 'I'm getting married!' she dashed the hopes of a former lover (perlocution)" (Ruitenberg 2015, 40).

Butler (1997) puts it thus: "the illocutionary speech act is itself the deed that it effects; the perlocutionary merely leads to certain effects that are not the same as the speech act itself" (3). In other words, the illocutionary speech act, under given social conventions, inevitably performs a certain act, as the act is, according to those social conventions, inherent in the very phrase uttered. By contrast, whether the perlocutionary speech act can be said to have performed an act is more contingent on variable circumstances. Referring back to the example above, *in* saying "I'm getting married!" the girl inevitably announced her engagement under the social convention that "engagement" means a couple's decision to get married; however, whether or not she dashed the hopes of a former lover *by* saying "I'm getting married!" is much less certain: perhaps she had no former lover, or none who had any interest in marrying her.

The distinction between illocutionary and perlocutionary effects is, thus, quite straightforward; deciding to which category to ascribe the kind of cyber violence I have

---

2 For a further discussion of the expansion of "speech act" to "discursive act," see Ruitenberg (2015).

been recounting is considerably more difficult. Butler explains the political significance of this distinction, specifically in the context of the United States, with its firm protections of free speech:

> legal precedents for the curtailment of "speech," broadly construed, are supported by the use of the illocutionary model of hate speech. The firmer the link is made between speech and conduct, however, and the more fully occluded the distinction between felicitous and infelicitous acts, the stronger the grounds for claiming that speech not only produces injury as one of its consequences, but constitutes an injury in itself, thus becoming an unequivocal form of conduct. ... [If] "speech" ... can be fully subsumed under conduct, then the first Amendment is circumvented. (1997, 23)

Butler's concern is with the way in which the collapse between speech and conduct in the case of the illocutionary utterance seems to reduce the agency of the person subjected to such hate speech. If a particular type of speech is considered inherently injurious, the person subjected to that speech cannot claim not to have been injured. One of the discursive genres in which this discussion arises is pornography, and Butler opposes the American legal scholar Catharine MacKinnon, who has argued that pornography is a discursive form of subordination of women and should be banned as hate speech. Butler notes that, "significantly, MacKinnon's argument against pornography has moved from a conceptual reliance on a perlocutionary model to an illocutionary one" (1997, 18).

Returning to the cases of misogynist online discourse I have discussed, it would appear that, on one hand, to argue that a certain utterance has illocutionary violent effects denies the possibility of insurrectionary speech, of speaking back, and the troller not autonomously deciding on victimization. On the other hand, to argue that the violent effects of an utterance are perlocutionary suggests that they are contingent on the recipient, who could also "choose" not to feel hurt.

I agree with Butler when she questions:

> the presumption that hate speech always works, not to minimize the pain that is suffered as a consequence of hate speech, but to leave open the possibility that its failure is the condition of a critical response. If the account of the injury of hate speech forecloses the possibility of a critical response to that injury, the account confirms the totalizing effects of such an injury. (1997, 19)

The effects of misogynist e-bile are not totalizing, and insurrectionary speech is always possible. However, I disagree with Butler that this means such discourse should be considered perlocutionary. Illocutionary discursive acts are not as totalizing as Butler makes them out to be.

Butler writes that understanding hate speech as illocutionary means that we understand hate speech as *performing injury*, but that is not necessarily the case: I see hate speech of the kind I have discussed in this chapter as performing *violence*, which is not the same as saying it performs *injury*. "Violence" is a description of the act and, using Garver's (1968) conception of violence I discussed earlier in this chapter, violence by definition involves a violation of the person or her rights; "injury," however, might better be reserved for a description of the further effects of that violence and violation on the subject. My claim that hate speech (or hateful discursive acts more generally) performs *violence* echoes the term used by Lawrence and colleagues in the opening line of *Words That Wound*: "This is a book about assaultive speech, about words that are used as weapons to ambush, terrorize, wound, humiliate, and degrade" (1993, 1). My claim that certain discursive acts constitute *violence* in an illocutionary manner echoes their claim that certain discursive acts constitute *assault* in an illocutionary manner, as "assault" is a description of the act, not its further effects. I can draw a parallel here with the illocutionary category of the threat. Certain utterances have the illocutionary force of constituting a threat. If I say to someone, "If you don't pay me that money back, I will beat you up," then that constitutes a threat. Whether that threat has the perlocutionary effect of actually frightening the person to whom I say this depends on a host of other factors, including that person's assessment of my credibility, their access to friends who can protect them, and so forth. Even if my threat does not end up frightening the person but, for instance, angers them instead, it no less constitutes a threat; the act does not, however, inherently produce fear in the target.

We can thus maintain that discursive violence is illocutionary *and* that the subject of this violence is agentic. Accounting for the injury of hate speech as violence, and thus accounting for hate speech as illocutionary utterance, does not foreclose the possibility of a critical response. The gendertrollers who targeted Sarkeesian and Beard committed acts of violence; that is, *in* sending the misogynist messages they sent, they subjected Sarkeesian and Beard to violence. However, both Sarkeesian and Beard show that being subjected to discursive violence does not confirm the "totalizing effects" of this violence. They clearly experienced the misogynist message *as* violence – and not, for example, as a joke; Beard (2013a) writes on her blog: "the whole 'cunt' talk and the kind of stuff represented by the photo on right is more than a few steps into sadism." However, Sarkeesian, Beard, and other women who stood up to gendertrollers did not in any way lose their ability to provide a critical response.

Butler (1997) writes: "I am not opposed to any and all regulations, but I am skeptical about the value of those accounts of hate speech that maintain its illocutionary status and thus conflate speech and conduct completely" (102). By contrast, I see value in an account of some forms of gendertrolling that sees these as performing violence as illocutionary effect. I say "some forms" because I would not go as far as to classify all individual messages by gendertrollers as performing violence in this illocutionary sense. The messages that Sarkeesian, Beard, and other women who have been the targets of gendertrolling have received can be a strange mixture of what appear to be plain (though likely still unwelcome) expressions of desire, violent rape and mutilation fantasies, and direct threats. Just as I disagree with MacKinnon that all pornography constitutes hate speech but agree that some does, I would say that not all messages by gendertrollers constitute violence, but some do. It seems to me unequivocal that "I'll ram a tire iron up your cunt," to give one graphic example from the messages Sarkeesian received and archived via screenshot, or "I'm going to cut off your head and rape it," to give an example of the e-bile Beard received (as cited in Mead 2014), perform misogynistic violence.

At the same time, I wonder if, on this point, the line between illocutionary and perlocutionary effects blurs. Surely even those who do not want to classify the misogynist e-bile as "violence" and who consider the pain experienced by Sarkeesian and

Beard a perlocutionary effect recognize that this pain is a *conventional* response to this type of discourse. I would argue that it is, in fact, hard to imagine how a person would *not* suffer ill effects, including physical ill effects, of hundreds or, in Sarkeesian's case, thousands, of threats, graphically violent images, and descriptions of rape and mutilation. If discursive violence is seen as perlocutionary, it can still be seen as constituting violence when it has many of the same features of conventionality that illocutionary utterances do.

After all, the patterns of misogynistic discursive violence in a social context make its effects if not wholly predictable, then certainly not idiosyncratic; these patterns are very similar to the "convention" category Austin uses for illocutionary effects. The patterns – a word that really does not do justice to the numbing repetitiveness – of gendertrolling reflect and amplify a pre-existing and "conventional" sexism that the trollers did not invent. Jane (2013) writes, "one of the most striking characteristics of e-bile is its interchangeability" (565). The same kinds of slurs, the same kinds of rape and mutilation threats, the same kind of outrage at women speaking at all rather than remaining silent gives e-bile what Jane calls a "quasi-algebraic quality" (565).

The Public Pedagogy of Insurrectionary Speech

Regardless of whether misogynist online discourse is considered illocutionary or perlocutionary, Sarkeesian, Beard, and others (Caroline Criado-Perez, Stella Creasy, Jessica Valenti, Brianna Wu, Randi Harper, and unfortunately the list goes on) show clearly that being its subject does not involve losing one's agency. They engaged in what Butler (1997) calls "insurrectionary speech," which she describes as "the necessary response to injurious language, a risk taken in response to being put at risk, a repetition in language that forces change" (163). Sarkeesian and Beard took risks in response to being put at risk, archived and recirculated the language that had violated them, and by doing so forced a conversation about the responsibility of social media platforms in regulating hater trollers.

In the final section of this chapter, I want to argue that the very psychic survival of these women – the fact that they speak and speak back at, their sheer refusal to go away or shut up – offers a resistant, feminist public pedagogy. In order not to exacerbate the "consternation" of Sandlin, O'Malley, and Burdick (2011) and other public pedagogy scholars "with the widespread practice of authors citing the term without adequately explicating its meaning, its context, or its location within differing and contested articulations of the construct" (339), let me indicate briefly how my claims about Sarkeesian's and Beard's feminist public pedagogy relate to existing public pedagogy scholarship. Sandlin et al. provide a typology of five kinds of public pedagogy to add some nuance and specificity to the very broad understanding of public pedagogy as all "educational activity and learning in extrainstitutional spaces and discourses" (2011, 338). My discussion of the feminist public pedagogy offered by Sarkeesian and Beard fits squarely in the category of public pedagogy through "popular culture and everyday life" (343) and, in particular, the intersection of "feminist constructions" of popular culture (343) and the understanding of "popular culture as a terrain of contestation" (347). Put more simply: both Sarkeesian and Beard use popular culture as an "extrainstitutional educational space and discourse" but also critique popular culture for its facilitation of sexism and misogyny.

In Sarkeesian's case, the gendertrolling began in response to an explicitly educational project, namely a series of videos intended to "explore, analyze and deconstruct some of the most common tropes and stereotypes of female characters in games" and "highlight the larger recurring patterns and conventions used within the gaming industry" (Sarkeesian 2012a). Since then, she has used other popular media, such as her blog, Twitter, and the TEDxWomen talk available from YouTube, not only to call attention to but also to analyze and critically discuss gendertrolling and the persistent sexism in the video game industry. In the TEDxWomen talk, for example, she uses "the analogy of an MMO (Massively Multiplayer Online Game) to explain how these types of large scale harassment campaigns operate" (Sarkeesian 2012c).

Beard's case is a little different, in that her main career is as a Cambridge scholar and educator, which means she also engages in the formal pedagogy of university education. Her ongoing contact with university students gave her a different motivation for taking on the e-bile. As Mead (2014) describes:

> Beard's object is not simply to embarrass offenders; it is to educate women. Before social media, she argues, it was possible for young women like those she teaches at Cambridge to enjoy the benefits of feminist advances without even being aware of the battles fought on their behalf, and to imagine that such attitudes are a thing of the past. Beard says, "Most of my students would have denied, I think, that there was still a major current of misogyny in Western culture."

In addition to her formal teaching, Beard also used her blog and spoke with various news media to discuss her experience with gendertrolling. Connecting her scholarly expertise in Classics and her personal experience, she gave a 2014 London Review of Books Winter Lecture entitled "Oh Do Shut Up Dear! Mary Beard on the Public Voice of Women: Language and Misogyny." The audio recording of the lecture and its full transcript are available online, thus supplementing her public pedagogy in the semi-formal setting of the British Museum (where the lecture took place) with the online platforms of the London Review of Books and the BBC. Beard has continued to use Twitter, and has commented on the medium: "if people say to me, why dont I just get out of the sphere if I dont like some of the harrassment; why do I spend time pointing it out or complaining? Then my answer is likely to be that we dont tend to respond to playground bullies, by leaving the bullies in charge of the playground" (Beard 2013b, absence of apostrophes in original).

Finally, Sarkeesian and Beard's sheer audacity to be educated women who are public intellectuals, and who refuse to shut up or go away, is not an insignificant part of the public pedagogy they offer. The value of their public pedagogy lies not just in what they teach but also in the fact that they have stuck around in public media and popular culture to teach. Their example does not teach others *how* to survive; that would be too simple an assumption, as each gendertrolling campaign and the circumstances of each victim are different, and victims should not be blamed for not learning Sarkeesian's and Beard's "lessons" on how to respond. However, their ongoing presence in public media and popular culture shows *that* it is possible to survive.

References

Abraham, B. 2016. "Maneka Gandhi Wants Trolling of Women Online Be Considered as Violence." *India Times*, May 18. http://www.indiatimes.com/news/india/maneka-gandhi-wants-trolling-of-women-online-be-considered-as-violence-255267.html (last accessed October 24, 2017).

Ashcraft, C. 2000. "Naming Knowledge: A Language for Reconstructing Domestic Violence and Systemic Gender Inequity." *Women and Language* 23(1), 3–10.

Austin, J.L. 1962. *How to Do Things with Words*. Oxford: Oxford University Press.

Beard, M. 2013a. "Internet Fury: Or Having Your Anatomy Dissected Online." *A Don's Life*, January 27. www.the-tls.co.uk/internet-fury-or-having-your-anatomy-dissected-online (last accessed November 2, 2017).

Beard, M. 2013b. "Why Tweet?" *A Don's Life*, September 13. www.the-tls.co.uk/why-tweet (last accessed November 2, 2017).

Betz, J. 1977. "Violence: Garver's Definition and a Deweyan Correction." Ethics 87(4), 339–351.

Bishop, J. 2013. "The Effect of De-individuation of the Internet Troller on Criminal Procedure Implementation: An Interview with a Hater." *International Journal of Cyber Criminology* 7(1), 28–48.

Butler, J. 1997. *Excitable Speech: A Politics of the Performative*. New York: Routledge.

Clark, K. 2015, March 10. "Clark Calls for Investigation and Prosecution Oo Online Threats against Women." http://katherineclark.house.gov/index.cfm/2015/3/clark-calls-for-investigation-and-prosecution-of-online-threats-against-women (last accessed October 24, 2017).

Day, E. 2013. "Mary Beard: I Almost Didn't Feel Such Generic, Violent Misogyny Was About Me." *The Guardian*, January 26. https://www.theguardian.com/books/2013/jan/26/mary-beard-question-time-internet-trolls (last accessed October 24, 2017).

De Haan, W. 2008. "Violence as an Essentially Contested Concept." In *Violence in Europe*, edited by S. Body-Gendrot and P. Spierenburg, pp. 27–40. Dordrecht: Springer.

Foucault, M. 1984. "What Is an Author?" Translated by J.V. Harari. In *The Foucault Reader*, edited by P. Rabinow. New York: Pantheon Books. Original work published 1979.

Foucault, M. 2002. *Archaeology of knowledge*. Translated by A.M. Sheridan Smith. New York: Routledge. Original work published 1969.

Garver, N. 1968. "What Violence Is." *The Nation* (June 24), 209, 817–822.

Hanssen, B. 2000. *Critique of Violence: Between Poststructuralism and Critical Theory*. London: Routledge.

Hardaker, C. 2010. "Trolling in Asynchronous Computer-Mediated Communication: From User Discussions to Academic Definitions." *Journal of Politeness Research. Language, Behaviour, Culture* 6(2), 215–242.

Jane, E.A. 2012. "'Your a ugly, whorish, slut.'" *Feminist Media Studies* 14(4), 531–546.

Jane, E.A. 2013. "'Back to the kitchen, cunt': Speaking the Unspeakable about Online Misogyny." *Continuum* 28(4), 558–570.

Katz, B. 2015. "What's It Like Being Subjected to Incessant, Misogynistic Trolling? Ashley Judd and Anita Sarkeesian Speak Out." *New York Times Live*, April 23. http://nytlive.nytimes.com/womenintheworld/2015/04/23/whats-it-like-to-be-subjected-to-incessant-misogynistic-trolling-ashley-judd-and-anita-sarkeesian-speak-out/(last accessed October 24, 2017).

Lawrence III, C.R., Matsuda, M., Delgado, R., and Crenshaw, K.W. 1993. "Introduction." In *Words That Wound: Critical Race Theory, Assaultive Speech, and the First Amendment*, edited by M. Matsuda, C.R. Lawrence III, R. Delgado, and K.W. Crenshaw, pp. 1–15. Boulder, CO: Westview Press.

Mantilla, K. 2013. "Gendertrolling: Misogyny Adapts to New Media." *Feminist Studies* 39(2), 563–570.

Mead, R. 2014. The Troll Slayer. *The New Yorker*, September 1. http://www.newyorker.com/magazine/2014/09/01/troll-slayer (last accessed October 24, 2017).

Redcliffe State High School. n.d. "Tech Talk … Cyber-bullying & Trolling What Is the Difference?" https://redcliffeshs.eq.edu.au/Supportandresources/Formsanddocuments/Documents/Parent%20Resources/Tech%20Talk-cyber%20bullying%20vs%20trolling.pdf (last accessed October 24, 2017).

Ruitenberg, C.W. 2015. "Performativity and Affect in Education." *Philosophical Inquiry in Education* 23(1), 38–52.

Ryan, M. 2014. "The Threats Against Anita Sarkeesian Expose the Darkest Aspects of Online Misogyny." *The Huffington Post*, October 15. http://www.huffingtonpost.com/maureen-ryan/anita-sarkeesian_b_5993082.html (last accessed October 24, 2017).

Sandlin, J.A., O'Malley, M.P., and Burdick, J. 2011. "Mapping the Complexity of Public Pedagogy Scholarship: 1894–2010." *Review of Educational Research* 81(3), 338–375.

Sarkeesian, A. 2012a. "Tropes vs. Women in Video Games." *Kickstarter*, May 17. https://www.kickstarter.com/projects/566429325/tropes-vs-women-in-video-games/description (last accessed October 24, 2017).

Sarkeesian, A. 2012b. "Harassment, Misogyny and Silencing on YouTube." *Feminist Frequency*, June 7. https://feministfrequency.com/2012/06/07/harassment-misogyny-and-silencing-on-youtube/(last accessed October 24, 2017).

Sarkeesian, A. 2012c. "TEDxWomen Talk about Online Harassment & Cyber Mobs." *Feminist Frequency*, December 5. https://feministfrequency.com/2012/12/05/tedxwomen-talk-on-sexist-harassment-cyber-mobs/(last accessed October 24, 2017).

Searle, J.R. 1969. *Speech Acts: An Essay in the Philosophy of Language*. Cambridge: Cambridge University Press.

UN Broadband Commission for Digital Development Working Group on Broadband and Gender. 2015. *Cyber Violence Against Women and Girls: A World-wide Wake-up Call*. http://www2.unwomen.org/~/media/headquarters/attachments/sections/library/publications/2015/cyber_violence_gender%20report.pdf?v=1&d=20150924T154259 (last accessed October 24, 2017).

25

Gender as a Factor in School Violence

Honor and Masculinity

Amy Shuffelton

In *Rampage* (2004), sociologist Katherine Newman and her coauthors identify five conditions for the kind of school shootings they term "rampages": episodes of gun violence in which the shooter intends to kill but does not target particular individuals. Newman et al. conclude that the following five conditions are necessary, though not sufficient:

1) The shooter perceives himself to be extremely marginal in the social world that matters to him.
2) The shooter suffers from psychological problems that magnify the impact of his perceived marginality.
3) Cultural "scripts," which function as prescriptions for behavior, are available to lead the way toward armed attack.
4) There is a failure of surveillance systems intended to identify troubled teens before their problems become extreme.
5) Guns are available.

Although national conversation about rampage shootings in the contemporary United States has focused mainly on conditions 2, 4, and 5 – that is, gun availability and mental illness – the remaining two conditions connect school shootings to a long-standing concern of legal, political, and ethical thinking about violence: the demands of honor. How ought a person respond to peers whose words and actions, in his perceptions, fail to recognize him as the person he is committed to being? What kind of action ought an agent take to maintain his ethical identity in the face of disrespect? These are questions of honor. School shootings are typically portrayed as "senseless violence," but the ethical demands of honor indicate their logic (for another interpretation of the "sense" in school shootings, see Keehn and Boyles, 2015). Nor is the compulsion of that logic exclusive to school shooters. Masculine honor, this chapter contends, also underlies resistance to the gun control and social welfare provisions that would be required to address the more technical problems of gun legislation and mental health care. An effective response to this resistance requires rethinking what masculine honor might demand. This inquiry focuses on rampage gun violence insofar as such incidents represent the extreme end of the range of violent actions in schools. In treating actual gun

The Wiley Handbook on Violence in Education: Forms, Factors, and Preventions, First Edition.
Edited by Harvey Shapiro.
© 2018 John Wiley & Sons, Inc. Published 2018 by John Wiley & Sons, Inc.

violence as an extreme response to a far more common set of concerns, the chapter's analysis of masculine honor's problematic connections to violence applies also to lesser and more mundane incidents of school violence.

In the wake of the Newtown, Connecticut rampage that killed 20 children and 6 teachers at Sandy Hook Elementary School, public outrage turned on the Bushmaster assault rifle advertisement that pictured a rifle with the caption "Consider Your Man Card Reissued." The outrage is understandable, yet the advertisement accurately captures crucial aspects of the connection between gun violence, masculinity, and honor. Masculinity is never an identity a man can establish permanently; it needs to be "reissued" by those in a position to judge a man's masculinity. This chapter begins with an exploration of honor as an ethical framework that treats identity as constantly in need of "reissue." Honor depends upon a peer group qualified to judge whether one deserves the identity-based respect one claims. Like the Bushmaster advertisement, this ethical framework is troubling, as it may divorce the demands of honor from other ethical standards. And yet, insofar as it attends to aspects of our identity that matter to us and to the relationships that give human lives meaning, an ethic of honor is as powerful as it is dangerous. The second section of the chapter asks what honor has to offer and what relation it has to notions of the good that stand beyond social convention. Along the way, it addresses one "reissue" of the "man card," namely Plato's revision of archaic notions of what it means to be a man. The third section of this chapter directly addresses the relationship between contemporary masculinity and gun violence, drawing on Douglas Kellner's correlation of gun violence, media spectacle, and a crisis in masculinity in his *Guys and Guns Amok* (2008). The final section turns to Adrienne Rich's "Women and Honor" (1980) to suggest a better reissue of identity cards.

Like an advertisement, honor has sometimes been thought a matter of mere surface appearance. Rich draws out deeper dimensions: honor's implication of honest speaking and listening. Honor is honesty's etymological root; to be honest was originally to be a person of honorable character, truly to be what one seems. Rich notes the gendered inflections of honor, and their entanglement of honor with deceit, and she calls for a reissue of honor as honest communication in relationships. In such a reissue, I see promise for addressing violence in schools. Given the association of "manly action" with violence, violence can seem a boy's only recourse for "saving face," a necessary tool for preserving threatened masculinity. Honest communication opens up alternative possibilities, including the expansion of available masculinities and the improvement of relationships between and among men and women.

What Is Honor?

In an influential 1970 essay, Peter Berger declared honor obsolete. Honor is an "ideological leftover" from premodern times, he declared, surviving within modern societies only in the consciousness of "obsolete classes, such as military officers or ethnic grandmothers" (1983, 172). In Berger's analysis, the obsolescence of the concept of honor is part and parcel of modernity, with its new moralities and political arrangements. These have replaced "honor" with "dignity," for better and for worse. Honor and dignity each supply a rationale for interpersonal respect, Berger argues, but they do so on importantly different grounds. Honor is often considered an aristocratic value, and it remains a feature of sociopolitical hierarchies, though a person of any status can lay claim to honor, provided his or her behavior conforms to the requirements of honor dictated by his or her position within a particular social hierarchy. "For all," Berger points out, "the qualities enjoined by honor provide the link, not only between self and community, but between self and the idealized norms of the community ... Conversely, dishonor is a fall from grace in the most comprehensive sense – loss of face in the community, but also loss of self and separation from the basic norms that govern human life" (Berger 1983, 174). In the rationale of honor, as Berger explains it, a person's claim to respect depends upon his or her ability to meet the norms prescribed by his or her "institutional roles" within a particular social system. Modernity, whose moralities and politics free the individual from institutional roles, has replaced honor with dignity, which is respect owed to a person qua person, who has dignity as such. Dignity rests on an altogether different conception of the self and its relationship with society. "Institutions cease to be the 'home' of the [modern] self," says Berger; "instead they become oppressive realities that distort and estrange the self" (179). The modern core self, which stands free of institutional roles that are always provisional, has become the moral self owed respect. In important ways, Berger notes, the replacement of honor with dignity has served people well, and there is no reason to turn the clock back.

Given honor's association with oppressively hierarchical systems, it is unsurprising that in recent decades few political and moral theorists committed to progressive politics – or simply to modernity – have wanted anything to do with it. It has been picked up by conservative theorists like Allan Bloom (1987) and Harvey Mansfield (2007) in their lamentations for the lost virtues of manhood, but otherwise relegated to the philosophical basement. There might seem to be little a committed egalitarian could say in its defense. All the same, Berger suggested, a rediscovery of honor by modern society was both empirically plausible and, with qualifications, desirable. "It seems clear to us," he writes, that "the unrestrained enthusiasm for total liberation of the self from the 'repression' of institutions fails to take account of certain fundamental requirements of man, notably those of *order* – that institutional order of society without which both collectivities and individuals must fall into a dehumanizing chaos" (Berger 1983, 180). Inevitably, Berger predicted, the tide would turn and institutions would come back into favor. "The ethical question," he supposed, "is what these institutions will be like." Arguably, instead institutions have become even more irrelevant, as liquid as the postmodern self. Indeed, from the vantage point of several decades into postmodernity, "unrestrained enthusiasm for total liberation of the self from institutions" seems another ideological leftover, the province of college sophomores and unreconstructed hippies tilting at windmills.

Honor may be salvageable, however, on grounds other than those Berger imagined and other than Bloom's and Mansfield's. Kwame Anthony Appiah, drawing on work on honor in and outside philosophy, emphasizes features of honor that flow from its definition as an ethical code that links the self to a community and its idealized norms: its attunement to identity, motivation, and interpersonal relationships (Appiah 2010). Honor, Appiah contends, is a "crucial" but "neglected" topic for contemporary moral philosophy, and crucial for the same theoretical and practical reasons as the philosophical consideration of race, ethnicity, gender and sexuality, and other social identities. "[L]ike our social identities, it connects our lives together. Attending to honor ... like noticing the importance of our social identities, can help us to treat others as we should and to make the best of our own lives" (Appiah 2010, xv).[1]

Appiah conceptualizes honor not in terms of institutional *roles* but of interpersonal *relationships*. Because having honor means being entitled to respect from others, it is relational from the ground up. Drawing on Stephen Darwall's (1977) differentiation of two kinds of respect – appraisal and recognition respect – Appiah delineates two types of honor. One type – which might also be called *esteem* – is accorded to persons based on others' appraisal that they have demonstrated excellence in some field deemed worthwhile. A person can be honored, for instance, as a superior musician, or warrior, or scientist. This type of honor, which rank-orders persons against a standard, is intrinsically competitive and hierarchical. The other type of honor, however, which Appiah (following Darwall) calls *recognition respect*, accords respect equitably on the grounds that a person meets certain standards of behavior that are expected of anyone so situated. All decent teachers, for instance, have a claim to honor as teachers (recognition respect), but this is different in kind from the honor we accord a "teacher of the year" (esteem). Frank Henderson Stewart's *Honor*, another source for Appiah's analysis, distinguishes between "vertical" and "horizontal" honor (Stewart 1994, 54–63). While the "vertical" honor that functions in hierarchies accords more honor/esteem to some persons than others, "horizontal" honor exists among peers. Berger's argument treats honor exclusively in its vertical/appraisal/esteem sense, ignoring honor in its horizontal/recognition aspect. Insofar as "dignity," post-Kant, implies a self whose claim to respect exists regardless of its social relationships, it denotes a kind of respect that is distinctly different from honor. Berger is correct that we have added the notion of freestanding dignity to our conceptual repertoire, but dignity has not rendered honor in its sense of recognition respect obsolete.

Although they are dealt out differently, esteem and recognition respect have core features in common. Honor of both kinds involves an honor code: a rationale for according or denying honor, based on expected standards of behavior. Both also rely upon the notion of a group qualified to accord and receive honor. Appiah calls this group one's "honor peers," and they are intrinsic to the accordance of respect. My honor peers are the people whose respect matters to me, in part because I believe they – and only they – are qualified to grant me respect worth having. For instance, a gentleman could never preserve his honor by accepting a challenge to a duel from a butcher. The butcher was not his honor peer; to accept the challenge would acknowledge him as a peer, and thereby undermine the gentleman's claim to honor as a gentleman (Appiah 2010, 3–51). In terms relevant to school violence, the honor peers of an adolescent boy are other members of the honor peer group of adolescent boys – other boys, or those recognized as legitimate constituents of that world (the basketball coach, perhaps, but probably not

---

1 A look at the eclectic sources that contemporary theorists of honor draw on confirms Appiah's claim that philosophers have neglected the topic. Berger's essay was first printed in a sociological journal. Appiah turns to historical sources and to anthropologist Frank Henderson Stewart's *Honor* (1994). *Honor* opens with anthropologist Julian Pitt-Rivers's claim that before the social sciences addressed honor in the 1960s, little was written outside literature. This is not quite true, Stewart says, although the philosophical literature has been undistinguished except for Italian theorists of the sixteenth century, but his counterexample is legal scholarship. Insofar as honor is a matter of social relationships and motivation, it makes sense that serious thinking about it would be spread across literature, social sciences, and law – fields in which these are central concerns – as well as philosophy.

mothers). Importantly, most people have multiple, partly but not entirely overlapping, sets of honor peers; for example, fellow professionals, local community members, aficionados of the same hobbies. This is less true of people in tightly integrated communities, such as Achaean princedoms and small-town American high schools, in which "honor groups" overlap such that a person's status in one realm carries into all the others. (On the importance of the school environment to young people, see Warnick, Kim, and Robinson 2015.)

Honor, in sum, is inherently a matter of person-relevant ethical standards maintained in relationship with others. As such, honor does not necessarily support hierarchical and politically retrograde notions of value, and it has never become obsolete. Its *potential* to support unjustified social conventions makes it a volatile ethical rationale, but theorists unfazed by instability can find in it plenty that merits further consideration. Like Appiah, I find honor worthy of philosophical analysis because it attends to features of human life that make it worth living: one's relations with others, commitment to ideals that give one's actions meaning, and obligations to others who have an equal claim to respect.

A fleshed-out notion of honor supports a richer understanding of what it means, existentially and ethically, for a person to perceive himself as marginalized by a community that matters to him. Marginalization at the hands of one's "honor peers" cannot be taken lightly. To be dishonored is to "lose face," which connotes the loss not only of one's visibility but, if "face" cannot be restored, one's very claim to personhood. Dishonor is both profoundly personal (as it threatens a person's sense of self) and profoundly relational (as the existence of that self depends on how one appears to, and has one's appearance reflected back by, others.) If honor enables us to "make the best of our own lives," the continual experience of dishonor makes it impossible to live well.

Honor and Agency

Why dishonor should be a reason for *violence*, however, calls for further exploration of the connections between honor and action. As Appiah understands honor, it "is, for us, what it has always been, an engine, fueled by the dialogue between our self-conceptions and the regard of others, that can drive us to take seriously our responsibilities in a world we share" (Appiah 2010, 179). Honor, that is, is a motivational force. Appiah claims honor as the engine driving ethical and political progress, and in chapters addressing dueling in Western Europe, foot-binding in China, and the Atlantic slave trade, he shows how a shift in public conceptions of what was honorable drove progressive social change. In all three cases, Appiah contends, reasonable arguments about the injustice of the institution gained limited traction until reformers shifted the public's understanding of what honor required, after which change came remarkably quickly. In China, for example, would-be reformers had for years provided reasons to end foot-binding – reasons that were understood and recognized as valid – but to no avail. The practice quickly ceased, however, after reformers emphasized that it made China appear uncivilized in the eyes of Europeans. National honor, not reason, drove change. Appiah makes a compelling case for addressing lingering injustices not by heaping rational argument on top of rational argument but by shifting majority opinion to align what honor demands with the aims of justice. This might seem no easier to pull off than reform through reason-giving, but note that, as in the case of China, a reconstitution of the honor peer group can spur change. In the late nineteenth century, Chinese elites came to see Western elites as their honor peers, and, from that new perspective, foot-binding seemed shameful. If this is so, revision of the "cultural scripts" that support school shootings and revision of the gun culture that supports easy access to guns could be effected by such a realignment. Before accepting that conclusion, however, two questions need to be addressed: Why is honor the "engine" of change, and what relation does honor have with genuinely *good* ends?

In *Shame and Necessity* (1993), Bernard Williams teases out the relationship between the two terms of his title and, although honor is not its explicit focus, his analysis connects honor to agency. Shame is not synonymous with dishonor, as shame is an emotion whereas dishonor is an ethical category, a descriptor of the ethical problem of rupture between an individual and his ideals that is recognized by the community that gives significance to those ideals, which is reflected back to and perceived by the individual. Shame is, however, the appropriate emotional response to dishonor.[2] As Williams shows, through an analysis of Greek drama and epic poems, the shame that characters feel in the wake of dishonor, or know they will feel if they behave dishonorably, drives their decisions and actions. This is not, he argues, merely a feature of the psyche of Ancient Greeks. The need to preserve one's honor, in Williams's account, remains a wellspring of agency.

In Sophocles' *Ajax*, the hero (who is supposedly the second strongest Greek, after Achilles – the proper recipient of esteem, as well as recognition respect) is slighted by the award of Achilles' arms to Odysseus. To keep him from killing the Greek army in revenge, Athena makes him mad, and he slaughters a flock of sheep and cattle, believing them to be the army. When he recovers from his temporary madness and realizes that he has made himself absurd, he resolves to commit suicide. He has been dishonored twice over: by the Greek decision and by his own mad actions. Williams homes in on his statement "I must go," the last words he speaks before killing himself. Why *must* he go? Because, Williams argues, given the (Achaean, heroic) ideals to which Ajax is dedicated, it has become clear to him that there is literally no way he can go on living:

> He knows that he cannot change his ethos, his character, and he knows that after what he has done, this grotesque humiliation, he cannot live the only kind of life his ethos demands ... Being what he is, he could not live as the man who had done these things; it would be merely impossible, in virtue of the relations between what he expects of the world and what the world expects of a man who expects that of it. (Williams 1993, 72–73)

Ajax's actions are strikingly similar to those of rampage shooters, and Williams's analysis of their ethical import shines some light on the sense in "senseless" violence. The boys who turn guns on their classmates and then often themselves are, like Ajax, motivated to act by the sheer impossibility of continuing to live without honor.

---

2 Philosophical and ethnographic analyses distinguish shame from guilt. Shame is tied to honor, guilt to having broken a rule or disobeyed a rightful authority. This distinction opens a host of corollary connections of shame to honor, relationality, and socially situated/practice-based ethics and guilt to disobedience and deontological/Kantian morality.

Newman describes school shooters Michael Carneal and Mitchell Johnson, for instance, as feeling their masculinity under siege. Carneal had been called gay in a middle school newspaper, and Johnson, who had been sexually abused as a child, was described by peers as intensely concerned with projecting a "hard," masculine image. Peer skepticism of their "man cards" led both to contemplate suicide, but suicide, in Newman's words, is "a weak way to die, one at odds with the script of masculinity. School shooters are looking for status-winning, manhood-enhancing departures" (Newman et al. 2004, 150). Their decision to shoot may, she suggests, be a choice of "death by cop" as a twofold escape from dishonor. As many adolescents have a limited comprehension of death's finality, this can also be accompanied by fantasies of enhanced post-shooting status. Carneal imagined himself walking through the halls of his high school after the shooting, when "maybe [other kids] would be scared and then no one would mess with Michael" (152). (On guns and men's experiences of shame, see O'Donnell 2015).

Rampage violence followed by suicide, however, is not the only possible response to a loss of face. Williams offers as a counterexample Euripedes' play *The Madness of Heracles*, but a somewhat more promising example (because Heracles does kill his children, though not himself) would be that of Achilles. In the pivotal scene in the *Iliad* where he considers killing Agamemnon after Agamemnon dishonors him by taking Briseis, his war prize and symbol of his personal worth, Achilles reconsiders. Instead of killing the king, he avenges his honor by publically showing restraint and then withdrawing himself and his Myrmidons from the fighting.

Achilles' reconsideration and restraint are, importantly, brought about through an internal dialogue between different "parts" of his psyche. When angered by Agamemnon's disrespect, Achilles is initially unsure what to do: "within his shaggy breast the heart was divided two ways, pondering whether to draw from beside his thigh the sharp sword ... or else to check the spleen within and keep down his anger." Note that both alternatives are portrayed as *actions*; Achilles must overcome either Agamemnon or the parts of him that are divided against other parts. While Achilles "weighed in mind and spirit" these two possible actions, Athena – the goddess of orderly warfare and wise judgment – "caught him by the fair hair" and gave him the additional information that, should he refrain from killing Agamemnon, "some day three times over such shining gifts shall be given you by reason of this outrage" (Homer 1962, 80). Achilles checks his spleen; Agamemnon lives. Yet although Achilles is a savvier preserver of his honor than Ajax, and presented as fully sane throughout this episode, he is hardly an exemplar of non-violent conflict resolution. His withdrawal from battle nearly destroys the Greek army, and by the end of the *Iliad* his actions have caused the deaths of the friend whose life he held most dear, countless Greeks and Trojans, and himself. Plato said as much, and in the *Republic* he simultaneously reconfigures the terms in which crises of honor are internally debated and opens up new ways of living.

The part of the soul associated with honor in Homer, Plato, and other Greek literature is the *thumos*, usually translated as "spirit."[3] As Achilles' internal debate between "mind

---

3 In English, "heart" has this sense of a body part that is the seat of feeling, as in "lion-hearted" or "wearing one's heart on one's sleeve," and perhaps "heartbroken." *Thumos*, unlike English "spirit," has to do with *worldly* human concerns and relationships, not supernatural entities, who may seize one's hair but not one's *thumos*.

and spirit" suggests, it was treated by the Greeks as one seat of deliberation, and in Plato it is the part of the soul that, in these internal dialogues, supports the aims of *time*, honor (Sharples 1983). The *Republic* first explicitly mentions *thumos* in Book II, when Socrates and Glaucon are considering the problem of warfare, and whether guardians can be sufficiently courageous to defend the city yet sufficiently loyal to avoid turning on it.[4] Although this is a brief section of the *Republic*, the question they raise resonates throughout the rest of the book and continues to haunt political life. It is the problem at the heart of contemporary gun violence, of rampage shootings but also chronic violence among the dispossessed and the militarization of the police force. How can a society that thrives on competition for consumer goods, and that relies upon force to protect insiders who have these goods from outsiders exploited to produce them, simultaneously cultivate defenders of its way of life and avoid becoming prey to these armed defenders? How can it defend itself against outsiders without creating outsiders within? As Glaucon exclaims, "By Zeus, it won't be easy."

Plato's resolution of this problem depends upon appropriate education of the spirit. Socrates notes living exemplars of this desirable alliance of courage and loyalty: dogs, who are gentle to familiars and fierce toward enemies. Like a dog, this analogy implies, the spirit is part of human purposes but less than completely human. Dogs, who defend property, are a necessary element in elevating a political community over the "city of pigs," in enabling citizens to live a fully human life, but they are still dangerous unless properly trained. By analogy, the spirit usefully keeps the appetite in check but needs to be put under the control of reason. This marks a shift from Homer, in which mind and spirit negotiated as equals (Koziak 2000). For Plato, the spirit remains a source of agency, but it should not select its ends. In *Phaedrus*, Plato uses another animal analogy that recognizes *thumos* as a crucial aspect of agency but not a guide to its direction. Socrates likens the soul to "the natural union of a team of winged horses and their charioteer." Without the horses, who represent spirit (the "beautiful and good" horse) and the appetites ("the opposite"), the chariot cannot move; if the charioteer does not direct the horses, the chariot veers off course. This analogy perhaps better captures how *thumos* works as an honor-focused engine, although the dog analogy better captures the prospect of violence and internal sabotage.

To direct the soul toward the aims of reason, which is the soul's proper ruler as the person is of the domestic animal, Plato turns to the arts to stamp the spirit with an impression of the good. Among the stories the young in the Republic will *not* be told is the story of Achilles. Achilles, driven by honor nearly to destroy his own army, can be no model for a guardian. The education Plato describes in the *Republic* will create a new kind of leader, the philosopher, whose spirit is dominated by reason such that honor aligns with justice.[5] When Plato traces the decline of the ideal republic through four lesser political arrangements in Books VIII and IX, the first stage of decline is "timocracy," a politics guided by honor, whose rulers are persons dominated by their

---

4 *Thumos* is evoked but not named in Book I when Thrasymachus leaps up in anger at Socrates and insists that justice is support of one's friends and harm to one's enemies. There, Thrasymachus is a case-study of what the *thumos* is capable of when unchecked by reason. His interpretation of justice, of course, correlates to the traditional notion of what honor demands. See Wilson (1995).

5 The connection between violence, state sovereignty, and individual self-rule is also analyzed in Shapiro (2015).

spirits. A timocracy is the best of the inferior modes of government but inferior all the same, as it represents the domination of honor over justice, spirit over reason, the dog over its master. In presenting the just Republic as a better alternative, Plato opens up new ways to be human and a new kind of sociopolitical order in which such persons could thrive. In doing so, he offers a way out of the shame-driven necessity that drove Ajax to suicide and Achilles to destruction. An Achaean warrior might *need* to kill for the sake of his honor because he could not change his character, but the philosopher would never need to do so. In envisioning an alternative rationale to convention, and alternative ways of being human, Plato counteracts the necessity of violent action.

Plato, that is to say, issues a new kind of "man card."[6] He does so in response to the question Glaucon and Socrates raise: how a wealthy society can be protected from attacks by both the outsiders it exploits and those inside who, seeing the opportunity to benefit, attack insiders. His resolution to the problem of honor – to respect it as a motivating force but require it to align it with justice rather than follow its own ends – might seem a promising basis for addressing gun violence, which proliferates in just such a situation. Yet Plato's answer raises new problems even as it resolves others. Above all, the "guard dogs" within any society – that is, those who are educated to use violence to achieve their ends but expected always to subordinate their own interests to the aims of persons higher in status – are not dogs but human beings and unlikely always to accept their subordination. In establishing a hierarchy of persons within society, and treating those moved by honor as destined to be fighters but not rulers, Plato creates the conditions for a militarized notion of honor that ties it even more firmly to violence. That hierarchy also creates the conditions for competitive, esteem-seeking honor at the expense of equitable relations among peers. And the demotion of spirit from its equal place at the table of decision making becomes grounds for dismissing certain kinds of people – those deemed too influenced by spirit in its various manifestations, such as "emotional" women, and "aggressive" men of color – from equitable access to authority. Insofar as Plato's "man cards" could only ever be issued to some men, they cannot serve as an alternative to honor to those deemed unqualified to receive them. Honor, having been associated with conventional masculinity and violent aggression, becomes an even more dangerous dog.

In more pragmatic terms, when people feel tugged in one direction by the demands of honor and another by the demands of reason, telling them one more time to listen to reason is unlikely to have much effect. This is what Appiah's historical-philosophical case studies establish. It frankly is no solution to gun violence at all to tell gun owners what reason demands. The judgment of school shooters may be clouded by mental illness, but reason is also of limited use where it might be thought better to apply: gun regulation. Although reason can clarify what kind of gun regulation a society might put in place to control internal violence, it can do little to convince citizens to support such regulation when honor tells them otherwise. And honor *does* tell them otherwise. Most gun owners say they keep a gun to protect themselves and their families against crime. Public health experts warn that keeping a gun in the household creates a risk far greater

---

6 Plato, famously, also offers guardian status to women. As Jane Roland Martin shows, however, women are allowed this status only insofar as the cards they carry are man cards. See Martin (1985, ch. 2).

than the risk of a violent intruder, but this logic has limited sway with those who stake their honor on being able to respond to potential violence with violence. What I hope the above analysis of honor as an engine (perhaps but not necessarily aiming toward the good) suggests is that rather than yet more *reasons* for laws and policies likely to reduce violence, progressive political reform requires a shift in the notion of what honor demands of a man.

Gun Violence and the Crisis in Masculinity

Douglas Kellner's *Guys and Guns Amok* (2008) provides a focused exploration of gun violence's connection to masculine identities in the contemporary United States. In accentuating "right-wing" extremism, his book obscures the continuity between violent extremists and moderate gun owners committed to gun rights, but it provides insight into how specifically *masculine* identity is implicated in US gun culture. Kellner argues that rampage violence in American public spaces, which he extends to include acts of domestic terrorism as well as school shootings, is fueled by a toxic brew of media spectacle, a crisis in masculinity, and the availability of guns. In referring to media spectacle, he adopts and adapts Guy Debord's conception of spectacle as "the overarching concept to describe the media and consumer society, including the packaging, promotion, and display of commodities and the production and effects of all media" (Kellner 2008, 3). Like Debord, Kellner treats media spectacle as relevantly one aspect of an economically stratified society. Kellner addresses the linkages between the actions of domestic terrorists, including school shooters, and the media, with the media serving both as the source of violent scripts addressed to culturally specific identity groups – for example, alienated white men – and as the public stage on which shooters expect their actions to be broadcast.[7]

Noting that contemporary youth are frequently portrayed as a menace (Plato's dogs again), other times as subject to unprecedented hazards, Kellner emphasizes the inequitable distribution of advantages and disadvantages among them. Young men, especially young white men, are still a privileged group, but they face diminished prospects as compared to earlier generations. Kellner explores the refuge some white men have taken in ultra-violent masculine identities. Cultural, political, and economic changes, Kellner notes, have "robbed white men of positive identities (as family providers, farmers, union members, and so on) and left them feeling besieged and confused." Some men, Kellner points out, have "made the transformation smoothly, expressing solidarity with other groups and identities in an egalitarian spirit, and constructed identities that were multiple, flexible, and politically progressive." Others, however, have created a "new strain of white male identity politics fueled by intense rage, resentment, paranoia, and apocalyptic visions, often exploding into violence" (Kellner 2008, 92). According to Kellner:

> The crisis in masculinity drove many men to seek solace in guns and weapons. Guns and military culture in particular fetishize weapons as an important part of

7 For a rich consideration of the media's link to gun violence, see O'Dea (2015).

male virility and power, treating guns as objects of almost religious veneration and devotion. In this constellation, the expression of violence through guns and the use of weapons is perceived as an expression of manhood. In recent years, however, gun culture has mutated into a more defuse [*sic*] military culture where explosives and more lethal weapons are deployed by extremist white male groups and individuals to try to reconstruct even more exaggerated hypermale identities. (Kellner 2008, 7–8).[8]

Kellner's account of white male identity politics and extremist groups provides useful social context for understanding the actions of school shooters and other domestic terrorists.

Guys and Guns Amok, however, is less useful for making sense of the wide middle ground between militant extremists and progressives committed to fluid, flexible, gender-egalitarian identities. Many men who disdain expressions of white male identity culture, such as foul-mouthed talk shows and militia movements, enjoy hyper-masculinized professional sports and video games. The "amok" metaphor, which connotes a state of battlefield madness, captures the problem of Ajax and school shooters, but not the problem of Achilles, the self-controlled and successful but ultimately more destructive man of honor. A polarized account like Kellner's, which divides men into the two camps of good progressives and bad right-wingers, is an unsatisfactory means of understanding the logic of men like Adam Winkler, a legal scholar whose *Gunfight* (2011) chronicles recent judicial interpretation of the Second Amendment. Winkler's analysis is even-handed and reasonable; the reader gets the sense that he is committed to expansive gun rights but is not one of the extremists he calls "gun nuts." In the last, affectionate words of his acknowledgments, he reveals why he favors the right to bear arms: his wife ("the love of my life") and his "beloved" daughter ("who made me want to make the world a better place"). "They embody," he says, "the reason a law-abiding person might want to own a gun" (Winkler 2011, 302). According to the American Academy of Pediatrics, "the absence of guns from children's homes and communities is the most reliable and effective measure to prevent firearm related injuries in children and adolescents,"[9] but *as a husband and father*, Winkler is apparently unconvinced. What the lens of honor provides that Kellner's analysis lacks is a way to understand why a rational and loving man might put his family at risk for the sake of his self-respect. The masculine ideal that a good man is the protector of his family, as staunch as any guard dog, is widely shared. It can seem benign, but it upholds the arguments of Winkler and other moderate proponents of expansive Second Amendment rights and thereby makes guns widely available within American communities, where they are terribly dangerous. In upholding their honor, such men sometimes find, as did Achilles, that they have inadvertently destroyed those they most love.

---

8 Would that it were defused instead of diffuse.

9 American Academy of Pediatrics, "Gun Violence Policy Recommendations." https://www.aap.org/en-us/advocacy-and-policy/federal-advocacy/documents/aapgunviolencepreventionpolicyrecommendations_jan2013.pdf.

Women and Honor and Human Beings

Plato's *Republic* and Kellner's *Guys and Guns Amok* both respond to a sharply perceived and persistent problem: the threat to good order posed by men of honor who are simultaneously empowered defenders and second-class beneficiaries of that order. Their solutions, however different, share a commitment to stabilizing honor by aligning it with right order, with that order founded on a "grand narrative." For Plato, the ideal Republic and its idealized constituents are based on metaphysical certainties, namely the order of the cosmos and the corresponding order of city and soul. After establishing that ideal city and soul in his readers' imaginations, Plato traces its historical decline, with honor/timocracy/*thumos* playing parallel roles as first steps down from the ideal. Kellner aligns his theory with cultural studies and Frankfurt School critical theory, and the Marxist influences on the latter continually surface in his references to "progressive" reforms, with "right-wing" men of honor functioning as a drag on that historical trajectory. For Plato and Kellner alike, honor can support good human purposes *because those purposes are stable, ascertainable, and historically situated.*

What, however, is to be done about honor if one is skeptical of grand historico-metaphysical narratives, unconvinced that there exists a clear path and a designated driver, to whose chariot honor should be hitched? One answer is to reissue honor afresh. In "Women and Honor: Some Notes on Lying" (1980), Adrienne Rich offers an alternative interpretation of honor that has several appealing features. Her account of honor as honest communication is harnessed to no grand narrative. It lends itself to an ameliorative rather than revolutionary, pragmatic rather than idealistic, approach to addressing gun violence.[10] Furthermore, in both Plato's and Kellner's accounts, the esteem/competitive sense of masculine honor predominates, with the mutual recognition sense of honor falling nearly out of sight. In contrast, Rich's essay parallels the *Iliad* and Appiah's *The Honor Code* in its awareness that honor also indicates peer-to-peer relationships of equality and respect. Rich reissues honor – masculine and otherwise – in terms that have something to offer those concerned about gun violence in schools.

Whereas "male honor" has had "something to do with killing," as she notes, and is "something needing to be avenged: hence the duel," women's honor has been "something altogether else: virginity, chastity, fidelity to a husband." Strictly gendered delineations of what honor requires are also evident in the realm of interpersonal communication. A man of honor could give his word to a personal or public commitment, and "a man's 'word' sufficed – to other men – without guarantee." Honesty has not been expected of women, however, and as Rich points out, women "have been expected to lie with our bodies: to bleach, redden, unkink or curl our hair, pluck eyebrows, shave armpits ... We have been required to tell different lies at different times, depending on what the men of the time needed to hear." Expected to lie, women have become, Rich laments, liars. Men, meanwhile, have been expected to tell the truth – but "about facts, not about feelings. They have not been expected to talk about feelings at all." Nor have men been expected to tell the truth to women, and Rich

---

10 Rich's piece is, indeed, "notes." It is an essay in the true sense of an exploratory foray, an attempt. In calling it pragmatic, I mean loosely to associate the ideas in this particular essay of hers with Dewey's invocation of "the better" rather than "the good," as well as with Appiah's look at what honor means in practice – and to suggest it as a practical approach.

accuses "patriarchal lying" of manipulating women "both through falsehood and through silence" (Rich 1980, 186–188).

The question that interests Rich in this piece is whether, through new commitment to honest communication in relationships, "a truly womanly idea of honor [is] in the making" (189). In reorienting honor from visual *spectacle* to (honest) *speech*, Rich's account of honor is at odds with the predominant metaphor of honor as a matter of surface appearances that runs through Plato, through the correlation of honor and "face," and through the Latin etymology of "respect" (to look back). Yet her correlation of honor with honest communication in relationships harks back to another scene in the *Iliad* on which Achilles' honor pivots: his meeting with Priam over the return of Hector's body. This scene is not conventionally read as about honor at all, but rather as about compassion overcoming rage. I would contend that it *is* about honor, though in its mutual recognition rather than its esteem aspect. As the recognition aspect of honor has been relatively neglected, the honor-relevant dimensions of this scene have also been overlooked. Recognizing these dimensions makes Rich's essay, like Appiah's analysis of honor as recognition respect within relationships, the reissue of older ideas rather than a complete novelty.

When Priam comes in supplication, Achilles has for 12 days been desecrating Hector's body by dragging it behind his chariot and refusing it proper burial. By overreaching in his use of violence, he stands to lose the honor on which he has staked everything he values. Even the gods are appalled by his behavior, which dishonors Achilles as much as it does Hector. Apollo and Hermes – both gods of good speech – therefore help Priam reach Achilles' tent, where the two men talk. Priam's honest account of his feelings for his son Hector, and his appeal to Achilles' feelings for his own father, finally move Achilles to pity. Their conversation starts with Priam catching Achilles' knees in a gesture of supplication, a display of esteem that recognizes Achilles as "dangerous and man-slaughtering," but after hearing Priam's grief Achilles "took the old man by the hand, and set him on his feet again," thereby recognizing Priam as a respect-worthy equal (Homer 1962, 510). Through honest communication in and about relationships between men, Achilles comes to treat the dead Hector and his kin as he ought to, thus re-establishing his honor. While Achilles' claim to esteem as the greatest of warriors is maintained through the public spectacle of his quarrel with Agamemnon and its eventual resolution, his *identity* as a good prince can only be maintained through this conversation (which takes place, appropriately, in his private tent).

Rich declares that honor's requirement of honest communication among peers has been shamefully neglected by men and is rightfully taken up by women. Although she explicitly states that "[t]hese notes are concerned with relationships between and among women," her insight need not be not limited by that focus. "The possibilities that exist between two people, or among a group of people," she concludes, "are a kind of alchemy." Rich associates the transformative potential of honest relationships with political, as well as personal, change. "Truthfulness, honor," she says, "has to be created between people. This is true in political situations. The quality and depth of the politics evolving from a group depends in very large part on their understanding of honor." Plato and Homer would concur.

> When relationships are determined by manipulation, by the need for control, they … are repetitive. The shock of human possibilities has ceased to

reverberate through them … It isn't that to have an honorable relationship with you I have to understand everything, or tell you everything at once, or that I can know, beforehand, everything I need to tell you. It means that most of the time I am eager, longing for the possibility of telling you. That these possibilities may seem frightening, but not destructive to me. That I feel strong enough to hear your tentative and groping words. That we both know we are trying, all the time, to extend the possibilities of truth between us. (Rich 1980, 193–194)

The reissue of honor along such lines would reissue man cards, perhaps even human being cards.

With regard to the problem of violence in schools, fostered by notions of masculine honor that legitimize aggression as a response to slights and marginalize some for the sake of upholding social hierarchies, this suggests a deceptively simple response. Masculine honor needs to involve listening to outsiders, recognizing them as equals even when their truths are painful to hear, and speaking honestly in response, about feelings as well as facts. Remember that Chinese elites ended foot-binding when their "honor peer" group expanded, and that rampage shootings happen rarely in urban schools, where adolescents have a varied range of social contacts. Boys who are exposed to a variety of ways of being a man, to peers with diverse aspirations and values, and to images of masculinity that align with a plurality of values, I suspect, have more ways to consider their man cards issued. The trick, of course, is that alternative masculinities are only plausible as honorable alternatives if they are recognized as such by those positioned to confer honor – by an honor peer group, that is. Feminist poets are well poised to envision social change, but it requires man card holders actually to change masculine honor. By Zeus, as Glaucon might say, it won't be easy. Why, after all, would those already holding those cards want to change the terms of their issue? Because, perhaps, not to do so puts at risk both the honor and the relationships that they, like all human beings, hold dear.

References

Appiah, Kwame Anthony. 2010. *The Honor Code: How Moral Revolutions Happen.* New York: W.W. Norton.

Berger, Peter. 1983. "On the Obsolescence of the Concept of Honor." In *Revisions: Changing Perspectives in Moral Philosophy*, edited by Stanley Hauerwas and Alasdair MacIntyre, pp. 172–181. Notre Dame, IN: University of Notre Dame Press.

Bloom, Allan. 1987. *The Closing of the American Mind.* New York: Simon & Schuster.

Darwall, Stephen. 1977. "Two Kinds of Respect." *Ethics* 88(1), 36–49.

Homer. 1962. *The Iliad.* Translated by Richard Lattimore, p. 80. Chicago: University of Chicago Press.

Keehn, Gabriel and Boyles, Deron. 2015. "Sense, Nonsense and Violence: Levinas and the Internal Logic of School Shootings." *Educational Theory* 65(4), 441–458.

Kellner, Douglas. 2008. *Guys and Guns Amok: Domestic Terrorism and School Shootings from the Oklahoma City Bombing to the Virginia Tech Massacre* (Boulder, CO: Paradigm Press.

Koziak, Barbara. 2000. *Retrieving Political Emotion: Thumos, Aristotle, and Gender.* University Park: Pennsylvania State University Press.

Mansfield, Harvey. 2007. *Manliness.* New Haven, CT: Yale University Press.

Martin, Jane Roland. 1985. "Plato's Female Guardians." In *Reclaiming a Conversation: The Ideal of the Educated Woman.* New Haven, CT: Yale University Press.

Newman, Katherine S., Fox, Cybelle, Harding, David J., Mehta, Jal, and Roth, Wendy. 2004. *Rampage: The Social Roots of School Shootings.* New York: Basic Books.

O'Dea, Jane. 2015. "Media and Violence: Does McLuhan Provide a Connection?" *Educational Theory* 65(4), 405–421.

O'Donnell, Aislinn. 2015. "Curriculum as Conversation: Vulnerability, Violence and Pedagogy in Prison." *Educational Theory* 65(4), 475–490.

Rich, Adrienne. 1980. "Women and Honor: Some Notes on Lying." In Adrienne Rich, ed. *Selected Prose* 1966–78. New York: Norton.

Shapiro, Harvey. 2015. "When the Exception Is the Rule: School Shootings, Bare Life and the Sovereign Self." *Educational Theory* 65(4), 423–440.

Sharples, R.W. 1983. "But Why Has my Thumos Spoken With Me Thus?" Homeric Decision-Making." *Greece and Rome* (Second Series) 30(1), 1–7.

Stewart, Frank Henderson. 1994. *Honor.* Chicago: University of Chicago Press.

Warnick, Bryan, Kim, Sang Hyun, and Robinson, Shannon. 2015. "Gun Violence and the Meaning of American Schools." *Educational Theory* 65(4), 371–386.

Williams, Bernard. 1993. *Shame and Necessity.* Berkeley: University of California Press.

Wilson, J.R.S. 1995. "Thrasymachus and the Thumos." *The Classical Quarterly* (New Series) 45(1), 58–67.

Winkler, Adam. 2011. *Gunfight: The Battle over the Right to Bear Arms in America.* New York: W.W. Norton.

26

Radical Truth Telling from the Ferguson Uprising

An Educational Intervention to Shift the Narrative, Build Political Efficacy, Claim Power, and Transform Communities

David Ragland

> *"Who the fuck you callin' violent?"*
> Ferguson demonstrators response to media and police narrative
> of Ferguson protests as violent

Introduction

This chapter describes the ideology and development of the Truth Telling Project of Ferguson, as an initiative responding to the sociopolitical environment of emerging social movement consciousness, the growing interest in restorative and transitional justice as strategies to educate and disrupt state-sanctioned police violence. The starting point for this inquiry is understanding the manifestations of structural violence as rooted in unaddressed historical trauma inducing violence and crime against African Americans, Indigenous and non-white people, that live invisibly in the current political, economic, and security apparatus of the United States. Truth telling, as an organic act and community initiative, is offered as one grassroots intervention that learns from history, critical frameworks, and authentic voices, to share stories to uncover systemic and direct violence, while initiating healing, and narrative change.

While political officials, law enforcement, mainstream media, and conservatives consider protests violent, there is little acknowledgment of police violence and the social conditions that make violence inevitable. At the same time, civil disobedience, while often considered violent, is not. In 2015, the year after Michael Brown was killed, the *Guardian* (UK) reported that the rate of African Americans murdered by police in the United States was three times that of any other racial group.[1] This rate of police violence leveled at black communities in the States raises the existential threat, making more visible the disposable nature of black bodies in this society. Recently, one of my students described how he paid less attention to black murders since they "happen all the time," given the instantaneous transmission of video that proliferates through social media. Despite video evidence (Sexton 2016), the US legal system rarely holds police

---

1 www.theguardian.com/us-news/ng-interactive/2015/jun/01/the-counted-police-killings-us-database.

The Wiley Handbook on Violence in Education: Forms, Factors, and Preventions, First Edition.
Edited by Harvey Shapiro.
© 2018 John Wiley & Sons, Inc. Published 2018 by John Wiley & Sons, Inc.

accountable (Madar 2014).[2] Given the legacy of injustice that characterizes US dealings with black folk, intergenerational harm, trauma, and structural and direct violence continue to teach marginalized communities about the value of their lives. These teachings simultaneously induce silence and continued violence because of the intransigence of racism and white supremacy in many institutions and policies that deal with marginalized communities. In the United States, Ferguson became the flashpoint in confronting the racist past that reverberates throughout of American life.

The treatment of blacks, people of color (POC), and those that identify differently from the "mainstream" provides the clearest example of continued and unacknowledged white supremacy and class and race privilege. For example, an Arizona legislator recently introduced a law to ban any "activity or course which discusses social justice, skin privilege, or racial equality" (King 2017). While many have become numb to state-sanctioned violence, those with *othered* identities feel an increased threat. It is troubling that more people are not deeply distressed by the suspension of citizens' rights in Ferguson, Baltimore, and cities around the country as protesters attempt to express constitutionally guaranteed rights to dissent. At the same time, the voices that are heard, most significantly impacting change are from those with identity privilege. Even thought urgently important, the students of Parkland merit white house visits within days of the tragic school shooting; and the #metoo movement sees the immediate high level investigations. In 2017 National Public Radio reported how sexual harassment and assault of black women are silenced. (https://www.npr.org/2017/12/03/568133048/women-of-color-and-sexual-harassment) Even the #metoo black woman creator was ignored when she initially launched the campaign. As well, the emergence of Columbine-like shootings resulted in zero tolerance policies in black and brown communities, where mass-school shootings were less likely (Stahl 2016). We might question if the United States, given its foundational violence of genocide, slavery, and colonialism, can recognize the full humanity of the black population and POC in the margins without an intervention that acknowledges and disrupts white supremacy, privilege, and history lived out in the current social landscape.

To be sure, state-sanctioned and racialized violence have always been present[3] since colonial times. This history and the images of Michael Brown lying on the ground in the simmering heat of August in Ferguson, Eric Garner being choked by officers, Sandra Bland being assaulted by Texas law enforcement, and the recent slew of footage showing violence against black people led to increased civil disobedience throughout the United States. The Ferguson protests initiated new kind of vibrancy characteristic of this generation of youth and protesters. The chants "fuck the police" and "the whole damn system is guilty as hell" reiterated a deep sense of frustration and distrust of the traditional authority and power located in the state apparatus that continuously violates the dignity of communities of color. With a consciousness recognizing the deep structural violence, victimized people refused to soften the truth, especially when that often meant denying the extent of traumatization caused by the slave trade and racism embedded broadly across US economic, political, and educational (and other) institutions.

---

2 In 2014, After Eric Garner was murdered by Pantaleo and other NYPD officers, Ramsey Orta, who filmed the deadly encounter, was the only one to face charge: https://www.democracynow.org/2016/7/13/two_years_after_eric_garner_s. Also see Park and Lee's (2017) *New York Times* article showing the absence of accountability for murder of blacks by police.

3 No law requires the United States to keep track of demographic information for police-involved shooting (Grothaus 2015).

While protests dramatize underlying issues that society has been unwilling to address, the truth telling in Ferguson has offered an alternative narrative; shedding light on contradictions, intentionally produced ignorance and silence, and unaddressed past wrongs that have contributed to current structural and direct violence too harsh for some to admit as reality. The waves of African Americans escaping the terrorism of the Jim Crow South in the Great Migration between 1916 and 1970 encountered structural racism in the form of housing covenants, redlining, predatory financial policies, and brutal policing to halt movement toward decent housing, schooling, and employment in suburban communities like Ferguson (Coates 2015; Rogers 2015; Rothstein 2014). Predatory policing, reinforcing this de facto segregation, was the catalyst sparking the radical truth telling that began in response to the humiliating murder of Michael Brown Jr. on August 9, 2014. The ensuing protest was a kind of revolutionary theater, attempting to teach America despite its refusal to learn. As LeRoi Jones (also known as Amiri Baraka) said: "The Revolutionary Theater … should stagger through our universe correcting, insulting, preaching, spitting craziness … but a craziness taught to us in our most rational moments" (1965). The truth telling in the protests, while angry, were demand-oriented cries to disrupt the comfort of the larger society in hopes they would address the injustices perpetrated on historically marginalized communities. Protestors and their demands for "black lives [to] matter" were characterized as violent. This myopic view is the default setting for media and many who side with abusive law enforcement, despite the realities of policing in black communities – which many of us consider remnants of slave patrols and "lingering colonialities" (Williams 2016) that reinforce white supremacy.[4]

In this context, the Truth Telling Project of Ferguson (TTP) emerged as a community initiative and educational intervention, rooted in restorative and transformative justice, to challenge narratives that justify harm leveled against black people, while building community efficacy through the telling of stories that reflect the experience of those most victimized by direct and structural violence.

New Movement, New Values

Despite the media and the broader public's disdain and critiques, we told our stories to anyone who would listen. Similar communities, experiencing the same kind of direct and structural violence, joined in solidarity immediately after the murders of Michael Brown and Eric Garner. The onslaught of news reporting contributed to an organic engagement in civil disobedience. People who had never protested took to the streets to confront police killings in their own cities. Ferguson and Baltimore provided the playbook for protests, and the hashtag #Black Lives Matter (BLM) encapsulated an idea and sentiment that came to articulate the sense of this political moment. Alicia Garza (2014) articulates the term when she states, "Black Lives Matter is an ideological and political intervention in a world where Black lives are systematically and intentionally targeted for demise. It is an affirmation of Black folks' contributions to this society, our humanity, and our resilience in the face of deadly oppression."

---

4 Part of the colonial project was valuing all things white and not valuing the indigenous. Williams (2016) describes the colonial structures in schooling which continued after the formal end of colonialism through institutions, systems, and behaviors. The lingering behavior is often reflected in preferences for persons with skin tone or hair texture similar to European phenotypes.

BLM is a global moral claim meant to address structures that posit black lives as less valuable, and thus dispensable. Garza (2014) continues:

> Black Lives Matter affirms the lives of Black queer and trans folks, disabled folks, Black-undocumented folks, folks with records, women and all Black lives along the gender spectrum. It centers those that have been marginalized within Black liberation movements ...
>
> When we say Black Lives Matter, we are talking about the ways in which Black people are deprived of our basic human rights and dignity. It is an acknowledgement [of] Black poverty and genocide is state violence. It is an acknowledgment that 1 million Black people are locked in cages in this country −one half of all people in prisons or jails − is an act of state violence. It is an acknowledgment that Black women continue to bear the burden of a relentless assault on our children and our families and that assault is an act of state violence.

The momentum and energy of Ferguson-like protests, with this ideology, expanded the sense that black worth extends beyond the respectability politics. The focus on the murders of black men, women, LGBTQ (lesbian, gay, bisexual, transgender, and queer) people, immigrants, and many other marginalized intersecting black identities, unleashed a global movement. In a forthcoming chapter, Arthur Romano and I write: "The statement "Black Lives Matter" came to represent a moral claim of human dignity and full personhood despite the generations denying the value of black life through systemic practices of indignity and humiliation. This moral claim for human dignity expresses the particularity of ethical requirements often denied by state power to communities of color" (Romano and Ragland, 2018).

Fuad Al-Daraweesh and Dale Snauwaert (2015) point out the specificity of human dignity as they describe the need for rights to acknowledge and be consistent with respect for identity. This line of thinking reinforces the sanctity of cultural identity and its needs, which cannot be reduced or generalized given the deep marginalization and disenfranchisement of various groups. This systematized treatment − that is, racial and economic discrimination and specific school-based structural violence of racial, ethnic, and sexual minorities − includes policies described in the *Color of Wealth* (Lui et al. 2006), which are structurally violent. As Al-Daraweesh and Snauwaert argue, "if we are moral equals, and if our identity is inseparable from our culture, then what follows in principle is a right to cultural recognition. In turn, if we have a right, justified claim, to cultural recognition, then the others are obligated to respect our cultural heritage (2015, 22).

The statement "Black Lives Matter" challenges rote equality present in color-blind approaches that fail to recognize the need for equity to account for the systematic denial of the rights (through voter suppression and ID laws, inequity in school funding, etc.), which disproportionately impact black and brown communities. To assert that "Black Lives Matter" expresses an awakened consciousness and sense of agency in seeking redress for centuries of systemic violence (Romano and Ragland 2018).

This moral claim about the value of black bodies is part of an uninterrupted expression of worth, continuing from early modern-era encounters of black and indigenous peoples with Europeans; from fighting against capture, to resistance on slave ships, to struggle throughout the Americas and Europe against imperialism, to civil rights movements, to black power, to decolonial struggles of past decades, and to the current movement for black lives, ecological justice, LGBTQ rights, Standing Rock, and many of the current intersecting social justice struggles.

Truth telling, as a process in this social movement ideology and context, provides a culturally rooted and theorized space for such expression. The denial of moral worth for these populations allows, reinforces, and structures conditions and spaces where internal community violence purportedly justifies the use of violence against black and brown bodies. In this sense, injustice is structurally violent and connected to direct violence. For example, Martin Luther King described the riots in the 1960s as a manifestation of people denied human dignity and forced into ghettos and poor communities.

Schools, which ought to be spaces that foster democracy, peace, and justice, for example (Apple and Beane 1995; Snauwaert 2009), are often both directly violent and structurally violent (Reardon 1988; Williams 2013). Public education policies and practices in the United States provide clear examples of structural violence and the importance of truth telling about the intersections of poverty, lack of equitable funding for urban schools, increased policing, arrests of black and brown students for minor infractions, deficit-based teaching, and pedagogies with little regard for student identity representation and acknowledgment.

From the perspective of Hakim Williams, Caribbean decolonization and critical peace education scholar, the violence embedded in schools and their colonial structures provides an example for how the worldview and European epistemological construction of knowledge and value are imposed in former colonies (2016).

In US communities of color, a similar relationship exists between the way education is administered and the way it is practiced. Instead of increased funding or recruiting more teachers that might relate to students, urban schools are more likely to have police, metal detectors and bars, teachers and administrations that utilize law enforcement to discipline students (Stoughton and Gupta-Kagan 2015), as well as high-stakes testing regimes that impact student behavior and teacher discipline (Au 2011; Figlio 2006; McIntosh et al. 2008). The rote pedagogies and policies (No Child Left Behind, zero tolerance, for example) imposed on the economically challenged, which often overlap with POC communities, reinforce a narrow way of learning and administering schools that have less to do with student intellectual development, ability to empathize with others, or the capacities to think critically. Most US students experience education as reinforcing the status quo, a situation that Hannah Arendt's (1954) prophetic essay "Crisis in Education" warned against (Arendt 2006). For students of color, this structural violence is multiplied through the Eurocentric lens constituting de facto colonized education, as highlighted in the critical scholarship of *Education for Extinction* (Adams 1995) and the *Mis-education of the Negro* (Woodson 1998).[5]

TTP and the organic truth telling about injustice in the protests, between neighbors, and on social media is a response to the humiliation of white supremacy, but more importantly, it is an expression of political efficacy challenging the lingering colonial narrative. Intergenerational trauma is present in the stories and bodies that bear witness to the daily replaying of history. The dialectic of elite violence and imposition of values onto black, indigenous, and POC personhood are embedded in American

---

5 *Education for Extinction* describes the imposition of white culture onto Native Americans in "Indian boarding schools," while *Mis-education of the Negro* adds to this description by pointing out how white supremacy is imposed on black persons through formal and informal modes of social education.

institutions, teaching American institutions how to re-enact violence, since the status quo offers complicity for some and a resulting unwillingness to consider other experiences. The ideological indoctrination supports public and institutional complicity, while TTP breaks the cycle, as organic informal education through expression and narrative sharing to reassert basic autonomy and democracy.

When faced with what our youth and the broader society learn from the hypocrisy in the expressed values of democracy and equality versus the reality of racism and denial of that racism, the ignorance and blindness to unjust conditions, while not condoned, is understandable. Yet the power elite utilize the blindness and ignorance of "all lives matter (and blue lives matter)" mantras for their benefit. This blindness is racist, and therefore structurally violent. Truth telling (as a process connected to transitional and restorative justice) is concerned, at theoretical and practical levels, with uncovering structural violence which leads to and is often reinforced by direct violence. TTP addresses police violence leveled against black and brown people, as the tip of an iceberg grounded in racism, white supremacy, and various forms of systematized injustice.

Framing Truth Telling and Violence through Coloniality, Critical Race Theory, and Peace Education

> each thousand years
> of our silence
> is examined
> with regret,
> and the cruel manner in which our values
> of compassion and kindness
> have been ridiculed
> and suppressed [must be]
> brought to bear on the disaster
> of the present time.
> The past must be examined closely, I believe, before we can leave
> it there ...
>
> Alice Walker, "Democratic Womanism"

Our attempts to come to grips with this troubling, oppressive, violent past and to understand the ongoing racial injustice and suppression of subaltern voices are often pacified and given cursory attention in efforts to "move on," "unify and bring people together," "provide a solution," and even "make peace." Attempts at discourse meant to address structural violence in communities experiencing systemic injustices often amount to what Amartya Sen describes as "cultural violence": marginalizing local voices in communities, imposing solutions to "fix" them. Sen writes: "[W]ell meaning attempts at pursuing global peace can have very counterproductive consequences when these attempts are founded on fundamentally illusory understandings of the world of human beings."[6] Because surface understandings of culture have enormous implications that

---

6 http://www.slate.com/articles/news_and_politics/politics/2006/03/what_clash_of_civilizations.html. Adapted from Sen (2006).

colonialism bears witness to, deeper understanding, expertise, and leadership from the local communities are imperative. In peace education (peace and conflict studies), the core problematic is violence (Barash and Webel 2009; Ragland 2015; Reardon 1988). The ultimate approach, as this section describes, relies on the critique of violence. As well, at their moral core, peace education, critical race, and decolonization approaches attend specificity of human dignity as expressed by current social movements. Human dignity is an urgent matter of justice, which, I argue, constitutes peace (Ragland 2015).

The elements of coloniality/decolonization and critical race theory are essential to understanding structural violence (Bajaj 2008; Diaz-Soto 2005; Fontan 2012; Ragland 2009, 2014, 2015b; Williams 2015). Peace education, peace and conflict studies, conflict resolution and transformation theory, restorative justice and human rights education have contributed analyses, but often are Eurocentric and global North-centric (Bajaj 2008; Ragland 2009, 2015b; Tandon 1989; Williams 2015). We pivot here to consider how peace education approaches embodying critical race theory and the subaltern/voices from the margins as reflexive lens respond to violence and offer framing for restorative community practice.

Peace Education and Violence

When we think of violence, we often stop at physical violence without thinking of structural violence. In the current social movement, people of color are being engaged across the globe to demand an end both to structural and to direct violence, seeking new acknowledgment, recognition, and reparation required by human dignity. Betty Reardon, who is known as the founder of the American approach to peace education, defines violence (within the context of peace education) as "avoidable, intentional harm, inflicted for a purpose or perceived advantage of the perpetrator or of those who, while not direct perpetrators, are, however, advantaged by the harm" (Reardon and UNESCO, 2001, 35). This definition has been used by numerous peace education scholars in their descriptions of violence and the role and purposes of peace education (Ardizzone 2007; Jenkins 2008; Navarro-Castro and Nario-Galace 2008; Snauwaert 2009). This peace education critique does the important work of characterizing structural injustice of capitalism as violent, impacting the lives of marginalized people in and outside of the United States. For instance, financial investments for many people are in companies that produce weapons used against innocent communities, inflicting long-lasting harm on natural habitats[7].

Peace educators consider violence the core problematic of *peace* and *education*. Reardon, drawing on Paulo Freire in *Pedagogy of the Oppressed* (1970), points out that

---

7 The processes of slavery and colonization transferred wealth, in terms of humans and resources, from Africa, the Americas, and Asia to Europe under the guise of civilizing the uncivilized. The colonial project was only about accumulating capital. Tandon (1989) argues that there is a direct relationship of disparity between poverty in the global South and wealth in Europe and the United States. Capitalism is not just the spread of Western products to the far corners of the globe, but the arms trade, which sees Western manufactured arms sold to the elite of the global South, not for any humanitarian reasons, but for money (Kisembo 1993; Mirra 2008).

no education is neutral and that underlying values of many societies go unquestioned. She writes:

> It is important to emphasize here that the peace knowledge field has identified various forms of violence. In addition to the politically organized violence of war and various forms of repression, and the structural violence of neocolonial economic institutions there is, as well, social violence such as racism, sexism and religious fundamentalism, and the cultural violence of patriarchal institutions, blood sports, and the glorification of violent historical events in national holidays and the banalization of violence in the media. And now, all of these forms of violence are being seen in their totality as a "culture of violence and war." (Reardon 2000, 8)

Violence is identified here as values, practices, and systems that devalue subaltern perspectives. Reardon points out how understanding the content, however, is not central to the understanding of most peace education.

Conceptually, peace education includes negative peace, positive peace and structural violence. Negative peace is the absence of violence or war. Positive peace is the absence of war and the presence of justice, moving toward the elimination of structural violence. Forms of structural or "indirect" violence include racism, sexism, homophobia, economic injustice, xenophobia, and cultural appropriation. While many in peace education study the forms of structural violence, the core of scholars, underlying theories, and the practice remain Eurocentric and uncritical of the deep complicity and trauma of racism and colonialism (Bajaj 2008; Diaz-Soto 2005). Azarmandi (2016, 158) writes: "Normative Peace Studies remains very much embedded in concepts of liberal peace, which are inherently state-centric and negative peace-oriented. Such an outlook is also inherently blind to questions of race and colonialism."

While the fields of peace education and conflict studies attempt to address physical violence and structural violence, the failure to acknowledge coloniality and racism continues to generate blind spots in analysis and development.[8] These blind spots can be used in neoliberal agendas that promote peace and non-violence abroad and in black and other POC communities, while failing to acknowledge state-sanctioned and state-inspired violence of the police, military, and global policy. US foreign policy planner George Kennan articulates a disinterested, even anti-human rights, orientation toward the relationship between the global South and the United States when he writes:

> We have about 50% of the world's wealth, but only 6.3% of its population ... In this situation, we cannot fail to be the object of envy and resentment. Our real task in the coming period is to devise a pattern of relationships, which will permit us to maintain this position of disparity without positive detriment to our national security. To do so, we must dispense with all the sentimentality and day dreaming: and our attention will have to be concentrated everywhere on our immediate national objectives. (Kennan cited in Abunimah and Arnove 2000, 11)

---

8 Many development, non-governmental organization, and international education workers rely on peace education and peace and conflict studies scholarship to ground their work.

While realism would absolve the immorality of this view, a critical race, coloniality, and peace education orientation would critique Kennan's principles as clear examples of structural violence and neocolonialism, which hides the reality of economic coercion and of graft in order to gain access for extractive development practices on natural resources and indigenous bodies (Fanon 1963).

When there is no pedagogy of acknowledgment or accurate representation of subaltern experience and identity, education is violent and unjust (Bajaj 2008; Lynn, Jennings, and Hughes 2013). Since the concept of structural violence has a normative- human rights framework, it is considered a form of violence because the conditions of structural violence often cause harm to mental and physical health and overall well-being, and provide the conditions for direct violence or war (Galtung 1969; Ho 2007; Montesanti and Thurston 2015; Ragland 2015; Rylko-Bauer and Farmer 2016; Steenkamp 2005).

Understanding Coloniality While Centering Critical Race Pedagogy and Womanism to Ground Truth Telling

> *The imperialist system is anti-truth and anti-science.*
>
> Yash Tandon, "Peace Education: Its Concepts and Problems
> and Its Application to Africa"

The extractive nature of colonization continues in the conduct of majority institutions toward racialized minority communities. This conduct maintains the status quo, hegemonic property rights, and the flow of capital. During the Ferguson protests, the protection of property was the justification given for the militarized policing. The historical parallel phenomena of slaves-as-property and current criminal justice systems and policing, of slave catcher patrols police practices, continue to be relevant (Alexander 2012; Mac 2016; Silverii 2014)[9]. Non-violent protests of the past and of the present are met with the full force of national guards, militarized police, and deputized security. In these actions, law enforcement and political officials communicate the value of social order over human needs and lives. Thus, the theoretical frameworks of coloniality/ decolonization and critical race theory and pedagogy (CRT/CRP), were natural connections informing the M4BL (Movement for Black Lives)[10] and TTP.

In part, the view from the subaltern, black, and brown experience recognizes race as a proxy for white elitist capitalism. Bell (1987, 1992) explains how the presence of African slaves became an identifiable distinction, allowing poor whites to identify more closely with elite white, male landowners. While natives could escape more easily, blacks and their offspring were slaves for life, highlighting the deplorable conditions of

---

9 http://www.democracynow.org/2016/7/14/ex_seattle_police_chief_condemns_systemic; http://www.blackagendareport.com/slave_patrols_police_terror; http://countercurrentnews.com/2015/04/police-originated-from-slave-catching-patrols/.

10 The Movement for Black Lives denotes many organizations, actions, and ideals focused on global black liberation, in this current political manifestation that grew initially from the Ferguson protests. Later, the term "Black Lives Matter" was problematically used by media to describe the entire movement – silencing voices from Ferguson, Baltimore, New York City, and communities around the world working toward the goals of black liberation.

slavery. Swartz (2015) describes the line of reasoning used by poor whites to express racial superiority: "At least I'm not a nigger." This retort speaks to the hierarchy of race created by the life-long conditions of black servitude. The superiority (both actual power superiority and perceptual) enjoyed by whites endures from the time blacks were property, free labor, or an easily exploitable class. As a litany of literature explains, although formal slavery ended, it persisted in different forms, such as sharecropping, debt discrimination, and so forth.[11] Each generation is re-traumatized by new iterations of previously used mechanisms (Alexander 2012; Blackmon 2008, Zinn 1990).

But alongside intergenerational trauma, resilience and knowledge of the impact of systems of oppression are also passed down. New understandings that make ideas like intersectionality, restorative justice, and womanism prominent offer counter-approaches to just transformation of our society.

Ferguson and the Truth Telling Project (TTP)

In the Truth Telling Project, we embrace that notion that storytelling is a form of resilience as well as dissent, as it shifts the narrative, centering marginalized voices. Formal education, adult learning, and community spaces often exclude the historical truth of struggle and trauma carried from generation to generation. Although peace education, in my own educational experience, helped me to question and deconstruct violence and contextualize racism, I began to see the frameworks, while useful, as limiting and only speaking to the experience of an audience. With the throwing asunder of respectability politics in the Movement for Black Lives, I started to connect the missing elements of peace education with the truth of coloniality, particularly because of the global implications of transitional justice. In describing the pedagogical approach of truth telling, Arthur Romano and I write:

> Critical race pedagogy, especially in this context, acknowledges the unsaid as a core part of transformational learning … Critical race pedagogy, applied to truth telling, seeks to challenge silence about racial oppression, to engage with structural racism, and to recognize the intersectional nature of systemic oppression by attending to ways of knowing that honor black culture and positions experience of community members as truth and connect them with other forms of marginalization and resistance. (Romano and Ragland 2018)

I had been informally studying restorative justice in K–12 circles and integrating the practice in my own teaching practices. I had also been writing about critiques of peace education as being too focused on and centering Eurocentric values, scholars, and research. Then, Pastor Cori Bush and I began working closely together. (She had been much more integrated in the protest community, supporting and providing leadership to the youth protesters.)

---

11 A Propublica report describes how debt is unequally and often fraudulently collected in black communities, with St. Louis as ground zero: https://www.propublica.org/article/debt-collection-lawsuits-squeeze-black-neighborhoods.

Responding to economic injustice and inequity, TTP focuses on capacity development for the most marginalized identities. It works to make its professional pedagogy
consistent with ideology, practices, and principles of leadership developed by the larger
social movement of Black Lives Matter as a way to maintain accountability for placing
the truth in the foreground. TTP came to represent a unity of ideas rooted in the experience and needs of the Ferguson/St. Louis protest community, beginning as a coalition
between St. Louis-based and other national community and advocacy groups, to support local truth and reconciliation efforts. While many were cautious of the idea of
reconciliation, because it was perceived to be focused on forgiveness, truth telling as an
idea and a focus on healing efforts was welcomed.

Weekly conversations with TRC (truth and reconciliation commission) experts led to
the Truth Telling Weekend in March of 2015, where experts and community members
came to learn more about truth and reconciliation and to decide if it was a useful strategy.
The mission statement developed in the months following the convening continues as:

> The Truth Telling Project implements and sustains grassroots, community-cen-
> tered truth-telling processes to share local voices, to educate America, and to
> support reconciliation for the purposes of eliminating structural violence and
> systemic racism against Black people in the United States.[12]

With consultation from the Greensboro Truth and Reconciliation Commission,[13] TTP
created a focused mandate and declaration of intent to hear testimony through 2016
that would be shared widely in order to document US state-sanctioned violence and
express experiences of marginalized communities. Rather than creating a formal
commission, TTP emerged as a community-based project because (i) most TRCs are
nation-state sponsored, with interests that are primarily state-centered; (ii) because of
the current conditions, distrust of the state was high due to perceived government
complicity in repression at local levels; (iii) the impact of Ferguson saw the creation of
many commissions that to date have not generated structural transformation; and
(iv) transitional justice suggests that there is a formal end of conflict, while police
violence continues and trauma, distrust, and resentment resurface among marginalized
people and communities.

The truth telling hearings began in November of 2015 in Ferguson, MO. Over 30
participants shared their experiences of police violence, and stated what they believed
to be its underlying causes, and what change they wanted to see. TTP sponsored local
discussion groups and forums with national activists, academics, artists, and advocates
to further the notion of truth telling as the first and most important step in any truth
and reconciliation processes.

TTP organizers developed educational materials and dialogue frameworks[14] to
support groups in other locales in understanding the tensions and commitments

---

12 http://thetruthtellingproject.org.
13 http://www.greensborotrc.org.
14 TTP Night of A Thousand Conversations – Guide and FAQ to support community dialogue after
watching testimony of those victimized by police violence. Conversation Guide: https://drive.google.com/
file/d/0B1RkIXhZFa0_UktIT0NmZGlPSTg/view?usp=sharing; FAQ for facilitators: https://drive.google.
com/file/d/0B1RkIXhZFa0_LWhjZ05TTUFZTE0/view?usp=sharing.

embedded in this emerging approach to truth telling. These materials were informed by the truth telling hearings and forums.

In addition to the hearings, community conversations, and a host of connected events sponsored by the Truth Telling Project, one primary concern continues to be with the importance of truth. By giving attention to black individuals who are victimized by police violence, TTP attempts to uplift the narrative of communities whose story is often not believed. This engaged narrative development attempts to resituate the notion of truth within oppressed communities instead of its more prevalent presence in white-dominated institutions.[15]

TTP emerged with the understanding that truth telling can be leveraged toward healing and structural change if rooted in a community's values and understandings of the world. The need for acknowledgment of shared experiences of racialized violence and their root causes can bring communities together.

Conclusions, Educational Implications, and Possibilities

We imagined that, like the Ferguson protests and the public testimonies held in South Africa, Colombia, Greensboro, and many other places, the public hearings needed to convey the drama of the political moment and incidents of violence to speak to the hearts of our citizens. At the core of this form of storytelling is an educational experiment and intervention aimed at disrupting the dominant narrative and explaining how POC movements must be understood by mainstream Americans as necessary to fulfill the promises of democracy and rights in the United States. The sharing of stories in this way connects the deeper reality of individual stories with larger systemic forms of violence, and makes more palpable the solidarity needed to end police violence and other related forms of structural violence.

To say "experiment" is not to dilute the project we have undertaken, but to express our willingness to deal with our own healing, stories, and capacious justice. From the perspective of a community with deep distrust of the US economic and justice systems, TTP, as a grassroots project, has been a necessary act of empowerment and validation. Truth tellers shared their experiences as an educative and loving act to reach out to as many people as possible, while healing and validating the similar experiences and pain of others.

When Toni Taylor, mother of Cary Ball Jr., described the amount of bullets in her son's body;[16] or when Michael Brown Jr.'s sisters talked of missing their big brother, the prankster, who was always smiling;[17] or when the sister of Sandra Bland, Shonda Needem, teared up at the thought of Sandra's nieces and nephews never seeing their Auntee again,[18] it was all to heal and to acknowledge the feelings of shared

---

15 https://medium.com/@dr538/
truth-lies-and-politics-dont-be-limited-by-mainstream-thought-lessness-2c6a2f890b41#.3z9h7mowd.
16 Toni Taylor spoke as a truth teller in November 2015 at the Truth Telling Initiative launch in Ferguson, MO; see article written about her testimony: https://medium.com/@thetruthtellingproject/listening-and-understanding-in-racist-america-3c814101a140#.i3favbize.
17 The sisters of Michael Brown spoke at the Truth Telling Hearing in August 2016 in Ferguson, MO
18 Shonda Needam spoke as a truth teller in November 2015 at the Truth Telling Initiative launch in Ferguson, MO.

experiences, to come together to prevent future police violence, and to connect empathetically.

Some critiques assert that truth telling can become an echo chamber or, if focused solely on racial justice without an outward posture (a particular aspect of restorative justice that confronts victimizers), might prevent healing and even re-traumatize truth tellers (King 2011). From another critique: "truth-telling easily devolves into retributive constructions of justice defeating the goal of reconciliation. Geared to looking backwards to focus on blame and punishment, this kind of 'truth' tends to leave the broader systems of injustice unchallenged" (Davis and Scharrer forthcoming).

While these critiques may hold much general truth, the core understanding of TTP emerged from Ferguson community members who understood that truth and reconciliation is desirable, but that reconciliation would not be possible without structural transformation, that is, ending the conditions that allow police violence to flourish. The beginning of any TRC process, according to Imani Scott (2014), author of *Crimes against Humanity in the Land of the Free: Can a Truth and Reconciliation Process Heal Racial Conflict in America?*, requires truth telling, which is a "searching moral inventory" that the entire society must undertake. This first step requires society to listen, learn, and make changes based on the understanding gleaned from truth telling.

Ferguson did teach society, but the wrong lesson was learned. For instance, the "Ferguson effect" has become a widely used phrase in law enforcement, referring to civil disobedience. In some instances, police claimed they were afraid to do their work. Many in law enforcement began suggesting there was a "war on cops" despite crime rates dropping by "50 percent from 1994 through the first half of 2014" (MacDonald 2016).[19] This rhetoric reinforces support for violent policing practices in communities of color because of negative attitudes toward communities claiming their rights. The recent election and vast right-wing sweep of political offices throughout the United States reflects an identification of mainstream America with law and order politics and conservative and sometimes racist values.[20]

Despite the current sentiments, the Truth Telling Project promotes a reconsideration of how we conceive of the notion of justice, which often is minimized in retributive terms and as maintenance of social order. Based on the healing and reconciliation possible in restorative and transformative approaches[21] that ground TTP on an interpersonal level, restorative justice is preferred (Latimer, Dowden, and Muise, 2005). TTP looks for the same kind of relational transformation at the structural level.

---

19 https://www.washingtonpost.com/news/volokh-conspiracy/wp/2016/07/21/more-on-the-ferguson-effect-and-responses-to-critics/?utm_term=.914795ffd926; also see https://www.policeone.com/community-policing/articles/194645006-4-ways-to-stave-off-the-Ferguson-effect/.

20 https://www.washingtonpost.com/news/wonk/wp/2016/03/03/researchers-have-found-strong-evidence-that-racism-helps-the-gop-win/?utm_term=.f1a95997ef82.

21 http://www.eastbaytimes.com/2014/12/09/guest-commentary-restorative-justice-program-has-become-a-vital-tool-for-public/; http://chicago.suntimes.com/news/cook-county-to-create-community-court-in-north-lawndale/.

Truth Telling as American Educational Intervention

Since the current political landscape is mired with "good intentions" and a fear of addressing racism in meaningful ways, few ways educate white allies and bystanders on the most marginalized perspectives. TTP is gathering the recorded testimony, launching an online learning platform, "the Truth Telling Commons," to go beyond official transitional justice reporting mechanisms. Through this platform, the Truth Telling commons will seek to equip learners with (i) deep listening skills to prepare learners for authentic hearing of video and audio personal accounts from individuals who experienced police brutality; (ii) the opportunity to begin reflection on white allyship with persons of color and their encounters with state-sanctioned direct and indirect violence and racism; and (iii) the capacity to follow listening, learning, and reflection with action.

We expect that the Truth Telling Commons will document inequity by bridging what is often a gap between data on racial injustices and empathic connections needed to act against racially charged direct and indirect violence enacted on people of color. We also hope it will foster political efficacy in communities through extending marginalized, authentic voices to educate and break through racial stereotypes, apathy, and inaction. Through sharing the experiences of black communities and our experiences with police violence, the online learning platform, "It's Time to Listen," is rooted in a community of healing and support, as it develops political strength. It seeks to foster and disseminate stories and testimonies, engaging with the local and national community of human rights and racial justice. While the platform assists in alternative narrative building, it also connects partner organizations by guiding users to issues that emerge from testimonies to become active with groups working on those same issues. The stories fill in the gaps for national and global audiences as they witness an empowered community that shares its testimony and informs the world of how their stories bring clarity to the larger landscape of police violence with structural racism at its core. Our stories illustrate the specificity of human dignity and this platform and its dissemination will connect learners to this orientation to inform their work.

The target audience is threefold: (i) adult and high school age educators, dialogue facilitators; (ii) adult and high school age learners; (iii) white allies for racial justice. While the primary purpose of this platform is to house testimony from the Ferguson Truth Telling Hearings, the educational outreach is a core focus for working toward racial justice, sharing stories widely per the wishes of community members telling them. The target audiences of adult and high school age educators and dialogue facilitators, including, but not limited to, educators/teachers, Sunday school/religious educators, professional social work circles, after-school community education groups and dialogue groups focused on racial justice, whiteness and similarly related groups will be introduced to the online learning toolkit through four regional workshops, webinars, and an online facilitation guide. The demographic of the adult learners and high school age learners the educators will reach out to are primarily white, aged 14–64, middle- to working-class socioeconomic status, liberal to moderate leaning, aware of some injustices, but with limited knowledge and wary of asking questions about racial issues.

The videos included in the online learning platform are of individuals sharing stories of loss and trauma that learners can use to connect ordinary experiences rooted in bias and their own personal narratives and families. The questions that emerge from videos are easily answerable with links, popups, cartoons, and lesson plans that educate users on terms like "structural racism" or "racial profiling." The learning platform humanizes subjects to connect with learner empathy and intellect. The online platform, the current Movement for Black Lives, and the work of this project represent critical voices and approaches from the margins, extending and reaching out to the broader public to offer authentic testimonies and narratives that inform us of the most pressing concerns of this society.

References

Abunimah, A. and Arnove, A. 2000. *Iraq under Siege: The Deadly Impact of Sanctions and War*. London: Pluto.

Adams, D.W. 1995. *Education for Extinction: American Indians and the Boarding School Experience, 1875–1928*. Lawrence University Press of Kansas.

Al-Daraweesh, F. and Snauwaert, D. 2015. *Human Rights Education Beyond Universalism and Relativism: A Relational Hermeneutic for Global Justice*. New York: Palgrave Macmillan.

Alexander, M. 2012. *New Jim Crow: Mass Incarceration in the Age of Colorblindness*. New York: The New Press.

Apple, M.W. and Beane, J.A. 1995. *Democratic Schools*. Association for Supervision & Curriculum Development.

Ardizzone, L. 2007. *Getting My Word Out: Voice of Urban Youth*. Albany, NY: SUNY Press.

Arendt, H. 2006. "The Crisis in Education." In *Between Past and Future*. New York: Penguin.

Au, W. 2011. "Teaching under the New Taylorism: High-stakes Testing and the Standardization of the 21st Century Curriculum." *Journal of Curriculum Studies* 43(1), 25–45.

Azarmandi, M. 2016. "Colonial Continuities." *Peace Review* 28(2), 158–164.

Bajaj, M. 2008. "Critical Peace Education." In *Encyclopedia of Peace Education*, edited by M. Bajaj. Charlotte, NC: Information Age Publishing.

Barash, D. and Webel, C. 2009. "Peace and Conflict Studies." In *The Meanings of Peace*, pp. 4–12. Thousand Oaks, CA: Sage.

Bell, D. 1987. *And We are Not Saved: The Elusive Quest for Racial Justice*. New York: Basic Books.

Bell, D. 1992. *Faces at the Bottom of the Well: The Permanence of Racism*. New York: Basic Books.

Blackmon, D.A. 2008. *Slavery by Another Name: The Re-enslavement of Black People in America from the Civil War to World War II*. New York: Doubleday.

Coates, T.-N. 2015. *Between the World and Me*. New York: Spiegel & Grau.

Davis, F. and Scharrer, J. forthcoming. Chapter excerpts in *Transforming Justice*. Indiana University Press.

Diaz-Soto, L. 2005) "How Can We Teach Peace When We Are So Outraged? A Call for Critical Peace Education." *Taboo: The Journal of Culture and Education* (Fall/Winter), 91–96.

Fanon, F. 1963. *The Wretched of the Earth*. New York: Grove Press.

Figlio, D.N. 2006. "Testing, Crime and Punishment." *Journal of Public Economics* 90(4), 837–851.

Fontan, V. 2012. *Decolonizing Peace*. World Dignity University Press.

Freire, P. 1970. *Pedagogy of the Oppressed*. New York: Continuum.

Galtung, J. 1969. "Violence, Peace, and Peace Research." *Journal of Peace Research* 6(3), 167–191.

Garza, A. 2014. "A Herstory of the #BlackLivesMatter Movement." The Feminist Wire, October 7. http://www.thefeministwire.com/2014/10/blacklivesmatter-2/(last accessed October 30, 2017).

Grothaus, M. 2015. "The U.S. Doesn't Track Deaths by Police, so Citizens Are Doing It." Fast Company, June 18. www.fastcompany.com/3045724/fatal-encounters-crowdsourcing-deaths-by-police (last accessed October 30, 2017).

Ho, K. 2007. "Structural Violence as a Human Rights Violation." *Essex Human Rights Review*, 4.

Jenkins, T. 2008. "The International Institute on Peace Education: Twenty-six Years Modeling Critical, Participatory Peace Pedagogy." *Factis Pax* 2(2), 166–174.

Jones, LeRoi [Amiri Baraka]. 1965. "The Revolutionary Theatre." *Liberator*, July 5, pp. 4–6. http://nationalhumanitiescenter.org/pds/maai3/protest/text12/barakatheatre.pdf (last accessed October 30, 2017).

King, R. 2011. "Healing Psychosocial Trauma in the Midst of Truth Commissions: The Case of Gacaca in Post Genocide Rwanda." *Genocide Studies and Prevention: An International Journal* 6(2), 134–151.

King, S. 2017. "Arizona Lawmaker Proposes New Bill Banning Classes or Events Discussing Social Justice on College Campuses." *Daily News*, January 13. www.nydailynews.com/news/national/king-rep-ban-social-justice-events-arizona-schools-article-1.2945382 (last accessed October 30, 2017).

Kisembo, P. 1993. *A Popular Version of Yash Tandon's Militarism and Peace Education in Africa*. African Asociation for Literacy and AdultEducation. Nairobi, Kenya.

Latimer, J. Dowden, C., and Muise, D. 2005. "The Effectiveness of Restorative Justice Practices: A Meta-Analysis." *The Prison Journal* 85(2), 127–144.

Lui, M., Robles, B., Leondar-Wright, B., Brewer, B., and Adamson, R. 2006. *The Color of Wealth: The Story Behind the U.S. Racial Wealth Divide*. New York: The New Press.

Lynn, M., Jennings, M.E., and Hughes, S. 2013. "Critical Race Pedagogy 2.0: Lessons from Derrick Bell." *Race, Ethnicity and Education* 16(4), 603–628.

Mac, L. 2016. Ferguson Response Network Podcast. http://fergusonresponse.org/author/lesliemac/.

MacDonald, H. 2016. "More on the "Ferguson Effect," and Responses to Critics." *Washington Post*, July 21. https://www.washingtonpost.com/news/volokh-conspiracy/wp/2016/07/21/more-on-the-ferguson-effect-and-responses-to-critics/?utm_term=.842943a0864f (last accessed November 6, 2017).

MacIntosh, K., Flannery, K., Sugai, G., Braun, D., and Cochrane K. 2008. "Relationships between Academics and Problem Behavior in the Transition from Middle School to High School." *Journal of Positive Behavior Interventions* 10(4), 243–255.

Madar, C. 2014. "Why It's Impossible to Indict a Cop." The Nation. www.thenation.com/article/why-its-impossible-indict-cop/(last accessed October 30, 2017).

Mirra, C. 2008. "Countering Militarism through Peace Education." In *Encyclopedia of Peace Education*, edited by M. Bajaj, pp. 93–98. Charlotte, NC. Information Age Press.

Montesanti, S.R. and Thurston, W.E. 2015. "Mapping the Role of Structural and Interpersonal Violence in the Lives of Women: Implications for Public Health Interventions and Policy." *BMC Women's Health* 15, 100.

Navarro-Castro, L. and Nario-Galace J. 2008. *Pathways to Peace.* Quezon City. Philippines. Center for Peace Education, Miriam College.

Park, H. and Lee, J.C. 2017. "Looking for Accountability in Police-Involved Deaths of Blacks." *New York Times*, May 3. www.nytimes.com/interactive/2016/07/12/us/looking-for-accountability-in-police-involved-deaths-of-blacks.html?_r=0 (last accessed October 30, 2017).

Ragland, D. 2009. "Recasting Classical and Contemporary Philosophies to Ground Peace Education: A Review Essay of James Page, Peace Education: Exploring Ethical and Philosophical Foundations." *Infactis Pax: Journal of Peace Education* 4(1).

Ragland, D. 2014. "Unsettling the Settled Concepts." *Peace Chronicle: Peace and Justice Studies Association* (Winter). https://www.peacejusticestudies.org/sites/default/files/PeaceChronicle%20Winter-2014.pdf.

Ragland, D. 2015. "Peace Education as an Ethical Framework to Situate Restorative Justice: Locating the Concerns of Communities of Color in Peace and Justice Discourse." In *Peace Studies between Tradition and Innovation.* Cambridge: Cambridge Studies Press.

Reardon, B. 1988. *Comprehensive Peace Education*: New York: Teachers College Press.

Reardon, B. 2000. Peace Education: A Review and Projection. In *International Companion to Education*, edited by B. Moon, S. Brown, and M.B. Peretz. New York: Routledge.

Reardon, B.A. and United Nations Educational Science, and Cultural Organization, Paris (France). Div. of Educational Policy and Planning. 2001. *Education for a Culture of Peace in a Gender Perspective.* UNESCO.

Rogers, J. 2015. *Ferguson Is America: Roots of Rebellion.* St. Louis, MO: Printed for the author by Mira Digital Publishing.

Romano, A. and Ragland, D. 2018. "Truth Telling from the Margins: Exploring Black-led Responses to Police Violence and Systemic Humiliation." In *Systemic Humiliation in America*, edited by D. Rothbart. Palgrave Macmillan.

Rothstein, R. 2014. "The Making of Ferguson." Economic Policy Institute. October 15. http://www.epi.org/publication/making-ferguson/(last accessed November 6, 2017).

Rylko-Bauer, B. and Farmer, P. 2016. "Structural Violence, Poverty and Social Suffering." In *The Oxford Handbook of the Social Science of Poverty*, edited by D. Brady and L.M. Burton. Oxford: Oxford University Press.

Scott, I.M. 2014. *Crimes against Humanity in the Land of the Free: Can a Truth and Reconciliation Process Heal Racial Conflict in America?* Santa Barbara, CA: Praeger.

Sen, A. 2006. *Identity and Violence: The Illusion of Destiny.* New York: W.W. Norton.

Sexton, J. 2016. "FBI Director Comey: Small Group of Videos Are Not "Proof of an Epidemic" of Police Brutality." Hot Air. http://hotair.com/archives/2016/10/17/fbi-director-comey-small-group-videos-not-proof-epidemic-police-violence/(last accessed October 30, 2017).

Silverii, S. 2014. *Cop Culture: Why Good Cops Go Bad.* Boca Raton, FL: CRC Press: Taylor & Francis Group.

Snauwaert, D. 2009. "Human Rights and Cosmopolitan Democratic Education." *Philosophical Studies in Education* 40, 94–103.

Stahl, Stephanie D. 2016. "The Evolution of Zero-Tolerance Policies." *CrissCross* 4(1), Article 7. http://digitalcommons.iwu.edu/crisscross/vol4/iss1/7.

Steenkamp, C. 2005. "The Legacy of War: Conceptualizing a 'Culture of Violence' to Explain Violence after Peace Accords." *The Round Table* 94(379), 253–267.

Stoughton, S. and Gupta-Kagan, J. 2015. "Why Are Police Disciplining Students?" *The Atlantic*, October 29. www.theatlantic.com/politics/archive/2015/10/when-should-police-discipline-students/413056/(last accessed October 30, 2017).

Swartz, O. 2015. "Gay Rights/African American Rights: A Common Struggle for Social Justice." *Socialism and Democracy* 29(2), 1–24.

Tandon, Y. 1989. "Peace Education: Its Concepts and Problems and Its Application to Africa." In *Militarism and Peace Education in Africa*, pp. 50–76. Nairobi: African Association for Literacy and Adult Education.

Williams, H. 2013. "Postcolonial Structural Violence: A Study of School Violence in Trinidad & Tobago." *International Journal of Peace Studies* 18(2).

Williams, H. 2015. "Decolonization Ain't Over: The Pressing Need for a Global Peace Education, Now!" *Global Campaign for Peace Education* 118. http://www.peace-ed-campaign.org/decolonization-aint-over-the-pressing-need-for-a-global-peace-education-now/(last accessed October 30, 2017).

Williams, H. 2016. "Lingering Colonialities as Blockades to Peace Education: School Violence in Trinidad." In *Peace Education: International Perspectives*, edited by M. Bajaj and M. Hantzopoulos, pp. 141–156. London: Bloomsbury.

Woodson, C.G. 1998. *The Mis-education of the Negro*. Trenton, NJ: Africa World Press.

Zinn, H. 1990. *A People's History of the United States*. New York: Harper & Row.

27

Emmanuel Levinas

Philosophical Exposures, and Responses to Systemic and Symbolic
Violence in Education

Gabriel Keehn and Deron Boyles

Introduction

One could be forgiven for wondering what a chapter on the philosophical thought of
Emmanuel Levinas is doing in a handbook on violence of any kind, let alone one on
violence as it specifically relates to educational concerns. Indeed, when Levinas is
considered in discussions of violence generally, it is often in the significantly more
abstract context of rehearsing the critique leveled against him by Jacques Derrida in
his essay "Violence and Metaphysics" (2001), which takes Levinas to task for various
assumptions made in Levinas's early work *Totality and Infinity*, and indeed characterizes these assumptions as ontologically violent in certain ways. Aside from the
Derridean critique, which will not figure prominently in the rest of this discussion,
Levinas's understandings and philosophical uses of violence have gone largely unaddressed in the interpretive literature, although there has been a significant resurgence
of interest within education in Levinas in a general sense (see Biesta 1999, 2000;
Chinnery 2000, 2001; Davis 2008; Joldersma 2008; Todd 2003). This is not entirely
unjustifiable, however, as the most obvious and profound influence Levinas's work
has had on the contemporary philosophical scene is manifested in the "ethical turn"
of recent political theory, a concept to which we will return shortly as it sets a very
important contextual backdrop for considerations of Levinasian thinking about
violence. What is important to note now is that we feel that Levinas's understandings
and applications of his theory of violence are not only worth studying as an interpretive matter, but can be brought to bear specifically on the concerns of the current
volume, namely the various manifestations of violence in educational settings. While,
as our title suggests, we find particularly relevant applications of Levinas's work in
thinking about symbolic and systemic violence, we also hope to argue that Levinas
can provide us with an important theoretical bridge between these types of violence
and the concretely real, murderous physical violence which has become something of

The Wiley Handbook on Violence in Education: Forms, Factors, and Preventions, First Edition.
Edited by Harvey Shapiro.
© 2018 John Wiley & Sons, Inc. Published 2018 by John Wiley & Sons, Inc.

an epidemic in American schools today.[1] Specifically, we see the various types of symbolic violence which exist in America schools (corporate intrusion, rote teaching and learning, terrible conditions in school buildings, the unprecedented sense of policing of these environments, and so on) to set the ontologico-ethical stage, as it were, for the outbursts of more obvious types of violence on which the media and much research tend to focus. That is, we see Levinas as providing the philosophical tools necessary to respond to what we see as a dominant myth about gun violence in American schools, and American society more generally. We are specifically referring to the idea that gun violence, generally, is senseless, absurd, and irrational; that there is no intelligible way to approach a discussion of gun violence in anything other than the very shallowest questions of proximate or material causes (e.g., "violent video games," "easy access to guns"). Beyond these types of claims lies an unbridgeable chasm of nonsense and the perpetually lurking madness in the human heart – the eruption of which can, in principle, never be understood or predicted. These sentiments are even stronger in cases of school violence, where the unquestionable innocence and vulnerability of the victims, as well as the sanctity of the spaces in which such violence takes place, add yet another layer of unfathomability to an already baffling act.[2] At the same time, where Levinas provides us with a trenchant and philosophically robust diagnosis of the relationship between these sets of problems, he also, we argue, provides us with promising avenues of resistance to structural violence and ways of rethinking educational relationships so as to foster educational relationships which proceed from respect and reverence for others, rather than from their exploitation and denigration. Key to our discussion will be the deployment of a number of Levinasian concepts ("the Other," "the Face," etc.), some of which will seem counterintuitive and strange when abstracted from their philosophical ecosystem of Levinas's thought. We will be utilizing a key distinction in Levinas's thinking between, on the one hand, violence, and on the other, murder. While the distinction will be explicated in much more detail below, it is important to acknowledge at the outset that the Levinasian usage of both of these terms has little to nothing to do with our everyday understandings of the terms. Put briefly, for Levinas, murder, rather than being a general subtype of violence as some larger category, is actually an act which can never be committed once one truly engages in ethical relation. As we will see, Levinas suggests that to take ethics seriously inherently means to be unable to commit murder. Our argument will be that our educational institutions perpetrate violence in the sorts of crude symbolic ways which Levinas suggests signal a lack of ethical understanding, and that a shift from this type of violent relation to a relationship which recognizes the ethical seriousness of murder, and hence is unable to perpetrate violence, is what is necessary in contemporary educational discourse.

---

1 For relevant comparative data on this point, see *Small Arms Survey* 2007: *Guns and the City* (Small Arms Survey 2007). While the data are not as recent as we would like, the data collected since the publication of the 2007 report do not indicate a radical shift in overall trends worldwide; see http://www.smallarmssurvey. org/publications/by-type.html (accessed August 16, 2014). See also Alpers and Wilson (2007) and Giblin (2014).

2 In some of what follows, we may occasionally lapse into speaking in general terms of "gun violence," without the qualifier "in schools." We maintain that in almost all cases the remarks we make about gun violence will apply a fortiori to gun violence in schools.

Levinas and Violence: Historico-Biographical Considerations

Stanley Cavell often made the point that philosophy is inextricably linked to biography, and for nobody is this claim more true than Levinas. Levinas's life and experiences can be seen as running in a quite close parallel with his philosophical development and any account of his understanding of violence, ontology, and related topics must engage with his experiences in both the political and philosophical milieu of World War II Europe. Born to Jewish parents in Lithuania (then part of pre-Revolutionary Russia), Levinas witnessed the various violences of the Russian Revolution and was forced to emigrate from a suddenly hostile environment to the Ukraine, only to return to Lithuania in the early 1920s after the country had gained independence from the Russian Revolutionary Government. However, it was the next two decades which would most profoundly shape the subsequent trajectory of Levinas's philosophical and spiritual life.

In order to study with Edmund Husserl, Levinas shifted the locus of his philosophical studies from Strasbourg, France to Freiburg in the late 1920s. Importantly, during this time, Levinas attended Martin Heidegger's inaugural seminar in 1928 after he took over the chair in philosophy from Husserl. Heidegger's philosophical thought would come to serve in many ways as the catalyst for Levinas's own philosophical positions, for example, on the nature and role of Being. However, it was Heidegger's well-known political affiliations during this time which made an even greater impact on Levinas. It is easy to forget in the seemingly perpetually recurring controversies and exposés regarding Heidegger's associations with National Socialism[3] that his political predilections were already well known in the early 1930s, and especially after his signing of the infamous "Loyalty Oath of German Professors to Adolf Hitler and the National Socialist State" in 1933 (Young 1997, 3). Indeed, this point is made by Levinas himself in "As If Consenting to Horror," a short essay appearing originally in *Le Nouvel Observatuer* in 1988. Levinas opens the piece writing, "I learned very early, perhaps even before 1933 and certainly after Hitler's huge success at the time of his election to the Reichstag, of Heidegger's sympathy toward National Socialism" (Levinas 1989, 485). Levinas's subsequent rejection of Heidegger's thought was not as simple or swift as one might assume, though he of course would have been on sound footing, as a deeply committed Jewish philosopher, if he had rejected Heidegger on simply political grounds. Indeed, this type of critique of Levinas's thinking in general, and his movement against Heidegger particularly, has been recently advanced by Alain Badiou, who had characterized Levinas's ethical thought as essentially politically impotent (a point to which we will return) and problematically "identitarian," rooted too deeply in Levinas's Jewish identity (Badiou 2001, 18–29). Levinas signals his difficulties grappling with the Heideggerian legacy, recalling his reaction after learning of Heidegger's Nazism, writing "I could not doubt the news, but took it with stupor and disappointment, and also with the faint hope that it expressed only the temporary lapse of a great speculative mind into practical banality" (Levinas 1989, 485). Rather than simply attributing Heidegger's Nazism to a momentary lapse of judgment, Levinas chose to examine the metaphysical traces of fascism within the tradition of European philosophy. He saw totalitarian complicity as rooted in the dominant

---

3 The best general volume on these topics is Wolin (1992).

Cartesian understanding of abstract human subjectivities (Descartes "cogito") as existing in isolation from one another in incorporeal space. In concluding his personal reflections on this difficult time in his philosophical life, and after praising the profound philosophical insights contained in Heidegger's *Being and Time*, Levinas plaintively asks of the book: "Can we be assured, however, that there was never any echo of Evil in it? ... the diabolical is endowed with intelligence and enters where it will ... Intellectual effort is needed to recognize it. Who can boast of having done so?" (Levinas 1989, 488).

It is particularly important here, in illustrating Levinas's commitment to a deep philosophical engagement with violent ideologies, to mention his article, published just a year after Heidegger's signing of the oath, "Reflections on the Philosophy of Hitlerism" (Levinas 1990a). Although Levinas later came to regret his writing of this article, claiming that he gave National Socialism too much credit in attempting to engage with it philosophically (Moyn 1998, 35), in many ways the discussion he offers in this piece sets the agenda for his later work, and indeed where the first glimpses of Levinas's thinking on violence make their appearance. Here, Levinas characterizes Nazism as a fundamental assault on the traditional Western understanding of the self, detranscendentalizing any sense of human subjectivity, ultimately grounding human existence in a type of biological bondage to "the mysterious urgings of the blood, the appeals of heredity and the past for which the body serves as an enigmatic vehicle" (Levinas 1990a, 69). For Levinas, there was a direct line to be drawn from the denial of any type of transcendental subjectivity through a metaphysically violent denial of human freedom and ethical relations and from there to out-and-out racist political movements (Moyn 1998, 38). That is, Levinas felt that a purely materialistic understanding of the human person would be unable to sustain the sort of ethical critique necessary to stave off the evils of National Socialism in Nazi Germany. If the individual is reduced to a purely material process, it is much easier, in Levinas's view, to justify the sorts of reductive and violent ideological maneuvers perpetrated by the Nazis. These reflections on the nature of Nazism and the specific types of ideological violence such a view does to the conception of the human person were undeniably important in Levinas's philosophical development in thinking about violence. Indeed, Samuel Moyn has gone so far as to assert that these prewar writings are actually the most philosophically important in understanding Levinas's general project, writing that "Levinas always remained a pre-Holocaust philosopher insofar as his thought continued to be governed by inter-war premises and directed at the interwar end of 'the other'" (Moyn 2005, 196). While this would certainly be a controversial claim among most scholars of Levinas, given the fact that Levinas lost much of his own family in the Holocaust and was himself captured and imprisoned by the Nazis, and given the fact that Levinas once characterized his whole corpus of work as "dominated by the presentiment and the memory of the Nazi horror" (Levinas 1990b, 291), there is an important kernel of truth in Moyn's characterization.[4] Specifically, Moyn's pointing out the enduring importance of Levinas's understanding of the other and otherness, a line of thinking which was developing in the face of pre-Holocaust National Socialism, would come to define Levinas's work and influence the rest of his

---

4 And if one looks carefully at the preceding quote from Levinas, one will see that he himself placed great emphasis on what he referred to as his "presentiment" of the Holocaust.

career. Since Levinas's particular understanding of otherness will come to greatly affect his thinking on violence, we will now turn to an examination of otherness in Levinas's thought generally.

The Grounds of Ethics: Otherness and The Other

In 1988, a Belgian graduate student at the University of Leuven uncovered a box containing hundreds of previously unknown articles written during World War II by celebrated literary critic and noted deconstructionist Paul de Man for the Belgian newspaper *Le Soir*. This was something of a scandal in both the literary and philosophical worlds, particularly in North America, not only because such a discovery is always an event, but because in the case of de Man, the content of the articles was often explicitly anti-Semitic and even more frequently implicitly so. Further complicating the issue was the fact that *Le Soir* was a well-known colloborationist newspaper, being one of the few papers in Belgium which opted to continue publishing under occupied Nazi censorship rather than continue publishing freely from underground.[5] The de Man affair raised serious questions about the fundamental program of the literary postmodernism of the moment, prompting many to question whether this philosophical approach was underwritten by a certain problematic blindness to history and, more importantly, to ethics. As R. Clifton Spargo suggests, there was a sense that "high theory's talent for suspending the ethical moment in favor of perpetual critique" had been exposed and now merited more significant scrutiny (Spargo 2006, 1). It was this self-critical end to what Geoffrey Galt Harpham refers to as the "Theoretical Era" (Harpham 1999, 18) and its orthodoxy of suspicion toward ethics which represents the so-called ethical turn in contemporary philosophy. Importantly, it was also around this time that the works of Emmanuel Levinas were beginning to be seriously examined and disseminated widely, and they were quickly seized upon as a potential answer to the perceived ethical weaknesses of deconstructionist postmodernism. Particularly attractive was Levinas's notion of "otherness" or "the other."

As with much of Levinas's writing, one constantly runs the risk of allowing his style and locution to interfere with the grasping of what are often essentially simple and ultimately relatable concepts and claims, and the same is generally true in the case of the Other. When Levinas speaks of the Other or Otherness or the radical alterity that accompanies the intrusion of the Other into our experience as the grounding of ethics and philosophy, he is referring to nothing more alien than our everyday face-to-face interactions with other human beings. To be sure, Levinas takes these interactions to bear a force and weight unlike any other interactions or objects in the world around us, and his work can be thought of as largely directed toward the end of getting us to realize the deep gravity of our interpersonal relations. Encountering the Other, as represented by a human body distinct from our own, is, for Levinas, a type of call, or summons, to take seriously and feel the force of the ethical relation between ourselves and that other. In this sense, Levinas's intersubjective phenomenology is descriptive, attempting to capture the experience of ethically engaging with a human being in their full

---

5 Facsimiles of some of these articles are reprinted in de Man (1988).

uniqueness. This is what leads Jacques Derrida, in his perceptive commentary on Levinas's mature work, to state that "Levinas does not seek to propose ... moral rules, does not seek to determine *a* morality, but rather the essence of the ethical relation in general" and to refer to Levinas's philosophical project at "an Ethics of Ethics" (Derrida 2001, 138). The Other, then, refers not to any particular physical person in any particular ethical situation, which would be the type of moral rule giving that Derrida so correctly points out is *not* Levinas's goal. Rather, the Other refers to the primary phenomenological feeling of ethical relationship. It is the feeling of being confronted with a being to which you must respond, and respond ethically. Levinas sometimes talks of this relationship as a type of call and response, where the ethical demand of Otherness is experienced by the subject as a call to act or speak, a demand. For Levinas, this feeling of being called upon is the beginning of all ethics. Ethical obligation comes primarily from our feeling of relatedness with others, rather than any sort of considered reflection on the nature of right and wrong. While we are always already thrown into relation with an Other, it is the ethical call of that Other which marks our subjectivity and at the same time troubles and puts that subjectivity into question. That is, once the call of the Other is felt, the Cartesian temptation of the isolated cogito is no longer a plausible view of our own subjectivity, and we must accept our foundational relatedness with others. It is this calling out from the Other which, for Levinas, constitutes the fundamental ethical relationship, a relationship which precedes ontological classification, the subsumption of the Other under the various labels and categories by which we normally navigate the world of other individuals, hence his famous characterization of ethics as first philosophy. Recognizing the primacy of ethics means realizing that the ontological labeling and categorizing of the Other always only comes as a reaction to the feeling of ethical relation. Importantly, Levinas also believes that our responses to these calls will always already be inadequate in certain senses, that we will never be able to fully live up to our ethical duties, making ethics a kind of perpetual, asymptotic struggle to honor the irreducible Otherness which calls us to respond.[6]

In a historical sense, we can situate Levinas's development of his concept of Otherness in these ways as a reaction to Heideggerian ontology, which he came to see as fundamentally aligned with the National Socialist project of reducing all human identity and relationship to bodily fettered-ness. Again, what we mean here is that Levinas is reacting against what he saw as a dangerous and crass materialism which denied any type of transcendent (i.e., non-material) selfhood in the name of a purely physical understanding of the human person as rooted finally in her body, and nothing else. Indeed, Levinas's move to situate transcendental ethical Otherness at the center of his philosophical system can be seen as a politicization of the dispute between Husserl, who had attempted to secure the image of the autonomous, sovereign self that Descartes never could, and Heidegger, who, at least to Levinas, problematically centers ontological, bodily concerns of "being-in-the-world" (Moyn 1998, 39). Levinas saw the Heideggerian view of ontological primacy as fundamentally underlying the political program of the Nazis, and so undertook to counter this philosophical move with an assertion of

---

6 Some have criticized Levinas on this point, suggesting that this vision of ethics ultimately leads to a view of ethics which is not only impossible to achieve, but actually also impossible for human beings to bear, as there seems to exist a certain Judeo-Christian kernel of self-abnegation in Levinas's ethical scheme. See Rajiva (2013).

transcendental (i.e., immaterial) selfhood against the pure materialism of National Socialism. While there is much more to be said regarding Levinas's understanding of the Other, it is here that the key question of violence becomes relevant to Levinas's thinking.

Violence and Murder

Levinas is neither methodical nor systematic in his development of a theory of violence, but the topic is one which permeates key pieces of his postwar thought. In his opening salvo against Heidegger, "Is Ontology Fundamental?," Levinas begins referencing the role which violence must play in any serious consideration of ethical relations. In doing so, he also begins to suggest what will become a critical distinction in his later work, namely that between violence and murder. Violence will come to represent partial negation, with murder signaling a more total form of negation:

> In relation to beings in the opening of being, comprehension finds a signification for them on the basis of being. In this sense, it does not invoke these beings but only names them, thus accomplishing a violence and negation. A partial negation which is violence. This *partiality* is indicated by the fact that, without disappearing, those beings are in my power. Partial negation, which is violence, denies the independence of a being: it belongs to me. (Levinas 1996a, 9, emphasis in original)

He goes on to note,

> It is not starting from being in general which he [the Other] comes to meet me. Everything which comes to me from the Other starting from being in general certainly offers itself to my comprehension and possession. I understand him in the framework of his history, his surroundings and habits. That which escapes comprehension in the Other is him, a being. I cannot negate him partially, in violence, in grasping him within the horizon of being in general and possessing him. The Other is the sole being whose negation can only announce itself as total: as *murder*. The Other is the sole being I can wish to kill. I can wish. (Levinas 1996a, 9, emphasis in original)

There are a number of important theoretical points in just these two short paragraphs. First, it is important to notice and carefully consider the dichotomies Levinas emphasizes – between partial and total negation, and between violence and murder. Each of these function as surrogates standing always in reference to the motivating distinction between the Same and the Other which guides Levinas's work and his critique of homogenizing Heideggerian ontology, which in his view worked by attempting to reduce transcendental alterity to the Sameness of bodily existence.[7] Heidegger's

---

7 It is worth noting here that there is widespread disagreement about how fair an interpreter of Heidegger Levinas turned out to be. Unfortunately, we do not have the space here to enter into this interesting discussion.

centering of the bodily self in his ontology was, to Levinas, dangerous in that it, in his view, reduced the possibilities of ethical relation. Without a transcendent self which calls us to ethical relationship, simple bodily groundedness will not be able to sustain any type of robust ethical stance or behavior, hence the vulnerability of Heideggerian philosophy (again, in Levinas's view) to appropriation by nationalist and racist ideologies. Clarence Joldersma brings out these dualities, and the critical role which naming plays in comprehension and assimilation to Sameness, when he suggests that "the far pole" of "totality, sameness, economy ... puts everything in the world into a conceptual totality, with myself, an I, at the center" (Joldersma 2001, 182). We modify Joldersma's positioning of the I at the center of the world of sameness slightly to suggest, rather, that the I is positioned at the periphery of the Same, assumed and able to gaze at and grasp all of the named objects which fall within the horizon of being. Picturing a circle, the periphery of which is the horizon of being – that is, existence – the Heideggerian ontology of bodily sameness and homogenization positions the self at the edge of the circle, looking over the rest of the space, taking it in and assimilating it to itself, that is, making it same, failing to respect difference, alterity. Levinas's use of the imagery of classical optics when he speaks of "the horizon of being" is not accidental and the metaphor can be extended even further. The horizon, the vanishing point, is traditionally the mirror image of the viewing I which rests at the terminus of the *axis visualis* and delineates the totality of the visual field. Levinas here taps into Ludwig Wittgenstein's observation in the *Tractatus* that "The subject does not belong to the world; rather, it is a limit of the world ... And nothing *in the visual field* allows you to infer that it is seen by an eye" (Wittgenstein 2002, 69). This is the world of the same, within which the I can survey and possess, or in Joldersma's economizing interpretation, transact with, all that I comprehend. The Other does not come from anywhere within the visual field and so cannot be grasped, cannot be transacted with. This is the duality of the world of the Same and that of the Other.

Intuitively, some of the proxy concepts which represent, respectively, Sameness and Otherness, appear to be deeply related to one another, perhaps even inextricably so, and yet Levinas appears to treat them all as Aristotelian pairs, each corresponding to one extreme polarity of a dyad. Perhaps the most vexing of these Janus-faced concepts is the violence–murder relation. Surely, we might think, murder is simply a subset of all possible violence. In murdering, can we help but do violence? Levinas seems to suggest otherwise in continuing to explicate violence and murder, writing that "The temptation of total negation, measuring the infinity of this attempt and its impossibility – this is the presence of the face. To be in relation with the Other face to face is to be unable to kill" (Levinas 1996a, 9). The concept of being face to face with an Other here perhaps needs some further explication. Drawing significant connections between Levinas's views of the face of the Other and his Judaism, Hilary Putnam suggests we read Levinas here as imputing some of the traditional features of God onto the Other in the sense of emphasizing the transcendent alterity of the Other. He notes that "Part of the idea [of the face-to-face ethical relation] is that even when I stare at your physical face, at your skin itself, I do not see you face to face in the Biblical sense, do not and cannot encounter the you that 'hides its wretchedness and orders me'" (Putnam 2004, 44). Relatedly, Putnam also suggests that this understanding of the face "is also connected with Levinas's emphasis on the neediness of others and the corresponding obligation on the 'me' who always has ... to sacrifice for others, to the point of substituting for them, to the point of martyrdom" (Putnam 2004, 45). Here, the connection between killing (murder) and total negation is explicitly drawn. Murder and total negation are one and the same, as are violence and partial negation, indicated in the first extended quote of Levinas above. Violence is possession within the horizon of being, where the Same resides, and possession is only possible if the thing to be possessed actually exists and can be comprehended. Only when the I is taken as the given, unquestioned observer and possessor of the world can violence occur. The Cartesian account of subjectivity presupposes certain rights of control of the self, for Levinas. The centering of the cogito in traditional metaphysics closes off the self-sacrificing ethical subject which is the precondition, for Levinas, of human relations themselves. This is why Levinas emphasizes the importance of the *partiality* of violence; if I were to ever totally negate and destroy that which I hoped to possess, that is, if it were ever outside the horizon of being, I would be undermining my own ambition. While this understanding of violence as possession or consumption of the Other may seem somewhat foreign to our everyday thinking about the term, there are important philosophical precedents for the idea, as well as intuitive ties to our contemporary understandings of symbolic violence. Levinas's close friend Roger Burggraeve links Levinas's ethical thinking in his first major work, *Totality and Infinity*, to the moral philosophy of Immanuel Kant (Burggraeve 1999, 36). Specifically, Burggraeve sees a parallel in Levinas's concern with the absolute prohibition of utilizing the Other as a means of any kind, an echo of Kant's famous categorical imperative, which holds, among other things, that human beings are never to be utilized as means, but always treated as ends in themselves. Concretely, Burggraeve suggests that the symbolic violence of negation "happens whenever I try to make the other person subordinate to me as 'food' or 'power', or to press him into one or another form of service, hence to 'consume' the other, to instrumentalize him and use him" (Burggraeve 1999, 36). Further, these types of reductive attempts to control, use, or otherwise categorize the Other via images, concepts, or themes inevitably leads me to "approach the other not according to his otherness itself, but from a horizon, or another totality" (36). In other words, to respond to the other in ways which ignore his unique here-and-now-ness in favor of subsuming him into our conceptual categories is both to do violence to the Other as he exists as well as to fail to heed his ethical call. For example, the simple case of an employer callously treating an employee not as an individual human being, with all that implies, and rather as another faceless object out of which the employer must extract this or that product, service, or profit would violate this Levinasian demand for respecting the Other *as* Other, rather than as a generic example of some category or other.[8]

Murder and total negation, on the other hand, are precisely the opposite of possession and, paradoxically, of violence. Murder is only even conceivable in the world of the Other. I can only be tempted toward total negation if I have confronted the face of the Other in all its immediacy. As Levinas reminds us on multiple occasions, however, I can only wish for the murder of the Other; I can never accomplish the task myself. If I have truly heard, and been called by, the voice of the Other, it will be impossible to murder her. On this

---

8 This type of Levinasian analysis of symbolic, or imagistic violence has recently been employed in political analyses of constructions of enemy figures to fascinating effect. See Cooper (2011).

point, Ann Chinnery contends that "the possibility always remains of responding to the appeal of the Other by way of violence and hatred" (Chinnery 2000, 71). This is correct, but the proviso must be added that to respond to the Other with violence is, in an important sense, not to respond to the Other at all, nor truly hear the appeal of the Other's ethical call, but only to draw the Other back into the horizon of being so that I may possess her, which is violence itself. As Levinas puts it, "When I have grasped the Other in the opening of being in general, as an element of the world where I stand, where I have seen him *on the horizon*, I have not looked at him in the face, I have not encountered his face" (Levinas 1996a, 16). Once the face is encountered, once the appeal is genuinely heard, the Other "through the nakedness and destitution of his defenseless eyes, ... forbids murder and paralyzes my impetuous freedom" (Levinas 1996a, 16). This is the paradox of Levinasian murder: I can only ever *conceive* of murdering and totally negating the Other, since she is fundamentally outside of my possession, and yet I could never possibly follow through on the murder of the Other without first drawing her back into the horizon of being, in which case I could only do her violence, a partial negation. Again, it is important to emphasize that Levinas in no way denies the possibility of doing violence and harm to others, as discrete individual physical bodies, but only that the total denial of the transcendent presence of the Other which he means to signify by the term "murder" is not possible if we confront the other person as Other. Again, it is important to keep in mind here that Levinas is explicitly attempting to move away from what he saw as the Heideggerian ontological centering of bodily, worldly experience. In a sense, Levinas sees physical, brute violence as less philosophically important than the symbolic violence of conceptual subsumption and negation discussed here. It is not that physical violence is somehow less urgent or the harms caused thereby less severe. Rather, Levinas sees the symbolic violence we have been discussing as a philosophical prerequisite for physical violence. That is, being able to do physical violence to another being implies a certain symbolic view of that being, a view which already must be symbolically violent in order to justify the subsequent physical violence.

Levinas is content, in 1951, to leave the question of "the temptation and the impossibility of murder" largely an open one (Levinas 1996a, 10), though the topic raises itself briefly on two occasions over the next few years: in "Ethics and Spirit," written in 1952, and "Freedom and Command," written in 1953. These two essays, both of which are among the less read of Levinas's works, are of less theoretical interest to us here as they have more to say about the specifically political implications of Levinas's ethical theory, rather than about his views on violence and murder specifically. He returns to the issue of the impossibility of murder most explicitly in *Totality and Infinity*, first published in 1961.[9] It is in this work that Joshua James Shaw proposes to locate the most important formulation of what he refers to as Levinas's "murder argument," which we have been leading up to.[10] Shaw sees the murder argument as the key justification of Levinas's

---

9 We are using a later edition: Levinas (1979).

10 Joshua James Shaw, *Emmanuel Levinas on the Priority of Ethics: Putting Ethics First* (2008). Shaw acknowledges that one might critique his focusing on the murder argument as "treating a passing idea as if it held the key to Levinas's entire philosophy" (33). He admits that he will be putting "*a lot* of interpretive weight" on the argument (32, italics in original), though he maintains that there is much that is relevant to Levinas's later thought in the murder argument. For our purposes, we make only the limited claim that Levinas's discussions of violence and murder are not undercut by anything he wrote subsequently and that the views he expressed on those subjects were never explicitly abandoned.

thesis regarding the transcendental incomprehensibility of the human Other. He suggests that the argument, in its simplest form, is that "there is something about acknowledging another person *as another person* that requires us to regard her as inviolable" (Shaw 2008, 32, italics in orginal). In situating the murder argument in the context of *Totality and Infinity*, Shaw rightly points out that the argument serves a particular purpose in the service of the overarching problematic of the book, which Levinas characterizes as an attempt to describe and argue for the possibility of a "relation with a reality infinitely distant from [our] own reality, yet without this distance destroying this relation and without this relation destroying this distance" (Levinas 1979, 41). The significance of the subtitle of the book, "An Essay on Exteriority," is thus illustrative. Levinas is after something which is demonstrably and irreducibly exterior to our own experience of the Same, something outside the horizon of being. The murder argument is meant to motivate the idea that it is our relations with transcendent Others that meet the criteria of the relationship Levinas describes.

Reading the murder argument as it is expressed in *Totality and Infinity*, we see a number of themes which were present in "Is Ontology Fundamental?" For example, Levinas writes, invoking the total-partial negation binary, "Murder still aims at a sensible datum, and yet it finds itself before a datum whose being can not [sic] be *suspended* by an appropriation. It finds itself before a datum absolutely non-neutralizable. The 'negation' effected by appropriation and usage remained always partial ... Murder alone lays claim to total negation" (Levinas 1979, 198). Similarly, Levinas invokes the idea that "The Other is the sole being I can wish to kill [murder]" (Levinas 1979, 198), the implication being that all we can ever do is wish, and furthermore, that this inability to ever actually carry out a murderous act against the Other is itself the precondition of ethical relation, and signals our viewing the Other as more than a member of some ontologically homogenizing category.

After rehearsing these rhetorical moves, however, Levinas poses a question which frames a significantly richer discussion than was provided in "Is Ontology Fundamental?" Levinas asks, "How does this disproportion between infinity and my powers differ from that which separates a very great obstacle from a force applied to it?" (Levinas 1979, 198). Levinas challenges himself to show that murder is not simply a very difficult task, a labor-intensive but ultimately practical challenge, but a conceptual impossibility; it is not simply the fact that I am unable to overpower the Other that prevents me from murdering her.

The answer to Levinas's question lies in his conception of what it means to take seriously ethics as first philosophy and "the epiphany of the face" that I encounter and am unable to assimilate into Sameness (Levinas 1979, 199). To truly hear the call of the Other and to open oneself to the "deeper, more ancient relationship" between the self and the Other means to see which Other for what she truly is, namely the very locus of all obligation and all ethics (Joldersma 2001, 181). The Other is, of necessity, the "fount of normativity," and as such cannot be violated murderously while maintaining her status *as* Other (Shaw 2008, 40). For Levinas, it is simply a category mistake to talk of the Other as being the victim of violence and murder. Only those things which have been subsumed and assimilated into the world of the Same can be done violence. Accordingly, they have ceased to be Other.

The Other can, at most, be the subject of murderous fantasy and temptation, but it is a part of her very nature to command against these acts ever manifesting themselves. Feeling the ethical call of the Other, seeing the vulnerability of the Other, and sensing the call for self-sacrifice which are the bases of ethical relation constitute an ethical demand of conscience which Levinas sees as absolutely primary to the human experience. The Other does not command in any direct or conscious way, but through its very presence. The self that would even attempt such an act against the Other would inevitably trap itself in an ethical catch-22. Shaw illustrates the difference between the violence done to objects and the murderous fantasies which can only be harbored against transcendent Others by invoking a parable from Frederick Douglass. Douglass relates the story of a slave owner who, knowing that his horses would work no harder for being whipped, refused to ever whip them. Thus, he demonstrated that he really did view the horses only as objects with which he interacted. The slaves, however, who were whipped quite theatrically, were by that very act shown to be objects of contradiction (Shaw 2008, 41). The abuse of the slave owner was a mechanism of removing the Otherness of the Other, to reduce the Other to the world of the Same, represented in this case by the horses. If the slave owner had truly been entirely unmoved by the eyes of the Other, and had truly never heard the call thereof, he would have no reason to treat the slaves any differently than the horses. In this connection, "Efforts to violate humanity have, then, a theatricality which reveals them to be contradictory" (Shaw 2008, 41), that is, that they are a type of performative contradiction in precisely the sense which Levinas wanted to demonstrate: "Murder [attempts to] exercise[s] a power over what escapes power" (Levinas 1979, 198).

Before moving to a discussion of the applications of Levinas's picture of violence and murder to the school, we want to clarify an aspect of Levinas's position which may up to this point have engendered skepticism. Levinas is perfectly clear that there is no *physical* or even *metaphysical* impediment to an individual ending the biological life of another individual. Speaking to the "banal" interpretation of murder, Levinas admits that in a straightforwardly corporeal sense,

> The Other who can sovereignly say *no* to me is exposed to the point of the sword or the revolver's bullet, and the whole unshakeable firmness of his "for itself" with the intransigent *no* he opposes is obliterated because the sword or the bullet has touched the ventricles or auricles of his heart. In the contexture of the world he is a quasi-nothing. (Levinas 1979, 199)

It would be a mistake, however, to move from the corporeal fact of murder to the ethical possibility thereof. Specifically, it would be to place ontology back at the center of the philosophical project in the face of Levinas's demands that it be supplanted by ethics. Though it is impossible to deny bodily death, violence, and pain, the consequence of Levinas's murder argument is that these things can never be present in the full light of the ethical, properly understood. That is, murder really is impossible in the ethical sense "insofar as the murderer purports to be able simultaneously to recognize her victim's humanity and violate her" (Shaw 2008, 43). To the degree that a murderer really does recognize the immediacy of the face, she will cease to be a murderer. To the degree that she succeeds in the ontological destruction of her victim, she has failed to recognize the face, in which case she will also cease to be a murderer in the ethical sense, and will herself be reduced to a doer of violence. In either case, again, murder is impossible.[11]

Possession, Negation, Reduction: Symbolic Violence in Schools

If the foregoing interpretive discussion is on the right track, one of the clearest implications for US schools is that, insofar as children are able to enact horrifying acts of physical violence against one another, often for seemingly trivial reasons (one thinks here not just of gun violence in schools, but also of day-to-day bullying behavior), the space of the school does not engender ethical engagement. That is to say, the fact that vulgar physical violence is so prevalent in schools today gives us a clue pointing toward the deeper symbolic forms of violence which are going on beneath this superficial (in Levinas's sense) outer layer. Levinas's theory of violence allows us to go beyond this outer layer of physical violence and explore the reasons why this type of violence appears to be so at home in American schools.

Levinas, to review, crucially equates violence with possession and consumption, suggesting that to attempt to possess or consume something precludes the very possibility of ethical action. It is worth unpacking this claim in more detail. The motivating idea for Levinas seems to be something like this: If I am to engage with you truly ethically, to take you seriously as a sovereign Other and recognize your alterity, I cannot in any sense be said to own or possess you. Relegating another person to the status of property or resource to be consumed renders ethical relationship impossible, and serves in parallel fashion, to set up the conditions for violence. I can only do violence to that which I possess, not in a simple property-owning sense, but in the sense of being able to exercise power over. This insight is, we believe, roughly analogous to the well-known objections to the process of objectification, whereby an individual is reduced from a full-fledged human being to an object (whether economic, sexual, or otherwise). The advance Levinas is making here comes in the idea (which, on reflection, seems intuitive) that objectification of this type is a kind of violence, or at least is a prerequisite thereof.

Taking Levinas's conception of violence as a type of possession and consumption which denies to another their full ethical status, we see a link to be made between Levinasian violence and the pervasive corporate intrusion into public education which has become more pronounced in recent years than ever before. That is, if school has become primarily a place of consumers and consumables (with children often serving as both simultaneously), and insofar as this process is one of objectification and replacing the humanity of individual children with a role in a market transaction, then it follows that the school will no longer be a place where ethics, in Levinas's sense, can possibly be instantiated. For example, the more children are seen as a type of captive market for companies to peddle their advertising to in the space of the school – that is, are seen as mere instances of the category "consumer" or "key demographic" or the

---

11 The distinction between murder and violence here might profitably be mapped onto a similar distinction in the thought of Walter Benjamin, which Harvey Shapiro touches on in his contribution to this volume, between divine and mythic violence. This analogy would have to be teased out in much more detail than we have the space to here, but see Shapiro's chapter for some insight into Benjamin's distinction.

like – the less they are valued as unique individuals, as Others in Levinas's sense. The empirical research in this area is extensive and few serious analysts now disagree on the fact of the matter, namely that, as Alex Molnar puts it, "In the ongoing quest to capture lifelong consumers, corporations are turning schools into servants of a marketing machine that represents the furthest development of capitalist society" (Molnar and Reeves 2002, 48; see also, Giroux 2001; Norris 2011; Saltman 2012). To get a sense of the trends which have been observed in the development of schoolhouse commercialism, it is helpful to examine the annual reports released by the Commercialism in Education Research Unit (CERU), of which Molnar is the director, at the National Education Policy Center. Since 1998, CERU has released annual reports on the state of commercialism in schools and developing trends in the relationship between corporations and public schooling.[12] The recent reports have illuminated some disturbing developments, including a legislative bias in favor of commercialism and a presumption that allowing advertisements and other forms of marketing in schools is beneficial; commercialism in public schools is related to adverse health effects on students, and, most importantly for our purposes here, does significant psycho-sociological damage to children which inhibits their relational development (see Molnar et al. 2013, 2014). Specifically, the 2009–2010 report found that commercialized school settings lead children to "think that their self-worth can and should come from commercial products" and that "it heightens their insecurities, distorts their gender socialization, and displaces the development of values and activities other than those associated with commercialism" (Molnar et al. 2011).

Various proposals for inoculating children against the pernicious influences of consumerism have been suggested, particularly as the research demonstrating the degrees of commercial incursion into children's lives has become more and more damning.[13] Little work has been done, however, in linking corporate influences specifically to violent behavior, or a lack of ethical relationships. A Levinasian analysis makes this link possible and clear. The logic of his theorizing is simple: as the degree to which public schools encourage those under its influence to view other human beings and themselves as objects to be consumed, economized, and commercially transacted increases, so too will "banal" physical violence increase. Because the sine qua non of violence is the denial of Otherness required for commodification; the ease with which violence can be done is precisely correlated with the difficulty of entering into an ethical relation with the Other. In a culture saturated with talk of children in the schoolhouse as a massive untapped market, future brand loyalists, drivers of household consumption through their influence on their parents, and so on, it cannot come as a surprise that children have internalized this social positioning and have come to see themselves and those around them in these ways, even if unconsciously so. When, as Molnar and

---

12 Our discussion of corporatism in public schools, though acutely related to issues of privatization more generally, is nonetheless distinct in important ways. Corporate incursions into public schooling are arguably a more nuanced and dangerous form of undermining truly *public* education than are out-and-out privatization schemes.

13 Norris optimistically envisions schools as sites of resistance to commercialism and teachers as enablers of critical media literacy and creative countercultural activity. See Norris (2011, 50n). Another proposal is suggested by Grace Roosevelt. She makes the Rousseauian argument for isolating and protecting children from the corrosive influences of contemporary commercial society, including corporatized schools. See Roosevelt (1990).

colleagues note, a child's self-worth is tied to his commercialized self, it is natural that the child's evaluation of the worth of others becomes tied exclusively to market logic in a parallel way.[14] Rather than viewing my classmate as a "partner in the heart of a relation which ought only have made him present to me" (Levinas 1996a, 7), I see him, and myself, only as subsumed under a universal ontological category – the very negation of Otherness Levinas sees as a short-circuit around the primacy of ethical relationships. Violence toward those who grasp this totalizing move is, on the Levinasian view, not only inevitable, but always already committed by definition.

Indeed, the "naturalness" of violence under these circumstances is addressed by Levinas in a transcribed conversation between himself and members of the French Society of Philosophy following his first public presentation of "Transcendence and Height." An interlocutor challenges Levinas's vision of violence by invoking a variation on the senselessness myth: "I believe that the formula that you used just now, 'acts of violence which can be commanded by Reason,' is something absolutely unintelligible: violence is to be found precisely outside of the world where Reason and Philosophy reign. Violence can never be at the service of Reason."[15] While the subsequent discussion veers off into the relationship between Levinas and Descartes, Levinas's response to the myth, thus articulated, is discernible in a response he gives to a previous question regarding the functioning of state hierarchies and the implicit violence in state domination:

> For me, the negative element of violence in the State, in the hierarchy, appears even when the hierarchy functions perfectly, when everyone submits to universal ideas. There are cruelties which are terrible because they proceed from the necessity of the reasonable Order. There are, if you like, the tears which the civil servant cannot see: the tears of the Other ... In such a situation, individual consciences are necessary, for they alone are capable of seeing the violence that proceeds from the proper functioning of Reason itself. (Levinas 1996b, 23)

The point here is that it is built into the definition of Reason and Order that Otherness be subsumed into pre-established categories, and so each unique Other is inevitably done violence. In this sense, the economic rationality of consumerist culture which necessitates the carving up of human existence into discrete universal categories of "consumer," "producer," "product," and the like, is by definition violent and can only engender further violence. When a child enters a school and perpetrates physical violence against other children, she fails to see them as the unique individuals which Levinas argues they irreducibly are. Instead, she enacts the logic of consumption, subsumption, and possession which has been materially normalized for her in the form of targeted advertisements in her cafeteria, commercial announcements in her home-room, sponsored messages broadcast on and in her bus ride home, and so on. To kill, for Levinas, is the ultimate assertion of ownership and possession.

---

14 This applies whether conceptualized in terms of economic class, brand loyalty, or other features of commercial image enculturation (e.g., "prep," "Goth," "jock," "nerd," etc.). See, in addition to Molnar et al. (2011, 2013, 2014), Fabricant and Fine (2013).

15 See the discussion in Levinas (1996b, 25).

A similar line of thinking helps illuminate the reasons for the failures of many of the proposed solutions to the problem of violence in US schools. Zero tolerance policies, metal detectors, dress codes, increased numbers of "school resource officers" (i.e., police), etc. have all been shown to be ineffective at curbing violence in public schools.[16] Approaching the issue from a different theoretical perspective, namely critical race theory, Ivan Watts and Nirmala Erevelles note that these policies flow from a type of rationality which reifies normative expectations for students in schools. Such policies also subsume individual students under specific category headings, like "violent," "deviant," or "disabled" (Watts and Erevelles 2004). It is precisely these types of homogenizing, reductive categorizations, derivative of the dictates of Reason, which Levinas would argue preclude the very possibility of ethical engagement with Others recognized as Other. In this sense, then, the solutions which are proposed by those interested in "what works" solutions to violence in schools, but who neglect the development of "relationships that support … trust and connection" (Watts and Erevelles 2004, 294), are actually instances of the very problem they purport to solve: namely, the homogenizing "ontological event" which "consists in suppressing or transmuting the alterity of all which is Other" (Levinas 1996b, 11). This is the act of violent negation through possession. The irony of this situation, where totalizing power is utilized to solve an ostensive problem of violence, was not lost on Levinas. He noted, in the context of the administration of state hierarchy in line with the dictates of Reason and Order, that "in order to suppress violence, it is necessary to have recourse to violence" (Levinas 1996b, 15). The same, we think, can be said of the contemporary approaches to solving the problem of school violence.

These are by no means the only examples of underlying symbolic violence that might be adduced in making a Levinasian analysis of contemporary education. Think of the various ways in which students are reduced to test scores, grades, or tracking levels. It seems to us that these are the very types of symbolic subsumptions of unique individual beings under pre-established categories and headings which Burggraeve suggests are the archetypical examples of Levinasian violence. The question suggested here by a Levinasian analysis is about how we are supposed to expect a deep ethical respect between individuals in schools when the very things that enable such relationships (a willingness to hear the ethical call of the Other, the humility to know that one's actions will never meet the impossible demand issued by the Other, etc.) are denied in favor of homogenizing, reductive conceptualizations which mask the unique transcendence required for ethics.

At this point we want to take a moment to make a clarification in our argument and respond to some potential objections that one might raise against it. First, it is crucial to emphasize that we are not making any type of direct causal claim about *the* cause or rationale behind school gun violence; such strong claims are almost always foolish (not to mention wrong). Rather, we hope to have identified a factor, no doubt one among many, which has contributed to setting the stage for the occurrence of school gun violence. Again, it is entirely possible, indeed nearly certain, that these events are always overdetermined, with influences coming from sources such as those we have identified

---

16 See Cassella (2001). The text is an extended critique of the types of "get tough" policies which proliferated in the United States after the signing of the Gun Free Schools Act of 1994.

here, individual psychological situations, individual family dynamics, local conditions in a town or particular school, and so on, and we do not mean to downplay the potential importance of these and other factors.[17] Perhaps a given shooter who was bullied would not have done what he did in the absence of corporatist logic permeating his school setting, but maybe the bullying itself was enough, and vice versa. Complex human behaviors can rarely, if ever, be attributed to one cause, and often the best we can hope to do is identify or hypothesize progressively more of the potential influences that brought themselves to bear on that behavior, and this is what we hope to have done here.

Second, one might object that our tying school violence to contemporary economic, neoliberal ideologies does not have as strong support as we suggest, since there have always been violent acts committed in schools of one type or another. There are two things to be said about this. First, and to echo a point from the previous paragraph, we do not mean to say that corporate ideologies and neoliberal rhetoric invading the school setting are the only possible causes of ethical malaise and subsequent violence. It is certainly possible that a spurned lover or social outcast might have enough emotional agitation, as it were, to motivate themselves to commit a violent act without any further influences. Again, we do not presume to have isolated the only or even the most important variable in this infinitely complex equation. This leads to the second point, which is to note that there has been a historical uptick in school violence since the late 1990s. Furthermore, this uptick has roughly coincided with the undeniable and similarly dramatic uptick in corporate involvement in schooling. This is not to make a causal claim, but simply to point out that if Levinas is correct that violence is tied to consumption and possession, then this correlation should not surprise us for the reasons we have given here.

Murder as a Solution to Violence?

Recall Levinas's argument for the ethical impossibility of murder. If I have come to a stage in my relationship to a unique Other where I can fathom murdering him, in the full ethical signification of that term as not the termination of a biological process, but as the total negation or rejection of a full subjectivity, an attempt to erase the subject from its existence entirely, at least two things follow: (i) I am in an ethical relationship with the Other, which, for Levinas, is also "the situation of discourse" (a formulation which is important when we think of the relationship between ethics and dialogue) (Levinas 1996a); and (ii) I will never be able to follow through on my imaginings and successfully murder him. To understand the concept of murder is to be face to face with the Other and my own ethical consciousness. The understanding of murder, and of the wish and temptation to it which Levinas mentions repeatedly, is, therefore, a desirable goal for human relationships (Levinas 1996a, 9–10). Indeed, it is a precondition of discourse and mutual edification. This is not to say that I will ever be tempted to attempt to murder another, but only that I have come to understand the full ethical import of what murder would entail. It follows that if our schools are to become sites of

---

17 See Chapter 23 in this volume for detailed discussions of these issues as relating to particular school gun violence events, and specifically the difficulty in attempting to trace a single cause to even one act of gun violence, let alone the entire phenomenon.

democratic engagement between ethically conscious individuals in the Levinasian sense, an understanding of murder in this precise sense must be foregrounded in our pedagogical relationships and practices. This is, clearly, an inflammatory way to put the point, but we think the underlying logic is sound. We must treat our children not as instantiations of universal, abstract categories like grades, tracks, brand loyalists, etc. but as the unique moral being they are, demanding of us as all Otherness does ethical participation and sacrifice; particular and irreducible to social categories, economic statistics, or corporate brands. When they see themselves as more than passive objects which oscillate between consumer and consumable, they will cease seeing others in that way as well, and will come to respect the unique Otherness which each being brings to the table of ethical relation.

It is overly optimistic to think that we could provide specific policy recommendations for instituting such a discourse on the full ethical import of murder, in the Levinasian sense, in US public schools. Levinas does not lend himself to concrete policy proposals more generally, either.[18] It seems clear to us, though, that insofar as the violence and dehumanizing environment of US schools can be tied to the radical intrusion of corporate logics as well as neoliberal rhetorics of performance and standardization, we should undermine and reverse that trend. Part of this reversal must be the admission that the outbursts of cold physical violence in US schools are *not* unintelligible or meaningless. They are trying to tell us something about the state of the ethical core of our educational system, which is itself cold and violent on a symbolic level. The goals should instead include making schools places of ethical relationship and fellowship, where the *sui generis* encounter between a Self and an Other organically evolves and develops unmediated by administrative distance or the hierarchical order of economic rationality which governs the various corporate intrusions into public schools discussed earlier. Otherwise, we will continue to fruitlessly, and violently, appeal to the very same totalizing, homogenizing categorizations which currently restrict human interaction and foment violence in schools.

References

Alpers, Philip and Wilson, Marcus. 2007. "Guns in Finland: Firearms, Armed Violence, and Gun Law." International Firearm Injury and Prevention. http://www.gunpolicy.org/firearms/region/finland (accessed February 12, 2014).

Badiou, Alain. 2001. *Ethics: An Essay on the Understanding of Evil*. Translated by Peter Hallward. London: Verso.

Biesta, Gert. 1999. "Radical Intersubjectivity." *Studies in Philosophy and Education* 18(4), 203–220.

---

18 See Gereluk, Donlevy, and Thompson (2015) for some more distinctly pragmatic approaches to increasing care in school settings, a solution which seems to respond at least in part to the lack of ethical understand we have pointed to here. It is also important to bear in mind that, despite his dramatic and sometimes convoluted language, Levinas's conception of the ethical relation, when put into practice, is not necessarily as complex as it may seem. He writes of small, commonplace actions, such as holding a door open, smiling at a stranger, and the like as possible reflections of ethical engagement with the Other.

Biesta, Gert. 2000. "Levinas and Moral Education." In *Philosophy of Education 2000*, edited by A.G. Rud and L. Stone, pp. 75–77. Urbana-Champaign: University of Illinois.

Burggraeve, Roger. 1999. "Violence and the Vulnerable Face of the Other: The Vision of Emmanuel Levinas on Moral Evil and Our Responsibility." *Journal of Social Philosophy* 30(1), 29–45.

Cassella, Ronnie. 2001. *At Zero Tolerance: Punishment, Prevention, and School Violence.* New York: Peter Lang.

Cedarberg, Carl. 2014. "Thinking Revolution With and Beyond Levinas." In *Jewish Thought, Utopia, and Revolution*, edited by Elena Namli, Jayne Svenungsson, and Alana M. Vincent, pp. 79–93. Amsterdam: Rodopi.

Chinnery, Ann. 2000. "Levinas and Ethical Agency: Toward a Reconsideration of Moral Education." In *Philosophy of Education 2000*, edited by A.G. Rud and L. Stone, pp. 60–74. Urbana-Champaign: University of Illinois.

Chinnery, Ann. 2001. "Asymmetry and the Pedagogical I-Thou." In *Philosophy of Education 2001*, edited by A.G. Rud and L. Stone, pp. 189–191. Urbana-Champaign: University of Illinois.

Cooper, Thomas. 2011. "The Uses of Adversaries: Normalising Violence through the Construction of the Other." *At the Interface* 75, 3–11.

Davis, Trent. 2008. "'The Tears That a Civil Servant Cannot See' – Rethinking Civic Virtue in Democratic Education: A Levinasian Perspective." In *Philosophy of Education 2008*, edited by Ronald D. Glass, pp. 256–263. Urbana-Champaign: University of Illinois.

de Man, Paul. 1988. *Wartime Journalism 1939–1943*. Edited by Werner Hamacher, Neil H. Hertz, and Thomas Keenan. Lincoln: University of Nebraska Press.

Derrida, Jacques. 2001. "Violence and Metaphysics." In *Writing and Difference*. Translated by Alan Bass, pp. 97–193. London: Routledge.

Fabricant, Michael and Fine, Michelle. 2013. *The Changing Politics of Education: Privatization and the Dispossessed Lives Left Behind*. Boulder, CO: Paradigm Publishers.

Gereluk, Diane, Donlevy, J. Kent, and Thompson, Merlin B. 2015. "Normative Considerations in the Aftermath of Gun Violence in Schools." *Educational Theory* 65(4), 495–474.

Giblin, Elizabeth Uliano. 2014. "Will Giving Up Our Guns Really Make Us Safer? An International Survey of Gun Laws and Violent Crimes." *Law School Student Scholarship*, Paper 477. http://scholarship.shu.edu/student_scholarship/477 (accessed August 16, 2014).

Giroux, Henry A. 2001. *Stealing Innocence: Corporate Culture's War on Children.* New York: Palgrave Macmillan.

Harpham, Geoffrey Galt. 1999. "Ethics and Literary Study." In Geoffrey Galt Harpham, *Shadows of Ethics: Criticism and the Just Society*, pp. 18–38. Durham, NC: Duke University Press.

Joldersma, Clarence W. 2001. "Pedagogy of the Other: A Levinasian Approach to the Teacher–Student Relationship." In *Philosophy of Education 2001*, edited by Suzanne Rice, pp. 181–188. Urbana-Champaign: University of Illinois.

Joldersma, Clarence W. 2008. "Ethics, Justice, Prophecy: Cultivating Civic Virtue from a Levinasian Perspective." In *Philosophy of Education 2008*, edited by Ronald D. Glass, pp. 264–267. Urbana-Champaign: University of Illinois.

Levinas, Emmanuel. 1979. *Totality and Infinity*. Translated by Alphonso Lingis. Hingham, MA: Martinus Nijhoff.

Levinas, Emmanuel. 1989. "As If Consenting to Horror" (trans. Paula Wissing). *Critical Inquiry* 15(2), 485–488.

Levinas, Emmanuel. 1990a. "Reflections on the Philosophy of Hitlerism" (trans. Sean Hand). *Critical Inquiry* 17(1), 62–71.

Levinas, Emmanuel. 1990b. "Signature." In Emmanuel Levinas, *Difficult Freedom: Essays on Judaism*. Translated by Sean Hand. Baltimore: The Johns Hopkins University Press.

Levinas, Emmanuel. 1996a. "Is Ontology Fundamental?" In *Emmanuel Levinas: Basic Philosophical Writings*, edited by Adriaan T. Peperzak, Simon Critchley, and Robert Bernsasconi. Bloomington: Indiana University Press.

Levinas, Emmanuel. 1996b. "Transcendence and Height." In *Emmanuel Levinas: Basic Philosophical Writings*, edited by Adriaan T. Peperzak, Simon Critchley, and Robert Bernasconi. Bloomington: Indiana University Press.

Molnar, Alex and Reeves, Joseph A. 2002. "The Growth of Schoolhouse Commercialism and the Assault on Educative Experience." *Journal of Curriculum and Supervision* 18(1), 17–55.

Alex Molnar, Boninger, Faith, Harris, Michael D., Libby, Ken M., and Fogarty, Joseph. 2013. *Promoting Consumption at School: Health Threats Associated with Schoolhouse Commercialism: The Fifteenth Annual Report on Schoolhouse Commercializing Trends, 2011–2012*. Boulder, CO: National Education Policy Center, 2013).

Molnar, Alex, Boninger, Faith, Libby, Ken M., and Fogarty, Joseph. 2014. *Schoolhouse Commercialism Leaves Policymakers Behind: The Sixteenth Annual Report on Schoolhouse Commercializing Trends, 2012–2013*. Boulder, CO: National Education Policy Center, 2014.

Molnar, Alex, Boninger, Faith, Wilkinson, Gary, Fogerty, Joseph, and Geary, Sean. 2011. *Schools and the Machinery of Modern Marketing: The Thirteenth Annual Report on Schoolhouse Commercializing Trends, 2009–2010*. Boulder, CO: National Education Policy Center.

Moyn, Samuel. 1998. "Judaism against Paganism: Emmanuel Levinas's Response to Heidegger and Nazism in the 1930s." *History and Memory* 10(1), 25–58.

Moyn, Samuel. 2005. *Origins of the Other: Emmanuel Levinas between Revelation and Ethics*. Ithaca, NY: Cornell University Press.

Norris, Trevor. 2011. *Consuming Schools: Commercialism and the End of Politics*. Toronto: University of Toronto Press.

Putnam, Hilary. 2004. "Levinas and Judaism," In *The Cambridge Companion to Levinas*, edited by Simon Critchley and Robert Bernasconi, pp. 33–63. Cambridge: Cambridge University Press.

Rajiva, Jay. 2013. "The Unbearable Burden of Levinasian Ethics." *Angelaki* 18(4), 135–147.

Roosevelt, Grace. 1990. *Reading Rousseau in the Nuclear Age*. Philadelphia, PA: Temple University Press.

Saltman, Kenneth J. 2012. *The Failure of Corporate School Reform*. Boulder, CO: Paradigm Publishers.

Small Arms Survey. 2007. *Small Arms Survey 2007: Guns and the City*. Cambridge: Cambridge University Press.

Shaw, Joshua James. 2008. *Emmanuel Levinas on the Priority of Ethics: Putting Ethics First*. Amherst, NY: Cambria Press.

Spargo, R. Clifton. 2006. *Vigilant Memory: Emmanuel Levinas, the Holocaust, and Unjust Death*. Baltimore, MD: The Johns Hopkins University Press.

Todd, Sharon. 2003. *Learning from the Other: Levinas, Psychoanalysis, and Ethical Possibilities in Education*. Albany, NY: SUNY Press.

Watts, Ivan Eugene and Erevelles, Nirmala. 2004. "These Deadly Times: Reconceptualizing School Violence by Using Critical Race Theory and Disability Studies." *American Educational Research Journal* 41(2), 271–299.

Wittgenstein, Ludwig. 2002. *Tractatus Logico-Philosophicus*. London: Routledge, 2002.

Wolin, Richard, ed. 1992. *The Heidegger Controversy: A Critical Reader*. Cambridge, MA: MIT Press.

Young, Julian. 1997. *Heidegger, Philosophy, Nazism*. Cambridge: Cambridge University Press.

28

Violence and Peace in Schools

Some Philosophical Reflections[1]

Hilary Cremin and Alex Guilherme

Introduction

The work tackling violence in schools does not concern solely the school as a particular establishment; rather, we must understand this work as concerning the role of the school as an institution within wider society. Any institution has values that must be translated into practice – for example, the ways in which families are welcomed and communicated with, and the ways in which violence is addressed (Meirieu 2011, 1). This means that we must look at the issue of violence in schools, and its possible solutions, not only within the walls of the establishment, but beyond and into society.

Historically, Meirieu (2011) points out that research into violence in schools appears to have started in the 1960s when the distinction between institutional violence and violence against the institution first emerged in educational research. In the 1970s, there was a further division with research into violence against adults and violence between peers, which was something that until then had been minimized. Soon afterwards, the educational discourse incorporated the idea that alongside the violence that is perceived, there are other kinds of violence that underpin it. It is important to note that research in this area, violence in schools, continued to grow steadily at an international level and with impetus (Bondu and Scheithauer 2014; Brown and Winterton 2010; Cowie and Jennifer 2007; Devine 1996; Harber 2004; Msibi 2012; NCES 2011; Olweus 1999; Silva and Salles 2010; Smith 2003), and it is pertinent, therefore, to consider which theoretical frameworks might be useful in understanding and responding to the issue of violence in schools. In this respect, we discuss different conceptions of violence, considering the views of Johan Galtung, Frantz Fanon, and Michel Foucault. Following from this, we connect these notions of violence to Buber's philosophy of dialogue, in order to make a case for an "epistemological shift" which

---

1 An earlier version of this text was published as "Violence in Schools: Perspectives (and Hope) from Galtung and Buber," *Educational Philosophy and Theory* 48(11), 1123–1137. © Philosophy of Education Society of Australasia, reprinted by permission of Taylor & Francis Ltd, www.tandfonline.com on behalf of Philosophy of Education Society of Australasia.

might enable individuals and communities to achieve "peace." Finally, we direct our argument to the education context and put forward some concrete proposals for peacemaking in schools.

Violence: A Philosophical View

Johan Galtung, a Norwegian scholar and one of the founders of the International Peace Research Association, is considered to be one of the most prominent figures in the field of Peace Studies. Peace education has a long history. Some scholars, for example, trace it back to as far as the work of Comenius, the Czech educationist, who argued in *A Reformation of Schools* (1969; first published in 1642) that peace could only be achieved through a universally shared knowledge; or Immanuel Kant (1970), who argued in his essay *Perpetual Peace* (first published in 1795) that violence could be controlled by a legal system with "checks and balances based upon courts, trials, and jails," thus advocating "peace through justice" (Harris 2002, 7). Some would argue that the origins of peace education lie even further back in religious traditions, and the works of Buddha, Baha'u"lla (the founder of the Baha'i), and Jesus Christ (Harris 2002, 5).

Galtung's work does, however, remain an important landmark in the field of Peace Studies. He argues that the best way to characterize peace is to contrast it to violence, its antithesis. Thus, Galtung makes a distinction between the notions of direct violence and indirect violence. *Direct violence* is conceived as physical aggression and violence, which can lead to severe injury and ultimately death and massacre; *indirect violence* finds expression in two ways, structural and cultural (Galtung 1969). Structural violence is the kind of violence that is present in societies, rendering them socially unjust (e.g., death by malnutrition). Cultural violence occurs in support of structural violence, masking it (e.g., indifference or support of domestic violence) (Cremin, Sellman, and McCluskey 2012, 430). It is arguable that structural and cultural violence are interdependent, as the structures of society provide the foundations for cultural violence (e.g., a section of the population being denied their rights, as happened to the Jewish community under the Nazi regime in Germany when in 1935 the Nuremberg Laws stripped German Jews of their citizenship and prohibited sexual relations and marriage between Jews and those of "German or related blood"); and cultural values might provide support for the continuation of structural violence (e.g., it being acceptable to discriminate against a section of society, such as happened to black South Africans under the apartheid regime in South Africa when racism encouraged discriminatory legislation like the Prohibition of Mixed Marriages Act of 1949).

Moreover, and depending on the context, violence against the Other always involves one or more of these three elements, namely, physical, structural, and cultural violence. Galtung's characterization of violence seems to be very similar to that of Frantz Fanon, one of the most prominent thinkers on African decolonization. Commenting on the issue of colonialism, Fanon argues that it makes use of physical, structural, and psychological violence to oppress native populations. *Physical violence* means injuring human beings, with death being the ultimate form of injury; for Fanon colonialism is preceded, established, and maintained by the use of physical violence, which is used to subjugate local populations into accepting the colonizer's rule and order. On writing about physical violence in *The Wretched of the Earth*, Fanon (1963, 40) says, "the foreigner coming from another country imposed his rule by means of guns and machines." *Structural violence* is a kind of social-economic violence. This kind of violence is implemented through the harvesting and plundering of local resources by the colonizers, who use these resources in their own favor and in favor of the metropole, to the detriment of local populations and of the colony. This generates a situation in which the local population lives in dire poverty and the colonizer in affluence. Fanon writes in *The Wretched of the Earth*: "The colonial world is a world divided into compartments. It is probably unnecessary to recall the existence of native quarters and European quarters, of schools for natives and schools for Europeans: in the same way we need not recall apartheid in South Africa" (1963, 37). *Psychological violence* is injury to a human being's psyche and includes brainwashing, indoctrination, and threats, which are used to appease and break the local population's will for self-determination. This kind of violence injures the very idea of selfhood and identity within local populations, and causes a pathological condition in which the local population only has a sense of self in the face of the colonizer; that is, the colonized only attain a sense of selfhood and of identity in the face of the master and colonizer. The implications for cultural confidence, self-value, and pride are wide-reaching (Fanon 1963; Jinadu 2003; Morgan and Guilherme 2013a, 59–61).On writing about psychological violence in *Black Skin, White Masks*, Fanon says:

> When the Negro makes contact with the White world, a certain sensitizing action takes place. If his psychic structure is weak, one observes a collapse of the ego. The black man stops behaving as an *actional* person. The goal of his behaviour will be the Other (in the guise of the white man), for the Other alone can give him worth. That is on the ethical level: self-esteem. (1967, 60)

Thus, and according to Fanon, the psychological impact of colonization on local populations is severe and long-lasting, as the damage done to the psyche cannot be easily healed, and requires a continuous process in which selfhood is asserted and reasserted (Morgan and Guilherme 2013b).

The difference between Galtung's and Fanon's accounts is that Galtung understands *cultural violence* to be connected to *structural violence*, and vice versa, both of which are typified by him as forms of *indirect violence*. Fanon, however, who was a trained psychiatrist, seems to consider all forms of violence – physical, structural, and psychological – as direct violence. He identifies the implications of *cultural and structural imperialism* on colonized populations by arguing that it is a direct form of *psychological violence*. That is, Fanon draws our attention not only to forms of violence, but also to the very real *psychological damage* they do to individuals, affecting their sense of identity and of pride.

Fanon understood that education is very often used as a weapon of domination by colonialists, who either outlaw local culture (e.g., banning traditional dance and music) or downgrade it (e.g., undervaluing local language and replacing it with the colonizer's language). An example of this is noted by Guilherme (2012), when he writes about missionary work in colonized lands. He notes:

> This negative attitude towards local customs was certainly not something particular to the Salesians or to their work in the region, but something quite common in early missionary work across the world (e.g., American Protestant

missionaries denounced the Hawaiian Hula as a dance performed by heathens), which led to the loss of invaluable cultural heritage (i.e., their myths, concepts and religion, as well as their knowledge about the local environment, its food and medicinal resources). (Guilherme 2012, 5)

Writing in a different context, Paulo Freire, the Brazilian educationist, also commented on how education was used by the elites of the country to "domesticate" the lower classes through "banking education," thus preventing them from questioning the *structural* and *psychological/cultural* violences present in their societies (Freire 1970). The above-mentioned are prime examples of the kinds of violence that might spring from society into the classroom and schools, and we must identify these, be critical, and learn to deal with them in an effective manner.

Understanding schools and education as instruments of violence is also supported by the work of Michel Foucault (1979), the French philosopher writing from a poststructuralist perspective, who argued that schools are "institutions of power" (*institutions de séquestre*) in his seminal work *Discipline and Punish*. According to him, relations of power objectify individuals, attacking their singularities and normalizing them at the same time, so that they become incapable of fighting against that which dominates them. This is a form of structural violence coercing individuals to behave in a particular way, conforming to their realities, and becoming incapable of questioning the status quo either because they are incapable of critically analyzing it because they are too embedded in the system or because they fear reprimand from those who have more power. Thus, there is always a tension between those who retain power and those who are being dominated. In the educational context, we could mention the tension that often exists between those who govern a school and its teachers, or teachers and students, or support staff and parents. This tension caused by structural and indirect violence can erupt as forms of physical and direct violence, which can deeply affect an individual's and institution's life. In his essay "The Subject and Power," Foucault characterized power relations in schools as deeply problematic. This is due to institutional and societal political structures, as well as totalitarian procedures that are sometimes cleverly concealed, restraining the individual's capacity to consider things critically and act. He says:

> Never ... in the history of human societies ... has there been such a tricky combination in the same political structures of individualization techniques and of totalization procedures. This is due to the fact that the modern Western state has integrated in a new political shape an old power technique which originated in Christian institutions ... Take, for example, an educational institution: the disposal of space, the meticulous regulations which govern its internal life, the different activities which are organized there, the diverse persons who live there or meet one another, each with [his][2] own function, his well-defined, character – all these things constitute a block of capacity–communication–power. The activity which ensures apprenticeship and the acquisition of aptitudes or types of behavior is developed there by means of a whole ensemble of regulated

---

2 The original French would not have indicated gender in this way.

communications (lessons, questions and answers, orders, exhortations, coded signs of obedience, differentiation marks of the "value" of each person and of the levels of knowledge) and by the means of a whole series of power processes (enclosure, surveillance, reward and punishment, the pyramidal hierarchy). (Foucault 1982, 782, 787)

That is to say, schools can be structured in such a way that relations of power work as a form of violence between individuals. However, this structurally violent foundation has implications not just for the way individuals relate to each other but also to the way they engage with their education. The way they learn and what they study is affected by these structures of power and this could give rise to a culture of ambivalence, fear, and ultimately a feeling of revolt against the system. To deal with this situation, as we will argue, is to encourage more democratic structures in the classroom and in schools so that individuals do not feel threatened by power structures. Meirieu (2011, 17) concurs with Foucault and perhaps goes further by asserting that the very architecture of the school functions as a form of structural violence. This architecture is an inheritance from the past, from the army and monasteries, and imposes forms of both normalization and medicalization on the individual. It forces a way of being in the world, and a way of behaving in society, that the individual must accept in order to avoid being corrected. This kind of architecture does not fit in with current times, marked as they supposedly are by the democratization of education, modern teaching and learning methodologies, and the digitalization of society. It thus becomes imperative to consider questions of geography and architecture of classrooms and schools whilst thinking about ways of reducing violence in schools.

Thus, we argue that understandings of violence (i.e., physical, structural, cultural/psychological), which are often applied within Peace Studies and political theory and analysis, can be useful within the field of education. Schools and education systems can be powerful and efficient instruments of violence, which leaves real questions about how violence plays out in schools.

Peace: A Philosophical View

Having outlined the ways in which we can understand violence, we now go on to review how these relate to notions of peace, as suggested by Galtung. Galtung linked direct, structural, and cultural violence with notions of *negative peace* and *positive peace*. *Negative peace* is achieved by averting war or by removing the threat of direct violence, but without resolving the issues of structural and cultural violence. *Positive peace* implies encouraging conditions in which the causes of violence, whether direct or indirect, are removed; and this requires the development of democratic relationships and structures that enable conflict to be dealt with in a constructive and just manner (Cremin, Sellman, and McCluskey 2012, 430). We quote Galtung (1975, 29): "two concepts of peace should be distinguished: negative peace, defined as the absence of organised violence between such major human groups as nations, but also between racial and ethnic groups of the magnitude that can be reached by internal wars; and positive peace, defined as a pattern of cooperation and integration between major groups." Further, Galtung (1975, 1976) connected the earlier notion of *violence* to that of *peace* by advocating a differentiation between *peacekeeping*, and *peacemaking*, *peace-building*. Gill and Niens (2014, 11) commented that Galtung:

> [i]ntroduced the notion of peacebuilding, and distinguished peacemaking and peacekeeping as the immediate responses to conflict from peacebuilding as a means to build a sustainable peaceful future. Peacebuilding thus goes beyond the notion of "negative peace" (as an absence of war) and involves the development of "positive peace" characterised by conditions in a society that promote harmony between people, including respect, justice and inclusiveness, as well as "sustainable peace" that incorporates processes to address the root causes of violent conflict.

That is to say, *peacekeeping* is something reactive and it is necessary when either (i) violence has already occurred or (ii) there is the potential for the occurrence of violence between parties, which are better kept apart because there is either a lack of willingness by one of the parties, or by both, to engage in *peacemaking* or *peacebuilding*. As such, *peacekeeping* is connected to *negative peace*, and the mere aversion of immediate conflict, without dealing with its roots.

Peacemaking is also something reactive and it involves helping conflicting parties to deal with violence that has already taken place, and it involves bringing about, and providing the right conditions for, the development of dialogue between them.

Finally, *peacebuilding* is something proactive which occurs after peacemaking because it requires engaging in a culture of peace, making the occurrence of violence less likely. Peacebuilding is characterized as overcoming structural violence (e.g., exploitation, marginalization) and cultural violence (e.g., subconscious beliefs supporting violence); it is a process of democratization, inclusion, and management of social conflict and human needs (Bickmore 2005a, 162). Peacebuilding is difficult because engaging in democratic processes requires that individuals participate in dialogic decision making and social justice initiatives as well as developing critical awareness and judgment. At the same time as developing personal morality and decision making, the individual is required to engage with the Other, including those whose views and dispositions may be very different. (Curle, Freire, and Galtung 1974 cited in Bickmore 2005b; Galtung 1996).

Both *peacemaking* and *peacebuilding* are connected to the notion of *positive peace* because they aim to deal with the very roots of violence (Cremin, Sellman, and McCluskey 2012). It is arguable that while each of these three manifestations of reducing conflict and violence emerge in different situations and moments, there is a real danger for long-lasting peace between parties if only *peacekeeping* is encouraged between them. As suggested above, this is because peacekeeping is a form of negative peace and as such it does not deal with the causes of the problem. *Peacekeeping* is to do with *safety and security*, *peacemaking* with *dialogue and conflict resolution*, and *peace-building* with *equity and relationship building*. They work as three distinctive, but often consecutive, moments.

It is unfortunate, therefore, that parties and interventions often only engage in *peace-keeping*, because it is connected to the kind of violence that is most visible: that is, physical violence. This is to the detriment of *peacemaking* and *peacebuilding*. When this happens, there is a risk that *peacekeeping* will become a tool for maintaining the status quo and the continuation of structural and cultural/psychological violences. In this connection, Kathy Bickmore has very usefully applied these ideas to the field of education (Bickmore 2005a, 2005b, 2011). She has shown how schools tend to favor peace-keeping through security interventions such as CCTV, security guards, and metal detectors to the detriment of peacemaking initiatives such as peer mediation, and peacebuilding through activities such as engaging students in dialogue about controversial issues. She has shown how structural and cultural violence in many schools have undermined many peacemaking and peacebuilding initiatives through, for example, a lack of teacher training, fear of diversity, and the need to perform well in high-stakes testing. Gur-Ze'ev (2010, 319) goes further to suggest that peace education is not only often a failed endeavor; it can become the opposite of itself when it is used to enforce homogenized, packaged peace. If its aim is to pacify and promote conformity, there is a danger that it can become "one of the most advanced manifestations of these violences and ... a serious threat to human edification." A prime example of this in the school setting would be to ask the victim of bullying not to create any issues and to try to ignore or avoid the bullies because *it would be better for everybody*. This means that without *peacemaking* and *peacebuilding*, which deal with structural, cultural, and psychological violence, *peacekeeping* can become a manifestation of violence because it only addresses physical violence.

Further, *peacemaking* can also become a tool for appeasing individuals in the sense in which Fanon would have argued. Fanon noted that the various forms of violence practiced by colonialism suppressed all avenues for debate and dialogue, and that even when the colonizer seems to offer dialogue, or is forced to do so, this is no more than an attempt to consolidate a position and to continue to dominate, keeping structural, cultural, and psychological violence in place. That is, there is an attempt to engage in discussions and dialogue as a way of maintaining the status quo; this is a real stratagem for the perpetuation of violence. In response to this, Fanon would argue, controversially, that only violence can put a stop to violence (Cherki 2000: 261–262; Morgan and Guilherme 2013b), so that the perpetrator of violence experiences the same forms of violence he or she inflicts on others. Thus, for dialogue to be truly effective and transformative, there is a need to deconstruct the conditions of power that maintain violence in all its forms, dealing with structural and cultural violence. This means that *peacebuilding* must involve discussions about power relations between individuals, while also analyzing the structures of the institution. Both Fanon and Foucault would maintain that only then can truly democratic and egalitarian relations and structures emerge.

Our position here is that, although these notions of violence, peacekeeping, peacemaking, and peacebuilding are very helpful for understanding conflict in individuals and communities, more work needs to be done to understand what we call the "epistemological shift" that is necessary for conflict transformation in educational settings. By "epistemological shift" we mean that for conflict resolution to happen, for some sort of closure to take please, the way the Other is perceived needs to be altered. That is to say, there has to be a change in the way parties perceive each other otherwise positive peace will not take place, and they will remain confined to negative peace, and perhaps even revert to aggression. This necessitates work at the individual and community level to ensure that the Other ceases to be viewed as an aggressor or enemy, and Buber's philosophy of dialogue is very helpful to us in explaining this epistemological shift (Guilherme and Morgan 2009; Morgan and Guilherme 2013a, 2013b). That is, Buber's views enable us to understand what takes place when we objectify the Other (e.g., an aggressor) as well as when we meet the Other as an equal, a person like us. This is something crucial for making sense of the idea of epistemological shift and it is to this that we turn our attention now.

Buber: Dialogue and Conflict Resolution

In *I and Thou* Buber (2004) establishes a typology describing different kinds of human relations. For Buber, human beings:

- are relational beings;
- are always in a relation with either other human beings, or the world, or God;
- possess a twofold attitude toward other human beings, the world, or God, which is indicated by the basic words I-It (*Ich-Es*) and I-Thou (*Ich-Du*).

The basic words are a "linguistic construct created by Buber as a way of pointing to the quality of the experience that this *combination of words* seeks to connote" (Avnon 1998, 39, emphasis added), so that I-It and I-Thou are read as "unities" indicating one's state of Being and attitude toward the *Other*, the *World* and *God*.[3] This means that there is no *I* relating to a *Thou* or to an *It*; rather, what exists is a kind of relation encapsulated by the unification of these words. Avnon (1998, 40) comments insightfully that "one may summarize this point by suggesting that the difference between the I-You and the I-It relation to being is embedded in the hyphen." The hyphen of I-Thou indicates the kind of relation that is inclusive of the Other whilst the hyphen of the I-It points to the sort of relation that is not inclusive of the Other, that in fact separates the Other. As such, these basic words are pivotal for a proper understanding of Buber's thought, and consequently of his views on education. Buber (2004, 3) characterized these basic words succinctly, and in accordance with what we have just said about them, as follows: "The primary word I-Thou can only be spoken with the whole being. The primary word I-It can never be spoken with the whole being."

In more detail, the I-Thou relation is an *inclusive* reality between individuals. Buber argues that the I-Thou relation lacks structure and content because infinity and universality are at the basis of the relation. This is so, since when human beings encounter one another through this mode of being, an infinite number of meaningful and dynamic situations may take place in that which Buber calls the Between. Thus, it is important to note that any sort of preconception, expectation, or systematization about the Other prevents the I-Thou relation from arising (Olsen 2004, 17; Theunissen 1984, 274–275) because they work as a "veil," a barrier to being *inclusive* toward the Other. Within I-Thou relations, the "I" is not sensed as enclosed and singular, but is present, open to, and inclusive toward the Other (Avnon 1998, 39) and Buber (1961, 22) comments that "no matter whether spoken or silent … each participant really has in mind the other or others in their present and particular being and turns to them with the intention of establishing a living mutual relation between himself and them." Despite the fact that it

---

3 For lack of space we are not able to deal with Buber's philosophy of dialogue in relation to the World and God.

is difficult to characterize this kind of relation, Buber argues that it is real and perceivable, and examples of I-Thou relations in our day-to-day life, at different moments in time, are those of two lovers, two friends, or a teacher and a student.

In opposition to this is the I-It relation, in which a being confronts another being, objectifies it, and in so doing *separates* itself from the Other. This is in direct contrast with I-Thou relations, because the "'I' of I-It relations indicates a separation of self from what it encounters" and

> [b]y emphasising difference, the "I" of I-It experiences a sensation of apparent singularity – of being alive by virtue of being unique; of being unique by accentuating difference; of being different as a welcome separation from the other present in the situation; of having a psychological distance ("I") that gives rise to a sense of being special in opposition to what is. (Avnon 1998, 39)

Thus, when one engages in I-It relations one separates oneself from the Other and gains a sense of being different, which can either be special – and, arguably, superior at the same time – or disconcerting, leading to a feeling of inferiority. For instance, a racist engages with people of other races through I-It relations and in doing so, believes he or she is special and somehow superior to them; likewise, victims of racism will feel unconformable and might gain a wrong sense of inferiority.

Buber understood that human existence consists of an oscillation between I-Thou and I-It relations and that the I-Thou experiences are rather few and far between. It is also important to emphasize that he rejects any sort of sharp dualism between the I-Thou and I-It relation. That is, for Buber there is always an interplay between the I-Thou and the I-It rather than an either-or relation between these foundational concepts. I-Thou relations will always slip into I-It relations because I-Thou relations are too intense and we live in a worldly reality, requiring us to use people to fulfil our basic needs; but I-It relations have always the potential of becoming an I-Thou relation, if we remain on the watch, open to and inclusive of the Other. This oscillation is very significant for it is the source of transformation; that is, through every I-Thou encounter, the I is transformed and this affects the I's outlook of the I-It relation and of future I-Thou encounters. Putnam (2008, 67) notes that "the idea is that if one achieves that mode of being in the world, however briefly ... then ideally, that mode of being ... will *transform* one's life even when one is back in the 'It world.'"

However, we argue that sociopolitical instability can easily lead to I-It relations gaining a stranglehold on human relations and thus suppressing I-Thou relations. Buber also understood that there are situations in which I-It relations become so prevalent that they suppress I-Thou relations and this has serious implications for human relationships. First, such situations devalue human beings and human existence because they do not account for the richness of the human condition; that is, they do not account for the fact that human beings are capable of both *dialogical I-Thou* relations and of *objectifying I-It* relations. Second, such situations have significant moral implications. That is, if one ceases to say *Thou* to fellow human beings then one ceases to see *Them* as *persons* and they become merely *objects*, they become *means to an end*, as we said earlier. As the *I-Thou* relation requires a mutual attitude of recognition, if one is unable to establish a *dialogue* with one's fellow human beings, if one is unable to say *thou* to one's fellow human beings, then one also becomes an object for them because one will not hear the call *Thou* from *Them* (Babolin 1965, 197; Morgan and Guilherme 2013a; Okshevsky 2001, 297–298; Tallon 2004, 62).

In the light of this, how does Buber's philosophy of dialogue help us make sense of the "epistemological shift" that takes place in Galtung's *peacekeeping, peacemaking,* and *peacebuilding*? The epistemological shift means to be able to switch from I-It to I-Thou relations; that is, *to cease seeing the Other as an It and realizing that the Other is a Thou*. It is only when this "shift" occurs that conflict resolution can take place. Accordingly, it is arguable that in *peacekeeping*, parties are already treating each other as Its, rather than Thous, and there is a real danger that this will worsen through the use of violent means; as such, parties need to be kept apart so that they do not hurt each other. In peacekeeping, the epistemological shift is not ready to occur, and parties seem to be incapable of seeing each other as Thous rather than Its. That is, in peacekeeping individuals continue to objectify each other as, for instance, the aggressor, and therefore there is a need for putting in place measures to prevent them from performing some sort of direct violence against one another.

In *peacemaking*, parties have treated each other as *Its*, and this may have deteriorated into violence, but they have now reached a stage in which they are capable of engaging in meaningful dialogue; that is, there is a need to provide the right conditions for I-Thou relations to arise so that they do not deteriorate again into I-It relations. Thus, in peacemaking parties are ready to experience the epistemological shift and to cease treating each other as Its. In conflict theory this is referred to as "non-adversarial dispute resolution" (Coleman, Deutch, and Marcus 2014; Fisher and Ury 2012). The work of mediators and others is to encourage the parties to move away from attacking each other toward attacking the problem at the heart of the conflict. It is a move away from competition and hostility toward cooperation and problem solving. Energies engaged in fighting are redirected toward communication, empathy, creativity, and resolution. However, in peacemaking the right conditions need to be in place for the epistemological shift to occur; that is to say, for seeing the Other not as an It but as a Thou.

Finally, in *peacebuilding* the conditions exist for the proactive prevention of destructive conflict, and the harnessing of the transformative power of constructive conflict. Parties are ready to engage even more in I-Thou relations, despite the challenges that they may face, and the inescapability of I-It relations at times. Thus, in peacebuilding the epistemological shift has already occurred as parties have ceased routinely treating each other as Its in favor of addressing each other as Thou. In this connection, measures need to be put in place to facilitate I-Thou relations to continue to arise and to be strengthened, thus providing solid foundations for positive peace.

Conflict and Violence in Schools

Research shows that direct violence in European schools is substantial, and this is even without taking account of indirect structural, psychological, and cultural violence. For instance, in 2003, Smith reviewed levels of violence in schools in Europe through an initiative of the European Commission under its Fifth Framework programme of research activities, which aimed to gain an overview of violence in schools in the 15 member states at the time, and two associated states. Smith's research showed increasing levels of student–student and student–teacher direct violence. In French secondary schools, for example, in 1999 a total of 240,000 incidents were registered with central government, with 6,240 of these regarded as serious. In Portugal, there was a 14% increase in reports of violence between 1995 and 1998. In Austria, studies from 1997 found that around 12% students admitted to bullying other students regularly or often. In the Netherlands, a nationwide random survey in 1994 found that 22% students had been victims of sexual harassment by boys at least once, and 43% had been a victim of intentional damage to property. More recent data reinforce these findings and trends reported by Smith. In Britain, in 2008, a survey by MORI found that 23% of 16-year-olds reported being victims of bullying, and another survey verified that 60% of teachers reported being verbally abused by students every week (Brown and Winterton 2010, 17, 32). And in the United States, the Institute of Educational Sciences established that 31% of students in grades 9–12 reported being in a physical fight at least once in the previous 12 months, with 27% of male students regularly carrying a weapon (NCES 2011). All these studies deal with the issue of direct violence but do not engage explicitly with indirect violence. Our question thus is: How then do we apply Galtung's and Buber's insights on conflict resolution in a school setting?

In the case of *peacekeeping* – that is, if violence has already occurred at the school, or may occur – strategies such as CCTV cameras, or separate "inclusion units" are often used to keep students safe. In connection to this, Taylor (2011) notes that 85% of schools in the United Kingdom have installed CCTV as a way of "controlling pupils' behaviour," "monitoring pupils' behaviour," and "tackling bullying." Cremin, Mason, and Busher (2010) found that the use of CCTV cameras, locks, fences, and surveillance of both pupils and teachers in a secondary school created a prison culture, and that pupils felt criminalized, marginalized and "forgotten." Cremin (2003) that other strategies such as zero tolerance and the use of inflexible sanctions and rewards are equally to blame for creating negative peace in schools through compliance, extrinsic motivation, and processes of pacification. As we have argued above, this involves teachers and students treating each other as Its, rather than Thous, and therefore this strategy avoids an escalation of violence without addressing its root causes. That is, it remediates it but does not solve it. Thus, it is arguable that through practicing peacekeeping only, schools generate an It-culture amongst students, missing opportunities to work toward more I-Thou relations in the student body. In addition, this It culture characterizes teacher–student relations, given that these will always be of an asymmetrical nature, with teachers favoring directive methods, such as authoritative power, rather than collaborative and educative methods, such as dialogue, to establish order within the school environment.

Peacemaking is different because it starts to deal with the causes of the problem, the source of violence, and as such, it is an important part of any education process. Galtung's notion of *peacemaking* has similarities with that which Jean Paul Lederach (e.g., 1995) has referred to as "elicitive conflict transformation." This means that the role of the teacher, facilitator, or mediator is to elicit solutions to conflict from the parties involved, rather than imposing a solution. Clearly, if this work can begin in schools, there are many advantages for wider society in having young people who have a certain degree of conflict literacy, and who are able to take responsibility and be flexible in conflict situations. This suggests that learning conflict resolution skills, such as the ones proposed in this chapter, would have a very positive impact outside the classroom, in the wider society. Lederach (2003) suggests that this can be done in three stages, which might help us visualize a concrete way of implementing peacemaking in schools. We quote:

- First, we need a lens to see the immediate situation.
- Second, we need a lens to see past the immediate problems and view the deeper relationship patterns that form the context of the conflict. This goes beyond finding a quick solution to the problem at hand, and seeks to address what is happening in human relationships at a deeper level.
- Third, we need a lens that helps us envision a framework that holds these together and creates a platform to address the content, the context, and the structure of the relationship. From this platform, parties can begin to find creative responses and solutions.

That is, we must evaluate the situation, consider foundational issues, and in the light of this seek innovative proposals. As per our previous discussion, in peacemaking parties are ready to stop treating each other as Its, and to starting addressing each other as Thous. One such strategy is *peer mediation* (Cremin 2007), which encourages young people to develop the skills, values, and attitudes to facilitate each other to resolve conflict cooperatively. Another is *restorative practice*, which enables young people in schools to be held to account for any harm that they have caused to others, and to make reparation for their actions (Sellman, Cremin, and McCluskey 2013). Building on concepts of shame, reintegration, and reparation in indigenous cultures, especially Maori culture, restorative justice (restorative practice or restorative approaches in schools) has been found to significantly reduce reoffending in criminal justice settings, and to build cultures of peace in schools. This is yet another important point demonstrating the porous condition that exists between schools and the wider society not only in terms of violence (e.g., structural violence such as malnutrition impacting on learning) but also in terms of solutions (e.g., indigenous culture notions of shame, reintegration, and reparation helping us construct a notion of restorative justice).

Examples of both of these strategies have been recorded by Cremin (2012) in her report of a restorative intervention in a secondary school in the United Kingdom. In one example, Jamie, a 13-year-old boy, had been cautioned by the police for assisting a burglary of his former primary school, and a restorative meeting took place between Jamie, his mother, and the head teacher of the primary school in the local community hall. The meeting was facilitated by a support worker attached to the secondary school who had been part of the restorative training program. Prior to the restorative meeting, Jamie had acknowledge the harm caused to his mother, his new school, and his old school, especially the head teacher. The meeting commenced with ground rules, and went on to ascertain that both Jamie and the head teacher wanted to repair the situation. There was further acknowledgment of the harm caused and an apology was given. Jamie's mother spoke of her feelings of shame, and was supported by people in the meeting, including Jamie. An agreement was reached whereby Jamie wished to clear litter from the school site and to talk with his friends about stopping the ongoing vandalism of the school. Formal legal proceedings were avoided, and all partiers were supported to move out of adversarial I-It relations in the interests of healing and community cohesion. Through dialogue all parties ceased "objectifying" each Other and were able to reconnect on a deeper and more meaningful level. An "epistemological shift" occurred in which horizontal I-Thou relations replaced adversarial and objectifying I-It relations.

As can be gathered, the establishment of a Thou culture seems to be taking root, grounding student–student as well as teacher–student relations. Authoritative power and threats are replaced by dialogue and more equitable relations.

Finally, *peacebuilding* builds on peacemaking as it seeks to be proactive about peace. That is, it seeks to tackle potential sources of violence and conflict even before they become an issue. As such, it is important that schools provide a good standard of education, which provides pupils with critical thinking skills, is inclusive, and avoids categorization of certain sections of the community of students. The use of talking circles and cooperative group work and problem solving generate a collegial atmosphere and a sense of interdependence between teacher and students and between students.

An example of peacebuilding was recorded as part of the restorative intervention in the secondary school highlighted above. A teacher engaged with the local primary schools prior to the new intake arriving in September in order to support students at risk of exclusion to make a successful transfer. This was a voluntary process supported by parents. Students who had been in trouble in their primary school were invited to workshops over the summer to reflect on ways of improving their behavior and making a fresh start in their new school. Strategies such as Circle Time[4] were used to promote empathy, cooperation, and creative problem solving. Students considered how they could be supported to make different choices in the future. These discussions were used by students to create individual behavior support plans. This resulted in a lower number of incidents being recorded for these students during transfer than had been the case for similar students in previous years, and no exclusions. This had been a real problem in the past. These ventures encourage and facilitate I-Thou relations, avoiding the permanent deterioration into I-It relations, the very source of violence and conflict. In peacebuilding, a more dialogical and democratic approach is developed, leading to more egalitarian power relations between students, and between teachers and students. This helps in dealing with the causes of conflict, whether structural or cultural/psychological, by creating and encouraging a culture of peace in the institution. The primary and obvious outcome of this is that the levels of violence in the school subside over time, providing a safer environment for both students and teachers. However, another outcome that is not always necessarily obvious to both teachers and students is that by engaging in building a culture of peace within the institution, they are actually creating a positive working environment for themselves, somewhere where they actually want to be and where they can study.

Final Thoughts

At the start of our discussion we mentioned that research into violence in schools has been growing steadily at an international level, suggesting a possible increase in levels of violence in schools, or at least a perception that this is taking place. This presents a serious problem for the education system to address. Finding positive ways to respond to violence has become imperative. As Meirieu (2011, 7) has argued, a crucial role of

---

4 Circle Time is a teaching strategy that involves students sitting in a circle to engage in various activities designed to develop social and emotional skills. Students use a talking object to symbolize trust and basic ground rules. These ensure that each person gets quality listening time and is not ridiculed or disrespected.

education is "to protect the student, particularly those who are from less favourable backgrounds, from those violences" (our translation). Meirieu is drawing our attention to the importance of protecting childhood, much as, we believe, Arendt had argued in *Reflections on Little Rock* and *The Crisis in Education* (Arendt 1954, 1957). But in the light of our discussion thus far, we could take this further and also argue that the teachers, support staff, and all those engaged in education also have to be protected from "those violences," namely direct and indirect violence.

In our discussion we also, however, drew attention to the multifaceted nature of "violence," demonstrating that it should not be understood as something merely direct and physical in nature, but as having structural, cultural, and psychological manifestations. We also argued, following Galtung, that there are three ways of responding to direct and indirect violence, namely *peacekeeping*, *peacemaking*, and *peacebuilding*, and that these understandings can usefully be applied to education.

It is our contention here that those involved with the education of others should become fully aware of all expressions of violence and peace in order to offer an education that is fit for purpose for the twenty-first century. This is a topic of utmost importance that Cremin extends in more detail elsewhere (Cremin and Bevington 2017), but it is enough at this stage to reassert that this is not just a matter for schools, and does not only concern direct forms of violence. In contemporary cultures of schooling, there is a propensity for direct physical violence to be identified at the expense of more indirect (but no less harmful) forms of violence. This has the result that *peacekeeping* is often pursued, to the detriment of other more positive and proactive forms of *peacemaking*. Such a strategy is problematic because it does not encourage the "epistemological shift" that enables individuals, or sections of society, to stop treating Others as Its, and to starting addressing them as Thous. Further, it does not build toward long-lasting peace, which necessitates a well-established culture of peace and democracy that can address power imbalances and structural and cultural violence. Finally, such a simplistic approach to the issue of violence (i.e., physical) and peace (i.e., *peacekeeping*) presents us with a major issue because, and to quote Gur-Ze'ev (2010, 319) again, peace education might become "one of the most advanced manifestations of these violences and is a serious threat to human edification." That is, this approach does not deal with the causes of the problem and perpetuates more nuanced, but nevertheless insidious, forms of violence.

References

Arendt, H. 1954. *The Crisis in Education*. http://www.thecriticalreader.com/wp-content/uploads/2016/07/ArendtCrisisInEdTable.pdf (last accessed November 1, 2017).

Arendt, H. 1957. *Reflections on Little Rock*. http://learningspaces.org/forgotten/little_rock1.pdf (last accessed November 1, 2017).

Avnon, D. 1998. *Martin Buber: The Hidden Dialogue*. Lanham, MD: Rowman & Littlefield.

Babolin, A. 1965. *Essere e Alterità in Martin Buber*. Padua: Editrice Gregoriana.

Bickmore, K. 2005a. "Foundations for Peacebuilding and Discursive Peacekeeping: Infusion and Exclusion of Conflict in Canadian Public School Curricula." *Journal of Peace Education* 2(2), 161–181.

Bickmore, K. 2005b. "Teacher Development for Conflict Participation: Facilitating Learning for 'Difficult Citizenship' Education." *International Journal of Citizenship and*

Teacher Education 1(2), 1–15. http://www.citized.info/ejournal/Vol%201%20 Number%202/007.pdf (last accessed November 1, 2017).

Bickmore, K. 2011. "Location, Location, Location: Restorative (Educative) Practices in Classrooms." Paper presented as part of the "Restorative Approaches to Conflict in Schools" seminar series, Edinburgh, February. http://www.educ.cam.ac.uk/research/ projects/restorativeapproaches/seminarfour/BickmoreSemianr4.pdf (last accessed November 1, 2017).

Bondu, R. and Scheithauer, H. 2014. "Leaking and Death-Threats by Students: A Study in German Schools." *School Psychology International* 35(6), 592–608.

Brown, J. and Winterton, M. 2010. "Violence in Schools: What Is Really Happening?" Macclesfield: BERA. https://www.bera.ac.uk/wp-content/uploads/2014/01/Insight1-web.pdf (last accessed November 1, 2017).

Buber, M. 2004. *I and Thou*. London and New York: Continuum.

Buber, M. 1961. "Dialogue." In *Between Man and Man*. London and Glasgow: Collins. First published 1929.

Cherki, A. 2000. *Frantz Fanon: Portrait*. Paris: Seuil.

Coleman, P.T., Deutch, M., and Marcus, E.C. 2014. *The Handbook of Conflict Resolution Theory and Practice*, 3rd ed. San Francisco: Jossey-Bass.

Comenius, J. 1969. *A Reformation of Schools*. Translated by S. Harlif. Menston, UK: Scholar Press. First published 1642.

Cowie, H. and Jennifer, D. 2007. *Managing Violence in Schools: A Whole-School Approach to Best Practice*. London: Paul Chapman Publishing.

Cremin, H. 2003. "Thematic Review: Violence and Institutional Racism in Schools." *British Educational Research Journal* 29(6), 929–939.

Cremin H. 2007. *Peer Mediation: Citizenship and Social Inclusion Revisited*. Buckingham, UK: Open University Press.

Cremin, H. 2012. "Report on a Restorative Intervention in a Secondary School." Unpublished. (Enquiries: hc331@cam.ac.uk.)

Cremin, H. and Bevington, T. 2017. *Positive Peace in Schools: Tackling Conflict and Creating a Culture of Peace in the Classroom*. London: Routledge.

Cremin, H., Mason, C., and Busher, H. 2010. "Problematising Pupil Voice Using Visual Methods: Findings from a Study of Engaged and Disaffected Pupils in an Urban Secondary School." *British Educational Research Journal* 37(4), 585–603.

Cremin, H., Sellman, E., and McCluskey, G. 2012. "Interdisciplinary Perspectives on Restorative Justice: Developing Insights for Education." *British Journal of Educational Studies* 60(4), 421–437.

Curle, A., Freire, P., and Galtung, J. 1974. "What can education contribute towards peace and social justice? Curle, Freire, Galtung panel," in Haavelsrud, M., (ed.), *Education for Peace: Reflections and Action*, Keele, UK: University of Keele, pp. 64–97.

Devine, J. 1996. *Maximum Security: The Culture of Violence in Inner City Schools*. Chicago: University of Chicago Press.

Fanon, F. 1963. *The Wretched of the Earth*. New York: Grove.

Fanon, F. 1967. *Black Skin, White Masks*. New York: Grove.

Fisher, P. and Ury, W. 2012. *Getting to Yes: Negotiating Agreement Without Giving In*. Boston, MA: Random House.

Foucault, M. 1979. *Discipline and Punishment: The Birth of Prison* New York: Vintage.

Foucault, M. 1982. "The Subject and Power." *Critical Inquiry* 8(4), 777–795.

Freire, P. 1970. *The Pedagogy of the Oppressed*. New York: Seabury Press.

Galtung, J. 1969. "Violence, Peace, and Peace Research." *Journal of Peace Research* 6(3), 167–191.

Galtung, J. 1975. *Peace: Research, Education, Action. Essays in Peace, Volume I.* Copenhagen: Christan Ejlers.

Galtung, J. 1976. "Three Approaches to Peace: Peacekeeping, Peacemaking, Peacebuilding." *Peace, War and Defense: Essays in Peace Research, Volume II*, edited by J. Galtung, pp. 297–298. Copenhagen: Christian Ejlers.

Galtung, J. 1996. *Peace by Peaceful Means: Peace and Conflict, Development, & Civilization*. London: Sage & International Peace Research Association.

Gill, S. and Niens, U. 2014. "Education as Humanisation: A Theoretical Review on the Role of Dialogic Pedagogy in Peacebuilding Education." *Compare: A Journal of Comparative and International Education* 41(1), 10–31.

Guilherme, A. 2012. "Language-death: A Freirian Solution in the Middle of the Amazon." *Educational Philosophy and Theory* 45, 1–14.

Guilherme, A. and Morgan, W.J. 2009. "Martin Buber's Philosophy of Education and Its Implications for Adult Non-formal Education." *International Journal of Lifelong Education* 28(5), 565–581.

Gur-Ze'ev, I. 2010. "Beyond Peace Education: Toward Co-poiesis and Enduring Improvisation." *Policy Futures in Education* 8(3 & 4), 315–339.

Harber, C. 2004. *Schooling as Violence*. Abingdon, UK: RoutledgeFalmer.

Harris, I.M. 2002. "Peace Education Theory." Paper presented at the Annual Meeting of the American Educational Research Association, New Orleans, Louisiana, April 1–5.

Jinadu, LA. 2003. *Fanon: In Search of the African Revolution*. London and New York: Kegan Paul.

Kant, I. 1970. "Perpetual Peace: A Philosophic Sketch." In *Kant's Political Writings*, edited by H. Reiss, pp. 93–143. Cambridge, MA: Cambridge University Press. First published 1795.

Lederach, J.P. 1995. *Preparing for Peace: Conflict Transformation Across Cultures*. New York: Syracuse University Press.

Lederach, J.P. 2003. "Conflict Transformation." Beyond Intractability. http://www.beyondintractability.org/essay/transformation (last accessed November 1, 2017).

Meirieu, P. 2011. "Quelle parole face à la violence?" *La nouvelle revue de l'adaptation et de la scolarisation* 3, 1–19.

Morgan, W.J. and Guilherme, A. 2013a. *Buber and Education: Dialogue as Conflict Resolution*. London: Routledge.

Morgan, WJ. and Guilherme, A. 2013b. "Martin Buber et Frantz Fanon – Le politique dans l'éducation: dialogue ou rebellion." *Diogène* 241, 35–57.

Msibi, T. 2012. "'I'm used to it now': Experiences of Homophobia Among Queer Youth in South African Township Schools." *Gender and Education* 24(5), 515–533.

NCES. 2011. "Indicators of School Crime and Safety: 2011." National Center for Education Statistics. https://nces.ed.gov/pubs2012/2012002rev.pdf (last accessed November 1, 2017).

Okshevsky, W. 2001. "Martin Buber's 'Sacred' Way and Moral Education." *Philosophy of Education*, 297–299.

Olsen, G. 2004. "Dialogue, Phenomenology and Ethical Communication Theory." In *Proceedings of the Durham–Bergen Postgraduate Philosophy Seminar*, II, 13–26.

Olweus, D. 1999. "Sweden." In *The Nature of School Bullying: A Cross-national Perspective*, edited by P.K. Smith, Y. Morita, J. Junger-Tas, D. Olweus, R. Catalano, and P. Slee. London and New York: RoutledgeFalmer.

Putnam, H. 2008. *Jewish Philosophy as a Guide to Life: Rosenzweig, Buber, Levinas, Wittgenstein*. Bloomington, IN: Indiana University Press.

Sellman, E., Cremin, H, and McCluskey, G. 2013. *Restorative Approaches to Conflict in Schools: International Perspectives on Managing Relationships in the Classroom*. London: Routledge.

Silva, J.M.A.P. and Salles, L.M.F., eds. 2010. *Jovens, violência e escola: um desafio contemporâneo*. São Paulo: Cultura Acadêmica.

Smith, P.K. 2003. *Violence in Schools: The Response in Europe*. London: RoutledgeFalmer.

Tallon, A. 2004. "Affection and the Transcendental Dialogical Personalism." In *Buber: Dialogue and Difference*, edited by P. Atterton, M. Calarco, and M. Friedman. Pittsburgh, PA: Duquesne University Press.

Taylor, E. 2011. "UK Schools, CCTV and the Data Protection Act of 1998." *Journal of Education Policy* 26(1), 1–15.

Theunissen, M. 1984. *The Other: Studies in the Social Ontology of Husserl, Heidegger, Sartre and Buber*. Translated by C. Macann. Cambridge, MA: MIT Press.

29

Critical Peace Education as a Response to School Violence

Insights from Critical Pedagogies for Non-violence

Michalinos Zembylas

Introduction

It is now officially recognized by the United Nations that schooling contributes to sustaining direct forms of violence (Pinheiro 2006) such as gendered violence, bullying, racial and ethnic prejudice, hatred, the use of corporal punishment, the physical and mental stress and illness caused by over-testing and examination of students, and the militarization of schooling and learning to kill as part of the curriculum (Harber and Sakade 2009). More importantly, Harber (2004) points out, schools play a role in the reproduction of "structural violence," that is, the existence of oppressive and unequal socioeconomic and political relationships. Considerable research in the last 30 years indicates that school violence contributes to damaged relationships, increased fear, anger, and hatred, poor student performance, and troubled emotional health for students, teachers, and their communities (Harris 2007). While violence is commonly thought of as physical, theorists describe violence as multifaceted – physical, psychological, structural, and cultural (Galtung 1969, 1990, 1996) – and as caused by thoughts, words, and deeds. As these various forms of violence infiltrate into schools or are perpetuated by schools, educators around the world attempt to respond to this challenging social problem in various ways.

Peace education, as both academic field and pedagogical practice, has emerged in the aftermath of the two world wars as a response to these various forms of violence and conflict. The field has since expanded to embrace issues related to international education, human rights education, non-violence, global studies, citizenship, democratic education, environmental education, multicultural awareness, peer mediation, and conflict resolution education (Burns and Aspeslagh 1996; Harris and Morrison 2003; Salomon and Nevo 2002). Interest in peace and non-violence education has grown considerably since the 1980s, especially in combination with efforts to address social inequalities. As Reardon states, "Teaching about or for peace necessitates teaching about and for economic and social justice" (2000, 409). Increasing calls over the last decade for "critical peace education" (Bajaj 2008, 2015; Bajaj and Brantmeier 2011; Brantmeier 2011; Diaz-Soto 2005; Trifonas and Wright 2013; Zembylas and Bekerman 2013), in particular, in direct acknowledgment of the link between peace and social

The Wiley Handbook on Violence in Education: Forms, Factors, and Preventions, First Edition.
Edited by Harvey Shapiro.
© 2018 John Wiley & Sons, Inc. Published 2018 by John Wiley & Sons, Inc.

justice, examine and challenge structural inequalities, aiming to transform students and teachers as well as schools and the communities that they serve. Part of the efforts to articulate critical peace education is to examine the ways in which "critical pedagogies" – that is, pedagogies in which both teachers and students recognize, challenge, and work to transform structures that sustain social inequities and injustice (Darder, Baltodano, and Torres 2003) – can be used to promote critical peace and non-violence in schools and to address problems of violence in broader society.

This chapter builds on and extends previous work on how "critical pedagogies for nonviolence" (Chubbuck and Zembylas 2011) may inform critical peace education. Working from the assumption that critical pedagogy must engage with the emotional complexities of the efforts to transform structures that sustain social inequities and injustice, I have been working in recent years to theorize critical pedagogy so that it considers emotional knowledge as a source of fruitful and responsive learning (Zembylas 2013a, 2015). This chapter asks, then, "How can critical pedagogies for non-violence that pay attention to emotion as potentially both constitutive of unjust structures and supportive of resistance to inequity, offer deeper understandings to peace education efforts?" To respond to this question, I will draw on my experience as a peace education researcher, scholar, and teacher in the last 15 years. As someone who has lived for most of his life in a conflict-affected, violent, and divided society, I always wondered how education – which seemed to have an important role in cultivating such negative emotions – might contribute to peacebuilding and reconciliation. The present chapter presents a series of conceptual propositions on what I have come to realize so far in relation to the question posed above.

A central argument of this chapter is that there is much to be learned from analyzing ways in which critical pedagogy can be used to promote non-violence and work toward peace, while keeping emotional complexities in the forefront of analysis. As such, the sections that follow (i) explore the rise of peace education, and especially critical peace education; (ii) offer a theoretical model of critical pedagogy for non-violence that takes into consideration the role of emotion; and (iii) discuss three aspects of critical pedagogy for non-violence based on my longtime research in which I show how critical peace education may be informed by critical emotional praxis (Zembylas 2015).

Point of Departure

A number of important questions can be raised in efforts to deepen our understandings of the entanglement of emotions, violence, and peace education in conflict-affected societies: Do students' and teachers' emotional responses to traumatic conflict and violence constitute insurmountable obstacles in peace education efforts? How do hegemonic narratives of conflict and violence shape the emotions of identity and collective memory, and what can be done pedagogically to transform the powerful influence of such narratives and emotions? Can peace education efforts that foreground emotion in critical ways become a productive pedagogical intervention to combat violence in conflicted societies? My ethnographic research in Cyprus over the last 15 years has taught me how teachers and students remain firmly emotionally rooted in the hegemonic narratives of their own community, even when these emotional practices are challenged and clearer alternatives to the reigning ones are being considered. At the same time, however, I have witnessed inspiring examples of pedagogical practices through which small but powerful transformations have taken place.

At stake in these struggles and small transformations is a tense and open-ended process of *politicization* of emotions. More often than not, emotions of traumatic conflict and violence are appropriated by social and political institutions, such as schools, to justify collective narratives and ideologies about the victims and perpetrators of a conflict (Bekerman and Zembylas 2012; Zembylas 2008, 2015). A classic example of how emotions of conflict and violence can be politically appropriated, not only in society at large (Bourke 2006) but also in schools (Giroux 2003), is the case of "fear." Schools seem to be particularly successful in passing down fear (Fisher 2006). Fear – for example, of the "evil other" who is deemed responsible for unspeakable trauma and violence against "us" – works both at the psychic level and the sociopolitical level, and it structures how the "other" is viewed through unconscious feelings, expectations, anxieties, and defenses. The emotion of fear, just like hatred and resentment, *does* something extraordinary, as Ahmed (2004) points out; it establishes a distance between bodies that are read as "similar" and those that are considered to be "different." In other words, fear is politicized by establishing affective boundaries between "us" (the "good") and "them" (the "bad"); the others are fearsome – and thus it is easier to dehumanize them – because in our thinking they are constructed as a danger to our very existence.

In general, much research in conflict-affected societies – "conflict" may be social, political, or war-like – provides evidence of how schools stimulate prejudices and stereotypes and contribute to the normalization of emotions of traumatic conflict and violence for political purposes (Bekerman and McGlynn 2007; McGlynn et al. 2009). Educators in such societies must confront the following question: How can the ideological appropriation of emotions of trauma and violence be critically challenged through peace education efforts, when schools themselves often contribute to this appropriation? This question is at the heart of this chapter.

(Critical) Peace Education[1]

"Peace education" is a term often used to denote a variety of programs, studies, and initiatives that are primarily empirically based. The first forms of peace education focused on non-violence, disarmament, and the prevention of war, as a result of both world wars, the Vietnam War, and the Cold War (Burns and Aspeslagh 1996). In Galtung's (1969) terms, the initial emphasis of "peace studies" (from which peace education developed as a field) was on "negative peace," that is, the absence of violence (e.g., war). "Positive peace," on the other hand, refers to the absence of structural violence, that is, systemic social injustices and inequities such as gender and racial discrimination. Burns and Aspeslagh (1996), Bar-Tal (2002), and Salomon and Nevo (2002), among others, refer to the growth of peace education as a field of academic knowledge as well as an area of program initiatives over the past 40–50 years. Because of the concerns

---

1 My discussion here draws on and extends the analysis of peace education, its origin and its "critical" version, provided in Zembylas, Charalambous, and Charalambous (2016).

about the devastating consequences of the atomic bombs dropped on Hiroshima and Nagasaki, in the decades immediately after World War II – the 1950s, the 1960s, and the 1970s – peace education focused more on nuclear disarmament, while in the 1980s it was mostly concerned with the issue of human coexistence (Burns and Aspeslagh 1996). In the 1990s, a more humanistic view of peace education came to prominence with an emphasis on how peace education could address various forms of violence (e.g., domestic, cultural, ethnic) and contribute to social justice. Thus there has been a shift from "negative peace" in previous decades to approaches aiming at "positive peace" and the development of a culture of peace that eradicates poverty and injustice (Burns and Aspeslagh 1996; Harris and Morrison 2003; Salomon and Nevo 2002).

Over these decades, a large number of peace education initiatives have been designed and implemented worldwide; yet, there are still varied views at the conceptual level as to what peace education is (Page 2008; Salomon and Nevo 2002). Part of the problem is that peace education programs all over the world differ considerably in terms of ideology, objectives, focus, curricula, and teaching practices (Bar-Tal 2002). As Bar-Tal writes:

> Whereas the content of traditional subjects is well defined (i.e. pupils in every part of the world identify the subject from its content), the content of peace education is of a wider scope and is less defined. Even though their objectives may be similar, each society will set up a different form of peace education that is dependent on the issues at large, conditions, and culture, as well as the views and creativity of the educators. (2002, 34–35)

Furthermore, program initiatives that could fit under the heading of "peace education" often carry different names (Lopes Cardozo 2008). Peace education takes different "faces" (Bush and Saltarelli 2000) as educators attempt to address various forms of violence in different social and political contexts: international education, human rights education, peacebuilding education, conflict resolution education, global education, education for democracy/citizenship, development education, environmental education (Davies 2004; Harris 2011). Each of these approaches has different foci, yet all of them align with many of the goals and values of peace education as a field and a movement. While these approaches continue to emerge and evolve, peace education also becomes diversified and therefore what seems to constitute "peace education" remains an open question.

Critical elaborations of peace education have been developed in recent years from a variety of political, theoretical, and methodological positions. Central to critical peace education projects is that they pay attention to issues of structural inequalities and aim at cultivating a sense of transformative agency to advance peacebuilding (Bajaj 2008, 2015; Bajaj and Brantmeier 2011; Brantmeier 2011; Trifonas and Wright 2013; Zembylas and Bekerman 2013). Bajaj (2008) discusses Diaz-Soto's (2005) approach to critical peace education as situated in consciousness-raising inspired by Freire. Bajaj and Brantmeier (2011) also argue that one of the most important features of critical peace education is its alignment with a counter-hegemonic paradigm for social change through education. The goal of critical peace education is to empower young people to engage in practices and activism that increase societal equity and justice, which, in turn, foster greater peace. As Bajaj and Brantmeier write: "What we term critical peace education ... is that which approaches the particularistic, seeking to enhance transformative agency and participatory citizenship, and open to resonating in distinct ways with the diverse chords of peace that exist across fields and cultures" (2011, 222). Both Bajaj's (2008) analysis and Brantmeier's (2011) identification of critical peace education as the cultivation of transformative agency highlight how injustice and conflict are linked. Hence, the transformation of unjust societal structures addresses conflict, just as the reduction of destructive forms of conflict fostered through critical peace education contributes to dismantling unjust structures and eliminating inequities.

I have entered the debates on critical peace education with Zvi Bekerman (see Bekerman, Zembylas, and McGlynn 2009; Zembylas 2015; Zembylas and Bekerman 2013) by arguing that "peace education" may often become part of the problem it tries to solve, if theoretical work is not used to interrogate the taken-for-granted assumptions about peace, conflict, and peace education. For this purpose, we have put forward a proposition consisting of four elements aiming to reclaim criticality in peace education: (i) reinstating the materiality of things and practices; (ii) re-ontologizing research and practice in peace education; (iii) becoming critical experts of design; and (iv) engaging in critical cultural analysis (Zembylas and Bekerman 2013). All of these four elements basically emphasize the idea of resisting rigid norms and standards for what peace education ought to be and suggest that contextualized forms of peace education need to be engaged in ongoing conversations with other fields and traditions of critical education.

Critical pedagogy, in particular, can be valuable in critical peace education efforts to develop pedagogies that promote non-violence and address social injustices. Critical pedagogy, although not monolithic, commonly promotes educational experiences that are transformative, empowering, and transgressive (Giroux 2004; Kincheloe 2005; McLaren 2003). The common ground of critical peace education and critical pedagogy is that they are both oriented toward enhancing transformative agency and praxis in resonance with the diverse manifestations of emotion and peace that exist across cultures. In the context of such theorizations, new concepts have emerged in recent years to articulate the interrelations among critical peace education, critical pedagogy, and transformative praxis.

For example, my analysis of "critical emotional praxis" (see Zembylas 2008, 2015) is an attempt to develop an overarching concept that is theoretically grounded in critical pedagogy in post-traumatic societies and that intersects with critical peace education. "Critical emotional praxis" is a theoretical and practical tool that recognizes how emotions play a powerful role in either sustaining or disrupting hegemonic discourses about past traumatic events. Critical emotional praxis is theoretically grounded in a psychoanalytic and a sociopolitical analysis of emotion and trauma and provides a platform from which teachers and students can critically interrogate their own emotion-laden beliefs. For instance, this practice encourages the identification, recognition, and critical analysis of emotions and affects that set certain boundaries within which teachers and students are socialized to reproduce those emotions and affects.

In general, there is now a growing consensus in what has become known as "critical peace education" that peace education should utilize critical pedagogies to teach for/ through/about peace; that is, pedagogical practices that provide spaces for experiential learning and reflective and critical dialogues through which students are not only engaged in critical discussions about social phenomena but are also encouraged to take specific action for change. Peace education initiatives around the world have developed numerous programs, activities, and teaching methods that are grounded in role-plays, games, and group activities through which children and youth are encouraged to learn about negotiation, conflict-resolution and conflict-transformation skills, and cooperation. Having discussed critical peace education, I will move on now to elaborate what "critical pedagogy for non-violence" entails and how it may be manifested in practice to promote critical peace education.

Critical Pedagogies for Non-violence[2]

As mentioned earlier, critical pedagogy promotes learning experiences that are transformative of the social and political status quo that is also perpetuated via institutions such as schooling (Giroux 2004; Kincheloe 2005; McLaren 2003). Drawn from many theoretical streams, critical pedagogy posits that institutions, including schools, inculcate Gramsci's notion of hegemonic commonsense conceptions of truth that privilege the oppressor and perpetuate domination (Darder, Baltodano, and Torres 2003). At its center, then, critical pedagogy engages educators in a critical examination of how power relations (particularly in relation to which and whose knowledge is legitimated) operate in schools and society, and then equips teachers and students to become transformative democratic agents who recognize, challenge, and transform injustice and unequal social structures (Freire 1970).

Educational efforts and programs grounded in critical pedagogy typically engage educators and students in a praxis of critical dialogue, that is, in a dialogical process which aims at *conscientization* (Freire 1970). Conscientization or critical consciousness focuses on achieving an in-depth understanding of the world through which oppressed individuals will become active agents who transform unjust societal structures and increase their own humanness and that of their oppressors, as well. This work is accomplished at two levels: the micro level of the classroom including curricular, instructional, and relational structures, and the macro level of district, state, and national structures (North 2006). Ideally, these levels weave together into pedagogies and policies that equip students' transgressive agency by developing their "ability to work collectively toward a better society" through an unabashed commitment to "fostering the attitudes, skills and knowledge required to engage and act on important social issues" (Westheimer and Kahne 1998, 2). Therefore, a holistic definition of critical pedagogy is embraced: the transformation and enactment of policies and pedagogical practices that improve the learning and life opportunities of typically underserved students while equipping and empowering all students to engage critically in the creation of a more socially just society themselves (Chubbuck and Zembylas 2008, 2011; Cochran-Smith 2004; Ladson-Billings 1994).

Peace education, as an attempt to reduce the many forms of violence by teaching about and for peace (Reardon 2000), complements critical pedagogy's goals of transforming societal structures to be more socially just. Peace theorist/researcher Johan Galtung (1969, 1990, 1996) defines violence as those circumstances that deprive humans

---

2 My analysis here builds on the work I have done with Sharon Chubbuck (see Chubbuck and Zembylas 2011).

of their life potential. Violence that produces that diminished potential can take several forms: direct violence (e.g., killing someone); structural violence (covert violence with no apparent actor, embedded in policies, institutions, and structures of society that produce unequal power); and cultural violence (symbolic violence through religion, ideology, language, art, science, media) (Galtung 1969, 1990, 1996). In his conceptualization of different forms of violence, Galtung explains that these forms constitute the points of a triangle of violence:

> Violence can start at any corner in the direct–structural–cultural violence triangle and is easily transmitted to other corners. With the violent structure institutionalized and the violent culture internalized, direct violence also tends to become institutionalized, repetitive, ritualistic … This triangular syndrome of violence should then be contrasted in the mind with a triangular syndrome of peace in which cultural peace engenders structural peace, with symbiotic, equitable relations among diverse partners, and direct peace with acts of cooperation, friendliness and love. It could be a virtuous rather than vicious triangle, also self-reinforcing. (Galtung 1969, 302)

Whether schooling or sites of education can address all forms of violence at all levels is an issue of debate in discussions of critical peace education (Bajaj 2015). In particular, this chapter seeks to bridge approaches that promote critical peace education with critical pedagogies that specifically pay attention to *non-violence*. The non-violent resistance and activism espoused by Mahatma Gandhi (1959, 1993), a rich resource to create social change by addressing the forms of violence described above (e.g., see Burrowes 1996; Jurgensmeyer 2002; Merton 1965), presents peace-oriented pedagogical perspectives that complement critical pedagogy. For Gandhi, the multiple forms of violence violate the truth of the unity of life; hence, the pursuit of non-violence is founded on his concept of *satygraha* (Gandhi 1993), a struggle to "hold onto the truth," which is expressed through a wide range of non-violent actions to secure justice for each and every individual. Gandhi's notion of "civil disobedience" is one example of non-violent resistance; another example is non-cooperation, such as strikes, economic boycotts, and tax refusals – measures that show refusal to submit to the injustice being fought. Thus Gandhi's *satygraha*, in part, implies the use of non-violent actions in a dialogic process – a process, though, that promotes non-violent communication with oppressors rather than involving violent actions (Allen 2007; Burrowes 1996). Non-violent communication is the avoidance of violent actions or behaviors that harm others; through critical pedagogy, non-violent communication can be taught as a process of communication to improve empathetic understanding and connection to others (Zembylas 2015).

Gandhi's approach to education also emphasizes "both the multidimensional nature of violence and the structural violence of the status quo" (Allen 2007, 295), that is, those commonsense, uninterrogated pedagogies and policies that normalize and reproduce multiple layers of inequity in the everyday life of schooling. Thus, physical violence that occurs in schools cannot be separated from other forms of violence – linguistic, psychological, cultural, political, and religious – that are expressed both directly/personally and indirectly/structurally and are normalized by cultural violence (Galtung 1996). For instance, words expressed person to person inside the classroom or written in texts originating outside the classroom "can serve as a violent weapon used to control, manipulate, humiliate, intimidate, terrorize, oppress, exploit, and dominate other human beings" (Allen 2007, 295). Gandhian thought, then, captures critical educators' responsibility to actively and non-violently resist and transform the ways educational goals and practices can inflict both overt and covert violence – whether found in the macro level of official curricula or the micro level of teachers' own body language and classroom practices (North 2006). The alignment of peace education goals and Gandhian thought with critical pedagogy – recognizing, challenging, and transforming, at all levels, those "iniquitous relations of power" (Giroux 1997, 313) in order to end the reproduction of inequity – is striking.

In response to both minor and major incidents of youth violence, schools traditionally have focused on "negative peace" efforts, most commonly through a peacekeeping effort to promote peace by controlling student behavior (Harris 1999). This approach primarily blames youth for dysfunctional behaviors, at least partially adopted from their social environment, instead of addressing the root violence at a wider social level (Harris 1999). Peacemaking promotes dialogue through conflict resolution and peer mediation programs that help students resolve conflict in a win–win manner (Harris 2002), by giving students the necessary attitudes and skills to end violence, such as explaining its roots, teaching alternatives, and empowering students "to redress the circumstances that can lead to violent conflict" (Harris 2004, 5). Though more proactive in empowering youth to respond to violence themselves rather than depending on external forces of control, this approach also can be criticized for locating the source of and solution to violence solely in young people themselves.

On the contrary, peacebuilding addresses the deeper roots of violence by teaching youth how to live peacefully through creating the conditions for peace such as attitudes, habits/behaviors, and dispositions conducive to positive peace and non-violent resistance and activism to transform unjust structures. This involves studying structural violence (Galtung 1969) and working to redress inequities and injustices produced by oppression and marginalization. Indeed, a critical component of positive peace education is the promotion of peace accompanied by social justice since that injustice frequently becomes the source and site of direct violence (Harris 2002). As Burns and Aspeslagh (1996) argue, one of the most important features of peace education is its alignment with a counter-hegemonic paradigm, that is, those efforts that critique, confront, and oppose the existing status quo. The goal, then, is not merely to stop violence reactively, but also to empower young people to engage in proactive behaviors such as non-violent communication (Harris 2002) and activism to increase societal equity and justice, which in turn, foster greater peace.

A Theoretical Framework of Critical Pedagogies for Non-violence

This brief analysis of critical pedagogy, critical peace education, and non-violence points to the potential of an emerging educational philosophy that we have called *critical pedagogies for non-violence* (see Chubbuck and Zembylas 2011) – in the plural because there are potentially many manifestations of "critical pedagogy for non-violence." My discussion here aims to extend the conversation on the theoretical assumptions that need to be clarified for this philosophy:

1) *Critical pedagogy for non-violence is a holistic, integrated way of life* that begins inside (Nhat 2004) and extends to every aspect of education. Just as non-violence needs to permeate a person's entire life from the inside out (Galtung 1996), non-violence is not a theoretical idea to be added on to critical pedagogy. In order to create conditions for social transformation, individuals need to transform their entire lives by rejecting violence in any form – direct/structural/cultural and physical/psychological – and embracing non-violent action. This holistic aspect, reflective of Ghandi's notion of the multidimensional aspects of violence, including the structural violence of the status quo (Allen 2007) and of peace educators' admonition to attend to all levels of violence (Galtung 1996), calls educators to integrate non-violence into every aspect of their practice and interactions with students and systems in their efforts to enact critical pedagogy. Rather than being compartmentalized, critical non-violent pedagogy offers a guiding framework for all aspects of life and work.

2) *Critical pedagogy for non-violence centrally acknowledges and engages power relations.* Power relations that support inequitable structures, are restrictive or owned by individuals, and are oppressive and violent against others need to be unmasked and dismantled (Kincheloe 2005; McLaren 2003). Power relations also, however, can be productive forces capable of fueling resistance and transforming relationships, practices, and policies for greater justice (Darder, Baltodano, and Torres 2003). Critical pedagogy for non-violence seeks to engage power as productive and distinct from violence. The notion of "power as productive" draws on Foucault's (1982) useful distinction that relationships of violence "force ... bend ... break ... [and] close possibilities" (220), while relationships of power are capable of opening up possibilities of resistance and transformation. In other words, power is not only "restrictive" but also "productive" in the sense that it produces new possibilities and openings for change. Integrally connected to the notion of power as productive is the role of "critical dialogue" mentioned earlier. The very nature of a dialogic process that critically interrogates our taken-for-granted assumptions and beliefs allows all individuals, even current perpetrators of violence, to become active agents with the potential to transform not only their lives but also their communities.[3]

3) Finally, *critical pedagogy for non-violence recognizes and navigates emotion as constitutive of unjust structures.* This recognition utilizes key elements of critical emotional praxis (Zembylas 2008, 2015) where teachers interrogate the historical/political power of emotion to support or resist unjust structures, and at the same time engage the transaction of emotions in local contexts to create openings for growth. For example, critical pedagogy for non-violence may very well evoke emotional discomfort among students and teachers (Boler 1999) in its challenge of long-cherished ideologies and practices and its problematizing of the ways deeply embedded emotions frame and attend daily routines; I discuss this possibility in the last part of this chapter. Discomfort, however, is not a negative; indeed, both Martin

---

3 As Martin Luther King (1958, 102) wrote, non-violent action "is directed against forces of evil rather than against persons who happen to be doing the evil. It is evil that the nonviolent resister seeks to defeat, not the persons victimized by evil."

Luther King and Gandhi maintained the importance of the will to suffer emotional pain in the struggle to transform unjust conditions. Thus, being willing to question and challenge the sustained, emotionally laden assumptions teachers and students hold on a wide range of issues (e.g., identity, culture, nation-state, religion, etc.), and being able to engage in interrogating these emotions and how they are evoked in everyday life, can create a critical tool to change those policies and practices that reproduce inequity. In addition, as students encounter examples of oppression and injustice, the emotions of sorrow and discomfort they experience can pierce apathy and provide the catalyst needed to act for change (Greene 1998).

In sum, critical pedagogies for non-violence – the holistic integration of non-violent attitudes and practices, the transformative use of power relations in the context of inequitable structures, and the utilization of the constitutive power of emotion to resist and transform unjust structures – can form an action-oriented pedagogical approach. Both critical pedagogy and critical peace education, then, focus on dismantling unjust structures and eliminating inequities. Hence, the transformation of unjust societal structures leads to a reduction of violence, and greater non-violence fostered through critical peace education similarly leads to critical pedagogy's goal of greater societal level justice and equity. This marriage of critical pedagogy and peace education is a potentially valuable resource for greater justice in both schools and society.

Three Elements of Critical Pedagogy for Non-violence: Entanglements with Critical Peace Education

In the last part of this chapter, I make an attempt to outline three aspects of critical pedagogy for non-violence through which critical peace education may be informed in order to promote transformative agency and praxis – or critical emotional praxis, as I call it. The three aspects I discuss here (clearly, they are not the only ones) are the following: (i) pedagogies of discomfort; (ii) the pedagogical principle of mutual vulnerability; and, (iii) compassion and strategic empathy. Each of these three aspects – along with their strengths and limitations – are briefly discussed below in terms of how they help navigate critical peace educators in ways that promote agency and solidarity.

Pedagogies of Discomfort

In recent years, there is increasing research that acknowledges how challenging students and teachers beyond their "comfort zones" and pushing them to deconstruct the ways in which they have learned to see, feel, and act constitutes a valuable pedagogic approach in social justice, citizenship, and anti-racist education (e.g., see Boler 1999, 2004; Boler and Zembylas 2003; Zembylas, Charalambous, and Charalambous 2016; Zembylas and McGlynn 2012). In fact, it has been argued that if a major purpose of teaching is to unsettle taken-for-granted views and emotions, then a "pedagogy of discomfort" is not only unavoidable but may also be necessary (Berlak 2004). "A pedagogy of discomfort begins," explains Boler, "by inviting educators and students to engage in critical inquiry regarding values and cherished beliefs, and to examine constructed self-images in relation to how one has learned to perceive others" (1999, 176–177).

For example, individuals who belong to a hegemonic culture experience discomfort when having to confront their privileges in relation to educational and social inequities (see, e.g., Leibowitz et al. 2010). Leibowitz and her colleagues, who write in the context of post-apartheid South Africa, demonstrate how a pedagogy of discomfort is valuable in uncovering and questioning the deeply embedded emotional dimensions that shape some individual and group privileges (e.g., those of white students) through daily habits and routines. By closely problematizing these emotional habits and routines and their attachments to structural injustices, it is shown that teachers and students, in a context in which there have been and still are serious human rights violations, can begin to identify the invisible ways in which they comply with dominant ideologies.

When examined through the lens of a theory that attempts to instill criticality, agency, and solidarity in peace education, then, it becomes clearer how and why certain features of pedagogic discomfort can be helpful in identifying the complexity and situatedness of "peace" and "conflict" and their consequences. Students and teachers come into the classroom carrying their troubled knowledge about "conquest and humiliation, struggle and survival, suffering and resilience, poverty and recovery, black and white" (Jansen 2009, 361). Unsettling this troubled knowledge demands emotional effort, careful listening to each other's traumatic experiences, and explicit discussion of the potential and the harm that troubled knowledge stimulates (Zembylas 2013b). The value of pedagogic discomfort thought cannot be overstated. This process should not be assumed to be always already transformative, and beyond question. In other words, there are no guarantees for change in the social and political status quo; a pedagogy of discomfort, especially in light of the challenges identified in this chapter, demands time and realistic decisions about what can and what cannot be achieved. Needless to say, not all students will respond in the same way or benefit from pedagogic discomfort in the same manner; some may adopt some sort of change, others may resist, and still others may experience distress (Kumashiro 2002). Therefore, the concern here is not simply about overcoming resistance or motivating students who express apathy or hostility; "it is, rather, a pedagogical commitment to locate, interrogate, and engage troubled knowledge ... in ways that permit disruption of received authority" (Jansen 2009, 267).

The Pedagogical Principle of Mutual Vulnerability

The second aspect which enriches pedagogical efforts toward criticality, agency, and solidarity in peace education concerns the pedagogical principle of "mutual vulnerability" (e.g., see Keet, Zinn, and Porteus 2009; Zembylas 2013a). The notion of mutual vulnerability is grounded in the idea that there is interdependence between human beings and that the recognition of all people as "vulnerable" has important pedagogical consequences concerning the possibility of assuming critical responsibility toward one's own life and the lives of others in a community. The argument that is developed here is grounded theoretically in the work of Butler (2004) and particularly her essay "Violence, Mourning, Politics."

Butler (2004) presents a number of examples to show that "each of us is constituted politically in part by virtue of the social vulnerability of our bodies ... Loss and vulnerability seem to follow from our being socially constituted bodies, attached to others, at risk of losing those attachments, exposed to others, at risk of violence by virtue of that exposure" (Butler 2004, 20). The social vulnerability of our bodies is evident, for instance, in the experience of losing someone whom one is attached to; thus, each one of us is mutually obliged to others because of this common vulnerability. The denial of such vulnerability unleashes violence against others whereas its acknowledgment creates openings for an ethical encounter with others. Consequently, "we might critically evaluate and oppose," Butler emphasizes, "the conditions under which certain human lives are more vulnerable than others, and thus certain human lives are more grievable than others" (2004, 30). Once we consider how hegemonic power relations determine "who will be a grievable human" and what "acts" are "permissible" for "public grieving" (37), then we may begin to realize how a prohibition of grieving others' lives extends the aims of violence and conflict. For example, as Butler says, hegemonic power relations in the United States make the grieving for Jews killed in the Middle East "permissible" in the public arena, while a similar act for Palestinians is treated with suspicion.

The notion of vulnerability has important pedagogical consequences for the entanglement of critical peace education, social justice education, and critical citizenship education, because the mutual experience of loss and mourning reveals the possibility of creating an alternative moral responsibility and sense of community in classrooms and schools (Vlieghe 2010). Butler's theorization of common vulnerability constitutes the point of departure for a renewed pedagogical politics of recognition in conflict-affected societies. The notion of mutual vulnerability enriches critical peace education, because it disrupts normative frames of community on the basis of rationality and self-advancement and puts forward the notion of community on the basis of loss; that is, the reconstitution of communities on the basis that all human beings suffer loss. This idea does not imply, however, an equalization of vulnerability, but the recognition that there are different forms of vulnerabilities.

Compassion and Strategic Empathy

Finally, the third aspect we want to share in this chapter concerns the value of compassion and strategic empathy in critical peace education praxis (e.g., Zembylas 2012, 2013a). Jansen (2009) argues that critical theory and pedagogy in post-traumatic contexts is severely limited "for making sense of *troubled knowledge* and for transforming those who carry the burden of such knowledge on both sides of a divided community" (2009, 256, emphasis added). "Troubled knowledge" is the knowledge of a traumatized past such as the profound feelings of loss, shame, resentment, or defeat that an individual carries from his or her participation in a traumatized community. As Jansen maintains, critical theory receives and constructs the world as divided (e.g., black/white, oppressors/oppressed) and then takes sides to free the oppressed. The focus of this concern is less on what to do with the racist or nationalist in the classroom and more to do with how to empower the marginalized. Yet, the challenge in traumatized communities is often how to deal with the student who resists or rejects critical perspectives and who openly expresses racist or nationalist views because his or her privileges are being threatened or lost; or the student who is so traumatized as a result of racism or nationalism that he or she feels that nothing can be done to rectify the situation.

In light of this discussion, then, it is evident that troubled knowledge provokes strong emotional reactions in the classroom – reactions that could be quite discomforting for teachers and students alike. Teachers have to find ways to handle constructively these reactions as well as the discourses that overly focus on one's own traumatic experiences and ignore the other's sufferings. Importantly, teachers need to establish trust in the classroom, develop strong relationships, and enact compassionate understanding in every possible manner. Jansen (2009) highlights two pedagogical tactics that are particularly useful in teaching students how to learn compassion by challenging these binaries: first, the acknowledgment of brokenness by all sides, that is, the idea that humans are prone to failure and incompleteness and as such we constantly seek a higher order of living which cannot be accomplished without being in communion with others. Second, a pedagogical reciprocity is also required, that is, everyone carrying the burden of troubled knowledge has to move toward each other. This movement toward each other, as Jansen explains, entails, for example, the following in the context of post-apartheid South Africa: "the white person has to move across the allegorical bridge toward the black person; the black person has to move in the direction of the white person. Critical theory demands the former; a postconflict pedagogy requires both" (2009, 268).

To promote the prospects of compassion in the classroom, we also argue that one of those pedagogical resources that will be needed is strategic empathy. Strategic empathy is essentially the use of empathetic emotions in both critical and strategic ways (Lindquist 2004); that is, it refers to the willingness of the critical pedagogue to make herself strategically skeptical (working sometimes against her own emotions) in order to empathize with the troubled knowledge students carry with them, even when this troubled knowledge is disturbing to other students or to the teacher. The use of strategic empathy can function as a valuable pedagogical tool that opens up affective spaces which might eventually disrupt the emotional roots of troubled knowledge – an admittedly long and difficult task (Zembylas 2012). Undermining the emotional roots of troubled knowledge through strategic empathy ultimately aims at helping students integrate their troubled views into compassionate and socially just perspectives.

Conclusions and Implications

Critical pedagogies for non-violence offer a framework in curricula, teaching, and teacher education that opens up possibilities for addressing injustice and exploring non-violent alternative responses, both of which can lead to a reduction of violence. For example, holistically interrogating violence at multiple levels and in multiple contexts, as part of the curriculum, opens the possibility of understanding how unjust systems and practices inform our everyday life (Harris 2007) and produce violence. Developing and embracing nonviolent resources, such as nonviolent communication, in curriculum and teaching creates openings for alternate responses, expressions, articulations, identities and visions regarding those systems and practices (Allen 2007). The process itself opens possibilities for change and growth for students and teachers to understand the differential effects of structural violence.

In particular, teacher education programs can introduce pre-service and in-service teachers to a critical pedagogy for non-violence by focusing on how power relations can be transformed into productive, positive expressions that promote social justice (see also Brantmeier 2011). As pre-service and in-service teachers explore the ways they can use their own power to support critical dialogue in the learning communities of their classrooms, they can recognize the power of students' voices and life experiences to inform knowledge and to critique societal structures. In that process, learning a productive rather than restrictive use of their power as educators can potentially support their understanding of how fragmented and partial our individual grasp of truth can be, opening the possibility of greater non-violence as each voice is honored as contributing to understanding (Chubbuck and Zembylas 2011).

Also, critical pedagogy for non-violence can illuminate the role of emotion in sustaining or dismantling structures of power, privilege, racism, and oppression (Zembylas 2015). Without that illumination, these structures of violence will remain unchallenged when particular emotional responses (such as grief, remorse, compassion, and caring) are withheld from groups of people deemed Other (Zembylas 2008). By analyzing school violence and its emotional basis, educators and students alike can recognize how violence teaches and sustains particular emotions – apathy, bitterness, disempowerment, hatred, anger, rage, humiliation, guilt, and shame – and how those emotions then sustain continued violence. Equally, in that recognition, teachers can create alternative pedagogies that may transform the emotional lives of themselves and their students, thus interrupting the cycle of violence. This process requires alternative pedagogies of emotion, marked by compassion, tolerance, caring, and empathy, which can critically empower teachers and students. Pedagogies that prevent/disrupt violence develop from affective connections and social relations constructed on critical interrogations of past emotional histories and experiences, especially of how those experiences are built around violence. These interrogations, derived from a critical pedagogy for non-violence, can serve as a foundation for activism for greater justice and non-violence.

In conclusion, it goes without saying that the approach discussed here has limitations, just as any other approach; some of these limitations have been identified and discussed in this chapter, and others will certainly find out more limitations. This debate is fruitful in terms of discovering whether this (or any other approach) "works" for the purposes described here, and specifically "how it works" in terms of pushing forward discussions of critical peace education and how it may combat violence. Future research may focus explicitly on making connections between the theoretical premises of critical peace education and specific pedagogical implications of critical pedagogy for non-violence in particular settings. The elements outlined in this chapter may certainly constitute an important point of departure for reconstructing some fundamental theoretical premises as well as important practical issues in critical peace education and articulating further how different versions of critical peace education may have a pragmatic impact in addressing school violence.

References

Ahmed, S. 2004. *The Cultural Politics of Emotion*. Edinburgh: Edinburgh University Press.

Allen, D. 2007. "Mahatma Gandhi on Violence and Peace Education." *Philosophy East and West* 57(3): 290–310.

Bajaj, M. 2008. "'Critical' Peace Education." In *The Encyclopedia of Peace Education*, edited by M. Bajaj. Greenwich, CT: Information Age Publishing.

Bajaj, M. 2015. "'Pedagogies of Resistance' and Critical Peace Education Praxis." *Journal of Peace Education* 12(2), 154–166.

Bajaj, M. and Brantmeier, E. 2011. "The politics, Praxis and Possibilities of Critical Peace Education." *Journal of Peace Education* 8(3), 221–224.

Bar-Tal, D. 2002. "The Elusive Nature of Peace Education." In *Peace Education: The Concepts, Principles and Practices in the World*, edited by G. Salomon and B. Nevo, pp. 27–36. Mahwah, NJ: Lawrence Erlbaum.

Bekerman, Z. and McGlynn, C., eds. 2007. *Addressing Ethnic Conflict through Peace Education*. New York: Palgrave Macmillan.

Bekerman, Z. and Zembylas, M. 2012. *Teaching Contested Narratives: Identity, Memory and Reconciliation in Peace Education and Beyond*. Cambridge: Cambridge University Press.

Bekerman, Z., Zembylas, M., and McGlynn, C. 2009. "Working Towards the De-essentialization of Identity Categories in Conflict and Post-Conflict Societies: Israel, Cyprus, and Northern Ireland." *Comparative Education Review* 53(2), 213–234.

Berlak, A. 2004. "Confrontation and Pedagogy: Cultural Secrets and Emotion in Antioppressive Pedagogies." In *Democratic Dialogue in Education: Troubling Speech, Disturbing Silence*, edited by M. Boler, pp. 123–144. New York: Peter Lang.

Boler, M. 1999. *Feeling Power: Emotions and Education*. New York: Routledge.

Boler, M. 2004. "Teaching for Hope: The Ethics of Shattering World Views." In *Teaching, learning and loving: Reclaiming passion in educational practice*, edited by D. Liston and J. Garrison, pp. 117–131. New York: RoutledgeFalmer.

Boler, M. and Zembylas, M. 2003. "Discomforting Truths: The Emotional Terrain of Understanding Differences." In *Pedagogies of difference: Rethinking education for social justice*, edited by P. Trifonas, pp. 110–136. New York: Routledge.

Bourke, J. 2006. *Fear: A Cultural History*. Emeryville, CA: Shoemaker Hoard.

Brantmeier, E.J. 2011. "Toward Mainstreaming Critical Peace Education in U.S. Teacher Education." In *Critical pedagogy in the 21st century: A new generation of scholars*, edited by C.S. Malott, and B. Porfilio, pp. 349–376. Greenwich, CT: Information Age Publishing.

Burns, R.J. and Aspeslagh, R. 1996. *Three Decades of Peace Education Around the World: An Anthology*. New York: Garland.

Burrowes, R. 1996. *The Strategy of Non-violent Defense: A Gandhian Approach*. Albany: SUNY Press.

Bush, K.D. and Saltarelli, D. 2000. *The Two Faces of Education in Ethnic Conflict: Towards a Peacebuilding Education for Children*. Florence: UNICEF.

Butler, J. 2004. *Precarious Life: The Powers of Mourning and Violence*. London: Verso.

Chubbuck, S.M. and Zembylas, M. 2008. "The Emotional Ambivalence of Socially Just Teaching: A Case Study of a Novice Urban School Teacher." *American Educational Research Journal* 45(2), 274–318.

Chubbuck, S. and Zembylas, M. 2011. "Toward a Critical Pedagogy for Nonviolence in Urban School Contexts." *Journal of Peace Education* 8(3), 259–275.

Cochran-Smith, M. 2004. *Walking the Road: Race, Diversity, and Social Justice in Teacher Education*. New York: Teachers College Press.

Darder, A., Baltodano, M., and Torres, R.D. 2003. "Critical Pedagogy: An Introduction." In *The Critical Pedagogy Reader*, edited by A. Darder, M. Baltodano, and R.D. Torres, pp. 1–21. New York: Routledge.

Davies, L. 2004. *Education and Conflict: Complexity and Chaos*. New York: Routledge.

Diaz-Soto, L. 2005. "How Can We Teach Peace When We Are So Outraged? A Call for Critical Peace Education." *Taboo: The Journal of Culture and Education (Fall-Winter)* 9(2), 91–96.

Fisher, R.M. 2006. "Invoking 'Fear' Studies." *Journal of Curriculum Theorizing* 22, 39–71.

Foucault, F. 1982. "The Subject and Power." In *Michel Foucault: Beyond Structuralism and Hermeneutics*, edited by H. Dreyfus and P. Rabinow, pp. 208–226. Chicago: The University of Chicago Press.

Freire, P. 1970. *Pedagogy of the Oppressed*. Translated by M.B. Ramos. New York: Continuum. First published1955.

Galtung, J. 1969. "Violence, Peace and Peace Research." *Journal of Peace Research* 6(3), 167–191.

Galtung, J. 1990. "Cultural Violence." *Journal of Peace Research* 27(3), 291–305.

Galtung, J. 1996. *Peace by Peaceful Means: Peace and Conflict, Development and Civilization*. Thousand Oaks, CA: Sage.

Gandhi, M. 1959. *Collected Works of Mahatma Gandhi, Volume 45*. Delhi: Publications Division, Ministry of Information and Broadcasting, Government of India.

Gandhi, M. 1993. *An Autobiography: The Story of My Experiments with Truth*. Boston, MA: Beacon Press.

Giroux, H.A. 1997. "Rewriting the Discourse of Racial Identity: Towards a Pedagogy and Politics of Whiteness." *Harvard Educational Review* 67(2), 285–320.

Giroux, H. 2003. *The Abandoned Generation: Democracy Beyond the Culture of fear*. New York: Palgrave Macmillan.

Giroux, H.A. 2004. "Critical Pedagogy and the Postmodern/Modern Divide: Towards Pedagogy of Democratization." *Teacher Education Quarterly* 31(1), 132–153.

Greene, M. 1998. "Introduction: Teaching for Social Justice." In *Teaching for Social Justice*, edited by W. Ayers, J.A. Hunt, and T. Quinn, pp. xxvii–xlvi. New York: New Press.

Harber, C. 2004. *Schooling as Violence*. London: RoutledgeFalmer.

Harber, C. and Sakade, N. 2009. "Schooling for Violence and Peace: How Does Peace Education Differ from 'Normal' Schooling?" *Journal of Peace Education* 6(2), 171–187.

Harris, I. 1999. "Types of Peace Education." In *How Children Understand War and Peace*, edited by A. Raviv, L. Oppenheimer, and D. Bar-Tal. San Francisco, CA: Jossey-Bass.

Harris, I. 2002. "Conceptual Underpinnings of Peace Education." In *Peace Education: The Concept, Principles and Practices Around the World*, edited by G. Salomon and B. Nevo, pp. 15–26. New York: Lawrence Erlbaum.

Harris, I. 2004. "Peace Education Theory." *Journal of Peace Education* 1(1), 5–20.

Harris, I. 2007. "Peace Education in a Violent Culture." *Harvard Educational Review* 77(3), 350–354.

Harris, I. 2011. "The Many Faces of Peace Education: From International Relations to Interpersonal Relations." In *Handbook of Research in the Social Foundations of Education*, edited by S. Tozer, B.P. Gallegos, A.M. Henry, M.B. Greiner, and P.G. Price, pp. 348–357. New York: Routledge.

Harris, I. and M. Morrison 2003. *Peace Education*, 2nd ed. London: McFarland & Co.

Jansen, J 2009. *Knowledge in the Blood: Confronting Race and the Apartheid Past*. Stanford, CA: Stanford University Press.

Jurgensmeyer, M. 2002. *Gandhi's Way: A Handbook of Conflict Resolution*. Berkeley: University of California Press.

Keet, A., Zinn, D., and Porteus, K. 2009. "Mutual Vulnerability: A Key Principle in a Humanising Pedagogy in Post-conflict Societies." *Perspectives in Education* 27(2), 109–119.

Kincheloe, J.L. 2005. *Critical Pedagogy*. New York: Peter Lang.

King, M.L. 1958. *Stride toward Freedom: The Montgomery Story*. New York: Harper & Row.

Kumashiro, K.K. 2002. "Against Repetition: Addressing Resistance to Anti-oppressive Change in the Practices of Learning, Teaching, Supervising, and Researching." *Harvard Educational Review* 72(1), 67–92.

Ladson-Billings, G. 1994. *Dreamkeepers: Successful Teachers of African American Children*. San Francisco: Jossey-Bass.

Leibowitz, B., Bozalek, V., Rohleder, P., Carolissen, R., and Swartz, L. 2010. "'Ah, but the whiteys love to talk about themselves': Discomfort as a Pedagogy for Change." *Race Ethnicity and Education* 13(1), 83–100.

Lindquist, J. 2004. "Class Affects, Classroom Affectations: Working Through the Paradoxes of Strategic Empathy." *College English* 67(2), 187–209.

Lopes Cardozo, M. 2008. "Sri Lanka: In Peace or in Pieces? A Critical Approach to Peace Education in Sri Lanka." *Research in Comparative and International Education* 3(1), 1935.

McGlynn, C., Zembylas, M., Bekerman, Z., and Gallagher, T., eds. 2009. *Peace Education in Conflict and Post-conflict Societies: Comparative Perspectives*. New York: Palgrave Macmillan.

McLaren, P. 2003. *Life in Schools: An Introduction to Critical Pedagogy in the Foundations of Education*, 4th ed. Boston, MA: Allyn & Bacon.

Merton, T., ed. 1965. *Gandhi on Non-Violence*. New York: New Directions.

Nhat, T.N.H. 2004. *Creating True Peace: Ending Violence in Yourself, Your Family, Your Community, and the World*. New York: Free Press.

North, C. 2006. "More than Words? Delving into the Substantive Meaning(s) of 'Social Justice' in Education." *Review of Educational Research* 76(4), 507–535.

Page, J. 2008. *Peace Education: Exploring Ethical and Philosophical Foundations*. Charlotte, NC: Information Age Publishing.

Pinheiro, P. 2006. *World Report on Violence Against Children*. Geneva: United Nations.

Reardon, B.A. 2000. "Peace Education: A Review and Projection." In *Routledge International Companion to education*, edited by B. Moon, S. Brown, and M. Ben-Peretz, pp. 397–425. New York: Routledge.

Salomon, G. and Nevo, B., eds. 2002. *Peace Education: The Concepts, Principles, and Practices Around the World*. Mahwah, NJ: Lawrence Erlbaum.

Trifonas, P. and B. Wright, eds. 2013. *Critical Peace Education: Difficult Dialogues*. Dordrecht, Netherlands: Springer.

Vlieghe, J. 2010. "Judith Butler and the Public Dimension of the Body: Education, Critique and Corporeal Vulnerability." *Journal of Philosophy of Education* 44(1), 153–170.

Westheimer, J. and Kahne, J. 1998. "Education for Action: Preparing Youth for Participatory Democracy." In *Teaching for Social Justice*, edited by W. Ayers, J.A. Hunt, and T. Quinn pp. 1–19. New York: New Press.

Zembylas, M. 2008. *The Politics of Trauma in Education*. New York: Palgrave Macmillan.

Zembylas, M. 2012. "Pedagogies of Strategic Empathy: Navigating through the Emotional Complexities of Antiracism in Higher Education." *Teaching in Higher Education* 17(2), 113–125.

Zembylas, M. 2013a. "The 'Crisis of Pity' and the Radicalization of Solidarity: Towards Critical Pedagogies of Compassion." *Educational Studies: A Journal of the American Educational Studies Association* 49, 504–521.

Zembylas, M. 2013b. "Critical Pedagogy and Emotion: Working through Troubled Knowledge in Posttraumatic Societies." *Critical Studies in Education* 54(2), 176–189.

Zembylas, M. 2015. *Emotion and Traumatic Conflict: Re-claiming Healing in Education.* Oxford: Oxford University Press.

Zembylas, M. and Bekerman, Z. 2013. "Peace Education in the Present: Dismantling and Reconstructing Some Fundamental Theoretical Premises." *Journal of Peace Education* 10(2), 197–214.

Zembylas, M., Charalambous, C., and Charalambous, P. 2016. *Peace Education in a Conflict-affected Society: An Ethnographic Journey.* Cambridge: Cambridge University Press.

Zembylas, M. and McGlynn, C. 2012. "Discomforting Pedagogies: Emotional Tensions, Ethical Dilemmas and Transformative Possibilities." *British Educational Research Journal* 38(1), 41–60.

Index

Page numbers in *italics* refer to figures and those in **bold** refer to tables.

The Wiley Handbook on Violence in Education: Forms, Factors, and Preventions, First Edition.
Edited by Harvey Shapiro.
© 2018 John Wiley & Sons, Inc. Published 2018 by John Wiley & Sons, Inc.